# PRINCIPLES OF INTERACTIVE COMPUTER GRAPHICS

**McGRAW-HILL**
**COMPUTER SCIENCE SERIES**

HAROLD S. STONE
*University of Massachusetts*

**McGRAW-HILL SERIES IN ARTIFICIAL INTELLIGENCE**

*Consulting Editor*
Edward A. Feigenbaum, Stanford University

**Aircraft simulation**

A simulated view from the flight deck of an aircraft, used in training pilots. Thirty such images are generated each second in order to simulate motion realistically. (Courtesy Evans & Sutherland Computer Corporation)

**Realism in computer graphics**

A computer-generated still life illustrating the use of curved surfaces and shading. (Courtesy of Information International)

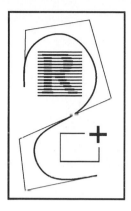

# PRINCIPLES OF

# INTERACTIVE

# COMPUTER GRAPHICS

## Second Edition

**WILLIAM M. NEWMAN**
Xerox Corporation

**ROBERT F. SPROULL**
Carnegie-Mellon University

McGRAW-HILL BOOK COMPANY

New York  St. Louis  San Francisco  Auckland  Bogotá  Düsseldorf
Johannesburg  London  Madrid  Mexico  Montreal  New Delhi  Panama
Paris  São Paulo  Singapore  Sydney  Tokyo  Toronto

**Library of Congress Cataloging in Publication Data**

**Newman, William M** 1939-
    Principles of interactive computer graphics.

    (McGraw-Hill computer science series) (McGraw-Hill series in artificial intelligence)
    Bibliography : p.
    Includes index.
    1. Computer graphics. 2. Interactive computer systems. I. Sproull, Robert F., joint author.
    II. Title.

T385.N48  1979            001.55            78-23825
ISBN 0-07-046338-7

PRINCIPLES OF INTERACTIVE COMPUTER GRAPHICS

7 8 9 0 **DODO** 8 3 2 1

The editors were Charles E. Stewart and Frances A. Neal; the production supervisor was Dominick Petrellese. R.R. Donnelley & Sons Company was printer and binder.

*To Bui Tuong Phong, 1942-1975*

# PREFACE

Computer graphics is a topic of rapidly growing importance in the computer field. It has always been one of the most visually spectacular branches of computer technology, producing images whose appearance and motion make them quite unlike any other form of computer output. Computer graphics is also an extremely effective medium for communication between man and computer; the human eye can absorb the information content of a displayed diagram or perspective view much faster than it can scan a table of numbers. All of this has been known for some years, but the high cost of computer graphics technology has prevented its widespread use. Now the cost is dropping rapidly, and interactive computer graphics is becoming available to more and more people.

This book has been written to help those interested in learning about computer graphics. Interest in computer graphics can of course take many forms; some readers will want to know how to use computer graphics in a particular application, some will be interested in the basic algorithms and techniques of computer graphics, and some will wish to design hardware or software graphics systems. Readers of every kind will, we hope, find material in this book to interest them.

The book's organization reflects a desire on our part to provide the reader with a thorough understanding of the basic principles and techniques of computer graphics, so that at the end he is well prepared to design graphics systems and application programs. Towards this end we have arranged the book in six parts:

*Part One: Basic Concepts.* These five chapters provide the reader with a general introduction to computer graphics as a whole, and explain basic techniques like clipping, geometric transformations, and incremental methods.

*Part Two: Graphics Packages.* This group of chapters explains how to build a package of graphics functions or subroutines to support the writing of application programs. The explanation starts with a very simple package design, and proceeds to cover the principal methods of modeling and structuring information for picture generation.

*Part Three: Interactive Graphics.* Many techniques and devices have been invented for graphical interaction with computers. The four chapters of Part Three describe input devices and techniques, and discuss the ways in which a graphics package may be extended to handle input and interaction.

*Part Four: Raster Graphics.* Up to this point, the book is concerned almost entirely with line-drawing graphics. The set of chapters in Part Four introduce a different approach to computer graphics that uses TV-based raster displays. This is a topic of increasing importance to interactive systems design.

*Part Five: Three-dimensional Graphics.* One of the principal uses of computer graphics lies in the modeling and display of three-dimensional objects such as automobile body parts and aircraft components. Some of the two-dimensional graphics techniques discussed in earlier chapters are extended to three dimensions in Part Five; some new topics are introduced, such as hidden surface removal, shading, and the modeling and display of curved surfaces.

*Part Six: Advanced Topics.* The final three chapters are devoted to topics of general interest that bring together much of the preceding material: display processors, device-independent graphics systems, and the design of user interfaces.

This organization has been chosen to help instructors in their use of the book as a text. Computer graphics is a popular classroom subject, for it touches on many other branches of computer science, and suggests lots of interesting and engrossing projects. At the same time, the unusual breadth of the subject makes it difficult to teach in a cohesive manner. To solve this problem, a strong emphasis is maintained throughout the book on *systems design:* the basic issues in graphics system design are introduced in Chapter 6, and each new topic is related back to the overall systems theme.

The book may be used as a text for a variety of different computer graphics courses; the only prerequisite is that the student have some programming experience, and be conversant with machine organization and data structures. A 10-week undergraduate course may be planned around Parts One, Two and Three, and will leave the student with a thorough understanding of two-dimensional, line-drawing computer graphics. A longer course can include Parts Four and Five, and will allow time for each student to complete a small project, always a valuable experience. A graduate course should be designed to cover the first half of the book fairly rapidly, and to concentrate on the material of Parts Four, Five and Six.

The book represents an extensive revision of the first edition, published in 1973. Much of the earlier edition was written in 1970 or 1971; computer graphics has developed and matured a great deal since then. Progress can be seen in all areas, perhaps most of all in raster graphics and in the overall design of graphics systems. We have therefore included a completely new group of chapters on raster graphics, and have completely revised the material of Part Two to cover graphics package design along more up-to-date lines. The other parts of the book reflect advances in display design, interactive programming, curved surface manipulation and display, and hidden-surface removal.

Despite these extensive changes, the book retains much of the overall structure of the first edition. Chapters are shorter, however, and material is sometimes presented in a slightly different order. More exercises have been included at the end of each chapter, and program examples are now written in PASCAL, a somewhat better-known language than SAIL, whose use in the first edition necessitated the inclusion of a 20-page user's manual!

While revising the book to reflect advances in computer graphics, we have also tried to incorporate as many as possible of the helpful suggestions we have received from readers of the first edition. In particular we would like to acknowledge the help of Ron Baecker, Robert Burton, Jim Clark, Steve Coons, Robin Forrest, Martin Newell, Kevin Weiler, and Rich Riesenfeld, who were kind enough to read and critique the manuscript of the second edition. Henry Bohl, Bert Herzog, Ronald Wigington, Henri Gouraud and others provided much useful advice on ways of improving the presentation of material in the first edition.

We are indebted to an equally long list of people who helped in the production of the second edition. The Xerox Palo Alto Research Center very generously made its facilities available for what turned into a somewhat ambitious project to produce camera-ready copy directly from the edited manuscript. The line illustrations were created with the aid of an interactive graphics system, and the text was edited on-line, formatted, combined with the line illustrations and printed on a xerographic matrix printer. This effort would not have succeeded without the considerable help of Michelle Sedlak, who typed and edited much of the manuscript and performed a large portion of the page layout, and of HayChan Sargent, who gave valuable assistance in the preparation of illustrations. The photographs that appear in the book were collected from many sources; among those who went to great lengths to help us were Gary Demos of Information International Inc., Mike Milochik of the University of Utah, and Louis Knapp and Ted Naanes of Evans and Sutherland Computer Corporation. Many members of the technical staff of Xerox Palo Alto Research Center provided assistance: Patrick Baudelaire developed the line-drawing illustration program, Dale Green built the printer that produced the camera-ready copy, and help was also received from Tom Hanna, Joe Maleson, Larry Tesler, Ron Pellar, Jan Murphy, Bob Taylor, and Dick Shoup. Lee Sproull helped with the Bibliography, and Karmen Newman with indexing; both were greatly supportive of this entire project.

William M. Newman
Robert F. Sproull

Palo Alto
November 1978

## Disclaimer

The use of generic masculine pronouns has been retained in text references to individuals whose gender is not otherwise established. It should be emphasized that this has been done solely for succinctness of expression and such references are intended to apply equally to men and women.

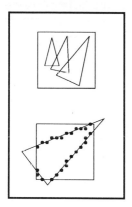

# PART ONE

## BASIC CONCEPTS

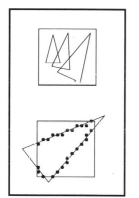

# 1

# INTRODUCTION

One of the most popular recent inventions for home use is the *video game*. One such invention, a simulated game of ping-pong, is shown in Figure 1-1; it is played by two people with a pair of levers and a home television set. When the game is switched on, a small bright spot, representing a ball, is seen bouncing to and fro across the screen. Each player uses his lever to position a "paddle" to bounce the ball back to his opponent. A player who hits the ball past his opponent wins a point; the game is won by the first player to reach 15 points.

Video games represent the first major use in the home of *computer graphics,* i.e., the creation and manipulation of pictures with the aid of a computer. Such pictures may be generated on paper or film, using a computer-controlled *plotter;* familiar examples of this form of computer graphics include the titles shown on TV and other forms of computer art (Figure 1-2). Images like these are examples of noninteractive or *passive* computer graphics; the observer has no control over the image. We can give the observer some control over the image by providing him with an input device, such as the lever of the ping-pong game, so that he can signal his requests to the computer. We then have an example of *interactive* computer graphics.

Interactive computer graphics involves two-way communication between computer and user. The computer, upon receiving signals from the input device, can modify the displayed picture appropriately. To the user it appears that the picture is changing instantaneously in response to his commands. He

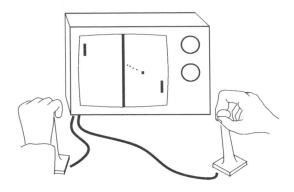

Figure 1-1 Computer graphics in the home: a video game based on ping-pong.

can give a series of commands, each one generating a graphical response from the computer. In this way he maintains a *conversation*, or *dialogue*, with the computer.

Interactive computer graphics affects our lives in a number of indirect ways; for example, it helps train the pilots of our airplanes. These pilots spend much of their training not in a real aircraft but on the ground at the controls of a *flight simulator*. The flight simulator is a mockup of an aircraft flight deck, containing all the usual controls and surrounded by screens on which are projected computer-generated views of the terrain visible on takeoff and landing. As the trainee pilot maneuvers his "aircraft," these views change so as to maintain an accurate impression of the plane's motion. A typical view is shown in the frontispiece. Flight simulators have many advantages over real aircraft for training purposes, including fuel savings, safety, and the ability to familiarize the trainee with a large number of the world's airports.

Figure 1-2 Computer-generated TV title. *Courtesy Information International, Inc.*

The electronics industry is even more dependent than the airlines on the use of interactive computer graphics. A typical integrated electronic circuit of the kind used in a computer is so complex that it would take an engineer weeks to draw by hand and an equally long time to redraw in the event of a major modification. Using an interactive graphics system, like the one shown in Figure 1-3, the engineer can draw the circuit in a much shorter time. He can then use the computer to help in checking the design and can make modifications to the design in a matter of minutes. Much of the trend toward low-cost electronic equipment can be attributed to such advances in integrated-circuit design.

These are examples of industries that have come to depend on interactive computer graphics to carry out tasks that would otherwise be prohibitively expensive to perform. Many other tasks can be made considerably easier or less expensive by the use of interactive graphics. For example, architects can explore alternative solutions to design problems at an interactive graphics terminal; in this way they can test many more solutions than would be possible without the computer. The molecular biologist can display pictures of molecules and gain insight into their structure. Town planners and transportation engineers can use computer-generated maps which display data useful to them in their planning work. Figure 1-4 shows examples of some of these applications.

The main reason for the effectiveness of interactive computer graphics in these applications is the speed with which the user of the computer can assimilate the displayed information. For example, the engineer designing an integrated circuit can see on the screen features that would never be apparent in

**Figure 1-3** Electronic circuit design using a tablet and graphics display. *Courtesy Calma Corp.*

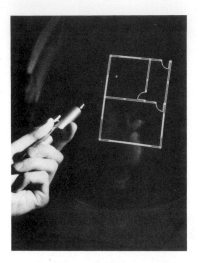
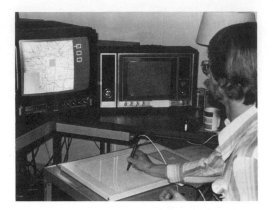

**Figure 1-4** Examples of interactive graphics applications: above, map display; left, architectural layout.

an ordinary numerical computer printout. With the ability to interact with the computer, the engineer can quickly correct a design error, and see a revised picture of the circuit. Thus interactive graphics improves the *bandwidth* of communication between the user and the computer in both directions.

## 1-1 THE ORIGINS OF COMPUTER GRAPHICS

Years of research and development have been necessary to achieve all these advances. In 1950 the first computer-driven display, attached to MIT's Whirlwind I computer, was used to generate simple pictures [166]. This display made use of a *cathode-ray tube* (CRT) similar to the one used in television sets. Several years earlier, a CRT had been used by the late F. Williams as an information storage device; this technique was to emerge years later, in the form of the storage CRT incorporated in many low-cost interactive graphic terminals (see Chapter 3).

During the 1950s, interactive computer graphics made little progress because the computers of that period were so unsuited to interactive use. These computers were "number crunchers" that performed lengthy calculations for physicists and missile designers. Only toward the end of the decade, with the development of machines like MIT's TX-0 and TX-2, did interactive computing become feasible, and interest in computer graphics then began to increase rapidly.

The single event that did most to promote interactive computer graphics as an important new field was the publication in 1962 of a brilliant thesis by Ivan E. Sutherland, who had just received his Ph.D. from MIT. This thesis, entitled *Sketchpad: A Man-Machine Graphical Communication System*, proved to many

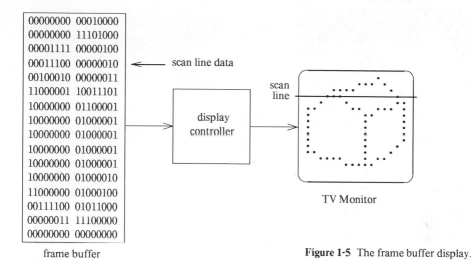

```
00000000 00010000
00000000 11101000
00001111 00000100
00011100 00000010
00100010 00000011
11000001 10011101
10000000 01100001
10000000 01000001
10000000 01000001
10000000 01000001
10000000 01000001
10000000 01000010
11000000 01000100
00111100 01011000
00000011 11100000
00000000 00000000
```

scan line data

scan line

display controller

TV Monitor

frame buffer

**Figure 1-5** The frame buffer display.

readers that interactive computer graphics was a viable, useful, and exciting field of research. By the mid-1960s, large computer-graphics research projects were underway at MIT, General Motors, Bell Telephone Laboratories, and Lockheed Aircraft; the Golden Age of computer graphics had begun.

If the 1960s represent the heady years of computer-graphics research, the 1970s have been the decade in which this research began to bear fruit. Interactive graphics displays are now in use in many countries and are widely used for educational purposes, even in elementary schools. The instant appeal of computer graphics to users of all ages has helped it to spread into many applications and will undoubtedly guarantee its continued growth in popularity.

## 1-2 HOW THE INTERACTIVE-GRAPHICS DISPLAY WORKS

The modern graphics display is extremely simple in construction. It consists of three components: a digital memory, or *frame buffer*, in which the displayed image is stored as a matrix of intensity values; a television monitor, i.e., a home TV set without the tuning and receiving electronics; and a simple interface, called the *display controller*, that passes the contents of the frame buffer to the monitor. The image must be passed repeatedly to the monitor, 30 or more times a second, in order to maintain a steady picture on the screen.

Inside the frame buffer the image is stored as a pattern of binary digital numbers, which represent a rectangular array of picture elements, or *pixels*. In the simplest case, where we wish to store only black-and-white images, we can represent black pixels by 1s in the frame buffer, and white pixels by 0s. Thus a 16 × 16 array of black and white pixels could be represented by the binary

**Figure 1-6** Raster image of a wheel, showing staircase-like quantization effects.

values stored in the 32 8-bit bytes shown in Figure 1-5 (a *byte* is an 8-bit binary unit of digital data).

The display controller simply reads each successive byte of data from the frame buffer and converts its 0s and 1s into the corresponding video signal. This signal is then fed to the TV monitor, producing a black-and-white pattern on the screen, like the wheel shown in Figure 1-6. The display controller repeats this operation 30 times a second and thus maintains a steady picture on the TV screen.

Suppose we wish to change the displayed picture. All we need do is modify the frame buffer's contents to represent the new pattern of pixels. In this way we can achieve such effects as a rotating wheel or a wheel that grows and shrinks.

We can now see how the ping-pong game might be programmed. Each of the sixteen possible positions of the right-hand paddle could be displayed by a different set of bit patterns; some of these are shown in Figure 1-7. The computer reads the position of the right-hand control lever and selects the appropriate pattern, substituting it for the right-hand column of 16 bytes in the frame buffer. It does the same for the left-hand lever and the left-hand column of the frame buffer. The position of the "ball" is computed, and the appropriate bits are set to 1 in the frame buffer. This entire process is repeated over and over again; meanwhile the display controller continues to pass the contents of the frame buffer to the TV monitor to maintain the moving picture on the screen.

## 1-3 SOME COMMON QUESTIONS

It should be pointed out, in fairness to those who have spent years of effort and millions of dollars of research money on computer graphics, that there is a great deal more to interactive graphics than the preceding example suggests. Some readers will already have questions about this example. The following are some of the more frequently asked questions about interactive graphics.

### How Do We Display Straight Lines?  How Are Curves Drawn on the Display?

The wheel picture in Figure 1-6 illustrates two of the problems in drawing curved and straight lines on a graphic display. First, we must choose which pixels should be black and which white; the choice is not always straightforward. Second, slanting lines and curves in our image will be far from smooth and will instead show unpleasant "staircase" effects.

The first problem is solved by using a procedure, or *algorithm*, that computes which pixels should be black from the equation of the line or curve. A number of such algorithms have been developed, some of which are described in the next chapter. Most of these algorithms are so simple that they can easily be implemented in hardware, leading to very fast line and curve generation.

The second problem of staircaselike *quantization* effects in the picture is much more difficult to solve. The most common solution is to use a different sort of display, called a *line-drawing display*, which plots continuous lines and curves rather than separate pixels. With a line-drawing display it is possible to draw lines that appear completely smooth to the unaided eye.

Until recently, line-drawing displays were the only widely used type of graphic display; the cost of digital memories made the frame buffer too expensive to consider. Although this situation is now changing, most computer graphics research has been oriented toward line-drawing displays; the frame buffer and its effective use are relatively unexplored topics.

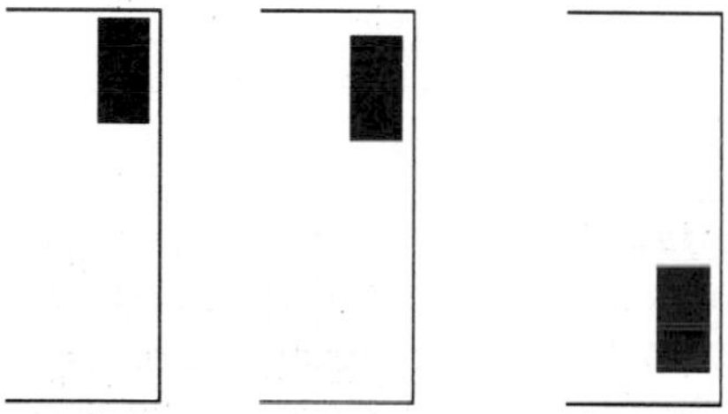

| | | |
|---|---|---|
| 00000011 | 00000000 | 00000000 |
| 00000011 | 00000011 | 00000000 |
| 00000011 | 00000011 | 00000000 |
| 00000011 | 00000011 | 00000000 |
| 00000000 | 00000011 | 00000000 |
| 00000000 | 00000000 | 00000000 |
| 00000000 | 00000000 | 00000000 |
| 00000000 | 00000000 | 00000000 |
| 00000000 | 00000000 | 00000000 |
| 00000000 | 00000000 | 00000000 |
| 00000000 | 00000000 | 00000000 |
| 00000000 | 00000000 | 00000011 |
| 00000000 | 00000000 | 00000011 |
| 00000000 | 00000000 | 00000011 |
| 00000000 | 00000000 | 00000011 |
| 00000000 | 00000000 | 00000000 |

**Figure 1-7** Frame buffer bit patterns for three of the 16 possible positions of the paddle.

### Why Is Speed So Important in Displaying Pictures?

Again there are two answers. In the first place, any display based on the CRT must be *refreshed* by repeatedly passing to it the image to be displayed. The image must be transmitted to the display point by point (or line segment by line segment, in the case of a vector display). Unless the entire image can be transmitted at least 25 times a second, it will begin to flicker in an unpleasant way. The longer it takes to transmit each element of the picture the fewer elements can be transmitted and the less information can be displayed. Early displays, like the one used by Sutherland to develop the *Sketchpad* system, could display only a few hundred dots before the onset of flicker; nowadays vector displays can show many thousands of lines flicker-free.

A second aspect to the problem of speed concerns the *response* of the computer program to actions by its user. Speed of response depends on the rate at which the computer can generate a fresh picture in response to each action by the user, and on the rate at which this picture can then be transmitted to the display. In many applications, fast response is of paramount importance. For example, if the flight-simulating computer were to respond to movements of the controls only once every few seconds, the displayed view would change sluggishly and in a noticeably jerky fashion. The trainee pilot would not get a realistic impression of flying the aircraft and might even have difficulty in maintaining control. Generally speaking, slow response always makes interactive graphics programs more difficult to operate, and this explains why so much research effort has gone into finding ways of improving the speed of interactive response.

### How Are Pictures Made to Grow, Shrink, and Rotate?

Many applications show various parts of the displayed picture changing in size and orientation. Our knowledge of how to apply such changes, or *transformations*, to pictures is based on standard mathematical techniques: coordinate geometry, trigonometry, and matrix methods. These techniques tell us how to compute the coordinates of a line segment's endpoints after scaling or rotating it. It is therefore relatively easy to apply the appropriate computation and to plot the line segment that results from the transformation. Problems arise only if the computation takes a long time; this can be prevented by using special hardware to perform the transformations.

### What Happens to Pictures That Are Too Large to Fit on the Screen?

Display screens are relatively small, and the pictures we wish to display on them are often too big to be shown in their entirety. If we were to enlarge the wheel of Figure 1-6, for example, it would no longer fit in the frame buffer. In this case, we would probably like to show as much of it as we could (Figure 1-8). A technique called *clipping* can be used to select just those parts of the picture that

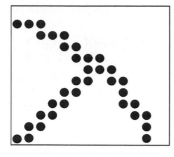

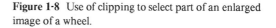

**Figure 1-8** Use of clipping to select part of an enlarged image of a wheel.

lie on the screen and to discard the rest. Clipping can be regarded as a special form of picture transformation, and is indeed often carried out by the same piece of software or hardware that performs other transformations.

### How Can the User of the Display Draw on the Screen?

The user's ability to create pictures directly on the display screen is perhaps the most irresistible aspect of interactive computer graphics. A number of different input devices—light pen, tablet, mouse—have been invented to make this kind of interaction more convenient; some of them can be seen in Figures 1-3 and 1-4. When we draw with these devices, we have the impression of making marks directly on the display screen. In fact the computer is following every movement of the input device and is changing the picture in response to these movements. It is the speed of the computer in changing the picture that creates the impression of drawing directly on the screen.

There are many more questions of an obvious nature that we could ask about computer graphics, and these too could be answered one by one. Some of the problems in computer graphics are not so obvious, however. In the chapters that follow, we shall be exploring some of these problems, discussing some of their solutions, and pointing out where these solutions are unsatisfactory. This chapter will close with short outlines of the four principal problems facing us in interactive graphics today.

### 1-4 NEW DISPLAY DEVICES

The CRT has always been the predominant display device for interactive computer graphics. For many years there was in fact no alternative. Now one or two other devices exist, but they are in many respects inferior to the CRT and have achieved only limited acceptance.

Why should we look for an alternative to the CRT? After all, the CRT is reliable, relatively inexpensive, and capable of displaying rapidly changing pictures. The main problems with the CRT as a computer display device are the very high voltages it requires, its bulkiness, and its weight. The device for which we are all searching could be powered by a 10-volt battery and would be no bulkier or heavier than a briefcase. Display devices with these attributes are just beginning to emerge from research laboratories in the United States and Japan; few of them, however, can compete with the CRT in performance and reliability. None of them solves the CRT's one other severe problem, its limited screen size.

Although we might consider this topic to be a branch of engineering rather than computer science, we cannot afford to ignore it, for it has an enormous impact on interactive computer graphics. We can see very clearly the impact of the CRT, for example, in the many articles that have been published either on ways to exploit the CRT's particular capabilities or on how to cope with its deficiencies. New display devices, as they are introduced to computer graphics, will undoubtedly have a similar impact.

## 1-5 GENERAL-PURPOSE GRAPHICS SOFTWARE

Many kinds of computer input and output are nowadays programmed in standard ways, using high-level programming languages. For example, languages like PASCAL include facilities for file input and output and for handling interactive text terminals. The ability to express such operations within a standard high-level language makes programming much easier and permits the resulting programs to be run on a wide variety of different computers. We would like our graphic application programs to be equally easy to write and equally portable. Unfortunately this is rarely the case.

We can gain ease of programming and portability of programs through the use of a *graphics package*, a set of subroutines that provides high-level access to the graphics input-output hardware. A good graphics package simplifies the programmer's task and makes it possible to write *portable* programs that can be run on different computers and with different displays. This greatly reduces the cost of writing software for graphics applications. Most such packages are *general-purpose*, allowing many different kinds of application program to be written.

The design of general-purpose graphics packages is a central issue in computer graphics. Since a package of this kind must provide a wide range of functions, its design involves almost every branch of computer graphics. In particular it involves consideration of graphic display devices and their characteristics, and this is where it becomes most difficult. As each new type of display is introduced, it creates new problems in the design of high-level graphics software. The diversity between devices makes it difficult to achieve portability in application programs. Some of the newer devices, including certain kinds of frame-buffer display, have not been in use long enough to permit the development of general-purpose programming techniques for their use. This is one of the problems that will continue to face us.

## 1-6 THE USER INTERFACE

Every interactive graphics program requires a period of training before the user can expect to operate the program proficiently. Very few are as easy to learn as the ping-pong game described earlier; instead they generally involve anything from hours to weeks of instruction and practice. During this period, the user is learning to understand the functions the program can perform, he is familiarizing himself with the various commands that invoke these functions, and he is learning to recognize the graphic representations used by the program to communicate the results of its computations. These are all aspects of the *user interface* of the program; they are the parts of the program that link the user to the computer and enable him to control it.

A good user interface makes the program not only easy to learn but also easier and more efficient to operate. Conversely, a bad user interface may make

**Figure 1-9** Computer-generated display of a simulated three-dimensional scene. *Courtesy University of Utah.*

things so difficult for the user that the program is unusable. Operating this sort of program is like trying to solve a puzzle of the kind that involves maneuvering several tiny steel balls through a maze: we try to work steadily toward our ultimate goal but keep making mistakes that cause us to lose all the ground we have gained.

When we try to use a program with a faulty user interface, it often seems as if the programmer has tried, as in the case of the puzzle, to create a bad user interface intentionally. In fact this kind of program is merely evidence of how difficult it is to design a good user interface. The programmer designing an interactive graphics program has few guiding principles upon which to base his user-interface design and even fewer ways to analyze his design and predict its performance. As we shall see in Chapter 28, we can learn a great deal from past experience, in particular from past mistakes. User-interface design, more than any other aspect of computer graphics, remains as much an art as a science.

## 1-7 THE DISPLAY OF SOLID OBJECTS

Look closely at the object shown in Figure 1-9. It appears to be a champagne glass standing on a checkerboard-patterned surface. In fact it is a computer-generated picture of an object that has never existed, except as a mathematical model stored in the computer's memory. Some extremely ingenious computational methods were employed in converting the computer-stored model into such a realistic displayed image.

The computer techniques we use to generate pictures like Figure 1-9 fall into three categories:

1.  We must model the curved surfaces of the object; this is done by splitting the surfaces into small *patches* and representing each patch by parametric equations in such a way that we can easily modify its shape.
2.  We must determine which parts of the object will be invisible, as they will be if they face away from the observer or are obscured by other parts of the object; this is called the *hidden-surface problem*, and is one of the classic problems of computer graphics.
3.  We must compute how to *shade* the visible surfaces of the object.

The technique used to shade Figure 1-9, developed at the University of Utah by the late Bui Tuong Phong, requires programming the computer to model how illuminated objects are perceived by the human eye.

Solid-object display is the most analytical branch of computer graphics and over the years has inspired some of the most original research work. The results of this research have been put to a number of uses, perhaps most effectively in the flight-simulation example described earlier. Solid-object display also has many potential uses in aircraft and automobile design, architecture, and planning. The extent to which it can be used in these applications depends on the development of faster and less expensive methods of solid-object display; this remains one of the most challenging research problems in interactive computer graphics.

## EXERCISES

**1-1** Make a list of the mechanical devices with whose user interfaces you are familiar, e.g., record players, automobiles, typewriters. How well are their user interfaces designed? How easy are they to learn? How could they be improved?

**1-2** The $16 \times 16$ display of Figure 1-5 uses a frame buffer of 32 bytes, or 256 bits of information. How many bits would be needed to produce an image on a TV screen with 525 scan lines (United States standard) or 625 lines (European standard)? To answer this question, you will need to know that the ratio of height to width of a TV screen (its *aspect ratio*) is 3:4; you should assume that the width of each dot is the same as its height.

**1-3** Examine Figure 1-9 carefully, and note any anomalies or flaws in the realism. Can you explain why they are there?

**1-4** In PASCAL, or any language of your choice, write a program that allows two people to play ping-pong using a pair of levers and a frame buffer display. You may set the contents of any pixel by means of the function *SetPixel* $(x, y, intensity)$ where *intensity* is either 0 (white) or 1 (black); also the positions of the two levers (values between 0 and 31) are constantly maintained in two locations *LeftLever* and *RightLever*. The program will need to loop continuously, reading the two lever positions, changing the positions of the paddles on the screen as described in the chapter, updating the position of the ball, and checking the ball for collision with the paddles.

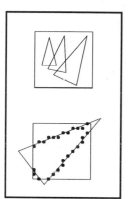

2

# POINT-PLOTTING

# TECHNIQUES

The frame-buffer display described in Chapter 1 is an example of a *point-plotting* display device. The smallest picture unit accepted by such displays is a single dot, variously termed a *point* or a *pixel*. To construct a useful picture on a point-plotting display we must build the picture out of many hundreds of pixels, each generated by a separate command from the computer. Lines and curves must be drawn with closely spaced pixels; to display a text character, i.e., a letter or a digit, we use a pattern, or *matrix*, of pixels. Figure 2-1 is an enlarged picture of lines and text characters constructed on a point-plotting display.

The very first graphical displays were of the point-plotting variety. They did not use frame buffers but were fed with a stream of point coordinates by the computer. Only a very limited number of points could be displayed in this fashion without flicker.

Point-plotting displays of this kind were made obsolete by the introduction of line-drawing displays in the mid-1960s. The line-drawing display can draw complete segments of straight lines without plotting each individual pixel on the line; it therefore has a much higher capacity than the point-plotting display for line drawings. It also does away with the need to compute the position of each pixel in the picture.

Despite the obsolescence of the original point-plotting displays, the techniques developed for programming them remain relevant today. The main

17

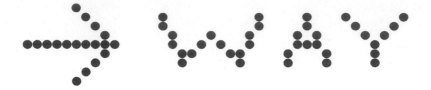

**Figure 2-1** Lines and text on a point-plotting display, enlarged to show individual pixels.

reason is that point-plotting techniques have become essential in programming frame-buffer displays, where once again the intensity of each dot must be separately computed. Point-plotting techniques also serve to introduce us to the *incremental methods* so frequently useful in computer graphics.

## 2-1 COORDINATE SYSTEMS

Point-plotting techniques are based on the use of a *cartesian coordinate system.* Points are addressed by their $x$ and $y$ coordinates; the value of $x$ increases from left to right and $y$ likewise from bottom to top (Figure 2-2).

Points are plotted in response to digital signals from the computer. This means that they cannot be positioned with infinite precision; instead we are limited by the precision of the digital values presented to the display. For example, if $x$ and $y$ are passed to the display each as a 10-bit binary number, there can be only 1024 ($= 2^{10}$) distinct $x$-coordinate values and only 1024 for $y$. The screen offers us a 1024 $\times$ 1024 array of positions, at any one of which a dot may be displayed.

What determines the precision of a display? In most cases precision is based on the *resolution* of the display screen. This is the number of visibly distinct dots that can be displayed in a given area of the screen. A typical display might have a resolution of 100 dots per inch, indicating that two dots 1/100 inch apart can just be distinguished from each other. Nothing is gained by increasing coordinate precision much beyond the resolution of the screen because the observer will not be able to tell the difference. If precision is much less than resolution, however, there will be resolvable points on the screen at which it is impossible to display a dot; this will cause visible gaps in lines. Hence when a display is designed, its coordinate precision is made approximately equal to screen resolution.

Given the coordinate precision and the size of the screen, we can arrive at the number of addressable points. A display with 100 dots per inch resolution cannot easily be built with a screen much larger than 12 inches square. Therefore most displays allow no more than 1200 points to be addressed in each direction. The value 1024 is popular, as it makes full use of ten-bit integer coordinates, but displays have been built with as many as 4096 $\times$ 4096 addressable points and with as few as 256 $\times$ 256.

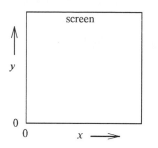

**Figure 2-2** The cartesian screen coordinate system.

To summarize, most interactive computer displays marketed today use a cartesian coordinate system, with 10 bits of $x$ and $y$ coordinate precision; display screens generally measure about 10 inches (30 centimeters) square. The practice of using integer coordinate values and of placing the origin at the lower left-hand corner of the screen, as shown in Figure 2-2, is fairly common; alternative coordinate systems are discussed in Chapter 5 in the context of viewing transformations.

## 2-2 INCREMENTAL METHODS

The newcomer to a city often finds his way about by an incremental method. If he is at 203 Main Street and is looking for number 735, he gets there by finding the house with a number greater than 203; this might be house number 205. Having found number 205, he proceeds in the same direction past number 207, and so on until the house number reaches 735. The use of house numbers and the arrangement of houses in numerical order make it much easier for him to find his way. If instead he were in Tokyo, where houses are numbered according to their date of construction, the simple incremental method would not work. Incremental methods are frequently used in computer graphics, where again they tend to simplify things. Later in this book we shall see how the introduction of incremental techniques has simplified both scan conversion and the shading of computer-generated pictures of solid objects. It is appropriate to begin our study of incremental methods in this chapter, as these methods are useful in generating lines on point-plotting displays.

Incremental computing techniques are a form of iterative computation, in which each iterative step is simplified by maintaining a small amount of *state*, or memory, about the progress of the computation. The visitor looking for house number 735 needs only three pieces of state information: the direction in which he is going, the number of the house he has just passed, and the number of the house he is looking for. If he reaches a house whose number lies outside the range of these two house numbers, his algorithm tells him to reverse direction. This algorithm, shown in the following PASCAL program, is an example of a simple incremental method.

$\Delta x$

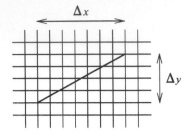

$\Delta y$

**Figure 2-3** A straight line segment connecting two grid intersections may fail to pass through any other grid intersections.

```
procedure FindHouse(houserequired: integer);
    var housepassed, t, direction: integer;
begin
    direction := 1;
    housepassed := ReadHouseNumber;
    while housepassed <> houserequired do begin
        MoveToNextHouse(direction);
        t := ReadHouseNumber;
        if (t > Max(housepassed, houserequired)) or
        (t < Min(housepassed, houserequired)) then
            direction := − direction;
        housepassed := t
    end
end;
```

Incremental methods come into their own when not only the final result but the intermediate results are of use. When we plot lines incrementally, we start at one end and finish by computing the coordinates of the other end; in between, the incremental technique generates the coordinates of all the dots that lie on the line. Thus one iterative process generates many useful results.

## 2-3 LINE-DRAWING ALGORITHMS

Straight-line segments are used a great deal in computer-generated pictures. They occur in block diagrams, bar charts and graphs, civil and mechanical engineering drawings, logic schematics, and architectural plans, to name a few

**Figure 2-4** Output from a poor line-generating algorithm.

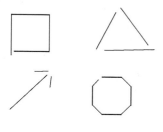

**Figure 2-5** Symbols drawn with lines that fail to connect accurately.

examples of commonly displayed pictures. Furthermore, curves can be approximated quite effectively by sequences of short straight-line segments. Since straight lines are so useful, it is worth taking care that they are well drawn.

What are the things a good line-drawing algorithm should do well? To answer this question, we should consider the skills a draftsman must develop in order to draw well. He must learn to make his lines straight, to ensure that they start and finish in exactly the right places, to maintain constant blackness, or *density*, along the length of each line, and to make sure that lines have matching density where appropriate. Given time, he will also learn to draw lines quickly.

Exactly the same criteria apply to computer-generated lines:

*Lines should appear straight.* Point-plotting techniques are admirably suited to the generation of lines parallel or at 45° to the *x* and *y* axes. Other lines cause a problem: a line segment, though it starts and finishes at addressable points, may happen to pass through no other addressable points in between. Figure 2-3 shows such a line. In these cases we must approximate the line by choosing addressable points close to it. If we choose well, the line will appear straight; if not, we shall produce crooked lines, as in Figure 2-4.

*Lines should terminate accurately.* Unless lines are plotted accurately, they may terminate at the wrong place. The effect is often seen as a small gap between the endpoint of one line and the starting point of the next or as a cumulative error (Figure 2-5).

*Lines should have constant density.* With bright lines plotted on a dark background, line density is observed as brightness; when the line is black and the background light, it is seen as blackness. In either case, line density is proportional to the number of dots displayed divided by the length of the line. To maintain constant density, dots should be equally spaced. This can

**Figure 2-6** Uneven line density caused by bunching of dots.

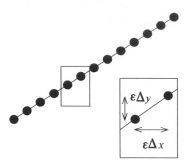

**Figure 2-7** Ideal incremental method for line generation.

be achieved only in lines parallel or at 45° to the axes. In other cases, we must attempt to achieve as even spacing as possible; bunching of dots will otherwise be visible as particularly bright or dark regions on the line (see the example of Figure 2-6).

*Line density should be independent of line length and angle.* This is a difficult requirement to satisfy. As we have just seen, to achieve constant line density we must maintain a constant number of dots per unit length. Before plotting the line we must therefore determine its exact length, which involves computing a square root. Also we must be able to control the rate, in terms of distance traveled, at which dots are plotted. Neither of these is easily done. Normally the best we can do is to compute an approximate *line-length estimate* and to use a line-generation algorithm that keeps line density constant to within the accuracy of this estimate.

*Lines should be drawn rapidly.* In interactive applications we would like lines to appear rapidly on the screen. This implies using the minimum of computation to draw the line; ideally, this computation should be performed by special-purpose hardware.

Since the line-generation methods described below are all incremental, they share certain features. In particular, each method basically generates two sets of signals; these signals step the $x$ and $y$ coordinates of the point that traces out the line. Thus to draw a vertical line we would issue only $y$ signals, and to draw a line at 45° we would issue $x$ and $y$ signals at an equal rate. For any given line, each of the following methods generates the same total number of $x$ signals and $y$ signals, since these signal totals must sum to the magnitudes of $\Delta x$ and $\Delta y$, the displacements in $x$ and $y$ of the finishing point of the line from its starting point (see Figure 2-3). The methods differ only in the order in which the signals are issued and in how they are generated.

**The Symmetrical DDA**

The digital differential analyzer (DDA) generates lines from their differential equations. As we shall see later in this chapter, we can build DDAs to draw curves as well as straight lines provided these curves can be defined by ordinary differential equations. The equation of a straight line is particularly simple:

$$\frac{dy}{dx} = \Delta y / \Delta x \qquad (2\text{-}1)$$

The line-generating DDA is correspondingly straightforward.

The DDA works on the principle that we simultaneously increment $x$ and $y$ by small steps proportional to the first derivatives of $x$ and $y$. In the case of a straight line the first derivatives are constant and are proportional to $\Delta x$ and $\Delta y$. Thus in the ideal case of an infinite-precision display we could generate a line by incrementing $x$ and $y$ by $\varepsilon \Delta x$ and $\varepsilon \Delta y$, where $\varepsilon$ is some small quantity (see Figure 2-7).

In the real world of limited-precision displays we must generate only addressable points. This can be done by rounding to the nearest integer after each incremental step; after rounding we display a dot at the resultant $x$ and $y$.

An alternative to rounding is the use of arithmetic overflow: $x$ and $y$ are kept in registers that have two parts, integer and fractional. The incrementing values, which are both less than unity, are repeatedly added to the fractional parts, and whenever the result overflows, the corresponding integer part is incremented. The integer parts of the $x$ and $y$ registers are used in plotting the line. This would normally have the effect of *truncating* rather than rounding, so we initialize the DDA with the value 0.5 in each of the fractional parts to achieve true rounding.

One advantage of this arrangement is that it allows us to detect changes in $x$ and $y$ and hence to avoid plotting the same point twice. The overflow indicator generated by the DDA produce the signals we need to reposition the point that traces out the line. Note that the precision of the incrementing values and of the fractional parts of the registers must be no less than the coordinate precision of the display; otherwise accuracy will be lost on long lines.

The appearance of lines generated by the DDA depends on the value chosen for $\varepsilon$. In the case of the *symmetrical DDA* we choose $\varepsilon = 2^{-n}$, where

$$2^{n-1} \leq \max(|\Delta x|, |\Delta y|) < 2^n \qquad (2\text{-}2)$$

In fact $\varepsilon$ is the reciprocal of the DDA's line-length estimate, in this case $2^n$. A line drawn with the symmetrical DDA is illustrated in Figure 2-8; the organization of a symmetrical DDA is shown in Figure 2-9.

The symmetrical DDA generates accurate lines, since the displacement of a displayed dot from the true line is never greater than one-half a screen unit. Logically the symmetrical DDA is simple; the use of a negative power of 2 for $\varepsilon$ means that the incrementing values can be determined by shifting the $\Delta x$ and $\Delta y$ registers rather than by a division. Each step in the line is computed with just two additions.

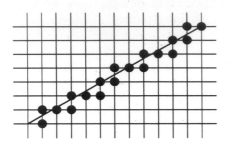

**Figure 2-8** Line drawn with a symmetrical DDA.

### The Simple DDA

The symmetrical DDA uses a power of 2 as a line-length estimate, since this simplifies the logic. The principle of the DDA tells us, however, that we may use any line-length estimate and any corresponding value of $\varepsilon$ provided neither $\varepsilon \Delta x$ nor $\varepsilon \Delta y$ exceeds unit magnitude.

For the *simple DDA* we choose a line-length estimate equal to the larger of the magnitudes of $\Delta x$ and $\Delta y$, so that either $\varepsilon \Delta x$ or $\varepsilon \Delta y$ is of unit magnitude. This allows us to replace one of the DDA's adders with a simple counter. The simple DDA therefore generates unit steps in the direction of greatest motion; Figure 2-10 shows an example. A PASCAL implementation of the simple DDA is as follows:

```
procedure DDA (x1, y1, x2, y2: integer);
    var length, i: integer; x, y, xincrement, yincrement: real;
begin
    length := abs(x2 − x1);
    if abs(y2 − y1) > length then length := abs(y2 − y1);
    xincrement := (x2 − x1)/length;
    yincrement := (y2 − y1)/length;
    x := x1 + 0.5; y := y1 + 0.5;
    for i := 1 to length do
```

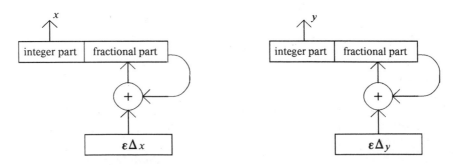

**Figure 2-9** Arrangement of the symmetrical DDA.

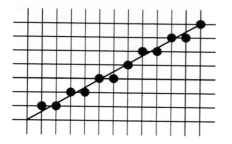

Figure 2-10 Line drawn with a simple DDA.

```
        begin
        Plot(trunc(x), trunc(y));
        x := x + xincrement;
        y := y + yincrement
        end
end;
```

The simple DDA is as accurate as its symmetrical counterpart but generates a different sequence of dots because of its different method of estimating line length. Logically it is simpler, except for the need to perform an initial division to determine the incrementing value. The simple DDA is an ideal basis for a software line generator, but the need for division logic makes it less suited to hardware implementation.

### Bresenham's Algorithm

An interesting line-drawing algorithm has been developed by Bresenham [73]. Like the simple DDA, it is designed so that each iteration changes one of the coordinate values by ±1. The other coordinate may or may not change, depending on the value of an error term maintained by the algorithm. This error term records the distance, measured perpendicular to the axis of greatest movement, between the exact path of the line and the actual dots generated. In

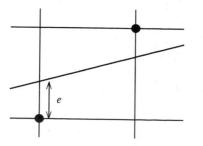

Figure 2-11 Bresenham's algorithm: error term $e$ measures distance between path of line and dots generated.

the example of Figure 2-11, where the $x$ axis is the axis of greatest movement, the error term $e$ is shown measured parallel to the $y$ axis. The following description of the algorithm assumes this particular orientation of the line.

At each iteration of the algorithm the slope of the line, $\Delta y/\Delta x$, is added to the error term $e$. Before this is done, the sign of $e$ is used to determine whether to increment the $y$ coordinate of the current point. A positive $e$ value indicates that the exact path of the line lies above the current point; therefore the $y$ coordinate is incremented, and 1 is subtracted from $e$. If $e$ is negative the $y$ coordinate value is left unchanged. Thus the basic algorithm is expressed by the following PASCAL program:

```
{ Note: e is real; x, y, deltax, deltay are integers }
e := (deltay/deltax) − 0.5;
for i := 1 to deltax do begin
    Plot(x, y);
    if e > 0 then begin
        y := y + 1;
        e := e − 1
        end;
    x := x + 1;
    e := e + (deltay/deltax)
end;
```

The weakness of this sequence of operations lies in the division required to compute the initial value and increment of $e$. This division can be avoided, however, since the algorithm is unaffected by multiplying $e$ by a constant: only the sign of $e$ is tested. Thus by multiplying $e$ by $2\Delta x$ we produce the following program, requiring neither divisions nor multiplications:

```
{ Note: all variables are integers }
e := 2 * deltay − deltax;
for i := 1 to deltax do begin
    Plot(x, y);
    if e > 0 then begin
        y := y + 1;
        e := e +(2 * deltay − 2 * deltax)
        end
        else e := e + 2 * deltay;
    x := x + 1
end;
```

A full implementation of Bresenham's algorithm involves allowing for other cases besides $0 \le \Delta y \le \Delta x$, the case discussed above. At the same time the algorithm can be somewhat simplified by using only integer arithmetic. Like the simple DDA, Bresenham's algorithm avoids generating duplicate points. Because it also avoids multiplications and divisions, it is well suited to implementation in hardware or on simple microprocessors.

## 2-4 CIRCLE GENERATORS

In certain classes of application, particularly those involving the display of mechanical engineering parts, circles and circular arcs are frequently displayed. A number of incremental methods have been invented to plot circles and arcs. These methods are valuable because most displays, although they have hardware for line generation, have none for circle drawing. Where line-generation hardware exists, incremental circle generators can be used to compute the endpoints of consecutive short line segments; where it does not, circle generators are capable of generating closely spaced dots, suitable for point-plotting displays. We shall discuss one circle-generation method, a variant of the DDA; other methods are adequately referenced in the Bibliography [72, 112, 373].

### The Circle-generating DDA

As we saw earlier, the principle of the DDA can be extended to other curves; one such curve is the circular arc. The differential equation of a circle with center at the origin can be written

$$\frac{dy}{dx} = -x/y \tag{2-3}$$

This suggests that we can implement a circle-plotting DDA by using $\varepsilon x$ and $\varepsilon y$ as incrementing values

$$x_{n+1} = x_n + \varepsilon y_n$$
$$y_{n+1} = y_n - \varepsilon x_n \tag{2-4}$$

This involves computing the incrementing values afresh at each step, but the computation can be reduced to a pair of shifts and a complement operation if $\varepsilon$ is chosen to be a negative power of 2; to prevent the spacing of consecutive points from exceeding one screen unit, $\varepsilon$ should equal $2^{-n}$, where

$$2^{n-1} \leq r < 2^n \tag{2-5}$$

$r$ being the radius of the circle.

Unfortunately the method just described plots a spiral, not a circular arc. Each step is made in a direction perpendicular to a radius of the circle; each point is therefore slightly farther from the center than the one before. This problem is easily solved, however, by using $x_{n+1}$ rather than $x_n$ to compute $y_{n+1}$:

$$\begin{aligned} x_{n+1} &= x_n + \varepsilon y_n \\ y_{n+1} &= y_n - \varepsilon x_{n+1} \end{aligned} \qquad (2\text{-}6)$$

This solution is based on the following reasoning: Equations 2-4 can be written in matrix form as

$$[\,x_{n+1} \quad y_{n+1}\,] = [\,x_n \quad y_n\,] \begin{bmatrix} 1 & -\varepsilon \\ \varepsilon & 1 \end{bmatrix} \qquad (2\text{-}7)$$

The determinant of the matrix on the right does not equal unity but $1 + \varepsilon^2$; this implies that the curve will spiral out. If the determinant can be reduced to unity, the curve will close. We achieve this effect by modifying the matrix as follows:

$$[\,x_{n+1} \quad y_{n+1}\,] = [\,x_n \quad y_n\,] \begin{bmatrix} 1 & -\varepsilon \\ \varepsilon & 1 - \varepsilon^2 \end{bmatrix} \qquad (2\text{-}8)$$

This is easily reduced to Equations 2-6.

Circles drawn by the DDA need not be centered on the origin, as they must for Equations 2-6 to hold. Instead the displacements in $x$ and $y$ from the circle's center of the point $(x_n, y_n)$ are used in determining $(x_{n+1}, y_{n+1})$. This algorithm is well suited to hardware implementation.

The reader will probably already have discovered that Equations 2-6 generate points on an ellipse, not on a circle. The eccentricity of the resulting curves may be quite noticeable when $\varepsilon$ is relatively large. Provided $\varepsilon$ is kept small, this effect is negligible, but the use of very small $\varepsilon$ values increases the computation considerably.

It is feasible to construct a DDA that draws an exact circle, using the equations

$$\begin{aligned} x_{n+1} &= x_n \cos\theta + y_n \sin\theta \\ y_{n+1} &= y_n \cos\theta - x_n \sin\theta \end{aligned} \qquad (2\text{-}9)$$

Since $\theta$ is generally small, values of $\cos\theta$ and $\sin\theta$ are relatively easy to compute and are then constant for any particular circle radius. This pair of equations can therefore be used to advantage if multiplications can be performed inexpensively. Cohen has extended this approach to the display of general conics [112].

Several other circle-generating methods have been extended to plot a wider class of curves [373, 317, 251]. These methods may be useful in specific cases, but they lack the generality and the power of some of the more recently developed curve generation methods described in Chapter 21.

# EXERCISES

**2-1** This chapter has hinted at other encoding schemes for cartesian coordinates besides positive binary integers. Without reading Chapter 5, can you suggest what some of these schemes might be and why they are not used? As a hint, consider in turn alternatives to the three words in the phrase *positive binary integer.*

**2-2** One well-known application of CRT displays uses a polar rather than cartesian coordinate system. In polar coordinates, points are addressed by the length and angle of a radius drawn to the point from a fixed origin. What is this well-known application, and why are polar coordinates used? What would be the disadvantages of a polar coordinate display for general applications, such as the ones described in Chapter 1?

**2-3** As we have seen, displays generally have a precision of about 100 dots per inch. Try to measure the precision of other graphical media, such as a TV screen, a newspaper photograph, a half-tone illustration in this book, or a glossy photographic print. Compare them with the 100 dots per inch figure. What do your results suggest about applications of interactive computer graphics?

**2-4** We can easily compute the density of points for the simple DDA with unit increment as the number of points plotted divided by the line's true length. Write down expressions for this density $d$ in terms of $s$, the slope of the line. Find the values of $s$ giving minimum and maximum density. Repeat for the symmetric DDA.

**2-5** Some of the line-generating algorithms described above will not draw 45° lines properly. Why? Can you suggest modifications that will correct this flaw?

**2-6** If a line is drawn from (0, 0) to (10, 5) with a symmetrical DDA, how many iterations are performed? How many distinct points are displayed? How many points did the DDA generate twice in succession? Will the same point ever be generated three times in succession? How does the initial line-length estimate affect the answers to these questions?

**2-7** Sketch the design of a hardware circular-arc generator based on Equations 2-6 to the same level of detail as the symmetrical DDA shown in Figure 2-9.

**2-8** Suppose you are using a display that has hardware for line generation but cannot draw lines of full screen width; instead lines are limited to a maximum of 31 units movement in $x$ and $y$. Design a routine based on the DDA capable of plotting lines of any length.

**2-9** Find expressions for the line-length estimates employed by (a) the symmetrical DDA, (b) the simple DDA. Suggest other line-length estimates that are simple to compute and more accurate than the DDA estimates.

**2-10** In section 2-3 we noted that line density is proportional to the number of dots displayed divided by the line length. What do we mean by "the number of dots displayed" in the case of (a) a bright line on a dark background, (b) a dark line on a bright background? What does this suggest about the applicability of the various line generators to drawing the two types of line?

**2-11** Explain the initial value of $e$ in Bresenham's algorithm. Does the algorithm generate the same points as the simple DDA?

**2-12** Suppose you are to construct from hardware a symmetrical DDA to plot points on a display screen whose coordinate system runs from 0 to 1023 in each direction. How many bits should be allocated to the integer and fractional parts shown in Figure 2-9? How many bits of adder will be required?

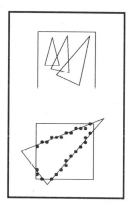

3

# LINE-DRAWING

# DISPLAYS

Computer-generated pictures may be divided into two classes, line drawings and continuous-tone images. Examples of each are shown in Figure 3-1, and others were shown in Chapter 1. Not only are these two classes of image very different in appearance, but they require very different techniques for their generation. Line drawings are in most respects easier to create because the algorithms for their generation are simpler, the amount of information required to represent them is less, and they can be displayed on equipment which (at least until very recently) has been more readily available. Continuous-tone images in fact could not be displayed at all until the advent in the late 1960s of the frame-buffer display, and algorithms for generating these images are still being developed. Since the display of line drawings is so much better understood, it forms a more appropriate focus for the first half of this book.

The frame-buffer display which we encountered in Chapter 1 is of course capable of displaying lines. Using one of the incremental methods described in Chapter 2 we can compute which pixels are intersected by a line segment, and can change the contents of the corresponding memory location in the frame buffer. This is a very practical way of displaying line drawings; in fact the line illustrations in this book were all prepared by drawing them on an interactive frame-buffer display. Nevertheless the frame buffer has some shortcomings: it cannot display very smooth lines, since the quantization effects on the screen are almost always noticeable; and it is unsuited to highly interactive image

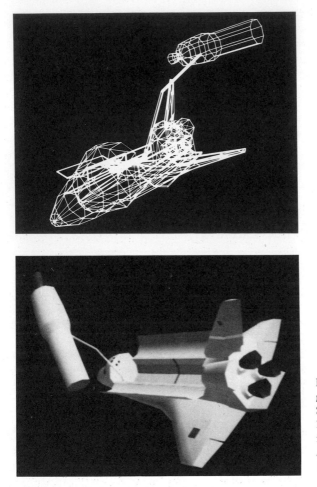

**Figure 3-1** Two computer-generated views of the Space Shuttle: above, a line drawing; left, a shaded, continuous-tone image. *Courtesy Evans and Sutherland Computer Corporation.*

manipulations. To avoid these problems we must use displays that have been designed expressly to draw striaght lines. A number of such displays are discussed in this chapter.

## 3-1 DISPLAY DEVICES AND CONTROLLERS

Two items of display hardware on which we shall focus our discussion are the *display device* and the *display controller*. The purpose of the display device is to convert electrical signals into visible images. The display controller sits between the computer and the display device, receiving information from the computer and converting it into signals acceptable to the device. Tasks performed by the display controller include voltage-level conversion between the computer and the display device, buffering to compensate for differences in speed of operation, and generation of line segments and text characters.

The display controller thus has the overall task of compensating for any idiosyncratic features or limitations that the display device may possess, so as to provide the computer, and its programmer, with a reasonably straightforward interface to the device. This is the original task for which the display controller was invented. Many display controllers are nowadays furnished with additional hardware to perform functions such as scaling and rotation that would otherwise be carried out by software; the purpose of this hardware is generally to improve speed of response. Chapters 19 and 26 will discuss various advanced forms of display controller. This chapter will concentrate on display devices and simple line-drawing display controllers.

## 3-2 DISPLAY DEVICES

In most applications of computer graphics the quality of the displayed image is very important. It is therefore not surprising that a great deal of effort has been directed toward the development of high-quality computer-display devices. When this work began in the 1950s, the CRT was the only available device capable of converting the computer's electrical signals into visible images at high speeds. In those days CRTs were small, dim, and rather expensive. Over the years, however, CRT technology has produced a range of extremely effective computer-display devices. At the same time the CRT's peculiar characteristics have had a significant influence on the development of interactive computer graphics. We shall see signs of this influence many times in the chapters that follow.

Along with the continuing development of the CRT there has been an intensive search for alternatives. This has led to the development of a number of new techniques for converting electrical signals into images. Many of the resulting new devices have been inspired by the needs of the alphanumeric display and television industries; nevertheless most of the new displays are applicable to computer graphics. None of them, however, has been able to displace the CRT as the dominant graphic display device.

## 3-3 THE CRT

The basic arrangement of the CRT is shown in Figure 3-2. At the narrow end of a sealed conical glass tube is an *electron gun* that emits a high-velocity, finely focused beam of electrons. The other end, the face of the CRT, is more or less flat and is coated on the inside with *phosphor*, which glows when the electron beam strikes it. The energy of the beam can be controlled so as to vary the intensity of light output and, when necessary, to cut off the light altogether. A

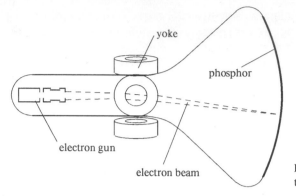

**Figure 3-2**  The basic construction of the CRT.

*yoke*, or system of electromagnetic coils, is mounted on the outside of the tube at the base of the neck; it deflects the electron beam to different parts of the tube face when currents pass through the coils. The light output of the CRT's phosphor falls off rapidly after the electron beam has passed by, and a steady picture is maintained by tracing it out rapidly and repeatedly; generally this *refresh* process is performed at least 30 times a second.

**The Electron Gun**

The electron gun makes use of *electrostatic fields* to focus and accelerate the electron beam. A field is generated when two surfaces are raised to different potentials (voltage levels); electrons within the field tend to travel toward the surface with the more positive potential. The force attracting the electron is directly proportional to the field potential.

The purpose of the electron gun in the CRT is to produce an electron beam with the following properties:

1.  It must be accurately focused so that it produces a sharp spot of light where it strikes the phosphor;
2.  It must have high velocity, since the brightness of the image depends on the velocity of the electron beam;
3.  Means must be provided to control the flow of electrons so that the intensity of the trace of the beam can be controlled.

The electron gun therefore contains a number of separate parts, shown in Figure 3-3. Electrons are generated by a *cathode* heated by an electric filament. Surrounding the cathode is a cylindrical metal *control grid*, with a hole at one end that allows electrons to escape. The control grid is kept at a lower potential than the cathode, creating an electrostatic field that directs the electrons through a point source; this simplifies the subsequent focusing process. By altering the control-grid potential, we can modify the rate of flow of electrons, or *beam*

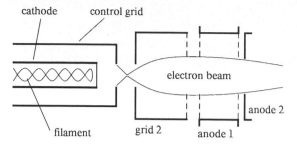

cathode    control grid

electron beam

filament    grid 2    anode 1    anode 2

**Figure 3-3** The electron gun of the CRT.

*current,* and can thus control the brightness of the image; we can even cut off the flow of electrons altogether.

Focusing is achieved by a *focusing structure* containing two or more cylindrical metal plates at different potentials. These set up a toroidal electrostatic field that effectively catches straying electrons and deflects them back toward the axis of the beam. The result is a beam that is extremely finely focused and highly concentrated at the precise moment at which it strikes the phosphor. An *accelerating structure* is generally combined with the focusing structure. It consists of two metal plates mounted perpendicular to the beam axis with holes at their centers through which the beam can pass. The two plates are maintained at a sufficiently high relative potential to accelerate the beam to the necessary velocity; accelerating potentials of several thousand volts are not uncommon.

The resulting electron-gun structure has the advantage that it can be built as a single physical unit and mounted inside the CRT envelope. Other types of gun exist, whose focusing is performed by a coil mounted outside the tube; this is called *electromagnetic focusing* to distinguish it from the more common electrostatic method described in the preceding paragraph. The electro-magnetic technique can result in finer focusing, but the electrostatic method is generally prefered in graphic displays because it leads to a cheaper gun construction.

## The Deflection System

A set of coils, or *yoke,* mounted at the neck of the tube, forms part of the deflection system responsible for addressing in the CRT. Two pairs of coils are used, one to control horizontal deflection, the other vertical. A primary requirement of the deflection system is that it deflect rapidly, since speed of deflection determines how much information can be displayed without flicker. To achieve fast deflection, we must use large-amplitude currents in the yoke. An important part of the deflection system is therefore the set of *amplifiers* that convert the small voltages received from the display controller into currents of the appropriate magnitude.

The voltages used for deflection are generated by the display controller from digital values provided by the computer. These values normally represent coordinates that are converted into voltages by *digital-to-analog* (D/A) *conversion* [136]. To draw a vector a pair of gradually changing voltages must be generated for the horizontal and vertical deflection coils. Several methods have been used, including the following:

1. *Integrators.* An integrator is a circuit which, if provided with a constant voltage input, generates a linearly increasing or decreasing voltage as output. Thus if the $\Delta x$ and $\Delta y$ values defining a vector are converted into voltages and used as inputs to a pair of integrators, the appropriate deflection signals will be generated.
2. *Digital methods.* A fast digital vector generator, such as a DDA, can be constructed from hardware and used together with a pair of D/A converters. Every time a fresh $x$ or $y$ coordinate is generated, the coordinate value is converted to a deflection voltage, and a dot is displayed.

These and other vector-generation techniques are described in references in the Bibliography [132, 136, 433].

### Phosphors

The phosphors used in a graphic display are normally chosen for their color characteristics and persistence. Ideally the persistence, measured as the time for the brightness to drop to one-tenth of its initial value, should last about 100 milliseconds or less, allowing refresh at 30-hertz rates without noticeable smearing as the image moves. Color should preferably be white, particularly for applications where dark information appears on a light background. The phosphor should also possess a number of other attributes: small grain size for added resolution, high efficiency in terms of electric energy converted to light, and resistance to burning under prolonged excitation.

In attempts to improve performance in one or another of these respects, many different phosphors have been produced, using various compounds of calcium, cadmium, and zinc, together with traces of rare-earth elements. These phosphors are identified by a numbering system, using names like P1, P4, P7, etc. The most popular phosphors for graphic displays are P7, a fairly long-persistence blue phosphor that leaves a green afterglow, and P31, which is green and has a much shorter persistence. Black-and-white television tubes generally use P4, a white phosphor with about the same persistence as P31. Phosphors with much longer persistence than any of these do exist but are rarely used because of smearing problems.

### The Beam-Penetration CRT

The normal CRT can generate images of only a single color, due to the limitations of its phosphor. A color CRT device for line-drawing displays has been developed, however; it uses a multilayer phosphor and achieves color control by modulating a normally constant parameter, namely the beam-accelerating potential.

The arrangement of the beam-penetration CRT is similar to that of normal CRTs; the only unusual component is the multilayer phosphor, in which a layer of red phosphor is deposited behind the initial layer of green phosphor. If a fairly low-potential electron beam strikes the tube face, it excites only the red phosphor and therefore produces a red trace. When the accelerating potential is increased, the velocity of the beam striking the phosphor is greater, and as a result the beam penetrates into the green phosphor, increasing the green component of the light output. A limited range of colors, including red, orange, yellow and green, can be generated in this way.

The principal problem with the beam-penetration CRT is the need to change the beam-accelerating potential by significant amounts in order to switch colors. When the accelerating potential changes, the deflection system must react to compensate. The hardware or software must be designed to introduce adequate delays between changes in color, so that there is time for voltages to settle. In order to prevent frequent delays and consequent flicker, it is necessary to display all the red elements of the picture consecutively, then change the accelerating potential and display the yellow elements, and so on through all the different colors.

## The Shadow-Mask CRT

The shadow-mask color CRT can display a much wider range of colors than the beam penetration CRT, and is used in the majority of color TV sets and monitors. Its construction is shown in Figure 3-4. Just behind the phosphor-coated face of the CRT is a metal plate, the *shadow mask*, pierced with small round holes in a triangular pattern. In place of the usual single electron gun, the shadow-mask tube uses three guns, grouped in a triangle or *delta*. These three guns are responsible for the red, green, and blue components of the light output of the CRT.

The deflection system of the CRT operates on all three electron beams simultaneously, bringing all three to the same point of focus on the shadow mask. Where the three beams encounter holes in the mask, they pass through and strike the phosphor. Since they originate at three different points, however, they strike the phosphor in three slightly different spots. The phosphor of the shadow-mask tube is therefore laid down very carefully in groups of three spots—one red, one green, and one blue—under each hole in the mask, in such a way that each spot is struck only by electrons from the appropriate gun. The effect of the mask is thus to "shadow" the spots of red phosphor from all but the red beam, and likewise for the green and blue phosphor spots. We can therefore control the light output in each of the three component colors by modulating the beam current of the corresponding gun.

Great improvements have been made in the performance of the shadow-mask tube since it was first demonstrated by RCA in 1950. Nevertheless it has

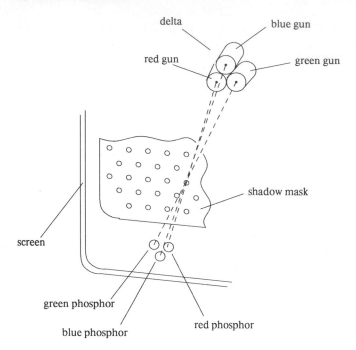

**Figure 3-4** The shadow-mask CRT.

remained relatively expensive compared with the monochrome CRT, and still has a relatively poor performance in all respects except color range. The shadow-mask CRT compares particularly unfavorably in resolution and in efficiency of light output. Both these effects are caused by the use of the shadow mask: the grain of the triangular pattern of holes sets a limit on attainable resolution, and the mask tends to block a large proportion of the available beam energy, reducing the total brightness. With the use of very high accelerating potentials it is, however, possible to match the brightness of monochrome CRT images.

A further, unique problem with the shadow-mask tube is that of *convergence*. It is extremely difficult to adjust the three guns and the deflection system so that the electron beams are deflected exactly together, all three converging on the same hole in the shadow mask. Where they fail to converge, the three component colors appear to spread in a manner reminiscent of a poorly-aligned color printing process. Often it is possible to achieve adequate convergence over only a limited area of the screen.

The convergence problem, together with the relatively poor resolution and light output of the shadow-mask CRT, have tended to discourage its use in line-drawing displays. It is, however, a very popular device for use with a frame buffer, as we shall see in Chapter 19.

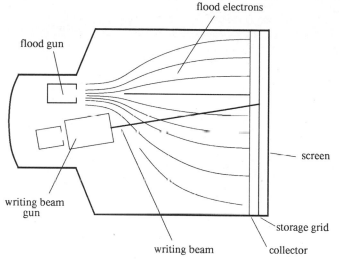

**Figure 3-5** The direct-view storage tube.

## 3-4 INHERENT-MEMORY DEVICES

Refresh line-drawing displays based on the CRT have the disadvantages of high cost and tendency to flicker when the displayed picture is complex. These two problems have led to the development of display devices with inherent image storage capability. The most widely used of these devices is the *direct-view storage tube* (DVST); others include the plasma panel and the laser-scan display.

### The Direct-view Storage Tube

Outwardly the DVST behaves like a CRT with an extremely long-persistence phosphor. A line written on the screen will remain visible for up to an hour before it fades from sight. Inwardly, too, the DVST resembles the CRT, since it uses a similar electron gun and a somewhat similar phosphor-coated screen. The beam is designed not to write directly on the phosphor, however, but on a fine-mesh wire grid, coated with dielectric and mounted just behind the screen. A pattern of positive charge is deposited on the grid, and this pattern is transferred to the phosphor by a continuous flood of electrons issuing from a separate *flood gun.* The general arrangement of the DVST is shown in detail in Figure 3-5.

Just behind the storage mesh is a second grid, the *collector*, whose main purpose is to smooth out the flow of flood electrons. These electrons pass through the collector at a low velocity, and are attracted to the positively charged portions of the storage mesh but repelled by the rest. Electrons not

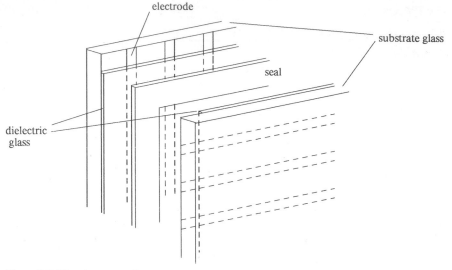

**Figure 3-6** The plasma panel.

repelled by the storage mesh pass right through it and strike the phosphor. In order to increase the energy of these relatively slow-moving electrons and thus create a bright picture, the screen is maintained at a high positive potential by means of a voltage applied to a thin aluminum coating between the tube face and the phosphor.

Until they pass through the mesh, the flood electrons are still moving fairly slowly and therefore hardly affect the charge on the mesh. One of the problems with the DVST is in fact the difficulty in removing the stored charge to erase the picture. The normal erasing method is to apply a positive voltage to the storage mesh for one second or more; this removes all the charge but also generates a rather unpleasant flash over the entire screen surface. This erase problem is perhaps the most severe drawback of the DVST, for it prevents the use of the device for dynamic graphics applications. Other problems are its relatively poor contrast, a result of the comparatively low accelerating potential applied to the flood electrons, and the gradual degradation of the picture quality as background glow accumulates; this glow is caused by the small amounts of charge deposited on the mesh by repelled flood electrons.

In terms of performance, the DVST is somewhat inferior to the refresh CRT. Only a single level of line intensity can be displayed, and only green-phosphor tubes are available. Until recently, the DVST used relatively small-screen tubes; now tubes with 19-inch and 25-inch diagonals are available. The smaller DVSTs have the advantage of a flat screen, not present in the larger variety. Some storage-tube displays possess the capability to refresh a limited number of vectors.

## The Plasma Panel

The plasma panel is an unorthodox display device. Images can be written onto the display surface point-by-point; each point remains bright after it has been intensified. This makes the plasma panel functionally very similar to the DVST even though its construction is very different.

Construction of the plasma panel is shown in Figure 3-6. It consists of two sheets of glass with thin, closely spaced gold *electrodes* attached to the inner faces and covered with a dielectric material. The two sheets of glass are spaced a few thousandths of an inch apart, and the intervening space is filled with a neon-based gas and sealed. By applying voltages between the electrodes the gas within the panel is made to behave as if it were divided into tiny cells, each one independent of its neighbors. By an ingenious mechanism, certain cells can be made to glow, and thus a picture is generated. A cell is made to glow by placing a firing voltage across it by means of the electrodes. The gas within the cell begins to discharge, and this develops very rapidly into a glow. The glow can be sustained by maintaining a high-frequency alternating voltage across the cell; the shape of this *sustaining signal* is shown in Figure 3-7. Furthermore, if the signal amplitude is chosen correctly, cells that have not been fired will not be affected. In other words, each cell is *bistable*: it has two stable states.

Cells can be switched on by momentarily increasing the sustaining voltage; this can be done selectively by modifying the signal only in the two conductors that intersect at the desired cell. Similarly, if the sustaining signal is lowered, the glow is removed. Thus the plasma panel allows both selective writing and selective erasure, at speeds of about 20 microseconds per cell. This speed can be increased by writing or erasing several cells in parallel.

The plasma panel produces a very steady image, totally free of flicker, and is a less bulky device than a CRT of comparable screen size. Its main disadvantages are its relatively poor resolution, of about 60 dots per inch, and its complex addressing and wiring requirements. Its inherent memory is useful but is not as flexible as a frame-buffer memory. Digital memories are now so inexpensive that a raster-scan display can cost less than a plasma panel. As a result, plasma panels are not used in very many of today's displays.

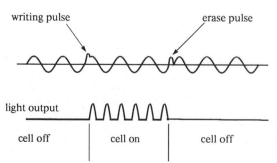

Figure 3-7  Plasma panel sustaining signal (above) and corresponding cell light output (below).

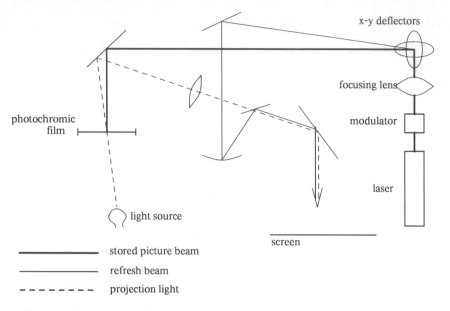

**Figure 3-8** Light beam paths in the laser-scan display.

### The Laser-Scan Display

The laser-scan display is one of the few high-resolution, large-screen display devices. It is capable of displaying an image measuring 3 by 4 feet and still has a relatively small spot size of about 1/100 inch. It has been used in displaying maps, high-quality text, and elaborate circuit diagrams [523].

The principle of the display is very simple: a laser is deflected by a pair of mirrors so that it traces out the desired image on a sheet of photochromic film. This material is usually transparent, but the light from the laser leaves a dark trace on it. A light-projection system is used to project onto a large screen the image thus deposited on the film. To produce a fresh image, the display simply winds the roll of film to bring a blank region under the laser.

The mirrors deflecting the laser are extremely small and are controlled by the electrical signals received from the display controller. A complex correction mechanism compensates for the inertia of these mirrors. For interactive purposes, a second laser displays a cursor nondestructively on the screen. The overall arrangement of the display is shown in Figure 3-8.

Many other devices besides the plasma panel and the laser-scan display have been proposed as solutions to the problem of generating high-quality images from a computer; none of these has yet been developed into a truly useful display device. The CRT and DVST remain the most popular and successful devices for computer graphics. The remainder of this chapter is devoted to a discussion of display hardware based on these two types of device.

## 3-5 THE STORAGE-TUBE DISPLAY

A typical storage-tube display, the Tektronix 4006-1, is shown in Figure 3-9. It incorporates a 7- by 10-inch DVST and a built-in alphanumeric keyboard. The screen coordinate system is divided into 1024 positions horizontally and 760 positions vertically.

The task of generating signals for the DVST from computer-supplied data is carried out by the display controller. The controller receives a series of instructions from the computer, each specifying a single element of the picture. For example, we can display a dot on the screen by supplying the controller with its $x$ and $y$ coordinates. The controller converts these coordinates into voltages that are applied to the deflection yoke to move the beam to the right spot; the energy of the beam is then increased momentarily to store the dot on the storage mesh. Complete line drawings can be decomposed into individual dots for display in this fashion, using the point-plotting techniques described in Chapter 2.

To reduce the computational overhead and improve performance, most storage-tube displays are designed instead to plot vectors, i.e., segments of straight lines. The computer supplies the two endpoints of the vector; the

**Figure 3-9** The Tektronix 4006-1 Computer Display Terminal. *Courtesy Tektronix Inc.*

| 0 0 1 1 1 0 1 |

ENTER GRAPHICS MODE

| 0 0 1 1 1 1 1 |

LEAVE GRAPHICS MODE

| 0 1 | $y$ (high) | 1 1 | $y$ (low) | 0 1 | $x$ (high) | 1 0 | $x$ (low) |

VECTOR

**Figure 3-10** Basic instruction repertoire for Tektronix storage tube display. The first VECTOR command following an ENTER GRAPHICS MODE command simply sets the current beam position, without drawing a vector.

display controller positions the electron beam at the first endpoint and moves it in a straight path to the other end. The beam's path is determined by a vector generator which feeds the deflection yoke with voltages that change at a steady rate as the vector is being traced out.

Vector-drawing instructions do not define both endpoints of the vector explicitly, but make use of the *current beam position*, the position reached by the electron beam after plotting the previous point or vector. Every vector starts at the current beam position and finishes at the specified endpoint, which then becomes the current beam position. This provides a convenient means of drawing connected vectors; disjoint vectors must be drawn by preceding each vector-drawing instruction with an instruction that moves the current beam position to the start of the vector.

A storage-tube display that uses 10-bit positive-integer coordinates must supply 20 bits of data with every instruction. At least one additional bit is required as an operation code to distinguish between the various kinds of instructions. To avoid feeding 21 or more bits at a time to the display controller, instructions are broken down into 7-bit instruction bytes. It is then possible to transmit instructions to the display in the same *serial asynchronous* fashion used to transmit alphanumeric data to text terminals. Almost all storage-tube displays will accept serial asynchronous instruction codes; this greatly simplifies the problem of attaching them to a computer.

The use of a 7-bit instruction byte leads to a somewhat complex instruction set for the display. The Tektronix 4006-1, for example, has the instruction set shown in Figure 3-10. The two commands ENTER GRAPHICS MODE and LEAVE GRAPHICS MODE permit the display to act both as an alphanumeric text terminal and as a graphic display. When the display is in graphics mode, instruction bytes are interpreted as vector-plotting commands. The LEAVE GRAPHICS MODE command switches the display to a mode in which it interprets instruction bytes as ASCII character codes; each character is displayed on the screen at the current beam position, which is then moved to the right by the width of the displayed character. After plotting characters, the ENTER GRAPHICS MODE command must be given before additional points and vectors can be plotted.

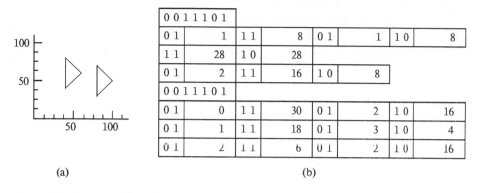

(a)                                    (b)

**Figure 3-11**  A simple picture (a) encoded for a storage-tube display, using the instruction set of Figure 3-10.

The Tektronix 4006-1 uses a vector instruction format that permits compact representation of pictures containing short vectors. If two successive endpoints have coordinates that differ only in their lower-order five bits it is unnecessary to transmit the higher-order bits. Figure 3-11 shows the encoding of a storage-tube representation of a simple picture.

## 3-6 THE REFRESH LINE-DRAWING DISPLAY

Before 1968, when the first storage-tube displays were introduced, virtually every graphic display used a refresh CRT. This type of display, although inherently more complicated and expensive than the storage-tube display, is still one of the most popular types of display for interactive work. Its popularity derives mainly from its ability to display dynamically changing pictures. In many applications, such pictures are extremely effective in presenting the results of simulations or in helping the user of an interactive program to operate it.

What are the characteristics that make a refresh display controller different? First and foremost, the controller must operate at high speed. The CRT can maintain a steady, flicker-free picture only if it is fed with a fresh description of the picture 30 or so times a second. The picture may contain as many as 5000 vectors, each of which must be passed to the controller during its 1/30-second refresh cycle. Thus the controller must be able to process 150,000 (30 × 5000) vector instructions per second. This lies well beyond the comfortable range of serial asynchronous transmission.

The refresh line-drawing display, like the storage-tube display, contains a display controller to convert the computer's output signals into deflection voltages for the yoke of the CRT. In some respects this controller is very similar to that of the storage-tube display; it accepts instructions to plot vectors, and it uses the current beam position to define their starting points.

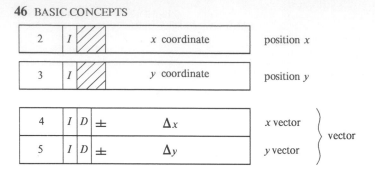

**Figure 3-12** Point-plotting and vector-drawing instructions for a refresh display. $I = 0$ for unintensified, 1 for intensified; $D = 1$ to draw vector. In a two-word vector, $D = 0$ in the first word, 1 in the second. Horizontal or vertical vectors may be drawn with a single instruction, with $D = 1$.

In the refresh display controller, speed of refresh is increased in two ways: by using a wider *data path* between the computer's memory and the controller, and by accessing memory more efficiently. The typical computer to which refresh displays are attached has a 16-bit memory word, and it is normal to pass instructions to the display in a 16-bit parallel fashion. This can be handled by a program executing in the computer's central processing unit (CPU) that transmits each instruction to the display upon request. To avoid taxing the CPU, however, the display controller will normally use *direct memory access*; it reads display data from memory independently of the CPU, from which it merely "steals" a memory cycle whenever it needs an instruction. The controller contains an *address register*, updated after each instruction has been fetched, and this register tells the controller where to find the next instruction. Instructions are stored in a contiguous sequence of memory locations and are collectively known as the *display file*.

The line-drawing display usually accept instructions for point-plotting as well as for vector-drawing. Typical formats for a set of point-plotting and vector-drawing instructions are shown in Figure 3-12. Note the use of *relative* endpoint coordinates, i.e., endpoints defined in terms of the current beam position, and the use of one bit to control intensification. Unintensified points may be used to reset the current beam position, and unintensified vectors move the beam position through the distance specified without producing a visible trace. Figure 3-13 shows the use of this instruction set to describe the picture shown in Figure 3-11a.

The refresh display needs *flexibility* in addition to high speed in order to take advantage of the CRT's dynamic properties. As we have noted, we can use images that change dynamically, either to display the state of a program during execution or to provide the operator of an interactive program with immediate graphic feedback. These changes are effected by means of corresponding changes to the display file. It is generally somewhat difficult to make rapid changes to a large contiguous block of display instructions, but if the display file can be broken into a number of disjoint sequences, changes can be made more

| 2 | 0    | 40  |
|---|------|-----|
| 3 | 0    | 40  |
| 4 | 0 0  | 20  |
| 5 | 1 1  | 20  |
| 4 | 0 0  | −20 |
| 5 | 1 1  | 20  |
| 5 | 1 1  | −40 |
| 2 | 0    | 80  |
| 3 | 0    | 30  |
| 4 | 0 0  | 20  |
| 5 | 1 1  | 20  |
| 4 | 0 0  | −20 |
| 5 | 1 1  | 20  |
| 5 | 1 1  | −40 |

**Figure 3-13** A display file representation of Figure 3-11a, using the instruction set of Figure 3-12.

easily. Most display controllers therefore provide an instruction to reset the contents of the address register. This is called a *jump instruction*, since its effect is analogous to a computer's jump or branch instruction.

A display controller that can reset its own address register by means of a jump instruction can of course store in this register the starting address of the display file whenever it reaches the end. This puts the controller in an endless loop, requiring no further attention from the computer; it is even possible to make changes to the display file without stopping the display. We generally use the term *display processor* for any display controller that can function entirely independently of the CPU. Nowadays almost all refresh line-drawing displays have this capability.

It is common to provide a *subroutine-jump* capability in addition to the basic jump instruction. The subroutine-jump instruction sets the display processor's address register to the specified address; a *return-jump* instruction restores the register's previous contents and in this way effects a return from the subroutine. To allow subroutines to call other subroutines we can use a *push-down stack* to store return addresses. This is an array of memory locations with a pointer addressing the top of the stack, i.e., the most recently used location. When a subroutine-jump instruction is executed, the return address is pushed into the stack, and the stack pointer is raised to point to the next location in which the return address is deposited. A subroutine jump instruction of this kind is often called a *push-jump*. To effect a return, the return address is popped off the stack, the contents of the top location are transferred to the address register, and the stack pointer is lowered. This is akin to "popping" the contents of the top location off the stack, and the return instruction is therefore called a *pop-jump*. Figure 3-14 shows the state of the stack at various points during the display of a set of nested subroutines.

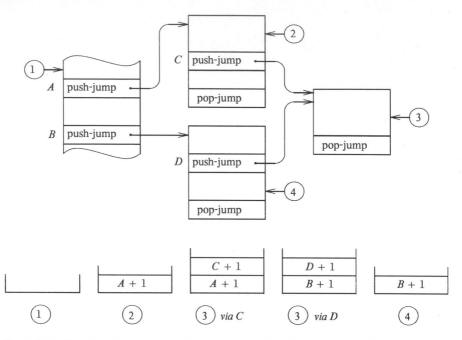

**Figure 3-14** Use of push-jump and pop-jump instructions to call a set of nested display subroutines. The state of the return address stack is shown at different points in the refresh process.

Display subroutines, like ordinary subroutines, offer a way of eliminating repetitive sequences of instructions; in applications that involve the display of repeated symbols, display subroutines can thus reduce the size of the display file. A pair of positioning instructions must be placed before the subroutine jump to set the position of the symbol; Figure 3-15 shows the use of subroutine-jump instructions to generate the picture of Figure 3-11a. The subroutine jump is also useful in constructing complex display-file structures, such as are described in Chapter 8.

An obvious use for the subroutine-jump instruction is in displaying text; each character is represented as a subroutine, and strings of characters are included in the display file as sequences of subroutine jumps. This method is wasteful of space since it uses one 16-bit word per displayed character. A more efficient approach involves the provision of a *text-display* instruction and the use of a hardware *character generator*, rather than a set of subroutines, to generate the characters. The text-display instruction allows each displayed character to be encoded in a single 8-bit byte. The character generator receives these bytes from the display processor and generates either sequences of short strokes or matrices of dots, which it reads from a small read-only memory.

The formats of the jump and text display instructions are shown in Figure 3-16. Most refresh line-drawing displays provide additional instructions to

| 2 | 0 | 40 |
|---|---|---|
| 3 | 0 | 40 |
| 6 | address | |
| 2 | 0 | 80 |
| 3 | 0 | 30 |
| 6 | address | |

| 4 | 0 0 | 20 |
|---|---|---|
| 5 | 1 1 | 20 |
| 4 | 0 0 | −20 |
| 5 | 1 1 | 20 |
| 5 | 1 1 | −40 |
| 0 | | 1 |

**Figure 3-15** Use of a display subroutine to represent the picture of Figure 3-11a.

allow control of brightness, display of short vectors or curves, and so on. These instructions are easily accommodated within the instruction repertoire.

## EXERCISES

**3-1** The instruction set shown in Figures 3-12 and 3-16 uses two words to draw a vector. Redesign or extend the instruction set to allow more compact representation of short vectors.

**3-2** Design an instruction set for a refresh display using instructions of (*a*) 12 bits, and (*b*) 24 bits.

**3-3** How efficient is the instruction set for the storage tube display shown in Figure 3-10, in terms of full utilization of the maximum bit-rate of the transmission line?

**3-4** The point-plotting and vector-drawing instructions we have discussed have used *immediate* data, i.e., data stored in the instruction itself. What would be the advantages and disadvantages of designing these instructions instead to *address* the data?

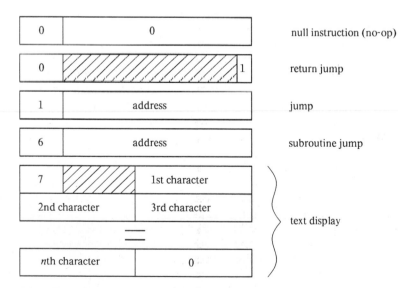

**Figure 3-16** Jump and text-display instruction formats.

**3-5** Instruction sets are given below for two hypothetical displays. Discuss their good and bad points.

*DISPLAY A:*

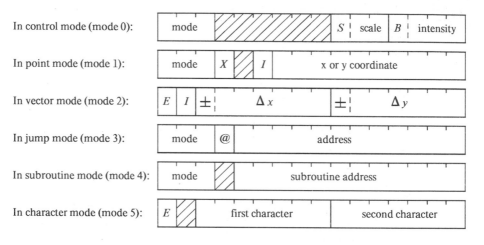

| | |
|---|---|
| In control mode (mode 0): | mode ///// $S$ \| scale $B$ \| intensity |
| In point mode (mode 1): | mode $X$ /// $I$ x or y coordinate |
| In vector mode (mode 2): | $E$ $I$ $\pm$ \| $\Delta x$ $\pm$ \| $\Delta y$ |
| In jump mode (mode 3): | mode @ address |
| In subroutine mode (mode 4): | mode /// subroutine address |
| In character mode (mode 5): | $E$ /// first character second character |

**Notes:**

*mode:* these bits determine how the next instruction will be interpreted; the display always starts in mode 0.

*S:* if this bit is set, the following 2 bits are interpreted as a scale setting: $00 = \times 1, 01 = \times 2, 10 = \times 4, 11 = \times 8$.

*B:* if this bit is set, the following 3 bits are interpreted as an intensity level between 0 and 7.

*X:* if this bit is set, the instruction sets the x coordinate; if the bit is cleared, the y coordinate is set.

*I:* this bit, if set, causes the point or vector to be intensified.

*@:* if this bit is set, the address refers *indirectly* to the jump address; i.e., the display jumps to the location whose address is stored in the location specified in the jump instruction.

During vector and character modes, the mode remains unchanged until an instruction is encountered with the $E$ bit set, whereupon the next instruction will be interpreted in control mode. When a subroutine jump is performed, the return address is deposited in the specified location, and the display commences execution of the instruction following this location.

*DISPLAY B:*

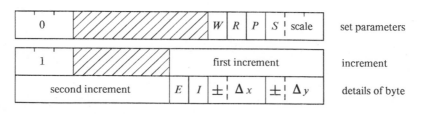

| | |
|---|---|
| 0 ///// $W$ $R$ $P$ $S$ \| scale | set parameters |
| 1 ///// first increment | increment |
| second increment $E$ $I$ $\pm$ \| $\Delta x$ $\pm$ \| $\Delta y$ | details of byte |

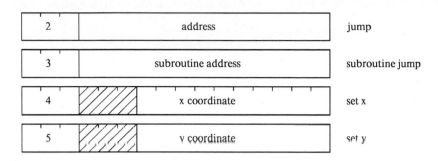

**Notes:**

*W:* if this bit is set, the display waits until the next 60 Hz interval.

*R:* if this bit is set, the display executes a return jump; a single level of subroutine calls is permitted.

*P:* if this bit is set, a point is intensified at the previously specified *x* and *y*.

*S:* as in Display A.

*E:* if this bit is set, the sequence of increment bytes terminates; until a byte is encountered with this bit set, each byte is treated as a short vector.

*I:* if this bit is set, a visible increment is drawn.

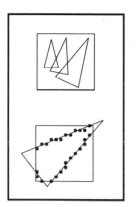

# 4

# TWO-DIMENSIONAL

# TRANSFORMATIONS

## 4-1 TRANSFORMATION PRINCIPLES

A graphics system should allow the programmer to define pictures that include a variety of transformations. For example, he should be able to magnify a picture so that detail appears more clearly, or reduce it so that more of the picture is visible. He should also be able to apply transformations to symbols. We have already discussed positioning of symbols in Section 3-6; this amounts to applying a *translation* to the symbol information. It is also useful to be able to change the *scale* of a symbol and to *rotate* it through some angle.

Two aspects of the formulation of transformations should be emphasized:

1. A transformation is a single mathematical entity and as such can be denoted by a single name or symbol;
2. Two transformations can be combined, or *concatenated*, to yield a single transformation with the same effect as the sequential application of the original two. Thus transformation $A$ might be a translation and transformation $B$ a scaling. The concatenation property allows us to determine a transformation $C = AB$ whose effect is to translate and then scale.

The principles of denotation and concatenation will pertain to all transformations described in this book: clipping, windowing, and three-dimensional and perspective transformations. Each of these transformations is used to generate a new point $(x', y')$ from the coordinates of a point $(x, y)$ in the original picture description. If the original definition includes a line, it suffices to apply the transformation to the endpoints of the line and display the line between the two transformed endpoints.

### Translation

The form of the translation transformation is

$$x' = x + T_x \qquad y' = y + T_y \tag{4-1}$$

As an example, consider a triangle defined by its three vertices (20, 0), (60, 0), (40, 100) being translated 100 units to the right and 10 units up $(T_x = 100, \quad T_y = 10)$. The new vertices are (120, 10), (160, 10), and (140, 110); the effect is shown in Figure 4-1.

### Rotation

To rotate a point $(x, y)$ through a clockwise angle $\theta$ about the origin of the coordinate system, we write

$$x' = x \cos \theta + y \sin \theta \qquad y' = -x \sin \theta + y \cos \theta \tag{4-2}$$

The triangle (20, 0), (60, 0), (40, 100) rotated 45° clockwise about the origin is (14.14, −14.14), (42.43, −42.43), (98.99, 42.43), and is shown in Figure 4-2. These equations can be used only if rotation is about the origin of the coordinate system.

### Scaling

The scaling transformations

$$x' = x S_x \qquad y' = y S_y \tag{4-3}$$

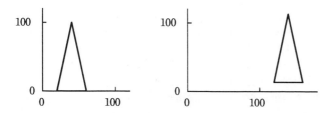

**Figure 4-1** Translation.

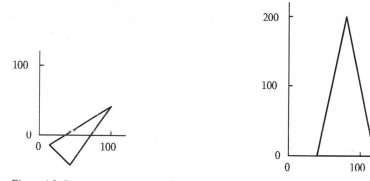

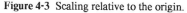

**Figure 4-2** Rotation about the origin.          **Figure 4-3** Scaling relative to the origin.

can be used for a variety of purposes. If the picture is to be enlarged to twice its original size, we might choose $S_x = S_y = 2$. Notice that the enlargement is relative to the origin of the coordinate system. The triangle (20, 0), (60, 0), (40, 100) becomes (40, 0), (120, 0), (80, 200), as shown in Figure 4-3.

If $S_x$ and $S_y$ are not equal, they have the effect of distorting pictures by elongating or shrinking them along the directions parallel to the coordinate axes. For instance, Figure 4-4a can be distorted as shown in Figure 4-4b or c.

The mirror image of an object can be generated by using negative values of $S_x$ or $S_y$. Mirror images of Figure 4-5a can be generated as shown in Figure 4-5b to d.

## 4-2 CONCATENATION

Sequences of transformations can be combined into one transformation by the *concatenation* process. These sequences occur frequently in picture definitions. Indeed it is fairly rare that we want to apply a simple transformation such as rotation about the origin or scaling relative to the origin. In general we need to perform more complex transformations like rotations about arbitrary points. Rotation about an arbitrary point can be performed by applying a sequence of

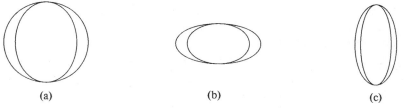

(a)                              (b)                              (c)

**Figure 4-4**      Independent scaling in x and y.

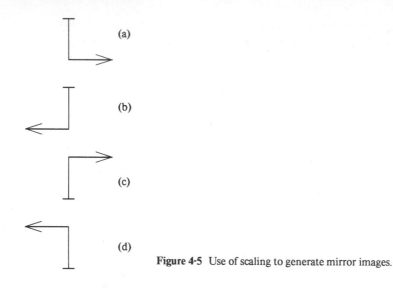

**Figure 4-5** Use of scaling to generate mirror images.

three simple transformations: a translation, followed by a rotation, followed by another translation.

Sequences of transformations also arise when subroutine calls are nested. If each call has a relative transformation associated with it, a graphic item specified in a subroutine may have to undergo several transformations before the item can be displayed.

The ordering of a sequence of transformations must not be destroyed by the concatenation. Consider the following sequence: rotate the triangle of Figure 4-1 through 90°, then translate it with $T_x = -80$, $T_y = 0$. The resulting triangle is shown in Figure 4-6a. If the order of application of the two transformations is reversed, the new figure is as shown in Figure 4-6b.

The main aim of concatenation is to represent a sequence of transformations as one transformation. The sequence above is

$$x' = y \qquad y' = -x \tag{4-4}$$

followed by

$$x'' = x' - 80 \qquad y'' = y' \tag{4-5}$$

The concatenation is simply

$$x'' = y - 80 \qquad y'' = -x \tag{4-6}$$

Use of the concatenated transformation has several advantages. We can represent it more compactly than a sequence, and we can generally compute the transformation with fewer arithmetic operations than if we were to apply each of the transformations in the sequence one after the other. However the rules for concatenating transformation equations are quite complex. They are much simpler if we use *matrices* to define transformations.

## 4-3 MATRIX REPRESENTATIONS

Two-dimensional transformations can be represented in a uniform way by a $3 \times 3$ matrix (see Appendix I for a discussion of matrix techniques). The transformation of a point $(x, y)$ to a new point $(x', y')$ by means of any sequence of translations, rotations, and scalings is then represented as

$$[x' \ y' \ 1] = [x \ y \ 1] \begin{bmatrix} a & d & 0 \\ b & e & 0 \\ c & f & 1 \end{bmatrix} \tag{4-7}$$

where the $3 \times 3$ matrix completely specifies the transformation. The matrix, a single entity, represents the transformation. When we name this matrix we gain the ability to denote the entire transformation by a single name.

The addition of the third element of unity to the $[x \ y]$ vector enables it to be transformed by the $3 \times 3$ matrix. The point vector and matrix must be in the form given above in order to specify all simple transformations and concatenations of simple transformations with one notation (see Appendix II for a complete discussion of the three-element vectors).

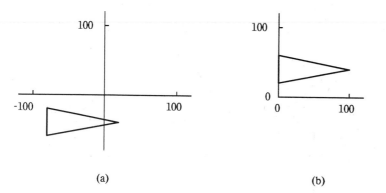

(a)  (b)

**Figure 4-6** Different ordering of transformations.

## Matrix Formulation of Transformations

The parameters of the 3 × 3 transformation matrix can be arranged to make the matrix represent the simple transformations of translation, rotation, and scaling:

$$\text{Translation: } [x' \quad y' \quad 1] = [x \quad y \quad 1] \begin{bmatrix} 1 & 0 & 0 \\ 0 & 1 & 0 \\ T_x & T_y & 1 \end{bmatrix} \tag{4-8}$$

$$\text{Rotation: } [x' \quad y' \quad 1] = [x \quad y \quad 1] \begin{bmatrix} \cos\theta & -\sin\theta & 0 \\ \sin\theta & \cos\theta & 0 \\ 0 & 0 & 1 \end{bmatrix} \tag{4-9}$$

$$\text{Scaling: } [x' \quad y' \quad 1] = [x \quad y \quad 1] \begin{bmatrix} S_x & 0 & 0 \\ 0 & S_y & 0 \\ 0 & 0 & 1 \end{bmatrix} \tag{4-10}$$

The reader can easily verify that these formulations are equivalent to Equations 4-1 to 4-3.

## Concatenation of Matrix Transformations

The matrix formulation has the conspicuous virtue of making the concatenation of transformation sequences particularly straightforward. Consider the following sequence: scale a point with $S_x = S_y = 2$; then translate it with $T_x = 10, T_y = 0$. We have

$$[x' \quad y' \quad 1] = [x \quad y \quad 1] \begin{bmatrix} 2 & 0 & 0 \\ 0 & 2 & 0 \\ 0 & 0 & 1 \end{bmatrix} \tag{4-11}$$

$$[x'' \quad y'' \quad 1] = [x' \quad y' \quad 1] \begin{bmatrix} 1 & 0 & 0 \\ 0 & 1 & 0 \\ 10 & 0 & 1 \end{bmatrix} \tag{4-12}$$

The result $[x' \quad y' \quad 1]$ is merely an intermediate one; we can eliminate it by substituting the first equation into the second

$$[x'' \quad y'' \quad 1] = [x \quad y \quad 1] \begin{bmatrix} 2 & 0 & 0 \\ 0 & 2 & 0 \\ 0 & 0 & 1 \end{bmatrix} \begin{bmatrix} 1 & 0 & 0 \\ 0 & 1 & 0 \\ 10 & 0 & 1 \end{bmatrix} \tag{4-13}$$

The two $3 \times 3$ matrices are independent of the $(x, y)$ points being transformed and are derived only from the parameters $(S_x, S_y, T_x, T_y)$ specified in the transformation sequence. We can therefore simplify the equation by multiplying the two $3 \times 3$ matrices to yield a new $3 \times 3$ matrix

$$[x'' \quad y'' \quad 1] = [x \quad y \quad 1] \begin{bmatrix} 2 & 0 & 0 \\ 0 & 2 & 0 \\ 10 & 0 & 1 \end{bmatrix} \tag{4-14}$$

Thus the product of two matrix transformations represents the concatenation of those transforms. Irrespective of the number of transformations in a sequence, we can always concatenate so that a single $3 \times 3$ matrix represents the entire sequence.

Complex transformations can be described as concatenations of simple ones. Suppose we wish to derive a transformation which will rotate a point through a clockwise angle $\theta$ about the point $(R_x, R_y)$. The rotation transformation (Equation 4-2 or 4-9) can be applied to rotate points only about the origin. Therefore we must first translate points so that $(R_x, R_y)$ becomes the origin

$$[x' \quad y' \quad 1] = [x \quad y \quad 1] \begin{bmatrix} 1 & 0 & 0 \\ 0 & 1 & 0 \\ -R_x & -R_y & 1 \end{bmatrix} \tag{4-15}$$

Then the rotation can be applied

$$[x'' \quad y'' \quad 1] = [x' \quad y' \quad 1] \begin{bmatrix} \cos\theta & -\sin\theta & 0 \\ \sin\theta & \cos\theta & 0 \\ 0 & 0 & 1 \end{bmatrix} \tag{4-16}$$

And finally, we translate the point so that the origin is returned to $(R_x, R_y)$:

$$[x''' \quad y''' \quad 1] = [x'' \quad y'' \quad 1] \begin{bmatrix} 1 & 0 & 0 \\ 0 & 1 & 0 \\ R_x & R_y & 1 \end{bmatrix} \tag{4-17}$$

These can be concatenated

$$[x''' \quad y''' \quad 1] =$$

$$[x \quad y \quad 1] \begin{bmatrix} 1 & 0 & 0 \\ 0 & 1 & 0 \\ -R_x & -R_y & 1 \end{bmatrix} \begin{bmatrix} \cos\theta & -\sin\theta & 0 \\ \sin\theta & \cos\theta & 0 \\ 0 & 0 & 1 \end{bmatrix} \begin{bmatrix} 1 & 0 & 0 \\ 0 & 1 & 0 \\ R_x & R_y & 1 \end{bmatrix} \tag{4-18}$$

If values for $R_x$, $R_y$ and $\theta$ are known, the three matrices can be multiplied to yield one transformation matrix.

### Efficiency

When generating a picture for display, we may need to apply a transformation to a large number of points. This application must be as efficient as possible. The computation

$$[x \quad y \quad 1] \begin{bmatrix} a & d & 0 \\ b & e & 0 \\ c & f & 1 \end{bmatrix} \tag{4-19}$$

seems at first glance to require nine multiplications and six additions. However, in the formulation given here, the third column of the $3 \times 3$ matrix will always be

$$\begin{bmatrix} 0 \\ 0 \\ 1 \end{bmatrix} \tag{4-20}$$

even if the matrix is the result of many concatenations. The computations for $x'$ and $y'$ thus reduce to

$$x' = ax + by + c \qquad y' = dx + ey + f \tag{4-21}$$

which requires fewer arithmetic operations (four multiplications and four additions) than the full vector multiplication. A matrix notation for this abbreviated computation is

$$[x' \quad y'] = [x \quad y \quad 1] \begin{bmatrix} a & d \\ b & e \\ c & f \end{bmatrix} \tag{4-22}$$

The transformation matrix is now a $3 \times 2$ matrix. Note, however, that we cannot concatenate two $3 \times 2$ matrices by multiplying them together; before we multiply them we must first return them to $3 \times 3$ form by attaching a third column.

### EXERCISES

**4-1** Prove the assertion that the transformation of a line between two points $A$ and $B$ is equivalent to the line between the transform of $A$ and the transform of $B$. Consider only the translation, rotation, and scaling transformations.

**4-2** The matrix formulation suggests other transformations that we have not considered, e.g., the transformation $x' = x + ay$ and $y' = y$. Can you characterize these transformations?

**4-3** Suppose we know a point $(x', y')$ and the fact that it was transformed from an unknown point $(x, y)$ by a known matrix $Q$. Describe a mechanism for finding the original point $(x, y)$. Is this mechanism likely to be useful in graphics?

**4-4** Suppose that successive points $P_i$ on a curve are generated by the formula, $P_{i+1} = P_i C$, where $C$ is a $3 \times 3$ matrix. Express the circle-generating DDA of Section 2-4 in this form. Now suppose we wish to generate points $Q_i$ on a curve which is a linear transformation of the original curve, i.e., $Q_i = P_i T$, where $T$ is a $3 \times 3$ transformation matrix. Find the matrix $C'$ such that $Q_{i+1} = Q_i C'$. Use this result to describe a method of incremental ellipse generation.

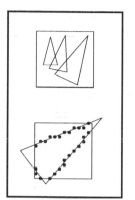

# 5

# CLIPPING AND

# WINDOWING

Many graphics application programs give the user the impression of looking through a window at a very large picture. Figure 5-1 shows the use of this effect in a program for viewing different portions of a large architectural plan at different scales. The program makes use of the scaling and translation techniques described in the previous chapter to generate a variety of different views of a single representation of a plan. Other applications, such as map display and circuit design, can make similar use of linear transformations.

To display an enlarged portion of a picture we must not only apply the appropriate scaling and translation but also identify the visible parts of the picture for inclusion in the displayed image. This selection process is by no means straightforward. Certain lines may lie partly inside the visible portion of the picture and partly outside. These lines cannot be omitted entirely from the displayed image because the image would become inaccurate, as can be seen in Figure 5-2. Likewise we cannot display each of these lines in its entirety; to do so would involve trying to display points that overflow the coordinate addressing scheme of the display, and this too would create anomalies. Figure 5-3, for example, shows the wraparound effect exhibited by certain displays when attempting to draw lines off the edge of the screen.

The correct way to select visible information for display is to use *clipping*, a process which divides each element of the picture into its visible and invisible portions, allowing the invisible portion to be discarded. Clipping can be

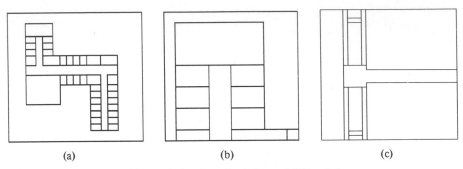

(a)                                    (b)                                    (c)

**Figure 5-1** Viewing an architectural plan through windows of different sizes.

applied to a variety of different types of picture element: points, vectors, curves of various kinds, text characters, and even polygons. The basis for these clipping operations is a simple pair of inequalities that determine whether a point $(x, y)$ is visible:

$$x_{\text{left}} \leq x \leq x_{\text{right}} \qquad y_{\text{bottom}} \leq y \leq y_{\text{top}} \tag{5-1}$$

where $x_{\text{left}}$, $x_{\text{right}}$, $y_{\text{bottom}}$, and $y_{\text{top}}$ are the positions of the edges of the screen. These inequalities provide us with a very simple method of clipping pictures on a point-by-point basis; we substitute the coordinates of each point for $x$ and $y$, and if the point fails to satisfy either inequality, it is invisible.

It would be quite inappropriate to clip pictures by converting all picture elements into points and using these inequalities; the clipping process would take far too long and would leave the picture in a form no longer suitable for a line-drawing display. We must instead attempt to clip larger elements of the picture. This involves developing more powerful *clipping algorithms* that can determine the visible and invisible portions of such picture elements as vectors, text characters, and polygons. The following sections discuss some of the algorithms that have been developed for clipping vectors. More recently, with the increasing emphasis on solid-area graphics, the need has arisen for algorithms to clip polygons; one such algorithm is described in this chapter.

**Figure 5-2** Effect of omitting partially visible lines from Figure 5-1c.

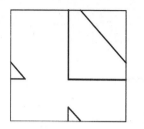

**Figure 5-3** Occurrence of wraparound in drawing a partially invisible triangle.

## 5-1 A LINE CLIPPING ALGORITHM

Figure 5-4 shows a number of different attitudes that a straight-line segment (abbreviated in this chapter to *line*) may take with respect to the screen. Notice that those lines which are partly invisible are divided by the screen boundary into one or more invisible portions but into only one visible segment. It is an extremely useful fact that clipping to a convex boundary, such as a square screen, never generates more than one visible segment of a straight line. This means that the visible segment of a straight line can be determined simply by computing its two endpoints. The following algorithm, invented by Dan Cohen and Ivan Sutherland, is designed not only to find these endpoints very rapidly but also to reject even more rapidly any line that is clearly invisible. This makes it a very good algorithm for clipping pictures that are much larger than the screen.

The algorithm has two parts. The first determines whether the line lies entirely on the screen and if not whether it can be trivially rejected as lying entirely off the screen. If it satisfies neither of these tests, then it is divided into two parts, and these two tests are applied to each part. The algorithm depends on the fact that every line either is entirely on the screen or can be divided so that one part can be trivially rejected.

The rejection test is implemented by extending the edges of the screen so that they divide the space occupied by the unclipped picture into nine regions, as shown in Figure 5-5. Each of these regions has a 4-bit code, and the two

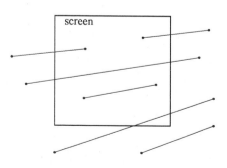

**Figure 5-4** Different attitudes of line segments to the edges of the screen.

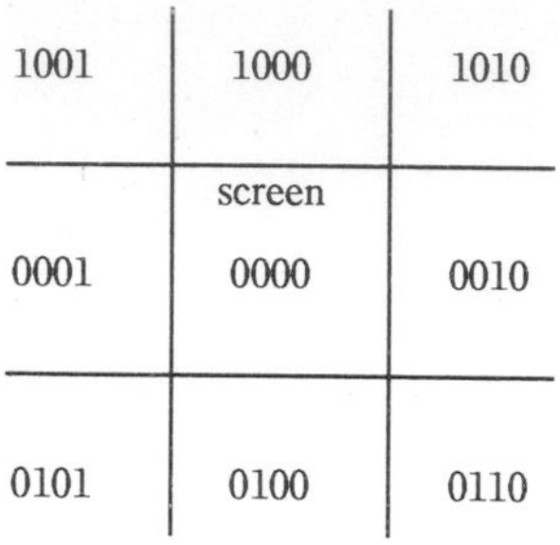

| 1001 | 1000 | 1010 |
|------|------|------|
|      | screen |    |
| 0001 | 0000 | 0010 |
| 0101 | 0100 | 0110 |

**Figure 5-5** The nine regions defined by the screen edges, showing their endpoint codes.

endpoints of the line are assigned codes appropriate to the regions they are in. The 4 bits in the code mean the following if set:

| | |
|---|---|
| First bit: | point is to the left of the left-hand edge. |
| Second bit: | point is to the right of the right-hand edge. |
| Third bit: | point is below the bottom edge. |
| Fourth bit: | point is above top edge of screen. |

Clearly if the 4-bit codes for both endpoints are zero, the line lies entirely on the screen. What is less obvious is that if the logical intersection of the two codes is not zero, the line must lie entirely off-screen.

If the line cannot be eliminated by either of these tests, it must be subdivided. A simple method of subdivision is to find the point of intersection of the line with one edge of the screen and to throw away the part that lies off-screen. For example, the line $AB$ in Figure 5-6 could be subdivided at $C$ and the portion $AC$ thrown away. We now have a new line $BD$, to which the trivial rejection tests are applied. The line still cannot be trivially rejected, and so we subdivide again at $D$. The resulting line $BD$ is found to lie entirely within the screen. It is not always easy to determine whether subdivision should be made first at $C$ or at $D$, but if we apply the rejection test in a repeated fashion, the order in which subdivisions are made does not affect the final result.

The inherent simplicity of this algorithm is demonstrated by the following implementation of it in PASCAL:

```
var Clipxl, Clipxr, Clipyb, Clipyt: real;

procedure Clip (x1, y1, x2, y2: real);
    label return;
    type edge = (left, right, bottom, top); outcode = set of edge;
    var c, c1, c2: outcode; x, y: real;

    procedure Code (x, y: real; var c: outcode);
    begin
        c := [ ];
        if x < Clipxl then c := [left] else if x > Clipxr then c := [right];
```

```
        if y < Clipyb then c := c + [bottom] else
              if y > Clipyt then c := c + [top];
    end;
begin
    Code(x1, y1, c1); Code(x2, y2, c2);

    while (c1 <> [ ]) or (c2 <> [ ]) do begin
        if (c1 * c2) <> [ ] then goto return;
        c := c1; if c = [ ] then c := c2;
        if left in c then begin { Crosses left edge }
            y := y1 + (y2 − y1) * (Clipxl − x1)/(x2 − x1);
            x := Clipxl end else
        if right in c then begin { Crosses right edge }
            y := y1 + (y2 − y1) * (Clipxr − x1)/(x2 − x1);
            x := Clipxr end else
        if bottom in c then begin { Crosses bottom edge }
            x := x1 + (x2 − x1) * (Clipyb − y1)/(y2 − y1);
            y := Clipyb end else
        if top in c then begin { Crosses top edge }
            x := x1 + (x2 − x1) * (Clipyt − y1)/(y2 − y1);
            y := Clipyt end;
        if c = c1 then begin
            x1 := x; y1 := y; Code(x, y, c1)
        end else begin
            x2 := x; y2 := y; Code(x, y, c2)
        end
    end;
    { If we reach here, the line from (x1, y1) to (x2, y2) is visible }
    ShowLine(x1, y1, x2, y2);
return: end;
```

## 5-2 MIDPOINT SUBDIVISION

We can subdivide the line at its midpoint and in this way avoid direct computation of the line's points of intersection with the edges of the screen.

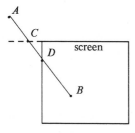

**Figure 5-6** Stages in the clipping of a line, using the Cohen-Sutherland algorithm.

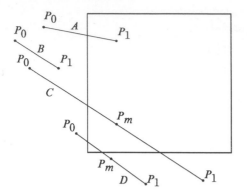

**Figure 5-7** Clipping lines with the midpoint algorithm.

This modification makes the algorithm more suitable for machines without hardware for multiplication and division. The midpoint variation of the algorithm has been implemented in hardware in the clipping divider [451].

Once again, the algorithm clips the line by finding the endpoints of its visible segment. Each endpoint is found by an identical process, and in the hardware implementation these two processes are carried out in parallel. The goal of this process is to find the visible point on the line segment $P_0P_1$ that is farthest from $P_0$. The steps in the process are as follows:

1. We test whether $P_1$ is visible; if so, it is the farthest visible point from $P_0$ and the process is complete (Figure 5-7, line $A$). If it is invisible (lines $B$, $C$ and $D$), we continue.
2. We check whether $P_0P_1$ can be trivially rejected, in which case the process is complete and no output is generated (Figure 5-7, line $B$). Otherwise we continue.
3. We divide $P_0P_1$ at its midpoint $P_m$. This is a guess at the farthest visible point. If the segment $P_mP_1$ can be trivially rejected, we have overestimated (Figure 5-7, line $D$) and we repeat from step 2 using the segment $P_0P_m$; otherwise we repeat from step 2 with segment $P_mP_1$ (Figure 5-7, line $C$).

This process may terminate during steps 1 or 2 in the manner indicated. It may also stop during step 3; this happens if the segment $P_0P_1$ becomes so short that its midpoint, computed in the integer coordinate system of the screen, coincides with one endpoint or the other. In this case $P_0$ is the farthest visible point.

While this process is determining the farthest visible point from $P_0$, an identical process is finding the farthest visible point from $P_1$ by applying the same sequence of steps to the segment $P_1P_0$. The overall effect is to perform a pair of parallel *logarithmic searches* for the endpoints of the visible segment of the line. The number of subdivisions that must be performed during each search is at most equal to the number of bits of precision in the representation of $x$ and $y$.

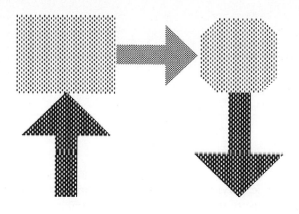

**Figure 5-8** Solid areas defined by polygons.

## 5-3 CLIPPING OTHER GRAPHIC ENTITIES

The pictures we display generally contain other kinds of graphic entity besides straight-line segments: they nearly always contain some alphanumeric characters, and they often include circular arcs or other forms of curve. Special methods have been developed to clip each such type of entity.

Characters are often clipped simply by omitting any character that is only partially visible. The test for visibility can be performed by examining the diagonal of the rectangle bounding the character. If the diagonal is completely visible, the character is displayed; otherwise it is omitted. When accurate character clipping is needed, characters can be represented as sets of short line segments, each of which is then clipped in the normal manner. This method cannot be used when characters are generated by hardware.

We can likewise clip curves by breaking them down into short straight-line segments and clipping each segment. This is not as inefficient as it sounds, for curves must in any case generally be broken down into vectors so that they can be passed to a line drawing display. Almost all other types of graphic entities can likewise be broken down into straight-line segments and can then be clipped with the aid of the Cohen-Sutherland algorithm.

## 5-4 POLYGON CLIPPING*

It is sometimes inconvenient to divide graphic entities into line segments in order to clip them; we would prefer the output of the clipping operation to be an entity of the same kind as the input. This is particularly true of polygons, i.e., closed outlines bounded by straight edges. For line-drawing applications it does not matter whether we subdivide polygons into lines before clipping them,

---

* This section may be omitted on first reading, but should be read before Part Four since it relates directly to raster graphics.

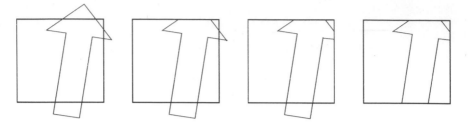

**Figure 5-9** Polygon clipping against each screen edge in turn.

but in images like Figure 5-8 we use polygons to define the outlines of solid areas of gray or color and we must ensure that these remain polygonal after the clipping process. We must therefore use a *polygon clipping algorithm.*

When we clip a polygon, we create an outline that is no longer closed; we must close it by piecing together appropriate sections of the screen boundary. It is quite difficult to compute which sections to use. Another problem is posed by concave polygons (those with at least one interior angle greater than 180°), which may be clipped into several smaller polygons. These two problems prevent us from clipping polygons simply by clipping each edge with a line-clipping algorithm. Fortunately, however, an elegant solution to the polygon clipping problem has been discovered by Ivan Sutherland and Gary Hodgman [465].

The Sutherland-Hodgman algorithm is based on the observation that it is relatively easy to clip a polygon against a single clipping edge. We can therefore clip the polygon against all four edges of the screen by clipping the entire polygon against one edge, then taking the resulting polygon or polygons, and clipping against a second edge, and so on for all four edges (Figure 5-9). This approach is unconventional and at first sight appears to require a considerable amount of storage to retain the intermediate polygons generated by the first three clipping operations. This is not so, however; the algorithm requires storage for only two pairs of coordinates for each clipping edge.

The algorithm operates on the vertices of the polygon rather than on its edges. These vertices we shall call $P_1, P_2, \ldots, P_n$. The $n$ edges of the polygon are formed by connecting $P_1$ to $P_2$, $P_2$ to $P_3$, and so on, closing the polygon with the edge $P_n P_1$. The output from the algorithm is a new sequence of vertices, $Q_1, Q_2, \ldots, Q_m$. We shall consider this sequence to represent a single polygon with $m$ edges, although it may in fact consist of several polygons connected by degenerate edges, as in the example of Figure 5-10. We shall see in Part Four that these degenerate edges do not interfere with the display of solid areas. Alternately we may use an algorithm, such as that of Weiler and Atherton [503], designed expressly to handle concave polygons.

The Sutherland-Hodgman algorithm tests each vertex $P_i$ $(i = 1, 2, \ldots, n)$ in turn against a clipping edge $e$. Vertices that lie on the visible side of $e$ are included in the output polygon the algorithm generates, while invisible vertices

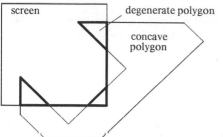

**Figure 5-10** Degenerate polygon formed by clipping a concave polygon.

are discarded. The algorithm also tests whether $P_i$ lies on the same side of $e$ as its predecessor $P_{i-1}$. If it does not, the point of intersection of $e$ with the line $P_iP_{i-1}$ is computed and added to the output polygon. This last step is omitted for the first vertex $P_1$; at the end, when $P_n$ has been tested, the algorithm tests $e$ for intersection with $P_nP_1$.

Figure 5-11 shows a flow chart of the algorithm to clip each vertex of the polygon against a single edge $e$. The algorithm is shown in two parts: the first part is applied to every vertex, while the second is a *closing routine,* applied only after processing the final vertex of the polygon. At various points the algorithm outputs a vertex; we may consider this process to add the vertex to a list of vertices representing the clipped output polygon. To clip against four successive edges we could use a four-step sequence, taking the output polygon from each step, and using its vertices as inputs to the next step. The result would be to clip the polygon against the four screen edges.

We have seen, however, that a large amount of storage may be required to store the intermediate polygons between steps. We can also see that such storage is unnecessary. The algorithm generates the vertices of the output polygon in sequential order and then feeds each of these vertices *in the same order* to the next step of the process. Instead of storing each output vertex until the step is complete, we can pass it directly to the next step by invoking the same algorithm in a recursive manner. The complete clipping process is then represented by four stages of the same algorithm, each stage clipping against one of the four edges of the screen. Output vertices from the first stage are fed to the second stage, vertices from the second are fed to the third, and so on; the vertices generated by the final stage form the clipped output polygon.

## 5-5 VIEWING TRANSFORMATIONS

In Chapter 4 we have seen how transformations can be applied to points and lines in order to change the scale and orientation of pictures in which they occur. This chapter has discussed ways of clipping pictures in order to remove invisible parts. In the remainder of this chapter we shall discuss how to combine the transformation and clipping processes so as to provide a very general viewing capability.

One of the great advantages we gain from the use of transformations is the opportunity to define pictures in the coordinate system of our choice. Until now, our discussions have used the display screen's coordinate system, but we can see how awkward this could become in practice. The hardware of the display allows us to address points on the screen by means of integer coordinates, typically in the range 0 to 1023. We might wish to use the display to plot a graph from a table of floating-point numbers. Even if we are lucky enough to find that these numbers all lie nicely within the range 0 to 1023, we

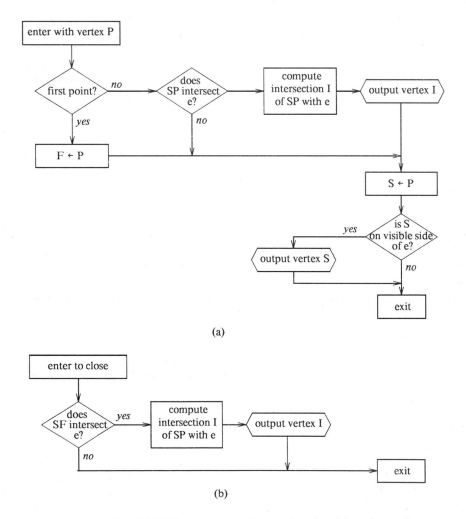

(a)

(b)

**Figure 5-11** The Sutherland-Hodgman polygon clipping algorithm: (a) routine to clip each polygon vertex; (b) polygon closing routine.

must still convert them all into integers; and if the range of numbers is altogether different, we must scale them. Sometimes we cannot predict the range of numbers when we start to generate the graph, for they may be the results of a real-time experiment. In such a case, the graph may very well end up looking like Figure 5-12, needing to be rescaled in order to be useful.

We can easily avoid these problems by defining our picture in a more convenient coordinate system and using the appropriate transformation to convert it into screen coordinates. In the graph-plotting example we would simply plot the graph using the floating-point values found in the table. In defining the architectural plan of Figure 5-1 we might use inches or meters as our units; in displaying the state of a chess-playing program we might define the board to measure $8 \times 8$ units. After choosing the coordinate system and defining the picture, we set up the appropriate transformation to convert the picture into screen coordinates. This transformation may have been chosen so as to fit the whole picture onto the screen, or it may make only a part of it visible, the rest being removed by a clipping routine. Thus we have the capability, as described at the start of this chapter, of viewing the picture through whatever window we choose.

We may consider this approach to involve the definition of a *world* to be viewed through our adjustable window. We therefore use the term *world coordinate system* for the space in which the picture is defined and the term *viewing transformation* for the transformation that converts this picture into screen coordinates. The world coordinate system is chosen to suit the application program; the screen coordinate system, on the other hand, is inherent in the design of the display. The viewing transformation forms a bridge between the two.

The general two-dimensional viewing tranformation allows any desired scaling, rotation, and translation to be applied to the world-coordinate definition of the picture. This transformation can be applied by setting up a $3 \times 2$ matrix to be applied to each point in the definition; each line whose endpoints have been transformed is then clipped, and any visible portion is added to the display file. Relatively few applications require such a general form of the viewing transformation, however; the need to rotate the world-coordinate definition rarely arises. The less general case, in which no rotation is applied by the viewing transformation, is extremely useful and is called the *windowing transformation*.

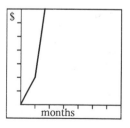

Figure 5-12 Example of an incorrectly scaled graph.

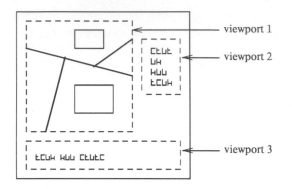

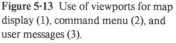

**Figure 5-13** Use of viewports for map display (1), command menu (2), and user messages (3).

## 5-6 THE WINDOWING TRANSFORMATION

The windowing transformation is so named because it involves specifying a *window* in the world-coordinate space surrounding the information we wish displayed. This is by no means the only way such a transformation can be specified; for example, we can define the scale factor and translation to be applied to the picture, or in place of the translation we can define a world-coordinate point we wish transformed to a certain spot on the screen, say the screen center. Each of these methods may prove convenient in certain circumstances; the windowing transformation has the advantage of letting us specify directly the rectangle of interest in the world-coordinate picture definition.

In addition to the window, we can also define a *viewport*, a rectangle on the screen where we would like the window's contents displayed. In doing so, we exploit the ability of our clipping algorithm to clip to any right rectangular boundary. It is often useful to specify a viewport smaller than the screen, for we can then leave room for command menus, system messages, and so forth. Each such part of the picture may be displayed in a separate viewport, as shown in Figure 5-13.

Figure 5-14 illustrates the full windowing transformation from world to screen. We use the window to define *what* we want to display; we use the viewport to specify *where* on the screen to put it. Thus we can scan over a large picture by keeping the window size constant and varying its position; changing the window size alters the picture magnification. Normally we shall take care to keep the window and viewport similar in shape. In Figure 5-14 however, we see the distortion that can be achieved by making the shapes different.

The actual transformation we apply to each point is very simple. Let us suppose that the edges of the window are at $x = W_{xl}$, $x = W_{xr}$, $y = W_{yb}$, and $y = W_{yt}$ (see Figure 5-14), all measured in *world coordinates*, and that the corresponding edges of the viewport are at $x = V_{xl}$, $x = V_{xr}$, $y = V_{yb}$, and $y = V_{yt}$, all measured in *screen coordinates*. Then the point $(x_w, y_w)$ in world coordinates transforms into the point $(x_s, y_s)$ in screen coordinates, as follows:

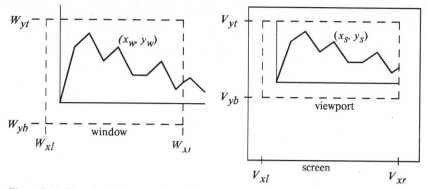

**Figure 5-14** The windowing transformation.

$$x_s = \frac{V_{xr} - V_{xl}}{W_{xr} - W_{xl}}(x_w - W_{xl}) + V_{xl}$$

$$y_s = \frac{V_{yt} - V_{yb}}{W_{yt} - W_{yb}}(y_w - W_{yb}) + V_{yb} \qquad (5\text{-}2)$$

These expressions are derived by determining the position of the point $(x_w, y_w)$ within the window as a fraction of full displacement from the bottom left-hand corner and interpreting this as a fraction of full displacement across the viewport. Adding the offset of the viewport's bottom left-hand corner gives the position of $(x_s, y_s)$ on the screen.

Equations 5-2 reduce to the form

$$x_s = ax_w + b \qquad y_s = cy_w + d \qquad (5\text{-}3)$$

We therefore arrange to compute the values of $a$, $b$, $c$, and $d$ when the window and viewport are defined, so that we can transform each point by a computation involving only two multiplications and two additions.

The complete windowing transformation can then be applied to a picture by transforming the endpoints of each line, using Equations 5-3, and clipping the line against the viewport boundary. In the interests of transforming the picture quickly we naturally wish to speed up the computation, and we can do so in a couple of ways. The first of these is based on the observation that the lines in a picture definition are often connected as a sequence of line segments with shared endpoints. We can avoid transforming each shared endpoint twice by comparing the world coordinates of each point and its predecessor.

A more dramatic improvement in the speed of transformation can be gained by transforming only visible lines. Since both window and viewport are right rectangles, and since both circumscribe the displayed information, we may use either of them as a clipping region. The more efficient implementation of the windowing transformation therefore clips *first*, using the window as clipping region, and then performs the transformation of Equations 5-3 on those lines which are at least partially visible. When a small portion of a very large picture is being viewed, the advantage of performing clipping before transformation is considerable.

## EXERCISES

**5-1** Program the Sutherland-Hodgman polygon clipping algorithm in the language of your choice, using recursion if possible.

**5-2** The Sutherland-Hodgman algorithm can be used to clip lines against a nonrectangular boundary. What uses might this have? What modifications to the algorithm would be necessary? What restrictions would apply to the shape of the clipping region?

**5-3** Some displays possess hardware for displaying circular arcs. Design an algorithm to clip circles and generate arcs suitable for passing to such a display.

**5-4** Extend the clipping program given on page 66 to perform the complete viewing transformation of a line from world coordinates to screen coordinates.

**5-5** Application programs often use floating-point numbers to define pictures, whereas the display uses integers. Should the conversion from floating-point to integer format be done before or after clipping? How should numbers be rounded? Does the decision whether to clip to the window or viewport depend on the relative speeds of integer and floating-point arithmetic?

**5-6** Under what circumstances would midpoint clipping be preferable to the use of the program on page 66?

**5-7** What additional logic is needed in the clipping algorithm to keep track of linked visible line segments?

**5-8** The Cohen-Sutherland clipping algorithm is optimized in favor of clipping pictures much larger than the window. What features would you look for in an algorithm to clip pictures only slightly larger than the window? Devise such an algorithm.

**5-9** Hand-simulate the polygon clipping alrithm to verify that it produces the same result as shown in Figure 5-9. Copy the figure of the arrow to graph paper and step through the flow chart of Figure 5-11.

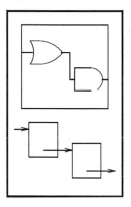

# PART TWO

## GRAPHICS PACKAGES

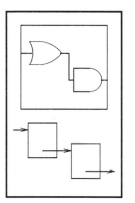

# 6

# A SIMPLE

# GRAPHICS PACKAGE

A *graphics system* may be defined as any collection of hardware and software designed to make it easier to use graphic input and output in computer programs. The design of graphics systems is a very important aspect of computer graphics. Without such systems, graphics application programs would be extremely difficult to write; only the most expert programmers would be competent to write them, and their rate of software production would be very slow. It is only by constructing graphics systems that we make it possible to exploit the potential uses of computer graphics.

This chapter and the others in Part Two are concerned mainly with the software component of graphics systems. The type of graphics software system we shall consider first is the most basic and essential of all, the *graphics package*. This is a set of subroutines or functions used by an application program to generate pictures on a plotter or display and to handle graphical interaction. We shall consider the graphical display rather than the plotter as our main output device, since we are concerned with graphics packages for interactive use. To start with, we shall employ a single form of output device, the storage-tube display described in Chapter 3, with the command repertoire shown in Figure 3-10. To permit true interactive use we shall extend our discussion during Chapters 7 and 8 to include techniques for output to refresh displays. Eventually we shall consider the design of graphic input software after covering the necessary background material of Chapters 11 and 12.

## 6-1 GROUND RULES FOR GRAPHICS SOFTWARE DESIGN

This chapter serves mainly to show how the basic concepts presented in Part One can be utilized in the design of a simple graphics package. The main difficulty in constructing such a package is to give adequate consideration to the many issues that affect the usefulness of the package. Some of the more important of these issues are:

*Simplicity.* Features that are too complex for the application programmer to understand will not be used. It is often difficult for the graphics package designer to detect potentially difficult aspects of his design. These aspects do, however, become more obvious when the user's manual is written. One way to avoid these difficult features is to try to write the user's manual before implementing the system. Anything difficult to explain will almost certainly be difficult to use.

*Consistency.* A consistent graphics system is one that behaves in a generally predictable manner. Function names, calling sequences, error handling, and coordinate systems all should follow simple and consistent patterns *without exceptions.* The application programmer is then able to build up a conceptual *model* of how the package functions. Again, inconsistencies often show up when the user's manual is written as small-print passages—sentences here and there, often overlooked by the reader, that warn of anomalies in the system.

*Completeness.* There should be no irritating omissions in the set of functions provided by the system; missing functions will have to be supplied by the application programmer, who may not have the necessary access to the computer's resources to be able to write them. Completeness does not imply comprehensiveness; i.e., the system need not provide every imaginable graphics facility. The system designer must try to design a reasonably small set of functions that can conveniently handle a wide range of applications.

*Robustness.* Application programmers are capable of extraordinary misuse of graphics systems, either through misunderstanding or through the mischievous enjoyment of trying everything once. The system should accept such treatment with a minimum of complaint. Trivial errors of omission or repetition should be corrected without comment from the system. When the programmer does something seriously wrong, the system should report the error in the most helpful manner possible. Only in extreme circumstances should errors cause termination of execution since this will generally cause the user to lose valuable results.

*Performance.* Graphics-system performance is often limited by such factors as operating-system response and display characteristics, factors beyond the system designer's control. There is nothing much to be done here by the graphics-system designer except to minimize the effect by omitting highly dynamic graphic functions that demand fast response or expensive hardware. Apart from this, the system designer should try to maintain consistent performance, so that application programs provide an equally consistent speed of response. It should be possible for the application programmer to achieve this consistency without resorting to special tricks. A really good graphics system offers no special advantages to those who understand the system's internal workings.

*Economy.* It is always frustrating to write an application program only to find that it is too bulky or too expensive to use. Graphics systems should be small and economical, so that adding graphics to an existing application program can always be considered.

These issues provide us with a number of *ground rules* of graphics software system design. Abiding by these rules is not always easy but is almost always worthwhile. We shall try wherever possible to invoke these rules during the exercises in graphics package design that occur in the next two chapters.

## 6-2 FUNCTIONAL DOMAINS

In the initial phase of graphics-system design the issue of completeness is more likely than any other to give the designer trouble. All of a sudden he finds himself inundated with conflicting requirements. He starts with a fairly simple design for a storage-tube display; then he decides to extend it to output to a refresh line-drawing display; he adds special input functions for dynamic graphics applications and three-dimensional transformations for displaying molecular models; then since his display equipment contains hardware for scaling but none for rotation, he omits the rotation function from the system. So he proceeds, never sure when he has reached a satisfactory resting place.

Anyone who designs a graphics package in this manner is ignoring two very important points. First, graphics package design must not be unduly influenced by hardware features or by highly specialized application requirements. Second, the functions in a graphics package can be separated into sets, each set concerned with a particular kind of task; it is then possible to address the issue of completeness, one set at a time. There are a number of such function sets to be considered in designing a system; in our first graphics package we shall provide the following two:

1. *Graphic primitives.* These are used to display straight lines, text strings, circular arcs, and other simple graphical items.
2. *Windowing functions.* These allow the programmer to choose his coordinate system for picture definition and to define the boundary of the visible portion of the picture.

Other function sets that we encounter in later chapters include *segmenting functions,* to permit easier modification of the picture; *two-dimensional transformation functions,* for rotation, translation, and scaling (see Chapter 4); and *input functions,* that allow the user to give commands with the help of a keyboard or graphical input device. In addition to the functions in these sets a number of miscellaneous utility functions for such things as initialization and inquiry always find their way into any graphics package.

The initial phase of system design, then, involves choosing a certain number of these sets to form the *functional domain* of the system. We then attempt to achieve a comprehensive collection of functions within each set while simultaneously attending to the other system-design ground rules.

The reasons behind our initial choice of two function sets are quite simple. In the first place, no system can do without graphic primitives; otherwise no lines can be drawn on the screen. Second, it is essential to provide windowing functions so that the user need not be concerned with details of the screen coordinate system. These are indeed the only two function sets essential to all graphics systems.

## 6-3 GRAPHIC PRIMITIVES

Graphic primitives are the functions that we use to specify the actual lines and characters that make up the picture. These functions must be chosen carefully to provide the application programmer with convenient methods of describing pictures and at the same time to take advantage of the capabilities of the display hardware. It is not sufficient, for example, to provide only a single function to display a dot at a specified coordinate position: this would be laborious to use and would not exploit the line-drawing capabilities of most displays. We shall use a set of three primitive functions in our graphics package:

| | |
|---|---|
| *MoveTo(x,y)** | set current beam position $(x,y)$ for the next line or text string |
| *LineTo(x,y)* | draw a straight line from the current beam position to the point $(x,y)$ and reset the starting point to $(x,y)$ |
| *DrawText(s)* | display the string $s$ with its lower left corner at the current beam position; then reset the current beam position to the string's lower right corner |

This is a much smaller set of graphic primitives than one normally finds in graphics packages. We shall purposely keep it small to simplify the following discussion. Normally the function set would be augmented with functions to display dots, to draw dashed and dotted lines, to specify lines by their length

---

*The function names used in this and following chapters adhere to modern programming language practice in using upper- and lowercase characters and in not restricting name length. Different names would be required in a graphics package for use with FORTRAN, for example.

rather than by their endpoint, to draw circular arcs, and so forth. The inclusion of too many primitive functions is a source of complexity and expense, however, and it is preferable to err in the direction of too few functions. Most of the graphic entities omitted can be drawn with combinations of the above set of three functions.

## 6-4 WINDOWING FUNCTIONS

It is convenient if window and viewport can be defined separately with a pair of functions:

*SetWindow* (*wxmin, wymin, wxmax, wymax*)
> define window position to extend from (*wxmin, wymin*) at the lower left to (*wxmax, wymax*) at the upper right

*SetViewport* (*vxmin, vymin, vxmax, vymax*)
> define viewport correspondingly

A single function could of course do the work of both of these functions, but it would then be more difficult to change the window independently of the viewport.

## 6-5 MISCELLANEOUS FUNCTIONS

To complete this simple graphics package, we need three utility functions:

*ClearScreen* — to clear the screen

*InitGraphics* — to be called once at the start of execution of every graphics program, to clear the screen, initialize the world-to-screen transformation, etc.

*Inquire* (*v*) — to determine essential terminal characteristics; returns with the following information in vector *v*:
> maximum screen *x* in *v.screenxmax*
> maximum screen *y* in *v.screenymax*
> width of text characters in *v.textwidth*
> height of text characters in *v.textheight*,
> etc.

The use of the package is illustrated in the following example program.

## 6-6 EXAMPLE: A GRAPH-PLOTTING PROGRAM

A general-purpose graph-plotting program is an example of the sort of simple but useful application program we can write with our graphics package. The program makes good use of windowing to perform automatic scaling of axes.

The program is written as a procedure, *GraphPlot*, called with five arguments:

1.  The number *n* of data points on the graph

```
procedure GraphPlot(n: integer; var vx, vy: array [1..100] of integer; var sx, sy: string);
    var xmax, ymax, xinterval, yinterval, i: integer; v: InquiryResponse; s: string;
begin
    InitGraphics; Inquire(v);
    xmax := vx[1]; ymax := vy[1];
    for i := 2 to n do begin { Find maximum data values }
        if vx[i] > xmax then xmax := vx[i];
        if vy[i] > ymax then ymax := vy[i]
    end;
    xinterval := RoundUpInterval(xmax/10); xmax := xinterval * 10;
    yinterval := RoundUpInterval(ymax/10); ymax := yinterval * 10;
    SetWindow(0, 0, xmax, ymax); { Region for graph }
    SetViewport(6*v.textwidth, 4*v.textheight,v.screenxmax,v.screenymax);
    MoveTo(0, ymax); LineTo(0, 0); LineTo(xmax, 0); { Draw axes }
    MoveTo(vx[1], vy[1]);
    for i := 2 to n do LineTo(vx[i], vy[i]); { Draw graph }
    SetWindow(0, 0, xmax, 4 * v.textheight); { Region for horizontal scale }
    SetViewport(6 * v.textwidth, 0, v.screenxmax, 4 * v.textheight);
    MoveTo(xinterval, 0); DrawText(sx);
    for i := 1 to 9 do begin
        MoveTo(xinterval * i, 4 * v.textheight);
        LineTo(xinterval * i, 3 * v.textheight);
        MoveTo(xinterval * i - 2 * v.textwidth, v.textheight);
        IntegerToString(xinterval * i, s); DrawText(s)
    end;
    SetWindow(0, 0, 6 * v.textwidth, ymax); { Region for vertical scale }
    SetViewport(0, 4 * v.textheight, 6 * v.textwidth, v.screenymax);
    MoveTo(0, 9.5 * yinterval); DrawText(sy);
    for i := 1 to 9 do begin
        MoveTo(6 * v.textwidth, yinterval * i);
        LineTo(5 * v.textwidth, yinterval * i);
        MoveTo(0, yinterval * i);
        IntegerToString(yinterval * i, s); DrawText(s)
    end;
end;
```

**Figure 6-1** Graph-plotting program written in PASCAL.

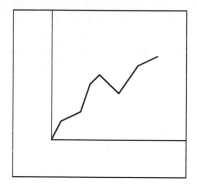

**Figure 6-2** Graph-plotting program: plotting the curve and axes.

2. A pointer to a vector *vx* containing *n* coordinate values for the *independent* variable
3. A pointer to a similar vector *vy* for the *dependent* variable
4. A string pointer *sx* for use in labeling the horizontal axis
5. A string pointer *sy* for the vertical axis

In this example we shall for simplicity assume that the origin (0,0) of the graph's coordinate system will always lie at the lower left corner of the graph plot. This allows us to make particularly effective use of windowing in labeling the axes.

The program is shown written in PASCAL in Figure 6-1. After calls to *InitGraphics* and *Inquire,* the program determines the maximum values in the two vectors *vx* and *vy*: these are stored in *xmax* and *ymax* and are used in a call to *SetWindow.* The viewport is set so as to leave a space at the left of the screen, 6 times the width of a displayed character and another at the bottom 4 times a character's height. These spaces are later used for axis labeling. The axes are then displayed, followed by the graph itself, plotted as a sequence of connected straight lines. The appearance of the display now resembles Figure 6-2.

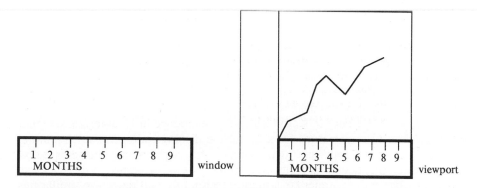

**Figure 6-3** Graph-plotting program: labeling the axes using separate viewports.

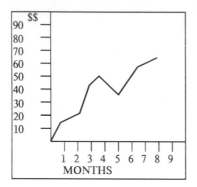

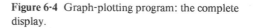

**Figure 6-4** Graph-plotting program: the complete display.

To label the horizontal axis we set window and viewport to the same widths as before, but we give them identical heights equal to four character heights (see Figure 6-3). Thus scaling in the horizontal direction is the same as for the graph and its axes, whereas in the vertical direction it is unity. This permits us to position text labels vertically independent of the graph's scaling. The labeling interval is determined as a function of the range of the independent variable, to give ten intervals across the graph. It is then easy to display the divisions, their labels, and the labeling string supplied. The vertical axis is labeled in a similar manner, with the labeling string at the top. Figure 6-4 shows the completed graph display.

## 6-7 IMPLEMENTATION OF THE FUNCTIONS

It is worthwhile to complete our first exercise in graphics system design by studying in some detail the internal design of each of the functions the system provides. Fortunately none of these functions is particularly complicated, thanks to the overall simplicity of the graphics package itself.

One important concept is involved in the functions' implementation, i.e., use of a separate *display-code generator*. As it happens, only three functions (*LineTo, DrawText,* and *ClearScreen*) actually issue commands to the display. We implement these functions by separating the procedures which have nothing to do with the display's characteristics, e.g. transformation functions, from those which generate the commands, or *display code,* for the display. The latter procedures form the display-code generator.

When we come later to study device independence in Chapter 26, we shall encounter some good reasons for keeping the display-code generator separate. Even if we ignore device independence, this separation represents good programming practice and results in a simpler overall structure to the package. Those familiar with compiler construction techniques will recognize similarities between this approach and the use of a separate code generator in a compiler.

## 6-8 THE TRANSFORMATION PROCESSOR

If we excise from the graphics package those parts which belong to the display-code generator, we are left with the *transformation processor*. Its internal design is shown in Figures 6-5 and 6-6. Note the following points:

1. *Windowing functions* (Figure 6-5). The parameters passed by *SetWindow* and *SetViewport* are always retained; then the transformation matrix is computed, using the latest window and viewport parameters. This mechanism permits these two functions to be called in either order. The use of *InitGraphics* to set up default window and viewport parameters ensures that pictures of some variety will still appear even if the user omits or forgets to set window or viewport.
2. *Primitive functions* (Figure 6-6). Only *LineTo* and *DrawText* are capable of generating display code; the arguments of *MoveTo* are merely transformed

```
type InquiryResponse = record
        screenxmax, screenymax, textwidth, textheight: integer;
        end;
var Wxl, Wxr, Wyb, Wyt, Vxl, Vxr, Vyb, Vyt: real;
    WVxm, WVxa, WVym, WVya: real;
    Clipxl, Clipxr, Clipyb, Clipyt: real;
    cx, cy: real;

procedure SetWindowViewport;
begin
        WVxm := (Vxr − Vxl)/(Wxr − Wxl);
        WVxa :− Vxl − Wxl * WVxm;
        WVym := (Vyt − Vyb)/(Wyt − Wyb);
        WVya := Vyb − Wyb * WVym
end;

procedure SetWindow(xl, yl, x2, y2: real);
begin
        Wxl := xl; Wxr := x2; Wyb := yl; Wyt := y2;
        SetWindowViewport
end;

procedure SetViewport(xl, yl, x2, y2: integer);
begin
        Vxl := xl; Vxr := x2; Vyb := yl; Vyt := y2;
        SetWindowViewport;
        Clipxl := xl; Clipxr := x2; Clipyb := yl; Clipyt := y2
end;
```

**Figure 6-5** Windowing functions of the transformation processor.

```
procedure WorldToScreen(x, y: real; var sx, sy: real);
begin
      sx := WVxm * x + WVxa; sy := WVym * y + WVya
end;

procedure MoveTo(x, y: real);
begin
      WorldToScreen(x, y, cx, cy)
end;

procedure LineTo(x, y: real);
      var nx, ny: real;
begin
      WorldToScreen(x, y, nx, ny);
      Clip(cx, cy, nx, ny); { Clip may call ShowLine in the code generator }
      cx := nx; cy := ny
end;

procedure DrawChar(c: char);
begin
      if (cx >= Clipxl) and (cx + v.textwidth − 1 <= Clipxr) and
       (cy >= Clipyb) and (cy + v.textheight − 1 <= Clipyt) then begin
            ShowChar(c, cx, cy);
            cx := cx + v.textwidth
      end;
end;

procedure DrawText(s: string);
      label return; var i: integer; c: char;
begin
      for i := 1 to MaxStringLength do begin
            c := s[i]; if c = '*' then goto return; { A string is terminated by * }
            DrawChar(c)
      end;
return: end;
```

**Figure 6-6**   Primitive functions of the transformation processor.  Note the use in *LineTo* of a call to the *Clip* routine of Chapter 5.


and stored in readiness for the next line or text string.  When *LineTo* and *DrawText* are called, the appropriate points are transformed into screen coordinates and clipping is then performed against the viewport boundary. The *Clip* routine given in Chapter 5 is used to clip line segments; *Drawtext* calls a routine *DrawChar* to plot each character, and this routine checks whether each character is wholly visible before plotting it.

## 6-9 THE DISPLAY-CODE GENERATOR

We have selected the storage-tube display as our output device. Before attempting to design the display-code generator for this device, we should familiarize ourselves with some of its characteristics:

*Modes.* Like most devices of this kind, our storage-tube terminal has two command modes, for graphics and text. A pair of special command codes permits mode switching. It is essential to ensure that all graphics functions always leave the terminal in the same mode.

*Transmission speed.* The performance of graphics-application programs is often limited by the speed at which commands can be transmitted to the display.

```
const EnterGraphicsMode = 29; LeaveGraphicsMode = 31;
var xlast, ylast: integer; v: InquiryResponse;

procedure TransmitCoords(x, y: real);
      var xi, yi: integer;
begin
      { Note: PutChar transmits a character of given ASCII code }
      xi := trunc(x); yi := trunc(y);
      if (yi div 32) <> (ylast div 32) then PutChar(32 + (yi div 32));
      if ((yi mod 32) <> (ylast mod 32)) or ((xi div 32) <> (xlast div 32))
            then PutChar(96 + (yi mod 32));
      if (xi div 32) <> (xlast div 32) then PutChar(32 + (xi div 32));
      PutChar(64 + (xi mod 32));
      xlast := xi; ylast := yi
end;

procedure ShowLine(x1, y1, x2, y2: real);
begin
      PutChar(EnterGraphicsMode);
      TransmitCoords(x1, y1);
      TransmitCoords(x2, y2);
      PutChar(LeaveGraphicsMode)
end;

procedure ShowChar(c: char; x, y: real);
begin
      PutChar(EnterGraphicsMode);
      TransmitCoords(x, y);
      PutChar(LeaveGraphicsMode);
      PutChar(ord(c));
      xlast := xlast + v.textwidth
end;
```

**Figure 6-7**   The display-code generator.

For this reason we should not add needlessly to the commands we transmit when each function is called.

*Teletype simulation\**. Storage-tube terminals often fill the dual role of drawing pictures and displaying text messages; the latter task is sometimes called Teletype simulation. If no special precautions are taken, these text messages will appear in the middle of the picture, a system feature likely to irritate the user.

Readers may already be questioning the choice of the storage-tube display in view of these programming problems. They will discover in the next chapter that the problems associated with refresh displays are much more severe. The storage-tube display is one of the most easily programmed graphics output devices, and has therefore been chosen as the basis for this section's discussion.

In the display-code generator shown in Figure 6-7 some effort has been made to solve these programming problems. Each routine assumes that the display is in text mode at the start and leaves it in text mode at the end. The display-code generator would also retain the screen coordinates of the last point visited by the display; before each line or text string is displayed, its starting point could be compared with the retained point, in case it should prove possible to avoid transmitting its screen position. This technique, which can approximately halve the amount of information needed to display connected lines cannot, however, be employed in displays like the Tektronix 4006-1, which requires a positioning command to be issued every time the display enters Graphics mode. The Teletype-simulation problem is not solved in this display-code generator design, but solutions will be developed in the next chapter.

## EXERCISES

**6-1** The graphics package just described is not completely robust. For example, a string containing the character code for ENTER GRAPHICS MODE would not be correctly handled by the *DrawText* function. Find as many such potential errors as you can and suggest remedies.

**6-2** In the same vein as Exercise 6-1, examine the graphics package in terms of the other ground rules of graphics-system design.

**6-3** Extend the set of graphics primitives to include other functions you consider useful, and add them to the design of Figures 6-5, 6-6 and 6-7.

**6-4** Suggest a solution to the Teletype-simulation problem suitable for use with the display-code generator of Figure 6-7.

**6-5** Suggest ways in which the storage-tube display might be redesigned to avoid the problems of mode and Teletype simulation.

**6-6** Extend the graph-plotting program to allow the origin of the graph to be placed arbitrarily with relation to the graph itself. Retain the same use of windowing to display the axis labels. This may suggest a useful additional function in the graphics package.

**6-7** Calculate the worst-case number of additions, multiplications, and divisions involved in a single call to *LineTo*. How can this number be reduced?

* Teletype is a trademark and service mark of the Teletype Corporation.

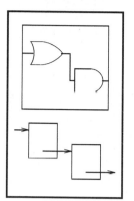

# 7

# SEGMENTED

# DISPLAY FILES

Dynamically changing displayed pictures appeal to everyone involved in computer graphics—user, programmer, system designer, or hardware expert. They attract because they are so unlike the static pictures we habitually draw on paper, because they suggest all sorts of intriguing uses, and because their creation is in itself such a challenging task. There is ample evidence of this attraction in the way the very first computer-graphics research workers immediately tackled the problems of dynamic computer graphics, ignoring until much later the simpler but equally useful subject of static computer graphics.

The graphics package we have discussed in Chapter 6 is basically unsuited to the display of dynamically changing pictures. One reason must at once be obvious to anyone who has sat in front of a storage-tube display. It is simply not possible to change the displayed picture fast enough to produce a smooth transition from one picture to the next. The lines appear one after the other; there is a short pause, followed by a brilliant green flash, and the picture vanishes; then the lines of the next picture start to appear.

Thus dynamic graphics demands *speed of regeneration* of successive pictures. Before we rush to invent ways of achieving this speed, however, we should consider what else is needed. Applications of computer graphics sometimes require that the complete picture be redrawn at each change, just as described; more frequently, however, only a small part of the picture changes, and the rest remains unchanged. For example, we might like to use a light pen

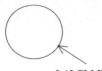

0.45 CM DIA.
0.001 MM. TOL.

**Figure 7-1** Positioning labels, illustrating the need for selective modifications.

or tablet to position the dimension of the hole in Figure 7-1 at the end of its arrow. Here it is essential that the arrow remain stationary while the text moves. The second major requirement for dynamic computer graphics is therefore the ability to make *selective modifications* to the picture, i.e., to add new parts, move them around, and delete them without disturbing the rest.

The storage-tube display is unsuited to dynamic graphics for two main reasons: First, the green flash that accompanies erasure destroys continuity; second, storage tubes cannot provide the full range of selective modification functions needed for dynamic graphics. The three basic functions we require are addition, replacement, and deletion of information. The storage-tube display can provide only the addition function; the other two require erasing the screen and redrawing the entire picture.

As we have seen in Chapter 3, the use of random-scan refreshed CRT displays provides all the characteristics we require for dynamic graphics. The picture is maintained on the screen by repeated regeneration from a stored *display file*, and this display file can be modified selectively and rapidly; no green flash accompanies modifications. Other types of display, such as raster-scan CRT displays and plasma panels, provide what is called *selective-erase* capability; portions of the picture can be deleted by retracing them, i.e., by redrawing them at the opposite intensity level. Since this is not as efficient as display-file modification for performing simple dynamic operations, we shall confine our discussion in this chapter to the random-scan CRT display.

## 7-1 SEGMENTS

It is easy to form the impression that the selective modification capability is all that is needed to achieve dynamic computer graphics. This impression is mistaken: it is like believing, as many did in the early 1960s, that to acquire a graphics display is to ensure its immediate and profitable use. Programming, as well as hardware, is involved. Before the selective-erase capability can be used, we must solve the question of *what* is erased: how do we provide the programmer with the ability to control which parts of the picture change and which parts stay still?

The first stage in solving this problem is obvious: we provide the programmer with the means to *name* the different parts of the picture. Having achieved a naming mechanism, we then furnish him with subroutines or functions that effect the desired modifications on the appropriate parts. The display file, provided it resides in addressable memory, possesses the two fundamental attributes we require: we can assign names or labels to sets of instructions, and these instructions are easily modified.

How should we choose our sets of display instructions for naming? One approach is to name each graphic primitive that we add to the display file. There is no reason, however, why these primitive entities should be a particularly appropriate choice; in almost all cases the unit of modification consists of several if not many such entities. So great, indeed, are the potential classes of pictures and of dynamic modifications that we cannot expect a single unit size to suffice. Instead we must let the programmer determine his own units.

In this chapter we shall discuss a simple approach to display-file manipulation. It is by no means the only such scheme, as we shall see in later chapters, but it is a widely accepted approach that is particularly appropriate to the concepts developed in the previous chapter. We shall use the term *segment* for the unit of picture that is named for modification purposes. The segment is a unit of the *display file*; thus the use of segments by the programmer requires him also to recognize the existence of the display file as a stored representation of the displayed image.

The segment is a *logical* unit, not necessarily contiguous either in the display file or on the screen. It is simply a collection of display-file instructions representing graphic primitives that we can manipulate as a single unit. We therefore need functions to perform these manipulations, and a naming scheme so that we can refer to each segment unambiguously.

## 7-2 FUNCTIONS FOR SEGMENTING THE DISPLAY FILE

In Chapter 6 we raised the notion that primitive graphic functions draw lines and text directly on the screen. We now modify that notion slightly by saying that they deposit display commands in a display-file segment representing the same lines and text. This slight modification to our model of the display process provides the basis for a set of functions for display-file manipulation.

Many readers will be familiar with the common methods of creating and modifying sequential disk files. We *open* a file before we add data to it, and we *close* the file when we have added the last data item and the file is complete. To change the contents of a file, we open it again, add the new data to replace the old, and close the new file. To get rid of a file, we *delete* it.

The very same operations are ideal for manipulating display-file segments. To create a new segment, we open it and then call graphic primitives to add to the segment the lines and text to be displayed; then we close the segment. The same sequence of operations applied to an existing segment will cause that

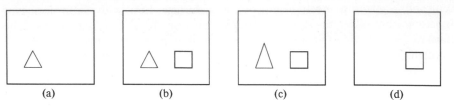

(a)　　　　　　　(b)　　　　　　　(c)　　　　　　　(d)

**Figure 7-2** Manipulation of triangle and square as separate segments.

segment to be replaced by a new one. To remove a segment from the display file, we delete it. Thus we need only three basic functions:

*OpenSegment* (*n*)　　open a display file segment named *n*
*CloseSegment*　　　　close the open segment
*DeleteSegment* (*n*)　remove from the display file the segment named *n*

To illustrate the use of these functions, suppose we wish to display a triangle, as shown in Figure 7-2a. We may use the following statements:

*InitGraphics;*
*SetWindow* (0, 0, 500, 500);
*OpenSegment* (*t*);
*MoveTo* (100, 100);
*LineTo* (150, 200); *LineTo* (200, 100); *LineTo* (100, 100);
*CloseSegment;*

The display file, if originally empty, now contains the single segment *t* (Figure 7-3a). We can add a square, as shown in Figure 7-2b, as follows:

*OpenSegment* (*s*);
*MoveTo* (300, 100);
*LineTo* (300, 200); *LineTo* (400, 200); *LineTo* (400, 100); *LineTo* (300, 100);
*CloseSegment;*

Now the display file contains the two segments *s* and *t*, as in Figure 7-3b. We can redefine the triangle as follows, to achieve Figure 7-2c:

*OpenSegment* (*t*);
*MoveTo* (100, 100);
*LineTo* (150, 250); *LineTo* (200, 100); *LineTo* (100, 100);
*CloseSegment;*

The original segment *t* has been replaced by a new one (Figure 7-3c). Note that we would like the original triangle to remain on the screen until the definition of the new one is complete. We shall encounter this requirement again in Chapter 8 when we discuss double buffering.

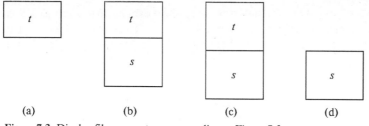

**Figure 7-3** Display file segments corresponding to Figure 7-2.

Finally we can erase the triangle (Figure 7-2d):

*DeleteSegment* (*t*)

The display file now contains only the single segment *s*, as shown in Figure 7-3d.

This is a minimal function set for manipulating segmented display files. The design of the functions shows the influence of the standards of simplicity, completeness, and robustness raised in Chapter 6. Thus there are no more functions than necessary, just enough to do what we want. Two different *OpenSegment* functions could have been provided, one for creating segments and one for replacing existing ones, but this would be capable of misuse — the programmer could try to open a new segment with the same name as an old one.* We could also have required an argument to be passed to *CloseSegment,* to indicate the name of the segment to be closed. This is unnecessary, however, since we can almost always construct display files without opening more than one at a time; thus *CloseSegment* closes the currently open segment and needs no argument.

## 7-3 POSTING AND UNPOSTING A SEGMENT

We can extend the usefulness of our graphics package considerably by allowing segments to become temporarily invisible. For this we need two additional functions. *Posting* is the action of including a segment in the display refresh cycle; thus posting makes a segment visible. *Unposting* removes the segment from the refresh cycle, so that it is no longer visible. The segment is not destroyed by unposting, and so it can be rendered visible again without redefining it, simply by posting it. The two functions to achieve this effect are

*PostSegment* (*n*)　　add segment *n* to the refresh cycle
*UnpostSegment* (*n*)　remove segment *n* from the refresh cycle

---

*File systems generally provide two separate functions here, partly to safeguard against accidentally overwriting a file. Such precautions are not necessary with display-file segments.

By convention, we assume that new segments are in the *unposted* state immediately after they have been defined and closed. Thus a *PostSegment* call is always necessary before a segment becomes visible. As we shall see in the next section, this need not be a significant extra burden to the programmer.

Posting and unposting are particularly useful in avoiding the need for repeatedly redefining graphic overlays, command menus, and other segments that are removed only temporarily from the screen. We can initially create all the menu or overlay segments and then switch between them by simply unposting the old segment and posting the new one.

## 7-4 SEGMENT NAMING SCHEMES

The most common scheme for naming segments is to provide each segment with a *unique integer name.* This is a departure from normal file-system practice, where text strings are more popular as names. Segment names are used only within the program, however, so they are essentially *internal names* unseen by the user of the program. Integers are not only more compact and more easily manipulated than strings but often more convenient as a means of relating segments of the display file to the items of data they represent.

Suppose, for example, we wish to use a graphical display in an air-traffic control center. We might present the air-traffic controller with a display like that shown in Figure 7-4, in which small symbols represent individual aircraft. From signals received in real time, a computer program maintains a data structure containing the identity, airspeed, heading in degrees, position, and altitude of each aircraft; Figure 7-5 shows a suitable list structure. Each aircraft symbol, together with the text labels showing identity, airspeed, and altitude, may be displayed as a single segment, greatly speeding up the task of modifying the picture. An appropriate name for each segment is then the index, in the main list, of the pointer to the vector defining the aircraft in the data structure. In this way we can easily determine the name of the segment representing any

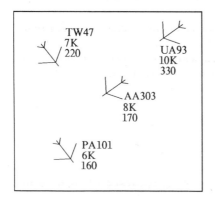

**Figure 7-4** An air traffic control display.

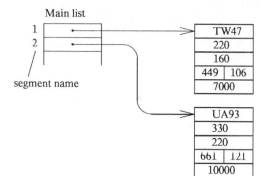

**Figure 7-5**  List-structure representation of air traffic control information.

particular aircraft in the data structure without using space in the data structure to define it.

## 7-5 DEFAULT ERROR CONDITIONS

Quite clearly, the programmer can make any one of a number of programming mistakes with the five functions *OpenSegment, CloseSegment, DeleteSegment, PostSegment,* and *UnpostSegment,* by issuing function calls in peculiar orders. For example, he can forget to close a segment, and then try to open another; or he can attempt to delete a nonexistent segment.

   There are several solutions to this class of problem.  It would obviously be quite simple and satisfactory to generate an error message on each such occasion.  Error messages are often superfluous during display-file construction, however.  Just the visible evidence on the screen is usually enough to indicate that the display file has been constructed incorrectly.  Consequently there is no need to do any more than perform the following default actions:

| | |
|---|---|
| *OpenSegment* (*n*) | any currently open segment is closed |
| *CloseSegment* | if no segment is currently open, no effect |
| *DeleteSegment* (*n*) | any currently open segment is closed; if segment *n* does not exist, no further effect |
| *PostSegment* (*n*) | any currently open segment is closed; if segment *n* is nonexistent or already posted, no effect |
| *UnpostSegment* (*n*) | any currently open segment is closed; if segment *n* is nonexistent or already unposted, no effect |

   Not only do these default actions take care of the more common mistakes of omission, but they simplify programming too.  It is no longer necessary both to close and to post a segment in order to make it visible; posting alone will suffice. Normal practice, therefore, is to use the following sequence to create a new, visible segment:

> *OpenSegment* (*s*);
> *MoveTo* (200, 200);
> *LineTo* (200, 300); *LineTo* (300, 300); . . .
> *PostSegment* (*s*);

The examples given in the earlier sections would therefore be rewritten with a call to *PostSegment* in place of each call to *CloseSegment.*

## 7-6 APPENDING TO SEGMENTS

It is sometimes inconvenient that a display-file segment, once it has been defined, cannot be incrementally modified but must always be completely rebuilt. Consider, for example, a program to display the results of two concurrent simulations in the form of two graphs plotted on the same axes, as shown in Figure 7-6. Every 2 minutes each simulation generates a fresh data point, and the graphs are extended.

One method of writing such a program would be to create a new segment for each addition made to either graph. This would be extremely inefficient, however, since a complete simulation might involve several hundred data points. On the other hand, any alternate approach, such as the use of a single segment for each graph, could involve reconstructing the entire segment after every step.

In situations like this, a function for appending to segments is useful:

> *AppendToSegment* (*n*)   open segment *n* for additions, leaving its present contents intact

Thus to add a line to a graph represented by segment *g* and leave the segment posted, we might write the following statements:

> *AppendToSegment* (*g*);
> *MoveTo* (*lastx, lasty*);
> *LineTo* (*newx, newy*);
> *PostSegment* (*g*);

The *AppendToSegment* function, although often useful in writing application programs, has some troublesome side effects. In view of these problems, which are discussed in the next chapter, the *AppendToSegment* function may involve more trouble than it is worth. In a few cases, like the example given, the lack of such a function will be felt by the application programmer; it is usually possible, however, to solve the problem by careful use of segments. Thus in the simulation example we can use a separate segment for each sequence of *n* data points, where *n* is in the range 20 to 50. We use a separate segment to represent each recent addition to either graph and redraw

**Figure 7-6** Plotting the results of two concurrent simulations.

these additions as a single segment each time the total number of the recent segments reaches *n*. Techniques of this kind are an indication of the complexity that can occasionally be avoided with the provision of an *AppendToSegment* function.

## EXERCISES

**7-1** What should the default error action be if the application program should call primitive functions without first opening a segment?

**7-2** Suppose we wished to be able to manipulate individual display primitives in the same manner as segments: what changes would be necessary to the graphics functions described in Chapters 6 and 7?

**7-3** What would be the advantages and disadvantages of permitting more than one segment to be open at a time?

**7-4** Although it is almost universal to use integers as segment names, it is feasible to use other types of data, such as strings and floating-point numbers. Can you think of reasons for using such names?

**7-5** Rather than divide the displayed image logically into segments, we could divide it physically, e.g., into small squares. What effect would this have on interactive programming?

**7-6** As we have seen, it is possible to provide two functions for opening segments, one to create a new segment, the other to redefine an existing segment. Does such a scheme have advantages? Illustrate your answer with some short program sequences.

**7-7** Some graphics packages implement posting and unposting as manipulation of an *attribute* of the segment, i.e. changing its visibility. Can you think of other useful segment attributes?

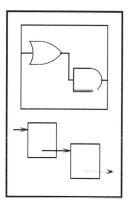

# 8

# DISPLAY FILE

# COMPILATION

It is by no means as easy to construct the display-code segments for a refresh display as it is to generate code for a storage-tube terminal. Since the display code must be stored for refresh, memory must be allocated for its storage; the space it consumes must be kept to a minimum, and care must be taken to ensure that it can be refreshed as fast as possible to reduce flicker. Furthermore, we would often like to reconstruct segments repeatedly in order to achieve dynamic picture changes; this suggests that we attempt to construct segments as fast as possible. All in all, the goals in display-file construction are very similar to those in compiling source programs into machine code. This has led to the use of the term *display-file compiler* for the refresh display-code generator. In this chapter we shall consider some of the issues in display-file compilation.

## 8-1 REFRESH CONCURRENT WITH RECONSTRUCTION

A display that periodically blinks or goes blank for a second or two is very annoying: it prevents the user from concentrating on the task at hand. Therefore we should try to construct our display-file compiler to ensure *uninterrupted refresh*. We should never stop the refresh process, even when we are reconstructing part of the display file, since a blink of even a fraction of a

| segment 1 |
| segment 2 |
| segment 3 |

**Figure 8-1** A three-segment display file.

second is noticeable to the user. Instead we should try to maintain constant refresh during all display-file modifications.

The problem thus raised is a classic one of *synchronization* of two concurrent processes. As the display file is being modified by one processor (the CPU executing the application program), it is being read by another (the display processor). This kind of operation, in which one process writes data while another process reads them, in general produces indeterminate results. For example, we might try to change segment 3 of the display file shown in Figure 8-1, simply by overwriting it with the new display code. Halfway through, the display processor might catch up with the display-file compiler, executing first an instruction from the new display segment and then one from the old segment. At best, the picture might appear momentarily to break up in a strange fashion; at worst, the display processor will be directed to the wrong part of memory, perhaps destroying the contents of certain vital memory locations.

We use the term *corruption* of the display file whenever the display file fails to represent a valid sequence of instructions for the display processor. A simple way to avoid corruption is to use *double buffering*. We construct the new segment in an unused area of memory, leaving the old version in the display file. When the new version is closed and posted, it takes the place of the old version and the vacated space is free for future use. Double buffering obviously creates discontinuities in the display file, which may eventually look something

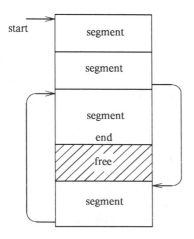

**Figure 8-2** Discontinuities in the display file caused by double buffering.

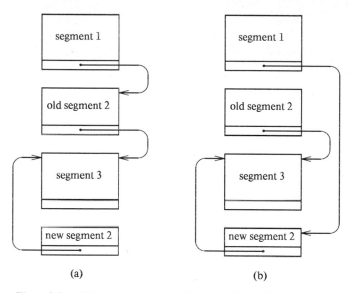

**Figure 8-3** Achieving a smooth transition in double buffering.

like Figure 8-2. Here each segment is followed either by the next consecutive segment or by a pointer (or jump instruction) to it. For generality, it is best if all segments terminate with a jump instruction that may simply address a segment starting at the next consecutive memory location.

There is a critical moment in the double-buffering operation when the new and old segments are exchanged. This must be done in the sequence shown in Figure 8-3. The new segment should be complete, including its final jump instruction pointing to the next segment in the display file, as shown in Figure 8-3a. Then the jump instruction in the preceding segment can be switched to point to the new segment, as in Figure 8-3b. In this way a smooth transition is ensured and corruption of the display file is prevented.

## 8-2 FREE STORAGE ALLOCATION

As we have just seen, the display-file compiler at frequent intervals needs blocks of unused memory in which to construct new segments. Just as frequently it discards blocks of memory for which it has no further use. A *free-storage allocation system* is therefore needed to supply blocks of free memory and to receive blocks that are vacated.

A display-file compiler makes somewhat unusual demands on a free storage allocation system. Three requirements are of particular importance:

1. The *amount* of memory required is unknown at the time of allocation; free

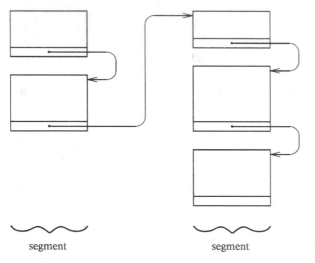

segment                    segment                    **Figure 8-4** Fractured segments.

storage is needed at the moment we open a segment, but the amount needed is not known until the segment is closed.

2.   *Speed of allocation* is important since any sizable delay adversely affects the program's response.

3.   *Blocks cannot immediately be reused* after they become free. Here again, we encounter a concurrency problem. If we reuse a block immediately, the display processor may still be executing instructions within it, and if we overwrite these instructions, we may corrupt the display file.

Although we do not know how much memory we need when a new segment is opened, it is always possible to make an estimate. In particular, when a segment is replaced, the new segment may be assumed to be approximately the same size as the old one. If we overestimate, we can simply return the unused memory to free storage. The situation caused by underestimating is less simple. We must fetch another block of free storage to accommodate the rest of the segment and include a jump instruction at the end of the first block pointing to the second block. This creates a *fractured segment,* which, as shown in Figure 8-4, may even contain three or more separate blocks.

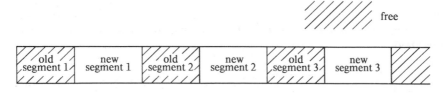

**Figure 8-5** Fragmenting effect on free storage of double buffering.

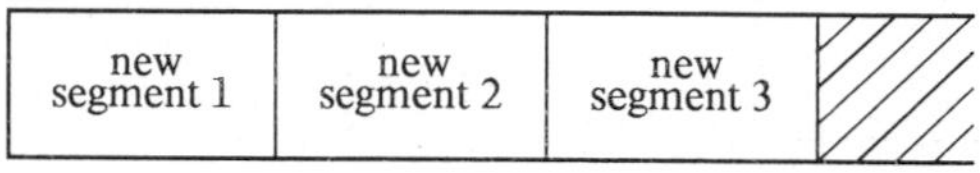

**Figure 8-6** Amalgamating free blocks by garbage collection.

Fractured segments are more troublesome to delete or replace since each of the blocks in the segment must be located and returned to free storage.

In an attempt to avoid fractured segments, we may choose instead always to overestimate the segment size. Thus we can always fetch the *largest* available block of memory, and later return the unused portion. When the program begins execution, the whole expanse of free memory (the *free-storage area*) is in the form of a single block, big enough to exceed all requests. Each time we construct a segment, we reduce the size of this block. We can try to maintain as large a block as possible by amalgamating it with any returned blocks that are contiguous in memory. Unfortunately the use of double buffering tends to prevent amalgamation. As Figure 8-5 shows, each new segment usually separates the main free block from the free block vacated by the old segment. Thus the main block becomes gradually smaller, until it is eventually too small to accommodate even one segment. Meanwhile many noncontiguous free blocks are scattered throughout the free storage area. We call this *fragmentation* of the free-storage area.

Fragmentation can be cured in one of two ways: by allowing segments to become fractured, hence permitting the use of fragments of any size; or by collecting all the fragments together into a single free block, by means of a process called *garbage collection*. To perform garbage collection we move all the blocks of display file toward one end of the free storage area, thus filling in all the unused fragments and creating a single free block at the other end (Figure 8-6). When each block is moved, all jump instructions or pointers to the block must be adjusted. Garbage collection may take a second or more to carry out; it is difficult to perform without stopping the display, which then blinks noticeably.

A simple approach to free-storage allocation is the use of *fixed-size blocks*. At the start we divide the entire free-storage area into blocks of, say, 32 words each. Segments are then constructed by chaining these blocks together. Any unused space at the end of the last block of a segment remains empty, rather than being returned to free storage. This method is extremely simple but somewhat wasteful because of these unused words. Furthermore, the use of fixed-size blocks is not always feasible, since free storage may be needed by other parts of the application program in blocks of other sizes. In such cases, the use is recommended of the *boundary-tag* allocation scheme described by Knuth [268].

Whichever allocation system we use, we must take care when blocks are released to delay their reuse until they are no longer being read by the display processor. The vacated blocks should be placed on a temporary free-storage list that is added to the main list only after the end of the refresh cycle has been

| name | address |
|------|---------|
| name | address |
| name | address |

Figure 8-7  Use of a vector as a name table.

reached. If the main list is completely exhausted, we may cause the program to wait until completion of the refresh cycle makes the temporary list available.

It is of course possible to exhaust all sources of free storage. This creates an error condition that should be handled gracefully by the graphics system. The currently open segment should be closed and all further graphic primitive-function calls should be ignored. For the benefit of application programmers who wish to handle this situation by deleting other segments or allocating more memory to free storage, the *Inquire* function should provide information about the amount of free storage available, and if free storage should be exhausted during compilation of a segment, the *Inquire* function should provide the name of the segment so that it can later be regenerated. A well-designed application program will inform the user when memory becomes scarce, advising him what steps to take.

## 8-3 DISPLAY-FILE STRUCTURE

Before we can implement segmenting functions, we must design the format of the display file. Display processors are frequently designed with little thought for ease of programming; sometimes it is very difficult to implement the set of functions for manipulating display-file segments. This is particularly true if the display processor possesses neither jump instructions nor a display subroutine

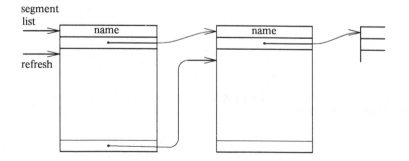

Figure 8-8  Names stored in segments, with linked-list pointers and jump instructions.

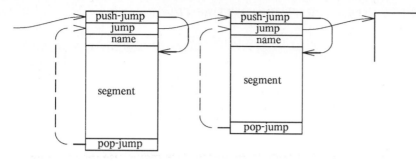

**Figure 8-9** Use of push-jump and pop-jump instructions to achieve single-pointer segment linkage.

mechanism. The following discussion of display-file organization will show how useful these two hardware features can be.

An essential part of the display file structure is the *name table,* which allows us to determine a segment's address in memory from its name. The name table may be stored in a vector, as shown in Figure 8-7, with two fields per entry, one for the name, the other for the segment address. A third field may be added containing the length of each segment to assist in garbage collection. A linear table like this can be searched rapidly for a given name and can be used in conjunction with most kinds of display processor. Its main drawback is that its size determines the maximum number of segments permitted in the display file unless provision is made to enlarge it when it fills up.

An alternate scheme is to store the segment name at the head of the segment itself, as shown in Figure 8-8. Space for names is then exhausted only with the exhaustion of free storage itself. We can locate any given segment by stepping along the linked list of segments. To speed up this search, we should include in the head of the segment a pointer to the next segment; this pointer is essentially a copy in a more easily located place of the jump instruction that terminates the segment.

Figure 8-9 shows a modification of this design, using push-jump and pop-jump instructions. The first instruction in each segment is a push-jump to the fourth instruction, followed by a jump to the next segment and the segment name. The push-jump directs the display over the following two words to the first word of display code. The pop-jump that terminates the segment returns the display processor to the jump instruction, which in turn directs it to the next segment. By eliminating the duplication of pointers, this scheme simplifies garbage collection and makes the display-file compiler more robust. Posting and unposting are very simple. A segment is unposted by copying into the first word the jump instruction contained in the second; it is posted by overwriting the contents of the first word with a push-jump to the fourth. This scheme has some further advantages when used with a light pen, which we shall explore in Chapter 13.

## 8-4 DISPLAY FILES FOR STORAGE-TUBE TERMINALS

Can display-file segmentation be applied to nonrefresh displays, such as the direct-view storage-tube terminal? Our initial reaction would probably be to guess not. The purpose of building a display file, segmented or not, is to refresh the display; the storage-tube display does not require refresh.

There are, however, three good reasons for using a segmented display file with a storage-tube terminal:

1. *To allow display regeneration without recomputation.* We often need to regenerate the display after a minor deletion. This could involve re-executing the parts of the program that generated the display in the first place. Thus the picture must be recomputed, retransformed and reclipped and the display code regenerated. None of this is necessary if we save the display code each time it is generated.
2. *To reduce the frequency of display regeneration.* If part of the picture is deleted, the display must be regenerated to show the effect. On the other hand, if more lines are added to the picture, no regeneration is necessary. It is tiresome for the programmer to have to remember when regeneration is required and when it is not. The method described below uses a segmented display file to ensure that the display is regenerated only when necessary.
3. *To achieve compatibility with refresh-display packages.* It is most convenient if we can run the same program unchanged on both refresh and nonrefresh displays. The addition of one function, the *Update* function, described below, makes this possible.

The display file for a storage-tube terminal consists of a number of separate segments, each containing the actual display codes to be transmitted to the terminal. As with refresh displays, a free-storage system is necessary, and we also need a name table. The methods described above for refresh displays are quite adequate. The problem of concurrency is no longer present, however, so double buffering and delayed reuse may be ignored.

Whenever a segment is closed or deleted, this display file is modified accordingly. No attempt is made to change the display, however. If we were to update the display automatically after every change, certain operations would become excruciatingly slow. For example, in order to delete five segments the user would have to wait through five complete regenerations of the display. So instead we ask the programmer to indicate when to update the screen, by calling the following function:

*Update*      update the display to reflect the current display file contents

Thus calling *Update* after making a batch of changes in the display file will cause the appropriate segments to be transmitted to the terminal. If no segment has been redefined, deleted, or unposted, only newly posted segments are transmitted; otherwise the screen is erased and the entire display file is sent (the GINO/F graphics package [522] draws a cross on the storage tube through each segment deleted). Typically the programmer will arrange for the *Update* function to be called before each request for user input.

Although the display file for a storage-tube terminal is simpler than a refresh display file, it requires one embellishment, a means of indicating whether any segment has changed since the last update. A simple solution is to mark each segment by means of a bit in its name-table entry either *painted* or *unpainted*, according to whether or not the segment in the display file matches its current representation on the screen. Thus immediately after a display-file segment has been defined and closed, it is marked *unpainted;* after it has been transmitted to the display, it becomes *painted;* immediately after redefining or deleting the segment becomes *unpainted* again. The *Update* function can determine whether to regenerate the display by the following algorithm:

1. If any segments are painted but unposted, or if any segment has been deleted since the most recent *Update,* erase the screen and transmit to the display all posted segments; otherwise transmit just those segments which are posted but unpainted.
2. Mark all posted segments painted and all unposted segments unpainted.

When this algorithm is employed, the effect of calling *PostSegment* and *UnpostSegment* is merely to change the setting of the segment's posted indicator. The segment's painted indicator is not changed until *Update* is called.

An issue has been raised in this section that will surface again in Part Six, namely *device independence* in graphics systems. By this is meant a system that allows programs to be used unchanged with different input and output devices. We can achieve a small but useful degree of device independence by always employing a segmented display file, whether or not we are using a refresh display, and by including an *Update* function that updates the nonrefresh display but has no effect on a refresh display. As mentioned earlier, this offers two other advantages in the case of the storage display, namely reduction in computation and fewer complete regenerations. One thing is lost, namely the ability to write huge numbers of lines onto the screen without using correspondingly huge display files. Solutions to this problem exist and will be discussed in Chapter 27.

## EXERCISES

**8-1** Suggest mechanisms for posting and unposting segments in the schemes illustrated in Figures 8-7 and 8-8; assume that no push-jumps are to be used.

**8-2** How does the fracturing of segments affect the schemes described above?

**8-3** Discuss ways in which display-processor design can simplify or complicate the task of the display-file compiler. For example, how would one cope with multiword instructions, or make use of short vector instructions? What special instructions might simplify display-file manipulation? What makes smooth transitions during double buffering difficult?

**8-4** Discuss modifications to the display file structure that would handle appending to segments.

**8-5** Above we have discussed the use of segmented display files for storage displays, containing actual display code for the terminal. Discuss the advantages and disadvantages of using a universal display-code format for all storage displays.

**8-6** Some displays permit segments to be erased by retracing them in erase mode. How would this capability affect the implementation of the graphics package and of the *Update* function in particular?

**8-7** What is the effect on the *Update* algorithm of including the *AppendToSegment* function in the graphics package?

**8-8** Some graphics packages include a *RenameSegment* (n1, n2) function, which changes the name of segment n1 to n2. Suggest uses for this function.

**8-9** Some graphics packages do not include implicit double-buffereing, but instead require the programmer to implement double-buffering using the *RenameSegment* function (see Exercise 8-8). Show how this would be done. What are the advantages and disadvantages of this method? Design a set of functions that make use of the *RenameSegment* function, and the others for segment manipulation, to provide double-buffered segment replacement.

**8-10** Review your answer to Exercise 7-7, Chapter 7. How easy would it be to implement the segment attribute manipulations you proposed?

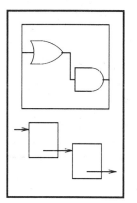

# 9

# GEOMETRIC MODELS

One of the most popular and effective uses of the digital computer is in the abstract representation of physical systems. The general term we use for this type of application is *modeling*. Computer models can be built of both physical objects and physical processes; some examples include:

*Electric circuits.* Power companies and authorities often model their power networks to predict loading and performance; designers of electronic circuits use computer models to help them in their design work.
*Buildings.* Computer models of buildings permit architects to test certain aspects of their designs and to generate plan and perspective views.
*National and world economies.* It is possible to develop programs that model the economic systems of the world in order to test the repercussions of currency devaluations and other financial strategies.
*Weather.* Some of the world's largest computers are involved in modeling weather conditions and helping forecast weather changes.

In several of these examples the computer model is used as a basis for *simulation,* i.e., to predict the behavior of the physical system under certain conditions. Simulation is a very important field of computing; a number of programming languages have been designed to help simulation by making it easier to build models, set up conditions, and observe the results. Nevertheless

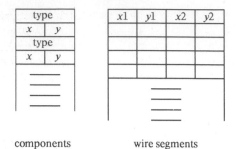

| type | | | x1 | y1 | x2 | y2 |
|------|--|--|----|----|----|----|
| x | y | | | | | |
| type | | | | | | |
| x | y | | | | | |
| | | | | | | |

components                    wire segments

**Figure 9-1** A simple data structure representing a circuit model.

simulation represents only one use of computer modeling. Another very important use is in computer-aided design: solid objects are modeled by computer so that their designers can generate machine-tool programs for their manufacture; integrated circuits are modeled so that they can be checked automatically against design rules and the masks for their manufacture can be generated by computer.

Computer graphics has long been associated with modeling. One obvious reason is that computer graphics offers a very convenient way to observe the behavior of computer models. When we simulate weather patterns, for example, we can plot pressure and temperature values on a displayed map, instead of printing them in tabular form; the resulting display is much more easily understood by the user of the model. We can also make use of interactive graphics in design applications, where the construction of the computer model represents a large part of the design process.

This chapter and Chapter 10 discuss ways in which computer graphics can be used in conjunction with modeling. The emphasis of these two chapters is on the generation of images from computer models. The actual techniques for building and manipulating models are not discussed in detail, except in the case of strictly graphical modeling techniques; modeling as a whole is too broad a subject to be covered in a few pages.

## 9-1  A SIMPLE MODELING EXAMPLE

In this section we shall use a simple example to present a few of the basic concepts of modeling and to discuss ways of displaying modeled information. Other examples of modeling will be used in a similar fashion throughout this chapter and Chapter 10.

Our example concerns modeling a digital electronic circuit. There are several reasons for modeling such circuits in a computer: we may wish to design them, to produce documentary diagrams of them, or to teach students about them. For each application we might construct a different type of model. Since we are not concerned here with the precise purpose of the model, we shall adopt a relatively simple and general one.

Many computer models consist of a mixture of data structures and procedures. In some cases, such as models of solid objects, we find a lot of data and very few procedures. In models of processes, such as weather systems and economics, it is the other way around. Very rarely do we find a model that is entirely in the form of a data structure or entirely procedural.

Our circuit model is no exception to the rule: it consists of a simple data structure supplemented by some procedures. The data structure defines each of the components and connecting wires in the circuit diagram. It does not contain any *relational* information, i.e., information describing relationships between these items, other than identification of the type of each component. This can be seen in the layout of the data structure in Figure 9-1, where each component is defined by an element of data containing its type and coordinate position on the diagram and each line segment of a wire is defined by the coordinates of its two endpoints. Relational information, such as the connections between components, is determined by procedures. Thus we can write a procedure to determine whether a wire and a component are connected by comparing coordinates; we can write another procedure to apply a similar connectivity test to any two wires; then by applying these two procedures iteratively to the contents of the data structure we can determine which components are connected together.

We can apply various processes to this basic model. For example, we can test for excessive *fan-out*, i.e., too many components with inputs connected to the output of a single component. This test will involve first determining all the wires leading from a given component's output connector, then counting how many of these are inputs to other components, and finally comparing this number with the manufacturer's recommended fan-out limit for the component. We can probably think of many other processes that would similarly help designers or students using the model. The most obvious and generally useful of these is a process to display the circuit diagram.

The representation we have chosen for our model makes it very easy to construct the circuit diagram on a display screen. The coordinate system in which component and wire endpoint positions are defined becomes our world

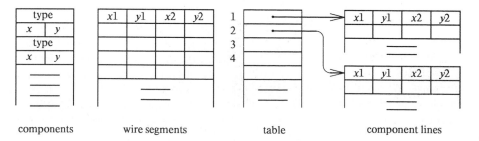

| components | wire segments | table | component lines |

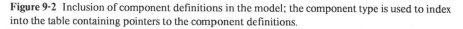

**Figure 9-2** Inclusion of component definitions in the model; the component type is used to index into the table containing pointers to the component definitions.

coordinate system. Line segments are then generated using the stored endpoints as parameters. The display of the components is slightly more complicated: we must define how each component is to be displayed on the screen. Figure 9-2 shows these definitions included in the model, by means of sets of lines to represent each type of component, and a table for use in addressing the appropriate set of lines. This approach is in keeping with the use of data structures, rather than procedures, to represent the geometry of connection lines. The following pair of procedures will scan the list of lines and components and display each at its appropriate position:

```
procedure ShowWires;
    var i: integer;
begin
    for i := 1 to nWires do begin
        MoveTo(Wires[i].x1, Wires[i].y1);
        LineTo(Wires[i].x2, Wires[i].y2)
    end;
end;

procedure ShowComponents;
    var i,j: integer; xt,yt: real; c: ↑component;
begin
    for i := 1 to nComponents do begin
        xt := Components[i].x;
        yt := Components[i].y;
        c := ComponentTable[Components[i].comptype];
        with c↑ do begin
            for j := 1 to nLines do begin
                MoveTo(Lines[j].x1 + xt, Lines[j].y1 + yt);
                LineTo(Lines[j].x2 + xt, Lines[j].y2 + yt)
            end
        end
    end
end;
```

If we examine this program for generating circuit diagrams, we can see several shortcomings. The program makes use of a data structure to represent the displayed form of each type of component, but it does not specify how this data structure is to be created, as must be done before the circuit diagram can be drawn. Also the program handles the translation of components in a very clumsy way; we shall shortly see how we can employ the transformation techniques of Chapter 4 to perform such operations in a much simpler fashion.

## 9-2 GEOMETRIC MODELING

Our digital-circuit model has the property of suggesting a specific geometric form for the circuit diagram. The line segments representing each component and each connection in the circuit are fully defined by the coordinates stored in the data structure. Models which have this property are called *geometric models;* they include a large proportion of the models we construct of physical objects. Nongeometric modeling is usually applied to physical processes, rather than objects; an economic model, for example, would not normally have any specific geometric form.

The conventional approach to geometric modeling is to place the geometry entirely in the data structure, as exemplified by the circuit model. It is not essential to follow this approach. We could, for example, store just the connectivity relationships of the circuit in the data structure and use a procedure to compute the geometry of the connecting lines. Thus if the data structure indicates that the output of component $A$ is to be connected to the input of component $B$ in Figure 9-3, we could use a procedure to determine the coordinates of a sequence of lines connecting the two components; one possible sequence, shown in the figure, would be generated by the following procedure:

```
procedure LinkPoints(x1, y1, x2, y2: integer);
begin
    MoveTo(x1, y1);
    LineTo((x1 + x2)/2, y1);
    LineTo((x1 + x2)/2, y2);
    LineTo(x2, y2)
end;
```

Taken to an extreme, this approach would allow us to omit all geometric data from the structure, since we could allocate coordinate positions to the components by means of a procedure. The next chapter discusses this kind of procedural approach in greater detail; in this chapter we consider the more conventional type of geometric model, whose geometry resides entirely in the data structure.

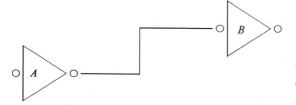

Figure 9-3  A pair of components connected by lines generated with the *LinkPoints* procedure.

### Displaying a Geometric Model

A model that defines the geometric form of an object or set of objects does not necessarily define how those objects should be displayed. In Figure 9-4, for example, we see three different displayed representations of the same three-dimensional object. The choice of method we use to display modeled objects depends partly on the purpose of displaying them and partly on the hardware and software available for their display. A great many techniques, some of them to be discussed in Part Five, have been developed to make the display of geometric models more effective. At the same time, certain basic methods exist that apply to the display of nearly all models. These methods are based on the existence of certain common features in nearly all geometric models:

*Basic elements of data* that typically appear as individual graphic entities on the screen. Examples include the lines and components in the circuit model and the edges or faces of the solid object shown in Figure 9-4. Sometimes the graphical representation of these entities is defined by means of additional data in the model, as in the component definitions of Figure 9-2; sometimes it is left undefined, as in Figure 9-1, in which case the display-generation process must supply it.

*Structure* imposing certain relationships between the basic data elements. Many different kinds of relationships can be expressed in models, using lists, arrays, sets, rings, and other kinds of structuring mechanisms. Thus we can model collections of similar objects by grouping elements together in lists, we can establish hierarchies by means of tree structures of elements, and we can attach property lists to elements to define their attributes. These are only a few of the wide variety of structuring methods used in computer models. In displaying modeled objects we are concerned principally with the task of traversing such structures in an efficient manner so as to display each of the elements in the structure.

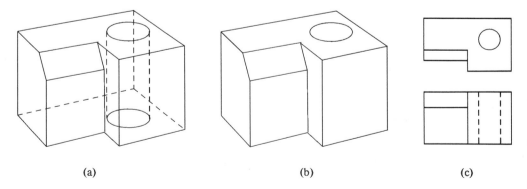

(a)                                  (b)                                  (c)

**Figure 9-4** Three different views of the same solid object: (a) a perspective view with hidden lines shown dashed; (b) the same view with hidden lines removed; (c) a pair of orthogonal projections.

*Transformations* that define the position and orientation of each part of the modeled object. In a model that includes many instances of the same component a transformation is applied to each one to place it appropriately in the modeling space. This can be seen in the circuit model of Figure 9-2, which includes translation factors to be applied to each instance of a component. Even when there is no repetitive use of the same component, we often use transformations to position the different parts of the modeled object.

Our earlier example of the digital circuit model exhibits all three of these features, and it also brings to light certain deficiencies in our ability to display such a model. Specifically it shows that while we possess adequate methods for traversing the structure of such models, we need more convenient methods for defining the graphical representation of each element of the model and for applying transformations to them. The next section shows how to add these capabilities to a graphics package.

## 9-3 SYMBOLS AND INSTANCES

The use of graphical symbols is very common in charts and graphs like the one shown in Figure 9-5. Here we see in the key of the chart a definition of each symbol, and multiple *instances* of each symbol in the chart itself. When we draw charts on a display, we must be able to define symbols so that we can include instances of each symbol in the displayed chart. The same capability is very useful in displaying plans of buildings, electric-circuit diagrams, and drawings of mechanical objects.

The way we define a symbol need not be very different from the way we define other images for display. There is a difference, however, in the choice of coordinate system. When we define a symbol, we do not know where it will be placed in the world coordinate system; indeed the whole point of the symbol is

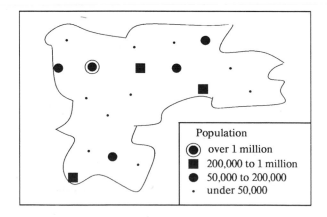

**Figure 9-5** Use of symbols in a population map.

that we can replicate it all over the world coordinate space. We must therefore define the symbol in a different coordinate system, called the *master coordinate system*. To display each instance of the symbol, we define an *instance transformation* to be applied to the master-coordinate definition to transform it into world coordinates.

Functions are needed for the specification of instance transformations. We therefore add three new *instance-transformation functions* that allow us to define the scaling, rotation, and translation to be applied to the symbol:

*Scale* (sx, sy)      scale the symbol by factors *sx* and *sy* in the *x* and *y* directions relative to the origin

*Rotate* (θ)          rotate the symbol through θ° degrees clockwise about the origin

*Translate* (tx, ty)   translate the symbol through distances *tx* and *ty* measured in the *x* and *y* directions

The use of this set of three functions follows naturally from the discussion of Chapter 4. Other ways of applying instance transformations are discussed in Chapter 10. By means of calls to one or more of these functions we can orient symbols in a variety of different ways, illustrated by the examples shown in Figure 9-6. As we have seen in Chapter 4, the order in which the functions are called affects the resulting instance transformation. We generally call *Scale* before *Rotate* and call *Translate* last of all. Other orderings can be used, but it is not so easy to predict the effects.

Since the instance transformation produces world coordinates, we must still invoke the viewing transformation on its results. In our simple graphics-package design we included the viewing transformation as a step in the primitive line-drawing function (Figure 9-7a); now we shall extend this function so that it effectively includes an instance transformation (Figure 9-7b). Thus we have augmented the ability of our graphics package to handle symbols by providing three extra functions and by redesigning our primitive graphic functions to incorporate both instance and viewing transformations.

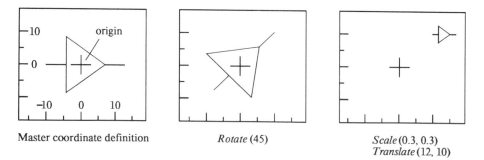

Master coordinate definition          *Rotate* (45)          *Scale* (0.3, 0.3)
                                                              *Translate* (12, 10)

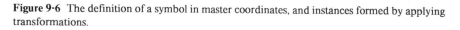

**Figure 9-6**  The definition of a symbol in master coordinates, and instances formed by applying transformations.

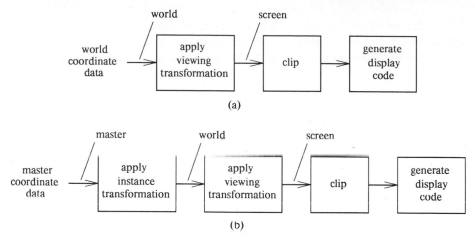

Figure 9-7 Steps in the transformation sequence: (a) without instance transformations; (b) with instance transformations.

How we define symbols and invoke instances of them is shown in the following example. Here we have taken the earlier example of a circuit diagram and, using the data structure of Figure 9-1, have included short sequences of function calls in the *ShowComponents* procedure to define the symbols to have the shapes shown in Figure 9-8. Each such sequence constitutes the master-coordinate definition of the symbol. It is preceded by a call to the *Translate* function that sets the position of the symbol for each of the instances defined in the data structure.

```
procedure ShowComponents;
     var i,j: integer; a: transform;
begin
     for i := 1 to nComponents do begin
          SaveTransform(a);
          Translate(Components[i].x, Components[i].y);
          case Components[i].comptype of
               1: begin MoveTo(0, −2); LineTo(0, 2);
                    LineTo(4, 0); LineTo(0, −2) end;
               2: begin MoveTo(0, −4); LineTo(0, 4); LineTo(6, 4);
                    LineTo(10, 0); LineTo(6, −4); LineTo(0, −4) end
          end;
          SetTransform(a)
     end
end;
```

In comparison with the earlier example on page 114, this program shows two improvements. First, it takes care of both the definition of each symbol and the generation of its instances; second, it handles instance transformations in a simple, straightforward manner. In retrospect we can see that the earlier example would have been quite unmanageable had it involved rotated symbols, whereas now they can be handled very easily with a call to the *Rotate* function.

The reader will have noticed two unexplained function calls to *SaveTransform* and *SetTransform*. These perform an essential part of the process of displaying symbols:

*SaveTransform* (*a*)     save in array *a* the current instance transformation
*SetTransform* (*a*)     set the instance transformation using the contents of array *a*

To understand why these functions are necessary we must realize that we have now redesigned our primitive functions as shown in Figure 9-7b so that they apply an instance transformation to every coordinate point they receive. At the outset this transformation is set to the identity matrix, and it remains so unless we specify otherwise by calling *Scale, Rotate,* or *Translate*. When we encounter a sequence of these function calls, we would like the transformations they specify to be concatenated with the current instance-transformation matrix. Within the loop of our program, however, a call to *Translate* is encountered during each iteration. We do *not* want to concatenate each translation with the previous one; instead we want to discard the previous one and concatenate the new translation with the original instance-transformation matrix. By calling *SetTransform* at the end of the loop we restore the original matrix, saved by an earlier call to *SaveTransform*.

The *SaveTransform* and *SetTransform* functions provide somewhat more power and generality than is needed for our simple example: we could get by with a simple function to reset the instance transformation to the identity function. The ability to save the instance transformation at any moment and to restore it later becomes very useful in the more complex situations described in the next chapter.

## 9-4 IMPLEMENTATION OF INSTANCE TRANSFORMATIONS

Chapter 4 has shown that the use of 3 X 3 matrices makes it very easy to concatenate transformations together. We would expect instance-transformation software to be equally straightforward. In conceptual terms it is indeed simple, as we saw in the block diagram of Figure 9-7b. In practice, however, there is need to add refinements to the process which make the implementation of instance transformations slightly more complicated.

## Concatenating the Instance and Viewing Transformations

Each of the two transformations shown in Figure 9-7b is a linear transformation that can be expressed as a 3 × 3 matrix. It is therefore possible to concatenate the two transformations into one, reducing the time taken to transform each line endpont. To do this we must represent the viewing transformation in matrix form, rather than as the two Equations 5-2 given in Chapter 5. This viewing matrix $V$ is premultiplied by the instance-transformation matrix $N$ to give a combined transformation matrix $M$.

## Forming the Instance-Transformation Matrix

When we call two or more instance-transformation functions in succession, we expect the transformations to be applied in the order specified. This means that we must be careful in forming the instance-transformation matrix from the individual matrices representing each function call. Thus if we wish to form a matrix $Q$ from a scaling matrix $S$, a rotation $R$, and a translation $T$, specified in that order, the three component matrices must be concatenated in the same order:

$$Q = SRT \tag{9-1}$$

When we perform this concatenation, we must allow for the possibility that the current instance transformation $N_0$, which we are about to update, is not the identity matrix. This happens in cases of *multilevel structure* where symbols are formed out of component parts, or are grouped together in *subpictures* (see Figure 9-9). Multilevel structures are discussed more fully in the next chapter; at this point we should understand that their display involves applying a separate instance transformation *at each level*. Thus to display the component rectangle indicated in Figure 9-9 we must first apply the instance transformation of the rectangle relative to the door, then concatenate this with the instance transformation of the door relative to the house, and finally concatenate the instance transformation of the entire house.

The implication of this to the matrix formation process is that after concatenating the individual transformations to form $Q$, we must use this

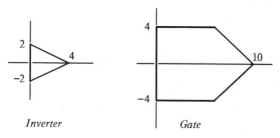

Inverter      Gate

**Figure 9-8** Inverter and gate symbols.

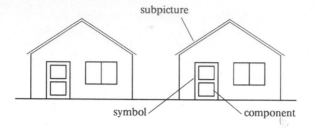

subpicture

symbol    component

**Figure 9-9** Picture with multilevel structure showing subpictures, symbols, and symbol components.

matrix to premultiply the current instance transformation $N_0$, yielding a new instance transformation $N_1$. We then multiply $N_1$ by the viewing transformation $V$ to obtain the combined transformation matrix $M$:

$$
\begin{aligned}
Q &= S\,R\,T \\
N_1 &= Q\,N_0 \\
M &= N_1\,V
\end{aligned}
\tag{9-2}
$$

We form the temporary matrix $Q$ by setting it to the identity matrix initially and postmultiplying it by each matrix formed from the parameters passed in function calls (in the above case, by $S$, $R$, and $T$). These matrices are themselves formed from templates based on Equations 4-8 to 4-10 given in Section 4-3.

Each time $Q$ is modified in this way, the combined matrix $M$ representing instance and viewing transformations becomes obsolete. The obvious remedy is to multiply the transformation matrices together after each instance-transformation function call, using Equations 9-2. This is an expensive solution, however, since several function calls are often grouped together, and in these cases we need compute the combined matrix only at the end of the sequence of calls. How can we detect the end of such a sequence?

The solution to this problem lies in modifying our primitive graphic functions to test whether $Q$ has changed since the previous primitive-function call; in cases of change, the matrices are combined and $Q$ is reset to the identity matrix. A simple 1-bit flag makes this check very easy to perform. For consistency the same check must be included in the *SaveTransform* function.

Thus the three steps in updating $M$ are

$$
\begin{aligned}
N_1 &= Q\,N_0 \\
M &= N_1\,V \\
Q &= I
\end{aligned}
\tag{9-3}
$$

Let us follow through the stages in building up the transformation of a symbol that forms part of a subpicture. We wish to apply to it the combination of two sets of instance transformations and a viewing transformation, followed by a clipping operation. We can trace the order in which these transformations are concatenated:

1.  At the outset, the combined transformation matrix $M$ is set equal to the viewing transformation $V$, and the current-instance transformation $N_0$ and the temporary matrix $Q$ are set equal to the identity matrix.
2.  As we encounter the instance-transformation functions for the subpicture, we postmultiply the temporary matrix $Q$ by each transformation.
3.  At the start of the subpicture we encounter a call to *SaveTransform*. Since $Q$ is no longer the identity matrix, we must update the combined matrix $M$ and reset $Q$ to the identity matrix, as in Equation 9-3.
4.  Primitives within the subpicture are transformed with $M$ and clipped.
5.  We encounter Instance-transformation functions to be applied to a symbol called by the subpicture definition. We postmultiply $Q$ by each of these transformations.
6.  At the start of the symbol procedure we encounter a graphic primitive function. As in step 3, $Q$ is no longer the identity matrix, so we update the combined matrix $M$ and reset $Q$ to the identity matrix.
7.  Lines within the symbol definition are transformed by the combined matrix $M$ before clipping.
8.  After displaying the symbol we return to the subpicture definition, where we encounter a call to *SetTransform*. We reset the instance transformation $N$ from the specified array and multiply it by $V$ to compute the combined matrix $M$. The temporary matrix $Q$ is reset, and we are now ready to proceed with the subpicture definition.

One of the lessons we can learn by following through this example is the importance of the *SaveTransform* and *SetTransform* functions. We can see now how necessary they are to the use of multiple levels of structure; without them we would be unable to restore intermediate values of the instance transformation $N$, as we must on returning to a subpicture from a symbol procedure call. A less obvious role played by *SaveTransform* is to update the combined transformation $M$. If this is not done between each set of instance-transformation function calls, two or more sets will be concatenated together in a single temporary matrix $Q$ in the wrong order.

### Clipping before and after Transformation

At the end of Chapter 5 we noted that clipping could be performed before applying the viewing transformation, with the advantage that invisible lines were not needlessly transformed. With the introduction of the instance transformation the situation must be reexamined. We now must choose between three possible positions for the clipping stage:

1.  Clipping after the viewing transformation (Figure 9-7b). This is the simplest choice, but it involves transforming all lines into screen coordinates, whether they are visible or not.
2.  Clipping between the instance and viewing transformations (Figure 9-10a).

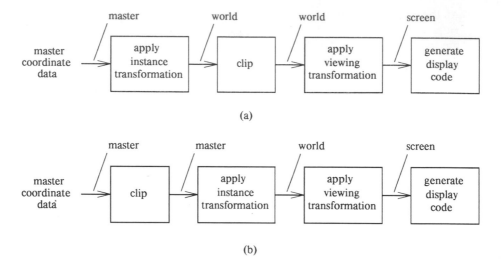

**Figure 9-10** (a) Clipping before the viewing transformation; (b) clipping before the instance transformation.

Whereas sequence 1 uses the viewport as a clipping region, this sequence uses the window. It still involves applying the instance transformation to every line but avoids the need to apply the viewing transformation to invisible lines. The overriding disadvantage of this sequence is that it prevents us from concatenating the instance and viewing transformations.

3. Clipping before the instance transformation (Figure 9-10b). This sequence allows us to avoid applying any transformations to invisible lines. It is a difficult process to implement, however, because it implies computing the window's position in master coordinates, which can be done only by applying the inverse of the instance transformation to the window. Worse still, the resulting clipping region will not be aligned with the axes if the instance transformation involves a rotation. Thus we may not be able to use the Cohen-Sutherland clipping algorithm.

It is possible to use sequence 3 in cases where symbols are not rotated. In these cases the inverse of the instance transformation is easily computed, and the clipping region is aligned with the axes. The transformation process must be *adaptive*, switching from sequence 3 to sequence 1 whenever rotated symbols are encountered. The resulting software is relatively complicated.

In most cases, the use of sequence 1 with its final clipping stage provides satisfactory performance. The transformation process is simple, and this reduces the amount of software required and the number of checks that must be invoked during the output process. We can expect to notice degradation in system performance when the amount of invisible information becomes very large. Methods of structuring the information to prevent such a degradation are discussed in the next chapter.

## EXERCISES

**9-1** The functions described in this chapter and Chapter 5 do not permit the entire picture, defined in world coordinates, to be rotated. Propose a change to the set of functions that would permit such rotations.

**9-2** In cases of multilevel structure, one might find it more convenient to save transformations on a stack, rather than in separate vectors as with *SaveTransform*. What advantages and disadvantages might this have?

**9-3** Discuss the advantages and disadvantages of replacing *Scale*, *Rotate*, and *Translate* with the single function *Transform*(*sx, sy, angle, tx, ty*).

**9-4** Discuss the use of the polygon-clipping algorithm, as described in Chapter 5, to permit clipping always to be performed in world or master coordinates.

**9-5** Implement the *Scale, Rotate, Translate, SaveTransform,* and *SetTransform* functions as suggested in this chapter, and modify the primitive function designs of Chapter 6 appropriately. Include in the redesign of the primitive functions the necessary changes to permit efficient formation of the combined transformation matrix $M$.

**9-6** As described in this chapter, the *SaveTransform* and *SetTransform* functions save and restore the instance transformation $N$. Discuss the advantages and disadvantages of instead saving and restoring the combined transformation matrix $M$.

**9-7** The use of a temporary matrix $Q$ can be avoided by having the programmer call *Scale, Rotate,* and *Translate* in the reverse of the order described in this chapter; each call simply computes $N_1 = PN_0$ and $M = N_1V$, where $P$ is the transformation specified. Discuss the advantages and disadvantages of this approach.

**9-8** Figure 9-11 shows a simple circuit diagram constructed from a single instance of a subpicture formed from the two symbol instances shown in Figure 9-6; the subpicture has been translated 10 units up and to the right. Using this example, work through the steps given on page 123, forming the transformation matrices, concatenating them, and applying them to the line segments of the symbol. Plot the line segments on graph paper to check the accuracy of your computations.

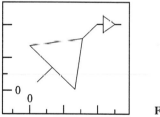

**Figure 9-11**

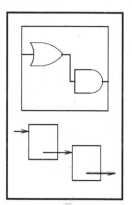

# 10

# PICTURE STRUCTURE

The pictures we construct from geometric models and other forms of data often have a clearly evident structure. This structure can be seen in the repeated use of certain symbols, in the connections drawn linking the symbols, and in the overall organization of the displayed image. Figure 10-1 shows various examples of visible picture structure. We use a variety of techniques to produce pictures with such structures. Some techniques make use of data structures, such as segmented display files (Chapter 7) or lists of lines describing symbols (Figure 9-2). Other techniques use a more procedural approach to picture structure. This chapter will discuss structured pictures and present techniques for their generation. We shall see how certain techniques apply to both categories of picture structure.

We can break down each of our categories further, to produce a list of four reasons for the occurrence of structure in pictures. The first two of these are forms of *inherent* structure that occur in many pictures; the other two are structuring techniques that are used by the programmer mainly for convenience.

*Repetition.* This is inherent in many pictures, where it is shown by means of repeated instances of symbols.
*Connectivity.* Pictures often show the relationships between elements by means of lines and arrows connecting them.

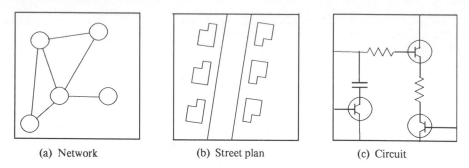

(a) Network                     (b) Street plan                    (c) Circuit

**Figure 10-1** Examples of pictures with clearly visible structures.

*Construction.* We can often find uses for transformations and symbols in constructing pictures, even though such structure is not clearly evident to the observer. For example, the transistor symbols shown in Figure 10-1c make use of various component parts, some of which are shown in Figure 10-2.

*Interaction.* As mentioned earlier, display-file segments simplify the design of interactive programs, and permit us to divide pictures in ways that sometimes have very little to do with their visible structure. A number of other structuring techniques have been developed to aid interaction.

Chapter 7 has already discussed segmentation, one of the simplest techniques for structuring pictures. This chapter will explore two other approaches to picture structure. The first part of the chapter picks up the modeling theme of Chapter 9 and develops it into a discussion of *display procedures.* The second part discusses the use of *structured display files* to represent picture structure, an approach that is in some respects a generalization of the use of segments. Throughout the chapter we shall try to relate these techniques to the uses of structure listed above.

## 10-1 DEFINING SYMBOLS BY PROCEDURES

In Chapter 9 we were concerned mainly with repetitive structures in pictures and with the use of symbols to represent these structures. We developed a method of defining symbols and invoking instances of them that made use of sequences of primitive function calls; before each sequence were the appropriate calls to instance-transformation functions. An example of such a technique was shown on page 119.

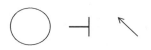

**Figure 10-2** Component parts used in constructing the transistor symbols used in Figure 10-1c.

In our example we used only two types of symbol. If we were to extend the program to use ten or fifty different symbols, the main loop containing all the sequences of primitives would become extremely long. We would be inclined to rewrite the program as a collection of procedures.

Figure 10-3 shows the earlier example rewritten as a shorter routine calling two small procedures. Each procedure contains the graphic primitive functions to represent one of the symbols shown in Figure 9-8. The run-time sequence of function calls is preserved unchanged. This reorganization of the program allows us to extend the symbol repertoire considerably without adversely affecting the clarity of the program. Indeed the use of procedures in this way tends to emphasize the structure of the picture in a way that the earlier routine given on page 119 did not.

## Multilevel Procedure Structure

Multilevel structure has already been mentioned in Chapter 9. In extending the set of symbols provided by our circuit-diagram program we are likely to encounter many symbols that make use of identical pieces or are similar in

```
procedure Inverter;
begin
     MoveTo(0, -2); LineTo(0, 2);
     LineTo(4, 0); LineTo(0, -2)
end;

procedure Gate;
begin
     MoveTo(0, -4); LineTo(0, 4); LineTo(6, 4);
     LineTo(10, 0); LineTo(6, -4); LineTo(0, -4)
end;

procedure ShowComponents;
     var i,j: integer; a: transform;
begin
     for i := 1 to nComponents do begin
          SaveTransform(a);
          Translate(Components[i].x, Components[i].y);
          case Components[i].comptype of
               1: Inverter;
               2: Gate
          end;
          SetTransform(a)
     end
end;
```

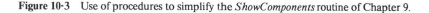

**Figure 10-3**  Use of procedures to simplify the *ShowComponents* routine of Chapter 9.

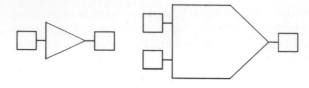

**Figure 10-4** Symbols with
multilevel structure.

other ways. For example, we might wish to include the two symbols shown in
Figure 10-4. Each of these incorporates one of the two original symbols
together with some small boxes at the terminal points. We could describe these
symbols by repeating the original sequence of primitive-function calls and
adding more calls to represent the boxes; it is much more convenient, however,
to use a set of procedures as shown in Figure 10-5.

   We have now added another level of structure to our system of procedures.

```
procedure Box;
begin
      MoveTo(0, 0); LineTo(−1, 0);
      LineTo(−1, 1); LineTo(−3, 1); LineTo(−3, −1);
      LineTo(−1, −1); LineTo(−1, 0)
end;

procedure InverterBox;
      var a: transform;
begin
      Inverter;
      Box;
      SaveTransform(a);
      Rotate(180); Translate(4, 0);
      Box;
      SetTransform(a)
end;

procedure GateBox;
      var a: transform;
begin
      Gate;
      SaveTransform(a);
      Translate(0, −2); Box;
      SetTransform(a);
      Translate(0, 2); Box;
      SetTransform(a);
      Rotate(180); Translate(10, 0); Box;
      SetTransform(a)
end;
```

**Figure 10-5**   Multilevel structure: construction of more complex symbols with the aid of procedure
calls.

The main loop calls the symbol procedures, which call other procedures to generate portions of each symbol. We can likewise extend the structure to include larger subpictures made up of collections of ordinary symbols and lines. One such subpicture is shown in Figure 10-6; the procedure to generate it is as follows:

```
procedure InverterGate;
    var a: transform;
begin
    InverterBox;
    SaveTransform(a);
    Translate(12, 2);
    GateBox;
    SetTransform(a);
    MoveTo(7, 0); LineTo(9, 0)
end;
```

These examples make extensive use of instance transformations. In some cases transformation functions are used as they were in Chapter 9, to transform from master to world coordinates. In other cases, such as the use of symbols within the definition of a subpicture, we use instance transformations to indicate how the symbol is to be oriented within the master-coordinate space of the subpicture; in other words, we are transforming from one master-coordinate space into another. This is a perfectly valid way of using instance-transformation functions, one we anticipated in the design of the functions in Chapter 9.

## 10-2 DISPLAY PROCEDURES

It will be clear from the example above and from the discussion of Section 9-4 that care is needed in the use of instance-transformation functions. We must apply the functions in the correct order, or symbols will be transformed incorrectly. In pictures with multiple levels of structure we must remember to include a call to *SaveTransform* before each set of calls to instance-transformation functions to make sure that the instance-transformation matrix is updated often enough.

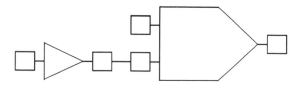

**Figure 10-6** Simple circuit constructed from symbols.

It is unwise to design a high-level programming system, such as a graphics package, in a way that exposes the programmer to undue sources of error. Generally we try to protect him against such errors by providing safe ways of expressing a full range of procedural steps. How can we provide a safer way of applying instance transformations?

Before attempting to answer this question, let us review the normal sequence of function calls involved in displaying a symbol. We shall use the following example:

> *SaveTransform* (*a*);
> *Scale* (2.5);
> *Rotate* (90);
> *Translate* (100, 200);
> *Inverter*;
> *SetTransform* (*a*);

We have seen enough other examples of invoking symbol procedures to recognize the pattern they follow:

1. The current-instance transformation is saved by means of a call to *SaveTransform.*
2. A sequence of one or more calls is made to instance transformation functions.
3. The symbol procedure is called.
4. On return from the symbol procedure, *SetTransform* is called in order to restore the original instance transformation.

Since this sequence of steps is so common, and since it is so important not to omit any of the steps, it is worth our while to provide the programmer with a more convenient way of defining the sequence. We notice that since steps 1 and 4 are invariant, we need only provide a means of specifying the parameters of steps 2 and 3. This can be done with a single statement:

> *Inverter* **scale** 2.5 **rotation** 90 **at** (100, 200);

We use the term *display procedure* to describe a procedure called in this manner; the call statement itself is termed a *display-procedure call.* This calling mechanism is the distinguishing feature of display procedures, which are in other repects like any other procedure. The display-procedure call is not a valid statement in PASCAL or any other common programming language. Extensions have in the past been made to various languages, such as EULER and LOGO, to permit the use of this type of statement [352, 348]. Where this cannot be done, it is sometimes possible to pass the procedure name and the other parameters to a special *Display* function:

> *Display* (*Inverter,* 2.5, 90, 100, 200)

Here we are passing the procedure name, *Inverter*, as an argument to another procedure. Certain languages, such as BCPL [390], permit this and therefore allow us to implement what might be called a *simulated* display-procedure call.

The effect of the display-procedure call, whether simulated or not, is to carry out the four steps listed above. The *SaveTransform* function is called; the appropriate instance-transformation functions are invoked; the procedure itself is called; and when it returns, a call is made to *SetTransform*. Thus the compiled code for the display-procedure call would be identical to the sequence of function calls given on page 132.

We show here the original *ShowComponents* procedure programmed with the aid of display procedures:

```
procedure ShowComponents;
    var i: integer;
begin
    for i := 1 to nComponents do begin
        case Components[i].comptype of
            1: Inverter at (Components[i].x, Components[i].y);
            2: Gate at (Components[i].x, Components[i].y);
        end
    end
end;
```

Note that if the rotation is zero or the scale factor unity, as in the display-procedure calls in this example, the corresponding part of the statement may be omitted. The statement syntax will normally allow the transformation parameters to be given in any order; whether or not this affects the resulting combined transformation depends on the way the statement is compiled.

## 10-3 BOXING

One of the privileges we reluctantly gave up when we introduced instance transformations was the ability to clip information before transforming it. We must now transform every line into screen coordinates before we can determine whether it is visible. When many lines are invisible this is a very wasteful process.

In looking for other ways to achieve faster transformation, it is worth considering two factors. First, we wish to avoid transforming invisible information; second, we would like to eliminate this information as rapidly as possible. Instead of applying a visibility test to every line in the picture, we should be able to test a collection of lines in a single step. This we can do by extending the display-procedure calling mechanism to incorporate such a test. Before we call a display procedure representing a symbol we test whether the

bounding box

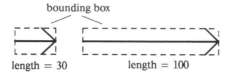

length = 30          length = 100

**Figure 10-7** Arrows drawn by a display procedure. Note that the shape of the arrowhead is unaffected by elongation.

entire symbol lies outside the clipping region; if it does, we proceed no further with the procedure call. We use the term *boxing* for this kind of visibility test, since it generally makes use of the bounding box of the symbol.

The display procedures we have discussed so far do not permit the application of a boxing test, since there is no means of determining the overall dimensions, or bounding box, of the symbol or subpicture they represent. We need a means of indicating these dimensions in the description of the symbol; therefore the dimensions must be added to the procedure itself. One way of achieving this is to extend the programming language to allow a *declaration* of the symbol's dimensions. The dimensions are conveniently represented by the coordinates of the lower left and upper right corners of the symbol's bounding rectangle, given in master coordinates:

> **procedure** *Inverter;* **dimensions** 0, 0, 100, 100;
> etc.

A more easily implemented extension is a dimension *statement*, which causes an immediate return from the procedure if the specified bounding rectangle lies competely outside the clipping region:

> **procedure** *Arrow(length: integer)*;
> **begin**
>     *Size*(0, − 10, *length*, 10);
>     *MoveTo*(0, 0);
>     *LineTo*(*length*, 0);
>     *LineTo*(*length*− 10, − 10);
>     *MoveTo*(*length*, 0);
>     *LineTo*(*length*− 10, 10)
> **end**;

In this procedure, the dimensions specified in the *Size* statement expand to enclose the arrow exactly, whatever its length (Figure 10-7).

How do we apply the boxing test? A particularly simple test can be used if the symbol is not rotated; we need only apply the Cohen-Sutherland clipping algorithm to a diagonal of the bounding rectangle, and if it is trivially rejected, we know that the rectangle lies entirely outside the clipping region. This is

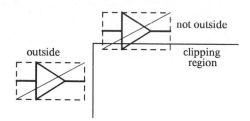

**Figure 10-8** Applying the boxing test, by checking a diagonal of each symbol's bounding box for trivial rejection.

illustrated in Figure 10-8. In general we must allow for rotated symbols, however, and it is not nearly so easy to detect whether a rotated rectangle intersects the clipping region. We could waste a lot of time trying to apply an accurate test, but it is better to make an approximate test, knowing that certain symbols will be included in the transformation process even though all their lines are invisible. A simple approximate test can be applied by constructing a larger bounding rectangle through the corners of the specified rectangle (Figure 10-9) and applying the trivial rejection test to one of its diagonals.

Apart from implementation difficulties, the main drawback of boxing is that it relies on the programmer to specify the bounding rectangle accurately. If he errs on the large side, the symbol will be transformed unnecessarily and the clipping routine will eliminate all its lines; thus no harm will be done to the displayed image. If he specifies too small a rectangle, the symbol may be omitted when it is partly visible and this will create unexpected effects on the screen.

## 10-4 ADVANTAGES AND LIMITATIONS OF DISPLAY PROCEDURES

Display procedures provide a convenient means of constructing pictures for display. In terms of our original list of types of picture structure, we have seen how they can handle repetition and the construction of complex subpictures. They have the useful property of allowing us to use different graphical representations for symbols by means of conditional statements within the procedure. For example, a single procedure could show a flip-flop component

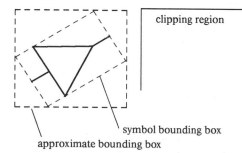

**Figure 10-9** Use of an approximate bounding box to check the visibility of a rotated symbol.

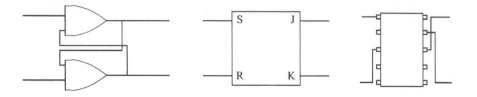

**Figure 10-10** Three different representations of a flip-flop symbol.

in any of the three ways shown in Figure 10-10, according to some global parameter governing the style of the circuit diagram or a parameter passed to the procedure. Display procedures also provide a convenient way of defining connectivity; indeed the *LinkPoints* procedure given on page 115 was a simple display procedure for connecting two symbols.

The main limitation to display procedures, and to any similar use of procedural descriptions to define picture parts, is in their ability to handle interactive picture manipulation. For example, we would like to be able to remove components from our circuit and add new components. Each time we do this we must invoke the routine that draws the entire circuit. This could make simple modifications to the circuit unbearably slow.

Two things come to our rescue here. First, we can continue to use the display-file segmentation techniques we developed in Chapter 7. We can create a separate segment for each component symbol, and when we wish to remove a symbol we need only delete its segment. Second, we can implement more than one set of procedures to operate on the same picture. Thus we can treat the routine shown on page 133 as the main routine for constructing the picture from the model, and we can write additional routines that make minor modifications to the picture.

A more serious problem with display procedures is the requirement that all symbols be predefined and compiled into the application program. In some cases we would like to provide the user of the program with the capability of creating new symbols at run time. A professional illustrator, for example, often designs special symbols for use in diagrams. This facility can be provided in one of two ways: we can use an interpretive language such as LOGO [348] that allows procedures to be constructed at run time from graphical input data, or we can revert to the technique we used in Chapter 9, in which symbols were defined in the data structure of the geometric model, as shown in Figure 9-2. The first of these solutions is obviously not much use to the FORTRAN or PASCAL programmer, but the second one fairly generally is useful. The next section discusses in some detail the use of data structures to represent displayed pictures.

## 10-5 STRUCTURED DISPLAY FILES

The display file, whose principal purpose is to refresh the displayed image, may also be used to define picture structure. We have already seen examples of the use of display file segments for this purpose. In Section 7-4, for example, we saw how an air traffic pattern may be displayed by assigning a separate segment to each aircraft; it is then possible to create, reposition and remove aircraft by small changes to the display file. Rather than define a procedure that generates the entire picture, we write several shorter and simpler procedures that manipulate the individual segments of the display file. For example, when an aircraft is to be handed off to another controller, and its symbol therefore removed from the screen, a simple procedure deletes the appropriate segment from the display file. By orienting the model and display procedures towards the effective use of segments we can achieve a highly interactive application program.

The same approach can be applied to applications that involve a more complex picture structure. Here, however, we require a more powerful structuring mechanism than is provided by segments. For example, we might wish to provide an artist with the ability to construct diagrams like Figure 10-6 out of symbols. He should be able to redefine the shape of any symbol, and have each instance of it change throughout the diagram. For this kind of application a single level of display file structure is inconvenient. We can represent certain objects by individual segments, but we cannot then easily modify component parts of these objects or collections of several objects. For such applications we require a display file with several levels of structure: a *structured display file.*

Structured display files may be built using many of the techniques discussed in Chapters 7 and 8 with reference to segmented display files. There is a fundamental difference, however, between the two types of display file. When we use a multilevel structure to represent pictures containing repeated symbols and subpictures, we must apply a different transformation to each repeated object. Each such transformation must be recorded in the display file, and must be applied by the display processor to the graphical information representing the object. In multilevel structures, several levels of transformation may be applied to certain objects; the appropriate transformations must be concatenated together so as to position each object correctly. Display processors have been constructed with the capability to apply general transformations in this way; we shall discuss them in Chapter 26. The display processors we have encountered in Chapter 3 have a limited transformation capability that restricts them to two-dimensional translation of symbols and subpictures. The following section describes a structured display file scheme designed for such display processors.

## Groups and Items

This section describes a structured display file technique based on a system built at MIT's Lincoln Laboratory as part of the LEAP language development [171]. The basic components of the structure are *items,* representing indivisible graphical units, and *groups,* consisting of collections of items or of other groups. If we were to use this structure for our earlier circuit problems, we would use a separate item to represent each type of component and would represent circuits and other collections of components by groups.

We define an item by listing the basic graphic entities (lines and text) that it is to contain. To do this we need a set of primitive functions to define the entities and a pair of functions to indicate the start and finish of the item:

| | |
|---|---|
| *Point* $(x, y)$ | insert a point at $(x, y)$ in the item |
| *Line* $(x, y)$ | insert a line from the previous point to $(x, y)$ |
| *Text* $(str)$ | insert the text string *str* at the previous point |
| | |
| *BeginItem* $(n)$ | start the definition of an item, to be named *n*; if an item with this name already exists, its definition will be replaced; |
| *EndItem* | terminate the definition of the item |

To build pictures out of items we create groups of them. A group can contain only references, or *calls,* to items and to other groups, i.e., basic graphic entities may not be included directly in a group. Each call specifies the name of the called group or item, the two-dimensional translation to be applied to it, and an additional name that identifies this particular call. It also specifies in which group the call is to be placed.

| | |
|---|---|
| *CallItem* $(g, n, c, x, y)$ | call item *n* from group *g* with translation $(x, y)$, and identify this call by the name *c* |
| *CallGroup* $(g, f, c, x, y)$ | call group *f* from group *g* in a similar manner |

Thus we do not define groups by the same *Begin-End* sequence we use when defining items. Instead we create a new group simply by referring to it in a call to an existing group or item. This is a more convenient mechanism than the use of *Begin* and *End;* it is feasible only because the order of the calls within a group cannot affect the picture.

The effect of these functions is to provide us with the ability to build hierarchic structures of groups and items. Figure 10-11 shows the hierarchy of a structure representing the circuit diagram of Figure 10-6. Note that each call generates a link in the structure with an attached transformation; this is the transformation of the called group or item *relative* to the calling group. The overall transformation of any item is found by tracing down to it from the

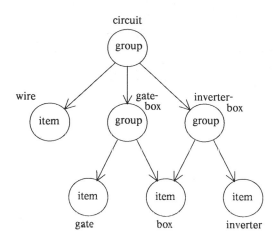

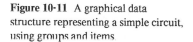

Figure 10-11  A graphical data structure representing a simple circuit, using groups and items.

group at the root of the tree, concatenating transformations together.  Note also that the root group is assumed always to exist and is given a reserved name.

To complete the set of functions for manipulating this structure we need the following functions for deleting groups, items and calls:

| | |
|---|---|
| *DeleteGroup* (*g*) | delete group *g* and all calls to it |
| *DeleteItem* (*n*) | delete item *n* and all calls to it |
| *DeleteCall* (*g, c*) | delete call *c* from group *g* |

The *DeleteGroup* function must of course be prevented from ever deleting the root group.

Figure 10-12 illustrates the use of the functions for building structures out of groups and items.  The program uses the same circuit diagram example of Figure 10-6.

## Implementation of Groups and Items

Many of the techniques for compiling display files described in Chapter 8 are applicable to the construction and manipulation of structured display files.  In particular we can use identical name tables and free-storage systems.  Many of the constraints that apply to display-file compilation apply here too since the display file is being refreshed by a display processor; for example, it is essential to perform double buffering when redefining a group or item.

Figure 10-13 shows a display-file organization for groups and items.  It can be refreshed directly by a display processor possessing relative line-drawing capability and a multilevel call mechanism for display subroutines.  In order to permit the individual calls within a group to be added and deleted independently, each one is represented by a separate 5-word block of memory, linked together by jump instructions.  Each block includes the call name, a pair of relative positioning instructions, and a push-jump to the called group or item. Items are represented as simple sequences of display instructions. A pair of lists link together all groups and all items.

With a structure like this the implementation of the functions is a relatively straightforward matter. The functions for item construction are similar to the segment-building functions of Chapter 7 and can be implemented along similar lines. The functions for calling groups and items simply add a block containing the appropriate name, pointer, and translation parameters to the list of blocks representing the parent group. The *DeleteCall* function locates the named call block and removes it from the list.

The most difficult functions to implement are *DeleteGroup* and *DeleteItem* since they must also delete all calls to the group or item in question. The

```
const Inverter=1; Gate=2; Box=3; Wire2=4;
     InverterBox=100; GateBox=101; InverterGate=102;

{ The four items are constructed first. }
BeginItem(Inverter);
     Point(0, −2); Line(0, 2); Line(4, 0); Line(0, −2);
EndItem;
BeginItem(Gate);
     Point(0, −4); Line(0, 4); Line(6, 4);
     Line(10, 0); Line(6, −4); Line(0, −4);
EndItem;
BeginItem(Box);
     Point(0, 0); Line(−1, 0); Line(−1, 1); Line(−3, 1);
     Line(−3, −1); Line(−1, −1); Line(−1, 0);
EndItem;
BeginItem(Wire2);
     Point(0, 0); Line(2, 0);
EndItem;

{ Build the three groups. }
CallItem(Inverter, InverterBox, 0, 0, 0, 1, 0);
CallItem(Box, InverterBox, 1, 0, 0, 1, 0);
CallItem(Box, InverterBox, 2, 4, 0, 1, 180);

CallItem(Gate, GateBox, 0, 0, 0, 1, 0);
CallItem(Box, GateBox, 1, 0, −2, 1, 0);
CallItem(Box, GateBox, 2, 0, 2, 1, 0);
CallItem(Box, GateBox, 3, 10, 0, 1, 180);

CallGroup(InverterBox, InverterGate, 0, 0, 0, 1, 0);
CallGroup(GateBox, InverterGate, 1, 12, 2, 1, 0);
CallItem(Wire2, InverterGate, 2, 7, 0, 1, 0);
```

**Figure 10-12**   Use of groups and items to build a simple circuit model.

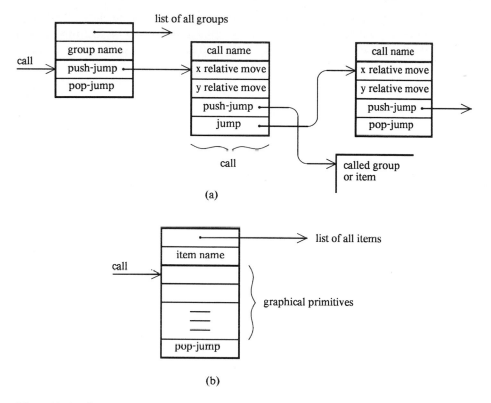

**Figure 10-13** Groups (a) and items (b).

structure shown in Figure 10-13 does not provide any simple means of determining the set of calls to a particular group or item. More pointers can be added to make this operation easier, but the maintenance of these pointers becomes a source of inefficiency. An alternative solution is to mark deleted groups and items and place them in a special list. We can then perform sporadic garbage collection, in which we scan the entire data structure, removing calls that address deleted groups or items; after this scan is complete we can discard the contents of the special list.

### Graphical Data Structures

In many applications of structured display files, whenever a change is made to the model a similar change is made to the display file. For example, if the user adds a symbol to a circuit, an entry is added to the model and a call is added to the display file. The application program performs many such parallel operations on the two data structures.

For the sake of economy we may try to combine the model and display file into a single structure, which we then call a *graphical data structure*. This approach was used by Sutherland in SKETCHPAD, and has since been tried in other systems [462, 104, 402, 468]. Non-graphical data may be included in the structure; these data are excluded from the refresh process by keeping them in separate blocks or storing them at the start of display blocks like the names in Figure 10-13. Guedj has described an interesting display processor for graphical data structures with a symbolically-addressed subroutine mechanism [213].

Graphical data structures have two conspicuous advantages over structured display files: they save space and they ensure that the displayed picture is an up-to-date representation of the modeled information. In general, however, the disadvantages of graphical data structures outweigh the advantages. Graphical data structures involve complex display file formats that are difficult for the application programmer to manipulate and difficult for the system designer to maintain. They also impose a fixed graphical representation on each of the modeled objects; once an object has been defined in the model, its display representation cannot be changed without altering the model. These disadvantages are avoided by the use of display procedures or a structured display file.

## Conclusion

This section has discussed the use of data structures for picture representation, and has described a simple graphics package for manipulating structured display files. Despite the lack of scaling and rotation, this type of graphics package is useful in a number of different applications and is particularly well suited to computer-aided electronic design. As a general approach to graphics system organization the use of a structured display file has a number of disadvantages, however. It requires a relatively large amount of software to support the manipulation of the display file; it depends on the use of a specific type of display processor, and therefore limits the range of displays on which we can run a particular application program; and it cannot handle the display of objects containing large numbers of separate entities since these objects produce very large display files. For these reasons it is preferable to use a transformed, segmented display file in any graphics system intended for general purpose use.

## EXERCISES

**10-1** The structured display file shown in Figure 10-13, since it makes use of relative positioning instructions in call blocks, requires that the beam position prior to the call be reset after the return from the call. A simple subroutine call mechanism of the kind described in Section 3-6 will not perform this. Suggest an extension to the subroutine call mechanism that rectifies this problem.

**10-2** Thomas [452, 479] has proposed an alternative to groups and items that has similar objectives. Compare the two approaches.

**10-3** Investigate methods of using display subroutines in a transformed, segmented display file to reduce display-file size.

**10-4** Suppose you were using the display procedure technique with a storage-tube display. What methods might you use to avoid regenerating the entire picture after every modification?

**10-5** Review your answer to Exercise 3-5 in light of what you have learned from the last six chapters.

**10-6** Can boxing be usefully applied to structured display files? If so, what is the simplest extension to the display instruction set of Figures 3-12 and 3-16 that would permit boxing of groups and items? Devise a method of computing the bounding boxes of groups and items during display file compilation. Can this method be applied to the automatic computation of bounding boxes of display procedures?

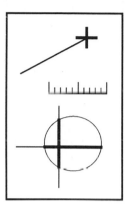

# PART THREE

## INTERACTIVE

## GRAPHICS

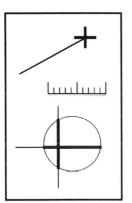

# 11

## GRAPHICAL

## INPUT DEVICES

### 11-1 POINTING AND POSITIONING DEVICES

Most display terminals provide the user with an alphanumeric keyboard with which to type commands and enter data for the program. For some applications, however, the keyboard is inconvenient or inadequate. For example, the user may wish to indicate one of a number of symbols on the screen, in order to erase the symbol. If each symbol is labeled, he can do so by typing the symbol's name; by *pointing* at the symbol, however, he may be able to erase it more rapidly, and the extra clutter of labels can be avoided.

Another problem arises if the user has to add lines or symbols to the picture on the screen. Although he can identify an item's position by typing coordinates, he can do so even better by pointing at the screen, particularly if what matters most is the item's position relative to the rest of the picture.

These two examples illustrate the two basic types of graphical interaction: *pointing* at items already on the screen and *positioning* new items. The need to interact in these ways has stimulated the development of a number of different types of graphical input device, some of which are described in this chapter.

Ideally a graphical input device should lend itself both to pointing and to positioning. In reality there are no devices with this versatility. Most devices are much better at positioning than at pointing; one device, the light pen, is the exact opposite. Fortunately, however, we can supplement the deficiencies of

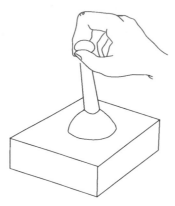

Figure 11-1 Joystick.

these devices by software and in this way produce a hardware-software system that has both capabilities. Nevertheless the distinction between pointing and positioning capability is extremely important.

Another important distinction is between devices that can be used directly on the screen surface and devices that cannot. The latter might appear to be less useful, but this is far from true. Radar operators and air-traffic controllers have for years used devices like the *joystick* (Figure 11-1) and the *tracker ball* (Figure 11-2), neither of which can be pointed at the screen. The effectiveness of these input devices depends on the use of visual *feedback:* the $x$ and $y$ outputs of the device control the movement of a small cross, or *cursor,* displayed on the screen (Figure 11-3). The user of the device steers the cursor around the screen as if it were a toy boat on the surface of a pond. Although this operation sounds as if it requires a lot of skill, it is in fact very easy.

The use of visual feedback has an additional advantage: just as in any control system, it compensates for any lack of *linearity* in the device. A linear input device is one that faithfully increases or decreases the input coordinate value in exact proportion to the user's hand movement. If the device is being used to trace a graph or a map, linearity is important. A cursor, however, can be controlled quite easily even if the device behaves in a fairly nonlinear fashion. For example, the device may be much less sensitive near the left-hand region of its travel: a 1-inch hand movement may change the $x$ value by only 50

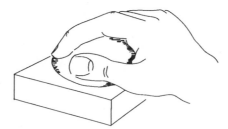

Figure 11-2 Tracker ball.

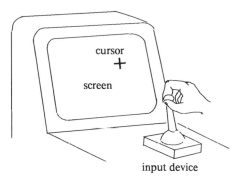

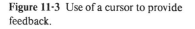

**Figure 11-3** Use of a cursor to provide feedback.

units, whereas the same movement elsewhere may change $x$ by 60 units. The user will simply change his hand movement to compensate, often without even noticing the nonlinearity. This phenomenon has allowed simple, inexpensive devices like the mouse to be used very successfully for graphical input.

## 11-2 THE MOUSE

The mouse consists of a small plastic box resting on two metal wheels whose axes are at right angles (see Figure 11-4). It was developed originally at Stanford Research Institute [158]. Each wheel of the mouse is connected to a *shaft encoder* that delivers an electrical pulse for every incremental rotation of the wheel. As the mouse is rolled around on a flat surface, its movement in two orthogonal directions is translated into rotation of the wheels. These rotations can be measured by counting the pulses received from the shaft encoders. The converted values may be held in registers accessible to the computer or written

**Figure 11-4** Mouse, showing push-buttons on top (left), wheels to detect motion (right). *Courtesy Xerox Corporation.*

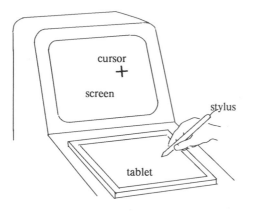

**Figure 11-5** Tablet and stylus.

directly into the computer's memory; the values are normally sampled 30 or 60 times a second by the computer. Push buttons may be mounted on top of the mouse, and the user can work them with his fingers as he moves the mouse. Ideally the computer should be able to read the position of these buttons whenever it reads the coordinates of the mouse.

In addition to its simplicity and low cost, the mouse has the advantage that the user need not pick it up in order to use it—the mouse simply sits on the table surface until he needs it. This makes the mouse an efficient device for pointing, as experiments have shown [159, 89]. The mouse has some unique properties that are liked by some and disliked by others. For example, if the mouse is picked up and put down somewhere else, the cursor will not move. Also the coordinates delivered by the mouse wrap around when overflow occurs; this effect can be filtered out by software, or can be retained as a means of moving the cursor rapidly from one side of the screen to the other. The mouse has two real disadvantages: it cannot be used for tracing data from paper, since a small rotation of the mouse or a slight loss of contact will cause a cumulative error in all the readings, and it is very difficult to handprint characters for recognition by the computer (see Chapters 12 and 14). For these types of application a tablet is essential.

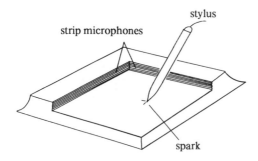

**Figure 11-6** The acoustic tablet.

## 11-3 TABLETS

The term *tablet* is used to describe a flat surface, generally separate from the display, on which the user draws with a *stylus* (see Figure 11-5). The similarity of the tablet and stylus to paper and pencil makes them a particularly natural combination for graphical input.

### Early Tablet Devices

The RAND Tablet was developed at the RAND Corporation [135], and was refined and marketed by Bolt Beranek and Newman, Inc. It provides a flat drawing area 10 inches square and rests on a table top. Embedded in the surface of the tablet are 1024 lines parallel to the $x$ axis and 1024 lines parallel to the $y$ axis. Each individual line carries a unique digitally coded signal that can be picked up by the stylus. Inside the stylus a sensitive amplifier detects the pulses from the lines, amplifies them, and delivers them via coaxial cable to decoding logic, which in turn deposits binary integer coordinates in the tablet's buffer registers. The stylus has a small switch in the tip, whose status is kept in an extra bit in the buffer register.

An alternative coordinate-input technique uses voltage gradients within a resistive plate. In the simplest configuration, a sheet of partially conductive material is used as the tablet surface. During successive time intervals, a potential is applied first horizontally and then vertically across the sheet. The stylus is kept in contact with the conductive sheet and senses a potential corresponding to its position. The $x$ and $y$ coordinates of the pen can be determined by measuring the potential during the horizontal and vertical time periods. Absence of any potential indicates that the pen is not in contact with the surface.

Sylvania Electronic Systems have developed a voltage-gradient tablet device in which the resistive sheet is a layer of stannous oxide fused into a glass plate and covered with another glass plate [474]. The signals in the plate are high-frequency alternating currents applied in such a way that the phase detected by the stylus varies for different positions on the sheet. Because high-frequency signals are used, considerable separation can be introduced between the stylus and the conducting surface; in fact the Sylvania tablet works quite acceptably through a book.

### The Acoustic Tablet

An ingenious tablet designed by the Science Accessories Corporation [431] works on an acoustic principle suggested by Brenner [71]. It depends on the use of *strip microphones*, which are mounted along two adjacent edges of the tablet, as shown in Figure 11-6. The stylus has a small piece of ceramic mounted close to its tip, and at regular intervals a small spark is generated across the surface of the ceramic between two electrodes. The microphones pick up the pulse of sound generated by the spark, and two counters record the delay between creating the spark and receiving the sound. These two delays are proportional to the stylus distance from the two edges of the tablet where the microphones are mounted. They can therefore be used as $x$ and $y$ values.

### The Electro-acoustic Tablet

Another acoustic technique has been employed in the *electro-acoustic tablet:* in this device, the writing surface is a sheet of magnetostrictive material acting like a row of delay lines. An electric pulse travels through the sheet, first horizontally and then vertically, and is detected by a sensor in the stylus as it passes by. A counter is used to determine the delay from the time the pulse is issued to the time it is detected; from this value the position of the stylus can be determined. Pulses may be issued at any frequency up to about 200 pairs per second, adequate to track the stylus at 5-millisecond intervals.

The electro-acoustic tablet is quieter in operation than its acoustic counterpart and is less affected by ambient noise or air movement. Both types of tablet can be constructed to sizes in excess of 1 meter square.


## 11-4 THE LIGHT PEN

The devices we have discussed so far are all *positioning* devices: they possess hardware to track the stylus or otherwise ensure that the $x$ and $y$ values in the buffer registers represent the current position of the device. At fairly regular intervals, perhaps whenever the internal clock generates an interrupt, the $x$ and $y$ values are read from the buffer register. These values can be used to reposition the cursor and to modify the display file in any desired fashion. If the device incorporates a tip-operated switch or a push button, it can be sampled at the same time and used to control branching within the program.

In contrast, the light pen is a *pointing* device. If it is pointed at an item on the screen, it generates information from which the item can be identified by the program. However, the light pen does not generally have any associated tracking hardware. Instead tracking is performed by software, making use of the output function of the display.

In concept the light pen is extremely simple. Two alternative arrangements are shown in Figure 11-7a. In each case the two main elements of the light pen are a photocell and an optical system which focuses onto it any light in the pen's field of view. A pen-shaped housing permits the light pen to be held in the hand and pointed at the display screen. On this housing is either a finger-operated switch or a shutter that must be depressed to allow light to reach the photocell. The output of the photocell is amplified and fed to a flip-flop which is set whenever the pen is pointed at a sufficiently bright source of light. This flip-flop can be read and cleared by the computer.

Pointing operations are easily programmed for the light pen, particularly if

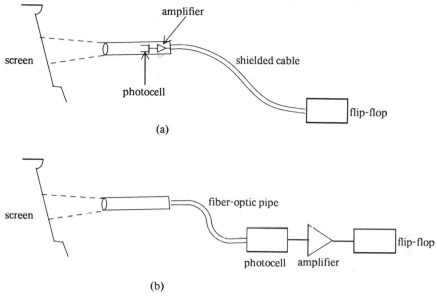

amplifier

screen

shielded cable

photocell

flip-flop

(a)

screen

fiber-optic pipe

flip-flop

photocell  amplifier

(b)

**Figure 11-7** The light pen: (a) using a hand-held photocell; (b) using a fiber-optic pipe.

we are using a point-plotting display: we can test the light-pen flip-flop after displaying each point and thus determine the exact spot at which the pen is pointing. Alternatively we can use an *interrupt* feature, like that described in Chapter 13, to indicate when the flip-flop is set. The computer can read the contents of the display's address register when an interrupt occurs and from them determine which item was seen by the pen. To make use of the light pen for positioning, some sort of *tracking program* must be running in the computer. Programs for pointing and positioning with the light pen are described in Chapter 13. As we shall see, they rely on the ability of the display processor to *enable* and *disable* the light pen during the refresh cycle, thus preventing certain parts of the picture from being seen by the pen.

All light-pen programs depend on a rapid response from the pen when it is pointed at the screen. A particularly fast response is required if the light pen is to be used with high-speed displays. Suppose, for example, a display executes one instruction every 2 microseconds but the delay between displaying a point or line and setting the light pen flip-flop is 3 microseconds. By the time this happens, the display will be processing either the next instruction or the one after that. The program may therefore incorrectly identify the seen item.

Fast-response light pens can be built by using a highly sensitive photocell such as a photomultiplier tube. However, this sort of device is too bulky to be held in the hand, so the light must be focused onto it by a fiber-optic pipe, as shown in Figure 11-7b. Transistor-type photocells, such as the photodiode, are cheap and small enough to be hand-held. However, photodiodes generally take

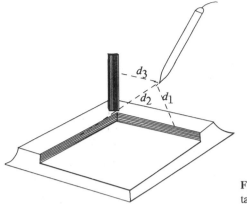

**Figure 11-8** A three-microphone acoustic tablet for three-dimensional coordinate input.

one or more microseconds to respond and are therefore more suited to light pens for slower displays.

## 11-5 THREE-DIMENSIONAL INPUT DEVICES

Input devices are very frequently used for interaction with a computer model, either to select items of information within the model or to add new information. The devices we have discussed, such as the mouse, tablet and light pen, are particularly well suited to interaction with two-dimensional models: models of electrical circuits, flow charts, geographic data, and traffic patterns.

The limitations of these input devices become noticeable when we try to use them to interact with a three-dimensional model. We need three coordinate values from the input device in order to define a point within the model; most input devices provide only two coordinates. This section describes some devices that have been developed for three-dimensional coordinate input.

### Acoustic devices

Perhaps the simplest of all three-dimensional input devices is the generalization of the acoustic tablet. To measure the stylus position in three dimensions, we can use three microphones aligned with the axes (Figure 11-8). The perpendicular distances of the stylus from these microphones can be determined from the three arrival times, and from these three distances the stylus coordinates can be computed (see Exercise 11-1).

A more compact input device can be constructed by mounting four strip microphones around the edges of a two-dimensional tablet, and using two pairs of timing counters. We then receive four distance measurements, shown in Figure 11-9 as $d_1$, $d_2$, $d_3$, and $d_4$. If the tablet dimensions are $2a$ by $2a$ and $x$ and $y$ are measured from the tablet center, we can show that

$$
\begin{aligned}
4ax &= d_1^2 - d_2^2 \\
4ay &= d_3^2 - d_4^2 \\
z^2 &= d_1^2 - (x + a)^2 \\
&= d_2^2 - (x - a)^2 \\
&= d_3^2 - (y + a)^2 \\
&= d_4^2 - (y - a)^2
\end{aligned}
\qquad \text{(11-1)}
$$

These yield the following values for $x$, $y$, and $z^2$:

$$
\begin{aligned}
x &= (d_1^2 - d_2^2)/4a \\
y &= (d_3^2 - d_4^2)/4a \\
z^2 &= \tfrac{1}{4}(d_1^2 + d_2^2 + d_3^2 + d_4^2) - \tfrac{1}{2}x^2 - \tfrac{1}{2}y^2 - a^2
\end{aligned}
\qquad \text{(11-2)}
$$

The acoustic tablet was not the first device to rely on the speed of sound as a basis for positioning in three dimensions. In 1966 a device called the *Lincoln wand* was developed at MIT's Lincoln Laboratory [405]. This device used a hand-held ultrasonic transmitter, emitting pulses of sound that were picked up by four microphones mounted at the four corners of the screen. The equations from which $x$, $y$, and $z$ were computed were almost identical to those given above. The TX-2 computer, to which the Lincoln wand was attached used about half a millisecond of computation every 40 milliseconds to compute $x$, $y$, and $z$. Nowadays a simple microprocessor-based interface could be used to perform the computation very rapidly.

## Mechanical devices

Three-dimensional coordinate input can also be achieved with the aid of mechanical linkages of various kinds. The simplest of these uses wires stretching from spring-loaded reels mounted at fixed positions (Figure 11-10). The distance from each reel to the hand-held input stylus can be determined from the rotation of the reel, and from these distances the coordinates of the stylus can be computed. Several articles have described the use of such devices

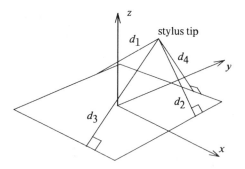

Figure 11-9 Computing the stylus position in three dimensions from distances to four microphones arranged along the edges of a tablet.

[108, 196]. Sutherland has described a more complex linkage system, designed to measure the head position of the user of a head-mounted display [459].

### The Twinkle Box

A device developed by Burton uses a light-emitting stylus whose position is determined by angular measurements [81, 82]. Sensors are mounted at various points in a room; each sensor consists of a high-speed photomultiplier tube, equipped with a wide-angle lens and mounted behind a rotating disk with slits around its periphery (Figure 11-11). As the disk rotates, each slit sweeps out a wide field of view, focusing onto the photomultiplier any light caught in its path. When the photomultiplier detects light from the stylus an electrical pulse is passed to the computer, and the position of the disk at this moment determines the angular position of the stylus. Angular measurements from three different sensors are sufficient to compute the stylus coordinates.

Burton mounted each disk with its axis of rotation horizontal, and placed two photomultipliers behind each disk, one above the axis of rotation and one to the side. These two sensors therefore measured the vertical and horizontal angular displacements of the stylus. Although two such assemblies on adjacent walls would be sufficient in theory, in practice it was found advisable to mount one on each of the four walls to provide redundancy in the position calculation and to track the stylus reliably when blocked from the view of one or more sensors. Several independent light sources could be tracked concurrently, by illuminating one source at a time for a complete scan time; the use of the device in this manner gave rise to the name "Twinkle Box." The high speed of rotation of the disks gave rise to an uncomfortable noise level in the room, but the device was successful in demonstrating the feasibility of measuring three-dimensional position by angular light sensing.

## 11-6 COMPARATORS

In this chapter we have described several different devices suitable for positioning and one device, the light pen, suitable for pointing. With the aid of special programming techniques, either of these two types of device can be made to perform both pointing and positioning. Chapters 13 and 14 describe these techniques.

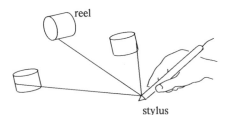

reel

stylus

**Figure 11-10**  Use of wires and spring-loaded reels to measure position.

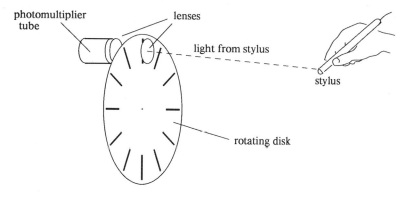

**Figure 11-11** The Twinkle Box.

One way to create a more versatile device is to add extra hardware. We can add *tracking hardware* to permit the light pen to be used as a positioning device; this is rarely done, however, because the hardware is quite complex and tends to interfere with the refreshing of the display. A positioning device can be used for pointing with the aid of a much simpler attachment called a *comparator.*

The comparator is a device that continuously compares the beam position with a pair of reference values. It may use *digital* reference values and compare them with the values in the display's $x$ and $y$ registers. However, this technique is applicable only to point-plotting displays. A comparator for use with an analog vector-drawing display uses a pair of reference *voltages* which are continuously compared with the display's deflection signals. These reference voltages are derived by digital-to-analog conversion from a pair of registers set by the computer. When both pairs of signals agree, the comparator issues a pulse which sets a flip-flop. The computer can change the reference position by reloading the comparator's $x$ and $y$ registers; normally the program will do this after sampling the stylus position. The comparator issues a pulse when the signals agree to within a certain tolerance, perhaps equivalent to 1/10 inch on the screen. This gives the effect of a small square region of interest around the tip of the stylus. A third register may be provided to permit the tolerance of the comparator to be reset by the program.

Notice that the $x$ and $y$ registers of the comparator need not be loaded directly from the coordinate registers of the graphical input device. If these two sets of registers are permanently wired together, a great deal of flexibility is lost in the way the comparator can be used. It should in general be possible to load the comparator registers with any desired transformation of the pen coordinates. It is sometimes helpful even to use coordinates that are completely unrelated to the pen's position. The comparator should be treated not as an input device but as an extension of the facilities offered by the display.

## EXERCISES

**11-1** Find an expression that is symmetrical in $d_1$, $d_2$, $d_3$, $d_4$, $a$, $x$, and $y$ that can be used to check the validity of the $x$, $y$, and $z$ values computed for the three-dimensional acoustic tablet.

**11-2** Derive the expressions relating the coordinates of the Lincoln wand to the distances $d_1$, $d_2$, $d_3$, and $d_4$ of the wand from the four corners of the screen where the microphones are mounted. Assume the screen measures $2a$ by $2b$. Derive also an expression for a value $E$ from which you could check the validity of the $x$, $y$, and $z$ values.

**11-3** What instructions would be needed in a display processor to permit a light pen to be used for pointing and tracking? Consider both display instructions and computer control instructions.

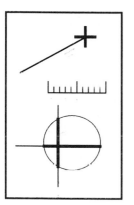

# 12

## GRAPHICAL

## INPUT TECHNIQUES

## 12-1 INTRODUCTION

Many of the input devices described in Chapter 11 bear a close resemblance to the pens and pencils we use to make marks on paper. This resemblance is intentional: the designers of light pens and tablets have gone to considerable trouble to provide us with devices we can grasp comfortably between our fingers. At the same time the resemblance is misleading, for it suggests that we should use graphical input devices in the same freehand fashion that we use pens and pencils. This we can do, and there have been some effective demonstrations of the use of freehand sketched input in which the user "paints" strokes of dots on the screen [287]. There are, however, many other very effective ways of using graphical input devices.

To understand how to make effective use of graphical input devices we must consider the user of the device and the environment in which the device is used. The user generally has a very specific task to get done on the computer and the faster and more easily he can accomplish it the more satisfied he will be. On the other hand he is not generally very skilled in the graphic arts, and we must look for ways to supplement his skills and reduce the need for great manual dexterity on his part. This is where the environment becomes relevant. Behind the input device is a digital computer, and connected to this computer is a graphical display; each can play an important part in improving the effectiveness of the input device.

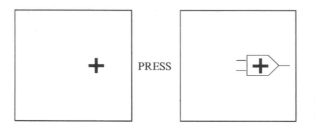

**Figure 12-1** Positioning a symbol.

Thus how we use graphical input devices should not be influenced purely by the way we use pens and pencils. We should instead consider the following three factors when we write programs for these devices:

1. What is the user trying to do?
2. What input information does the application program need?
3. How can the display and computer help the user?

Each of these questions has many different answers according to the situation, and for each set of answers we program the input device in a different way. The result is that we develop certain programming techniques for the use of input devices in each environment.

Some of the more effective and well-tried techniques for graphic input are described in this chapter. These are the techniques from which the programmer must choose when he designs an interactive graphics application program. Through his choice of techniques he provides the user of the program with a set of commands, sometimes called a *command language*. Chapter 28 will discuss some of the issues involved in selecting this set of commands.

The techniques are described here as they appear to the user. Each description attempts to say a few words about the application areas in which the technique is useful and about the general level of computing resources needed to implement the technique. When nontrivial algorithms are involved in the implementation of a technique, they are described in the next two chapters.

### The Use of Feedback

Many of the techniques described in this chapter make use of the display to provide an immediate response to the user's input action. We have already seen an example of such a technique in Chapter 11, in the use of a displayed cursor to help in the control of such input devices as the mouse and tablet. This is called *feedback* and is a very important ingredient of graphical interaction.

In many cases we shall find feedback employed to reduce the user's uncertainty about the effects of his actions. For example, if he presses a button, he may receive no response from the computer for several seconds. An immediate displayed confirmation saves him from wondering whether the button has malfunctioned. If he points to a symbol in order to erase it, he may not be sure what other parts of the picture will be erased along with it. Graphical feedback can show him the parts that will be affected before he commits himself to the action. In either case if feedback were not provided, the user's uncertainty would of course eventually be dispelled, but his efficiency of interaction would be greatly reduced.

Graphical feedback does more than just reduce the user's uncertainty. In the case of cursor feedback, for example, feedback is an indispensable part of the input process. Feedback is also extremely important to novice users, who need additional responses to help them use an unfamiliar program. As the user becomes more experienced, many of these responses become unnecessary and can be omitted.

## 12-2 POSITIONING TECHNIQUES

Positioning, sometimes known as *locating*, is one of the most basic graphical input techniques. The user indicates a position on the screen with an input device, and this position is used to insert a symbol or to define the endpoint of a line. The need for positioning occurs very often in geometric modeling applications, where the user frequently wishes to define a new element of the model or to reposition an existing one.

Positioning involves the user in first moving the cursor or tracking cross to the desired spot on the screen and then notifying the computer by pressing a button or key. Most graphical input devices incorporate buttons or pressure-activated switches for this purpose. A single positioning operation can be used to insert a symbol, as shown in Figure 12-1, and two in succession can define the endpoints of a line (Figure 12-2). Other geometric constructions, such as rectangular boxes and arcs of circles, can be defined by sequences of two or more positioning steps.

Although graphical input devices provide the easiest method of positioning, it is nevertheless possible to position without one by using a keyboard-propelled cursor. A set of four keys may be assigned to step the cursor vertically and horizontally, and a fifth key can be held down to move it through larger steps (Figure 12-3).

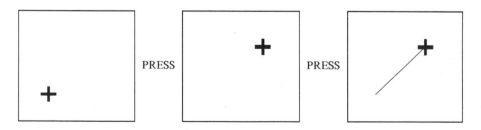

**Figure 12-2** Line endpoint positioning.

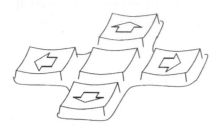

Figure 12-3 Stepping keys for cursor movement. The central key is held down for larger steps.

## Positioning Constraints

In many graphical applications the user must align input information with other information already on the screen. This is very difficult for the user without some assistance from the computer. However steady his hand, there is normally enough jitter to throw off his attempts at accurate positioning; the error may be only a few hundredths of an inch, but this is often enough to invalidate the positioning operation. We therefore use the computer to help achieve accurate positioning.

The mechanism we use is the geometric *constraint*. A constraint is a rule that we wish certain information, in this case the input coordinates, to obey. We enforce the constraint by applying a transformation to the input coordinates, generating a new pair of coordinates that satisfy the constraint. The most common form of constraint is the *modular constraint*, which forces the input point to the nearest intersection on a grid. This can be applied both to symbols (Figure 12-4) and to line endpoints (Figure 12-5). The spacing of the grid is selected by the application program but may be changed if necessary by the user. Note that it is not necessary to display the grid in order for modular constraints to be used effectively.

Another useful and relatively simple constraint is the *directional constraint* applied to straight lines. Many applications use only horizontal and vertical lines and are easier to operate if all input lines are constrained to be either horizontal or vertical. As shown in Figure 12-6, the user specifies two endpoints; the program determines whether the line they specify is more nearly horizontal or vertical and draws a line parallel to the corresponding axis. The

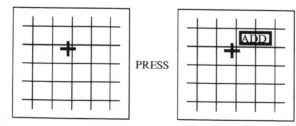

PRESS

Figure 12-4 Modular constraint applied to positioning a symbol.

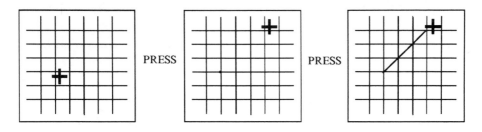

Figure 12-5 Modular constraint applied to line endpoint positioning.

length of this line is the distance between the two input points, measured parallel to the axis.

A slightly different form of the directional constraint requires the user to select either horizontal or vertical before defining the endpoints. The line will then be drawn in this direction no matter which axis is most nearly parallel to the line through the specified endpoints. This technique simplifies certain alignment tasks, as can be seen in Figure 12-7.

We may wish to attach a line or symbol to a point in the existing picture that does not lie on a grid intersection. We cannot use a modular constraint and must instead use a *gravity-field effect,* so-called because it simulates a gravitational pull between the lines on the screen and the input point. Around each of the lines we define an invisible region, shaped approximately like either a dumbbell or a sausage (Figure 12-8); if the input point lies within the region, we replace it by the nearest point on the line itself, as shown in Figure 12-9. The size of the invisible region must be chosen carefully to make attachment easy without increasing the chance of attaching to the wrong line. The dumbbell-shaped gravity field is more satisfactory in this respect, since it improves discrimination along the length of each line while making it easy to attach to endpoints.

## Scales and Guidelines

It is often helpful to display a grid on the screen, so that the user can select a grid intersection rather than rely on a modular constraint to select it for him.

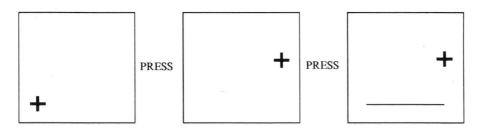

Figure 12-6 Horizontal/vertical line constraint.

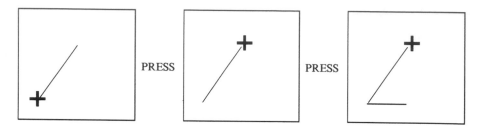

**Figure 12-7** Use of a horizontal line constraint to align endpoints vertically.

The grid display also helps him to input points at specific distances from each other, measured in grid units.

Precise measuring is also made possible by the use of a *scale,* as shown in Figure 12-10. The user gives a command to cause the scale to be displayed and after using it gives another command to erase it. A *guideline* can be displayed in a similar fashion, to assist the user in alignment (Figure 12-11). Both techniques are useful in applications where a full-screen grid might increase flicker or obscure essential parts of the picture.

**Rubber-Band Techniques**

Positioning operations can benefit in a number of ways from the use of feedback. One of the earliest examples of positioning feedback to be demonstrated was the *rubber-band line.* The user specifies the line in the normal way by positioning its two endpoints. As he moves from the first endpoint to the second, the program displays a line from the first endpoint to the cursor position (Figure 12-12); thus he can see the lie of the line before he finishes positioning it. The effect is of an elastic line stretched between the first endpoint and the cursor; hence the name for this technique.

Rubber-band lines are helpful in applications where lines must be positioned to pass through or near other points. It is a good idea to use rubber-band lines if several other commands use a similar sequence of two positioning actions; if the user accidentally invokes the line-drawing command, he will discover his mistake before it is too late.

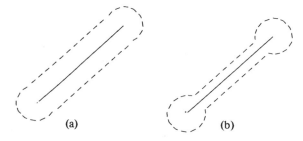

(a)　　　　　(b)

**Figure 12-8** Gravity fields: (a) uniform, (b) with increased field strength at line endpoints.

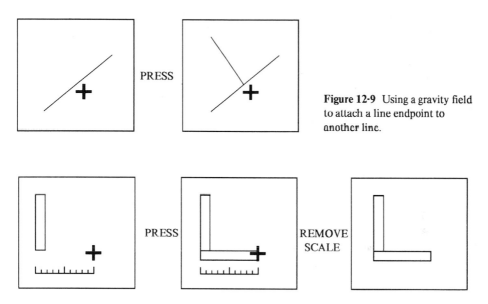

Figure 12-9 Using a gravity field to attach a line endpoint to another line.

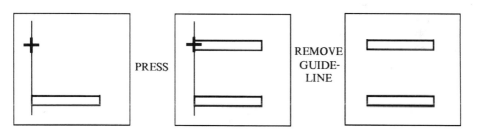

Figure 12-10 Scale used for precise measuring.

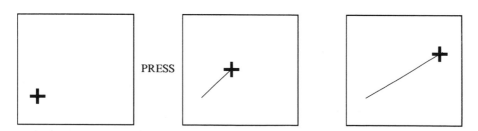

Figure 12-11 Guideline used for alignment.

Figure 12-12 Rubber-band line.

Other geometric entities can be drawn in a rubber-band fashion: examples include horizontally or vertically constrained lines, rectangles, and arcs of circles (Figures 12-13, 12-14). The technique is very helpful in drawing relatively complex entities such as rectangles and arcs, for here the shape of the entity cannot always be easily judged from the positions of the input points.

Rubber-band techniques make fairly heavy demands upon computing resources, and this prevents their use in certain circumstances. A rubber-band line must be redrawn 5 times a second or more in order to appear to move smoothly; if drawn less frequently, or on an irregular basis, it jerks around in a manner that is distracting rather than useful. On certain kinds of displays it is often difficult to regenerate the line fast enough; these include point-plotting displays and most of the raster displays described in Chapter 19.

Line-drawing displays are well suited to the use of rubber-band techniques but require local processing capability to compute the line each time the cursor moves. If the application program is running on a computer remote from the graphics terminal, it is usually difficult to update the line often enough. If the terminal can be programmed, however, the rubber-band line function can be provided as a built-in input technique. A generalized rubber-band capability to support rectangles, arcs, and so forth is more difficult to provide in this manner.

### Dragging

Feedback can be very helpful in positioning symbols; if the symbol is attached to the cursor, the user can *drag* it into position, and can make sure that it is aligned with the rest of the picture before giving the command to insert it (Figure 12-15). In many applications dragging can save the user from having to make several positioning attempts. Consider, for example, the task of positioning a circle so that it passes through two points (Figure 12-16). Extremely accurate positioning can be achieved if the movement of the symbol is scaled down from the cursor movement (Figure 12-17). It is also possible to achieve accurate positioning by applying a modular constraint after dragging the symbol to within the vicinity of the desired position; it then appears to snap into position.

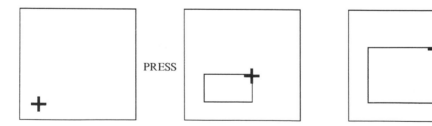

**Figure 12-13**  Drawing a rectangle in a rubber-band fashion.

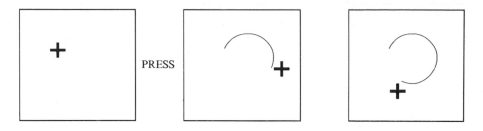

Figure 12-14  Rubber-band arc drawing.

Like rubber-band techniques, dragging requires some local processing to update the picture as the input device moves. If the symbol is defined in relative coordinates, very little processing is involved in updating its position. It is therefore quite easy to provide a dragging function in a graphics terminal for use by a remotely-run application program.

## Positioning Text

Many applications, particularly those relating to graphic arts and design, require the inclusion of text in the picture. Sometimes the position of text items is selected automatically by the program; for example, text may be placed in a box by typing it before positioning the box and letting the program center it once the box has been defined. In other cases the user is the best judge of where to place the text and should be allowed to position it himself.

Text strings can be treated in the same fashion as graphical symbols for positioning purposes. The user can specify the text position by defining the lower left corner of the first character of the string. In some cases, however, the user is more concerned about the position of the center or right-hand edge of the string, and should be allowed to choose the point on the string that he wishes to use for positioning purposes; Figure 12-18 shows the positioning of text by its center. It is also useful to be able to drag text into position, and it is often worthwhile to provide fine control by scaling down the cursor movement.

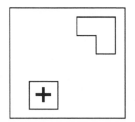
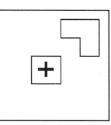
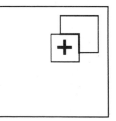

Figure 12-15  Dragging an object into position.

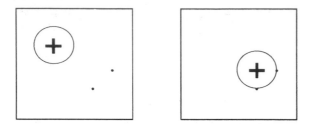

**Figure 12-16** Dragging a circle into intersection with two points.

## Dimensioning Techniques and Graphical Potentiometers

It is often helpful to display the dimensions or coordinate position of an item that is being manipulated by one of the feedback techniques just described. For example, we can display the dimensions of a line while drawing it in a rubber-band fashion (Figure 12-19); the text representing the dimensions is easily computed during the process of regenerating the line. The same technique can be used to display the dimensions of a box (Figure 12-20) or the coordinate position of a symbol during dragging (Figure 12-21). If two or more dimensions are displayed simultaneously, they should be positioned close together, as shown in the figures, so that the user can watch them both without constantly shifting his gaze. When the item has been positioned, the dimensions may be removed but they should remain on the screen long enough for the user to verify that he has positioned accurately.

A similar technique may be used for the input of numerical data. Suppose we display the $y$ coordinate of the pen position as we move the pen around. We then have a mechanism similar to a *potentiometer*, which can be adjusted to any value we choose between 0 and 1023. This value can then be used by the program as an input parameter (Figure 12-22). Furthermore we are not restricted to the range 0 to 1023 since the pen coordinate can be scaled by any factor we choose.

Input to the potentiometer may be scaled logarithmically so as to achieve better accuracy at the lower end of the scale. Alternately the output value may be changed at a rate proportional to the square or exponential of the pen velocity. This gives very fine control at low pen speeds.

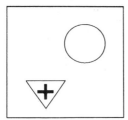 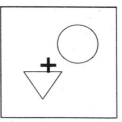 

**Figure 12-17** Scaled-down cursor movement for accurate positioning.

**Figure 12-18**  Positioning a text string by its center.

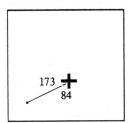

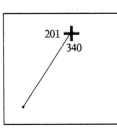

**Figure 12-19**  Displaying the dimensions of a rubber-band line.

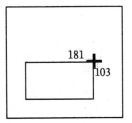

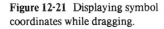

**Figure 12-20**  Dimensioning a rubber-band box.

**Figure 12-21**  Displaying symbol coordinates while dragging.

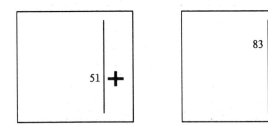

**Figure 12-22**  Graphical potentiometer.

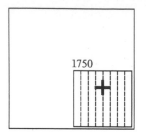

**Figure 12-23** The light handle.

Unless rate control is used, the linear potentiometer is limited in resolution to one part in 1000 or less. A device which does not suffer from this limitation is the *light handle* [344], effectively eight potentiometers arranged side by side, as shown in Figure 12-23. The rightmost potentiometer is for extremely accurate adjustment, and each of the others has a scale factor of twice that of the potentiometer to the right of it. The displayed value remains constant as the pen is moved horizontally. Thus it can be adjusted coarsely by moving up and down one of the left-hand potentiometers and more accurately by one of the right-hand ones. A circular pen motion winds the value up or down.

Dimensions and potentiometers are simple to program except where the displayed numbers are liable to be obscured by the line or object being drawn. In such cases the program should be capable of choosing an unobscured position for the numbers. The light handle is not a complicated program, but its parameters require careful adjustment before it can be used with ease. Like rubber-band drawing, all of these techniques depend on a system organization and language that permit a user program to be run every time the pen moves. Rate control is even more demanding, requiring inputs from the pen that represent points equally spaced in time.

## 12-3 POINTING AND SELECTION

Graphical input devices play a very important role in allowing the user to point to information on the screen. In many applications pointing, rather than positioning, is the basis for interaction. The user may have no need to add more information to the picture and may be interested solely in studying and asking questions about the information already displayed. Even in cases where positioning does occur, the user generally makes extensive use of pointing techniques to select picture parts that need modification and to issue commands with the aid of *command menus*.

### Selection

Programs that provide the user with the ability to interact with a data base, such as interactive modeling applications, must provide the user with a means of *selecting* parts of the data base or model. The user can then move, delete, or copy the selected part, or can apply nongraphical operations such as inquiring about its attributes or its relationships with other parts. Selection is such a useful tool in the hands of the user that it is well worthwhile to find efficient techniques for carrying it out.

The design of selection techniques poses several problems not encountered in positioning. Most of these problems are due to the fact that input devices provide only a pair of coordinates. This information is adequate for positioning purposes but is insufficient for selection in a number of respects. In the first place, the input point rarely lies exactly on one of the lines representing the selected item; the program must search for the nearest line. The use of a light pen helps to solve this problem but does not resolve ambiguous cases where two or more lines pass close to the selected point.

A second problem in selection is to determine *how much* is being selected. When the user points at the line indicated in Figure 12-24, he may wish to select a point on the line, the line itself, all four lines of the box to which the line belongs, or the complete assemblage of symbols including the box. In order to resolve this ambiguity, the user must define a certain *grain* of selection.

Several techniques can be used to help the user achieve unambiguous selection:

1.  *The use of selection points.* In order to select a graphical unit the user points to a specific spot, such as the center of a circle or an endpoint of a line. Selection points can be provided for symbols and larger subpictures. By choosing selection points with care the application programmer can reduce the likelihood of overlap. To help the user, selection points can be emphasized by highlighting or increased brightness (Figure 12-25).
2.  *Defining a bounding rectangle.* The user can define two opposite corners of a rectangle and in this way select an object that lies within the rectangle (Figure 12-26). This technique is useful mainly for multiple selection, as described below.
3.  *Multiple keys for selection.* When the user has positioned the cursor over the item he wishes to select, he can press one of several keys according to the type of item. Thus he might use one key to select a line, another to select a point, and a third to select a symbol. The multiple buttons on the mouse are appropriate for this method of selection.

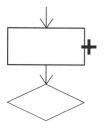

**Figure 12-24** Ambiguous selection: pointing to the box may have several different interpretations.

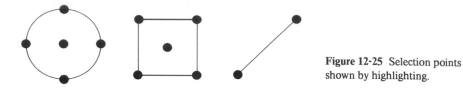

**Figure 12-25** Selection points shown by highlighting.

4. *Prefix commands.* The type of item to be selected can be determined by the user's prior choice of command. The command is given before the selection and may specify which type of item is to be selected. Thus three different DELETE commands might be provided, DELETE POINT, DELETE LINE, and DELETE SYMBOL.

5. *Modes.* The user may be able to change the selection mechanism by setting different modes of operation. In one mode the program might allow only line selection and in another just symbol selection.

These are only a few of the many techniques for graphical selection. The choice of which technique to use depends on the overall design of the command language and will be discussed further in Chapter 28.

## Selection Feedback

The ambiguity inherent in the selection process is a potential source of uncertainty on the user's part, and it is therefore appropriate to provide reassurance through the use of feedback. A simple form of selection feedback involves the use of brightness modulation: by increasing the brightness of a selected item we can distinguish it from other items. If brightness has been assigned another meaning, such as depth in a multilayer circuit board, then some other highlighting technique can be used, such as blinking the item on and off or drawing a box around it.

Selection feedback is particularly useful *before* the selection has been completed; the user can move the cursor around in the region of interest and

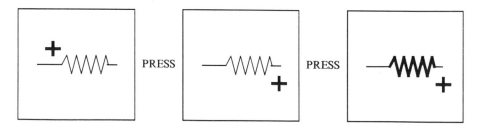

**Figure 12-26** Selecting a symbol by defining a bounding rectangle.

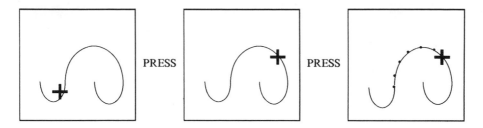

**Figure 12-27** Selecting points on a curve by indicating the first and last of the sequence.

see each possible selection highlighted in turn. When the item of his choice is highlighted, he completes the selection operation. This technique requires very rapid feedback: each item must light up as soon as the user points to it. If the data base is very large or the computer's response slow the use of this techniques may not be feasible.

## Multiple Selections

It is helpful to allow the user to select more than one item at a time. In this way he can issue a single command that operates on several items and need not invoke the command once per item.

This *multiple selection* capability can be provided in a number of ways. The easiest method, suitable for selection from a set of items that form a linear contiguous sequence on the screen, is to indicate the first and last items in the sequence that are to be selected, Figure 12-27 shows the use of this technique in selecting points on a curve. If the items are not ordered linearly but lie in close proximity, it is often possible to select them by specifying a bounding rectangle (Figure 12-28). If neither technique is applicable, the user must select each one in turn. Since this may take some time, and since he may make mistakes, the program must allow him to edit the set of selections before issuing the command that is to operate on all of them.

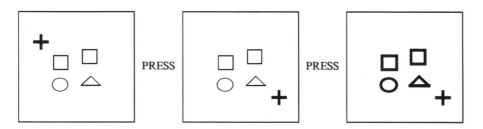

**Figure 12-28** Multiple selection by drawing a bounding rectangle.

**Figure 12-29** Menus: (a) for item selection, (b) for mode change, (c) for command selection.

## Menu Selection

Menu selection is a very powerful technique for interactive control. It is quite effective even in the simplest keyboard-operated programs, which can display a list of alternatives prefixed by numbers, one of which the user types to make his selection. Interactive graphics makes menu selection much simpler and faster. The menu is displayed on the screen, and the user points to his selection with a graphical input device. Menus can be used for a variety of purposes: they allow the user to choose an item for insertion (Figure 12-29a), to change the mode of operation of the program (Figure 12-29b), or to issue a command (Figure 12-29c). The use of menus helps the user to understand the range of alternatives open to him; at the same time it protects him from making an invalid selection, since only valid choices are included in the menu.

Menus are often constructed from short text strings displayed either down one side of the screen (Figure 12-30) or along the bottom (Figure 12-31). It is usually possible to accommodate more menu items along the side than along the bottom. This is not a particularly important consideration, however, because lengthy menus force the user to spend more time searching for the required menu item. It is better to try to keep menus short, dividing them if necessary into sets of submenus that require a sequence of two or more selections. Figure 12-32 depicts selection from such a tree-structured set of menus.

Graphic symbols may be used in place of text for menu items. This is appropriate where the user wishes to select a symbol for insertion in the picture (Figure 12-33). Command menus can similarly be displayed as a set of graphical *icons*, each representing a command (Figure 12-34). The novice user may require longer to learn to use a set of command icons than a text menu, but once he is familiar with the icons he is likely to make fewer selection errors than with a text menu. Icons have the added advantage that they generally use less screen space than text and therefore lead to more compact menus.

An interesting idea, proposed by Wiseman [520], is the use of a movable menu displayed close to the cursor (Figure 12-35). The user can make selections from such a menu with the minimum of hand movement. Movable menus should be displayed only when the user needs to make a menu selection; otherwise they tend to obliterate important parts of the displayed image.

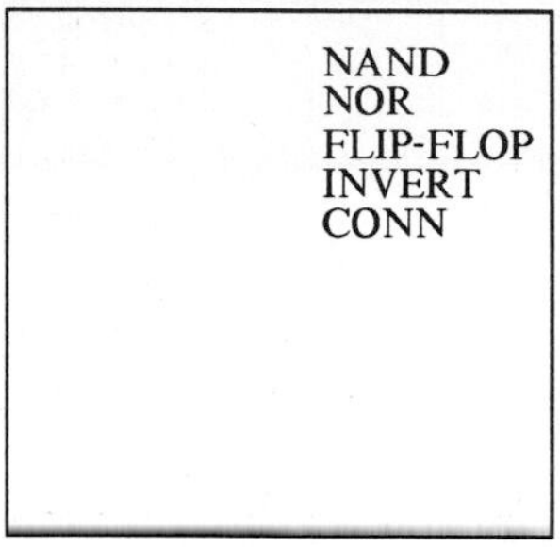

NAND
NOR
FLIP-FLOP
INVERT
CONN

**Figure 12-30** Menu items arranged along a vertical screen edge.

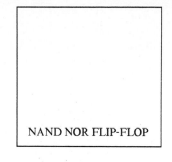

NAND NOR FLIP-FLOP

**Figure 12-31** Menu items arranged along the bottom of the screen.

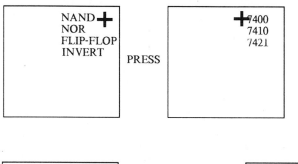

NAND
NOR
FLIP-FLOP
INVERT
PRESS
7400
7410
7421

**Figure 12-32** Selection by means of a two-level menu.

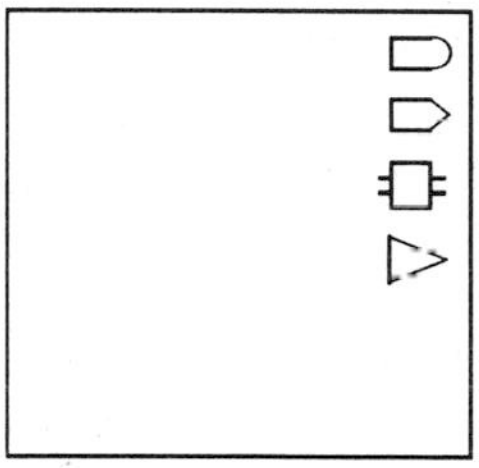

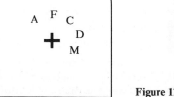

**Figure 12-33** Item menu displayed graphically.

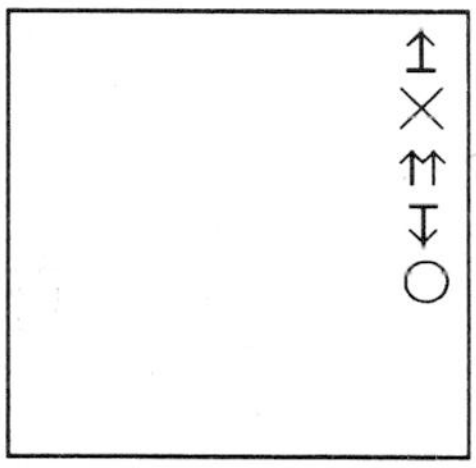

**Figure 12-34** Graphical command menu.

A
F
C
D
M

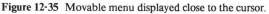

**Figure 12-35** Movable menu displayed close to the cursor.

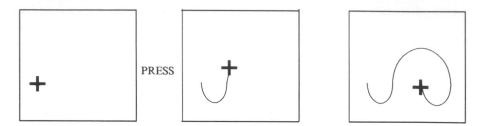

**Figure 12-36** Freehand inking.

The implementation of menus is usually quite straightforward. If a light pen is used for selection, the selected item is directly identifiable; with other devices, a very simple check on the device coordinates will identify the item. Menus are easy to construct and are often best represented as separate display-file segments so that menus can be switched by unposting one segment and posting another.

## 12-4 INKING AND PAINTING

If we sample the position of a graphical input device at regular intervals and display a dot at each sampled position, a trail will be displayed of the movement of the device (Figure 12-36). This technique, which closely simulates the effect of drawing on paper, is called *inking*. For many years the main use of inking has been in conjunction with on-line character-recognition programs (see Section 2-5). With the advent of high-quality raster displays the technique has found wider use for *painting* purposes.

**Figure 12-37** Image drawn by painting freehand on the screen. *Lance Williams.*

**Figure 12-38** Painting with a thick brush.

## Painting

A raster display incorporating a random-access frame buffer, like that described in Chapter 1, can be treated as a painting surface for interactive purposes. As the user moves the cursor around, a trace of its path can be left on the screen. The user can build up freehand drawings of surprisingly good quality. Figure 12-37 shows a picture drawn in this manner.

It is possible to provide a range of tools for painting on a raster display; these tools take the form of *brushes* that lay down trails of different thicknesses and colors. For example, instead of depositing a single dot at each sampled input position, the program can insert a group of dots so as to fill in a square or circle; the result will be a much thicker trace, as shown in Figure 12-38. On a black-and-white display the user needs brushes that paint in both black and white, so that information can be both added and removed (Figure 12-39). When a color display is used for painting, a menu of different colors can be provided (Figure 12-40).

## Constrained Painting

Freehand painting on display screens is useful for animated movie production, but it has relatively few other applications. With the addition of a modular constraint, however, painting is transformed into a technique useful for producing block diagrams and other kinds of technical illustration.

We apply a modular constraint to painting by dispensing dots only when the cursor moves from the vicinity of one grid intersection to the vicinity of

**Figure 12-39** Erasing with a white brush.

**Figure 12-40** Use of a menu of colors for painting.

another. We then draw the appropriate grid line segments to join the intersections. Thus as the cursor moves, the displayed trail follows the nearest grid lines (Figure 12-41). Different thicknesses of line can be dispensed, and white brushes can be used to erase lines and to achieve various special effects (Figure 12-42). This technique can be extended to permit diagonal line drawing as well, but greater skill is required.

When using this technique to permit line drawing with thick lines, care must be taken in constructing corners; otherwise ugly effects occur that spoil the quality of the image. A solution to this problem will be presented in Chapter 17.

## 12-5 ON-LINE CHARACTER RECOGNITION

Most positioning techniques are designed so that the user specifies in two separate steps what he wants to define and where he wants to position it. Thus he draws a line by giving the DRAW LINE command and defining two endpoints; he draws an arc by giving the DRAW ARC command followed by three

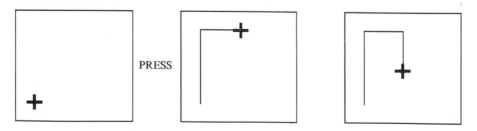

**Figure 12-41** Constrained painting.

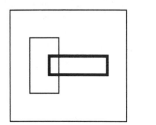

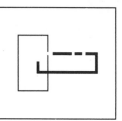

**Figure 12-42** Erasing with a constrained brush.

coordinate positions, he positions a character by first typing it and then indicating its position on the screen. We may ask whether it is always necessary to define explicitly what we wish to draw before defining its geometry. Could we not provide a few more features of the geometry so that the identity of the object is obvious?

This is the reasoning behind on-line character recognition, one of the most interesting of all interactive graphical techniques. Using the inking technique described in the previous section, the user draws several freehand strokes that define the character or symbol he wishes to insert. The computer then attempts to recognize the character by analyzing these strokes. As it recognizes each character, it erases the strokes and replaces them by a neatly drawn symbol (Figure 12-43). Some very successful character-recognition programs have been developed that have been used in a number of design applications.

The main problem in designing an effective recognition algorithm is to cope with the variation in the way different users draw the same character and also in successive attempts by a single user to draw the same character. The algorithm must tolerate a reasonable degree of variation without losing its ability to discriminate between characters that are intended to be different. Some recognizers do not to solve this problem completely but are designed on the assumption that all users will draw characters in approximately the same way. In other words the program trains the user to draw characters in a recognizable way.

Another approach to the design of recognizers has been to let the user train the program. These recognizers are designed in two parts. A training program conducts a dialog with the user, during which a data base is constructed that

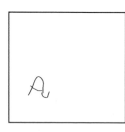

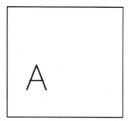

**Figure 12-43** On-line character recognition.

**Figure 12-44** Training an on-line recognizer.

decribes how this particular user draws each character. The data base is then used by a recognition routine included in the application program. The training dialogue is very simple. The user draws a character, and the program tries to recognize it, indicating its guess to the user (Figure 12-44). The user corrects the program's guess if necessary and redraws the character until the program can recognize it reliably. When the full set of characters has been taught in this way, the data base is complete and the application program can be run. If the user later encounters difficulty in drawing recognizable characters, he can return to the training program and redefine the shape of the characters in question.

One advantage of on-line character recognition is that a complete character or symbol can be defined in a single operation. In drawing the character the user defines what character it is, where it is to be positioned, and, if appropriate, how big it is to be. The technique can be used for both alphanumeric characters and graphical symbols. There is no need for the strokes the user draws to resemble the shape of the displayed symbol. A couple of strokes, for example, are enough to specify a transistor symbol (Figure 12-45).

Character recognition requires a fairly substantial amount of computing resources: at least 2000 16-bit words of memory are likely to be taken up by the recognizer program and its data base, and the program must run in a processor local to the display. There are other problems associated with this technique. It is not suitable for highly accurate graphical input, nor does it allow very rapid interaction since each character takes several seconds to draw and recognize. This relatively slow interaction cycle rules out the use of certain kinds of feedback, particularly in selection. Nevertheless on-line character recognition

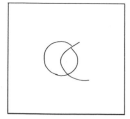 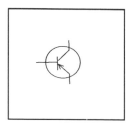

**Figure 12-45** A complex item may be specified by drawing a simple symbol.

has proved its usefulness in a number of applications as a method of specifying graphical information [11, 288].

## 12-6 CONCLUSION

As we have seen, a great many techniques have been developed for interaction with the graphical display. Some of these are sparing in their use of computing resources, while others make full use of the capabilities of an interactive display coupled to a dedicated computer. In the latter case, the close coupling of the computer to the display makes possible the use of various forms of feedback, and in many cases leads to more effective interaction. As it becomes increasingly feasible to provide displays with their own dedicated processors, interest in this style of interaction is likely to increase.

As new interactive techniques are invented, the repertoire available to the applications programmer increases. This is a mixed blessing. The programmer generally benefits from new and improved techniques, but the task of selecting appropriate techniques for the application may become more difficult as the range of selection widens. The programmer cannot choose randomly within this range; interactive techniques must be selected carefully so as to produce a consistent command language. Other issues are involved; in particular the user must develop a conceptual model of the objects he is manipulating, and the program must generate a displayed image consistent with this model. It is important to choose interactive techniques that are in keeping with the user's model and the techniques used for information display. Chapter 28, in its discussion of user interface design, will return to these issues.

## EXERCISES

**12-1** Program the Light Handle (Section 12-2), and experiment with it by modifying parameters such as the ratio of adjacent potentiometers, and by introducing velocity effects.

**12-2** Write a program to display a rubber-band arc of a circle in such a way that the user can dynamically change the angle subtended by the arc (Figure 12-14). Use the DDA circle generator described in Chapter 2. In designing the program, consider alternative ways in which the user might specify the arc, e.g., by the center and a point on the arc, by two tangents, etc.

**12-3** Although some of the techniques described above are more costly than their alternatives in their use of processing power, they are often more convenient and effective. Program some experiments along the lines of those of Card *et al* [89], to compare the effectiveness of some of these techniques, e.g. rubber-band versus endpoint positioning for line-drawing.

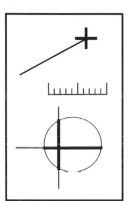

# 13

# EVENT HANDLING

## 13-1 INTRODUCTION

The last chapter described some of the interactive techniques made possible by the use of graphical input devices. These techniques are many and varied. Some of them, such as positioning with a tablet or mouse, are very easy to program; others are quite complicated, and their implementation involves a considerable investment in programming. This variation in ease of implementing the techniques has a direct bearing on their popularity; positioning is used very often, while on-line character recognition, one of the more difficult techniques to implement, is rarely used. Application programmers frequently avoid using some of the more effective interactive techniques because of problems in implementing them.

How can we solve this problem and provide application programmers with a wider choice of techniques? The answer lies in following the approach we took with graphic output. We must attempt to provide, with the aid of software, a set of functions that gives the programmer easy access to the capabilities of input hardware and that protects him from its peculiarities. If these functions are properly designed, even the most complicated techniques can be used with relative ease.

Designing a set of interactive input functions is not a straightforward task. Three factors make it particularly difficult. The first is the wide variety of techniques the functions must be able to implement (Chapter 12 has described only a selected few). To provide enough flexibility in the set of functions we may have to sacrifice simplicity, creating difficulties for the inexperienced programmer. The second factor is the variation between input devices. Despite our concern to hide the peculiarities of input devices from the application programmer, we cannot always do so. Sometimes the device has specific limitations of which the programmer must be aware; in other cases it has special capabilities that he may wish to exploit. The light pen illustrates this point in both respects; it has a wide field of view that makes it unsuitable for accurate freehand drawing, but it has the ability to see lines on the screen and hence to provide a very fast response to pointing operations.

The third factor we must consider in designing input software is the unpredictable nature of interactive input. Graphical input devices are controlled by human beings, not by computers; this sets them apart from conventional input devices like card readers, paper-tape readers, and magnetic-tape drives. If a computer program needs to read a character from a paper tape, for example, it issues a READ command to the tape reader and within a few milliseconds the character is delivered. The computer has control over the tape reader and can therefore rely on receiving a character within a few milliseconds of issuing the READ command (except in the special case where there is no tape in the reader).

Now consider the problem of reading a character from an alphanumeric keyboard. The keyboard is controlled by its user, not by the computer, and there is no way to force this user to type a character for the computer to read. Thus the program may have to suspend execution indefinitely, waiting for the user to strike a key. In the meantime the user may change his mind and press a function button, for which no READ command has been issued and to which the computer therefore does not respond. Thus conventional programming techniques do not handle interactive devices very successfully. In the following pages we shall discuss more appropriate ways of handling them and develop a set of input functions that addresses the issues raised in this section.

## 13-2 POLLING

The problem we encountered in programming an alphanumeric keyboard in fact consists of two problems, both fundamental to interactive input devices. First, the user often has more than one device at his disposal, and the program cannot predict which one he will use next. Second, even if we restrict the user to a single device, we cannot predict when he will use it. The danger is not so much that the program may have to wait indefinitely but that it may miss the input data altogether because it is busy with some other task when the user decides to do something.

Taken together, these problems rule out the use of a simple READ command to collect data from a device. Instead we resort to a technique known as *polling:* we periodically check the status of each device. As we have seen in Chapter 11, input devices are connected to the computer by means of registers whose contents the computer can read. A keyboard usually has two registers, one to indicate whether a key has been struck, the other to identify the key by its character code. A tablet has three registers, two of which contain the $x$ and $y$ coordinates of the stylus while the third indicates the status of the switch in the tip of the stylus. If the program periodically checks the contents of these registers, it can determine when the user has struck a key, pressed on the stylus, or performed some other such action.

A simple *polling loop* can be used to check the status of each device in a repetitive manner and to pass on to the program the first item of data received. Figure 13-1 shows such an arrangement. Whenever data are received by the program, they are processed, possibly generating a fresh display; the program then returns to the polling loop. Simple interactive programs are often constructed in this fashion.

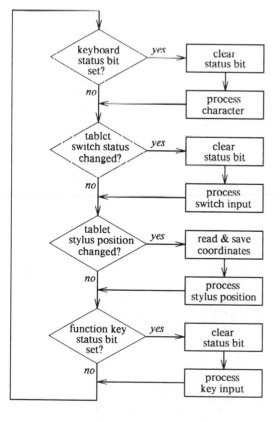

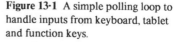

**Figure 13-1** A simple polling loop to handle inputs from keyboard, tablet and function keys.

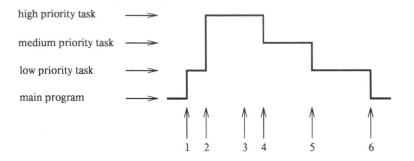

**Figure 13-2** Switching of control between tasks of different priorities, in response to traps and interrupts. Events shown are (1) low-priority interrupt, (2) high-priority trap, (3) medium-priority interrupt, (4) completion of high-priority task, medium-priority task begins, (5) completion of medium-priority task, low-priority task resumes, (6) completion of low-priority task.

## 13-3 INTERRUPTS

The simple polling loop solves the first of our problems, making it possible to use several input devices in conjunction. It does not address the second problem, however: input data will still be lost if entered by the user at a moment when the program is not in its polling loop. Thus if the user presses and releases a function button while the program is in the process-character routine of Figure 13-1, this action will go undetected by the program. During lengthy computations it is easy for several successive inputs to go unnoticed in this way. Clearly we need to arrange to check the status of each device more frequently. We can do this by inserting checks at various points in the program, but this is a tedious programming task and does not guarantee that input devices will be checked sufficiently frequently. Ideally we would like to interrupt the execution of the program at frequent, regular intervals to check the input devices.

Fortunately most computers are designed with this problem in mind: they possess hardware that makes it easy for the central processor to switch rapidly between two or more programmed tasks. Tasks are assigned different *priorities* so that higher-priority tasks may interrupt tasks of lower priority. Tasks may be associated with specific peripheral devices in such a way that when a signal, or *interrupt,* is received from a device, control passes to its task. If the interrupt is received while a lower-priority task is running, switching is immediate, and control passes back to the lower-priority task when the other task has run to completion. If the interrupt is of insufficient priority to cause immediate switching, its task is run when all higher-priority interrupts have been processed. The central processor may itself cause switching by means of *traps,* signals caused by special events such as arithmetic underflow or execution of an illegal instruction. In Figure 13-2 we see how control is passed between several tasks of different priorities in response to various traps and interrupts.

Computers are often equipped with a device, known as a *clock*, that generates an interrupt every 1/50 or 1/60 second. Clock interrupts thus provide us with a very simple way of ensuring that input devices are checked on a regular basis. We write the polling-loop routine as a high-priority task and arrange for this *polling task* to be invoked after every clock interrupt. The effect, shown in Figure 13-3, contrasts with the somewhat irregular task switching shown in Figure 13-2. A 50- or 60-hertz clock frequency is high enough to ensure that none of the user's actions will be overlooked by the polling task.

Other devices besides the clock may be permitted to cause interrupts. Separate tasks may be programmed for the keyboard, function buttons, and tablet stylus, to be invoked when interrupts are received from one of these devices. In general, however, it is sufficient to use a single device-polling task invoked by clock interrupts; the need for an additional task arises only when light-pen tracking must be performed (see Section 13-7).

## 13-4 THE EVENT QUEUE

When the polling task detects a change in the status of an input device, it must read the input data from the device registers and pass the data to the main program. This may happen at any moment. The main program may be in an idle state waiting for input from the user, or it may be in the midst of a lengthy computation. In the latter case, the input data must be saved until the computation is complete. Sometimes the user will have time to perform several input actions before the computer can attend to them; for example, he may type the first few characters of some alphanumeric data. Each such input action must be passed to the main program in the order of receipt by the polling task.

We employ an *event queue* to pass input data from the polling task to the main program in the correct order. The queue is a list of blocks, each representing one user action, or *event*. The polling task adds event blocks to the tail of the queue, storing in each block the type of device causing the event and the contents of the device registers. The main program takes events off the head of the queue and invokes the appropriate process in response. Typical events include pressing an alphanumeric or function key, pressing or releasing a mouse or stylus switch, and moving a graphical input device.

To implement the event queue we usually employ a *circular buffer*. This is a vector of memory in which the event blocks are stored contiguously. The

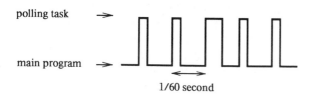

polling task

main program

1/60 second

**Figure 13-3** A polling task invoked every 1/60 second. Note that the duration of the task may vary, but its frequency of invocation remains constant.

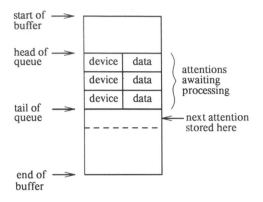

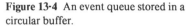

**Figure 13-4** An event queue stored in a circular buffer.

polling task maintains a pointer to the tail of the queue, i.e., to the next available position for an event block; meanwhile a pointer to the first event block indicates the head of the queue. The main program removes events from the queue by reading the information in the first event block and advancing the head-of-queue pointer to the next block. The polling task adds an event to the queue by storing data at the position indicated by the tail-of-queue pointer, which it then advances. If either pointer is advanced beyond the end of the buffer, it is repositioned at the start of the buffer. Figure 13-4 shows the arrangement of the circular buffer.

The circular buffer has a limited capacity for events, and if the user generates events faster than the program can handle them, the buffer will fill up. The polling task can detect a full buffer by checking whether the tail pointer, when advanced, will coincide with the head pointer. If the two pointers are allowed to overlap, an extra status bit is needed to indicate whether the queue is full or empty, since these two conditions are otherwise indistinguishable; a simpler solution is always to leave at least one event block empty.

As we shall see, it is necessary to take special precautions to prevent devices from generating events so rapidly that they fill the buffer up. This cannot always be prevented; the user may issue a flurry of keystrokes or stylus inputs without waiting to see the effect of each one. The only solution is for the polling task to ignore the events that would cause the buffer to overflow and to provide feedback to the user by flashing a message or ringing a bell.

Although the circular buffer is a simple and effective mechanism for handling events, it is not the only such mechanism. We can instead provide a pool of free blocks of memory in which to store event data; these blocks are linked together to form the event queue. Whether we use a linked list, a circular buffer, or some other method, we must pay adequate attention to the fact that *concurrent tasks* are accessing the event queue: while the polling task is adding events, the main program is removing them. Care is needed to ensure that the queue cannot be improperly accessed when in an inconsistent state.

## 13-5  FUNCTIONS FOR HANDLING EVENTS

When it is not busy processing the user's inputs, the main program sits in an idle state waiting for the next input event. When an event appears in the event queue, the main program removes it, checks to see which device caused it, and then *dispatches* control to the appropriate routine. When this routine has been executed, the program resumes its idle state.

A single function can be provided that checks the state of the queue, loops until an event arrives, and then unpacks the contents of the event block:

> *GetEvent* (*e*)          wait for an event to occur, and then return the event data in record *e*.

The use of a function to receive events is preferable to allowing the application programmer to manage the circular buffer himself; there is always a danger that he may forget to advance the head pointer or may advance it by the wrong amount. The *GetEvent* function hides all irrelevant details of event handling from the programmer.

Since the *GetEvent* function contains its own idle loop, the main program can call it whenever it requires input from the user. When the function returns, control is dispatched according to the event type. Thus we might implement a line-positioning routine as follows:

```
type action = (pendown, penmove, penup);
     event = record typ: action; x, y: integer end;

procedure LineInput;
     var e: event; x0, y0: integer;
begin
     GetEvent(e);
     if e.typ = pendown then begin
          x0 := e.x; y0 := e.y;
          GetEvent(e);
          if e.typ = pendown then begin
               MoveTo(x0, y0);
               LineTo(e.x, e.y)
          end
     end
end;
```

This program uses a record *e* of type *event* to retain the event data and uses a constant *pendown* to check the event type. These must be defined within the graphics package of which *GetEvent* forms a part.

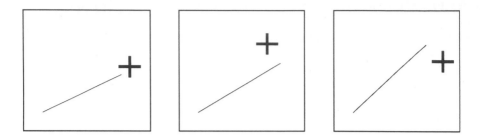

**Figure 13-5** Effect of lag in processing input coordinates while drawing a rubber-band line.

## Repetitive Events

Many of the techniques described in Chapter 12 depend on frequently reading the coordinates of a graphical input device. The polling task can very easily read the position of such a device and pass the coordinates to the main program by means of an event block. The main program then uses the coordinates to construct a rubber-band line, reposition a dragged symbol, or otherwise update the display.

How often should the polling task generate such an event? Should it pass the coordinates to the main program every 1/60 second or only when the coordinates change? In answering these questions we must remember the danger that the event buffer may overflow if events are generated too fast. If we allow pen-position events to be generated 60 times a second, we must be sure that the main program can process each such event in less than 1/60 second; if it cannot, the displayed response will lag farther and farther behind the user's hand movement and eventually the event buffer will overflow. Figure 13-5 illustrates the effect.

To prevent this kind of occurrence we must control the rate at which pen-position events and other events of a similarly repetitive nature enter the event queue. Ideally we would like to ensure that the event queue never contains more than one pen-position event; if it contains two or more, by the time the second event is processed its coordinates will be out of date. Provided we ensure that there is no interruption in the stream of pen-position events, we are quite justified in limiting the generation of these events so that the queue never contains more than one.

A simple method of achieving this control is to have the application program indicate when it is ready for an event. This is done with the following function:

> *PermitEvent* (*t*)     allow the polling task to add an event of type *t* to the event queue

This function may be called as soon as the main program has received a pen-position event, and will allow another event of this type to be added to the queue. The following example illustrates the use of this function in programming a rubber-band line:

```
procedure RubberBand;
    var e: event; x0, y0: integer;
begin
    repeat GetEvent(e) until e.typ = pendown;
    x0 := e.x; y0 := e.y;
    PermitEvent(penmove);
    repeat
        GetEvent(e);
        if e.typ = penmove then begin
            PermitEvent(penmove);
            OpenSegment(100);
            MoveTo(x0, y0); LineTo(e.x, e.y);
            PostSegment(100)
        end
    until e.typ = pendown
end;
```

This program calls *PermitEvent* once when the pen is initially pressed down, to start the flow of pen-position events, and then once after each such event is received. When a second pen switch event is received, the flow of position events ceases. One such event remains in the queue after the program has terminated; the next routine to call *GetEvent* must flush this event from the queue using a loop of the kind shown on the fifth line of the rubber-band program.

To implement the *PermitEvent* function we must provide the polling task with a set of status bits, one for each event type. When a status bit is set, events of the corresponding type are permitted to occur. Whenever a repetitive event such as a position event is generated, its status bit is cleared and no further events of this type are generated until the status bit is set by the *PermitEvent* function. Other kinds of events, such as keyboard and pen-switch events, have status bits that remain permanently set.

## 13-6 POLLING TASK DESIGN

The design of the polling task is in most respects very simple. Each input device must be checked in turn. If its status has changed, or if it is capable of generating repetitive events, the appropriate status bit is checked. If the status bit is set, an event block is added to the event queue, and finally the status bit may require clearing. In many cases a simple polling routine of this kind is adequate. Certain devices and certain kinds of event require special treatment, however, making the design of the polling task a more complex matter.

### Repositioning the Cursor

Most graphical input devices require the display of a cursor that follows the movement of the device. The cursor is represented by a short display-file sequence starting with a pair of positioning instructions. One of the responsibilities of the polling task is to update these instructions every time the input device is moved, so that the cursor moves to the corresponding position on the screen. This can normally be achieved by a couple of simple substitutions. Sometimes, however, it is appropriate to perform computations such as scaling, smoothing to remove input noise, clipping to screen or viewport boundaries. Often this processing is application-dependent and therefore cannot be carried out by hardware.

In some graphics packages the cursor is defined as a separate display-file segment, and whenever the input device moves, the segment is redefined. This allows the application program to change the shape of the cursor as a special form of feedback to the user. While conceptually elegant, this method is sometimes infeasible in practice since it depends on being able to invoke the segment-repositioning process often enough to achieve smooth motion. A more practical solution is offered by the use of symbol-definition facilities of the kind described in Chapter 10. A special symbol can be reserved as the cursor definition. When this symbol is redefined by the application program, the display-file sequence representing the cursor is replaced. Meanwhile the polling task can perform cursor repositioning.

### Inking

Inking is a second example of a process that cannot normally be carried out by the main program. There are two main reasons for this: first, unless the graphics package provides functions for appending to segments, it is virtually impossible for the main program to perform inking. Second, even if appending is permitted, it is rarely possible to perform it rapidly enough to generate smoothly inked strokes.

It is therefore more satisfactory to perform inking within the polling task. As the input device moves, "ink" is generated by adding dots or short vectors to the display file. Simultaneously a vector of coordinate pairs representing the trajectory of the inked stroke is created for use by the application program. The ink is deposited in a special portion of the display file that is later automatically erased (the *Update* function may be assigned to perform this task). The stroke trajectory can likewise be stored in a reserved vector of memory, or it can be placed in an array passed to the polling task by the application program. The latter method is the more convenient, for it does not require dedication of a large amount of memory to stroke storage; instead the stroke array is allocated only when needed. To save space the polling task may perform *thinning* of the stream of coordinates, discarding data points when the input device is stationary or moving slowly.

The action of inking a stroke may be treated as a special class of event. It is then feasible to pass a stroke storage array to the polling task when calling *PermitEvent* to invoke inking:

   *PermitEvent* (*ink, strokearray, strokewords*)

Note that the length of the array must be passed to the polling task so that it can prevent the array from overflowing. An array of 100 or 200 words is normally sufficient for short strokes like those used in writing characters for on-line recognition. The event block created when the stroke is complete should indicate the number of coordinate pairs it contains.

## 13-7 LIGHT-PEN INTERRUPTS

The light pen communicates with the computer through a single 1-bit status register that is set whenever the light pen sees an intensified spot on the screen. The identity of the spot is determined by reading the display address register as soon as the status bit is set. Instead of relying on the computer to respond immediately, the display processor halts when the status bit is set, thus ensuring that the address register will still be valid when the computer reads it. Nevertheless it is important for the computer to respond quickly to a change in the status bit; if the display remains off for more than a millisecond or two, the user will notice a flickering effect. This rules out checking the status bit by means of the polling task, which runs only once every 1/60 second. Instead the status bit generates an interrupt when it is set, and this invokes a high-priority task that reads the display address register and restarts the display.

Two kinds of light-pen interrupts may occur. The user may point the pen at an item on the screen in order to select it; this results in a *selection interrupt*. When the user is positioning with the pen, a *tracking pattern* is displayed in order to follow the pen's movement and *tracking interrupts* are generated when the pen sees the pattern. The light-pen task must distinguish between selection and tracking interrupts. This can be achieved by checking the display address register to see whether the display has been stopped while displaying the tracking pattern. If it has, the polling task proceeds with the tracking process; if it has not, the interrupt is treated as a selection interrupt and a selection event is generated.

### Light-Pen Tracking

When the light pen is used for positioning, a tracking pattern is displayed in the vicinity of the pen's field of view. When the pattern is seen by the pen a tracking interrupt is generated, from which the position of the pen is determined. If the pen has moved since the previous interrupt, the tracking pattern is moved to the new pen position. Thus the pattern follows the pen's movement around the screen.

center of spiral

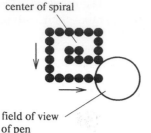

field of view
of pen

**Figure 13-6** A spiral light-pen tracking pattern.

As long as the pen is moved relatively slowly, this simple tracking technique will work, and some portion of the tracking pattern will always lie within the pen's field of view. As the pen is moved faster, however, it gets farther and farther ahead of the pattern until at a certain speed of hand movement tracking fails altogether. The hand speed at which this occurs depends on the size of the pattern and the frequency with which it is displayed. Tracking can therefore be made more reliable by increasing the size of the pattern and by displaying it more often. Neither of these methods is altogether beneficial, however. A large pattern can obscure important details of the picture, and frequent display of the tracking pattern tends to promote flicker. Instead when tracking fails, a larger pattern, the size of the screen if necessary, can be employed to find the pen. One solution to the problem of tracking failure is to track the pen with a spiral pattern that grows until it finds the pen (Figure 13-6).

Most tracking patterns, including spirals and simple rasters, cause inaccurate tracking. The part of the pattern seen by the pen may lie anywhere in the pen's relatively large field of view. To achieve accurate tracking a cross-shaped pattern should be used. The arms of the cross are drawn inward, starting at the extremity of each arm. They are drawn point by point so that the light pen will interrupt at the moment each arm of the cross emerges into the field of view. If the coordinates of the most recent point are read after each interrupt, four points $p_1$, $p_2$, $p_3$, $p_4$ will be found which lie on the circumference of the field of view (Figure 13-7). The center of the field of view is the point

$$(\tfrac{1}{2}(x_1 + x_2), \ \tfrac{1}{2}(y_3 + y_4)).$$

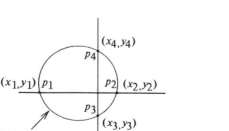

field of view

tracking cross

**Figure 13-7** Use of a tracking cross for accurate light-pen positioning.

Thus after receiving four interrupts, corresponding to the four arms of the cross, the light-pen task computes the coordinates of the center of the field of view, repositions the cursor, and stores the coordinates in a pair of memory locations that are read by the polling task.

The following refinements to the tracking process will lead to more reliable and effective tracking:

1.  Draw each arm from one side of the cross to the other in case the center of the cross is outside the field of view.
2.  Draw each arm of the cross several times if necessary, to increase the pen's chance of detecting it.
3.  Disable pen interrupts from other parts of the displayed picture while pen tracking is in progress, to protect these parts from accidental selection.

In an attempt to improve the performance of tracking programs *predictive* schemes have been used. Instead of displaying the cross at the latest pen position, these programs display it where the pen is *expected* to point the next time tracking is performed. Simple *linear prediction* assumes constant pen speed, while more complex second-order prediction schemes assume constant acceleration.

## Selection Interrupts

Selection interrupts occur when the light pen is pointed at an item on the screen other than the tracking cross. When the light-pen task receives such an interrupt, it performs the following three steps:

1.  It determines as much information as necessary about the item seen by the pen. This information is passed to the main program in an event block.
2.  It makes the item invisible to the pen to prevent further interrupts.
3.  It restarts the display.

*Identification of the item* normally requires the use of a segmented or structured display file. The multilevel structure shown in Figure 13-8 uses the push-jump technique described in Section 8-3 to provide the name of the selected item. Note that more than just this item's name is provided: all the ancestors of the item can be identified from the data in the subroutine return stack. As we have seen in Chapter 12, not all of this information need be passed back to the main program.

*Rendering the item invisible* is usually easy, since most displays designed for use with light pens have instructions for enabling and disabling pen interrupts from within the display file. Therefore a *disable pen* instruction placed before the call to the item will have the desired effect. The *PermitEvent* function may be used for this purpose.

*Restarting the display* is also quite straightforward provided the state of the

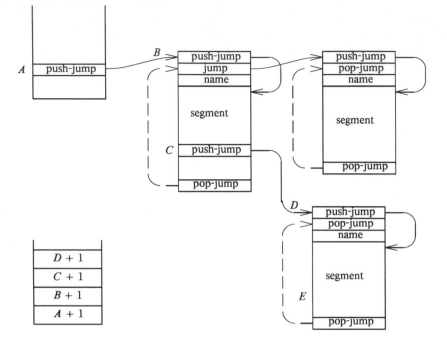

**Figure 13-8** Use of a structured display file to determine the identity and hierarchy of the selected segment. The diagram at lower right shows the state of the return address stack when the instruction at *E* is being executed.

display is not disturbed by the interrupt routine; in fact some displays have a *resume* instruction just for the purpose. Note that in one respect the state of the display must be changed: the light pen must be disabled for the rest of the current item since otherwise it will immediately generate another interrupt.

## EXERCISES

**13-1** Design a polling task for handling keyboard and stylus inputs, using status bits to prevent all forms of buffer overflow.

**13-2** Using the *GetEvent* and *PermitEvent* functions, write PASCAL routines that implement line drawing with directional constraints, with and without continuous feedback as the line is drawn.

**13-3** Program the light handle (see Section 12-2) using the *GetEvent* and *PermitEvent* functions.

**13-4** The polling task may be designed to watch for pen movement and to generate pen-position events only when the pen moves or alternately to generate events every 1/60 second (both, of course, subject to status bit control). Discuss the relative merits of these two approaches.

**13-5** In neither of the foregoing program examples are the input coordinates converted from screen to world coordinates. Discuss the relative merits of performing this conversion *(a)* in the *GetEvent* function or *(b)* in the program itself.

**13-6** One of the problems with light-pen tracking is that positioning in the extreme corners of the

**Figure 13-9** A tilted tracking cross.

screen is difficult due to the size of the tracking pattern. What modifications must be made to the tracking-cross method to allow positioning in the extreme corners of the screen?

**13-7** A tracking algorithm developed by A. Armit at Cambridge University used a cross whose arms were not parallel to the axes (Figure 13-9). What computation must this algorithm have performed to obtain the coordinates of the center of the field of view?

**13-8** Since the light-pen task adds selection events to the event queue, it may try to add an event block concurrently with the polling task. What methods can be used to prevent this from corrupting the queue?

**13-9** What is the appropriate action for the light pen task to take if it receives fewer than four interrupts from the pen during tracking?

**13-10** When a selection interrupt is received from the light pen, it is useful to record the pen coordinates in the event block. How would you determine these coordinates from the display address of the seen item?

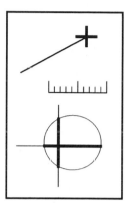

# 14

# INPUT FUNCTIONS

One of the advantages of the event queue as a mechanism for programming input devices is its flexibility. With the aid of the *GetEvent* and *PermitEvent* functions we can program any of the techniques described in Chapter 12. Most of them require little more programming than the two examples of Section 13-5. Nevertheless there are situations where the two event-handling functions are inadequate. In particular, novice programmers may have difficulty using them, and even experienced programmers need ways of writing input routines more compactly.

For these reasons it is worthwhile to provide the application programmer with a small set of functions that implement some of the more commonly used techniques. These *high-level functions* can be programmed using the *GetEvent* and *PermitEvent* functions. Most of the techniques described in Chapter 12 can be provided through high-level functions, but a large proportion of them involve feedback that must be provided through the use of display-file segments. These functions will therefore require the application programmer to observe certain conventions in the naming of segments. The following three functions do not impose this requirement and are therefore more appropriate for general-purpose use:

> *ReadPosition* (*p*)      wait for a pen switch input and then return the pen's coordinates in the two-element record *p*.

*Ink (inkarray, length)*      wait for the user to draw a stroke with the pen and return the stroke trajectory in *inkarray* (an array of *length* words); the number of points on the trajectory is returned as the function's value.

*Recognize*      wait for the user to draw a character and then return the code of the character that most closely matches the character drawn.

These functions, although described in terms of a tablet and stylus as input devices, could be programmed to use inputs from any graphical input device.

Three other functions are extremely useful in interactive programming, even though they do not operate directly on input devices:

*HitDetect (x, y)*      returns the name of the segment whose lines pass closest to (*x, y*) given in screen coordinates; if no segment passes within a certain tolerance, the function returns zero.

*Drag (s)*      causes segment *s* to move with the input-device cursor.

*Fix (s)*      terminates the dragging operation.

The *ReadPosition* and *Ink* functions are extremely easy to implement and will be left to the reader as programming exercises. The four functions *Drag, Fix, HitDetect,* and *Recognize* are less straightforward and are discussed in the sections that follow.

## 14-1 DRAGGING AND FIXING

The *Drag* and *Fix* functions can be implemented only on refresh displays that permit segments to be constructed entirely in relative coordinates. A single pair of absolute coordinates at the start of the segment defines the segment position. To move the segment we simply alter these coordinates.

The *Drag* function is therefore very easily implemented. It sets a status word that is examined on a regular basis by the polling task; it also provides the polling task with the name of the segment to be dragged. While the status word is set, the polling task updates the segment position when it repositions the cursor. The *Fix* routine clears the status word and therefore causes dragging to cease.

If the cursor position is substituted for the starting coordinates of the segment, the initial effect will be for the segment to jump across the screen in an unexpected and unpredictable fashion. It is therefore best to translate the cursor coordinates by the appropriate amount so as to achieve a smooth transition from the stationary position. The first time the polling task repositions the segment it must therefore read the segment starting coordinates, subtract the current cursor coordinates from them, and store the results in a pair of memory locations. This displacement is then added to the cursor position whenever the cursor moves, giving a fresh pair of coordinates for repositioning the segment.

Although only those segments which are to be dragged need be constructed in relative coordinates, the display-code generator cannot tell in advance which these segments are. Therefore *all* segments are constructed in relative form; generally this is a relatively small additional burden for the display-code generator. At the same time, a record must be kept of each segment's bounding box, and this information must be stored with the segment; it can then be used to prevent the segment from being dragged off the edge of the screen.

## 14-2 HIT DETECTION

The *HitDetect* function can be implemented in a number of ways. A particularly elegant technique makes use of the output transformation and clipping process, as follows:

1. A small square region of interest is defined surrounding the position of interest.
2. The coordinates of this square are transformed back from screen to world coordinates.
3. Using this square as a window, the display file is regenerated, omitting the final display-code generation stage.
4. If any line or other entity is found to lie within the window, it represents a hit; the regeneration process stops, and the appropriate information is passed to the program.

This technique is costly in CPU time unless the boxing test is used to good effect in the picture definition, in which case very few lines reach the clipping stage. However this technique has two significant points in its favor:

1. It can be implemented by means of a minor extension to any standard windowing routine.
2. When the process encounters a hit it will have traced the picture hierarchy to the exact point corresponding to the indicated item; therefore the required ancestry information is readily available.

This technique can also be used with display procedures (see Section 10-2). The picture is regenerated by executing each of the main display procedures of the program until a hit is detected. In this case, the process stops at the entry in the data base corresponding to the indicated item. In order to execute the display procedures, a list must be kept of those procedures used in generating the current picture. Note that this technique may fail if the data base is altered between generating the picture and processing the hit. This is considered by some people to be a disadvantage of the technique.

If this hit-detection technique cannot be used, there are basically two alternatives: either to interpret the display file or to trace through the data base looking for a hit. The first technique may be assisted by compiling extra data into the display file. For example, we could include data at the start of each segment indicating its overall dimensions (see Figure 14-1). The second technique is somewhat more cumbersome, particularly in cases where complex transformations are involved; in some applications, however, quite simple special-purpose routines may be written to trace through the data structure and perform hit-detection.

Once a hit has been detected, the question arises of how much ancestry data should be passed to the program. System designers should avoid the *ambiguity fallacy,* which postulates that since an item may have several levels of ancestry, it is impossible to determine to which level the user is referring when he points at the item. This problem is often posed using a circuit as an example: if the user points at a resistor, is he trying to indicate the resistor, or the circuit of which the resistor forms a part, or just a certain line within the resistor? This situation should never occur in a well-constructed program, which should always either *know* the level in which the user is interested or should *ask* him to state the level. It is an indication of serious deficiencies in the command language if the user is able to make an ambiguous pointing action.

Ideally the user should precede each pointing action with a command such as DELETE ITEM or DELETE LINE. It is then possible for the hit-detection process to restrict its search to the appropriate level. If the user is permitted to point first and indicate the level afterward, the entire ancestry must be determined and passed to the program, which takes action only after the level information is received.

## 14-3 ON-LINE CHARACTER RECOGNIZERS

On-line character recognizers have been the focus of considerable research activity ever since the development by Teitelman in 1964 of the first trainable recognizer. This research has led to the development of a large number of recognition techniques, some of them quite ingenious. Recognizers have been used with success in a number of applications, including the GRAIL programming system developed at The RAND Corporation in the late 1960s. More recently a recognizer developed by Ledeen in 1967 has been widely used in circuit design and other applications. Ledeen's recognizer is based on the earlier design of Teitelman and has the merit of being simple and sparing in its use of resources. This section describes how the Ledeen recognizer is implemented.

In its overall structure the Ledeen recognizer is identical to all other trainable recognizers, which contain the following four components:

1.  A *tablet-polling routine,* which reads the stylus position at regular intervals, applies whatever smoothing is necessary, and builds a list of coordinate pairs representing each stroke of the character;
2.  A *feature-extraction routine,* which extracts from each stroke a small number of basic properties, or *features,* that can be used as a basis for recognition;
3.  A *dictionary-lookup routine,* which searches through a dictionary of characters for a set of features matching those of the input strokes;
4.  A *training routine* used to construct the dictionary.

### Tablet Polling

The inking technique described in Section 13-6 may be used to pass strokes to the feature-extraction routine. It is necessary, however, to determine when the user has completed drawing the character. Most recognizers use a timer to detect lengthy pauses between strokes, and consider the character complete when a pause of longer than about half a second is detected.

The timing-out of stroke input may be performed by the polling task, which can generate a *time-out event* when a half-second pause is detected. This event is enabled by means of the *PermitEvent* function:

> *PermitEvent* (*timeout, msec*)  causes a time-out event to be generated when the polling task detects a pause longer than *msec* milliseconds between strokes

Thus one of the first actions of the *Recognize* function should be to issue such a call to *PermitEvent.*

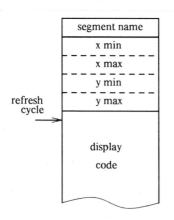

Figure 14-1 Inclusion in the segment of its overall dimensions.

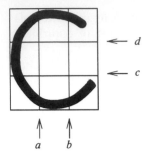

**Figure 14-2** Division of the stroke's bounding rectangle into nine regions for encoding purposes.

## The Feature-Extraction Routine

The main difference between recognizers lies in their choice of features to extract from the input strokes. For speed and economy, these features should be easy to extract and should be compact when stored in the dictionary. They should also permit the dictionary-lookup routine to discriminate easily between different characters without discriminating between different examples of the same character. Recognizers have used curvature, directional changes, inflexion points, and drawing speed as features. A recognizer designed by Berson [42] extracts features that correspond closely to the muscular movements involved in drawing the stroke; Herbst and Liu have described a similar system [220].

In Ledeen's recognizer, as in most other recognizers based on Teitelman's program, features are extracted by detecting the regions through which the stroke passes. For this purpose a rectangle is fitted around the stroke and is divided into nine regions of equal size by four dividing lines (see Figure 14-2). The features by which the stroke is defined when it is stored in the dictionary are these:

1.  The region in which the stroke begins;
2.  The number of times the stroke crosses each of the four dividing lines;
3.  The stroke's position in relation to the other strokes that make up the character.

The first two properties are extracted very simply by computing the positions of the dividing lines, establishing the starting region, and then

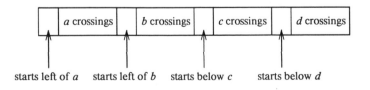

**Figure 14-3** Format of a 16-bit word containing an encoded stroke.

stepping along the stroke, counting intersections with the dividing lines. The properties are then encoded in a single 16-bit word as four components, one 4-bit component for each dividing line. One of the 4 bits indicates on which side of the dividing line the stroke starts; the remaining 3 bits record the number of crossings. Figure 14-3 shows the format of the complete 16-bit word, and Figure 14-4 shows some typical strokes and their encoded representations.

Horizontal and vertical strokes are difficult to encode in this fashion because the enclosing rectangle has such a high aspect ratio. The feature-extraction routine therefore checks the aspect ratio and when it exceeds about 4:1, it assigns a standard encoding to the stroke. The same action is taken if the stroke is very small. The standard encodings are as follows:

| | |
|---|---|
| Horizontal, drawn left to right | 9-9-0-8 |
| Horizontal, drawn right to left | 1-1-0-8 |
| Vertical, drawn downward | 0-8-1-1 |
| Vertical, drawn upward | 0-8-9-9 |
| Dot | 0-8-0-8 |

The reader may wish to check that no other stroke shapes can generate these encodings.

The technique used to encode the relative positions of the strokes is very similar to the encoding technique for the strokes themselves. A rectangle encloses the entire character, and a pseudo stroke is constructed joining the centers of all the surrounding rectangles of the component strokes. This pseudo stroke is then encoded in the same manner as the other strokes. The actual method by which the relative positions are encoded is somewhat simpler than this description implies: each stroke center is assigned a four-component code according to the region in which it lies (Figure 14-5); starting with the first two strokes, each successive pair of codes is exclusive-ORed together to yield a set of *transition codes.* These transition codes are summed component by component to give the crossings components, which are combined with the starting-region

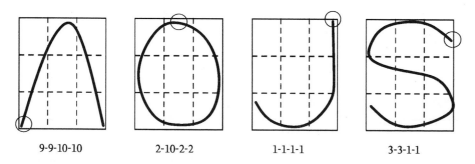

| 9-9-10-10 | 2-10-2-2 | 1-1-1-1 | 3-3-1-1 |

**Figure 14-4** Examples of strokes and their 4-component encodings; the start of each stroke is indicated by a small circle.

| 1-1-0-0 | 0-1-0-0 | 0-0-0-0 |
|---------|---------|---------|
| 1-1-0-1 | 0-1-0-1 | 0-0-0-1 |
| 1-1-1-1 | 0-1-1-1 | 0-0-1-1 |

**Figure 14-5** Codes assigned to each of the nine regions, used in generating relative-position descriptions.

bits by an inclusive-OR operation. This technique may also be used to compute stroke encodings; it produces the same result as the crossing-count method, but may in certain circumstances involve more processing.

The encoding of the relative stroke positions thus yields one additional 16-bit value that is added to the list of 16-bit values for the strokes themselves. Thus the letter F, drawn as shown in Figure 14-6, would generate the following four 16-bit values:

| | |
|---|---|
| 0-8-1-1 | Vertical stroke |
| 9-9-0-8 | Upper horizontal stroke |
| 9-9-0-8 | Lower horizontal stroke |
| 9-8-0-10 | Relative positions |

Only multistroke characters require inclusion of relative position information, which is therefore omitted in the case of single-stroke characters.

### The Dictionary-Lookup Routine

The feature-extraction phase is now complete, and the strokes may be looked up in the dictionary. In creating dictionary entries, the Ledeen recognizer rearranges the information generated by the feature extracter, grouping

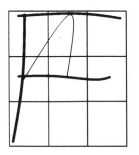

**Figure 14-6** The letter F drawn as three strokes. The thin curve represents the trajectory of the stroke centers, and its 4-component encoding defines the relative positions of the strokes.

together the corresponding components of each of the values. The result is always to produce four sequences, each sequence containing a variable number of 4-bit components. Thus the letter F would generate the following sequences:

| | |
|---|---|
| 0-9-9-9 | First components |
| 8-9-9-8 | Second components |
| 1-0-0-0 | Third components |
| 1-8-8-10 | Fourth components |

The dictionary is divided into four parts, corresponding to these four sequences. Thus the first part of the dictionary contains sequences of first components; each sequence is padded with trailing 0s to produce a standard sequence length. To each sequence is attached a list of the characters matched by this sequence, with weighting values for use in resolving ambiguous cases. Thus the dictionary might include the following entries:

| | |
|---|---|
| 9-9-0-0-0 | (A, 3) (F, 3) |
| 0-12-9-0-0 | (B, 3) |
| 2-0-0-0-0 | (C, 3) |
| 0-10-9-0-0 | (D, 3) |
| 0-9-9-9-9 | (E, 3) |
| 0-9-9-9-0 | (E, 4) (F, 4) |
| 2-9-0-0-0 | (G, 3) |
| 0-0-9-9-0 | (H, 3) |
| 0-0-0-0-0 | (I, 3) |
| 1-9-0-0-0 | (J, 3) |

| | |
|---|---|
| 9-9-8-0-0 | (A, 3) (F, 3) |
| 8-12-8-0-0 | (B, 3) |
| 2-0-0-0-0 | (C, 3) |
| 8-10-8-0-0 | (D, 3) |
| 8-9-9-9-8 | (E, 3) |
| 9-9-9-8-0 | (E, 4) |
| 8-9-9-8-0 | (F, 4) |
| 2-9-9-0-0 | (G, 3) |
| 8-8-9-9-0 | (H, 3) |
| 8-0-0-0-0 | (I, 3) |
| 1-9-1-0-0 | (J, 3) |

| | |
|---|---|
| 10-0-0-0-0 | (A, 3) |
| 2-0-0-0-0 | (F, 3) (G, 3) |
| 1-1-0-0-0 | (B, 3) (D, 3) (H, 3) (J, 3) |
| 1-0-0-0-0 | (C, 3) (F, 4) (I, 3) |
| 1-0-0-0-1 | (E, 3) |
| 2-0-0-1-0 | (E, 4) |

| | |
|---|---|
| 10-8-8-0-0 | (A, 3) |
| 1-1-8-0-0 | (B, 3) (D, 3) |
| 1-0-0-0-0 | (C, 3) |
| 1-8-8-8-10 | (E, 3) |
| 2-8-8-8-0 | (E, 4) |
| 1-8-8-10-0 | (F, 4) |
| 2-8-8-0-0 | (F, 3) |
| 1-8-8-0-0 | (G, 3) |
| 1-1-8-8-0 | (H, 3) |
| 1-0-0-0-0 | (I, 3) |
| 1-8-1-0-0 | (J, 3) |

Note that a single character, such as F, may have been drawn in several different ways during the training session and may therefore appear several times in each part of the dictionary.

The dictionary-lookup routine scans each of the four parts of the dictionary and if successful will find one entry in each part matching the corresponding input sequence. Each entry may list several characters that the sequence can represent; the lookup routine determines which character appears in all four lists or if there is no such character, which character appears in the most lists. In cases where two or more characters score equally, their weights are used to make a decision. If matching entries are found in fewer than two of the four parts, the recognizer reports failure to recognize the character.

### The Training Routine

The training routine is responsible for setting up the dictionary tables. The design of this routine is a good exercise in interactive programming. The user should be able to control the program with one input device, the tablet stylus. He draws several strokes, and as he does so the inking technique is used to show the strokes on the CRT screen. When the stroke set is complete the recognizer is called to try to recognize the character using whatever dictionary has already been built. The program may then display to the user the results of the recognition; this has been shown in Figure 12-44 on page 180. If no candidate character is found, the recognizer declares it does not know the character. If characters were found but the final decision was close, the recognizer may say it thinks it has made a correct recognition and display the character. If the final decision is overwhelming, it may say it is sure of the identity of the character.

In any case, the user may wish to cause information about the character he just drew to be added to the data structure. If the recognizer correctly identified the character, he may use the YES menu item to increase the weights associated with the recognition of the character from the stroke set. If the recognizer failed to identify the character, the user may reply with the NO menu item, which causes a menu of all possible characters to appear; he uses the stylus to point to the correct character. If the user decides that he does not want to change the dictionary entry for this character, he can use an ABORT menu item to ignore this character. This process is repeated until the recognizer achieves an acceptable identification rate. Then the data structure can be output, as in the list above, so that the training need not be repeated.

This particular training scheme only *increases* the weights associated with a property set. If a character is correctly recognized and the YES response given, four weights are increased, one for each of the four property sequences recorded for the character. It is not possible to decrease the weight of a property set; the user must instead increase the weights of other property sets so that the relative weights change in the desired manner. An additional FORGET command that expunges an entire set of entries from the dictionary may be provided in order to undo the effects of training.

## 14-4 CONCLUSION

This chapter has discussed input functions of various types, ranging from the very simple *ReadPosition* function up to complex processes like on-line character recognition. The purpose of these functions is to simplify the application programmer's task in constructing interactive programs. They enable him to define the interactive command language of a program by means of a small number of calls to a few high-level functions.

The overall design of the interactive component of application programs is somewhat more complex than this suggests, however. To support the user in giving commands, the program must provide feedback and must display information in such a way that the user can interact effectively. For example, the user cannot select or modify items if they are displayed too closely together to be distinguishable. Many other issues are involved in creating an effective interactive partnership between man and computer; some of these are discussed further in Chapter 28, which addresses the topic of user interface design.

## EXERCISES

**14-1** Find some pairs of characters that would appear identical to the Ledeen recognizer.

**14-2** A dictionary for a Ledeen-type recognizer might be constructed by simply storing a list of 4-component values for each character, together with a weight, thus:

    A (3): 9-9-10-10  9-9-0-8  0-8-0-8
    B (3): 0-8-1-1  12-12-1-1  9-8-0-8
    C (4): 2-2-1-1
    etc.

Comment on the advantages and disadvantages of this approach, compared with the approach described in the text.

**14-3** The Ledeen encoding technique allocates 3 bits to represent each crossing-count. What would be the effect of reducing this to 2 bits per count? Given that 16 bits are still used to represent each stroke, how would you utilize the extra 4 bits saved in this manner? In answering the last question, give consideration to the recognition deficiencies of the Ledeen algorithm that you identified in answering Exercise 14-1.

**14-4** The use of windowing in hit-detection, as described in Section 14-2, involves regenerating and re-transforming the entire picture, in a way that is difficult for simple graphics packages to carry out. How could the design of such a package be changed so as to permit this form of hit-detection?

**14-5** Design a set of symbols for use by a designer in (a) laying out an electronic circuit, (b) drawing an architectural plan, (c) designing pipework for a chemical plant. Try to use symbols that convey the necessary geometric information, that are easy to draw, and that are easily distinguished by the recognizer.

**14-6** Program the Ledeen recognizer in PASCAL.

**14-7** The *Drag* function permits a two-dimensional translation to be applied to a segment for feedback purposes. What would be the advantages of permitting scaling and rotation to be carried out in the same way? Why are these functions difficult to provide in a graphics package?

**14-8** After a segment has been dragged and fixed, its displacement must be recorded in the model. How is this displacement determined? Why is it not necessary for the *Fix* function to return a final segment position?

**14-9** A recognizer for a limited set of characters can sometimes be very useful. Design a program that will recognize horizontal strokes drawn in either direction, vertical strokes, any of the four possible diagonal strokes, and a dot. Assume that each stroke is passed to the recognizer as a pair of stroke endpoints.

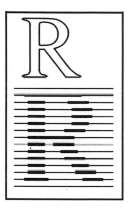

# PART FOUR

## RASTER GRAPHICS

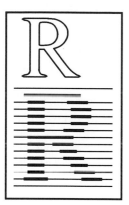

# 15

# RASTER GRAPHICS

# FUNDAMENTALS

## 15-1 INTRODUCTION

In this chapter we turn our attention away from random-scan vector drawing displays to a type of display whose popularity has gradually been increasing since the late 1960s, the *raster-scan display*. This type of display has already been mentioned in Chapter 1, where the *frame-buffer display* was described. Raster-scan displays differ in many fundamental respects from random-scan displays, and it is therefore not surprising that they require rather different programming techniques. This chapter and the others in Part Four present some of the techniques for programming such displays.

The raster-scan display differs from the random-scan line-drawing display chiefly in how displayed data are represented. A display file for a line-drawing display contains only information about lines and characters to be drawn; the void areas of the screen are ignored. The raster-scan display, however, controls the intensity of each dot, or *pixel*, in a rectangular matrix, or *raster*, of dots that covers the entire screen. Strictly speaking, raster scan implies in addition that the image is scanned onto the screen surface in a raster sequence, i.e., as a succession of equidistant *scan lines*, each scan line made up of pixels. Several other types of display are nevertheless included under the heading raster scan, even though no such scanning out takes place. An example is the plasma-panel display. It would be more correct to use the term *raster display* to encompass all these devices, but the phrase *raster scan* has become widely used and appears firmly established in the computing vocabulary.

Raster-scan displays owe their increase in popularity to two causes. The first of these is the need for greater realism in pictures, especially in applications involving three-dimensional objects. The frontispiece to this book indicates the high degree of realism attainable with the aid of advanced shading and hidden-surface techniques. Such images would obviously be somewhat difficult to produce on a line-drawing display. They are instead generated as a raster of intensity values, plotted on the surface of a raster-scan display.

While applications for these high-quality displayed images have been increasing, the cost of raster-scan display equipment has been decreasing, a second reason for wider acceptance of raster-scan graphics. Whereas in the mid-1960s a raster-scan display would have been prohibitively expensive, now it is possible to build one for a few thousand dollars. Sharply decreasing memory costs have caused this trend and will continue to make raster-scan displays increasingly competitive with random-scan vector displays.

### Applications of Raster-Scan Graphics

As raster-scan displays increase in capability and drop in price, their range of usefulness increases. Already the raster-scan display can be used for many of the purposes for which the random-scan display was developed; in addition, particular properties of the raster-scan display have enabled it to address new graphics applications. The following list indicates the range of uses of this type of technology:

1. *Flight simulation.* The use of computer-based flight simulators saves airline companies huge sums of money. Daylight flight simulators, simulating the conditions of takeoff and landing during daylight hours, use raster-scan color displays to generate realistic images of the view the pilot would expect to see from the flight deck. Chapters 20 to 25 describe some of the special hardware and software techniques used to generate dynamically moving images of this kind.
2. *Animation.* The raster-scan display can also be used as a "painting" surface, on which are prepared the individual frames for animated sequences. Film is then produced as direct output from the computer. Many of the more repetitive steps in animation, such as "in-betweening" to interpolate motion sequences, can be assisted by the computer.
3. *Design.* Realistic views of solid objects—machined parts, glass bottles, buildings—can be generated on the raster-scan display using stored geometric descriptions of the objects. These images can assist designers greatly in their work. Simpler and more conventional design applications of raster-scan graphics include logic-circuit design, integrated-circuit layout, and chemical pipework design.
4. *Technical illustration.* The surface of the raster-scan display can be used as

an interactive drafting table for the preparation of technical illustrations. The particular strength of the raster-scan display in this application is its ability to handle solid shaded areas, color, lines of varying thickness, and high-quality, variable-typeface text.

5. *Printing and plotting.* Several forms of raster-scan printer have been designed for generating hard-copy output of text and images. These include electrostatic plotters that print a raster of about 200 pixels per inch. Printers with higher resolutions exist: most of the pages of this book were produced on a high-resolution xerographic printer. Many of the techniques for image generation discussed in the following pages are applicable to raster-scan printers and plotters as well as to raster-scan displays.

6. *Image processing.* New techniques are constantly being developed for dealing with sampled images of real-world scenes. For example, the Landsat satellite transmits raster-scanned pictures to earth for display, processing, and analysis. The images are viewed on a raster-scan display, often using artificial coloring techniques to show normally invisible patterns such as infrared radiations.

For some applications, the random-scan display remains advantageous. High-precision engineering drafting, highly interactive solid-object design, and real-time computer animation are examples. The two drawbacks of the raster display in these applications are its generally low resolution, preventing display of fine detail, and the sometimes slow speed of *scan conversion,* i.e., of computing the pattern of dots that most closely matches a stored definition of the image. Much of this chapter is devoted to a discussion of such scan-conversion techniques.

## 15-2 GENERATING A RASTER IMAGE: THE FRAME BUFFER DISPLAY

A raster-scan image is generated not by tracing out a sequence of geometric items such as lines and characters but by plotting point-by-point the intensity value of each pixel in a two-dimensional *raster* or matrix of pixels. Complex images are constructed by creating appropriate patterns of pixel illumination. To display an image, the intensity or color of every pixel in the raster matrix must be determined.

An image represented as a raster can be displayed on a CRT by means of the *frame-buffer display,* introduced in Chapter 1. As we have seen, this device consists of three components:

1. The frame buffer itself, a large random-access memory in which the intensity of each pixel is stored as a binary intensity value;
2. A TV monitor, on which the image is displayed;
3. A display controller, whose purpose is to scan repeatedly through the

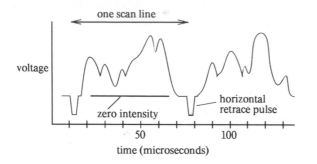

**Figure 15-1** Typical video signal waveform, showing two scan lines' data.

matrix of intensity values stored in the frame buffer and to produce from them a signal that can be fed to the TV monitor.

The TV monitor requires a very specific form of signal from the display controller, known as a *video signal*. This is a continuously varying voltage that specifies the intensity along each scan line of the image; a portion of such a signal is shown in Figure 15-1. Within the CRT of the TV monitor, the electron beam traces out each scan line in succession, returning quickly at the end of each scan line to commence scanning the next. The video signal modulates the beam current and in this way produces a trace of varying intensity; during the *horizontal retrace* period the beam's intensity is lowered to an invisible level. When the bottom of the screen is reached, the scan begins at the top again.

Most TV monitors use *interlace* to reduce the flickering effect of the top-to-bottom scan. After scanning each line, the electron beam skips to the next scan line but one; the scan lines thus omitted are scanned on the next cycle. The effect of interlace is to generate the image as two separate *fields*, one containing the even-numbered scan lines, the other the odd-numbered (Figure 15-2). This is a more "random" sequence than the non-interlaced scan, and the eye is therefore less aware of the scan sequence. The display controller is usually constructed to skip automatically through the intensity values for even-

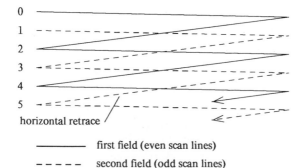

first field (even scan lines)
second field (odd scan lines)

**Figure 15-2** Interlaced TV scan sequence.

numbered scan lines, and then through the odd-numbered, thus permitting the intensity values to be stored as a continuous sequence, or *frame*.

A standard American TV screen is divided into 480 scan lines. It has an *aspect ratio* (height-to-width ratio) of 3:4; thus if we divide the scan line into square pixels, there are about 640 pixels per scan line. The frame buffer contains intensity values for each of the pixels forming the image, i.e., 480 × 640, or 307,200. The number of bits per intensity value varies with displays. Inexpensive frame buffers often allocate only one bit per pixel, providing two intensity levels (black and white) that are adequate for simple line drawings. At the other end of the scale, we find frame buffers with 8 or sometimes 24 bits per pixel; these are expensive devices, capable of generating high-quality continuous-tone images.

The capacity of the frame buffer depends on the number of bits representing each pixel, on the number of pixels per scan line and on the number of scan lines. The scan line count is generally chosen so as to permit the use of one of the 'standard' video line rates: 525, 625, 813, 875 and 1023 lines are the most popular rates. These values do not indicate the number of visible scan lines; they are derived by dividing the refresh cycle time by the time taken to draw each scan line. Part of the refresh cycle is occupied by the *vertical retrace* period, when the electron beam returns from the bottom to the top of the screen to commence the next field. No scan lines can be displayed during this period, which occupies up to 10 per cent of the refresh cycle. This is the reason why only 480 visible scan lines can be displayed on a 525-line TV monitor.

## 15-3 REPRESENTING A RASTER IMAGE

The frame buffer provides not only a means of generating raster images, but a representation for them as well, as a matrix of intensity values. To produce an image on a frame-buffer display, we need only provide a function for setting the value of a pixel:

*SetPixel*(*raster, x, y, intensity*)

This function stores a value, *intensity*, into the byte in the frame buffer corresponding to the pixel identified by coordinates (*x, y*). A *raster* is listed as an argument so that the function can be applied to several different raster matrices. The special raster *FrameBuffer* refers to the raster representation used to refresh the display.

It is also convenient to retrieve pixel values from a raster representation. The function *GetPixel*(*raster, x, y*) returns the intensity value corresponding to the pixel at (*x, y*).

### The Raster Coordinate System

A careful choice of the coordinate system used to address pixels in a raster will simplify many of the scan-conversion and raster-manipulation procedures. The most natural coordinate system is a two-dimensional scheme with $x$ increasing to the right, $y$ increasing upward, and the units chosen equal to the pixel spacing. Figure 15-3 illustrates a small raster that conforms to these conventions. It is 5 pixels wide and 6 high; the pixel at (3, 1) is darkened. A pixel is addressed by integral values of $x$ and $y$, and represents the intensity value for a square region of the screen whose lower left corner is at $(x, y)$. Thus the call *SetPixel*(*FrameBuffer, ix, iy, intensity*), for integers *ix* and *iy*, controls the light emitted over the region $ix \leq x < ix + 1, iy \leq y < iy + 1$.

The $x$ and $y$ coordinate values passed to the *SetPixel* and *GetPixel* functions must be converted into the address of the byte in the raster array that holds the pixel value. This conversion is performed so often it should be as simple as possible. If we let *BaseAddress* represent the address of the first byte in the raster array, corresponding to the pixel in the lower left corner of the raster, the address $p$ of the pixel at $(x, y)$ is given by

$$p = BaseAddress + (xmax - xmin)(y - ymin) + (x - xmin) \qquad (15\text{-}1)$$

where *xmin, xmax, ymin,* and *ymax* are integers that give the coordinates of the boundaries of the rectangular raster. For the raster shown in Figure 15-3, $xmin = 1$, $xmax = 6$, $ymin = -2$, and $ymax = 4$. This calculation can be simplified by performing a few substitutions to derive the following:

$$p = a + by + x \qquad (15\text{-}2)$$

where $b = xmax - xmin$, and $a = BaseAddress - b\,ymin - xmin$. In some frame buffers the raster is stored differently, with the upper left-hand pixel first in memory. An equation of the same form as Equation 15-2 can be used to calculate addresses for these displays. Very often the complexity of the address calculation in Equation 15-2 can be reduced still further by using incremental methods (see Exercise 15-3).

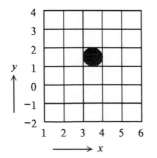

Figure 15-3 A raster and its associated coordinate system. The pixel at (3, 1) is shown black.

Because the raster dimensions are required for address calculations, they should be retained as part of the description of a raster. More precisely, a raster might be defined as a PASCAL type:

**type** *raster* = **record**
  *xmin, xmax, ymin, ymax: integer; a, b: integer;*
  { Perhaps more information, such as the byte size of a pixel or a }
  { pointer to the raster array }
  **end**;

Routines such as *GetPixel* and *SetPixel* that manipulate rasters use the values stored in this record to perform address calculations and to verify that coordinates lie within the legal ranges. The raster is similar to a two-dimensional array representation as provided in most programming languages, and can be represented and addressed by means of the same techniques that have been developed for handling arrays.

## 15-4  SCAN CONVERTING LINE DRAWINGS

In order to display vectors on a frame-buffer display, each vector must be converted from a conventional geometric representation into a raster representation using a process called *scan conversion.* Figure 15-4 shows the result of scan converting a straight-line segment on a small 16 × 16 raster. Most of the pixels are white, the color of the background; those in the path of the line segment are black, the color of the line. Figure 15-4 will remind us immediately of the methods described in Chapter 2 for generating lines on a point-plotting display. This is no coincidence; the raster shown in Figure 15-4 is in fact generated with a DDA algorithm like those described in Section 2-3.

A small modification must be made to the DDA algorithm to adapt it to scan conversion. After computing each dot coordinate position (x, y), the

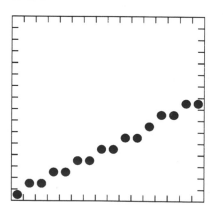

**Figure 15-4** A line drawn on a raster using an incremental point-plotting algorithm of the kind described in Chapter 2.

algorithm plots the point, not by adding a dot to the display file but by calling *SetPixel*(*FrameBuffer*, *x*, *y*, *intensity*), where *intensity* is the shade of the line. Any of the incremental point-plotting techniques described in Chapter 2 can be similarly adapted to scan conversion. These algorithms can be applied repeatedly to build up images containing many lines.

A graphics package of the sort described in Chapters 6 to 8 can easily be adapted to drive a frame-buffer display. The simplest approach is to treat the display as the logical equivalent of a storage-tube terminal. Thus we can add to its contents, but we cannot selectively erase. The only changes to the graphics package are in the display-code generator, where the following must be done:

1. The routine to clear the screen is changed to store an appropriate background value into every byte in the frame buffer.
2. The routine to add a line to the display, which previously generated commands to the storage-tube terminal, is changed to call a DDA routine that sets the appropriate pixels in the frame buffer.

These two changes are easily made, and the result is a graphics package that allows line drawings to be displayed on a raster-scan display. The solution is far from optimal, however, and provides no better performance than a storage tube.

Somewhat better performance can be achieved by allowing selective modifications to the frame buffer. To erase an individual line, for example, the same DDA algorithm can be used, but each call to *SetPixel* will specify the intensity of the background. Thus all the pixels altered when the line was originally drawn with the DDA are now reset to the background value. This selective erasure can be used to delete all the lines in a display-file segment whenever the segment is unposted or deleted, a strategy that is often faster than clearing the buffer and scan converting lines from all posted segments. Although line erasures may leave holes in remaining lines, the holes can be filled in by a small amount of additional scan conversion (see Exercise 15-6). This strategy first makes the important changes to the display (lines are erased) and later touches up the image to remove defects introduced by the erasing method.

Even if a graphics system uses selective erasure, it has not fully used the facilities of a raster display. Further advantages derive from the ability to place arbitrary patterns in the frame buffer and from the capability of any raster display to show solid areas of tone. These capabilities require further extensions to the scan-conversion process.

## 15-5 DISPLAYING CHARACTERS

The frame buffer's ability to present arbitrary patterns of intensities makes it ideal for displaying characters. It is no longer necessary to force each character

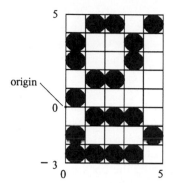

**Figure 15-5** A character mask represented as a raster. Note that the origin lies on the baseline of the character.

to be composed of short straight lines; instead, the frame buffer can contain characters of different sizes, different typefaces, and different colors.

In order to modify the frame buffer's contents to show a particular character, we need to know the pattern of pixels that will display the proper character shape. Although this pattern could be represented as a long list of calls to *SetPixel*, it is more compactly described by a *mask raster*. This raster, exemplified by Figure 15-5, contains binary values. A 1 value denotes a pixel that is part of the character shape, whereas a 0 value identifies a pixel that is to remain unaltered when displaying the character.

To insert a character into the frame buffer we must specify the displacement to be applied to the character mask. For this purpose every character mask has an *origin*. In Figure 15-5 the origin is on the left-hand side of the character mask, level with the *baseline*, i.e., the horizontal line that touches the base of uppercase characters. The position of each character inserted in the frame buffer is defined in terms of the origin of each character's mask. Thus if we place a character at $(x, y)$, we displace each of the mask pixels by an amount $(x, y)$. The next character in a string of text will lie at $(x + w, y)$, where $w$ is the *width* of the first character (in Figure 15-5, $w = 5$).

The mask-raster representation leads to a very simple algorithm for adding characters to the frame buffer. The procedure *WriteMask*, given below, writes into the frame buffer at location $(x, y)$ a character defined by the raster *MaskRaster:*

```
procedure WriteMask(var MaskRaster: raster; x, y, intensity: integer);
    var i, j: integer;
begin
    for j := MaskRaster.ymin to MaskRaster.ymax − 1 do
        for i := MaskRaster.xmin to MaskRaster.xmax − 1 do
            if GetPixel(MaskRaster, i, j) <> 0 then
                SetPixel(FrameBuffer, x+i, y+j, intensity)
    end;
```

**Figure 15-6** A character displayed on a reverse field.

This procedure is parameterized to allow the character to be written with a specific intensity. Characters can then be erased by using the background color as intensity. Characters can be displayed on a reverse field (Figure 15-6) by first setting a rectangular area black and then scan-converting text characters using white color.

Various character appearances can be created from a single mask by altering the procedure for writing the character into the frame buffer. Some of the possibilities are illustrated in Figure 15-7. Using the single character mask shown in Figure 15-7a, a scan-conversion algorithm can generate rotated characters (Figure 15-7b), approximations of boldface characters by displaying the character twice at adjacent $x$ positions (Figure 15-7c), and italic characters by applying a progressively increasing displacement to successive rows of the mask (Figure 15-7d).

There is no need to require the intensity or color of a character to be the same for all pixels in the character. It is possible, for example, to define a colored logo for a company letterhead. Each character can be represented by a raster that records the color of each pixel, reserving a special *transparent* value to indicate pixels that should not be modified. This raster then serves the dual purpose of specifying where the character pattern lies (its mask) and what color values to use. The *WriteColor* procedure shows the effect of this change:

```
procedure WriteColor(var ColorRaster: raster; x, y: integer);
    var i, j: integer;
begin
    for j := ColorRaster.ymin to ColorRaster.ymax − 1 do
        for i := ColorRaster.xmin to ColorRaster.xmax − 1 do
            if GetPixel(ColorRaster, i, j) <> transparent then
```

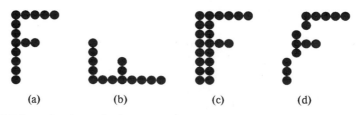

(a)  (b)  (c)  (d)

**Figure 15-7** Several variants of a character can be displayed using one mask: (a) the mask; (b) rotated character; (c) boldface effect; (d) italic effect.

$$SetPixel(FrameBuffer, x+i, y+j, GetPixel(ColorRaster, i, j))$$
**end**;

The distinguished value *transparent* can be associated with each raster or can have a constant value throughout the program.

## 15-6 SPEED OF SCAN CONVERSION

Although the algorithms for generating raster images of lines and characters are simple, they are used so often when composing a complex image that their efficiency is critical. Consider, for example, the simple act of clearing the display:

```
for y := FrameBuffer.ymin to FrameBuffer.ymax − 1 do
    for x := FrameBuffer.xmin to FrameBuffer.xmax − 1 do
        SetPixel(FrameBuffer, x, y, background);
```

For typical sizes of the frame buffer raster, this loop will require many thousands of calls to *SetPixel*. Each call checks coordinates and computes the frame-buffer address of the pixel to be modified. These calculations are very wasteful, because a very simple operation is being performed, namely setting every pixel in the frame buffer to *background*. It is wise to provide a separate function *Clear* that avoids the redundant checking and replaces frame-buffer values as fast as the hardware will allow.

Similar problems arise in other scan-conversion algorithms. For example, the calls to *SetPixel* can be removed from the inner loop of the DDA and replaced by incremental calculations to determine the address of the byte in the raster that needs modifying. Similar optimizations can be applied to *WriteMask* and *WriteColor*.

All the scan conversion algorithms share a common property: *they need fast access to the frame-buffer memory.* If this access is impeded by inefficient function calls, by slow hardware interfaces, or by latency due to lack of random access to the frame buffer memory, the effectiveness of the frame buffer is seriously impaired.

## 15-7 NATURAL IMAGES

One of the strengths of raster-scan displays is their ability to show *natural images*, images that look like photographs rather than geometrical figures. The original light image is *sampled* by recording its intensity on a grid of points and then reproduced by passing these intensities to a raster display. Television images are generated in this fashion. A camera performs the sampling, and a television receiver acts as the raster display.

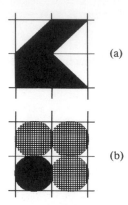

(a)

(b)

**Figure 15-8** Proper sampling of a geometric figure requires displaying pixels with intensities intermediate between black and white.

Sampling natural images with digital measurements allows a computer to operate on the image, improve its quality, compare it with other images, store its digital representation for later retrieval, and so forth. Entire disciplines have grown up to investigate techniques for image processing, pattern recognition, and image understanding. Although these applications were once time-consuming, increasing hardware speeds are beginning to bring some kinds of image manipulation within reach of interactive systems. References in the Bibliography point to a number of sources of image-manipulation techniques.

### Sampling

The theory of sampling images contains important lessons for raster graphics. A pixel displayed on a raster display is not a mathematically infinitesimal point but emits light over a small area, roughly the size of a square of the raster grid. The intensity value of this pixel must represent the light from all sources falling on the corresponding small area of the image. Thus the black-and-white image of Figure 15-8a, when sampled, yields intensities shown in Figure 15-8b. The brightness of the upper left dot, for example, is about half the maximum brightness, because half of the area sampled by the dot is fully bright and half is completely dark.

If such *area sampling* is not performed properly on lines and other geometric objects, edges of the objects will exhibit irregular staircase patterns similar to the one shown in Figure 15-4. If a frame-buffer display can show more than two intensities, the scan-conversion algorithm for lines should be modified to place gray pixels along edges to reflect proper area sampling [129, 440]. Figure 15-9 shows how lines are properly sampled on a raster-scan display. The enlarged image clearly shows gray shades at the edges of lines.*

---

*Those familiar with the sampling theorem will find these remarks unsurprising. The area-sampling argument amounts to applying a low-pass filter to the image before sampling is performed. A rectangular filter is an adequate approximation to the exact filter matched to the characteristics of the display's spot.

## Halftoning

Often it is necessary to present a natural image that has pixels of a great many different intensity values on a display with a limited range of output values. Solutions to this problem are called *halftoning techniques*, developed largely in order to print photographs using black ink on white paper. The basic idea is to use patterns of black and white to give the impression of intermediate intensities. Consider a "pattern technique" that uses a $3 \times 3$ array of binary pixels to display one of ten intensities. To achieve intensity $i$ $(0 \le i \le 9)$, we set $i$ of the 9 pixels to white, and $9 - i$ to black. Figure 15-10a shows a set of ten patterns that might be acceptable for this purpose. Figure 15-10b shows patterns for $i = 3$ that are less satisfactory because they will produce a pattern of horizontal stripes if repeated many times. Patterns must be carefully designed to avoid generating annoying textures when they are placed next to each other. Because most natural images require more than ten intensities, patterns larger than $3 \times 3$ pixels are generally required.

Another class of halftoning techniques is based on the idea of *thresholding:* if the image intensity of a pixel exceeds a threshold, white is displayed for that pixel, otherwise black. In this simple form, thresholding fails to show intensity

(a)                  (b)

**Figure 15-9** Proper sampling of lines on a raster-scan display: (a) viewed from a distance; (b) an enlargement of the upper left corner of (a). *Courtesy Evans & Sutherland Computer Corp.*

details present in the original image because the display of either a white or a black pixel introduces errors in the display. Two techniques can be used to reduce the errors. To explain them some additional notation is required. Suppose the image to be displayed at $(x, y)$ is represented by intensity $I(x, y)$, which ranges between a black value $b$ and a white value $w$, where $b \leq I(x, y) \leq w$. Let $g = (b + w)/2$ be a threshold in the middle of the range.

**Modulation.** The first technique modulates the intensity signal with a signal $M(x, y)$ whose values range from $-g$ to $g$, with average value 0. The pixel at $(x, y)$ is made white if $I(x, y) + M(x, y) > g$; otherwise it is set to black. Suitable functions for $M$ are sinusoids, for example, $g \sin \alpha x \sin \beta y$, or pseudo-random-number generators with appropriate ranges.

**Error distribution.** Floyd and Steinberg devised a scheme that records the error introduced by a thresholding operation and compensates for the error by distributing it to neighboring pixels [175]. The algorithm given below selects an intensity for display at $(x, y)$ and distributes the error to three neighbors: three-eighths of the error is propagated to the right neighbor, three-eighths to the bottom neighbor, and one-fourth along the diagonal. The program fragment must be embedded in a loop to examine all pixels in the image.

```
if I[x,y] > g then begin
    SetPixel(FrameBuffer, x, y, 1); { Make pixel white }
    error := I[x,y] − w
end else begin
    SetPixel(FrameBuffer, x, y, 0); { Make pixel black }
    error := I[x, y] − b
end;
I[x + 1, y] := I[x + 1, y] + (3 * error)/8;
I[x, y − 1] := I[x, y − 1] + (3 * error)/8;
I[x + 1, y − 1] := I[x + 1, y − 1] + error/4;
```

The error-distribution method above is designed so that a top-to-bottom left-to-right scan of the image to generate pixel values never requires backing up.

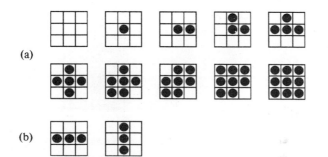

(a)

(b)

**Figure 15-10** Halftone patterns: (a) a set of ten patterns; (b) two patterns that will generate geometric patterns if they are repeated many times.

(a)                                         (b)

(c)                                         (d)

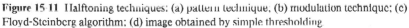

**Figure 15-11** Halftoning techniques: (a) pattern technique, (b) modulation technique; (c) Floyd-Steinberg algorithm; (d) image obtained by simple thresholding

Figure 15-11 includes examples of three different halftoning methods applied to one image. The resolution for these examples is made fairly low in order to illustrate the differences in the methods and to avoid artifacts introduced by the printing technique used to reproduce this book. Many additional halftoning methods have been developed to cope with various properties of displays or printers, various characteristics of the image being displayed, and different physical processes available to implement the methods. A survey of some of these techniques can be found in [241].

## EXERCISES

**15-1** The simplest form of frame buffer provides only two intensities (typically black and white) and therefore stores only one bit per pixel. Write the *SetPixel* procedure for use with such a frame buffer, in which 16 pixel values are packed into each word, i.e., the frame buffer is organized as a vector of 16-bit words. Be sure to check that values of $x$ and $y$ lie within the raster limits.

**15-2** Which of the techniques described in Chapter 2 for generating straight lines is best suited to scan conversion into a frame buffer?

**15-3** Consider scan converting lines for a frame buffer that records 1 bit per pixel, packing 16 pixel values into a word. How could the address calculations performed in *SetPixel* be folded into the incremental DDA algorithm? You should be able to avoid multiplications and divisions in the inner loop. Show how to check that points generated by the DDA lie within the raster limits without changing the inner loop.

**15-4** Suppose that each access to a frame buffer can read or write several adjacent pixels on the same scan line. What steps would you take to minimize frame-buffer accesses when scan converting lines? What changes to the DDA algorithm would be required?

**15-5** Explain how to implement the graphics system described in Chapter 7 with a frame-buffer display using selective erasure capabilities. Note that in some cases it may be faster to erase the screen and redraw existing segments than to erase a large number of individual lines. How can you design the system to make such choices properly? Is it appropriate for the system to make this choice?

**15-6** Selective erasure of a line may leave holes in other lines that cross the one erased. In a graphics system that maintains a segmented display file, the holes can be filled in after each erasure by scan converting lines from all posted segments. How might the computational requirements of this technique be reduced?

**15-7** Think of some applications of scan-conversion techniques outside the realm of computers. How is this scan conversion performed? Could computers help perform it, and if so, how?

**15-8** Early raster-scan displays used a drum in place of a random-access memory, with a separate sector of the drum devoted to each scan line; the smallest unit of data that could be modified was a complete sector. Discuss how this would affect the performance of scan conversion. What techniques could be employed to make scan conversion faster?

**15-9** Design an algorithm for displaying a character from a single mask, capable of displaying characters using different tones, at different $90°$ rotations, and with optional bold or italic effects.

**15-10** Design a set of scan-conversion algorithms for displaying lines and text and for clearing the screen. Explore opportunities to make them fast by appropriate choices of representation and by careful coding of critical loops.

**15-11** Make a list of special computer instructions that would help make scan-conversion algorithms more efficient. Try to order the list by importance.

**15-12** The sampling observation suggests that we should not be representing character patterns with binary masks, as shown in Figure 15-5. Instead we must use a representation that defines the fraction of the area of each pixel covered by the character. How can such information be represented? How is the scan conversion of characters altered by this change? What is the proper procedure if the eventual output is on a binary display?

**15-13** Write a scan-conversion algorithm for black lines that properly handles edge effects, using pixels of intensities intermediate between white and black, as in Figure 15-9.

**15-14** When two lines cross, what intensities should be displayed in pixels near the intersection if sampling is done properly? Can you offer an exact solution? Can you offer a simple approximation that has the property that the scan conversion of a line does not require knowledge of other lines that may intersect it? What procedure should be followed to erase a line from the frame buffer?

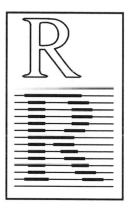

# 16

## SOLID-AREA

## SCAN CONVERSION

One reason for the increasing popularity of raster-scan displays is their ability to display images containing *solid areas* along with lines and text. Solid areas may represent lines of various thicknesses, colored geometric shapes appearing in diagrams, or facets of three-dimensional objects. Solid-area images are used in many applications, including technical illustration, creation of animated sequences, and rendering scenes of three-dimensional objects.

Generating a display of a solid area requires determining three properties of the area, its mask, its shading rule and its priority. The *mask* of an area is a representation that defines which pixels lie within the solid area. A common representation of a mask is a matrix of binary values in which a 0 indicates a pixel outside the area and a 1 indicates a pixel within it. The task of computing an area's mask from a geometrical description of the shape of the object, called *solid-area scan conversion,* is the main topic of this chapter.

A *shading rule* specifies how to compute the intensity of each pixel within the area. Different kinds of shading rules can be applied to an area, causing a shadowed effect on the displayed object by making one side darker than the other, by varying the coloration across its surface, or by simulating a textured pattern "painted" on it. Variable shading is useful principally in generating realistic displays of three-dimensional objects, a topic covered in Part Five.

If an image should contain more than one solid area, the *priority* of each area determines which area is displayed when two or more areas overlap.

Suppose a circle and a square overlap. The relative priority of the two overlapping areas determines which is obscured. If the circle has higher priority than the square, it appears to be on top; otherwise it appears underneath. In some cases, priority information is not needed to generate the display: if two areas do not overlap, their relative priority is unimportant; if two areas have the same uniform intensity, the display is independent of priority assignments. This last property allows us to create images consisting of black lines and black text without requiring priority information.

The techniques for displaying solid areas are best explained by first separating the three aspects of mask, shading, and priority and later considering their interaction. We shall first address the problem of scan converting an area to determine its mask. Then methods are described for resolving priorities. Finally the two computations are considered together. Throughout this chapter we shall consider only the simplest form of shading, where each area is shaded with a uniform intensity. More general shading techniques are discussed in Chapter 25.

## 16-1 GEOMETRIC REPRESENTATIONS OF AREAS

How solid areas are scan-converted depends to a large extent on their representation, i.e., how they are stored in the computer's memory. From a solid area's representation it must be possible to determine the three essential attributes of the area, its mask, its shading rule, and its priority. In this chapter we are concerned only with uniform shading, so a single intensity value or color specification suffices. As we shall discover, priority can similarly be represented as a single scalar value. Mask representation is a more complex issue since there are several different approaches from which to choose, each representation involving a different scan-conversion process to compute the pixels of the mask. A very simple representation is a matrix of binary values. This requires no scan conversion and is often used to represent alphanumeric character shapes. Large areas require a more compact representation, however, and are often represented geometrically.

Some geometric figures have very simple representations and need only simple scan-conversion algorithms. For example, a line described by its

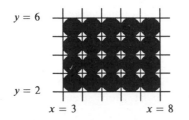

Figure 16-1 The raster coordinate system labels the lines dividing pixels with integer coordinates. The illustration shows a rectangle of width 5 and height 4 with lower left corner at (3, 2).

**Figure 16-2** A solid area with a curved boundary and a rectangular hole.

endpoints can be scan-converted with a DDA. Another easily scan-converted figure is the *rectangle* aligned with the coordinate axes. The following procedure displays a rectangle of a given width and height with lower left corner at $(x, y)$:

```
procedure WriteRectangle(x, y, width, height, intensity: integer);
    var i, j: integer;
begin
    for j := y to y + height − 1 do
        for i := x to x + width − 1 do
            SetPixel(FrameBuffer, i, j, intensity)
end;
```

This procedure recalls an important point about coordinate systems: the boundaries between pixels have integral coordinate values. Thus *SetPixel(FrameBuffer, a, b, intensity)* operates on the pixel representing the area $a \leq x < a + 1$, $b \leq y < b + 1$. This convention is chosen to make boundaries intuitive. The call *WriteRectangle*(3, 2, 5, 4, *intensity*) should affect areas of the screen $3 \leq x \leq 8$, $2 \leq y \leq 6$, as shown in Figure 16-1.

Because simple geometries such as the rectangle are few, a more versatile geometric representation is required. A more general representation that includes the rectangle as a special case is the *polygon*. Many of the shapes that we wish to display can be represented precisely as polygons or can be approximated by polygonal figures. For example, a circle can be approximated by a regular polygon with as many sides as necessary to obtain a good approximation. The polygon can be further generalized to allow curved sides or to permit holes inside the polygon; these additions are extremely useful for representing special symbols (Figure 16-2).

All these geometric representations describe objects by the *boundaries*, or *outlines*, of the solid area. Scan-conversion algorithms require a precise representation of the boundary in order to compute the area's mask. For a polygon, we can represent the outline by an ordered list of *vertices*. The example shown in Figure 16-3 might be represented by the list (1, 7) (9, 7) (9, 2) (5, 5) (1, 1). Although it does not matter which vertex is listed first, the vertices are ordered so that adjacent vertices in the list represent edges of the polygon. The edge from (9, 2) to (5, 5) is part of the outline because (9, 2) and (5, 5) are adjacent in the list. The last vertex is, by convention, adjacent to the first vertex, so an edge of the polygon runs from $(1, 1)$ to $(1, 7)$. An alternative representation is to list the *edges* of the polygon: Figure 16-3 might then be represented as the list $((9, 7)(9, 2))$, $((9, 2)(5, 5))$, $((5, 5)(1, 1))$, $((1, 1)(1, 7))$, $((1, 7)(9, 7))$. Either of these representations suffices to drive the scan-conversion techniques discussed below.

## 16-2  SCAN-CONVERTING POLYGONS

The scan conversion of a polygon involves finding all pixels that lie inside the polygon boundaries and generating a display by appropriately setting the intensities of these pixels. From a description of the outline of a polygon it is possible to decide whether a given point lies inside or outside the polygon by counting intersections of the boundary with an imaginary line extending from the point to some other point far outside the polygon. If an odd number of intersections is encountered, the point lies inside the boundary; otherwise it lies outside. For example, these techniques applied to Figure 16-3 show that the point $(3.5, 6.5)$ is inside the polygon and $(3.5, 2.5)$ is outside.

These observations suggest a simple scan-conversion algorithm. A function *Inside(polygon, x, y)* tests to see if the point $(x, y)$ lies within the polygon by counting intersections of the line from $(x, y)$ to $(-\infty, y)$ with each edge of the polygon and returning *true* if the count is odd or *false* if it is even. The following simple routine then generates the image (note that the *Inside* test is invoked on the center of the pixel):

> **for** $y := FrameBuffer.ymin$ **to** $FrameBuffer.ymax - 1$ **do**
>     **for** $x := FrameBuffer.xmin$ **to** $FrameBuffer.xmax - 1$ **do**
>         **if** $Inside(polygon, x + 0.5, y + 0.5)$ **then**
>             $SetPixel(FrameBuffer, x, y, intensity)$

This algorithm is simple but is unacceptably slow. Many thousands of points are tested, and testing each point requires intersecting a test line with each edge of the polygon. The number of points tested can be reduced by considering only pixels that lie inside the polygon's bounding box. Even this refinement does not greatly speed up the algorithm. A large polygon or one with many edges will be processed very slowly.

### Coherence

The performance of the scan-conversion algorithm can be improved substantially by taking advantage of a *coherence* property. If a given pixel is inside the polygon, immediately adjacent pixels are likely to be inside as well; a similar coherence holds for pixels outside the boundary. The visibility of adjacent pixels differs only if a boundary of the polygon passes between them, a relatively rare occurrence.

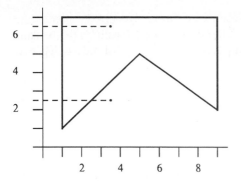

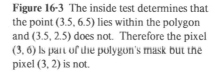

**Figure 16-3** The inside test determines that the point (3.5, 6.5) lies within the polygon and (3.5, 2.5) does not. Therefore the pixel (3, 6) is part of the polygon's mask but the pixel (3, 2) is not.

The coherence property suggests that a number of adjacent pixels should be tested together; a convenient group to test is an entire scan line. If we compute intersections of the scan line $y = 6.5$ with the edges of the polygon in Figure 16-3, we find two intersections, $x = 1$ and $x = 9$. These two points divide the scan line into three regions, the region $x < 1$, which contains pixels that lie outside the polygon; the region $1 \le x \le 9$, inside; and $x > 9$, outside. Thus the pixels with lower left corners from (1, 6) through (8, 6) all lie within the polygon.

Often there are more than two intersections of a scan line with the polygon boundaries. The scan line $y = 3.5$ intersects the polygon at $x = 7, 9, 1$, and 3.5. These intersections must be sorted by $x$ value to determine the regions of the scan line that lie inside the polygon. Sorting results in the list (1, 3.5, 7, 9). Adjacent intersections are then paired together, giving two pairs (1, 3.5) (7, 9); each pair represents a region of the scan line in which visible pixels should be displayed. Note that this algorithm uses the same criterion for visibility as the *Inside* algorithm given above: any pixel within the region of the scan line delimited by the pair of $x$ values will experience an odd number of boundary intersections between the pixel center and the point $x = -\infty$ on the scan line.

This discussion leads us to an algorithm substantially better in performance than the first one. The steps given below introduce only one new observation, namely that the intersections can all be computed first, and sorted out later.

### (YX) *Algorithm**

1.  For each edge of the polygon, compute all intersections of the edge with scan lines, remembering that scan lines are centered between integral values of $y$; a DDA algorithm can be used for this purpose. Build a list of the $(x, y)$ intersections.

*The names of scan-conversion algorithms are derived from the order in which sorting is performed. Parentheses group sorting steps. Thus the (YX) algorithm uses a single sort for both $y$ and $x$ values, while a Y-X algorithm sorts twice, first in $y$ and then in $x$. In conversation we use the phrases "YX" and "Y-then-X" to describe these algorithms.

2. Sort the list so that intersections for each scan line are grouped together and $x$ values within a scan line increase. That is, if two intersections $(x_1, y_1)$ and $(x_2, y_2)$ are in the list, $(x_1, y_1)$ should precede $(x_2, y_2)$ if and only if $(y_1 > y_2$ or $(y_1 = y_2$ and $x_1 < x_2))$.
3. Remove elements from the list in pairs, say $(x_a, y_a)$ and $(x_b, y_b)$. Since each pair represents a region of a scan line inside the polygon, we know that $y_a = y_b$ and $x_a \leq x_b$. Call $SetPixel(FrameBuffer, x, y_a - \frac{1}{2}, intensity)$ for integer values of $x$ such that $x_a \leq x + \frac{1}{2} \leq x_b$.*

A key feature of this algorithm is that it *sorts* intersections by $(x, y)$ values in order to find coherent groups of pixels. The sorting order is not particularly important; the roles of $x$ and $y$ could be interchanged in this algorithm without greatly changing its performance. Another way to look at the sorting is from the point of view of an individual pixel. Pixels are sorted into groups that have similar topological properties (inside or outside the polygon) and similar geometrical properties (adjacent on the same scan line).

Although the sorting order will not affect the final solution, it does affect the order in which pixels are discovered to lie inside the polygon. It therefore affects how the display appears to change if pixels are written directly into a frame buffer as scan conversion proceeds. The algorithm as stated will update the display from top to bottom, giving the appearance that the solid area is growing downward. A trivial change in the ordering criterion in step 2 will cause updates to flow from bottom to top. Interchanging the roles of $x$ and $y$ will make the growth of the polygon appear left-to-right.

Several variations on this algorithm are possible, based chiefly on different ways of performing the sorting. The sort in step 2 can be improved by separating the $y$ and $x$ sorting. The value of the function $Floor(y)$, i.e., the greatest integer less than or equal to $y$, is used to index a table to find a pointer to a linked list of $x$ intersections in sorted order (Figure 16-4). As an intersection $(x, y)$ is inserted into this structure, $y$ is sorted with a *bucket sort* and $x$ by an *insertion sort*. Still more sorting organizations will crop up in scan-conversion algorithms later in the chapter. First, however, two important aspects of our present algorithm must be examined.

## Singularities

Both the *Inside*-test and (YX) scan-conversion algorithms depend on calculating the coordinates of intersections between edges and scan lines. This calculation becomes difficult when a vertex of the polygon lies exactly on a

---

*Notice that all of the $\frac{1}{2}$ terms can be removed by a simple transformation. If at the outset we subtract $\frac{1}{2}$ from all $x$ and $y$ coordinates of the polygon, centers of pixels will thereafter fall at integral $(x, y)$ positions, simplifying the intersection calculations, the sorting, and the calls to *SetPixel*.

y bucket

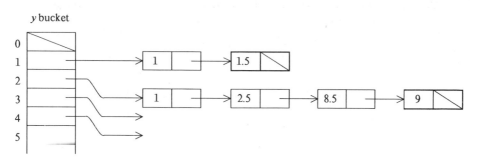

**Figure 16-4** The *y*-bucket insertion sort. Each scan line is described by a list of intersections sorted by *x*. The lists shown here correspond to the polygon in Figure 16-3.

scan-line center. In this case it is crucial for the proper number of intersections of the polygon boundary and the scan line to be recorded, for it is only by counting intersections that the scan-conversion algorithm determines whether a point lies inside or outside the polygon. Figure 16-5 illustrates two cases of such singularities. It is essential that one intersection be recorded for (4, 3.5) and that either two intersections or none be recorded for (7, 3.5). Failure to treat these vertices properly will cause the scan-conversion algorithm to turn the polygon inside out: it will find exterior points that are inside and vice versa.

One solution to this problem is to displace slightly each polygon vertex that lies exactly on a scan-line center so that it will lie just above the center. This method introduces a slight distortion in the shape of the polygon's outline. Furthermore, it depends critically on the ability to detect that an edge endpoint lies exactly on a scan-line center. If the *y* value of the ending point of one edge and that of the starting point of the next edge are calculated slightly differently, a small roundoff error could cause the point to be treated incorrectly. If vertices are represented carefully, using only integer arithmetic, this method is satisfactory.

A reliable way to process singularities relies less on the numerical precision of calculations and more on the topology of the polygon. It makes use of the

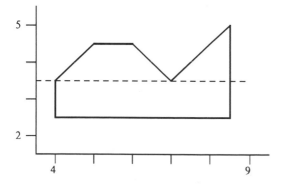

**Figure 16-5** Polygon vertices that lie exactly on a scan-line center require careful determination of intersections. The vertex at (4, 3.5) generates one intersection, while that at (7, 3.5) must generate either none or two.

*direction* of successive edges of the polygon. If the polygon boundary progresses monotonically upward or downward, only a single intersection with each scan line should be recorded. When the direction changes from downward to upward or from upward to downward, an intersection must be repeated. Thus the vertex $(4, 3.5)$ in Figure 16-5 generates one intersection because edges progress monotonically through the vertex, whereas the vertex $(7, 3.5)$ generates two intersections because the vertical direction of the boundary changes at the vertex. These observations are captured in the following algorithm, which also handles horizontal edges properly:

*Singularity Algorithm*

1. Assume the variable *yPrev* has been set in the process of generating intersections for an edge.
2. Retrieve the next edge of the polgyon. If there are no more edges, exit.
3. If this edge has no intersections with scan-line centers it is horizontal or very nearly so. Go to step 2.
4. Calculate *dy*, the difference between *y* at the ending vertex of the edge and the value at the starting vertex. If $dy > 0$, go to step 5, otherwise to step 6.
5. Since $dy > 0$, the first intersection generated must have $y = yPrev + 1$. After generating all intersections for the edge, record the *y* coordinate of the last intersection generated in *yPrev*. Go to step 2.
6. Since $dy < 0$, the first intersection generated must have $y = yPrev$. After generating all intersections for the edge, record the *y* coordinate of the last intersection generated in *yLast*. Set *yPrev* to $yLast - 1$. Go to step 2.

This algorithm deals with all singularities of the sort described above. The variable *yPrev* must be initialized properly by feeding edges into the loop until detecting one that reaches step 5 or 6. These steps cannot actually generate intersections because *yPrev* has not been set, but they can be used to set *yPrev* based on the *y* value of the last intersection that would have been generated. Once the algorithm is initialized, it can proceed. These initial edges must of course be passed to the algorithm at the end, so that intersections can be generated for them as well.

## Sampling

Our polygon scan-conversion algorithms fail to observe a dictum of Chapter 15: they do not calculate the area of the polygon that falls under each pixel but are concerned only with mathematical points that lie at the *center* of each pixel. Raster masks generated with these algorithms will therefore have unnecessarily jagged edges, like those illustrated in Chapter 15. To remedy this shortcoming, more precise calculations are required at the edges of the polygon in order to determine what *fraction* of each pixel is covered by the polygon. This fraction then modulates the tone value displayed at the pixel.

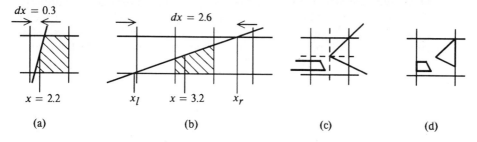

**Figure 16-6** Four methods for sampling a pixel: (a) steep edge; (b) shallow-angle edge; (c) increased resolution; (d) polygon clipping.

Since a precise calculation of the overlapping area can be quite costly, approximate methods are desirable. If we are using a display with very few intensity levels, there is no point in determining a precise value for the fractional area, because we shall be unable to make use of it. For binary displays we may choose to ignore the area-sampling refinements altogether.

We shall briefly describe four methods for calculating what area of a polygon falls within a pixel near the polygon's edge. The methods are listed in order of increasing difficulty and increasing precision.

*Method 1* (*Figure 16-6a*). We hypothesize that if a single edge passes through the pixel at a steep angle, the precise location of the $x$ intersection determines the fractional area $f$ covered. If the edge is at the left of a visible part of the polygon (as in the illustration), we might set $f = Floor(x) + 1 - x$, or 0.8 in the example. If the edge is at the right of a visible portion, $f = x - Floor(x)$.

*Method 2* (*Figure 16-6b*). If the edge passes through the pixel at a shallow angle, several pixels on the scan line will require fractional intensities. If we denote by $dx$ the change in the edge's $x$ position from scan line to scan line, i.e., the reciprocal of the slope of the line, then $|dx| > 1$ implies that the shallow angle condition holds. The fractional area covered is simply a linear interpolation from 0 at $x_l = x - |dx|/2$ to 1 at $x_r = x + |dx|/2$, where $x$ is the coordinate of the intersection of the edge and the scan-line center. The fractional area covered by the pixel at $i$ is thus $f = ((2i + 1) - (2x - |dx|))/2|dx|$, which evaluates to 0.6 for $i = 3$, as in the illustration. This expression must be modified for pixels that lie at the ends of the interval $[x_l, x_r]$.

*Method 3* (*Figure 16-6c*). Neither of the first methods copes properly with vertices falling within a pixel or with extremely narrow polygons that have no intersections with scan lines. If we require only a rough estimate of the area within the pixel, we can scan convert at, say, twice the resolution ultimately required, and then average four pixel fractions to approximate the answer at the original resolution.

*Method 4* (*Figure 16-6d*). A precise method for calculating overlapping area is to use the polygon-clipping algorithm (Chapter 5) to clip all polygons against the edges of the pixel area. The fraction is the sum of the areas of the resulting polygon or polygons; these areas are easily calculated. To perform such an operation for a large number of pixels, even for those known to lie at the edge of a polygon, is a considerable undertaking.

The intricate nature of these calculations unfortunately means that they are all too often neglected; the resulting pictures, produced with scan-conversion techniques that ignore the sampling problem, can be extremely annoying. The effect of jagged edges shows up dramatically in any sequence of slowly changing images, such as is often seen in animation. Extremely small polygons also cause problems if they are so thin that occasionally no edges intersect scan lines and the polygon is therefore not displayed at all. If a sequence of images is generated to depict motion, a small moving polygon will occasionally intersect scan lines and be seen, only to vanish again on the next frame. The best remedy for this problem is to avoid extremely small polygons or to change them into slightly larger polygons with reduced brightness.

In practice, methods 1 and 2 taken together suffice as a sampling technique. Because the two methods are similar, they can be treated together and inserted together into a scan-conversion algorithm. Rather than recording a single intersection $x$, we record $x_l = x - |dx|/2$ and $x_r = x + |dx|/2$, the interval over which the edge intersects pixels on the scan-line. This interval must be

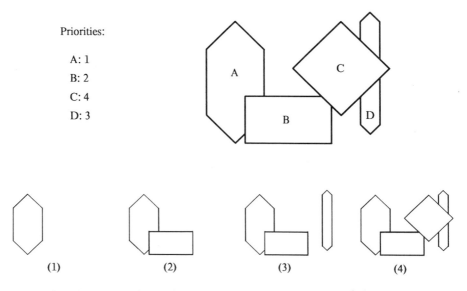

Priorities:

A: 1
B: 2
C: 4
D: 3

(1)          (2)          (3)          (4)

**Figure 16-7** The painter's algorithm for resolving priorities. Polygons are displayed in order of increasing priority. Although the figure shows only outlines, all polygons are opaque.

reduced near vertices so that neither $x_l$ nor $x_r$ extends beyond the vertices that bound the edge. After sorting by $y$ and $x_l$, these intervals are used to calculate the fractional coverage of each pixel on the scan line, using the following algorithm [128].

*Fraction Algorithm*

1. Assume an array *fraction*$(x)$ holds the fractional coverage for each pixel $x$. Set *fraction*$(x) = 0$ for all pixels on the scan line. Set $s = 1$.
2. Remove an interval $[x_l, x_r]$ from the list of intersections for this scan line. If no intervals remain, the scan line is finished and the *fraction* array holds the answers.
3. Use one of two methods to calculate the fractional area $f$ to the right of the edge:
   a. If *Floor*$(x_l) = $ *Floor*$(x_r)$, method 1 is used to calculate a fractional area $f$ covering pixel $x = $ *Floor*$(x_l)$. Then the fraction vector is updated: *fraction*$(x) := $ *fraction*$(x) + s \times f$. Go to step 4.
   b. If *Floor*$(x_l) \neq $ *Floor*$(x_r)$, method 2 is used to calculate a fractional area $f$ covering all pixels $x$ such that *Floor*$(x_l) \leq x \leq $ *Floor*$(x_r)$. The fraction vector is then updated for each of these $x$ values: *fraction*$(x) := $ *fraction*$(x) + s \times f$. Go to step 4.
4. For all $x > $ *Floor*$(x_r)$, set *fraction*$(x) := $ *fraction*$(x) + s$. Set $s = -s$. Go to step 2.

This method negates contributions of alternate left and right edges by changing $s$ and therefore does not require prior knowledge of whether an edge is a left edge or a right edge of the polygon. One of the strengths of this combination of methods 1 and 2 is that it is easily integrated into a scan-conversion algorithm.

## 16-3 PRIORITY

In order to generate displays of many polygons, it is necessary to resolve the problem of priority. When two polygons overlap, which one obscures the other? The artist solves this problem with ease. Each new opaque figure he paints on his canvas covers figures painted earlier. Thus the priorities of the artist's figures are related to the order in which they are painted. If the first figure painted is numbered 1, the second 2, and so forth, figures with higher numbers have higher priority.

The painter's algorithm is an effective way to resolve priorities on a raster display (Figure 16-7). Each polygon to be displayed is first assigned a priority number, and the polygons are sorted by priority. The screen is next cleared, and polygons are scan-converted and displayed in turn, starting with the polygon of lowest priority. Because polygons of high priority are processed after polygons of low priority, the high-priority polygons will cover the low-priority ones wherever polygons overlap.

Priority solution thus appears to involve sorting by priority value, just as scan conversion involves sorting by $x$ and $y$. The painter's algorithm is characterized as a P-(YX) algorithm because two sorting steps are performed: first, polygons are sorted by priority; second, the scan-conversion algorithm performs a (YX) sort.

This simple priority-solving algorithm has some minor disadvantages. The visual effect of the algorithm may not be appealing. The screen is cleared, and polygons appear in priority order. The most important polygons, those with highest priority, appear last.

In interactive applications, the order in which parts of the image appear on the screen is often important. It can be quite distracting to the user if polygons appear one-by-one in a random order as in the painter's algorithm. Updating is much less distracting if it proceeds steadily from top to bottom of the screen, or from left to right (Figure 16-8). This effect can be achieved by scan-converting on a row-by-row basis, rather than polygon-by-polygon as in the painter's algorithm. Because of the orientation of the frame buffer, we use horizontal rows, or scan lines, as the unit of scan conversion. The sorting steps must be rearranged to bring together intersection information for all polygons required to generate the display of a particular scan line. The following (YPX) algorithm achieves this effect.

1. For each polygon, compute all intersections of edges with scan lines. Enter the triple $(x, y, p)$ in a list, where $x$ and $y$ locate the intersection, and $p$ is the priority of the polygon.
2. Sort the list by $y$, $p$, and $x$. That is, $(x_1, y_1, p_1)$ precedes $(x_2, y_2, p_2)$ if and only if $(y_1 > y_2$ or $(y_1 = y_2$ and $(p_1 < p_2$ or $(p_1 = p_2$ and $x_1 < x_2))))$.
3. Remove pairs of triples from the list, operating as in step 3 of the (YX) algorithm. Whenever a new $y$ value is encountered, clear the corresponding scan line before processing intersections for it.

The difficulty with this algorithm is the large list of triples, which causes the sorting step to become unacceptably slow. The key to improving the performance of scan-conversion and priority calculations is to use more efficient sorting techniques.

## 16-4 THE Y-X ALGORITHM

The performance of a scan-conversion algorithm is determined largely by the sorting steps it uses. The (YX) and (YPX) algorithms both build large lists that require substantial effort to sort. The $y$-bucket insertion sort (Figure 16-4) will speed up either algorithm by separating the $y$ and $x$ sorting and by using a particularly efficient $y$ sort. This improvement, however, does nothing to reduce the storage required to retain lists of intersections.

What is needed is an approach that generates intersections only as they are needed to update the display, one scan line at a time. To generate the pixels for each scan line, we must first compute the intersections that lie on that scan line; then these intersections are sorted by $x$ coordinate to determine pixel intensity values. This may be termed a Y-X algorithm, since the computation of intersections in a given scan line involves a $y$ sort followed by an $x$ sort.

The principal data structure used by the Y-X algorithm is a list of polygon edges, sorted by maximum $y$ value. This is called the *y-bucket list*, because it is generated by a *bucket sort* in which each edge is entered in the "bucket" corresponding to its maximum $y$ value (Figure 16-9a). Each edge record contains the information needed to generate intersections: $x$, the location of the intersection on the topmost scan line; $dx$, the amount by which the $x$ value changes from scan line to scan line; and $dy$, the number of intersections that the edge will generate. This description is the result of applying the singularity algorithm to the edges of the polygon and then sorting edges into the $y$ bucket.

The Y-X algorithm generates the image from top to bottom, one scan line at a time. As it does so, it maintains an active-edge list, sorted by $x$, listing all edges that cross the scan line being prepared (Figure 16-9b). Successive pairs of these edges demarcate portions of the scan line in which the polygon is visible and are used to generate the display for the scan line. After displaying a scan line, each edge record is updated for the next scan line ($x := x + dx$; $dy := dy - 1$). These updates may occasionally require edges in the active edge list to be interchanged so that the list remains sorted by $x$. Some edges will terminate ($dy = 0$) and be removed from the list. Any edge records cited in the $y$ bucket for the new scan line need to be added to the active list.

The Y-X algorithm is attractive because it reduces sorting time, largely as a result of keeping the active edge list sorted by $x$. The effort required to keep the list sorted is very small because of the relative infrequency with which edges cross, necessitating changes in the order. Although the effort to sort a new edge into the list may be noticeable, this is also an infrequent occurrence.

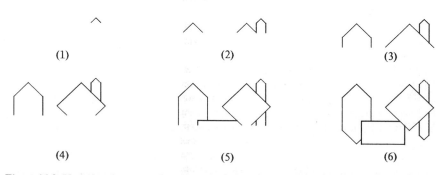

(1)  (2)  (3)

(4)  (5)  (6)

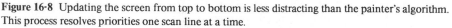

**Figure 16-8** Updating the screen from top to bottom is less distracting than the painter's algorithm. This process resolves priorities one scan line at a time.

**Interleaving Scan-Conversion and Priority Decisions**

The Y-X algorithm can be adapted to become a Y-(PX) algorithm that scan converts a number of polygons concurrently and makes priority decisions on each scan line. The algorithm begins by inserting into the $y$ bucket edge records for all polygons to be displayed. The active-edge list contains records for all polygons intersecting the current scan line, sorted first on priority and then on $x$ coordinate. As a scan-line is displayed, low-priority polygon intersections are found first in the active list, and are therefore superceded by the display of higher priority polygons farther down the list.

The Y-X algorithm can also be used for scan-conversion in the painter's algorithm to yield a P-Y-X algorithm. Polygons are first sorted by priority. Then each polygon is scan-converted in turn using the Y-X algorithm.

These algorithms all take advantage of a new coherence property, the coherence of edges. Whereas the (YX) algorithm involves a large sort to untangle $x$ intersections, the Y-X algorithm and its elaborations take advantage of the fact that edges are coherent, i.e., their order in $x$ rarely changes.


## 16-5  PROPERTIES OF SCAN CONVERSION ALGORITHMS

Although the discussion in this chapter has emphasized the performance of the sorting steps required in scan conversion and priority calculations, the comparisions apply only to the *growth* properties of the algorithms. An algorithm that sorts $n$ intersections in time C $n \log n$ will, as $n$ grows, eventually perform better than any algorithms with C $n^2$ performance. For many applications $n$ is small, however, and growth properties are less important than the overhead required to maintain complex data structures. Moreover, numerous optimizations can be applied to the algorithms presented in this chapter to reduce the coefficient C. The scan-conversion algorithms presented are summarized below:

*Scan conversion of single polygons:*
  (YX)    Simplest practical scan-conversion algorithm
  Y-X     Efficient sorting, taking advantage of edge coherence

*Scan conversion and priority resolution:*
  P-(YX)  Painter's algorithm, the simplest way to resolve priority conflicts
  (YPX)   Update appears to flow down the screen but sorting inefficient
  P-Y-X   Painter's algorithm using faster Y-X sorting
  Y-(PX)  Efficient sorting, with the update progressing down the screen

The choice of scan-conversion algorithm should take into account not only performance and storage requirements but also the way the algorithm is used in a graphics system. It may be used frequently or infrequently, for one polygon

(a)

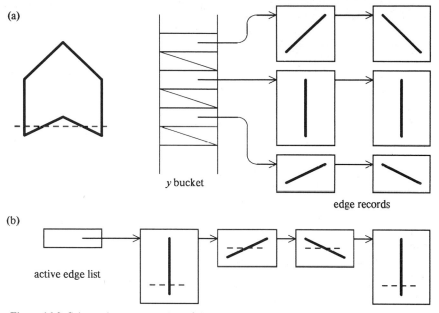

y bucket

edge records

(b)

active edge list

**Figure 16-9** Schematic representation of the data structures for the Y-X algorithm: (a) a polygon and associated y-bucket list of edge information; (b) the active edge list as it appears while processing a scan line (dashed line).

or for many. It may be necessary to adapt the algorithm for incremental use in order to make rapid, small changes to the display. The way in which the algorithm updates the screen may be the most important consideration because it influences the interactive effect of the system.

## EXERCISES

**16-1** The polygon scan-conversion algorithms can be used to display thick lines of the sort shown in Figure 16-10 by operating on appropriate polygons. Devise an algorithm that converts the endpoints $(x_1, y_1)$ and $(x_2, y_2)$, together with the width $w$ into an appropriate four-vertex polygon. Do not use trigonometric functions in your solution.

**16-2** Without writing any computer programs, try to estimate the relative performance of the *Inside*-test algorithm and the (YX) algorithm in its two versions (one-list version and a bucket-sort—insertion-sort version). Assume a typical polygon has $e$ edges and covers roughly $a$ pixels.

**16-3** What modifications are required so that the scan-conversion algorithms will properly compute masks for polygons with holes in them? Start by defining a representation for such extended polygons.

**16-4** How can scan conversion ideas be used to cross-hatch a polygon with lines, as illustrated in Figure 16-10?

**16-5** If we wish to display a polygon boundary with thick lines as shown in Figure 16-11, we must scan-convert a polygon with a hole in it. Devise an algorithm that computes the vertex coordinates of the new polygon and hole.

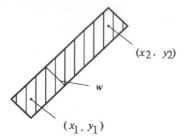

**Figure 16-10** A schematic representation of a thick line described by two endpoints and a width.

**16-6** If step 1 of the (YX) scan-conversion algorithm does not compute intersections properly near singularities, how are the errors manifested in the rest of the algorithm? What check can be installed that will catch such errors? What are the visual effects of an error?

**16-7** Show how the singularity algorithm can be implemented without requiring any edge to be passed to it more than once. To do this, the algorithm will have to "remember" at most one edge.

**16-8** How can sampling methods 1 and 2, used to compute proper sampling of pixels, be modified to cope with more than one edge of the polygon intersecting the same pixel area?

**16-9** Work out the details of the calculation of $f$ in steps $3a$ and $b$ of the combined sampling algorithm. How can some of the work in step 4 be saved?

**16-10** Make plots of *intensity* vs. $x$ dimension along a scan line for some polygon that has been properly sampled. How might you represent such a signal economically?

**16-11** How does the solution to the sampling problem change when more than one polygon is to be displayed?

**16-12** If a small change is made to a display image consisting of many polygons, it is possible to avoid clearing the entire screen and scan-converting each polygon anew. Explain how to achieve this reduction in computing time. *Hint:* If polygon $C$ in Figure 16-7 is moved one centimeter to the right, how much of the display must be updated?

**16-13** Suggest a modification to the painter's algorithm in which polygons of highest priority are painted first. Can the initial erasure of the screen be avoided? *Hint:* Keep a boolean array *Occupied*[$x, y$] that indicates whether a polygon has been displayed at the pixel ($x, y$).

**16-14** If a polygon has been scan-converted with careful attention to sampling, pixels at the edges will specify only fractional involvement with the polygon. In the painter's algorithm, how are these edge points to be handled? What problems arise? Devise a convincing example of the problems using colored polygons.

**16-15** Consider a shading rule that paints each pixel on the boundary of a polygon black and each pixel in the interior of the polygon white. What is the effect of such a rule when several overlapping

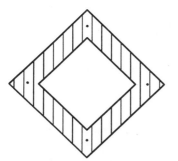

**Figure 16-11** A polygon that is best described as four thick lines connected together.

polygons are displayed? How might scan-conversion algorithms be modified to implement such a shading rule?

**16-16** Show how to modify step 3 of the (YPX) algorithm so that a scan line is displayed only after its *final* appearance has been determined.

**16-17** It might appear that the active-edge list of the Y-(PX) would become so long that the insertion of new edges from the *y* bucket would be unacceptably slow. Explain how the insertion of new edges can be achieved as the active-edge list is scanned to generate the display of the scan line.

**16-18** The idea of *depth number* is used to characterize the average number of polygons that lie over a given pixel. If the screen is largely empty, the depth number is almost zero. If the screen is nearly covered with nonoverlapping polygons, the depth number is 1. If, in addition, polygons overlap, the depth number grows above 1. Assume that $n$ polygons, each of area $a$ pixels, are displayed on the screen. Roughly, what is the relationship between $n$, $d$, $a$, and the screen dimensions? Estimate the execution time of the painter's algorithm P-(YX), including the scan-conversion step, as a function of these variables.

**16-19** Analyze all the scan-conversion and priority algorithms presented in this chapter, using the same framework as Exercise 16-18. What do you conclude about the relative performance of the algorithms?

**16-20** Suppose that an image contains so many objects that geometric descriptions of all of them are too large to fit in memory. What can be done? Which scan-conversion algorithms can be best adapted to deal with this problem?

**16-21** Extend the (YX) algorithm to handle "polygons" with curved edges. How does the representation of curves interact with the intersection calculation and with the detection and handling of singularities?

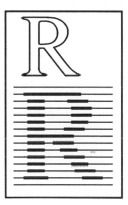

# 17

## INTERACTIVE

## RASTER GRAPHICS

Interactive computer graphics relies for its effectiveness on rapid display modifications. Random-scan displays lend themselves to a wide variety of dynamic changes involving very little computation. In the case of raster-scan displays, however, changes generally involve large amounts of processing; it is therefore difficult to achieve the speed of modification required for effective interaction. This chapter explores some general techniques for changing displays rapidly, together with some methods specifically suited to the frame-buffer display.

The problem of supporting interactive techniques on a raster-scan display is best illustrated by considering some examples. Figure 17-1 shows two images generated by interactive programs; each image is defined by 480,000 1-bit pixels in a frame buffer. Figure 17-1a shows a set of windows into a large programming system [464]. The program is operated with the aid of a mouse input device that propels a cursor over the screen. The mouse is used to identify program text to be manipulated or edited. Striking a key causes a menu to appear; it may be removed later if the screen becomes too cluttered. Both menus and windows can be moved to other positions on the screen and can be changed in size. Window priorities can change. A window that is partially hidden can be placed over those hiding it. The text within the window is displayed in several typefaces, and may "scroll" upward as new text is added at the bottom. In order for this system to be useful, all actions must occur smoothly, with delays well under ½ second.

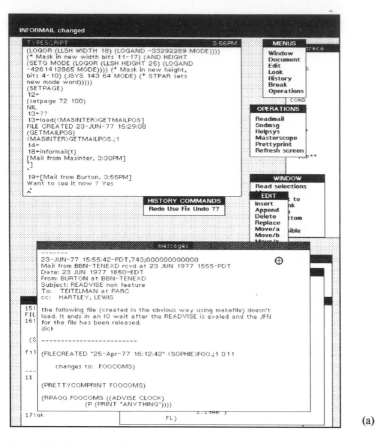

(a)

**Figure 17-1** Examples of interactive raster-scan application programs: (a) an interactive programming system using multiple windows and menus; (b) an interactive illustration program; note the menu at upper right.

Figure 17-1b shows an illustration being prepared with an interactive program. The user adds or erases straight lines of various thicknesses, text characters in various typefaces, and halftone images. An illustration can be rearranged by moving sections to new locations on the screen. All operations are controlled by a menu that is displayed near the cursor when it is needed but is removed quickly to leave the illustration undisturbed on the screen. This application must provide even faster response than the first. The judgments needed to design an illustration, to choose proper line thicknesses, and to position or align objects on the screen require rapid response.

The need for rapid image changes is thus just as real for raster displays as it is for random-scan displays. Sometimes it is necessary to supplement the computer's power with special hardware in order to achieve the necessary

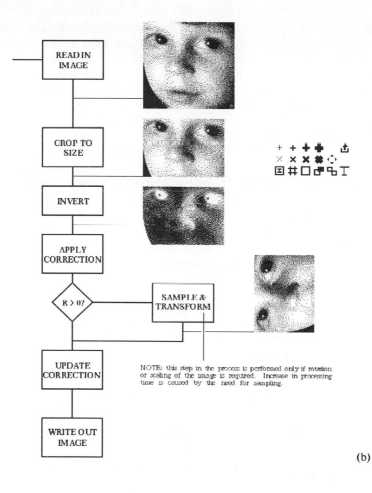

(b)

performance. For simple, low-cost applications this approach is too expensive, and methods must be found that provide rapid response on a raster display without depending on extra hardware.

## 17-1 UPDATING THE DISPLAY

Updating a raster-scan display is particularly difficult because of the volume of information that must be computed. When the picture is modified, each of a large number of individual pixels in the frame buffer may need to be changed. The quest for speed suggests a number of approaches, some general-purpose and some tailored specifically to the raster-scan display:

1. *Reducing the complexity of the displayed image.* To achieve speed, we try to limit the number of lines, characters, or solid objects displayed. The display may be restricted to objects that do not overlap, in order to avoid priority calculations. Solid objects may be disallowed altogether because scan conversion from geometric descriptions is so time-consuming. Unfortunately these restrictions often interfere with the needs of the application, which may depend upon the use of complex images.

2. *Designing special-purpose hardware* to update the display at high speed. For applications like daylight-flight simulation, which demand a complex image to be generated many times a second, special hardware is essential. Even if only part of the image changes rapidly, special hardware may be the best solution. For example, frame-buffer displays often make special provisions for cursors, which change position frequently. The various hardware organizations that support rapid display changes are discussed in Chapter 19.

3. *The use of incremental algorithms to update the display,* concentrating computing resources on causing changes, not on regenerating unaltered parts of the image. An example of this approach has already been seen in the use of a segmented display file for random-scan displays; the idea is to limit changes to a fraction of all segments. The frame-buffer display requires a somewhat different approach. The large number of pixels suggests that we try to reduce the number that must be changed, perhaps by confining our attention to areas of the screen where changes are occurring.

The techniques described in this chapter are elaborations of the incremental approach. The essence of this approach lies in updating images by using intermediate results obtained during previous updates. The frame buffer itself stores the pixel values from the previous image. The image of an individual object may be preserved by saving its mask, derived from a scan-conversion process. Still other objects, such as characters, are already represented in raster form. Some of these representations may have originally involved considerable amounts of computation for their generation. The incremental approach concentrates on preserving these representations and using fast, simple algorithms to achieve rapid change.

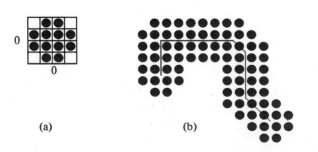

Figure 17-2 Painting with a brush and trajectory: (a) a brush mask with origin at the center; (b) a pattern of pixels created by moving the brush along the trajectory (thin line).

(a)

(b)

## 17-2 THE PAINTING MODEL

Imagine building up an image using a painter's brush. If the brush is applied to the canvas, it adds a blob of paint. If it is steered over a *trajectory*, it leaves behind a trail of paint. Brushes of different sizes and shapes, together with paints of different colors and shades, are used to create an image. The painter builds the image incrementally, changing only the small portion directly under the brush.

The brush and trajectory scheme can be modeled easily with a frame-buffer display. The scheme is illustrated in its simplest form in Figure 17-2. The brush is simply a small raster that describes the shape that each imprint of the brush will leave in the frame buffer. The trajectory is a list of points at each of which the brush is painted into the frame buffer by changing pixel values to reflect the color of the paint. Erasing material is simply a matter of painting with the background color. These painting operations are identical to the *WriteMask* procedure of page 221 for writing characters into the frame buffer. Extensions illustrated in *WriteColor* (see page 222) to represent the color of the character in the raster can be used to provide multicolored brushes.

The painting algorithm is unaffected by the exact shape of the brush and thus allows the use of a wide variety of brush shapes: rectangles, circles, ellipses, or arbitrary hand-generated patterns. The brush raster can be generated by a number of methods—it can be scan-converted from a geometric description, generated by an algorithm (suitable for simple geometries such as rectangles and circles), specified interactively by the user, or provided as pre-defined data by the program. Because the performance of the painting method is dominated by the repeated invocations of the painting subroutine, the efficiency of the technique used to generate the brush is relatively unimportant.

The painting trajectory may likewise be derived from any one of a number of different sources. Perhaps the most common painting method uses a graphical input device to specify the trajectory. The user moves the stylus and watches paint appear on the screen. A very simple painting program can be constructed using this paradigm, together with a menu of brushes and brush colors. If trajectory points are provided directly by the input device, the user can sometimes move the stylus rapidly enough to cause wide separation of successive points and therefore to leave gaps in the trail of paint generated. If this effect is unattractive, the painting program can interpolate additional trajectory points to fill in the gaps.

Computed trajectories are often used to govern painting. The DDA is an example of a computation that generates points on the trajectory of a straight line and paints with a brush one pixel in diameter. Larger circular brushes can be used similarly to produce thick lines. Displaying curves is also easy, using a trajectory computed from a mathematical description of the curve and a circular brush that will give the curve the appearance of uniform thickness regardless of its slope (Figure 17-3).

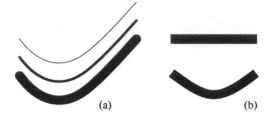

**Figure 17-3** Curved trajectories traced with various brushes: (a) circular brushes give the appearance of uniform thickness; (b) a rectangular brush rotates to follow the curve direction.

(a)          (b)

## Painting Constraints

Considerable skill may be required to operate an interactive painting program, especially if it is used to draw straight lines. The program can however be modified to apply *constraints*, similar to those described in Chapter 12, to make drawing easier. With the aid of such constraints we can construct images consisting of thick straight lines parallel to the $x$ or $y$ axes. As the cursor is moved over the screen, line segments appear, turning corners whenever the direction of cursor motion changes markedly. Each line segment lies on a grid line. Only when the cursor has moved from one grid intersection to an adjacent one will a new portion of the line appear on the screen. The new portion will be vertical or horizontal, depending on the general direction of motion of the cursor as constrained to the grid. Figure 17-4 illustrates vertical and horizontal brushes for line drawing and shows a sample display.

Figure 17-4 also illustrates a problem with this technique: the corners are not sharp. This small error can be corrected with a method shown in Figure 17-5, where both lines are conceptually extended beyond the corner grid point. Any pixel covered by *both* extensions is included in the image of the corner. In the example of Figure 17-5 this construction results in adding the missing pixel to the corner. This idea can be applied to lines of equal thickness meeting at any angle. Figure 17-6 shows a 45° corner on a 3-unit grid, where the crosses indicate pixels that become part of the corner as a result of the extension of the lines.

This method for drawing lines is suited to interactive applications because it builds the lines incrementally. Although solid-area scan conversion from a geometric description of the thick lines would yield the same result, the

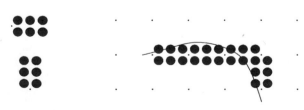

**Figure 17-4** Constraining a trajectory (thin line) to a grid (small dots). Either the horizontal or vertical brush is used, depending on the direction of motion of the trajectory.

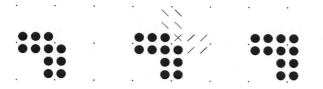

**Figure 17-5** Filling in corners. Each line is conceptually extended (diagonal marks). Wherever both extensions mark pixels to be displayed (cross), a pixel is filled in.

incremental method is substantially faster. Speed is gained by pre-computing masks for short line segments and using a simple logical operation to fill in corners.

## Filling Areas

A powerful painting tool is a function to fill a region of one color with a new color. A user of a painting program can first paint the outline of an object, and then use the filling function to spread paint in the interior of the object. The filling operation starts by replacing the value of a single pixel, and then spreads throughout the raster, replacing the value of any pixel that contains the old color. The spreading operation stops whenever it encounters a pixel that does not contain the "old" color. The technique is best expressed by the following recursive procedure:

```
procedure Fill(x, y, oldintensity, newintensity: integer);
begin
    if GetPixel(FrameBuffer, x, y) = oldintensity then begin
        SetPixel(FrameBuffer, x, y, newintensity);
        Fill(x + 1, y, oldintensity, newintensity);
        Fill(x − 1, y, oldintensity, newintensity);
        Fill(x, y + 1, oldintensity, newintensity);
        Fill(x, y − 1, oldintensity, newintensity)
    end
end;
```

A user invokes the filling function by pointing to a pixel within the region to be filled, and indicating a new color. The fill operation spreads this color throughout the region.

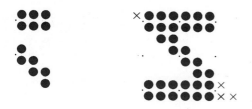

**Figure 17-6** Filling in corners of diagonal lines.

## 17-3 MOVING PARTS OF AN IMAGE

An important class of display changes are those which simply move part of an existing image to a new position on the screen. The applications illustrated in Figure 17-1 both make extensive use of such changes. When parts of an image are to be moved, we would like to avoid lengthy scan-conversion calculations and instead simply add a translation to the coordinates of each pixel in the frame buffer.

One approach to moving part of an image is to retain a separate raster description of pixel values for the portions of the image that must move. The *WriteColor* algorithm is then used to place the raster at the desired location in the frame buffer. This approach is ideal for small objects, but the storage required to save raster descriptions of large objects may become excessive.

In many cases the frame buffer itself can be used to hold the raster representation of the object. If the object of interest is already visible on the screen, it must have been written into the frame buffer. When the object is to be moved, we simply copy pixel values from one part of the frame buffer to another. Some efficient copying techniques have been developed that cause the object to appear to move very quickly.

In order to copy the object we must specify which pixels are relevant to the display of the object. Although this information could be defined by a mask, we would like to avoid allocating storage for this mask. A satisfactory compromise is to copy rectangular areas of the screen. This works well as long as object bounding boxes do not overlap. Where overlap occurs a more careful algorithm must be used.

The primitive copy operation thus copies a *source rectangle* in some *source raster* into a *destination rectangle* in a *destination raster*. This copy operation has many applications in reorganizing raster-scan images. The programs illustrated in Figure 17-1 use it extensively to move windows and portions of illustrations. It is also used in scrolling the contents of a window up or down. Instead of scan converting the entire window contents for each scrolling operation, we copy the rectangular portion that remains visible after scrolling and use scan conversion only to fill in the newly visible information (see Figure 17-7). Scan conversion is generally a slower operation than copying images since it involves accessing data structures in the application program, retrieving character masks, and repeatedly calling routines to modify the frame buffer. The use of copying therefore permits faster scrolling.

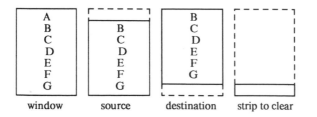

window     source     destination     strip to clear

**Figure 17-7** Scrolling a window involves copying part of the image (source) to a new place (destination), followed by clearing a strip of the screen. The same general method will also scroll down, left, or right.

**Figure 17-8** Inverting the intensity of pixels can be used to provide selection feedback.

## 17-4 FEEDBACK IMAGES

Perhaps the most stringent requirements for rapid display changes occur in the provision of feedback for interactive techniques. As we have seen in Chapter 12, these techniques rely for their effectiveness on an immediate graphical response on the display. Unfortunately some of the simplest forms of feedback, such as dragging a picture across the screen, require a considerable amount of computation on a raster-scan display and hence are difficult to perform at a sufficiently rapid rate. In many cases, however, we can use feedback techniques suited specifically to the raster-scan display. For example, selection feedback, which on a random-scan display might use intensity highlighting, can be performed on a raster-scan display by inverting the intensity of each pixel within the selected item's bounding box. The effect is shown in Figure 17-8.

Feedback techniques for raster-scan displays face a serious problem that is absent in random-scan displays. When a temporary feedback image is removed or repositioned to another place on the screen, the original image must be restored. For example, if a cursor is moved across the screen, the image across which it moves must not change. Three general methods for restoring the original image are special hardware, raster copying, and making reversible changes.

**Special hardware.** The frame buffer contents are not modified when the temporary image is displayed. Instead a special small frame buffer is provided that is dedicated to holding rapidly moving information. This small image can be positioned arbitrarily on the screen and will override the pixel values extracted from the frame buffer whenever the two overlap (Figure 17-9). Although this technique is very popular for implementing cursors, it lacks flexibility because of the generally limited size of the special frame buffer.

**Copying rasters.** Before the feedback image is displayed, the relevant portion of the frame buffer is copied; the copy is used later to restore the original image. Only those pixel values which will be modified by the feedback image need be

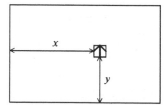

**Figure 17-9** A cursor raster is positioned at an arbitrary location on the screen by giving $x$ and $y$.

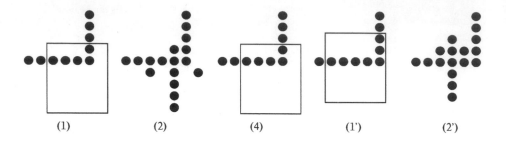

| (1) | (2) | (4) | (1') | (2') |

**Figure 17-10** A cursor implementation that copies rasters. The cursor is shown at the left. Numbers correspond to steps described in the text.

copied (it is common to copy all pixels within the bounding box of the feedback image). To illustrate this method, consider a cursor with a bounding box $Cw$ pixels wide and $Ch$ pixels high to be displayed with lower left corner at $(Cx, Cy)$, as shown in Figure 17-10:

1. Copy the rectangle $(Cx, Cy, Cw, Ch)$ from the frame buffer into a temporary array.
2. Display the cursor image at $(Cx, Cy)$ using *WriteMask*.
3. Wait until the cursor must be moved, say to $(Cx', Cy')$.
4. Restore the image in the rectangle $(Cx, Cy, Cw, Ch)$ from the temporary array.
1'. Copy the rectangle $(Cx', Cy', Cw, Ch)$ into the temporary array.
2'. Display the cursor image at $(Cx', Cy')$ using *WriteMask*.
3'. ...

As described, this technique may cause the feedback image to flash on and off because step 4 removes the feedback image from the frame buffer and 1' inserts it again. The flashing is avoided if the copying is properly synchronized to the display refresh cycle; steps 4, 1' and 2' are performed quickly while the refresh process is not accessing that region of the frame buffer. Alternatively, the flashing can be reduced by copying the new image into the frame buffer before removing the old one, although this requires care if the two images overlap.

**Making reversible changes in the frame buffer.** In order to display the feedback image we make a reversible change in the frame buffer; the original image is restored by reversing the change. For example, we could change the image to its

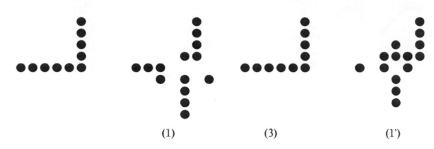

(1)                           (3)                           (1')

**Figure 17-11** Displaying a cursor by making reversible changes to a frame buffer. The numbers correspond to steps described in the text.

negative, as in photography, and later restore it to its positive form. To achieve this transformation, we simply apply to each pixel value $x$ the function $f(x) = a - x$, where $a$ is the maximum value that the frame buffer can record for a pixel. Then the function $f^{-1}(x) = a - x$ will invert the transformation.

This technique can be used to display a moving cursor. Suppose that the cursor is represented as a mask raster, to be displayed at $(Cx, Cy)$. Three steps are performed (see Figure 17-11):

1. Apply the function $f(x)$ to all pixel values that are specified by the mask, as positioned at $(Cx, Cy)$. The cursor image will now appear.
2. Wait until the cursor must be moved, say to $(Cx', Cy')$.
3. Apply the function $f^{-1}(x)$ to all pixel values that are specified by the mask, as positioned at $(Cx, Cy)$. The cursor now disappears.
1'. Apply the function $f(x)$ to all pixel values that are specified by the mask, as positioned at $(Cx', Cy')$.
2'. ...

The invertible function technique is convenient because no auxiliary storage is required to save pixel values. Its main disadvantage is the rather imprecise rendition of the feedback image. Although $f$ is chosen so that the image generally contrasts with the surrounding image, the actual "color" of the feedback image will vary as it moves across the screen.

These three feedback techniques are all applicable to displaying *temporary imagery*, information that must be quickly displayed and later removed quickly to leave the original image unchanged. The techniques are useful not only for showing moving cursors but also for implementing other interactive effects. The following list illustrates some of the many possibilities:

*Selection.* Figure 17-8 has shown a selection operation using the inversion technique to modify the bounding box of the selected objects. The objects can been seen even while they are selected.

*Rubber-band lines.* The rubber-band method for describing a line requires

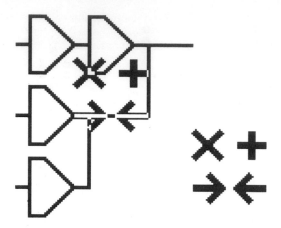

**Figure 17-12** A temporary menu can be readily displayed and removed by making reversible changes to a frame buffer. The figure shows two copies of the menu, one of which is placed over part of the permanent display.

repeated regeneration of the line as the cursor is moved. The line is drawn and removed in a repetitive sequence similar to the ones described above for drawing cursors.

*Menus.* Often a menu display is needed to allow the user to select an option; it can be removed from the display as soon as the choice is made. Chapter 12 describes a menu that appears near the cursor location and later disappears to avoid interfering with other images on the screen. Figure 17-12 illustrates the inversion technique used to display such a menu.

There are, of course, many other useful feedback techniques for raster-scan displays. The list above provides examples of some methods suitable for use with a frame buffer. All these techniques, as well as those covered earlier in the chapter for updating the display, require efficient implementation of the routines that change the frame buffer. The next chapter discusses how these routines are written.

## EXERCISES

**17-1** The method of copying rasters to provide feedback images has the disadvantage that the feedback image appears to flash as it is copied into the frame buffer and later destroyed. How can the loops in steps 4 and 1′ be combined to require at most one pixel to flash? Does your method work to reduce flashing of the reversible change method as well?

**17-2** The method for displaying rubber-band lines in a frame buffer will cause the line to flash on and off as it is moved across the screen. Suggest a method that will reduce this flashing considerably. In particular, if the line does not move, you should be able to avoid the flash altogether.

**17-3** Consider the brush shown in Figure 17-13 as an alternative to the one shown in Figure 17-4. If this brush is used to display 2-pixel-wide lines on a 3-pixel grid, there will be no missing pixels at right-angle corners. Is this approach generally a good idea?

**17-4** Show that the technique for filling in corners of thick lines gives exactly the same solution that scan conversion would give.

**17·5** Define in detail the algorithm discussed for correctly drawing the corners where thick lines meet. Pay particular attention to problems that arise when the lines meet at a very acute angle.

**17·6** As a practical matter, it may be wise to precompute masks for pixels that must be filled in at corners of lines. How many different masks are needed? How does your answer vary with the number of different line thicknesses and the number of different angles of lines?

**17·7** Interesting effects can be achieved by varying the size or shape of a brush as it is moved along a trajectory. Consider a brush whose size changes with speed. As the input device moves faster, the brush becomes smaller. What will be the effect? Can you suggest other, useful ways to modify shape or size?

**17·8** Investigate the visual effects of other invertible functions. For example, consider adding a feedback image value $t$ to the existing image value $i$: $f(t, i) = (t + i) \bmod (a + 1)$, where $a$ is the maximum value that the frame buffer can record for a pixel.

**17·9** Consider the functions $f(x) = x + b$ and $f^{-1}(x) = x - b$, proposed to be used as reversible functions for displaying temporary imagery. The value $b$ lies between 0 and the maximum permissible value in the frame buffer, $a$. Under what conditions will these functions work properly? Are these functions better than $f(x) = f^{-1}(x) = a - x$? (N. Negroponte calls this technique "transparent ink.")

**17·10** Devise additional functions $f(x)$ that are reversible. For each one, characterize the visual change they will cause on the screen.

**17·11** What is the maximum depth of recursion in the *Fill* procedure? Devise an implementation that is considerably more efficient than the one given in this chapter.

**17·12** Can you devise useful generalizations of the filling technique given in Section 17-2?

**Figure 17·13**

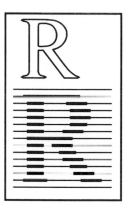

## 18

# RASTER-GRAPHICS

# SYSTEMS

The last three chapters, covering techniques and algorithms for raster image generation, have perhaps tended to emphasize the differences between raster-scan and line-drawing graphics. There are indeed many characteristics of raster graphics that set it apart: these include the special quality of raster-scan images, the particular hardware required, and the dominant problem of scan conversion. Nevertheless raster graphics has much in common with line-drawing graphics. In particular there is the same strong requirement for a software *system* to bind together the techniques and algorithms in a form the application programmer can use. We have now reached the point where it is appropriate to discuss the design of raster-graphics systems.

## 18-1 REPRESENTATIONS

One of the most basic problems in raster-graphics system design is the choice of *representation* of graphic items. This is an equally important question in line-drawing systems but is relatively easily answered: we represent graphical items as dots and lines, defined by their cartesian coordinates. More complex items, such as curves and composite symbols, can of course be represented in a variety of ways, but there is little argument against the use of dots and lines as basic entities.

In raster graphics systems we can choose between three different representations for basic items of graphical information:

1. *Rasters,* or rectangular arrays of intensity samples
2. *Lines and dots,* i.e., the same representation as in line-drawing systems
3. *Solid areas,* defined by the geometry of their outlines

The choice of representation has a significant impact on the overall design of the system. A system to handle lines and dots is likely to be very similar to a line-drawing graphics system and indeed can offer an identical function set and can use much the same software. A solid-area graphics system is rather different; internally it must incorporate scan-conversion software, and it must provide functions that permit the programmer to define each solid object's mask, shading, and priority. A complete contrast is provided by systems using raster representation, for here the programmer is concerned with operations on arrays of intensities; the operations include moving and copying arrays, applying half-toning or enhancing algorithms, and so on. This type of system is sufficiently different to require treatment as a separate system design topic. Systems based on lines and solid areas have certain features in common and are discussed later in this chapter.

## 18-2 RASTER MANIPULATION FUNCTIONS

The preceding chapters have presented a number of useful operations for manipulating rasters. They include the following:

1. *WriteRectangle:* storing a constant value in each pixel in a rectangular region of a raster. This is used to clear the screen or to display rectangular objects such as horizontal and vertical lines.
2. *WriteMask:* painting into the frame buffer objects described by a mask raster, using a constant pixel value. Objects are erased with a painting operation using the background color. This function is used to display characters and to implement painting programs.
3. *WriteColor:* painting objects of varying color into the frame buffer.
4. *CopyRaster:* copying a rectangular region of the frame buffer into another region on the screen or copying a region of the frame buffer into a temporary raster (not part of the frame buffer) and back again.
5. *InvertMask:* applying an inverting function $f(x)$ or $f^{-1}(x)$ to pixels identified by a mask raster.
6. *InvertRectangle:* applying the inverting function to an entire rectangular region of a raster. This function can be used to implement selection feedback.

All these operations fit a common pattern: a rectangular region of a *destination raster* is modified, using values extracted from a *source raster*. The value of a pixel in the destination raster can be computed as a function of the current pixel value $d$, the value $s$ of a corresponding pixel in the source raster, and a constant pixel value $c$. We apply a function $g(d, s, c)$ to determine the new value $d$ of each pixel. Different versions of this function can be used to implement the six operations listed above:

1. *WriteRectangle:* $g(d, s, c) = c$. The new destination value is constant throughout the raster.
2. *WriteMask:* $g(d, s, c) = $ (if $s \neq 0$ then $c$ else $d$).
3. *WriteColor:* $g(d, s, c) = $ (if $s \neq transparent$ then $s$ else $d$).
4. *CopyRaster:* $g(d, s, c) = s$.
5. *InvertMask:* $g(d, s, c) = $ (if $s \neq 0$ then $f(d)$ else $d$).
6. *InvertRectangle:* $g(d, s, c) = f(d)$.

Of course an appropriate loop must be written to iterate over all pixels in a rectangular region of the destination raster, applying $g$ and changing destination pixel values accordingly. Note that the frame buffer is like any other raster: operation 4 will copy rectangular regions to and from the frame buffer, depending on whether the frame-buffer raster is the destination or source. It will move images within the frame buffer if both source and destination rasters are located in the frame buffer.

A procedure can be defined that performs all these operations; its design requires careful attention to the order in which destination raster values are altered. If the order is wrong, copying a region of a raster to a new location in the same raster may destroy the image; this will happen if the source and destination regions overlap and if the order of operations alters a destination value *before* it is copied to its new location. The procedure *RasterOp* given in Figure 18-1 shows the proper sequencing. The destination rectangle is specified as a raster *destination*, together with the lower left corner $(x_d, y_d)$ of the destination rectangle and the width $w$ and height $h$ of the rectangle. The source is specified as a raster *source* and lower left corner $(x_s, y_s)$; the width and height are the same as for the destination.

The details of the *RasterOp* procedure can be varied to accommodate additional operations, to make execution more efficient, or to specialize the procedure for particular raster formats. For example, if raster arrays record only 1 bit per pixel, the six operations can be simplified to avoid conditional expressions and to use logical operations instead: the following list assumes *transparent* $= 0$ and $f(d) = 1 - d$; $\oplus$ is the exclusive-OR operation, $\vee$ is inclusive-OR, $\wedge$ is AND, and $\neg$ is NOT:

1. *WriteRectangle:* $g(d, s, c) = c$
2. *WriteMask:* $g(d, s, c) = d \vee s$ (if $c = 1$)
   $g(d, s, c) = d \wedge (\neg s)$ (if $c = 0$)
3. *WriteColor:* $g(d, s, c) = d \vee s$

4. *CopyRaster:* $g(d, s, c) = s$
5. *InvertMask:* $g(d, s, c) = d \oplus s$
6. *InvertRectangle:* $g(d, s, c) = d \oplus 1$

This simplification allows $g$ to be applied to many pixels in parallel using logical operations on entire words extracted from the raster arrays. The parallel operations greatly increase the speed of *RasterOp*.

Another useful enhancement to *RasterOp* is clipping. If either source or destination rectangles extend beyond the limits of their respective raster arrays, the rectangles are clipped so that *RasterOp* covers only coordinates that are legal in both source and destination rasters (Figure 18-2).

```
procedure RasterOp(operation: integer;
          var destination: raster; xd, yd, w, h: integer;
          var source: raster; xs, ys, c: integer);
      var xdir, ydir, i, j: integer;
begin
      xdir := 1; ydir := 1;
      if xs < xd then begin
          xdir := −1; xd := xd + w − 1; xs := xs + w − 1
      end;
      if ys < yd then begin
          ydir := −1; yd := yd + h − 1; ys := ys + h − 1
      end;

      for i := 1 to h do begin
      for j := 1 to w do begin
          case operation of
      1:   SetPixel(destination, xd, yd, c);
      2:   if GetPixel(source, xs, ys) <> 0 then
              SetPixel(destination, xd, yd, c);
      3:   if GetPixel(source, xs, ys) <> transparent then
              SetPixel(destination, xd, yd, GetPixel(source, xs, ys));
      4:   SetPixel(destination, xd, yd, GetPixel(source, xs, ys));
      5:   if GetPixel(source, xs, ys) <> 0 then
              SetPixel(destination, xd, yd, a − GetPixel(destination, xd, yd));
      6:   SetPixel(destination, xd, yd, a − GetPixel(destination, xd, yd))
          end;
          xd := xd + xdir; xs := xs + xdir
      end;
      xd := xd − xdir ∗ w; xs := xs − xdir ∗ w;
      yd := yd + ydir; ys := ys + ydir
      end
end;
```

**Figure 18-1**   The *RasterOp* procedure for operating on rectangular regions of rasters.

*RasterOp* is only a primitive function and must often be called several times to complete a modification to the screen. The scrolling operation illustrated earlier in Figure 17-7 will require two calls, one to copy a portion of the window upward and a second to clear out the bottom strip of the window. Afterwards additional calls to *RasterOp* can be used to generate text or lines in the new bottom strip of the window. These calls might use a clipping facility to prevent modifying portions of the screen outside the window.

A procedure like *RasterOp* plays a central role in an interactive graphics program: it is used not only to change feedback images rapidly but also to alter major portions of the screen. Although the procedure offers no assistance to the scan conversion of arbitrary lines or polygons, it can be applied to the raster representations of these objects that scan conversion produces. Thus the *RasterOp* function offers an opportunity to deal with images in ways that differ dramatically from the geometric approach used to specify random-scan images. Once a raster is generated, it can be manipulated in many different ways without recourse to the data structures or algorithms originally used to generate it.

## 18-3 SYSTEMS USING RASTER REPRESENTATIONS

A simple graphics system can be constructed around a set of operations for manipulating rasters. The rasters can be combined in numerous ways to produce many special effects. Natural images and shades images of 30 objects can be displayed. Images can be merged, used as masks to paint into other rasters, used to erase information, added to other images to produce an overlay effect, and so on. All the functions that make video mixers a powerful composition and special-effect tool for a television broadcaster can be performed as well by manipulating raster descriptions. Unfortunately, arbitrary translation, rotation, and scaling of rasters are generally very difficult operations that require digital filtering [129]. Certain special cases, such as translation by an integral number of pixels, rotation by 180°, and scaling up by an integral factor, are much simpler.

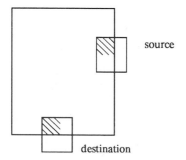

**Figure 18-2** Clipping the source and destination rectangles before copying a raster. The shaded region is legal in both source and destination.

A graphics package based on raster representations will need two kinds of facilities—representations and operations.

**Raster representations.** The system must provide a way to create and name rasters. It should provide a special raster *FrameBuffer* whose contents are displayed on the screen. Defining representations for rasters will require conventions for representing colors, for designating the "transparent" color, and so forth. Different rasters may be represented differently, depending on the kind of image information they contain.

It should be possible to save rasters in a file system and to load them from files. This mechanism can be used to initialize often-used rasters such as masks for characters and brushes.

It is not essential to provide many separate rasters in order to allow combination operations to be performed. Instead we can provide one large raster, only part of which is actually displayed. The application program can build raster images anywhere in this space and identify them by location. To be rendered visible, an image is copied into a region of the *FrameBuffer* raster that is actually being displayed.

**Raster operations.** Primitive operations are included in the system to modify and combine rasters. Functions such as *SetPixel* and *GetPixel* are clearly necessary. Even more helpful is the *RasterOp* function, with a full repertoire of raster combination operations [280, 236, 448]. Additional functions may be implemented to provide scaling and rotation of rasters, although these depend on the use of sampling and filtering techniques.

Designing and building a raster-based graphics package can be an intricate task. The operations on rasters must be efficient enough to make display changes or feedback images appear rapidly. At the same time, raster representations may grow very large, requiring some images to be saved on disks and "paged" into memory when access is required. As a result, the performance of these systems will tend to be very sensitive to the amount of memory available, to the suitability of the computer architecture for implementing raster operations, and to the speed with which the frame buffer can be accessed.

Raster-graphics systems are easily understood and used by application programmers. The raster is a simple, intuitive, natural representation of an image. The direct relationship between pixel values and the visual image makes it clear to the programmer what pixel modifications are required to achieve the desired image. Priority, for example, needs no explanation; the frame buffer displays the image most recently written into it. Composing a raster image using such operations as moving existing parts of the image to new locations or erasing parts of the image is as natural as composing a page by cutting, pasting, and erasing.

## 18-4 SYSTEMS USING GEOMETRIC REPRESENTATIONS

The main disadvantage of using geometric descriptions is the need to perform scan conversion. This process, if performed by software, will tend to slow down the generation of images. A major concern in designing systems of this kind is therefore to select algorithms and data structures that permit rapid scan conversion.

### Line-Based Raster Systems

One of the properties of the raster display is its ability to imitate a point-plotting display in many respects. Section 15-4 has discussed this property and has shown how a conventional graphics package can be modified to drive a frame buffer display.

This limited form of raster graphics system uses only a simple kind of scan conversion, the DDA algorithm, and can therefore achieve relatively good performance. The raster display behaves in many respects like a storage-tube terminal, for each dot generated is stored in the display's memory. As with a direct-view storage tube, we can represent the displayed image as a number of separate segments. Segment deletion can be achieved by blanking the screen and redrawing the posted segments, or by retracing the segment to be deleted, switching each pixel to the background color.

A line-based raster-graphics system can offer several useful capabilities, such as the ability to display high-quality text using raster copying and the option of colored lines and text. Its functional similarity to the systems described in Chapters 6 to 10 makes it easy to implement and allows applications written for line-drawing displays to be used with a raster display. We must recognize, however, that this approach to raster-graphics systems fails to take full advantage of the capabilities of the raster display.

### Solid-Area Raster Systems

A graphics package based on segmented display files can be extended to allow solid areas to be represented and displayed along with normal lines and text. Three kinds of extensions will be required: functions for specifying the geometry of the *outline* of the area, mechanisms to specify the *priority* of an area with respect to others, and a function that gives the *shading rule* for each area. With these three extensions, we can construct a system that manipulates lines, text, and solid shaded polygons.

Because the outline of a polygon is a series of connected line segments, it is natural to extend the *MoveTo* and *LineTo* functions to specify outlines. We require two additional functions, *BeginOutline*, which is called to indicate the start of a sequence of primitives defining an outline, and *EndOutline*, called to indicate the end of the outline. Using these functions, a solid triangle might be specified by:

*BeginOutline;*
    *MoveTo*(0, 0);
    *LineTo*(100, 0);
    *LineTo*(50, 50);
    *LineTo*(0, 0);
*EndOutline;*

These functions add to the currently-open display-file segment a suitable description of the polygon, just as a normal *LineTo* adds a description of a line. The last *LineTo* in this example could be made optional by requiring *EndOutline* to close the outline.

If areas are to be shaded with constant color, a shading rule can be given by a single function, *Intensity(value)*, which sets the intensity of a polygon. The call defines the intensity to be used for all objects subsequently added to the display file; further calls can of course change the intensity.

Extensions to handle priority are perhaps the hardest to devise. In principle, the priority of every object in every segment could be specified separately. A simpler approach often suffices:

1. If two or more objects are described in the same segment, an object added to the segment later has higher priority.
2. If two objects are described in different segments, the object from the segment with the larger segment name (as defined in the call to *OpenSegment*) has higher priority.

Since segment names are used to specify priorities, it must be possible to change the name of a segment in order to redefine priorities or to allow a new segment of intermediate priority to be generated. To meet these needs a function *RenameSegment(oldName, newName)* is provided to rename the segment *oldName* to have name *newName*.

A conventional graphic package thus requires only four new functions, *BeginOutline, EndOutline, Intensity,* and *RenameSegment,* to permit the application programmer to define solid-area objects.

## Internal Design of a Solid-Area Graphics System

Although only a few new functions are required to extend a graphics package to deal with solid areas, many changes result in the implementation of the package. Priority detection and scan conversion of polygons must be provided, using techniques like those illustrated in Chapter 16. These calculations are not simple and may make screen updating unacceptably slow unless work-saving techniques are used:

1. The *Update* function, described in Chapter 8, helps to reduce the number of screen updates to the minimum necessary to allow the user to see the results of each interaction.

2.  Incremental techniques are extremely helpful. Generally only a portion of the screen must be updated, namely the portion in which material has been added, deleted, or changed in priority. The area requiring updating can be identified by a *bounding box* that includes the bounding boxes of all objects (or segments) changed since the last update.
3.  The screen-updating algorithms can be streamlined to avoid much of the scan-conversion work each time the screen is updated. For example, if an object is deleted, no changes occur to the masks of the remaining objects: only priority decisions need be recomputed. We can therefore keep in the display file a representation of the mask of each object, built by a scan-conversion algorithm from data passed by *BeginOutline, MoveTo, LineTo,* and *EndOutline* calls. Then the screen-updating operation need only make priority decisions.

The first of these three points suggests that we incorporate a display file, serving the same purpose as in a storage-tube graphics package, i.e., allowing previously defined segments to be regenerated when other segments are deleted. With the storage tube this regeneration is required because it provides the only mechanism for selective erasure. With a raster display we can erase on a pixel-by-pixel basis, but we still need the ability to regenerate segments that may have been partially or wholly obscured by the deleted segment.

The choice of scan-conversion algorithm and display-file format are central to the design of the package as a whole. The requirements for the display file are somewhat different compared with those of a line-drawing display file, not just because solid objects must be represented but because it is advantageous to represent these objects in a scan-converted form for the reason given in point 3 above. In simple terms, we can either use a geometric display-file representation, applying the scan-conversion process in the *Update* function (Figure 18-3a), or we can apply scan conversion before adding information to the display file in scan-converted form (Figure 18-3b). Obviously the second approach requires less frequent scan conversion since we usually apply *Update* many times to each segment stored in the display file. On the other hand scan-converted information tends to be bulky; furthermore we must store it in the display file in such a way that we can distinguish the segments from each other.

One solution to these conflicting requirements is to split the scan-conversion process into two parts, applying part of the process before constructing the display file and part of it after, during *Update*. We attempt to include as many as possible of the time-consuming components of scan conversion in the first stage, in this way permitting the second stage to be performed very quickly. Thus the choice of how to split the process is a matter of selecting a sequence of execution of the following four processes and breaking the sequence into two suitable parts:

*Process C.* Calculating the intersections of each edge with the scan lines it crosses, and building a list of $(x, y)$ intersections
*Process Y.* Sorting the intersections by $y$ value

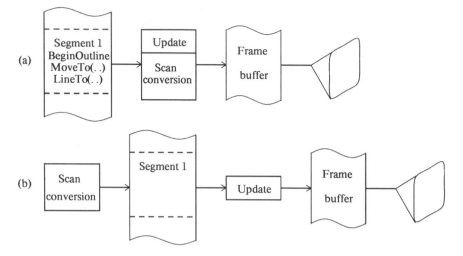

**Figure 18-3** Two approaches to solid-area graphics systems: (a) a segmented display file contains geometric information; (b) a segmented display file contains information in scan-converted form.

*Process X.* Sorting the intersections by *x* value
*Process P.* Sorting by priority and excluding parts of the picture obscured by higher-priority parts

The Y-(PX) algorithm described in Chapter 16 offers a particularly straightforward means of splitting the process. Before the *Update* process the edges are sorted by maximum *y* value, a step which performs part of Process Y. During the *Update* operation the image is scan-converted, one scan line at a time, by computing intersection points (Process C), sorting them by *x* coordinate (Process X), and determining priority (Process P).

If the image being generated contains polygons with a large number of short edges, the Y-(PX) algorithm will require large amounts of memory for the edge data structure. Such images are not uncommon if polygons have been used to model character shapes or to approximate curved objects by polygonal outlines. In these cases, it is sensible to compute intersections (Process C) before *Update* and to store intersections in the display file [450]. This leaves only Processes X and P to be performed during *Update*. We therefore define each edge, not by the *x, dx,* and *dy* values given in Chapter 16 but by a list of coordinate values representing points along the edge. These values can be defined relative to the starting point of the edge, permitting the segment containing the edge to be repositioned without recomputing the intersections.

Representation of edges by lists of intersection coordinates can be bulky; a compact representation can be achieved by *chain encoding* [188]. In this encoding technique, the edge is represented as a series of steps from one

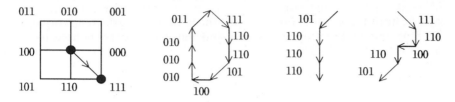

**Figure 18-4** Chain encoding the outline of a figure. A three-bit code records the direction of unit increments in the *x* and *y* directions.

intersection point to the next, where adjacent intersection points are on neighboring raster positions. Thus each step must be one of only eight possible steps to neighboring raster positions and can be represented by a 3-bit *chain code* (Figure 18-4). Still more compact chain encoding techniques can be achieved by taking advantage of the *monotonic* nature of edges (see Exercise 18-8).

The use of a chain-encoded edge representation leads to a display-file format of the kind shown in Figure 18-5, a variant of the data structure for the Y-X algorithm illustrated in Figure 16-9. Edges are sorted by maximum *y* value into *y* buckets; in addition the edges representing objects in each display-file segment are linked together by pointers. When a fresh segment is added to the display file, its edges are chain-encoded, linked together, sorted by maximum *y* value, and entered into the appropriate *y* buckets. The remainder of the scan-conversion process, performed during *Update,* is similar to the Y-(PX) algorithm, except that intersections are determined by the chain encodings rather than by incremental line equations.

This approach to scan conversion offers several advantages. Relatively little computation is required during *Update* because intersection points are precomputed, and the sorting of these points by *x* value can be performed very quickly, using a bubble sort that takes advantage of coherence from one scan line to the next. Incremental updates, covering part of the screen, can be performed by limiting the range of the process in *x* and *y*. In all cases the image is updated from top to bottom, generating a pleasing interactive effect.

## 18-5 CONCLUSION

Our discussion of raster-graphics systems has offered neither a prescription for a general-purpose design nor a detailed description of implementation issues. Experience with raster-graphics systems is simply too limited to justify offering an authoritative design. The brief exploration of some approaches can serve as a starting point for specific designs and for innovations that will deepen our understanding of the design of these systems. Above all, we must not abandon the objectives of any good graphics system, outlined in Chapter 6:

*Simplicity, consistency, completeness.* The tempting ambition to provide a bag of tricks for generating raster images should be avoided in favor of a few simple, flexible concepts. For example, the notion of a *raster* helps organize all functions of the graphics system and make it understandable to the programmer.

*Performance, economy.* Because raster-graphics systems manipulate large raster representations, application programmers will be especially concerned with performance. It may be preferable to offer low-level functions with consistently good performance rather than high-level functions that can do nothing quickly.

Even with a carefully designed software system, the speed of interaction provided by an application program may be unacceptably slow simply because the computer cannot make changes to the frame buffer fast enough. Some applications, such as real-time animation, require enormous amounts of computing to generate raster images. The next chapter describes how special hardware can be applied to the task of generating raste rimages more quickly.

## EXERCISES

**18-1**  Work out the details of implementation of *RasterOp* on a 16-bit machine with a frame buffer that records 1 bit per pixel but accesses 16 pixels at a time in a 16-bit word. How must the control structure of the subroutine be altered? What features do you find necessary that are missing from many high-level languages? From computer instruction sets? From ways to access frame buffers?

**18-2**  *RasterOp* is specified assuming that *masks* are binary arrays. Chapters 15 and 16 point out that a mask should allow other fractional values as well, in order to record correctly the area that falls over a pixel near the edge of the object. What changes to *RasterOp* can you suggest to accommodate such fractional masks?

**18-3**  Explore generalizations of the role of *c* in the *RasterOp* procedure. If *c* varies with position, we can represent repeating texture patterns such as stripes or half-tones. That is, *c* could itself be extracted from a raster array. Is such a facility useful? Instead of storing such rasters in huge arrays, it might be better to represent them as *procedures* that calculate pixel values from coordinates. Design such a scheme. Does it have other uses in raster-graphics systems?

**18-4**  Devise an algorithm for clipping rectangular regions of rasters against the legal limits of the raster. What information should be kept in the data structure for describing rasters that will speed this computation?

**18-5**  Explain how to design a video mixer that performs the *RasterOp* functions dynamically, perhaps without ever storing results back into a buffer. Is it practical? Are there any worthwhile special cases?

**18-6**  What conventions can you devise so that the *BeginOutline, MoveTo, LineTo,* and *EndOutline* functions can be used to describe polygons with holes in them?

**18-7**  Work out the details for updating incrementally a display that includes solid objects specified in a segmented display file. How do your methods impact the design of the display file?

**18-8**  A display-file representation of polygon masks can be encoded in several ways. Edges can be represented with incremental equations, as in the Y-X algorithm. Run coding is another choice: for each scan line $y$, we record $(x_l, \delta)$, the left edge of the polygon and a *run length*. Another choice, chain coding, records the change in the $x$ position of a polygon boundary from one scan line to the next. The fact that all edges progress monotonically downward in $y$ can reduce the number of bits used to encode chains. Design display-file formats based on these encodings. Discuss their advantages and disadvantages. How should a system designer choose among them?

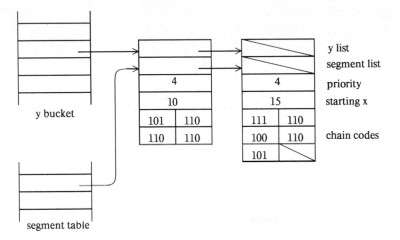

y list

segment list

priority

starting x

chain codes

y bucket

segment table

**Figure 18-5** A data structure for chain-encoded edges in a segmented display file. Edges of all solid areas in a segment are linked together. Edges are sorted by maximum *y* value into the *y* bucket table for use by the *Update* function.

**18-9** Discuss how the data structure illustrated in Figure 18-5 should be changed to simplify repositioning a segment, i.e., translating all information in it by $(\Delta x, \Delta y)$. What changes are needed to delete segments easily?

**18-10** Often a raster image is so large that it cannot fit entirely in memory; such is the case for images destined for raster hard-copy printers. How can a graphics system be designed to generate these images? How does your answer depend on the application?

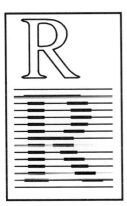

# 19

# RASTER DISPLAY

# HARDWARE

Interest in raster displays can be traced back to the mid-1960s, when the random-scan refresh CRT was the universal graphic-display device. It had two serious shortcomings: it flickered badly when displaying complex pictures, and it could not produce realistic images of solid objects. The raster display promised to solve both problems, since it had a large capacity limited only by screen resolution and could generate video images of extreme realism.

In modern raster displays we can see this promise fulfilled: these displays are used in a number of simulation and design applications where the realism of the displayed images is crucial to the applications' success. TV-based graphic displays are quite inexpensive, and can supply the needs of a very wide range of applications. Nevertheless the raster display is not without its own set of limitations. In particular the frame-buffer display is not as well suited as the refresh line-drawing display to dynamic interactive graphics, and it generally has rather low resolution. Many of the techniques described in Chapters 15 through 18 have been developed to cope with such limitations. The designers of display hardware have likewise been at work to try to improve the performance of raster displays. This chapter discusses some approaches to the design of raster displays.

## 19-1 RASTER DISPLAY DEVICES

We often discuss raster graphics as if it concerned only a single kind of display device. In fact there are a considerable number of such devices, as we have seen in Chapter 3. These devices form two distinct classes:

1. *Video devices.* These devices, of which the TV monitor is the most common, do not have any inherent image-storage capability. The displayed image must therefore be passed repeatedly to the device, at a high enough refresh rate to prevent flicker. The image is therefore passed as a *video signal,* a continuously fluctuating voltage that specifies the intensity variation along each scan line of the display. Color video devices can be fed with three separate video signals, one for each of the primary colors, or with a single signal in which the three color components are encoded together.

2. *Matrix-addressed storage devices.* The plasma panel is the best known of these devices. The screen is divided up into a matrix of cells, each one of which can be individually turned on or off to produce the desired image. Once turned on, the cell remains lit until turned off. Cells are addressed by row and column.

These two classes of display are similar in the sense that they use a rectangular array of pixels to generate images. Most of the raster techniques described in the preceding chapters can therefore be applied equally well to either class of display. The main difference between the two kinds of display lies in the absence of image storage in video displays and its presence in matrix displays like the plasma panel. Displays of the latter variety, since they possess inherent memory, require only a simple controller that turns cells on or off in response to signals from the computer. Video displays require an external memory and a controller capable of converting the contents of the memory into a video signal. Many different designs have been proposed for video-display controllers and memories; several of these designs are described in this chapter.

Before proceeding to discuss video-display hardware, we should perhaps pause to consider why so much effort has been put into the design of this hardware when a simpler alternative exists in the form of matrix devices with inherent memory. The problem is that these devices have not reached as advanced a level of development as the raster-scan CRT. Areas of particular weakness are:

*Resolution.* Most inherent-memory display devices are limited to a resolution of 60 lines per inch or less, whereas a CRT display can achieve double this resolution.

*Color and intensity.* Few devices can offer the range of color and intensity available on a CRT.

*Writing speed.* The cells of the plasma panel take several microseconds to fire, and a complete image may therefore take a second or more to display; on a CRT the entire image can be changed 30 or more times a second.

*Interactive properties.* The memory inherent in these devices is not as flexible as a frame buffer, and this limits the degree of interaction that can be achieved.

The last of these four points is perhaps the least obvious. The difficulties we have in using the plasma panel interactively are due in part to our inability to determine the contents of its inherent memory. Many interactive operations involve saving the state of part of the image so that it can be restored later; an example is the cursor-repositioning operation shown in Figure 17-10. The *RasterOp* function that we have found so useful in interactive raster graphics also involves determining the contents of the raster memory. These techniques can be applied to a plasma panel only if a copy of the contents of the panel is kept in a separate memory accessible to the computer. The need for special algorithms and extra memory detracts from the convenience and simplicity of the inherent-memory matrix display.

## 19-2 FRAME BUFFERS

Most raster-scan displays use video display devices based on the use of a large digital memory, or *frame buffer,* to store the displayed image. Many different kinds of memory have been used in frame buffers: drums, disks, integrated-circuit shift registers, and core stores. The number of bits assigned to each pixel may be as few as 1 or as many as 24. Nowadays most frame buffers are constructed from random-access integrated-circuit memories, with between 1 and 8 bits assigned to each pixel. The following sections discuss some of the earlier approaches to frame-buffer construction and show why random-access memories have become popular.

### Rotating-Memory Frame Buffers

The earliest frame buffers made use of disks and drums for image storage. The rotational frequency of these devices can be made to coincide with the frequency generally chosen for TV refresh. It is therefore possible to read intensity values from the drum or disk, convert them into analog voltage values, and thus construct a video signal. Each track of the memory device provides a single stream of bits; therefore one bit of memory represents each pixel. For more intensity precision several tracks must be used in parallel. Figure 19-1 shows the use of four tracks in parallel to provide a frame buffer with 16 different intensity levels.

Frame buffers of this type were used in the late 1960s to drive clusters of displays; in this way the relatively high cost of the rotating memory could be spread among a number of terminals. In The RAND Corporation's video graphics system [485] intensity values were stored on the disk in analog form. By the early 1970s the cost of integrated-circuit shift registers had dropped to a

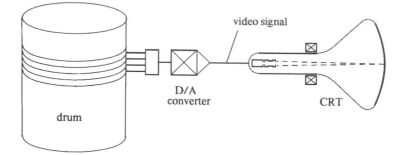

**Figure 19-1** A rotating-memory frame buffer in which 4 tracks are read in parallel to provide 16 different intensity levels.

point where it became cost effective to employ them in frame buffers, and rotating memories lost favor as interactive frame buffers.

### Shift-Register Frame Buffers

To generate a video signal from a digital memory we must read the contents of the memory at a constant high frequency. A fresh intensity value is required each time the CRT's electron beam moves to a new pixel; on a standard TV monitor this occurs every 90 nanoseconds, and on a high-resolution display the time drops to 25 nanoseconds or less. The rotating memories described in the previous section had considerable trouble producing streams of bits at such speeds, and those that could do so were quite expensive. Integrated circuits are better able to achieve the high memory bandwidths needed.

The *shift register* is a particularly appropriate circuit for use in a frame buffer: every time a pulse is applied to the shift register, its contents are shifted by one place, displacing one bit from one end of the register and allowing one bit to be added at the other end. As each bit emerges from the shift register, it can be used as an intensity value and then inserted into the other end of the register to keep the contents circulating. Several shift registers in parallel can be used where more than one bit of intensity per pixel is required.

In contrast to rotating memories, the shift register's contents need not be circulated at high speed. We construct the frame buffer out of a number of shift registers, each one representing one column of pixels on the TV screen. Thus if the screen image has 256 scan lines each of 340 pixels, we use 340 shift registers of 256 bits each. Each shift register is shifted once per horizontal scan and contributes one bit to the scan line. The registers are shifted in a carefully staggered sequence so that they produce bits of data at the exact moment they are needed to contribute to the video signal.

The use of circulating memories, such as disks, drums, and shift registers, poses a serious *latency* problem. In order to use the frame buffer in interactive applications we must be able to change its contents rapidly. Unfortunately any given spot on the screen can be changed only when the frame-buffer memory has circulated to a position where the appropriate bit in the memory is accessible; this happens once per revolution of a disk or once per cycle through a shift register's contents. Thus we must wait an average of 1/50 or 1/60 of a second to change each spot on the screen. At this rate even minor changes can take several seconds.

## 19-3 THE RANDOM-ACCESS FRAME BUFFER

The modern frame buffer uses random-access integrated memory circuits. Each pixel's intensity is represented by 1, 2, 4, 8 or more bits of memory; one bit is sufficient for text and simple graphics and leads to a relatively inexpensive display; 2 and 4 bits are useful in applications that require the display of solid areas of gray or color; and 8 or more bits are needed for high-quality shaded pictures.

Several different methods can be used to encode colored pictures for storage in a frame buffer. The simplest method is to define the color components of each pixel. The bits representing the pixel can be divided into three groups of bits, each indicating the intensity of one of the three primary color components. In an 8-bit byte, 3 bits are normally allocated to red, 3 to green, and 2 to blue. The three components are then fed to the three guns of the color TV monitor. This arrangment is shown in Figure 19-2.

### Color Mapping

The simple color-component encoding scheme has the disadvantage of limiting the range of colors. A more flexible scheme involves the use of a *color map*. The values stored in the frame buffer are treated as addresses into a table of colors defined by their red, green and blue, components. Thus an 8-bit-per-point frame buffer could address a 256-color table. Each of the color

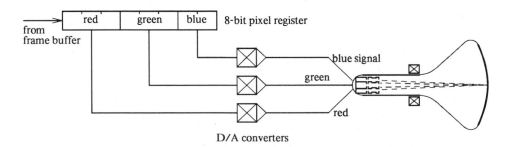

Figure 19-2 Decoding color values stored in a frame buffer.

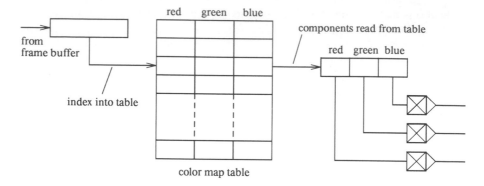

**Figure 19-3** Frame buffer pixel values used to index a color map.

components can be defined to high precision, thus providing very accurate control over the colors displayed. Figure 19-3 shows the organization of the color map.

For maximum utility, the color map should use read-write memory. It is then possible to assign a different set of colors to different application programs and to mix a set of colors interactively for painting purposes. A read-only color map, although simpler in construction, is far less flexible.

### Multiple-Plane Frame Buffers

The provision of multiple bits per pixel is not only useful in representing intensity and color but allows the frame buffer to be treated as several *planes,* each containing a separate image. Division into planes can be made in several different ways; for example, an 8-bit-per-pixel frame buffer can represent a single image to 8 bits of intensity precision, two images to 4 bits of precision, four images to 2 bits of precision, or eight separate black-and-white images. Other assignments of the bits can also be made, such as 4-2-2.

By dividing the frame buffer into planes we can apply a variety of different kinds of *video mixing.* One plane can be used to show a static picture and another to show a symbol or picture part that the user wishes to drag around the screen. In animation systems, several moving objects can be displayed as separate planes. A one-bit plane can be used as a mask to select certain regions of another plane for display.

To cater to such applications, a multiple-plane frame buffer should provide the following capabilities:

1. Each plane should be provided with a pair of registers to indicate the coordinate position of the plane relative to the screen coordinate system;
2. It should be possible to define planes of less than full screen size in order to economize on memory use;

3.  A full range of logical functions should be provided for concatenating the contents of the planes. Thus it should be possible to inclusive-OR two planes together to combine their images, or to apply a logical AND to perform masking.

The use of planes of less than full screen size is a convenient way of providing a cursor that follows the movement of a graphical input device. If a separate plane cannot be assigned to the cursor, special cursor display hardware may be needed in its place.

### Strengths and Weaknesses of the Frame Buffer

The frame buffer is one of the most versatile display devices. Given 8 or more bits of intensity precision, it can produce color and monochrome images whose quality and complexity are limited only by the performance of the TV monitor on which they are displayed. For applications that involve shading, solid areas of color, high-quality text, or any type of image processing the frame buffer offers the only satisfactory form of display.

The frame buffer is not without its problems, however. It does not offer the most compact way of representing an image; the large amounts of memory it uses make it expensive, and the time taken to fill this memory or change its contents makes interactive response sluggish at times.

Several solutions have been proposed to the high memory utilization of the frame buffer and to the slow speed of update. The most popular of these solutions, real-time scan conversion, is discussed in the next section. Other solutions based on compact image-encoding techniques are discussed at the end of this chapter.

### 19-4  REAL-TIME SCAN CONVERSION

The inefficiency of the frame buffer becomes most noticeable when we use it to display simple line drawings. Consider, for example, the cube shown in Figure 19-4. This is a very simple image, yet storing it in a frame buffer consumes considerable quantities of time and memory. Time is consumed in scan-converting the lines and in making the necessary memory accesses to modify the frame buffer's contents. Memory consumption is high because the frame buffer's design makes no attempt to capitalize on the simple geometry of the image. The inefficiency of the frame buffer is in striking contrast to the efficiency of the refresh line-drawing display, in whose display file this image can be stored in about 1% of the time using about 0.2% of the memory space.

Real-time scan conversion offers us the opportunity to achieve the efficiency of the line-drawing display while continuing to use a raster TV monitor as the output device. Images are stored not as arrays of intensity values but as geometric descriptions in a display file, and the entire display file is

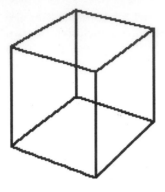

**Figure 19-4**   Raster-scan image of a cube.

scanned one or more times per refresh cycle to generate a video signal. Modifications to the geometry of the image are easily incorporated in the display file and are instantly visible on the display; hence the use of the term *real-time* scan conversion.

There has been considerable interest in real-time scan conversion since the early 1970s, but very few successful systems have been constructed. The difficulty lies in building hardware capable of performing the scan-conversion process fast enough to keep up with the refresh of the TV monitor. The most spectacular successes have been in the construction of real-time simulators for training aircraft pilots and ships' captains: these are huge hardware systems capable of scan converting complex three-dimensional scenes at a rate of 30 or more frames per second. Simpler scan-conversion processors have been built to display line drawings; the construction of such a processor is an interesting exercise in high-speed digital-hardware design.

## Scan Conversion of Line Segments

The problem of scan conversion in real time can be reduced to the task of determining, for a given scan line, whether any line segment in the display file crosses the scan line and if so at what precise point. In the general case we must assume that any of the line segments may cross the scan line; therefore before displaying each scan line we must test every line segment in the display file for intersection with the scan line. If intersection is detected, it is easy to determine the intersection point and to display a dot at that point on the scan line.

This is obviously a wasteful process, since each scan line crosses only a few of the line segments in the display file. We can greatly increase the capacity of the hardware by maintaining a list of *active* line segments that lie in the vicinity of the current scan line (see Figure 19-5). Although additional hardware is required to maintain this list, the performance requirements for intersection testing are considerably less.

The process of testing for intersections must nevertheless be performed rapidly enough to keep up with the refresh process. In other words, we must

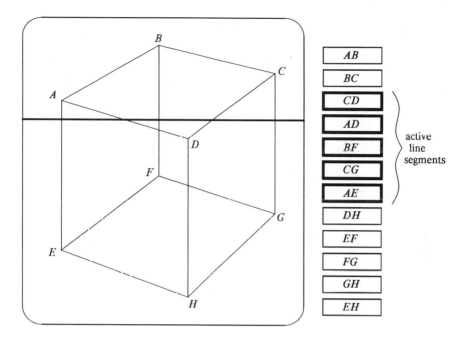

**Figure 19-5** A cube image constructed from line segments, showing a scan line and the active line segments it intersects.

scan the entire list of active line segments in the amount of time it takes to display a single scan line. On a 525-line TV refreshed at 30 hertz the horizontal scan period is 64 microseconds. Clearly the active list must either be very short or be stored in very fast memory. Even if there are only 256 active line segments, we must be able to read them from the display file at a rate of one vector every 250 nanoseconds. High-speed digital memories can offer considerably higher bandwidths than this, but it is difficult to make effective use of them because of the amount of processing that must be applied to each vector.

As each vector is read from the active list, the $y$ coordinates of its endpoints are checked to see whether the vector crosses the current scan line. If it does, the point of intersection must be computed. We first determine the slope $s$ of the vector and then compute the $x$ coordinate of the point of intersection:

$$x = x_0 + (y_{sl} - y_0)/s \tag{19-1}$$

where $(x_0, y_0)$ is the line endpoint from which the slope $s$ is measured and $y_{sl}$ is the $y$ coordinate of the current scan line (Figure 19-6). Derivation of the slope $s$ involves a division, and another division is involved in computing $x$; both divisions can be avoided, at the cost of a single multiplication, if the reciprocal

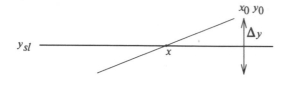

**Figure 19-6** Determining the point of intersection of a vector with the current scan line.

of the slope is stored in the display file, as shown in Figure 19-7. Note that the slope reciprocal is a signed double-precision fraction.

Equation 19-1 yields an $x$-coordinate value that determines which bit on the scan line should be turned on. The scan converter employs two *scan-line buffers,* each large enough to represent a full scan line's set of pixels. As one scan-line buffer is being filled, the other's contents are being converted into a video signal. At the end of every scan line the two buffers switch roles.

Although this form of scan converter correctly handles lines at more than 45° to the horizontal, other lines are incorrectly drawn because the process generates only one dot on each scan line for any given vector. Lines that are nearly horizontal must be represented by several dots on each scan line. To determine how many dots to insert in the scan-line buffer we compute the intersection point for *two* consecutive scan lines and fill in enough dots to connect the two intersection values.

### Maintaining the Active List

In the simplest form of real-time scan converter, no separate active list is maintained. Instead the entire display file is processed during every scan line. This severely limits the size of the display file: pictures containing more than about 500 vectors cannot be displayed.

The construction of an active list requires sorting the display file. A list of $y$-buckets can be maintained, as in the Y-X scan conversion method described on page 240. This requires a relatively complex display file structure; a simpler one is generated if we sort by the maximum $y$ coordinate of each line segment, as shown in Figure 19-8. We can then quickly eliminate from the active list all lines lying below the current scan line; only lines that extend above the scan line need be tested.

As the scan-conversion process moves down the screen, more and more line segments are added to the active list. We need a way of eliminating lines that lie entirely *above* the current scan line. This we can do by means of two pointers into the display file, one indicating where to start reading line segments

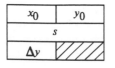

**Figure 19-7** Display file storage of vector parameters.

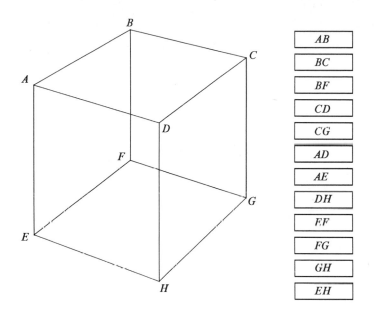

**Figure 19-8** Line segments sorted by maximum $y$ coordinate

and the other where to stop; these two pointers define the start and finish of the active list. Initially the start pointer is set to the beginning of the display file and the finish pointer to the first line segment that does not intersect the topmost scan line. Each pointer can be advanced at the end of every scan line: the finish pointer is advanced to include additional line segments that begin on the next scan line, while the start pointer is advanced to exclude all line segments that lie above the scan line. The start pointer is repositioned only if the scan-conversion process detects that one or more of the initial line segments tested lie entirely above the scan line; in such a case, the start pointer is reset to the first intersecting line segment. Figure 19-9 shows several steps in the scan-conversion process.

Techniques like the use of start and finish pointers enable more complex pictures to be scan-converted, but they do not guarantee that the scan converter will be able to process line segments fast enough under all conditions. If picture complexity is allowed to increase beyond certain limits, the scan-conversion process will begin to lag behind the refresh process, creating anomalies in the displayed image. The effect is in some ways more objectionable than the flicker that besets refresh line-drawing displays under similar circumstances, for the breakup of the image during scan conversion happens suddenly and actually destroys part of the image. It is therefore essential to take steps, using software if necessary, to prevent the displayed image from becoming too complex.

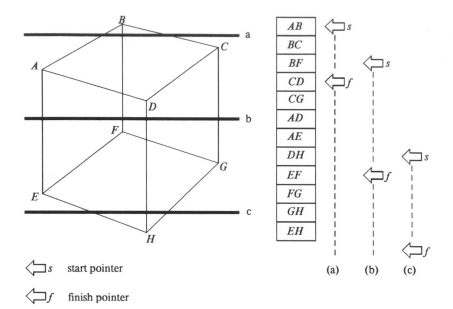

s    start pointer

f    finish pointer

(a)    (b)    (c)

**Figure 19-9** Use of start and finish pointers to shorten the active list; the positions of the pointers are shown for three scan lines.

### Real-Time Scan Conversion of Polygons

It is possible to make a minor extension to the real-time scan converter that permits it to display solid shaded polygons. Each line segment in the display file includes a color specification, indicating the color to be shown to the *right* of the segment. When the scan-line buffer's contents are generated, this color is applied to all pixels from the point of intersection up to the next line-segment intersection (or the right-hand end of the scan line). Figure 19-10b shows a simple display file defining the picture shown in Figure 19-10a.

To generate the display file of Figure 19-10b, all priority decisions must be made before the display file is constructed. This limits the speed at which picture changes can be made. To solve this problem, elaborate real-time scan converters have been constructed, in which a full Y-(PX) algorithm is implemented in hardware. These devices are used in simulators for training aircraft and ship pilots. Part Five will describe some of the three-dimensional image-generation techniques used in these devices.

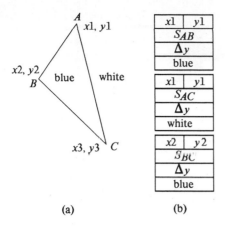

| x1 | y1 |
|---|---|
| $S_{AB}$ | |
| $\Delta y$ | |
| blue | |

| x1 | y1 |
|---|---|
| $S_{AC}$ | |
| $\Delta y$ | |
| white | |

| x2 | y2 |
|---|---|
| $S_{BC}$ | |
| $\Delta y$ | |
| blue | |

(a)          (b)

**Figure 19-10** Display file representation of a solid shaded polygon.

## 19-5 OTHER ENCODING SCHEMES

In terms of encoding and updating efficiency, the real-time scan converter lies at the opposite end of the spectrum from the frame buffer. In between the two lie a number of other schemes that achieve better storage efficiency than the frame buffer and that are easier to implement than real-time scan conversion. Two such schemes are mentioned here briefly.

### Run-Length Encoding

Run-length encoding is a technique for more compact storage of images involving solid areas of gray tone or color. An example of such an image is shown in Figure 19-11a. If we examine a typical scan line from this image, we notice that many consecutive pixels have the same intensity (Figure 19-11b). Instead of storing each intensity value separately we can store the length and intensity of each run of identical pixels. Thus the scan line shown in Figure 19-11a can be run-length-encoded as shown in Figure 19-11b. Each encoded scan-line consists of one or more instructions, each instruction defining a run length and intensity value.

The use of run-length encoding can offer considerable savings in the amount of memory needed to store certain kinds of images. For images like Figure 19-11a the memory requirements can be as little as 1% of the requirements for a frame buffer. The hardware to read the run-length-encoded information, decode it, and generate a video signal is relatively simple; Laws [279] has described a processor capable of generating high-quality gray scale images from run-length-encoded descriptions.

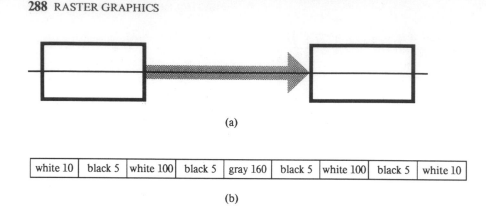

(a)

| white 10 | black 5 | white 100 | black 5 | gray 160 | black 5 | white 100 | black 5 | white 10 |

(b)

**Figure 19-11** Run-length encoding. The scan line indicated in (a) is shown encoded in (b).

### Cell-Organized Raster Displays

It is common knowledge that simple pictures can be drawn on alphanumeric displays using horizontal and vertical bars and other suitable characters from the alphanumeric repertoire. Some text displays include special characters that extend their ability to construct simple images. Jordan and Barrett [249, 30] have investigated ways of extending this approach to permit a general class of line drawings to be displayed by means of a special character set. They have proposed the term *cell-organized display* to describe hardware that operates on this principle.

The cell-organized display constructs images out of strings of square characters, each one either blank or containing one or more short line segments. The character size chosen by Jordan and Barrett was 8 × 8 pixels. Of course a very large repertoire of characters would be required to display line drawings in this way; Jordan and Barrett used masking, concatenation, and mirror imaging of characters to reduce the number of different characters required and were able to design a set of 104 characters that would handle a full range of line drawings.

### The Limitations of Encoding Techniques

Neither run-length encoding nor the use of character cells is a satisfactory approach to the construction of an interactive display. Both approaches make modification of the displayed image difficult. In run-length-encoded images the sequence of run-length codes must be rearranged every time a scan line is modified, and the need for instruction sequences of variable length puts a heavy load on the free-storage system that provides blocks of memory to store the sequences. The cell-organized display has a very similar problem, although Jordan and Barrett included a jump code in addition to the normal character codes to make modification easier.

In addition to problems of an interactive nature, these displays suffer from the same problem of complexity limitation as the real-time scan converter. Both the run-length-encoded display and cell-organized display have performance limits beyond which they begin to create distorted images. Only the frame buffer provides a display capability without complexity limits.

## EXERCISES

**19-1** Discuss the capabilities of the video devices described in this chapter to generate an interlaced video signal.

**19-2** Make a list of all the boolean functions that can be applied to the bits in two planes of a frame buffer and describe the effect of applying each function. Which functions do you think would be most useful?

**19-3** How could an 8-bit-per-point frame buffer and a read-write color map be used to generate simple animated sequences without changing the frame buffer contents?

**19-4** Discuss the problems involved in using a segmented display file with real-time scan-conversion hardware. Suggest modifications to the scheme described in this chapter that would help solve these problems.

**19-5** How would you design a real-time scan converter that could display both straight-line segments and arcs of circles?

**19-6** Describe in detail the visual effects caused by excessive picture complexity in (a) a real-time scan converter, (b) a run-length encoded display, (c) a cell-organized display. Devise algorithms to detect excessive complexity for use when constructing the display file.

**19-7** The real-time scan converter must perform a multiplication in determining each intersection point. Design an incremental scheme in which this multiplication step is eliminated.

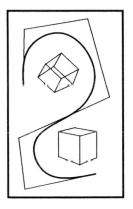

# PART FIVE

## THREE-DIMENSIONAL

## GRAPHICS

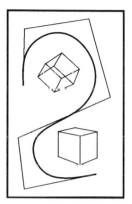

# 20

# REALISM IN

# THREE-DIMENSIONAL

# GRAPHICS

Many computer graphics applications involve the display of three-dimensional objects and scenes. For example, computer-aided design systems allow their users to manipulate models of machined components, automobile bodies and aircraft parts; simulation systems present a continuously moving picture of a three-dimensional world to the pilot of a ship or aircraft. These applications differ from two-dimensional applications not only in the added dimension: they also require concern for *realism* in the display of objects. In applications like simulation, a high degree of realism may be essential to the program's success.

Producing a realistic image of a three-dimensional scene on a two-dimensional display presents many problems. How is depth, the third dimension, to be displayed on the screen? How are parts of objects that are hidden by other objects to be identified and removed from the image? How can lighting, color, shadows, and texture contribute to the rendering? Indeed, how is the three-dimensional world to be modeled in a computer so that images can be generated? A growing number of techniques have been developed to address these questions; the following six chapters describe many of them.

The need for modeling and image-generation techniques stems from requirements imposed by applications. To communicate information to a user, the application program generates an image, which must show the information clearly, without ambiguity, and with as little extraneous information as possible.

The range of imaging requirements is illustrated by the following list of applications:

1. *Molecular modeling.* Chemists wish to build three-dimensional models of molecules in order to understand better their behavior. These models are usually obtained indirectly, by observing the three-dimensional electron density in a crystal and then inferring where atoms of the molecule must lie. The model is built interactively by adding atoms one at a time, orienting bonds according to the electron-density information. Realism is not an important objective in generating images of atoms in molecules—no one has ever seen such a structure! An abstract "stick" model communicates the essential spatial relationships between atoms. Sometimes more realistic spherical models are used to indicate the size of an atom's electron shell. It is important, however, that these images display *depth* relationships between atoms in order to communicate to the chemist the precise three-dimensional structure of the molecule.

2. *Computer-aided design* (CAD). Computer-generated images are used to help design automobiles, ships, airplanes, oil refineries, mechanical parts, etc. Images used in these applications must offer enough realism for the designer to evaluate a design: the airframe designer must visualize the shape of a wing to judge aerodynamic properties; the designer of a car body is concerned with both aesthetic and aerodynamic properties of its shape. These two applications thus require realistic portrayals of shape. Other CAD uses may present different needs: the designer of a part for a lawn mower may be more concerned with how the part fits with its neighbors than with details of its shape.

3. *Animation.* Sequences of pictures that educate or explain may require images of three-dimensional objects. Although animation uses graphics as much for art as for realism, it depends heavily on motion to substitute for realism of an individual image. Inexpensive animation communicates depth information with "2½-dimensional" images—opaque images painted on a few transparencies that slide relative to each other, thus allowing one image to appear closer to the observer than another.

4. *Simulation.* Some simulation applications require extreme realism, including moving images. A daylight flight simulator that uses computer-generated images of the view from the cockpit must generate very realistic pictures—pilots seem to depend for depth perception on subtle visual cues, such as skid marks on a runway. A similar form of simulator is used to train ship captains to maneuver their ships in a harbor; a complex harbor scene, including other ships in motion, sometimes obscured by fog, is presented on a very large display in front of a simulated bridge of a ship. Not all simulation applications demand such realistic images. A simulation of the motion of a collection of atoms governed by interatomic forces might produce images in which atoms are shown simply as circular profiles of spheres.

These applications indicate the range of image types required of a graphics display. In the next sections, we take up the individual techniques used to generate the images.

## 20-1 TECHNIQUES FOR ACHIEVING REALISM

On a graphics display, as on a painter's canvas, it is simply impractical to produce an image that is a perfectly realistic representation of an actual scene. Instead, we need techniques that take into account the different kinds of realism needed by applications, the amount of processing required to generate the image, the capabilities of the display hardware, the amount of detail recorded in the model of the scene, and the perceptual effects of the image on the observer. These five aspects will appear throughout our brief catalog of techniques. As applications change, as display hardware improves, or as processing becomes less expensive, we can expect new techniques for visualizing three-dimensional scenes to emerge.

The basic problem addressed by visualization techniques is sometimes called *depth cueing*. When a three-dimensional scene is projected onto a two-dimensional display screen, information about the *depth* of objects in the images tends to be reduced or lost entirely. Techniques that provide depth cues are designed to restore or enhance the communication of depth to the observer.

The list below enumerates several popular visualization techniques, approximately in order of increasing complexity of implementation. Detailed information about the implementation of these techniques is included in subsequent chapters.

1.  *Parallel projections.* Fundamental to the production of a two-dimensional display of a three-dimensional scene is the notion of *projection.* Many different kinds of projection techniques have been developed, mainly to ease the draftsman's task in generating images. Some of these techniques, such as *orthogonal projection,* are relatively simple. When a computer is available to perform the calculations, the simplicity of the projection technique is not as critical, however, and for this reason graphics applications tend to use more complicated but more realistic projections. A simple technique, the *parallel projection,* is illustrated in Figure 20-1, where a point on the screen is identified with a point in the three-dimensional scene by a line perpendicular to the screen. An architect often draws three such parallel projections to illustrate a house, a plan view and two elevation views. This technique depends on the viewer's ability to reconstruct the scene from the multiple projections; most people find this difficult.

2.  *Perspective projection.* The perspective projection, illustrated in Figure 20-2, is perhaps the most common projection technique, familiar to us because the images formed by the eye and by lenses on photographic film are perspective projections. The perspective projection conveys depth

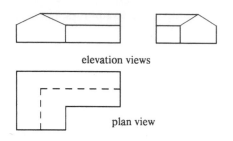

elevation views

plan view

**Figure 20-1** Several parallel projections can be used to show the structure of a three-dimensional object.

information by making distant objects smaller than near ones. If objects have only limited depth variation, however, the perspective foreshortening may not provide an adequate depth cue and an ambiguity appears. Figure 20-3a shows a "wire-frame" drawing of a block that is ambiguous: the block could be oriented as in Figure 20-3b or as in Figure 20-3c. The ambiguity seems to disappear if the perspective effect is exaggerated as if the image were generated with a wide-angle lens (Figure 20-3d). The exaggeration has some undesirable side effects in dynamic graphics applications: people are unaccustomed to viewing the world through a wide-angle lens, and the displayed objects may therefore appear distorted as they move about.

3. *Intensity cues.* One depth cue that is not expensive to implement in hardware is a modulation of the intensity of lines with depth; lines far away appear fainter than those near the viewer (Figure 20-4). On a raster display, a line can be made wider near the observer than it is when far away. These techniques are useful for simple objects. As the complexity of the image increases, the effectiveness of the cue usually decreases. In addition, if the range of depths of nearby lines is small, the intensities or widths may not vary enough to be noticeable.

4. *Stereoscopic views.* A dramatic depth cue is provided by generating two stereoscopic images. One image is shown to the left eye and is generated from a view appropriate to the location of that eye, while the other is generated analogously for the right eye (Figure 20-5). Several techniques can be used to permit each eye to see only the image intended for it. Two

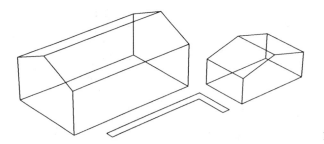

**Figure 20-2** A perspective view.

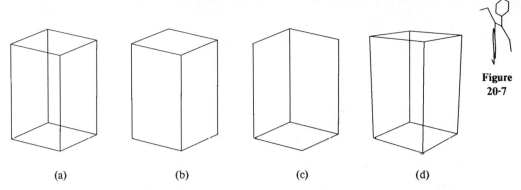

**Figure 20-7**

(a)  (b)  (c)  (d)

**Figure 20-3** Ambiguities can arise from wire-frame drawings. The object (a) could be either (b) or (c). Exaggerated perspective (d) suggests the figure resembles object (b).

separate screens can be used, one for each eye [459]. In another method, the two images are alternately flashed on a single screen about 20 times per second, in synchrony with shutters held in front of the eyes. Still another method polarizes the light from the two images in different directions and has the viewer wear glasses with polarizing material that admits only one image to each eye (Figure 20-6). Some people can "fuse" two separate stereo images like those in Figure 20-5 without the aid of any separation mechanism.

5.  *Kinetic depth effect.* Depth relationships can be understood by watching an object move. A very revealing motion is rotation about a vertical axis. Lines near the viewer move more rapidly than those far away; lines on opposite sides of the rotation axis appear to move in opposite directions, like a merry-go-round. Figure 20-7 illustrates the effect: flip the pages of the book and watch the image rotate. If you stop flipping, the relative depths can no longer be determined. On a display, the effect requires fairly rapid generation of a sequence of rotated images and may require special hardware to perform the calculations.

6.  *Hidden-line elimination.* The relative depth of objects in a scene is readily apparent if the lines that are hidden from view by opaque objects are

 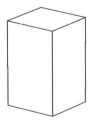 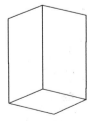

probably       probably not

**Figure 20-4** Intensity modulation is used to brighten parts of the image closer to the observer.

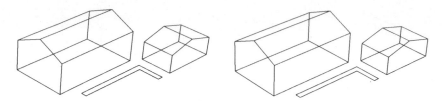

**Figure 20-5** A stereo pair. To help fuse the two images, place a piece of paper perpendicular to the page so that the left eye sees only the left image and the right eye only the right image.

removed from the image (Figure 20-8). Most of the ambiguities of wire-frame images disappear if hidden lines are removed. This technique requires considerable computation but is nevertheless useful for producing finished pictures of a scene.

7. *Shading with hidden surfaces removed.* On a raster-scan display, showing the color and intensity of surfaces helps to convey the depth and shape of an object. The frontispiece illustrates images in which the colors of surfaces, the direction of incident light, and the orientation of the surface with respect to the viewer are used to calculate a realistic intensity. Additional illustrations of shading effects are presented in Chapter 25.

8. *Three-dimensional images.* Someday it may be possible to generate synthetically a three-dimensional image of a scene directly from a computer model—an automatic model shop! Two existing methods, although limited, illustrate the potential of such models. A milling machine controlled by a computer can be used to carve complex shapes in wood or foam (Figure 20-9) [178]. Such a model conveys subtle shape information far better than a display image can. Another example is the vibrating varifocal mirror: together with a display, it generates a true three-dimensional virtual image [386]. The viewer can move around the image, observing it from different distances and directions, positioning himself to explore spatial relationships that interest him (Figure 20-10).

None of the visualization techniques listed above can be recommended as

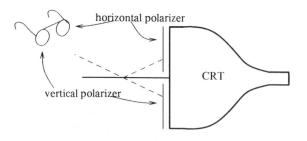

horizontal polarizer

CRT

vertical polarizer

**Figure 20-6** Polarizers used to show the image on the bottom half of the CRT to the right eye only and that on the top half to the left eye only. A horizontal half-silvered mirror is used to combine the polarized images. Note that the upper image is displayed upside down.

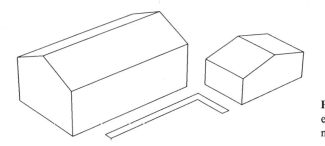

**Figure
20-7**

**Figure 20-8** Hidden-line elimination gives a line-drawing a more realistic appearance.

the "best" one. Each application will require a trade-off of realism, computation time, hardware suitability, and perceptual effectiveness. Many applications involving three-dimensional models may not require realism at all and are better served by special visualization techniques. For example, the draftsman creates three parallel projections of a mechanical part, not because he is unable to achieve greater realism, but because he can better illustrate construction details in the separate views. In three-dimensional display applications, the same objectivity is needed in the choice of visualization techniques.

## 20-2 MODELING THREE-DIMENSIONAL SCENES

The techniques used to generate different kinds of images of three-dimensional scenes all start from a *model* of the scene. The model is needed for two purposes. First, it is used by viewing algorithms, together with information about the location of the viewer, to synthesize images of the scene. Second, it is

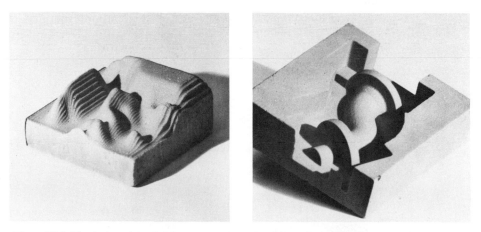

**Figure 20-9** Physical models of objects constructed from computer models with a numerically controlled milling machine. *Courtesy Cambridge University.*

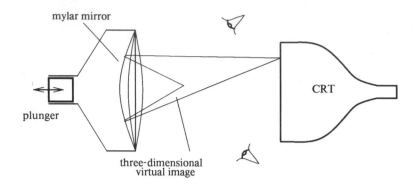

Figure 20-10 A three-dimensional virtual image is formed by a mirror that vibrates and changes focal length.

used to modify and analyze the objects in the scene, activities usually considered part of the application program. Models of two-dimensional scenes also serve these two purposes, as we saw in Chapter 9. The remainder of this section is devoted to the particular aspects of three-dimensional models required to implement different viewing techniques.

The information in a model of a three-dimensional scene can be divided into two important classes, geometry and topology. Geometry is concerned with measurements, such as the location of a point or the dimensions of an object. Topological information records the structure of a scene: how points are aggregated to form polygons, how polygons form objects, and how objects form scenes. Auxiliary information such as colors of surfaces may also be recorded in the model if the viewing techniques require it.

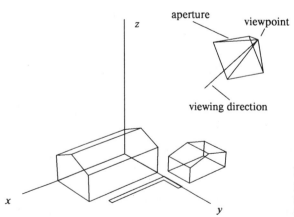

Figure 20-11 Three kinds of viewing parameters describe the view of a scene: the viewpoint, the viewing direction, and the aperture.

## Coordinate Systems

The geometric model of a three-dimensional scene must in some way record locations of points in a three-dimensional coordinate system. We shall choose this system, termed the *world coordinate system,* to be a right-handed three-dimensional cartesian coordinate system (Figure 20-11). Thus the location of a point, or the endpoint of a line, is specified by three numbers $(x, y, z)$. The origin of the world coordinate system, the directions of its axes, and units of measurement may be freely chosen, often for convenience in the application program. A model of buildings in downtown Salt Lake City, for example, might place the origin at the Mormon Temple, the $x$ axis pointing east, the $y$ axis north, and the $z$ axis up. This choice simplifies the modeling of common features: streets are parallel to axes and surfaces of many buildings are perpendicular to axes.

When a view of a three-dimensional scene is generated, a *viewpoint, viewing direction,* and *aperture* must be specified. These parameters are analogous to the adjustments made by a photographer when taking a picture of a real scene: he selects a location for the camera, a direction in which to point it, and a lens that determines how much of the scene will be included in the picture. By altering the viewing parameters, the photographer and the viewer of a graphics display can change the image to suit their requirements. These parameters are thus similar to the windowing parameters of Chapter 5 that select the portion of a two-dimensional model to be viewed. The mechanisms for specifying and using three-dimensional viewing parameters are discussed in Chapter 22.

## Modeling Objects

In three dimensions, just as in two dimensions, a set of primitives is needed to build models of objects. A convenient primitive to use as the basis for modeling objects is the *polyhedron*. This permits the modeling of familiar objects such as cubes, parallelepipeds, wedges, and polygonal prisms. By increasing the number of faces, a polyhedron can be constructed that will approximate any solid object; this completeness property makes the polyhedron particularly attractive as a primitive representation.

An arbitrary polyhedron can be modeled by defining its *faces;* each face is a planar *polygon* that can in turn be modeled by an ordered listing of the *vertices* of the polygon or by a similar list of its *edges.* For generating wire-frame displays, the edges of the polyhedron assume primary importance. For generating hidden-line or hidden-surface displays, the most important aspect of the polyhedron is the face: it is the face that is opaque and causes other objects to be hidden; it is also the face that models a reflective surface and must be shaded properly. The reasons for using polygons to model faces are thus analogous to those for choosing polygons in Chapter 16 to represent two-dimensional solid areas.

A face has two "sides" that must be distinguished: one side cannot be seen

## Table 20-1  Cube Representation

| Geometry | |
| --- | --- |
| Vertices<br>x, y, z coordinates | Plane equations<br>$ax + by + cz + d > 0$ means outside |
| V1    (1, 1, 1)     | F1    [0, 0, 1, −1] |
| V2    (1, 1, −1)    | F2    [−1, 0, 0, −1] |
| V3    (1, −1, −1)   | F3    [0, 0, −1, −1] |
| V4    (1, −1, 1)    | F4    [1, 0, 0, −1] |
| V5    (−1, 1, 1)    | F5    [0, −1, 0, −1] |
| V6    (−1, 1, −1)   | F6    [0, 1, 0, −1] |
| V7    (−1, −1, −1)  | |
| V8    (−1, −1, 1)   | |

| Topology | |
| --- | --- |
| Faces<br>List of vertices counterclockwise<br>when viewed from outside | Edges<br>Can be derived from faces<br>but duplicates are removed |
| F1    V1, V5, V8, V4 | V1, V4     V7, V8 |
| F2    V5, V6, V7, V8 | V4, V3     V8, V5 |
| F3    V6, V2, V3, V7 | V3, V2     V5, V1 |
| F4    V1, V4, V3, V2 | V2, V1     V8, V4 |
| F5    V8, V7, V3, V4 | V5, V6     V6, V2 |
| F6    V6, V5, V1, V2 | V6, V7     V7, V3 |

| Auxiliary information |
| --- |
| Colors<br>Red, green, blue components |
| F1    (0.4, 0, 0) |
| F2    (0.4, 0, 0) |
| . . . all faces are the same color |

because it faces the interior of the polyhedron; the other faces outward and is visible. To make this important distinction, several conventions can be used in the representation of faces. One method requires that the vertices of the face be

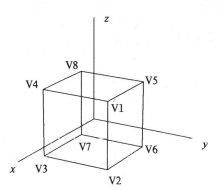

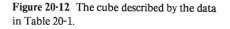

**Figure 20-12** The cube described by the data in Table 20-1.

listed in counterclockwise order when the face is viewed from outside the polyhedron. Equivalently, we can record a description of the *face normal*, a vector perpendicular to the plane of the face, directed outward from the polyhedron.

The face normal is closely related to another important attribute, the *plane equation* of the face. A plane is represented by four numbers $[a \ b \ c \ d]$, chosen so that $ax + by + cz + d = 0$ is true if and only if the point $(x, \ y, \ z)$ lies in the plane. If a point does not lie in the plane, the sign of the nonzero expression $ax + by + cz + d$ will determine on which side of the plane the point lies. This property allows us to establish the convention that points "outside" the face will have positive values of $ax + by + cz + d$. It turns out that the components of the normal vector can be determined from the plane equation; the vector is $[a \ b \ c]$. Calculations using the plane equation and the normal vector will play an important role in algorithms for hidden-line elimination and for shading (see Appendix II for more information on plane equations).

## Representing Topology and Geometry

The topological and geometrical aspects of a scene model must be represented in the computer in a form that allows convenient access by the algorithms that generate images. Although the precise choice of a data structure cannot be made until a viewing algorithm has been selected, we can nevertheless summarize the essential information required to describe a polyhedron.

Table 20-1 shows a definition of a cube, with dimensions $2 \times 2 \times 2$, centered at the origin (see Figure 20-12). The information is divided into three sections: geometric measurements, topological information, and auxiliary information. It is readily apparent that not all visualization algorithms require all the information in Table 20-1. Shading information is superfluous for constructing hidden-line images. A wire-frame visualization requires even less information; it need only enumerate edges of the polyhedron and retrieve coordinates of the vertices of each edge. As an extreme example the molecular-modeling application records coordinates of each atom explicitly, but much of the edge information can be recorded implicitly by ordering the atoms in a list that describes the molecule.

In general, a model will have considerably more information than we have illustrated, to be used not in generating images but in implementing the application. For example, a program that builds and modifies representations of complex three-dimensional shapes may keep additional structural information such as the relationship of the edges arriving at a vertex or of the faces meeting at an edge [34, 462].

### Structured Three-dimensional Models

It is often useful to include hierarchic structure in a model of a three-dimensional object. This structure serves the same purposes as in the two-dimensional models discussed in Chapters 9 and 10. It helps in modeling any inherent geometric repetition or connectivity in an object, and it simplifies the construction of the model and the user's subsequent interaction with it. Thus in a three-dimensional model of an automobile, we would normally represent the four wheels as four instances of the same three-dimensional symbol, each instance transformed appropriately to position it. This would lead to a more compact model and at the same time make it easy to construct the model and to change the attributes of all four wheels. Either a procedural model or a hierarchic data structure may be used to build such a model; the techniques described in Chapter 10 require only the extension of transformations to three dimensions.

### Constructing Models

One aspect of the modeling problem that is often overlooked is the difficulty of constructing a complex model. Some of the difficulty stems from the sheer size of a model: a model of New York harbor used in a ship navigation simulator has over 20,000 faces in it! A more serious problem is *consistency*. If a face is inadvertently omitted from the description of a polyhedron, the image will be incorrect. Errors will also arise if the vertices of a face do not all lie in the same plane, i.e., if the vertex coordinates are not consistent. Still more problems are caused by objects that should abut but in fact have small gaps between them. When the point of view is moved very close to one of these gaps, the viewer can see through the gap to parts of the model that he would expect to be obscured.

The task of enforcing consistency can be performed in large measure by appropriate data-entry programs. In effect, these programs will not allow the construction of inconsistent models. They can check face planarity and try to suggest missing polyhedron faces. One of the most effective measures to improve consistency, however, is to record structural information in the model properly. Although it is tempting to add a new object to a scene by inserting a new description, independent of existing objects, it is safer to tie the new object structurally to the old ones. For example, if we wish to add a pyramid to the cube of Figure 20-12, we should describe its faces in terms of the vertices already defined:

| Geometry | | | |
|---|---|---|---|
| **Vertices** | | **Plane equations** | |
| V9 | (0, 0, 1.3) | F7 | [0, 0.6, 2, 2.6] |
| | | F8 | [0.6, 0, 2, 2.6] |
| | | F9 | [0, −0.6, 2, 2.6] |
| | | F10 | [−0.6, 0, 2, 2.6] |
| | | F11 | [0, 0, −1, 1] |

| Topology | | | |
|---|---|---|---|
| **Faces** | | **Edges** | |
| F7 | V9, V1, V5 | V1, V9 | V5, V9 |
| F8 | V9, V4, V1 | V6, V9 | V2, V9 |
| F9 | V9, V8, V4 | | |
| F10 | V9, V5, V8 | | |
| F11 | V1, V4, V8, V5 | | |

The structural ties to existing points in the scene reduce the chances for errors—the roof will not become inadvertently separated from the cube if some geometrical information is changed.

The data-entry program used to construct a model is usually highly interactive and is, in effect, a computer-aided design program. The program tries to reduce the tedium of entering vast quantities of data and to provide good feedback to help the designer see flaws in the model. Complex models are usually constructed by assembling simpler primitives, often with built-in operations that perform the more routine constructions. Some systems provide primitives for defining arbitrary polyhedra in terms of faces, edges, and vertices, while others provide a small number of pre-defined primitive objects. Systems of this second type concentrate on *shape operations* that form complex objects by taking the union, intersection, and difference of primitive shapes. Three systems of Braid, Baumgart, and Sutherland illustrate the different approaches:

Braid's system [70, 69] is intended to aid the design of mechanical parts. A complex shape is built by assembling instances of primitive solid elements:

cubes, wedges, cylinders, fillets. Instances can be scaled and positioned appropriately. Solids may be added or subtracted. For a similar system, see [493, 494].

Baumgart [35] built a "geometric editor," to ease the construction of complex polyhedra. Polyhedra are edited by such operations as moving vertices; inserting new vertices, edges, or faces; joining faces, etc. Another set of operations allows a polygon to be converted into the corresponding solid of revolution. The program guarantees that each modification will preserve topological consistency.

Sutherland's system [464] uses a digitizer to extract coordinate information from engineering drawings of complex shapes such as ships. The digitizer can also be used to build models from several perspective pictures of an object; the models for the objects in Figure 25-5 were constructed with such a technique. Geometric information is computed by undoing the transformation used by the draftsman or the camera to make the drawing. The program also performs considerable bookkeeping to help build the complex topological information.

No single paradigm is ideally suited to all applications. If the data-entry program is to reduce the time required to construct models, it must be customized in places to accommodate specific problems faced in building individual models. For example, a road could be entered into a general-purpose modeling system as a single polygon with a rather large number of vertices, but a more convenient entry technique would be to specify only the width of the road and a sequence of points on its centerline, leaving the program to calculate the required polygon. The difficulties in building models—the consistency problems, the economy of specification by the user, the topological and geometric constraints that link objects together—all make the model-generation problem as interesting today as it was in the days of Sketchpad.

## 20-3 MODELING AND REALISM

Realism is as much an objective of model building as it is of image generation, because realism in an image cannot be attained without corresponding realism in the model of the scene. Although the image-generation technique used influences the realism of the image, much of the realism depends on the complexity of the model used. A building appears less real when its model is a simple parallelepiped than when the model includes window frames.

The range of detail in a model can be illustrated by considering a model of a barn. A simple model might be a polyhedron, as shown in Figure 20-13a. Details can be added to depict windows and doors (Figure 20-13b). Finally, some of the articulation of individual beams can be added (Figure 20-13c). Generally, the more complex model affords more realistic images. A detailed

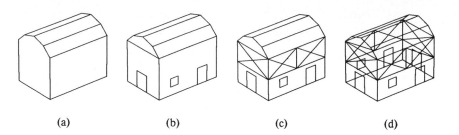

(a)               (b)               (c)               (d)

**Figure 20-13** Adding details to a model increases the realism of the image. Excessive detail may become confusing.

model can be a liability, however. If hidden lines are not removed, the image may be cluttered with details of windows and beams that should not be visible (Figure 20-13d). In addition, a more complex image may slow interaction or rule out applying the kinetic depth effect because too much computation is required to generate the different views. To cope with these problems, models may contain two or more descriptions of the same object at different levels of detail. One, a crude description, is used when computation must be reduced or when the object is viewed from far away; the other, a more precise definition, is used when a more realistic image is required.

Attempts to increase the realism in a model unfortunately add to its complexity. And as the complexity increases, so do the problems of building and maintaining a consistent model. One approach to reducing the complexity of models is to seek more compact, intuitive, self-consistent primitives from which to build the models. An example of this approach is Newell's use of *procedural models* that can contain more information than a topological-geometric model. For example, rows of windows on a building are modeled not as separate polygons but as an iterative algorithm invoked to shade the window regions dark [341]. Another example is the use of *surface models* that provide more compact and precise descriptions of complex shapes than a polyhedral approximation can. The next chapter summarizes some techniques used in these surface models.

## EXERCISES

**20-1** Show how to compute the *face normal* from a list of vertices of a face, given in counter clockwise order when viewed from outside the face.

**20-2** How would you represent a "thin" polyhedron, such as a piece of paper? Clearly, we would like to model the paper as one face, rather than six. How must the plane equation be interpreted?

**20-3** A model of a molecular structure can be viewed as a graph structure in which each node has an $(x, y, z)$ location and $n$ successors ($n$ is often 1). Show how the topological information could be compactly recorded for such a structure.

**20-4** Devise a data structure for modeling objects as illustrated in Table 20-1. Make a careful list of model-building operations that your data structure will support.

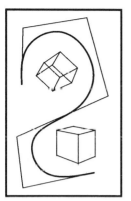

# 21

## CURVES

## AND SURFACES

Because objects with complex shapes occur frequently in our three-dimensional world, special techniques to model them properly and to generate realistic images of them have been developed. Although these objects can be approximated to arbitrarily fine precision as plane-faced polyhedra, such representations are bulky and intractable. For example, a polyhedral approximation of a coffee cup might contain 1000 faces and would be difficult to generate and to modify—many coordinate values would need changing in order to make a seemingly simple modification to the shape of the cup. We need a more direct representation of shapes, tractable both to the computer and to the person trying to manipulate the shapes.

## 21-1 SHAPE DESCRIPTION REQUIREMENTS

Our approach to shape representation depends on the application. Generally, shape representations have two different uses, an *analytic* use and a *synthetic* use. Representations are used analytically to describe shapes that can be measured; just as a curve can be fitted to a set of data points, a surface can be "fitted" to the measured properties of some real object. The objective of such representations may be to achieve a precise fit, to minimize the number of measurements required, to represent the shape in a very compact form, to simplify the computation of derived properties such as areas and volumes, etc. Synthetic uses of shape representation are encountered in design. A designer interactively creates or modifies a model of a shape, examining and improving the design until it is acceptable. The resulting model may be used to generate images of the new shape, or it may provide information to numerically controlled manufacturing equipment that will produce a real object. The objectives for synthetic uses of shape differ from analytic objectives: we are primarily concerned with assisting in the design process, with expressing shape modifications easily to an interactive program, with the freedom to explore many very different alternative shapes, and with the precision needed to capture the designer's wish exactly.

In this chapter, our brief treatment of the mathematical techniques applied to the modeling of shape will concentrate on the synthetic approach. We take this approach because synthetic techniques are the more demanding: they require a clear understanding of the user's needs and of the constraints of the application. In addition, synthetic methods can often be applied to analytic fitting problems, whereas analytic methods are rarely useful in design.

Before exploring mathematical properties of shape representations, it is helpful to keep in mind the requirements of the designer who must use these methods to build and modify models of shapes. The modeling system must support a class of shapes that is matched to the designer's application. To design a mechanical part for a typewriter, shapes limited to plane-faced polyhedra and sections of cylinders may be adequate. On the other hand, to design an automobile body, we need a more versatile selection of shapes and techniques to keep the surface "smooth." Small discontinuities that are tolerated or even desirable for a mechanical part are anathema to the body designer.

When a designer begins to use an interactive shape-modeling system, more requirements appear. The design process is iterative: the designer carefully observes the shape he has specified to see what it looks like, to see how it performs, and to formulate ideas for changes to it. Then he expresses the modifications he wants to an interactive computer program. The first step of this process requires us to generate images of shapes that have sufficient realism to communicate to the designer the shape information needed to evaluate the design. The second step is more difficult, because the designer must express the required changes in a limited vocabulary of modifications that the mathematical shape representations support. Ideally, the designer need change only a small number of parameters of the shape model to achieve the desired result. He is sufficiently familiar with the shape representation to be able to estimate which parameters need changing by how much and to anticipate exactly the shape changes that will result. This step illustrates one of the problems in selecting a shape representation: if only a small set of parameters is provided, the designer's task is simplified but the range of shapes that can be represented is likely to be limited. If there are many parameters, the designer can achieve more varied and more accurate models of his design but may be overwhelmed

**Figure 21-1** Control points (indicated by dots) govern the shape of a curve.

by the flexibility offered. Fortunately, some shape representations are able to accommodate a variable number of parameters: the designer can use as many or as few as necessary to create an acceptable model.

In addition to the user's requirements, any scheme for modeling curves and surfaces must be mathematically tractable, computationally convenient, and economical of storage. Computational needs sometimes conflict with those of the user; indeed, researchers in this area are still trying to devise mathematical representations of curves that match a designer's "feel" for how shapes should behave.

The requirements of the user and of the computer combine to suggest a number of properties that our representations must have. We list below some of the important properties for designing curves. The requirements for designing surfaces are very similar; as we shall see, surfaces can be represented using simple extensions of techniques for representing curves.

1. *Control points.* A common way to control the shape of a curve interactively is to locate points through which the curve must pass or points that control the curve's shape in a predictable way (Figure 21-1). These points are called *control points*, or sometimes *knots* when they lie on the curve itself. A curve is said to *interpolate* the control points if it passes through them (as in Figure 21-1). In the illustrations in this chapter, we shall often connect the control points with straight lines to show the "polygon" that defines a curve or surface.
2. *Multiple values.* In general, a curve is not a graph of a single-valued function of a coordinate, irrespective of the choice of coordinate system (Figure 21-2).
3. *Axis independence.* The shape of an object must not change when the

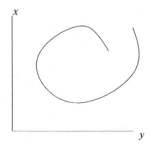

**Figure 21-2** A curve can be multivalued with respect to all coordinate systems.

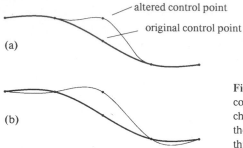

(a)

(b)

**Figure 21-3** Curve shapes are modified by moving control points. Curves having local control (a) change shape only near an altered control point; those with global control (b) change shape throughout.

control points are measured in a different coordinate system. If, for example, the control points are rotated 90 degrees, the curve should rotate 90 degrees but not change shape. Some mathematical formulations will cause a curve's shape to change if the reference coordinate system is changed.

4.  *Global or local control.* As a designer manipulates a control point, a curve may change shape only in the region near the control point, or it may change shape throughout (Figure 21-3). This last behavior, called *global control,* may be annoying to the designer trying to make fine adjustments to just one portion of the curve.

5.  *Variation-diminishing property.* Some mathematical representations have an annoying tendency to amplify, rather than smooth, any small irregularities in the shape outlined by control points (Figure 21-4a). Others, possessing a *variation-diminishing* property, always smooth the designer's control points. Figure 21-4b shows a sequence of knot points and an associated variation-diminishing curve. This curve will never cross an arbitrarily chosen straight line more often than a sequence of lines that connect the knot points (dashed line).

6.  *Versatility.* A curve representation that allows only a limited variety of shapes may frustrate a designer. A framework that provides only arcs of circles, for example, lacks sufficient versatility to model most designs. More flexible techniques allow the designer to control the versatility of a curve representation, often by adding or removing control points. For example, a

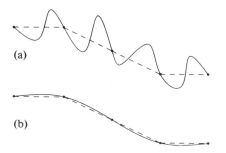

(a)

(b)

**Figure 21-4** (a) A curve that oscillates about its control points is usually undesirable. (b) Variation-diminishing curves tend to smooth out a sequence of control points.

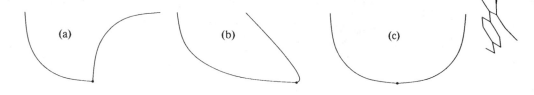

**Figure 21-5** Orders of continuity at joints: (a) zero-order continuity; (b) first-order continuity (slope); (c) second-order continuity (curvature).

curve specified by two control points might be a straight line connecting the points; introducing a third control point allows the curve to take on a large number of additional shapes, depending on the location of the control point.

7. *Order of continuity.* A complex shape is usually not modeled by a single curve, but by several curves pieced together end-to-end. Such joints are used to introduce sharp corners which might be difficult to represent within a curve framework. In other cases, a joint is introduced to increase versatility: a shape that cannot be described by a single curve can often be described by several curves joined together. When creating joints, the designer often wants to control the order of continuity at the joint (Figure 21-5). Zero-order continuity means simply that two curves meet; first-order continuity requires the curves to be tangent at the point of intersection; second-order continuity requires that curvatures be the same.

With these requirements in mind, we can begin to develop the basic techniques used in curve and surface representation. These are the basis for the Bézier and B-spline formulations of curves and surfaces we shall present in some detail.

## 21-2 PARAMETRIC FUNCTIONS

The dominant form used to model curves and surfaces is the *parametric* or *vector-valued* function. A point on a curve is represented as a vector:

$$P(u) = [x(u) \ y(u) \ z(u)]$$

For surfaces, two parameters are required:

$$P(u, v) = [x(u, v) \ y(u, v) \ z(u, v)]$$

As the parameters $u$ and $v$ take on values in a specified range, usually 0 to 1, the

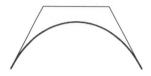

**Figure 21-6** A Bezier curve and the four control points used to define it.

parametric functions $x$, $y$, and $z$ trace out the location of the curve or surface. Functions of this sort easily meet multivalued requirements.

The parametric functions can themselves take many forms. Indeed, a single curve can be approximated in several different ways. The following two-dimensional functions all trace parts of a circle of unit radius centered at the origin:

$$\mathbf{P}(u) = [\cos u \quad \sin u]$$

$$\mathbf{P}(u) = [(1 - u^2)/(1 + u^2) \quad 2u/(1 + u^2)]$$

$$\mathbf{P}(u) = [u \quad (1 - u^2)^{\frac{1}{2}}]$$

$$\mathbf{P}(u) = [0.43u^3 - 1.466u^2 + 0.036u + 1 \quad -0.43u^3 - 0.177u^2 + 1.607u]$$

The last function is only an approximation, but its simple polynomial form makes it particularly easy to evaluate and to manipulate. Both Bézier and B-spline curve formulations use polynomial parametric functions.

Generally, it is not possible to devise a simple function that specifies the shape of an entire curve or surface, let alone four different functions such as we found for circular arcs. It is not so difficult if the function applies only for a small piece of the shape; the entire shape is then defined by a series of functions, pieced together. Such *piecewise* approximations require methods to give the designer control over the continuity at joints. If a joint must be inserted only to achieve more flexibility in the shape of the curve, the designer will want the joint to appear smooth, perhaps by requiring curvature to be continuous at the joint. Piecewise approximations help achieve the desirable local control property by defining a piece in terms only of control points near it and of the continuity requirements at its joints.

Even using simple parametric functions, we cannot expect the designer to achieve a desirable curve by changing coefficients of parametric polynomial functions or of any other functional form. Instead, we must find ways to determine the parametric functions from the locations of control points that are manipulated by the designer. This relation cannot be arbitrary; it must be chosen so that the designer can anticipate how changes to control point locations will be reflected in changes to curve shapes.

The following two sections present two of the many solutions to this problem. Bézier and B-spline formulations both use control points that lie off the curve but nevertheless provide remarkably effective control of the curve shape. A variant of B-splines uses control points that lie on the curve [200].

## 21-3 BEZIER METHODS

P. Bézier, of the French firm Régie Renault, pioneered the use of computer modeling of surfaces in automobile design. His UNISURF system, used by designers since 1972, has been applied to define the outer panels of several cars marketed by Renault [46].

### Bézier Curves

Bézier defines the curve $P(u)$ in terms of the locations of $n + 1$ control points $p_i$

$$P(u) = \sum_{i=0}^{n} p_i \, B_{i,n}(u) \qquad (21\text{-}1)$$

where $B_{i,n}(u)$ is a *blending function*

$$B_{i,n}(u) = C(n, i)u^i (1 - u)^{n-i}$$

and $C(n, i)$ is the binomial coefficient, $C(n, i) = n!/(i!(n - i)!)$. Equation 21-1 is a vector equation; it could be expressed by writing equations for the $x$, $y$, and $z$ parametric functions separately:

$$x(u) = \sum_{i=0}^{n} x_i \, B_{i,n}(u)$$

$$y(u) = \sum_{i=0}^{n} y_i \, B_{i,n}(u)$$

$$z(u) = \sum_{i=0}^{n} z_i \, B_{i,n}(u)$$

where the three-dimensional location of the control point $p_i$ is $[x_i \; y_i \; z_i]$. We shall continue to use the vector notation as in Equation 21-1, with the understanding that the equations can always be expressed using separate scalar functions.

Figure 21-6 shows an example Bézier curve in the plane; the $z$ coordinate of each control point is zero. The particular curve shown uses four control points, connected in the illustration to form an open "polygon."

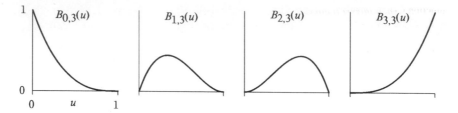

**Figure 21-7** The four Bezier blending functions for $n = 3$.

The blending functions are the key to the behavior of Bézier curves. Figure 21-7 shows the four blending functions that correspond to a Bézier curve with four control points. These curves represent the "influence" that each control point exerts on the curve for various values of $u$. The first control point, $p_0$, corresponding to $B_{0,3}(u)$, is most influential when $u = 0$; in fact, locations of all other control points are ignored when $u = 0$, because their blending functions are zero. The situation is symmetric for $p_3$ and $u = 1$. The middle control points $p_1$ and $p_2$ are most influential when $u = 1/3$ and $2/3$, respectively.

The equations that define Bézier curves can be readily converted into a program for drawing the curves. A PASCAL program is given in Figure 21-8 that computes $P(u)$ from a vector of control points. The program is designed to correspond to our formulation above; it can easily be made more efficient.

We can evaluate Bézier curves in terms of our list of important properties:

1. *Control points.* At first, it might seem that Bézier curves are hard to use because not all control points lie on the curve. However, the curve is predictably related to the locations of control points—each seems to exert a "pull" on the portion of the curve near it. The control points also satisfy two important mathematical properties: the curve *does* pass through the two endpoints ($p_0$ and $p_n$), and the curve is tangent at the endpoints to the corresponding edge of the polygon of control points (e.g., the curve at $p_0$ is tangent to the vector joining $p_0$ and $p_1$).
2. *Multiple values.* The parametric formulation of the Bézier curve allows it to represent multiple-valued shapes. In fact, if the first and last control points coincide, the curve is closed (Figure 21-9).
3. *Axis independence.* A Bézier curve is independent of the coordinate system used to measure the locations of control points.
4. *Global or local control.* These curves do not provide localized control: moving any control point will change the shape of every part of the curve. This can be seen from the blending functions illustrated in Figure 21-7: all functions are nonzero almost everywhere (the two values $u = 0$ and $u = 1$ are exceptions), and consequently the location of each control point will influence the curve location almost everywhere.
5. *Variation-diminishing property.* Bézier curves are variation-diminishing. In

```
function C(n, i: integer): integer;
        var j, a: integer;
begin
    a := 1;
    for j := i + 1 to n do a := a * j;
    for j := 1 to n - i do a := a div j;
    C := a
end;

function BBlend(i, n: integer; u: real): real;
        var j: integer; v: real;
begin
    v := C(n, i);
    for j := 1 to i do v := v * u;
    for j := 1 to n - i do v := v *(1 - u);
    BBlend := v
end;

procedure Bezier(var x, y, z: real; u: real; n: integer; var p: xyzArray);
        var i: integer; b: real;
begin
    x := 0; y := 0; z := 0;
    for i := 0 to n do begin
        b := BBlend(i, n, u);
        x := x + p[i, 1] * b; y := y + p[i, 2] * b; z := z + p[i, 3] * b
    end
end;

procedure DrawCurve;
        var ControlPoints: xyzArray; i: integer; x, y, z: real;
begin
    for i := 0 to 3 do ControlPoints[i, 3] := 0;
    ControlPoints[0, 1] := 0; ControlPoints[0, 2] := 0;
    ControlPoints[1, 1] := 1; ControlPoints[1, 2] := 2;
    ControlPoints[2, 1] := 3; ControlPoints[2, 2] := 2;
    ControlPoints[3, 1] := 4; ControlPoints[3, 2] := 0;

    for i := 0 to 40 do begin
        Bezier(x, y, z, i / 40, 3, ControlPoints);
        if i = 0 then MoveTo(x, y) else LineTo(x, y)
    end
end;
```

**Figure 21-8**   Procedures for drawing the Bézier curve in Figure 21-6.

addition a curve is guaranteed to lie within the convex hull of the control points that define it [200, 277]. Thus the Bézier curve never oscillates wildly away from its defining control points.

6.   *Versatility.* The versatility of a Bézier curve is governed by the number of

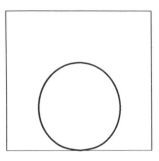

**Figure 21-9** A closed Bezier curve specified with six control points. The first and last control points coincide.

control points used. In the example of Figure 21-6, four control points are used ($n = 3$) to determine two parametric cubic polynomial functions that specify $x$ and $y$ values. More control points can always be used to describe more complex shapes, but eventually the high-order polynomial equations become difficult to use because of the lack of localized control.

7. *Order of continuity.* Bézier curves of modest order can be pieced together to describe a more complex curve. In these cases, the joints between the curves must be smooth. To achieve zero-order continuity at a joint, it is necessary only to make the end control points of the two curves coincide (Figure 21-10a). To achieve first-order continuity, the edges of the two polygons adjacent to the common endpoints must lie in a line, as shown in Figure 21-10b (i.e., points $p_{n-1}$ and $p_n$ of one curve and $p_0$ and $p_1$ of the next curve must all be collinear). Thus it is rather easy for the curve designer to locate control points so as to achieve first-order continuity. Higher-order continuity can also be ensured by geometric constraints on control points, but beyond first-order continuity the constructions become complex.

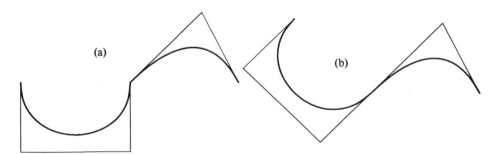

**Figure 21-10** Continuity at joints between Bezier curves: (a) zero-order continuity; (b) first-order continuity.

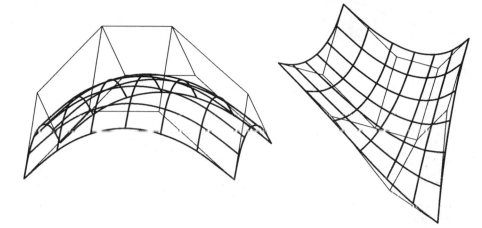

**Figure 21-11** Two Bezier surface patches. The mesh of control points is shown with thin lines. Both patches have $n = 2$, $m = 3$.

## Bézier Surfaces

The formulation of the Bézier curve extends easily to describe three-dimensional surfaces by generating the *cartesian product* of two curves. Two similar blending functions are used, one for each parameter:

$$P(u, v) = \sum_{i=0}^{n} \sum_{j=0}^{m} \mathbf{p}_{i,j} B_{i,n}(u) B_{j,m}(v) \qquad (21\text{-}2)$$

Figure 21-11 shows a view of two Bézier surfaces with $(n + 1) \times (m + 1)$ control points, arranged in a mesh. Adjacent control points are connected with lines in order to show the mesh. The surface itself is shown by drawing two sets of curves: one set holds the $u$ parameter constant and allows $v$ to range from 0 to 1; the other set holds $v$ constant and varies $u$. These curves of constant $u$ and $v$ are in fact Bézier curves. Consider the curve shown for $v = 0$. Because $B_{j,m}(0)$ is 1 if $j = 0$, and 0 otherwise, we can rewrite Equation 21-2 as

$$P(u, 0) = \sum_{i=0}^{n} \mathbf{p}_{i,0} B_{i,n}(u)$$

Thus the $n + 1$ control points $\mathbf{p}_{i,0}$ are exactly the control points for the $v = 0$ curve. Control points for other curves of constant $v$ will not generally coincide with the mesh control points $\mathbf{p}_{i,j}$.

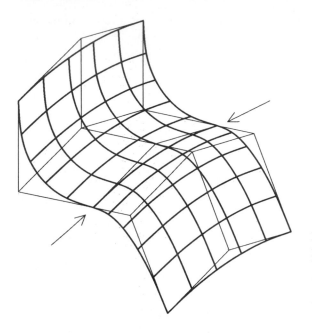

**Figure 21-12** Two Bezier surface patches joined together at a boundary indicated by arrows. Control points are chosen to yield first-order continuity across the boundary.

As with curves, an entire surface is not always best described as a single Bézier surface. Surfaces can be pieced together from individual patches, as shown in Figure 21-12. Continuity at the joint between two patches is achieved in much the same way as continuity at the joint between curves. Zero-order continuity is assured by making coincident the control points that describe the boundary curve of one patch and the control points that describe the boundary curve of the adjacent patch. Achieving first-order continuity across a boundary requires not only that first and last edges of the joining polygons be collinear but that the ratio of the lengths of all these edge pairs be constant.

The extension of curves to surfaces leaves the properties of the Bézier formulation listed above unaltered. The intuitive feel of control points, the variation-diminishing property of the curves, and the control of continuity all make Bézier curves and surfaces convenient for interactive design.

## 21-4 B-SPLINE METHODS

Although Bézier curves and surfaces are well suited to many shape-modeling problems, complex geometric constructions are required to guarantee continuity when piecing curves together. The use of *spline functions* avoids this problem by using mathematical constraints to allow only those curves that possess the required continuity at joints. The most common spline techniques provide this convenience at the expense of local control. The *B-spline* formulation avoids this problem by using a set of blending functions that have *local support* only—the location of the curve depends only on a few neighboring control points.

The overall formulation of the B-spline curve is much like that of the Bézier curve in that a set of blending functions is used to combine the effects of the control points:

$$P(u) = \sum_{i=0}^{n} p_i N_{i,k}(u) \tag{21-3}$$

The key difference lies in the formulation of the blending functions $N_{i,k}(u)$. Figure 21-13 shows the six blending functions for six control points ($n = 5$). The parameter $k$ controls the order of continuity of the curve: $k = 3$ in the illustration. The parameter $u$ varies over a wider range than for Bézier functions: it ranges from 0 to $n - k + 2$ in the illustration. The most important feature of the B-spline blending functions is that they are nonzero in only a portion of the range of the parameter. Thus, for example, control point 2 influences the curve shape only in the range $0 \leq u \leq 3$, because $N_{2,3}$ is zero for all other values of $u$. Similarly, we observe from the figure that at most three blending functions are nonzero for any value of $u$. Thus at most three of the six control points influence the local shape of the curve.

The B-spline blending functions of degree $k - 1$ (also called the B-spline basis functions) may be defined recursively as follows:

$$N_{i,1}(u) = \begin{matrix} 1 & \text{if } t_i \leq u < t_{i+1} \\ 0 & \text{otherwise} \end{matrix}$$

$$N_{i,k}(u) = \frac{(u - t_i) N_{i,k-1}(u)}{t_{i+k-1} - t_i} + \frac{(t_{i+k} - u) N_{i+1,k-1}(u)}{t_{i+k} - t_{i+1}} \tag{21-4}$$

Because the denominators can become zero, this formulation adopts the convention $0/0 = 0$.

Equation 21-4 requires choosing a set of *knot values* $t_i$ that relate the parameter $u$ to the control points. The relation offers control over the curve shape in addition to the information provided by the locations of control points. Two choices of knot values are used most frequently: the *uniform non-periodic B-spline* and the *uniform periodic B-spline*.

The non-periodic B-spline is used to model open curves like that shown in Figure 21-14. The knot values $t_0$ to $t_{n+k}$ are chosen with the following rule:

$$t_i = \begin{matrix} 0 & \text{if } i < k \\ i - k + 1 & \text{if } k \leq i \leq n \\ n - k + 2 & \text{if } i > n \end{matrix} \tag{21-5}$$

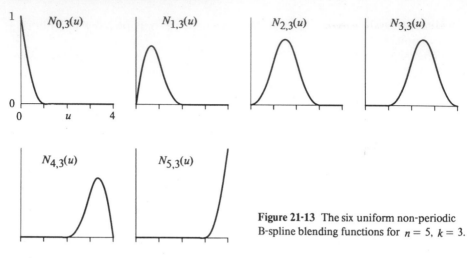

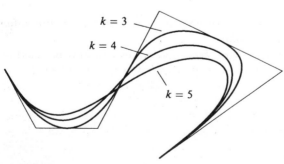

**Figure 21-13** The six uniform non-periodic B-spline blending functions for $n = 5$, $k = 3$.

The B-spline blending functions illustrated in Figure 21-13 are non-periodic, with $n = 5$, $k = 3$. The knot values $t_0$ through $t_8$ are, by the rule above, 0, 0, 0, 1, 2, 3, 4, 4, 4. The parameter $u$ ranges from 0 to $n - k + 2$. Figure 21-15 gives a PASCAL program that uses Equation 21-4 to evaluate uniform non-periodic B-splines. Other evaluation methods presented in the literature require less computation and are more stable [200, 138].

   The periodic B-spline is used to model closed curves (Figure 21-16). All blending functions have a canonical shape such as that illustrated by $N_{2,3}$ in Figure 21-13. One way to generate the blending functions is to choose knot values $t_i = i$ and reduce all blending functions to one:

$$N_{i,k}(u) = N_{0,k}((u - i + n + 1) \bmod (n + 1)) \qquad (21\text{-}6)$$

The parameter $u$ takes on values $0 \le u \le n + 1$.

   The local control of shape guaranteed by B-splines allows us to introduce "corners" (Figure 21-17). This effect can be achieved with *multiple control*

**Figure 21-14** Several non-periodic B-spline curves derived from six control points. Each of the three curves has a different order.

```
var knotK, knotN: integer;

function Knot(i: integer): integer;
begin
    if i < knotK then Knot := 0 else
    if i > knotN then Knot := knotN − knotK + 2 else
        Knot := i − knotK + 1
end;

function NBlend(i, k: integer; u: real): real;
    var t: integer; v: real;
begin
    if k = 1 then begin
        v := 0;
        if (Knot(i) <= u) and (u < Knot(i + 1)) then v := 1
    end else begin
        v := 0;
        t := Knot(i + k − 1) − Knot(i);
        if t <> 0 then v := (u − Knot(i)) * NBlend(i, k − 1, u) / t;
        t := Knot(i + k) − Knot(i + 1);
        if t <> 0 then
            v := v + (Knot(i + k) − u) * NBlend(i + 1, k − 1, u) / t
    end;
    NBlend := v
end;

procedure BSpline(var x, y, z: real; u: real; n, k: integer; p: xyzArray);
    var i: integer; b: real;
begin
    knotK := k; knotN := n;
    x := 0; y := 0; z := 0;
    for i := 0 to n do begin
        b := NBlend(i, k, u);
        x := x + p[i, 1] * b; y := y + p[i, 2] * b; z := z + p[i, 3] * b
    end
end;
```

**Figure 21-15**  Procedures for drawing B-spline curves.

*points,* i.e., by placing several consecutive control points at exactly the same location. Figure 21-17b shows two control points located together; the control point is said to have *multiplicity* 2. Multiple knot values can also be used to alter the local shape and continuity of a B-spline curve [200]. Multiple control points can be used with Bézier curves, but the non-local shape properties cause the shape of the entire curve to be affected by the multiplicity.

B-splines share many of the advantages of Bézier curves: the control points affect curve shape in a natural way, the curve is variation-diminishing, axis-independent and multivalued. The chief advantange of the B-spline

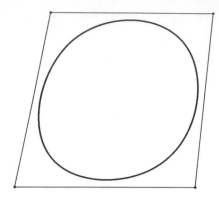

**Figure 21-16** A uniform periodic B-spline and its four control points ($k = 4$).

formulation over the Bézier curve is local control of the curve shape. Figure 21-18 shows two B-spline curves in which only a single control point has been moved. Portions of the curve that lie far from the altered control point do not change.

B-splines also reduce the need to piece many curves together to define a shape. Control points can be added at will without increasing the *degree* of the curve, which would make the curve more difficult to control and to calculate accurately. As a consequence, cubic B-splines ($k = 4$) suffice for a large number of applications. The B-spline offers a few more parameters to the designer than the Bézier curve: the degree can be selected, as can multiplicities of control points or knots.

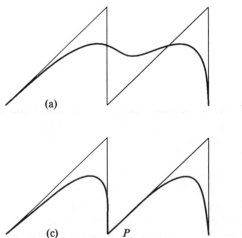

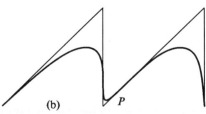

**Figure 21-17** Multiple control points induce regions of high curvature: (a) normal curve; (b) two control points at $P$; (c) three control points at $P$ ($k = 4$).

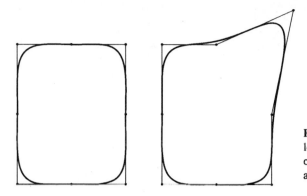

**Figure 21-18** B-spline curves have local control. The shape of the curve changes only in the vicinity of a changed control point.

## B-Spline Surfaces

B-splines extend to describe surfaces by the same cartesian product method used with Bézier curves:

$$P(u,v) = \sum_{i-0}^{n} \sum_{j=0}^{m} \mathbf{p}_{i,j} N_{i,k}(u) N_{j,l}(v) \tag{21-7}$$

Figure 21-19 shows an example of B-spline surfaces and their mesh of control points.

## 21-5 DISPLAYING CURVES AND SURFACES

Displaying a space curve or a surface to a designer is not an easy task; the designer may need to inspect small details of shape that are hard to make visible on a graphics display. The depth cues surveyed in Chapter 20 are barely sufficient to display realistic images of coarsely defined three-dimensional objects. They are generally inadequate for subtly curved surfaces.

The simplest method for displaying curves and surfaces is the wire-frame technique used for the illustrations in this chapter. To display a curve, its coordinates are evaluated for many closely spaced values of the parameter $u$, the points are displayed and are connected by short straight-line segments. A complete surface is displayed by generating a mesh of such curves, holding one parameter constant at a time. Figure 21-11, for example, shows seven curves that have constant values of $u$ ($u = 0, 1/6, \ldots, 1$) and seven more that have constant values of $v$. This method is not entirely satisfactory because it imposes a "ruled" appearance on the surface that may obscure shape details.

Some of the depth-cueing techniques described in Chapter 20 are effective in displaying curves and surfaces. Intensity modulation is helpful when a

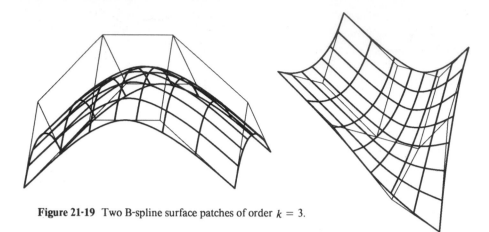

**Figure 21-19** Two B-spline surface patches of order $k = 3$.

simple wire-frame image of a surface would cause confusion between curves close to the observer and those much farther away, as might be the case in the display of a sphere. Kinetic depth, or the ability to "move around" a wire-frame display of a surface, can be an effective way to view a surface. With dynamic techniques like these, the designer can manipulate the viewing position or the position of the surface to find shape anomalies. By contrast, perspective foreshortening, a useful technique for viewing collections of polyhedra, is not very effective in conveying shape information.

Specific details of shape can often be best communicated by specific visualization techniques. An example is the *hedgehog,* illustrated in Figure 21-20 [180]. Here in addition to a wire-frame display of the surface, vectors normal to the surface are displayed. The normals unambiguously depict the orientation of the surface. If the normal vectors are made fairly long, even small variations in shape become evident (Figure 21-20b).

The visualization technique that corresponds most precisely to our own perception of shape is shading, as illustrated in the frontispiece. The position and orientation of a large number of points on the surface are used to determine intensities on a raster image. These techniques, which will be explored more fully in Chapter 25, require considerably more computation than methods that generate line drawings of surfaces. As a consequence, shaded images are not often used in interactive design applications: designers seem to prefer to examine a large number of carefully chosen but rapidly generated views of a surface rather than a high-quality image of a single aspect.

### Evaluating Points on Curves and Surfaces

All methods for displaying curves and surfaces require the computation of the location of the curve or surface for a large number of different values of the parameters. The calculation techniques illustrated in the programs given above

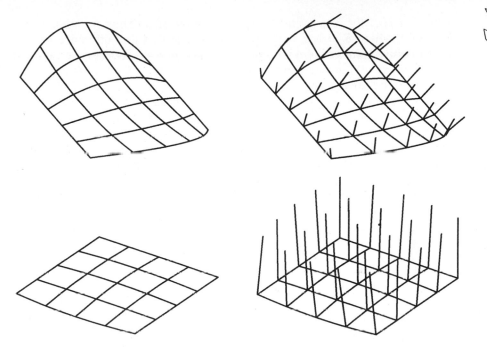

**Figure 21-20** The hedgehog visualization technique uses normal vectors to illustrate the shape of a surface. Long normal vectors help to show very small surface fluctuations.

can be economized considerably. Many curve and surface methods, including Bézier and B-spline formulations, express $x$, $y$, and $z$ as parametric polynomial functions. Thus the problem of calculating points on a curve can be reduced to that of evaluating a polynomial.

A simple technique for evaluating polynomials is Horner's rule. Let $p(u) = au^3 + bu^2 + cu + d$, a cubic polynomial. This equation can be rewritten to use only three multiplications and three additions: $p(u) = ((au + b)u + c)u + d$. Although this technique economizes on computation, the multiplications required make it unattractive for implementation in hardware or on small computers.

More efficient evaluation methods make use of *incremental methods* to calculate the coordinates of a curve for successive values of its parameter. This same idea is incorporated in the DDA and circle generator described in Chapter 2. For curves and surfaces, the *polynomial* character of the parametric functions makes incremental techniques simple and attractive.

The most common incremental method is the use of *forward differences* to evaluate a polynomial at equal intervals of its parameter. The technique is most easily illustrated for evaluating a linear equation, $p(u) = cu + d$. Consider evaluating $p(u)$ for $n + 1$ equally spaced values of $u$. Thus we want to find $p_i = p(i\delta)$, where $\delta = 1/n$, $0 \le i \le n$. We notice that the difference between two successive values of $p(u)$ is constant: $p_{i+1} = p_i + c\delta$. Successive values are thus found by adding the constant $c\delta$ to the previous value. This is precisely the technique used by the line-drawing DDA.

The method of forward differences can be applied to polynomials of any degree. Consider the cubic polynomial $p(u) = au^3 + bu^2 + cu + d$. The forward difference, $p_{i+1} - p_i = \Delta_{1,i}$ is not a constant, but rather a quadratic polynomial in $i$. If we can evaluate $\Delta_{1,i}$ easily, we can then evaluate $p_i$ rapidly. Applying the same reasoning to $\Delta_{1,i}$, we find that the forward difference $\Delta_{1,i+1} - \Delta_{1,i} = \Delta_{2,i}$ is a linear equation in $i$. As we saw in the preceding paragraph, a linear equation has a constant forward difference, and is indeed easily evaluated.

An algorithm for evaluating the cubic polynomial is found by carrying out the algebra to combine the three levels of forward differences. We initialize four variables as follows:

$$
\begin{aligned}
p &:= d \\
\Delta_1 &:= a\delta^3 + b\delta^2 + c\delta \\
\Delta_2 &:= 6a\delta^3 + 2b\delta^2 \\
\Delta_3 &:= 6a\delta^3
\end{aligned}
\tag{21-8}
$$

The initialization yields the value $p = p_0$. To calculate $p_1$, three additions are required:

$$
\begin{aligned}
p &:= p + \Delta_1 \\
\Delta_1 &:= \Delta_1 + \Delta_2 \\
\Delta_2 &:= \Delta_2 + \Delta_3
\end{aligned}
\tag{21-9}
$$

These three additions are repeated $n$ times, generating $p_1$ through $p_n$. Although simple methods for evaluating cubic polynomials require several multiplications for each evaluation, this method requires only three additions for each point. The forward difference technique can be applied to polynomials of any degree, resulting in an inner loop that uses $n$ additions for polynomials of degree $n$.

The difficulty with the forward-difference technique is that the parameter $\delta$ must be selected carefully to ensure that enough points are evaluated to make the curve appear smooth. Another approach is to take smaller and smaller steps along the curve until the difference between successive evaluations falls below some threshold, such as the resolution of the display device. The basic idea is to subdivide the parameter range by halves and develop simple expressions for the location of the curve at the midpoint.

Figure 21-21 illustrates this technique applied to a Bézier curve. The original curve, defined by four control points, is divided into two smaller curves, each defined by four control points. The calculation of the new control

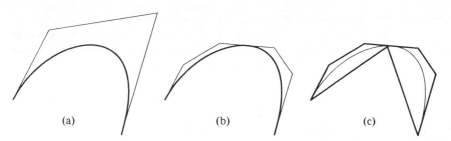

**Figure 21·21** Subdividing a cubic Bezier curve. (a) the original curve with four control points; (b) subdivision into two cubic curves at $u = 1/2$; (c) the convex hulls of the two smaller curves.

points is fairly simple. For example, the four new control points $\mathbf{p}_i{'}$ for the first half of the curve can be derived from the original control points $\mathbf{p}_i$:

$$
\begin{aligned}
\mathbf{p}_0{'} &= \mathbf{p}_0 \\
\mathbf{p}_1{'} &= \mathbf{p}_0/2 + \mathbf{p}_1/2 \\
\mathbf{p}_2{'} &= \mathbf{p}_0/4 + \mathbf{p}_1/2 + \mathbf{p}_2/4 \\
\mathbf{p}_3{'} &= \mathbf{p}_0/8 + 3\mathbf{p}_1/8 + 3\mathbf{p}_2/8 + \mathbf{p}_3/8
\end{aligned}
\tag{21-10}
$$

Each of the two curves resulting from the subdivision can be subdivided again, yielding still smaller curve segments. This process can be continued until the curves become small enough to be approximated by a straight line segment or to be displayed as a single dot on a raster. The *convex hull property* of Bézier curves helps to decide when the process should terminate: because a curve always lies within the convex hull defined by the control points (Figure 21-21c), the size of the convex hull is an upper bound on the size of the curve. Subdividing curves in this way is a remarkably useful technique. The method can be applied to any cubic polynomials, after first transforming the polynomial into the Bézier basis (Exercise 21-16).

The strength of both the forward difference and subdivision algorithms is that they perform only additions, subtractions, and divisions by powers of 2, which can often be implemented as shifts. (For example, the multiplication by 3/8 in Equation 21-10 may be implemented as 1/4 + 1/8.) They are therefore suitable for implementation in hardware or in computers without fast floating-point arithmetic. These techniques by no means exhaust methods for evaluating polynomials (see [268], vol. 2, sec. 4.6.4).

## 21-6 CONCLUSION

Modeling and display of curves and surfaces is a rich and fascinating subject, only briefly surveyed here. Many formulations have been developed in addition to Bézier and B-spline methods—quadric surfaces, natural splines,

Coons surfaces, and many more. For successful application in computer-aided design, a thorough understanding of the mathematical properties of shape representations is essential. This understanding also helps in the design of interactive systems that permit the designer to refine the model to his satisfaction. But curve and surface techniques are also useful in less formal settings. An interactive curve-drawing program for the construction of illustrations with curved shapes is a powerful interactive tool. Many of the illustrations in this book were created with the aid of just such a program.

## EXERCISES

**21-1** How do the four circle parameterizations differ? What criteria can you suggest for a "good" parameterization?

**21-2** Sometimes it is useful to *reparameterize* a curve in order to alter the relationship between parameter value and location along the curve but not to alter the shape of the curve. Consider a reparameterization $v = (au + b)/(cu + d)$. (a) How must $a$, $b$, $c$, and $d$ be related to ensure that $v = 0$ when $u = 0$ and $v = 1$ when $u = 1$? Given these constraints, reduce the reparameterization expression to an expression in $u$ and a single parameter $\alpha$. (b) The second parametric form for a circle quadrant given in the text unfortunately does not place the point $u = 0.5$ halfway along the curve. Find the reparameterization parameter $\alpha$ that will reparameterize this function so that $v = 0.5$ will be halfway along the curve. What are the new parametric functions?

**21-3** Prove that a Bézier curve in the plane is axis-independent.

**21-4** Suppose that a Bézier curve has been defined by $n + 1$ control points. Suppose we want to increase the degree of the curve, i.e., add a control point, but we do not want the shape to change. What are the locations of the $n + 2$ new control points? Such a degree-increasing operation is a convenient one to provide in a modeling system. The designer first asks that the degree be increased without changing the curve; then he can move the new control points to take advantage of the extra flexibility of the higher-degree curve.

**21-5** Derive Equation 21-10. Also derive similar expressions for the four control points of the other curve that results from the subdivision.

**21-6** Develop an expression for the curve through a Bézier surface $P(u, v_0)$, where $v_0$ is a constant, in a form similar to Equation 21-1. That is, find the set of control points for the curve of constant $v$ in terms of the original control points $p_{i,j}$ of the surface.

**21-7** Derive an expression $N(u, v)$ for a vector normal to a Bézier surface at a point given by the two parameters.

**21-8** Consider a B-spline curve with large $n$, and choose $i$ to be approximately $n/2$. Show that $N_{i,k}(u) = N_{i+1,k}(u + 1)$ for both periodic and uniform cases. Thus in the "interior" of a B-spline, the basis functions are simply translations of one another. How, precisely, is the "interior" characterized? How can this observation be exploited when displaying B-splines?

**21-9** Suppose $n + 1$ control points are given. Show that the uniform B-spline curve with $k = n + 1$ is equivalent to a Bézier curve using the same control points.

**21-10** Explore improvements to the algorithm given for computing points on a uniform non-periodic B-spline curve. The improvements should take advantage of the fact that $N_{i,k}(u) = 0$ for $u \leq i - k + 1$ or $u \geq i + 1$. Exercise 21-8 provides another idea for an improvement. The improvements should also eliminate the redundant evaluations performed by the recursive formula.

**21-11** Extend the forward-difference method so that it can be used to generate wire-frame drawings of *bicubic surfaces*. A bicubic surface is one in which both blending functions are cubic polynomials.

**21-12** Generalize the forward-difference technique to apply it to polynomials of any degree.

**21-13** A joint between two curves is said to have "geometric continuity of order $n$" if a geometric property is continuous: for $n = 1$, the tangent must be continuous at the joint; for $n = 2$, the curvature is continuous. A joint is said to have "parametric continuity of order $n$" if the $n$th derivative of the parametric function with respect to the parameter is continuous at the joint. Which is the stronger condition? What kinds of continuity are provided at joints between the Bézier curves shown in Figure 21-10b? How can a joint be constructed to give first order parametric continuity?

**21-14** Suppose a complex curve is described by four cubic Bézier curves ($n = 3$) pieced together in such a way that the entire curve has continuous curvature. If the control point at the middle joint is moved, what is the fewest number of control points that must be moved in order to guarantee that the entire curve has continuous slope? Continuous curvature?

**21-15** Write the blending functions shown in Figure 21-7 as cubic polynomials. Write polynomials that describe the blending functions in Figure 21-13.

**21-16** Four vectors **a**, **b**, **c**, and **d** are given. Each has an $x$, $y$ and $z$ component, as for control points. A curve is defined as $P(u) = au^3 + bu^2 + cu + d$. What are the four control points $p_i$ that define an identical Bézier curve?

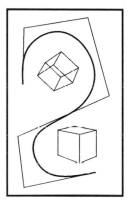

# 22

# THREE-DIMENSIONAL

# TRANSFORMATIONS

# AND PERSPECTIVE

Geometric transformations play an important role in generating images of three-dimensional scenes. They are used in modeling to express locations of objects relative to others. In generating a view of a scene, they are used to achieve the effect of different viewing positions and directions. Finally, the perspective transformation is used in many three-dimensional visualization techniques to project the three-dimensional scene onto a two-dimensional screen. In applications where the viewpoint changes rapidly or where objects move in relation to each other, transformations must be carried out repeatedly. It is therefore necessary to find efficient ways of performing three-dimensional transformations.

## 22-1 TRANSFORMATIONS

The techniques we shall develop in this chapter for expressing three-dimensional transformations are extensions of the two-dimensional techniques presented in Chapter 4. Two important aspects of the earlier formulation are retained: a transformation is expressed as a single entity, the *transformation matrix;* complex transformations, expressed as a sequence of primitive transformations, can be *concatenated* to yield a single transformation matrix that has the same effect as the sequence of primitives.

## Translation

The transformation which translates a point $(x, y, z)$ to a new point $(x', y', z')$ is:

$$[x' \ y' \ z' \ 1] = [x \ y \ z \ 1] \begin{bmatrix} 1 & 0 & 0 & 0 \\ 0 & 1 & 0 & 0 \\ 0 & 0 & 1 & 0 \\ T_x & T_y & T_z & 1 \end{bmatrix} \qquad (22\text{-}1)$$

where $T_x$, $T_y$, and $T_z$ are the components of the translation in the $x$, $y$, and $z$ directions, respectively.

## Rotation

Three-dimensional rotation transformations have more complexity than two-dimensional rotation transformations: we must determine a three-dimensional *axis* about which to rotate. As in two dimensions, the simplest form of the transformation occurs when the axis passes through the origin and is aligned with a coordinate axis. To rotate about an arbitrary point, we must concatenate three transformations: the first translates the point to the origin, the second performs the rotation, and the third translates the origin back. To complicate matters further, we must cope with axes of rotation that are not aligned with the coordinate axes: in these cases we can concatenate two or three primitive rotation transformations to form a matrix that performs rotation about the desired axis. Section 22-7 presents an example of such rotation about an arbitrary axis.

In three dimensions, it is helpful to devise transformations for rotation about each of the three coordinate axes. Rotation about the $z$ coordinate axis, through an angle $\theta$, is achieved with the following transformation (Figure 22-1a):

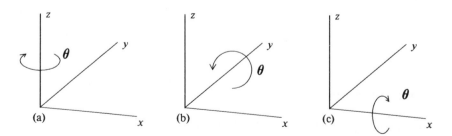

**Figure 22-1** The three primitive three-dimensional rotations. Angles are measured clockwise when looking along the rotation axis toward the origin.

$$[x' \ y' \ z' \ 1] = [x \ y \ z \ 1] \begin{bmatrix} \cos\theta & -\sin\theta & 0 & 0 \\ \sin\theta & \cos\theta & 0 & 0 \\ 0 & 0 & 1 & 0 \\ 0 & 0 & 0 & 1 \end{bmatrix} \quad (22\text{-}2)$$

The rotation angle $\theta$ is measured clockwise about the origin when looking at the origin from a point on the $+z$ axis. Notice that the transformation matrix affects only the values of $x$ and $y$ coordinates.

Rotation about the $y$ coordinate axis (Figure 22-1b) is given by:

$$[x' \ y' \ z' \ 1] = [x \ y \ z \ 1] \begin{bmatrix} \cos\theta & 0 & \sin\theta & 0 \\ 0 & 1 & 0 & 0 \\ -\sin\theta & 0 & \cos\theta & 0 \\ 0 & 0 & 0 & 1 \end{bmatrix} \quad (22\text{-}3)$$

Rotation about the $x$ coordinate axis (Figure 22-1c) is given by:

$$[x' \ y' \ z' \ 1] = [x \ y \ z \ 1] \begin{bmatrix} 1 & 0 & 0 & 0 \\ 0 & \cos\theta & -\sin\theta & 0 \\ 0 & \sin\theta & \cos\theta & 0 \\ 0 & 0 & 0 & 1 \end{bmatrix} \quad (22\text{-}4)$$

All three rotation primitives are minor variants of a single schema. Matrices expressing rotation about the $x$ and $y$ axes are obtained from the $z$-axis rotation matrix by permuting the axes in a cyclic fashion.

## Scaling

A scaling transformation can be used to scale dimensions in each coordinate direction separately:

$$[x' \ y' \ z' \ 1] = [x \ y \ z \ 1] \begin{bmatrix} S_x & 0 & 0 & 0 \\ 0 & S_y & 0 & 0 \\ 0 & 0 & S_z & 0 \\ 0 & 0 & 0 & 1 \end{bmatrix} \quad (22\text{-}5)$$

## Inverse Transformations

Many of the transformations given above have an inverse, which performs the symmetrically opposite transformation. The inverse of matrix 22-1 is

$$[x' \quad y' \quad z' \quad 1] = [x \quad y \quad z \quad 1] \begin{bmatrix} 1 & 0 & 0 & 0 \\ 0 & 1 & 0 & 0 \\ 0 & 0 & 1 & 0 \\ -T_x & -T_y & -T_z & 1 \end{bmatrix} \quad (22\text{-}6)$$

which undoes the effect of the translation of Equation 22-1. The inverse of 22-2 is simply

$$\begin{bmatrix} cos-\theta & -sin-\theta & 0 & 0 \\ sin-\theta & cos-\theta & 0 & 0 \\ 0 & 0 & 1 & 0 \\ 0 & 0 & 0 & 1 \end{bmatrix} \quad (22\text{-}7)$$

which is a rotation of the same magnitude and about the same axis as 22-2 but in the opposite direction.

We shall denote the inverse of transformation $T$ by $T^{-1}$. The two examples suggest this matrix can be obtained by choosing appropriate values for the parameters of a primitive transformation. If $T$ is an arbitrarily complex transformation, however, this approach will not work. Instead, $T^{-1}$, the *matrix inverse* of $T$, can be determined by a computer program (see Appendix I and [179]). Although some matrices are difficult to invert accurately, this is generally not a problem with matrices encountered in geometric applications.

## Concatenation

The successive application of an number of transformations can be achieved with a single transformation matrix, the *concatenation* of the sequence. Suppose two transformations $T_1$ and $T_2$ are to be applied successively. The same effect can be achieved by the application of a single transformation $T_3$, which is simply the product of the matrices $T_1$ and $T_2$. This can be readily demonstrated: the point $(x, y, z)$ is transformed into $(x', y', z')$ by $T_1$:

$$[x' \quad y' \quad z' \quad 1] = [x \quad y \quad z \quad 1] \, T_1 \quad (22\text{-}8)$$

The point $(x'', y'', z'')$ is then generated by applying $T_2$:

$$[x'' \quad y'' \quad z'' \quad 1] = [x' \quad y' \quad z' \quad 1] \, T_2 \quad (22\text{-}9)$$

Substituting Equation 22-8 into Equation 22-9 gives

$$[x'' \quad y'' \quad z'' \quad 1] = ([x \quad y \quad z \quad 1]T_1) \, T_2 = [x \quad y \quad z \quad 1] \, (T_1 T_2) \quad (22\text{-}10)$$

The *order* of application of the transformations must be preserved when the transformation matrices are multiplied together.

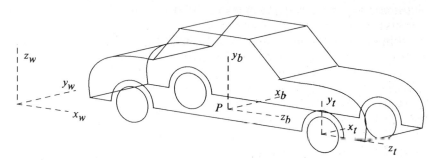

**Figure 22-2** Modeling an automobile by placing instances of symbols with transformations.

## 22-2 TRANSFORMATIONS IN MODELING

When transformations are used in modeling and viewing, they may be treated in two slightly different ways: as a way to move an object by changing its coordinates, or as a way to move the coordinate system that measures the position of the object. These are symmetrical approaches, but the distinction is helpful when determining primitive transformations and when specifying the order in which transformations should be applied.

The distinction between transforming objects and transforming a coordinate system involves a change in sign. If the point $P$ shown in Figure 22-2 is translated by a vector $(T_x, T_y, T_z)$ the new coordinates of $P$ become $(x + T_x, y + T_y, z + T_z)$. On the other hand, if the origin of the coordinate system is translated by an identical vector, the new coordinates of $P$ are $(x - T_x, y - T_y, z - T_z)$. Thus, if we have need to translate the coordinate system, the inverse translation is applied to objects to obtain measurements in the new coordinate system. The same reasoning holds for other transformations. For example, to derive a new coordinate system rotated 90° clockwise about the $z$ axis, we choose $\theta = -90°$ in Equation 22-2.

Figure 22-2 illustrates an automobile with four tires. Several coordinate systems are also shown: the *world* coordinate system $(x_w, y_w, z_w)$, which is the main reference coordinate system; the *body* coordinate system $(x_b, y_b, z_b)$, fixed to the body of the car; and the *tire* coordinate system $(x_t, y_t, z_t)$, fixed to a tire. Consider first the model of the automobile body, which records geometric measurements in the body coordinate system. In order to obtain the world coordinates of a location known in body coordinates, we apply a transformation $T_{bw}$, a transformation that specifies the location of the body coordinate system relative to the world coordinate system. If we denote a point measured in system $i$ by $P_i$, we can write this observation as

$$P_w = P_b T_{bw}$$

The subscript on the transformation $T$ indicates the change of coordinate system: the matrix converts measurements in system $b$ to measurements in system $w$.

Now suppose that the automobile travels forward along the $z_b$ direction and we wish to change the transformation $T_{bw}$ to reflect this motion. Let $T_{bb}$ represent a primitive translation transformation with an appropriate translation in the $z$ direction. The point $P_b$ is now moved to $P_b T_{bb}$. This transformation is used to change the location of a point, and not to change the coordinate system in which coordinates are measured. The conversion to world coordinates becomes

$$P_w = (P_b T_{bb}) T_{bw} = P_b (T_{bb} T_{bw})$$

The parenthesized expression, in which $T_{bw}$ is premultiplied by $T_{bb}$, might be called $T_{bw}'$, since it is the new body-to-world transformation.

On the other hand, suppose that the model is to be changed to reflect the motion of the automobile in the world coordinate system. If the car is to be moved 10 meters north, the transformation is conveniently expressed in world coordinates by a translation $T_{ww}$ along the direction $y_w$ (assuming $y_w$ points north):

$$P_w = P_b (T_{bw} T_{ww})$$

In this case, $T_{bw}$ is postmultiplied by the transformation that represents the change. These two examples illustrate that the transformation order is determined by the coordinate system in which the change is most conveniently expressed.

Modeling transformations are also used to place instances of a symbol at different locations in a model. To continue the example slightly further, consider the four tires. We can use a single model of the geometry of a tire and perform four different transformations to specify how tires are to be located with respect to the body coordinate system. The right front tire, for example, is described by the transformation $T_{tb}$ that converts coordinates measured in the tire system into the body system:

$$P_b = P_t T_{tb}$$

If the tire is rotated about its $x_t$ axis, as might happen when the automobile moves forward, the transformation to auto coordinates becomes

$$P_b = (P_t T_{tt}) T_{tb} = P_t (T_{tt} T_{tb})$$

where $T_{tt}$ is a primitive rotation matrix that rotates about the $x$ axis. What is really required, of course, is to convert the tire's coordinates to the world coordinate system. Concatenating all the relevant transformations, we obtain

$$P_w = P_t (T_{tt} T_{tb} T_{bw})$$

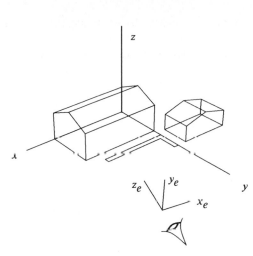

z

$z_e$    $y_e$    y

$x_e$

**Figure 22-3** The eye coordinate system has its origin at the viewpoint and $z_e$ axis along the viewing direction. The coordinate system is left-handed.

Transformations that relate several parts of a geometric model are an integral part of the model. Although an object's geometry and topology need be defined only once using the methods of Chapters 20 and 21, transformations allow us to include many *instances* of these objects in a scene. Thus the structure of a complex three-dimensional scene could be represented as primitive objects, together with a tree structure of "calls" to these primitives that include transformation information. Such a structure is illustrated for two-dimensional objects by the display procedure and graphical data structure techniques described in Chapter 10.

## 22-3 TRANSFORMATIONS IN VIEWING

Transformations are extremely helpful in establishing the effect of different viewing parameters on the display of a scene. In order to calculate the position on the display screen of the image of a point on some object, we must first transform the point from the world coordinate system into the *eye coordinate system*, which has its origin fixed at the viewpoint and its $z_e$ axis pointed in the direction of view (Figure 22-3).

A transformation $V$, the *viewing transformation*, is used to convert points in the world coordinate system $(x_w, y_w, z_w)$ into points in the eye coordinate system $(x_e, y_e, z_e)$

$$[x_e \quad y_e \quad z_e \quad 1] = [x_w \quad y_w \quad z_w \quad 1] V \qquad (22\text{-}11)$$

This transformation may be built up from several translations and rotations that are determined from the viewing parameters. Section 22-7 provides an example of the derivation of $V$ from viewing parameters.

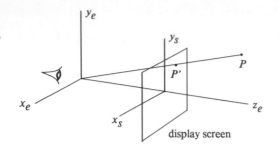

**Figure 22-4** The perspective projection of point $P$ onto the display screen.

We adopt the convention that the eye coordinate system is a *left-handed* cartesian coordinate system: the $z_e$ axis points forward from the viewpoint, the $x_e$ axis to the right, and the $y_e$ axis up. These conventions are chosen so that the $x_e$ and $y_e$ axes will align with the $x$ and $y$ axes of the display screen (see Figure 22-4). The name "left-handed" arises from a method for remembering the axis relationships. If the left hand is held flat with the thumb extending out, so that the thumb and first finger align with the $x$ and $y$ directions, respectively, the $z$ direction points outward from the palm and can be indicated with the second finger.

The world coordinate system is normally represented as shown in Figure 22-1 with *right-handed* conventions. Consequently it is necessary at some point to convert from one convention to another. This can be achieved with a transformation matrix; the example below inverts the sign of $z$ coordinates to make the change:

$$\begin{bmatrix} 1 & 0 & 0 & 0 \\ 0 & 1 & 0 & 0 \\ 0 & 0 & -1 & 0 \\ 0 & 0 & 0 & 1 \end{bmatrix} \qquad (22\text{-}12)$$

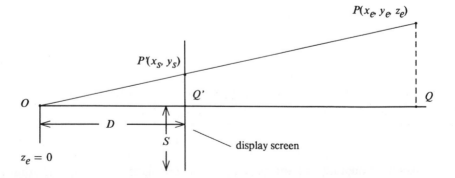

**Figure 22-5** The $(y_s, z_s)$ plane showing details of the perspective projection.

## 22-4 THE PERSPECTIVE TRANSFORMATION

A perspective display can be generated by simply *projecting* each point of an object onto the plane of the display screen, as in Figure 22-4. The coordinates $(x_s, y_s)$ of the projected image of the point $P$ measured in eye coordinates $(x_e, y_e, z_e)$ are easily computed.

Consider the $y_e z_e$ plane drawn in Figure 22-5. The triangles $OQ'P'$ and $OQP$ are similar, giving the relation $y_s/D = y_e/z_e$. A similar construction in the $x_e z_e$ plane yields $x_s/D = x_e/z_e$. The numbers $x_s$ and $y_s$ can be converted into dimensionless fractions by dividing by the screen size:

$$x_s = \left(\frac{Dx_e}{Sz_e}\right) \qquad y_s = \left(\frac{Dy_e}{Sz_e}\right) \tag{22-13}$$

Alternatively, we can convert to screen coordinates by including a specification of the location of the viewport in which the image is displayed

$$x_s = \left(\frac{Dx_e}{Sz_e}\right) V_{sx} + V_{cx} \qquad y_s = \left(\frac{Dy_e}{Sz_e}\right) V_{sy} + V_{cy} \tag{22-14}$$

The four viewport parameters are given in *center-size* notation: the viewport is centered at $(V_{cx}, V_{cy})$, is $2V_{sx}$ units wide and $2V_{sy}$ units high. These four parameters can be determined from the viewport parameters explained in Section 5-6. For example, $V_{cx} = (V_{xl} + V_{xr})/2$ and $V_{sx} = (V_{xr} - V_{xl})/2$.

The perspective transformation is fundamentally different from those for rotation, translation, and scaling: it involves *dividing* by the $z_e$ coordinate value, whereas the others involve only multiplication and addition. *Generating a true perspective image requires dividing by the depth of each point.*

Fortunately, however, a perspective image of a line can be generated easily by transforming only its endpoints and drawing the line between the two transformed endpoints. The process of generating a wire-frame perspective display thus involves retrieving the world coordinates of the endpoints of each line, using Equation 22-11 to obtain the eye coordinates of the endpoints and then Equation 22-14 to obtain screen coordinates of each endpoint. A vector generator can then generate lines from the endpoint information.

Equation 22-14 reflects the independence of the eye coordinate system from the screen coordinate system. Values chosen for the viewport parameters are given in the same coordinate system the display hardware uses to address locations on the screen. The values for the eye coordinate points, however, can be in a completely different form because a dimensionless ratio is formed in Equation 22-14. This independence is analogous to that of the two-dimensional world and screen coordinate systems described in Chapter 5.

The units of measurement of the parameters $D$ and $S$ are similarly

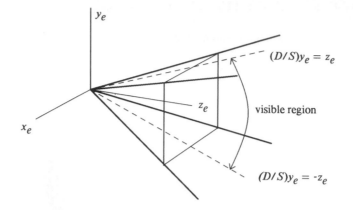

**Figure 22-6** The viewing pyramid specifies a region of the eye coordinate system in which objects must lie if they are to be visible.

independent of the other coordinate systems; only the ratio $D/S$ is involved in Equation 22-14. If this ratio is small, the aperture will be broad, thus producing an image similar to that of a wide-angle lens. A large value of $D/S$ specifies a narrow aperture, corresponding to a telephoto view.

## 22-5 THREE-DIMENSIONAL CLIPPING

The simple application of Equations 22-11 and 22-14 to produce a perspective image has two undesirable effects: objects behind the viewpoint may appear on the screen, and objects may exceed the prescribed limits of the viewport given in Equation 22-14. These effects can be eliminated by testing each point in eye coordinates against a *viewing pyramid,* which defines the portion of eye-coordinate space which the viewer can actually see (Figure 22-6).

Two conditions must be met for an individual point to be visible within the pyramid:

$$ -z_e \leq (D/S)x_e \leq +z_e \qquad \text{and} \qquad -z_e \leq (D/S)y_e \leq +z_e \qquad (22\text{-}15)$$

Note that these conditions exclude points behind the viewpoint ($z_e \leq 0$). If a point fails the test, it is not displayed. If it satisfies the two conditions, Equation 22-14 is applied to the eye coordinates to determine the position of the point on the display screen.

Lines cannot be processed as easily as points and must be *clipped* against the limits of the viewing pyramid defined in Equation 22-15. A line may be rejected as invisible if no part of it intersects the pyramid. Otherwise, the endpoints of the visible portion of the line are calculated in the three-dimensional eye coordinate system (Figure 22-7). Equation 22-14 is then

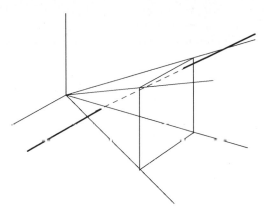

**Figure 22-7** Lines that penetrate the viewing pyramid must be clipped. The dashed portion of the line lies inside the pyramid and is visible.

applied to these endpoint coordinates, and the line is drawn on the screen. The clipping process must operate on three-dimensional descriptions of lines rather than on the screen coordinate values after Equation 22-14 is applied (see Exercise 22-5).

For the convenience of the clipping task, we define a new coordinate system (the clipping coordinate system, subscript $c$) in terms of the eye coordinate system:

$$[x_c \ y_c \ z_c \ 1] - [x_e \ y_e \ z_e \ 1] N \qquad (22\text{-}16)$$

$$N = \begin{bmatrix} D/S & 0 & 0 & 0 \\ 0 & D/S & 0 & 0 \\ 0 & 0 & 1 & 0 \\ 0 & 0 & 0 & 1 \end{bmatrix}$$

The conditions of Equation 22-15 become simply

$$-z_c \le x_c \le +z_c \qquad \text{and} \qquad -z_c \le y_c \le +z_c \qquad (22\text{-}17)$$

A three-dimensional clipping algorithm can be derived by extending the two-dimensional scheme described in Chapter 5. The algorithm determines whether an endpoint of the line lies outside the limits of Equation 22-17 by computing a 4-bit code for each endpoint:

| | |
|---|---|
| First bit: | $x_c$ is to left of pyramid, that is, $x_c < -z_c$ |
| Second bit: | $x_c$ is to right of pyramid, that is, $x_c > z_c$ |
| Third bit: | $y_c$ is below pyramid, that is, $y_c < -z_c$ |
| Fourth bit: | $y_c$ is above pyramid, that is, $y_c > z_c$ |

If the codes for both endpoints are zero, both endpoints lie within the pyramid and the line is trivially accepted. If the logical AND of the codes is not zero, both endpoints lie on the invisible side of one of the planes and the entire line is trivially rejected. Otherwise, the line must cross one or more of the pyramid planes. The algorithm computes the point of intersection of the line and this plane and uses this point to replace the endpoint that was on the invisible side of the plane. The point of intersection of the line and the plane is computed using a parametric form:

$$((1 - t)[x_1 \quad y_1 \quad z_1] + t[x_2 \quad y_2 \quad z_2]) \begin{bmatrix} \alpha \\ \beta \\ 1 \end{bmatrix} = 0$$

where $\alpha$ and $\beta$ have different values for the different planes. For example, the plane $x = z$ has $\alpha = 1$ and $\beta = 0$. The algorithm is shown in Figure 22-8.

If the clipping process yields a visible line segment, we must still apply the inverse of transformation 22-16 followed by the perspective transformation (Equation 22-14) to calculate the screen coordinates of the endpoints of the line. Equation 22-14 can be rewritten to perform both operations:

$$x_s = (x_c/z_c) V_{sx} + V_{cx} \qquad y_s = (y_c/z_c) V_{sy} + V_{cy} \qquad (22\text{-}18)$$

## 22-6 THREE-DIMENSIONAL GRAPHICS PACKAGES

The transformations we have discussed so far form the basis for a transformation system for generating wire-frame images of three-dimensional scenes. This process involves:

1.  A matrix multiplication that performs all the transformations used in modeling the objects in the scene.
2.  A matrix multiplication to transform from world coordinates to the clipping coordinate system. The matrix used is a concatenation of a viewing matrix $V$ (Equation 22-11) and the matrix $N$ of Equation 22-16.
3.  A clipping step, using an algorithm such as the one above.
4.  A "proportional division" shown in Equation 22-18.

These four steps can be performed by a graphics package to provide functions for generating views of three-dimensional scenes. A package like that described in Chapters 6 through 10 can be easily adapted for three-dimensional viewing by modifying a few functions.

*MoveTo, LineTo.* These functions need to take a third argument, in order to specify a $z$ value. Each line specified by these calls will be transformed by a

```
procedure Clip(x1, y1, z1, x2, y2, z2: real);
  label return;
  type edge = (left, right, bottom, top); outcode = set of edge;
  var c, c1, c2: outcode; x, y, z, t: real;
    procedure Code(x, y, z: real; var c: outcode);
    begin
      c := [];
      if x < -z then c := [left] else if x > z then c := [right];
      if y < -z then c := c + [bottom] else if y > z then c := c + [top];
    end;
begin
    Code(x1, y1, z1, c1); Code(x2, y2, z2, c2);
    while (c1 <> []) or (c2 <> []) do begin
        if (c1 * c2) <> [] then goto return;
        c := c1; if c = [] then c := c2;
        if left in c then begin { Crosses left edge }
            t := (z1 + x1) / ((x1 - x2) - (z2 - z1));
            z := t * (z2 - z1) + z1;
            x := -z;
            y := t * (y2 - y1) + y1
            end else
        if right in c then begin { Crosses right edge }
            t := (z1 - x1) / ((x2 - x1) - (z2 - z1));
            z := t * (z2 - z1) + z1;
            x := z;
            y := t * (y2 - y1) + y1
            end else
        if bottom in c then begin { Crosses bottom edge }
            t := (z1 + y1) / ((y1 - y2) - (z2 - z1));
            z := t * (z2 - z1) + z1;
            x := t * (x2 - x1) + x1;
            y := -z
            end else
        if top in c then begin { Crosses top edge }
            t := (z1 - y1) / ((y2 - y1) - (z2 - z1));
            z := t * (z2 - z1) + z1;
            x := t * (x2 - x1) + x1;
            y := z;
            end;
        if c = c1 then begin
            x1 := x; y1 := y; z1 := z; Code(x, y, z, c1)
            end else begin
            x2 := x; y2 := y; z2 := z; Code(x, y, z, c2)
            end;
    end;
    { If we reach here, the line from (x1, y1, z1) to (x2, y2, z2) lies within the viewing
    pyramid. We may now pass this line to a procedure to make a perspective display of it. }
    ShowLine(x1, y1, z1, x2, y2, z2);
return: end;
```

**Figure 22-8** A three-dimensional clipping algorithm.

4 × 4 transformation matrix (the concatenation of the modeling and viewing transformations), clipped with a three-dimensional clipping algorithm, and mapped onto the viewport with Equation 22-18.

*Translate, Rotate, Scale.* These functions need to be extended to modify the modeling transformation matrix by concatenating primitive three-dimensional transformations.

*View specification.* The viewing transformation $V$, the ratio $D/S$, and a viewport must all be established to specify the perspective view to be generated. The viewport is given by a call to *SetViewport,* as described in Chapter 6. The viewing transformation can be established by calls to the modeling transformation primitives *Translate, Rotate,* and *Scale* because the viewing and modeling transformations are concatenated to form a single matrix. A new primitive function, *Perspective(D/S),* can be called to concatenate the transformation given in Equation 22-16.

The graphics package can also be designed to separate the functions that control viewing transformations from those for modeling. The package provides functions that accept a viewing position and viewing direction and calculate the proper viewing transformations (see Exercises 22-12 and 22-13).

Three-dimensional transformations are an integral part of visualization techniques used to generate images of three-dimensional scenes. The kinetic depth effect, for example, requires that transformations and clipping be performed rapidly to produce a sequence of changing views. For applications like these, special hardware for transformations and clipping is usually required. The organization of some of these high-performance displays is discussed in Chapter 26.

## 22-7 EXAMPLES

We conclude this chapter with a pair of examples that illustrate the use of three-dimensional transformation methods. The first develops the matrix representation of rotation about an arbitrary axis in three dimensions. The second example shows how to generate a wire-frame perspective view of a simple object.

### Rotation about an Arbitrary Axis

The rotation about an arbitrary axis through an arbitrary point can be derived from combinations of the primitive transformations (Equations 22-1 to 22-5). Let us define $(x, y, z)$ as a point through which the rotation axis passes, and $(a, b, c)$ as the direction cosines of the axis, i.e., a unit vector along the rotation axis. The steps in the rotation through an angle $\theta$ about this axis are:

1. Translate the object into a new coordinate system where $(x, y, z)$ maps into the origin $(0, 0, 0)$ (matrix $T$).

2. Perform appropriate rotations about the $x$ and $y$ axes of this coordinate system so that the unit vector $(a, b, c)$ is mapped into the unit vector along the $z$ axis (matrices $R_1$ and $R_2$).
3. Perform the desired rotation $\theta$ about the $z$ axis of the new coordinate system. The matrix 22-2 gives the form of this transformation (matrix $R_\theta$).
4. Apply the inverse of step 2 (matrices $R_2^{-1}$ and $R_1^{-1}$).
5. Apply the inverse of step 1 (matrix $T^{-1}$).

The purpose of steps 4 and 5 is to return the object to its original coordinate system. The provisional coordinate systems created by steps 1 and 2 are used only as intermediate steps in the process. The complete transformation representing the five steps is thus $TR_1R_2R_\theta R_2^{-1}R_1^{-1}T^{-1}$.

If we let $v = (b^2 + c^2)^{\frac{1}{2}}$, the matrices are

$$T = \begin{bmatrix} 1 & 0 & 0 & 0 \\ 0 & 1 & 0 & 0 \\ 0 & 0 & 1 & 0 \\ -x & -y & -z & 1 \end{bmatrix} \tag{22-19}$$

$$R_1 = \begin{bmatrix} 1 & 0 & 0 & 0 \\ 0 & c/v & b/v & 0 \\ 0 & -b/v & c/v & 0 \\ 0 & 0 & 0 & 1 \end{bmatrix} \tag{22-20}$$

$$R_2 = \begin{bmatrix} v & 0 & a & 0 \\ 0 & 1 & 0 & 0 \\ -a & 0 & v & 0 \\ 0 & 0 & 0 & 1 \end{bmatrix} \tag{22-21}$$

$$R_\theta = \begin{bmatrix} \cos\theta & -\sin\theta & 0 & 0 \\ \sin\theta & \cos\theta & 0 & 0 \\ 0 & 0 & 1 & 0 \\ 0 & 0 & 0 & 1 \end{bmatrix} \tag{22-22}$$

*Notes on the derivation of Equations 22-19 to 22-22.* The direction cosines of the rotation axis have a very simple interpretation. Suppose one point on the rotation axis is $(x, y, z)$ and another is $(x', y', z')$. A vector along the axis is thus $A = [(x' - x) \quad (y' - y) \quad (z' - z)]$. If this vector is normalized, it is the vector of direction cosines:

$$[a \quad b \quad c] = \frac{A}{\{(x' - x)^2 + (y' - y)^2 + (z' - z)^2\}^{\frac{1}{2}}}$$

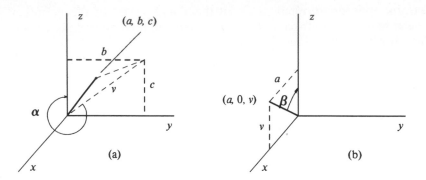

**Figure 22-9** Two rotations are used to align the point ($a$, $b$, $c$) with the $z$ axis: (a) a rotation about the $x$ axis; (b) a rotation about the $y$ axis.

After the translation given by matrix $T$, we must align the ($a$, $b$, $c$) unit vector with the $z$ axis. This is done in two steps: a rotation about the $x$ axis and a rotation about the $y$ axis (see Figures 22-9a and 22-9b). The components of the unit-length axis vector $[a \ b \ c]$ in the $yz$ plane are $b$ along the $y$ axis and $c$ along the $z$ axis, that is, $\cos \alpha = c/v$ and $\sin \alpha = -b/v$. These are precisely the parameters inserted into Equation 22-4 to yield the matrix of Equation 22-20.

The situation after the first rotation is shown in Figure 22-9b. The rotation angle $\beta$ is defined by $\cos \beta = v$ and $\sin \beta = -a$ (recall that because the direction cosines are normalized, the length of the hypotenuse in Figure 22-10b is 1). These parameters used in Equation 22-3 yield Equation 22-21.

### Perspective View of a Cube

Consider a cube centered at the origin of the world coordinate system, defined by the following points and lines:

| Lines | Points | | | |
|---|---|---|---|---|
| | | $x$ | $y$ | $z$ |
| AB, BC, | A | −1 | 1 | −1 |
| CD, DA, | B | 1 | 1 | −1 |
| EF, FG, | C | 1 | −1 | −1 |
| GH, HE, | D | −1 | −1 | −1 |
| AE, BF, | E | −1 | 1 | 1 |
| CG, DH | F | 1 | 1 | 1 |
| | G | 1 | −1 | 1 |
| | H | −1 | −1 | 1 |

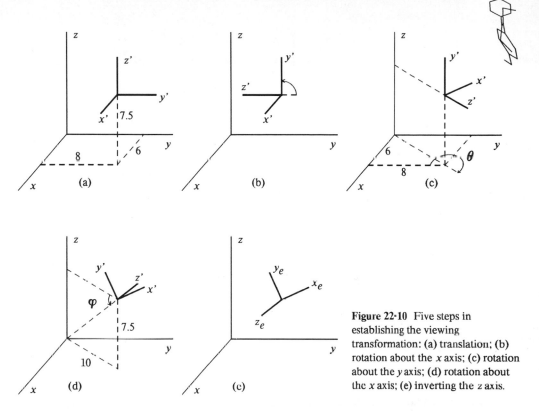

**Figure 22-10** Five steps in establishing the viewing transformation: (a) translation; (b) rotation about the $x$ axis; (c) rotation about the $y$ axis; (d) rotation about the $x$ axis; (e) inverting the $z$ axis.

We shall observe this cube from a point (6, 8, 7.5), with the viewing axis $z_e$ pointed directly at the origin of the world coordinate system. There is still one degree of freedom left, namely an arbitrary rotation about the $z_e$ axis; we shall assume that the $x_e$ axis lies in the $z = 7.5$ plane.

The viewing transformation is established by a sequence of changes of coordinate systems. Recall that a transformation that moves a coordinate system is the inverse of the corresponding transformation that moves points.

1. The coordinate system is translated to (6, 8, 7.5), as shown in Figure 22-10a. The point (6, 8, 7.5) in the original coordinate systems becomes the origin:

$$T_1 = \begin{bmatrix} 1 & 0 & 0 & 0 \\ 0 & 1 & 0 & 0 \\ 0 & 0 & 1 & 0 \\ -6 & -8 & -7.5 & 1 \end{bmatrix}$$

2. Rotate the coordinate system about the $x'$ axis by $-90°$, as shown in Figure 22-10b. Because we require the inverse transformation, we substitute $\theta = 90°$ into Equation 22-4:

$$T_2 = \begin{bmatrix} 1 & 0 & 0 & 0 \\ 0 & 0 & -1 & 0 \\ 0 & 1 & 0 & 0 \\ 0 & 0 & 0 & 1 \end{bmatrix}$$

3. Rotate about the $y'$ axis by an angle $\theta$ so that the point $(0, 0, 7.5)$ will lie on the $z'$ axis, as shown in Figure 22-10c. We have $\cos -\theta = \cos \theta = -8/10$ and $\sin -\theta = -\sin \theta = 6/10$:

$$T_3 = \begin{bmatrix} -0.8 & 0 & 0.6 & 0 \\ 0 & 1 & 0 & 0 \\ -0.6 & 0 & -0.8 & 0 \\ 0 & 0 & 0 & 1 \end{bmatrix}$$

4. Rotate about the $x'$ axis by an angle $\varphi$ so that the origin of the original coordinate system will lie on the $z'$ axis, as shown in Figure 22-10d. We have $\cos -\varphi = \cos \varphi = 10/12.5$ and $\sin -\varphi = -\sin \varphi = -7.5/12.5$:

$$T_4 = \begin{bmatrix} 1 & 0 & 0 & 0 \\ 0 & 0.8 & 0.6 & 0 \\ 0 & -0.6 & 0.8 & 0 \\ 0 & 0 & 0 & 1 \end{bmatrix}$$

5. Finally, reverse the sense of the $z'$ axis in order to create a left-handed coordinate system that conforms to the conventions of the eye coordinate system, as shown in Figure 22-10e. A scaling matrix is used:

$$T_4 = \begin{bmatrix} 1 & 0 & 0 & 0 \\ 0 & 1 & 0 & 0 \\ 0 & 0 & -1 & 0 \\ 0 & 0 & 0 & 1 \end{bmatrix}$$

This completes the five primitive transformations needed to establish the viewing transformation $V = T_1T_2T_3T_4T_5$.

Suppose that we wish to fill a 30- by 30-centimeter display screen, designed to be viewed from 60 centimeters away, and that the coordinate system of the screen runs from 0 to 1023. Thus, $D = 60$, $S = 15$, and $V_{sx} = V_{cx} = V_{sy} = V_{cy} = 1023/2$. The transformation 22-16 is therefore

$$N = \begin{bmatrix} 4 & 0 & 0 & 0 \\ 0 & 4 & 0 & 0 \\ 0 & 0 & 1 & 0 \\ 0 & 0 & 0 & 1 \end{bmatrix}$$

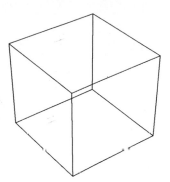

**Figure 22-11** The perspective view of a cube generated by the example calculations in the text.

and Equation 22-18 becomes

$$x_s = 511.5\,(x_c/z_c) + 511.5 \qquad y_s = 511.5\,(y_c/z_c) + 511.5 \qquad (22\text{-}23)$$

All the details of the transformations have now been specified. Each vertex of the cube is transformed by the matrix $VN$, clipped, and converted to screen coordinates using Equation 22-23.

$$VN = T_1T_2T_3T_4T_5N = \begin{bmatrix} -3.2 & -1.44 & -0.48 & 0 \\ 2.4 & -1.92 & -0.64 & 0 \\ 0 & 3.2 & -0.6 & 0 \\ 0 & 0 & 12.5 & 1 \end{bmatrix}$$

We can now apply this transformation to the eight vertices of the cube:

|   | $x_c$ | $y_c$ | $z_c$ |
|---|---|---|---|
| A | 5.6 | −3.68 | 12.94 |
| B | −0.8 | −6.56 | 11.98 |
| C | −5.6 | −2.72 | 13.26 |
| D | 0.8 | 0.16 | 14.22 |
| E | 5.6 | 2.72 | 11.74 |
| F | −0.8 | −0.16 | 10.78 |
| G | −5.6 | 3.68 | 12.06 |
| H | 0.8 | 6.56 | 13.02 |

Although the clipping routine must be applied to each line in the cube, it is apparent from the table that all of the vertices lie within the viewing pyramid, and the clipping algorithm will trivially accept each line. The screen coordinates of the line endpoints are calculated with Equation 22-23, and the lines are drawn as shown in Figure 22-11.

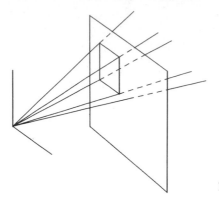

**Figure 22-12** An off-axis viewing pyramid.

## EXERCISES

**22-1** Show that the perspective projection of a three-dimensional line is the same as the two-dimensional line drawn between the perspective projections of its endpoints. If this were not true, the calculation of the perspective view of a line would be quite complicated. You are essentially asked to prove that the display formed by projecting endpoints and drawing two-dimensional lines (usually with display hardware) between them is an accurate perspective image.

**22-2** In conventional photography, the image formed by the lens (focal length $f$) is on a small negative. Typical equipment (50-millimeter lens focal length and 24- by 36-millimeter film) would give $D/S = 2$. Then an enlargement of the negative is made. The scaling is often by a factor of 5 to 50 and affects only the $x$ and $y$ locations of points. You would suspect that $D/S$ controls only the "perspective" of the image and viewport size the actual size of the screen. What is the relation between $D/S$ and viewport size so that a particular three-dimensional point always appears on the same spot on the screen? Does the relation depend on the coordinates of the three-dimensional point? The results of your analysis are useful in implementing a facility to control the perspective of the picture: you may have to zoom in or out but will want to keep the image size on the screen about constant.

**22-3** We have assumed that the user wants a viewing pyramid which is symmetric about the $z_e$ axis. Suppose she wants only to see a smaller, off-axis view, placed appropriately on the display screen, as shown in Figure 22-12. How would you generate such an image? Is it equivalent to simple perspective generation as described in this chapter using (1) a smaller viewport, (2) a smaller ratio $S/D$ and (3) a suitably rotated eye coordinate system?

**22-4** Extend the discussion of three-dimensional instances to perform a function analogous to two-dimensional boxing, i.e., describe how we might be able to say "no part of this three-dimensional instance will be visible inside the viewing pyramid" and thus avoid clipping any of the lines of the instance. We could pass over those instances which cannot appear and thus save considerable processing time.

**22-5** Why can we not project three-dimensional lines onto a two-dimensional plane and then clip them against a two-dimensional window? *Hint:* Consider a line from (1, 1, 4) to (1, 1, −4) as measured in eye coordinates in a viewing pyramid with $D/S = 1$.

**22-6** Rework the first example in Section 22-7 using transformations that alter coordinate system locations and orientations rather than transformations that move points. How is your answer related to the book's example?

**22-7** How might you exaggerate the perspective of an object?

**22-8** Write a midpoint-division version of the three-dimensional clipping algorithm.

**22-9** How can the polygon clipping algorithm described in Section 5-4 be adapted to clip polygons against the three-dimensional viewing pyramid?

**22-10** Art students are often taught to draw perspective pictures of city blocks and the like with a *vanishing point* method (see Figure 22-13). Under what conditions, if any, is the picture a true perspective drawing? What are the vanishing points of the perspective transformation (Equation 22-14)?

**22-11** The derivation of Equation 22-14 assumes that the image on the screen plane is square, i.e., that $V_{sx}$ is the same as $V_{sy}$. Suppose this is not the case. What modifications to the procedure are required for generating a display?

**22-12** Generalize the scheme used in the example of a perspective display of a cube to compute a viewing transformation $V$ given a viewpoint $(x, y, z)$, the viewing direction cosines $(a, b, c)$, and the perspective ratio $a/b$. Suggest a good convention for the remaining degree of freedom.

**22-13** Design a set of high-level functions that help to specify the viewing parameters and corresponding viewing transformation. Your design should include a description of how the viewing matrix $V$ is computed by the functions. Following are three schemes to serve as starting points.

(a) A function *LookFrom*$(x, y, z)$, which specifies the viewpoint, and a function *LookAt*$(x, y, z, r)$, which indicates that a sphere of radius $r$ and center $(x, y, z)$ should just about fill the field of view. What calculations transform these seven parameters into a viewing transformation? Is any more information required?

(b) A function *LookAt*$(x, y, z, r)$ as described above, and a function *LookFrom*$(r, \theta, \varphi)$ that gives the viewing position in spherical coordinates relative to the *LookAt* point.

(c) Functions to modify the current viewing parameters, perhaps specified initially by schemes (a) or (b). These functions are patterned after the motions of a movie camera: *Pan, Tilt, Zoom,* and *Roll* (move the camera forward or backward along the direction in which it points).

**22-14** A transformation $M$ of one three-dimensional space into another can be constructed if you know how four points transform: $AM = A'$, $BM = B'$, $CM = C'$, $DM = D'$. How is the transformation matrix $M$ actually computed? Is there any redundant information in the eight vectors $A, A', B, B',$ etc.? That is, can the same transformation matrix be derived with less information?

**22-15** In some applications, it is important to determine the inverse of the transformation matrix. Suppose that we keep two matrices at all times, the transformation matrix and its inverse. Show how when a primitive transformation (translation, rotation, scaling) is concatenated with the current transformation, the inverse can be updated. It is not necessary to use standard matrix inversion techniques.

**22-16** Section 22-2 shows uses for both premultiplication and postmultiplication of transformation matrices. How do these needs affect the design of a graphics package? How does the presence of the viewing matrix $V$ influence your answer?

**22-17** The recommendations for a three-dimensional graphics package given in Section 22-6 make no mention of the conversion from right-handed to left-handed coordinate systems. Discuss ways of handling this conversion within the package.

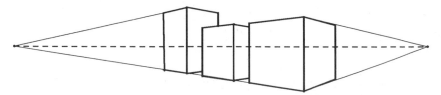

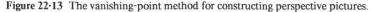

**Figure 22-13** The vanishing-point method for constructing perspective pictures.

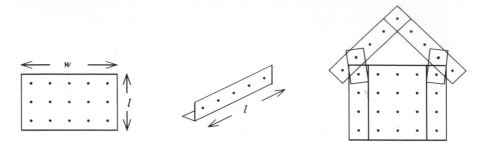

**Figure 22-14** Modeling a house using modular sheets and angle brackets.

**22-18** Imagine building a model of a house similar to the one in Figure 22-3 from a child's mechanical construction set. The set has two sorts of components, plates and angles, shown in Figure 22-14. Components of all sizes are available; the dimensions $w$ and $l$ must be an integral number of centimeters. Holes are drilled in the plates at 1-centimeter intervals for inserting fasteners. Write a computer program that first models the house, using the two components as geometrical primitives, and then generates a perspective view of it. The program must use modeling and transformation techniques to represent the structure of the house.

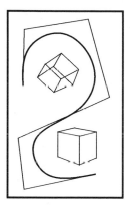

# 23

## PERSPECTIVE

## DEPTH

The operation of removing hidden lines or surfaces requires a perspective transformation with special properties. The image we wish to produce is a perspective view, but the *depth* of each point in the perspective image must be available for making decisions about which surfaces hide lines and other surfaces. Depth calculations must be performed correctly to avoid anomalies in the displayed image.

We shall augment the screen coordinate system introduced in Chapter 22 to be a three-dimensional system $(x_s,\ y_s,\ z_s)$. The $x_s$ and $y_s$ coordinates of a point in this system specify the location of a perspective view of the point on a two-dimensional screen. In the three-dimensional screen coordinate system, a $z_s$ coordinate will be calculated so as to retain depth information, without altering the interpretation of the $x_s$ and $y_s$ values. Thus, to display a point $(x_s,\ y_s,\ z_s)$ on a two-dimensional screen, we use the values of $x_s$ and $y_s$ directly, as shown in Figure 23-1, and ignore the $z_s$ coordinate. This display is an *orthographic projection* of the screen coordinate system, one in which the original point and its image lie on a line perpendicular to the plane of the screen.

Figure 23-1 illustrates how the three-dimensional screen coordinate system simplifies the hidden-surface problem. The perspective images of points $P$ and $Q$ are identical because they have identical values of $x_s$ and $y_s$. However, it is clear that point $P$ lies closer to the observer because its depth, $z_s = 0.3$, is less than the depth of point $Q$, $z_s = 0.6$. A similar comparison could be performed

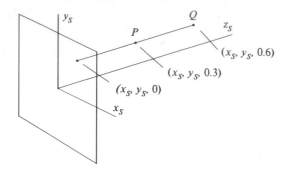

**Figure 23-1** The three-dimensional screen coordinate system simplifies comparing the depths of two points $P$ and $Q$ that project to the same point on the screen.

in the eye coordinate system, but it would be complicated by the fact that projections of points onto the viewing screen involve rays emanating from the viewpoint at various angles.

## 23-1 THE SCREEN COORDINATE SYSTEM

The calculation of the depth coordinate $z_s$ must be carefully performed if the results are to be helpful in hidden-surface calculations. In particular, we shall need to be able to calculate the depth of a line not only at its endpoints but also at intermediate points along it. To keep such depth interpolation simple, it is essential that *straight lines in the eye coordinate system transform into straight lines in the screen coordinate system.* It is equally essential that planes transform into planes. Thus we need to transform $z_e$ values so that a plane equation in eye coordinates transforms into a plane equation in screen coordinates:

$$ax_e + by_e + cz_e + d = 0 \quad \Rightarrow \quad a'x_s + b'y_s + c'z_s + d' = 0 \qquad (23\text{-}1)$$

The values for $x_s$ and $y_s$ are obtained by dividing the $x_e$ and $y_e$ coordinates by the distance $z_e$ from the observer to the point, as we showed in Chapter 22. Thus, $x_s = x_e/z_e$ and $y_s = y_e/z_e$, assuming for the moment that $D/S = 1$, $V_{sx} = V_{sy} = 1$, and $V_{cx} = V_{cy} = 0$. Given values for $x_s$ and $y_s$, we find that a value for $z_s$ of the form

$$z_s = \alpha + \frac{\beta}{z_e} \qquad (23\text{-}2)$$

will satisfy Equation 23-1. We can choose $\alpha$ and $\beta$ almost at will to yield a convenient range of $z_s$ values. Choosing $\beta < 0$ has the advantage that the intuitive notion of depth is preserved: if one point has a larger $z_e$ value than another, it will also have a larger $z_s$ value.

A prime consideration in choosing parameters for the perspective transformation is *depth precision.* If we know that $z_e$ values lie in the range $D \leq z_e \leq F$, we can maximize depth resolution by choosing $\alpha$ and $\beta$ so that $z_e = D$ maps into the smallest $z_s$ value and $z_e = F$ into the largest. Values outside this range will have no representation in the screen coordinate system. For convenience, we shall adopt the convention $0 \leq z_s \leq 1$.

These conventions modify the viewing pyramid by adding planes to limit the range of $z_e$ values (Figure 23-2). The perspective transformation maps this *truncated viewing pyramid* into a *standard viewbox* in the screen coordinate system. This box is characterized by values of $x_s$ and $y_s$ that lie in the range $-1$ to 1 and values of $z_s$ in the range 0 to 1. These values can be further mapped to display hardware coordinates by a viewport transformation, as in Equation 22-18.

The perspective transformation that accomplishes the mapping is:

$$x_s = \frac{x_e}{w} \qquad y_s = \frac{y_e}{w} \qquad z_s = \frac{S \ (z_e/D - 1)}{(1 - D/F) \ w}$$

$$w = \frac{S z_e}{D}$$

(23-3)

The value of $w$ is directly related to the depth of a point from the viewpoint along the $z_e$ axis. If a point lies in the plane of the viewpoint ($z_e = 0$), $w = 0$. Points with $w > 0$ lie in front of the viewpoint, and those with $w < 0$ lie behind. The quantity $w$ should be viewed as a fourth coordinate in the eye coordinate system for representing a point, a coordinate that contains "perspective information." Because $w$ is a linear function of $z_e$, we can interpolate values of $w$ with a line equation, just as we do for $x_e$, $y_e$, and $z_e$.

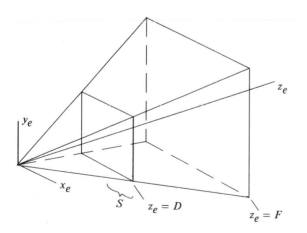

**Figure 23-2** The truncated viewing pyramid in the eye coordinate system. Visible points must have $z_e$ values between $D$ and $F$.

These equations are more easily represented as a 4 × 4 matrix to perform the linear parts of the calculation, and a separate division step:

$$[x \quad y \quad z \quad w] = [x_e \quad y_e \quad z_e \quad 1]P$$

$$P = \begin{bmatrix} 1 & 0 & 0 & 0 \\ 0 & 1 & 0 & 0 \\ 0 & 0 & S/\{D(1 - D/F)\} & S/D \\ 0 & 0 & -S/(1 - D/F) & 0 \end{bmatrix} \qquad (23\text{-}4)$$

$$x_s = \frac{x}{w} \qquad y_s = \frac{y}{w} \qquad z_s = \frac{z}{w} \qquad (23\text{-}5)$$

The matrix in Equation 23-4 contains all the parameters of the perspective transformation and can be concatenated with the viewing transformation to yield a single matrix that transforms coordinates in the world coordinate system into the system $[x \quad y \quad z \quad w]$. Equation 23-5 then yields the screen coordinate system by performing *the division that is essential to generate a perspective image.*

## Clipping before Division

Clipping can be performed after the application of Equation 23-4 but must be performed before the division in Equation 23-5. The clipping limits become

$$-w \leq x \leq +w \qquad \text{and} \qquad -w \leq y \leq +w \qquad (23\text{-}6a)$$

These inequalities guarantee that lines will be limited to the portion that lies in front of the eye ($w > 0$) and within the viewing pyramid. A clipping algorithm similar to the one given in Section 22-5 or the polygon clipper in Section 5-4 is used to enforce these limits. The algorithm takes the four coordinates $x, y, z,$ and $w$ of each endpoint and clips against the four limiting planes given in Equation 23-6a. The result is a new line, with endpoints also given by four coordinates, but guaranteed to lie within the clipping planes.

The formulation of the screen coordinate system in Equations 23-4 and 23-5 also allows us to use clipping to limit the extent of lines in depth. If lines are restricted to the interior of the truncated viewing pyramid in Figure 23-2, that is, $D \leq z_e \leq F$, we can be assured that $z_s$ values will lie between 0 and 1. An additional clipping limit is used to enforce these limits:

$$0 \leq z \leq +w \qquad (23\text{-}6b)$$

The clipping algorithm extends easily to clip against these two new planes.

## Window-Edge Coordinates

The clipping algorithm can be simplified by the use of a special coordinate system that records a point's position by giving the distance between the point and each of the clipping planes [451]. The point $(x, y, z, w)$ is represented by the 6-element vector $[w + x, w - x, w + y, w - y, 0 + z, w - z]$, which records distances from the planes given in Equation 23-6. If no components of this vector are negative, the point lies within the clipping planes. A negative distance indicates that a coordinate lies outside the permissible region and must be clipped.

A line is described by two endpoints in the window-edge coordinate system. Because the transformation into the new system is linear, intermediate points along the line can be interpolated between the endpoints. This property simplifies the calculations of the point of intersection of the line and one of the clipping planes. Suppose that the first endpoint lies within the limits because $w_1 + x_1 \geq 0$, but that the second point lies off the screen, $w_2 + x_2 < 0$. These two quantities record the distances from each endpoint to the $x = -w$ plane. The point of intersection of the line and the plane is readily computed from these distances.

$$ t = \frac{(w_1 + x_1)}{(w_1 + x_1) - (w_2 + x_2)} \tag{23-7} $$

The quantity $t$ records distance along the line: $t = 0$ at the first endpoint and $t = 1$ at the second. Using $t$, the $x, y, z$, and $w$ values at the point of intersection are calculated. For example, $x = t(x_2 - x_1) + x_1$.

Figure 23-3 shows a clipping procedure based on window-edge coordinates. It records two values for $t$: $t1$ locates the visible point on the line closest to one endpoint, and $t2$ the visible point closest to the other endpoint. The algorithm performs the interpolation step only if necessary, that is, if $t1 \neq 0$ or $t2 \neq 1$.

## 23-2 PROPERTIES OF THE SCREEN COORDINATE SYSTEM

The properties of the screen coordinate system differ greatly from those of the eye coordinate system. The viewpoint at $z_e = 0$ is undefined in the screen coordinate system but can be thought of as being infinitely far away along the $-z_s$ direction. Thus "rays" emanating from the eye are all parallel to the $z_s$ axis.

Examination of Figure 23-4 reveals the reasons why the screen coordinate system is used for hidden-line computations. Consider polygon $Q$, the face of a cube that has been transformed into the screen coordinate system. Any point inside a box with $Q$ as cross section will be hidden, as shown in Figure 23-4a. This box corresponds to the "shadow" cast by the polygon if a light source were

```
procedure Clip(x1, y1, z1, w1, x2, y2, z2, w2: real);
    type edge = 1..6; outcode = set of edge;
    var wc: array [1..2, 1..6] of real; c1, c2: outcode;
        dx, dy, dz, dw, t, t1, t2: real; i: integer;

procedure MakeWindowCoords(p: integer; x, y, z, w: real; var c: outcode);
    var i: integer;
begin
    wc[p, 1] := w + x; wc[p, 2] := w − x;
    wc[p, 3] := w + y; wc[p, 4] := w − y;
    wc[p, 5] := z; wc[p, 6] := w − z;
    c := [ ];
    for i := 1 to 6 do
        if wc[p, i] < 0 then c := c + [i];
end;


begin
    MakeWindowCoords(1, x1, y1, z1, w1, c1);
    MakeWindowCoords(2, x2, y2, z2, w2, c2);
    if (c1 * c2) = [ ] then begin
        t1 := 0; t2 := 1;
        for i := 1 to 6 do if (wc[1, i] < 0) or (wc[2, i] < 0) then begin
            t := wc[1, i] / (wc[1, i] − wc[2, i]);
            if wc[1, i] < 0 then begin if t > t1 then t1 := t end
                else begin if t < t2 then t2 := t end
        end;
        if t2 >= t1 then begin
            dx := x2 − x1; dy := y2 − y1;
            dz := z2 − z1; dw := w2 − w1;
            if t2 <> 1 then begin
                x2 := x1 + t2 * dx; y2 := y1 + t2 * dy;
                z2 := z1 + t2 * dz; w2 := w1 + t2 * dw
            end;
            if t1 <> 0 then begin
                x1 := x1 + t1 * dx; y1 := y1 + t1 * dy;
                z1 := z1 + t1 * dz; w1 := w1 + t1 * dw
            end;
            ShowLine(x1, y1, z1, w1, x2, y2, z2, w2)
        end
    end
end;
```

**Figure 23-3** Clipping algorithm using window-edge coordinates.


placed at the viewpoint. Two calculations are sufficient to show that a point $P$ is inside this box: the first calculation shows that the orthographic projection of $P$ is inside the boundaries of the orthographic projection of $Q$, and the second shows that $P$ is farther away from the viewpoint than $Q$. These calculations are as follows (see Figures 23-4b and 23-4c):

1.  *P* is inside polygon *Q*. The orthographic projection onto the screen allows this question to be answered with a two-dimensional calculation. This is similar to deciding whether a pixel lies inside a polygon boundary, as described in Chapter 16.
2.  We compare the $z_s$ coordinates of $P$ ($z_s = \varepsilon$) and the intersection of a line from $P$ to the viewpoint with the plane $Q$ ($z_s = z_d$); $z_d$ can be calculated easily if the plane equation of $Q$ is known in the screen coordinate system

$$ax_s + by_s + cz_s + d = 0$$

Substituting $x_s = \gamma$ and $y_s = \delta$, we solve for the desired $z_d$.

The properties of the screen coordinate system aid these calculations. Computing the intersection of a ray from the viewpoint and a surface is simple because all rays from the viewpoint are parallel to the $z_s$ axis. The corresponding calculation in the eye coordinate system is complicated by the various angles at which rays emanate from the viewpoint.

### Straight Lines Transform into Straight Lines

One of the most important properties of the screen coordinate transformation 23-4 and 23-5 is that straight lines in the eye coordinate system are converted into straight lines in the screen coordinate system. If this were not true, the screen coordinate system would be quite useless, because hidden-line

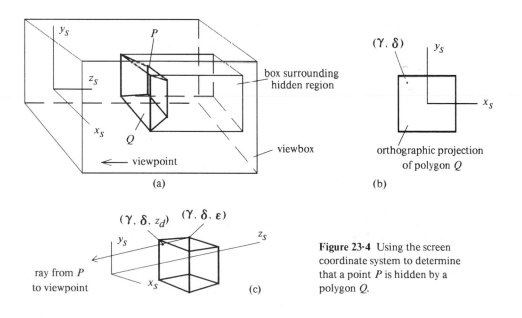

(a)

(b)

(c)

**Figure 23-4** Using the screen coordinate system to determine that a point *P* is hidden by a polygon *Q*.

algorithms need to compute the depth ($z_s$ values) of lines and planes at many points intermediate between endpoints and vertices. Because lines transform into lines and planes into planes, the depth of an intermediate point can be determined from a line or plane equation.

We shall represent a straight line in the eye coordinate system as

$$
\begin{aligned}
x_e &= (1-\alpha)x_{ea} + \alpha x_{eb} \\
y_e &= (1-\alpha)y_{ea} + \alpha y_{eb} \\
z_e &= (1-\alpha)z_{ea} + \alpha z_{eb}
\end{aligned}
\tag{23-8}
$$

where $(x_{ea}, y_{ea}, z_{ea})$ and $(x_{eb}, y_{eb}, z_{eb})$ are the line endpoints, and $0 \le \alpha \le 1$. This line transforms into a line in the screen coordinate system:

$$
\begin{aligned}
x_s &= (1-\beta)x_{sa} + \beta x_{sb} \\
y_s &= (1-\beta)y_{sa} + \beta y_{sb} \\
z_s &= (1-\beta)z_{sa} + \beta z_{sb}
\end{aligned}
\tag{23-9}
$$

where the points $(x_{sa}, y_{sa}, z_{sa})$ and $(x_{sb}, y_{sb}, z_{sb})$ are the transforms of $(x_{ea}, y_{ea}, z_{ea})$ and $(x_{eb}, y_{eb}, z_{eb})$, respectively.

The parameters $\alpha$ and $\beta$ are not identical, but are related by

$$
\beta = \frac{\alpha w_b}{(1 - \alpha)w_a + \alpha w_b}
\tag{23-10}
$$

This relation is derived from Equations 23-4 and 23-5, where $w_a$ is the value of $w$ at endpoint $a$ and $w_b$ at endpoint $b$. When $\alpha = 0$, $\beta = 0$; when $\alpha = 1$, $\beta = 1$. If $w_a$ and $w_b$ are of the same sign, then as $\alpha$ ranges from 0 to 1, so does $\beta$ although the ratio $\alpha/\beta$ is not constant. Thus, the line between eye coordinate points $(x_{ea}, y_{ea}, z_{ea})$ and $(x_{eb}, y_{eb}, z_{eb})$ maps into the line between $(x_{sa}, y_{sa}, z_{sa})$ and $(x_{sb}, y_{sb}, z_{sb})$.

However, this mapping fails for lines which pass through the $w = 0$ plane because $w = 0$ is a pole of the transformation in Equation 23-5. Equation 23-10 reflects this effect: the denominator will be zero for some value of $\alpha$ if the line passes through $w = 0$. In this case values of $\alpha$ between 0 and 1 do not yield values of $\beta$ in the range $0 \le \beta \le 1$ and hence do not represent points on a line between $(x_{sa}, y_{sa}, z_{sa})$ and $(x_{sb}, y_{sb}, z_{sb})$. Instead, the line maps into *all other* points on the infinite line that passes through $(x_{sa}, y_{sa}, z_{sa})$ and $(x_{sb}, y_{sb}, z_{sb})$. As an example, consider the line in eye coordinates from (1, 1, 6) to (1, 1, −6), which has the aspect shown in Figure 23-5a to a viewing pyramid with $S = 1$, $D = 4$, $F = \infty$. The endpoints of this line transform into the screen coordinate system as (2/3, 2/3, 1/3) and (−2/3, −2/3, 5/3), but the transform of the line looks like the diagram in Figure 23-5b.

Thus, if a line passes through the $w = 0$ plane, its image is two semi-infinite rays in the screen coordinate system. In this case, the transformed line cannot be found by connecting the transformed endpoints. The clipping algorithm must therefore exclude portions of a line with $w < 0$ *before* the division of Equation 23-5 is performed. Only in this way can the correct visible portion of the line be displayed.

## 23-3 HOMOGENEOUS COORDINATE REPRESENTATIONS OF PROJECTIVE TRANSFORMATIONS

A *homogeneous coordinate system* is a mathematical tool which aids describing projective transformations. The point $(x, y, z)$ in three dimensions is represented by a vector of four numbers: $[a\ b\ c\ d]$. The four components of this vector are interpreted as coordinates in a four-dimensional space. In order to transform a point $(x, y, z)$ in *ordinary* three-dimensional coordinates into a homogeneous representation, we merely choose some nonzero number $w$ and form the vector:

$$[wx \quad wy \quad wz \quad w] \tag{23-11}$$

The number $w$ is called the scale factor or the homogeneous coordinate. For example, the point $(1, 2, 3)$ will become $[1\ 2\ 3\ 1]$ if we choose $w = 1$, or $[2\ 4\ 6\ 2]$ if we choose $w = 2$, or $[-3\ -6\ -9\ -3]$ if we choose $w = -3$. A point in three-dimensional space thus has an infinity of representations in homogeneous coordinates, each corresponding to a different value of $w$.

A homogeneous point $[a\ b\ c\ d]$ can be converted back to ordinary three-dimensional coordinates by dividing by the scale factor: the point is $(a/d, b/d, c/d)$. The three homogeneous vectors above clearly reduce to the same ordinary three-dimensional point. From a geometric standpoint, the division means that undefined points in three dimensions (the points at infinity)

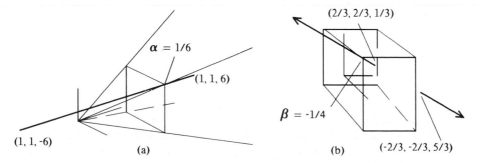

**Figure 23-5** Lines that pass through the plane $w = 0$ must be clipped before the perspective division is performed. The transform of the line shown in (a) is *not* the line connecting the transformed endpoints (b).

are well defined in the homogeneous coordinate system. For example, the homogeneous vector [0 0 −1 0] has no image in the three-dimensional system. However, we can get a feeling for such points by considering [0 0 −1 ε] as ε → 0. The ordinary coordinates of the point are $(0, 0, -1/\varepsilon)$: the point becomes infinitely far away along the − z axis as ε → 0.

The homogeneous representation can be viewed as a 4-space which is related to 3-space by the conversions described above:

$$(x, y, z) \Rightarrow [wx \quad wy \quad wz \quad w]$$
$$[a \quad b \quad c \quad d] \Rightarrow (a/d, b/d, c/d) \tag{23-12}$$

The division by the fourth coordinate suggests that the 3-space is the projection onto the $w = 1$ hyperplane of the 4-space. This projection generally alters the topology of an object that passes through the $w = 0$ plane [395].

Transformations such as translation, rotation, and scaling, which are defined as they apply to ordinary coordinates, can also be performed on the homogeneous representations of the points. In fact, the matrix notations outlined in Chapter 22 are precisely those for homogeneous representations: the introduction of the fourth vector element 1 simply represents the formation of the homogeneous vector for $w = 1$. The transformations will have the same effect regardless of the choice of $w$. For example, if we apply the translation:

$$\begin{bmatrix} 1 & 0 & 0 & 0 \\ 0 & 1 & 0 & 0 \\ 0 & 0 & 1 & 0 \\ 4 & 5 & -1 & 1 \end{bmatrix}$$

to two homogeneous representations of the ordinary point (2, 3, 0), [2 3 0 1] and [4 6 0 2], we get [6 8 −1 1] and [12 16 −2 2], respectively, both of which represent the same point in 3-space. Hence all the techniques of transformation, inverses, and concatenation developed in Chapter 22 can be applied directly to homogeneous representations of 3-space.

Homogeneous representations are particularly useful in three-dimensional graphics because the perspective transformation (Equations 23-4 and 23-5) is a homogeneous transformation. Equation 23-4 starts with the ordinary point $(x_e, y_e, z_e)$, chooses $w = 1$, and applies a 4 × 4 homogeneous transformation. The resulting value of $w$ is no longer 1 but instead contains the depth information critical to generating a perspective view. Equation 23-5 then transforms the homogeneous coordinates $x, y, z,$ and $w$ back into ordinary 3-space to yield screen coordinates of the point.

The clipping operation that operates on the limits shown in Equation 23-6 is sometimes called *homogeneous clipping* because it uses $x, y,$ and $z$ symmetrically [59]. The limits are stated so as to guarantee that $w$ is always positive. But we indicated above that negative values of $w$ are possible, which means that another region of the homogeneous coordinate space will also map into the viewbox as well as the one specified in Equation 23-6. Thus we have two regions in homogeneous space that will map into the viewbox:

Positive $w$:

$$-w \leq x \leq +w$$
$$-w \leq y \leq +w$$
$$0 \leq z \leq +w$$

Negative $w$:

$$-w \geq x \geq +w$$
$$-w \geq y \geq +w \qquad (23\text{-}13)$$
$$0 \geq z \geq +w$$

A clipping algorithm that deals properly with all homogeneous definitions of lines should find visible portions of lines in either region. After clipping, some lines may have *two* visible portions, one in each space; these are lines that have "wrapped around" through points infinitely far away in the eye coordinate system but at finite distances in the homogeneous coordinate system. Such lines arise primarily when displaying *rational parametric* curves [184, 119, 282, 283].

In practice, the clipping algorithm can discover easily which of the two regions is applicable to a line. If both endpoints have positive $w$ values, clearly it can enter only the region with positive $w$. If both endpoints have negative $w$ values, the line must be clipped against the region with negative $w$. This can be achieved simply by multiplying the homogeneous coordinates for both endpoints by $-1$ and clipping against the region with positive $w$ values. This technique takes advantage of the fact that scaling homogeneous coordinates does not change the corresponding ordinary coordinates. If the two values of $w$ differ in sign, the line must be processed twice to clip once against the region of positive $w$ and once against the region with negative $w$.

## 23-4 SUMMARY

The transformations developed in this chapter are an essential part of all hidden-surface and hidden-line algorithms. The geometric information from a model of a scene must be transformed and clipped before the hidden-surface algorithm begins its processing. We can summarize this process with the schema

$$[x \quad y \quad z \quad w] = [x \quad y \quad z \quad 1]\, VP(clip)S$$

$$(23\text{-}14)$$

$$x_S = x/w \qquad y_S = y/w \qquad z_S = z/w$$

The viewing transformation $V$ transforms coordinates into a left-handed system with origin at the center of the screen and viewing direction along the $+z$ axis. The matrix $P$, given in Equation 23-4, describes the perspective transformation. The *clip* step is applied to homogeneous representations of lines or polygons to limit them to the viewbox, the analog in the screen coordinate system of the viewing pyramid in the eye coordinate system. Finally, an optional transformation $S$ is used to expand the boundaries of the standard viewbox to an arbitrary viewport on the screen:

$$S = \begin{bmatrix} V_{sx} & 0 & 0 & 0 \\ 0 & V_{sy} & 0 & 0 \\ 0 & 0 & 1 & 0 \\ V_{cx} & V_{cy} & 0 & 1 \end{bmatrix} \qquad (23\text{-}15)$$

After the division specified in Equation 23-14, the coordinate information is in a convenient form to pass to hidden-surface algorithms. The values of $x_s$ and $y_s$ correspond to the hardware screen coordinate system, and the value of $z_s$ preserves depth information necessary to eliminate hidden parts of objects.

## EXERCISES

**23-1** Prove that a perspective transformation that preserves planarity must compute $z_s$ values with an equation of the form given in Equation 23-2.

**23-2** Derive the value for $z_s$ given in Equation 23-3 from the assumptions about the ranges of $z_e$ values.

**23-3** This exercise explores the issue of depth precision in the screen coordinate system. Suppose $z_e$ is represented by an $n$-bit 2's complement integer. Consider two points which are as close together as possible in the eye coordinate system: point $A$ has $z_e = d$, point $B$ has $z_e = d + 1$, $D \le d \le F - 1$. Derive an expression for the difference between the $z_s$ values of $A$ and $B$ in terms of $D$, $F$, and $d$. Derive an expression for $m$, the number of bits required for a fixed-point representation of $z_s$ if the difference in depth between $A$ and $B$ is to be non-zero for the entire range $D \le d \le F - 1$. If $D = 1$ and $F = 2^{n-1} - 1$, what is $m$? To reduce $m$, is it better to increase $D$ or to decrease $F$?

**23-4** Does the perspective transformation 23-3 have an inverse? That is, if $x_s$, $y_s$, and $z_s$ are given, can $x_e$, $y_e$, and $z_e$ be calculated? If an inverse exists, can it be expressed as a homogeneous transformation matrix?

**23-5** Prove that Equation 23-7 and the calculations used in the window-edge clipping program correctly interpolate lines.

**23-6** What is the reason for the test "if $t2 >= t1$" in the window-edge clipping program?

**23-7** Apply the window-edge coordinate system to clipping against the three-dimensional viewing pyramid in the eye coordinate system. This algorithm will have the same effect as the clipping algorithm given in Chapter 22.

**23-8** Derive Equation 23-10.

**23-9** Show that if we use Equation 23-14, in which $V$ is a concatenation of primitive translations, rotations, and scalings described in Section 22-1, we need clip only in regions of positive $w$.

**23-10** Martin Newell has remarked that a stereo transformation can be applied to screen coordinates after clipping. For example, the viewing transformation is arranged to produce an image for the left eye. Each line in the scene is transformed, clipped, and projected into the viewbox. The line is then drawn on the screen, to be shown to the left eye. Now the endpoints of the line, measured in the screen coordinate system, are transformed using a matrix $R$ to become the coordinates of the line that should be shown to the right eye. This new line is drawn on the screen, to be shown to the right eye. Show how $R$ is computed.

**23-11** If two lines are parallel in the eye coordinate system, are they parallel in the screen coordinate system? If not, give a simple counterexample.

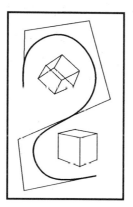

# 24

# HIDDEN-SURFACE

# ELIMINATION

One of the most challenging problems in computer graphics is the removal of hidden parts from images of solid objects. In real life, the opaque material of these objects obstructs the light rays from hidden parts and prevents us from seeing them. In the computer generation of an image, no such automatic elimination takes place when objects are projected onto the screen coordinate system. Instead, all parts of every object, including many parts that should be invisible, are displayed. In order to remove these parts to create a more realistic image, we must apply a *hidden-line* or *hidden-surface algorithm* to the set of objects.

In the early 1960s, when the first of these algorithms were developed, displays were exclusively line-drawing devices; effort was therefore focused on hidden-line removal. The earliest such algorithms, of which Roberts' was the most prominent, were extremely slow [404]. When raster displays became available, attention shifted to hidden-surface removal and many techniques, both hardware and software, were developed. Recently developed hardware processors for hidden-surface elimination are capable of generating realistic views at a rate of 30 images per second.

Despite the existence of many algorithms, there is no single answer to the hidden-surface problem, no best algorithm. Many of the differences between algorithms stem from different requirements: the algorithms operate on different kinds of scene models, generate different forms of output, or cater for images of different complexities. An algorithm designed to produce images in real time has very different objectives from an algorithm designed to achieve highly realistic shaded surfaces.

In spite of the wide variation in the details of their design, these algorithms share several characteristics. All use some form of geometric *sorting* to distinguish visible parts of an object from those that are hidden [466]. Just as alphabetical sorting is used to differentiate words near the beginning of the alphabet from those near the end, geometric sorting locates objects that lie near the observer and are therefore visible. Geometric sorting is much more complicated than alphabetical sorting because complex objects do not always have a simple ordering. We cannot, for example, state categorically that a bead is closer to us than the string on which it is threaded; parts of the bead are closer than certain parts of the string, and vice versa.

Hidden-line and hidden-surface algorithms also capitalize on various forms of *coherence* in order to reduce the computing required to generate an image. Different forms of coherence are related to different forms of order, or regularity, in the image. Scan-line coherence, for example, arises because the display of a scan line in a raster image is usually very similar to the display of the preceding scan line. Frame coherence, in a sequence of images designed to show motion, recognizes that successive frames are very similar. Object coherence results from relationships between different objects or between separate parts of the same object. Hidden-surface algorithms are generally designed to exploit one or more of these coherence properties to increase efficiency.

Hidden-surface algorithms designed to produce images on a raster-scan display bear a strong resemblance to two-dimensional scan conversion, described in Chapter 16. Both kinds of algorithm emphasize sorting and coherence. We shall discover that two-dimensional scan conversion plays an essential role in many three-dimensional algorithms.

## 24·1  TWO APPROACHES

Algorithms for hidden-surface removal work either in *object space* or *image space*. An object-space algorithm concentrates on the geometrical relationships among the objects in the scene in order to determine which parts of which objects are visible. An image-space algorithm, on the other hand, concentrates on the final image, and asks what is visible within each raster pixel.

An object-space algorithm performs geometric calculations with as much precision as possible, usually the precision available in floating-point hardware of the computer. Since the precision of the solution is much greater than that of a display device, the image can be displayed enlarged many times without losing accuracy. By contrast, image-space algorithms perform calculations with only enough precision to match the resolution of the display screen used to present the image. These algorithms simply calculate an intensity for each of the 250,000 or 1 million distinct dots on the screen.

The two approaches generally lead to algorithms with different performance characteristics. The computation time of an object-space algorithm will tend to grow with the number of objects in the scene, whether visible or not, while the image-space computation tends to grow with the complexity of the visible parts of the image. Generally, the cost of image-space algorithms will grow more slowly than that of object-space algorithms as the complexity of the scene increases.

Most of the algorithms described in this chapter are image-space algorithms, because we shall concentrate on hidden-surface algorithms. Object-space methods are used primarily in hidden-line algorithms, which are surveyed in [466].

## 24-2 THE DEPTH-BUFFER ALGORITHM

Of all image-space algorithms, the depth-buffer algorithm is the simplest. For each pixel on the display screen, we keep a record of the depth of the object within the pixel that lies closest to the observer. In addition to the depth, we also record the intensity that should be displayed to show the object. In this respect, the depth buffer is an extension of a frame buffer.

The depth-buffer algorithm given below requires two arrays, *intensity* and *depth*, each of which is indexed by pixel coordinates $(x, y)$.

*Depth-Buffer Algorithm*

1. For all pixels on the screen, set *depth*$[x, y]$ to 1.0 and *intensity*$[x, y]$ to a background value.
2. For each polygon in the scene, find all pixels $(x, y)$ that lie within the boundaries of the polygon when projected onto the screen. For each of these pixels:
   a. Calculate the depth $z$ of the polygon at $(x, y)$.
   b. If $z < depth[x, y]$, this polygon is closer to the observer than others already recorded for this pixel. In this case, set *depth*$[x, y]$ to $z$ and *intensity*$[x, y]$ to a value corresponding to the polygon's shading. If instead $z > depth[x, y]$, the polygon already recorded at $(x, y)$ lies closer to the observer than does this new polygon, and no action is taken.

After all polygons have been processed, the *intensity* array will contain the solution.

The depth-buffer algorithm illustrates several features common to all hidden-surface algorithms. First, it requires a representation of all opaque surfaces in the scene, polygons in this case. These polygons may be the faces of polyhedra recorded in the model of the scene or may simply represent thin opaque "sheets" in the scene. Any model that permits an enumeration of the (x, y) points on opaque surfaces would serve as well for the depth-buffer algorithm. Such enumeration techniques have been developed for the smooth-surface models described in Chapter 21 [96, 95].

The second important feature of the algorithm is its use of the screen coordinate system. Before step 1, all polygons in the scene are transformed into the screen coordinate system described in Chapter 23, using a matrix multiplication that accounts for the viewing and perspective transformations. The polygons must also be clipped with a polygon clipper (see Section 5-4 and [465]) to ensure that they all lie completely within the standard viewbox. Depth clipping should be included because it permits choosing a fixed-point representation for the *depth* array that is guaranteed to accommodate any possible value. After clipping, a viewport transformation is applied to map x and y into the display's raster coordinate system.

The depth-buffer algorithm, then, operates on polygons that have been converted into the screen coordinate system. Two important properties of this coordinate system are exploited. First, because a perspective display of any object is an orthographic projection of the screen coordinates, enumerating the pixel coordinates (x, y) that lie within the boundaries of the projected polygon is precisely the scan-conversion task described in Chapter 16.* The x and y screen coordinates of the polygon vertices are passed directly to a scan-conversion algorithm to perform step 2 of the depth-buffer algorithm.

The second virtue of the screen coordinate system is that the calculation of the depth z of a polygon at an arbitrary point (x, y) is simplified because we can record a plane equation for each polygon in the screen coordinate system. This equation can be solved afresh for each (x, y) coordinate encountered, or can be evaluated using incremental methods (see Exercise 24-2).

### Limitations of the Depth Buffer

The depth-buffer algorithm is not always practicable because of the enormous size of the *depth* and *intensity* arrays. Generating an image with a raster of 500 × 500 pixels requires 250,000 storage locations for each array. Even though a frame buffer may provide memory for the *intensity* array, the *depth* array remains large.

To reduce the amount of storage required, the image can be divided into many smaller images, and the depth-buffer algorithm is applied to each in turn. For example, the original 500 × 500 raster can be divided into 100 rasters, each 50 × 50 pixels. Processing each small raster requires arrays of only 2500 elements, but execution time grows because each polygon is processed many times. Alternatively we can use 100 horizontal bands, each 5 scan lines high and 500 pixels wide. At the extreme, we might provide a depth buffer for a single scan line and process all 500 scan lines separately.

Subdivision of the screen does not always increase execution time; instead

---

*In hidden-surface algorithms, scan converting a polygon in this way is often called *tiling*.

it can help reduce the work required to generate the image. This reduction arises because of coherence between small regions of the screen. If computations are performed on these regions in a particular order rather than in a random sequence, savings are considerable. An example is scan-line coherence, the property that the image on a scan line is similar to the image on the preceding scan line. It has given rise to a number of *scan-line algorithms.* Area coherence, the property that a small region of the display tends to show an image of a single polygon, likewise gives rise to *area algorithms.*

## 24-3 GEOMETRIC COMPUTATIONS

Many of the coherence properties require a more elaborate geometric analysis for their exploitation than the depth-buffer algorithm does. Many hidden-surface techniques, for example, need to compare two polygons to decide which one obscures the other. These calculations can be time-consuming unless they are done carefully.

### Plane Equations

We use the equation of a polygon's plane in the screen coordinate system to compute the depth of the polygon at various $(x, y)$ coordinates on the screen. Using the conventions established in Section 20-2, we express the equation as $ax + by + cz + d = 0$, and adopt the convention that $ax + by + cz + d > 0$ if a point lies outside the object of which the plane is a face. The plane's equation in screen coordinates can be determined from its equation in world coordinates by a suitable transformation (see Appendix II).

The plane equation is used to identify *back faces,* polygons that cannot possibly be visible because they lie on the side of an object facing away from the viewpoint. A back face is implied if a negative value results from substituting the screen coordinates of the viewpoint $(0, 0, -\infty)$ into the plane equation (the test $c > 0$ is thus equivalent). Back-face elimination, a simple use of object coherence, typically halves the number of polygons that need consideration during the generation of a hidden-surface image.

In some cases, eliminating back faces solves the hidden-surface problem. If the scene consists of exactly one convex polyhedron, the elimination of back faces eliminates *all* the hidden surfaces. A cube, for example, can be displayed simply by removing back faces. This is an extreme example of object coherence that makes processing convex polyhedra particularly easy.

### Overlap Tests

If two polygons do not overlap in $x$ and $y$, they cannot possibly obscure each other. A fast method to rule out overlap greatly reduces the number of polygons that require careful testing with respect to each other. *Minimax tests*

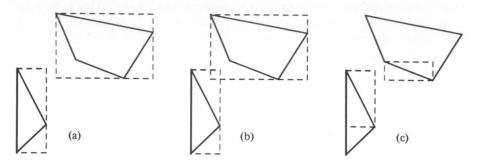

**Figure 24-1** Minimax tests: (a) test shows polygons do not overlap; (b) test inconclusive; (c) test applied to individual edges.

have this property. If the minimum $x$ coordinate of one polygon is greater than the maximum $x$ of another, the two cannot possibly overlap (Figure 24-1a). The same argument applies for $y$ values and may also be applied to $z$ values if depth overlap is a consideration. The two-dimensional $xy$ minimax test is often called the *bounding box* test, a technique used frequently in this book.

If a minimax test fails to show separation, it is still possible that the polygons do not overlap (Figure 24-1b). In this case, a more lengthy test must be applied to determine whether the $xy$ aspects of two polygons intersect. Each edge of one polygon is compared against each edge of the other to detect intersections. Minimax tests on edges can help speed this process by determining quickly that two edges cannot possibly intersect (Figure 24-1c). For extremely large polygons, sorting is helpful [436].

### Surrounding Polygons

Some area-coherence algorithms depend on testing whether a polygon completely surrounds a rectangular window on the screen, as illustrated in Figure 24-2. If all four corners of the window are inside the polygon, the entire window must be surrounded. We can determine whether an individual corner of the window is surrounded by applying the *Inside* test, described in Section 16-2. Alternatively, the sum of the angles subtended by the edges of the polygon can be computed. If the sum is zero, the corner lies outside the polygon; if it is $\pm 2\pi$, the point lies inside. The angles can be computed with extremely low precision (2 bits) without affecting the reliability of the algorithm [451].

### 24-4 SCAN-LINE COHERENCE ALGORITHMS

Scan-line algorithms solve the hidden-surface problem one scan line at a time, usually processing scan lines from the top to the bottom of the display. The algorithm successively examines a series of *windows* on the screen; each window is one scan line high and as wide as the screen. The simplest scan-line algorithm is a one-dimensional version of the depth buffer. We require two arrays, *intensity*[*x*] and *depth*[*x*], to hold values for a single scan line.

*Scan-Line Coherence Algorithm*

For each scan line perform steps 1 through 3.

1.  For all pixels on a scan line, set *depth*[*x*] to 1.0 and *intensity*[*x*] to a background value.
2.  For each polygon in the scene, find all pixels on the current scan line *y* that lie within the polygon. This step uses the Y-X scan-conversion algorithm described in Section 16-4. For each of these *x* values:
    a.  Calculate the depth *z* of the polygon at (*x*, *y*).
    b.  If $z < depth[x]$, set *depth*[*x*] to *z* and *intensity*[*x*] to the intensity corresponding to the polygon's shading.
3.  After all polygons have been considered, the values contained in the *intensity* array represent the solution, and can be copied into a frame buffer.

In effect, the algorithm concurrently scan converts all polygons in the scene, one scan line at a time. This is a simple extension of the Y-X scan-conversion algorithm described in Section 16-4; here a depth value must be computed and compared with the value already recorded in the depth buffer.

**Span-Coherence Algorithms**

Scan-line algorithms can capitalize on a one-dimensional form of area coherence, known as *span coherence*. Short spans, or sequences of pixels, on a scan line will lie within the same polygon. The algorithm searches for a span, in which it need then make only a few depth comparisons to identify the polygon

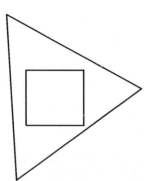

**Figure 24-2** Triangular polygon surrounding a square.

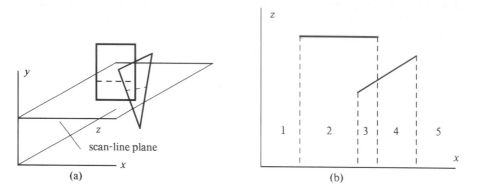

**Figure 24-3** Scan-line algorithm calculations; (a) scene in screen coordinate system; (b) segments of polygons in the *xz* plane divide the scan line into *spans.*

visible throughout the span. This technique is illustrated in Figure 24-3, which shows how *segments* of polygons are created by intersecting the polygons with the plane represented by a scan line.

Calculations in the *xz* plane are used to determine the relationships between the segments of all polygons intersecting the scan line and to decide which segments are visible in which spans. The locations of the segments are generated by the concurrent scan conversion of polygons, just as for the scan-line coherence algorithm. The *x* and *z* coordinates of endpoints of a segment may be computed in an incremental manner because they are linear functions of *y*, that is, the equation of a polygon's edge can be written as $x = \alpha y + \beta$ and $z = \gamma y + \delta$.

The spans of a scan line are identified by sorting all segment endpoints by *x* and examining regions delimited by these *x* values (Figure 24-3b). A span will fall into one of three classes:

1.  No segments appear within the span (spans 1 and 5). The background intensity is displayed in this region.
2.  A single segment falls within the span (spans 2 and 4). Clearly, the segment is visible, and the polygon's shade is displayed throughout the span.
3.  Several segments extend across the entire span (span 3). The segment closest to the eye, the one with smaller *z* values, is found by comparing the depths of all segments at one *x* coordinate, such as the left edge of the span. Once the visible polygon is identified, appropriate intensities can be determined for the span.

The algorithm takes advantage of coherence to reduce the *x* and *z* sorting. A single active edge list, sorted by *x*, contains edge descriptions for all polygons that intersect the scan line. As it is updated incrementally from scan line to scan line (as in the Y-X algorithm of Section 16-4), it is resorted. The identification of spans is a simple matter of extracting edges from this list.

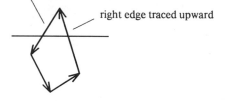

left edge traced downward

right edge traced upward

**Figure 24-4** The left-right sense of edges can be determined by examining the tracing direction.

During the processing of each scan line, which proceeds from left to right, the edges are used to keep a list of active polygons. The edge that starts a span will be either a polygon's left edge and cause the polygon to become active (e.g., start of span 2 in Figure 24-3b) or a right edge that terminates a polygon (e.g., at start of span 4). The left-right nature of edges can be distinguished (1) by associating with a polygon a single bit to record whether the polygon is currently active, and by complementing the bit each time an edge of the polygon is encountered; or (2) if polygons are always drawn in a consistent way (e.g., counterclockwise when viewed from outside the object), by letting the edge's direction determine its parity: a downward-moving edge is a left edge (Figure 24-4).

At the left edge of a span, the active polygons are searched to find the one with smallest $z$ and consequently closest to the observer. To simplify the search, the active polygon list can be kept sorted by $z$, with polygons entering and leaving the list as we move from span to span. Although the $z$ values must be recalculated for each span, the new values rarely alter the depth ordering of the polygons. In fact, order never changes after a polygon is inserted in the active list if we do not allow *penetrating faces*, in which a face of one object penetrates through a face of another (Figure 24-5). Handling penetrating faces will also require augmenting the three cases described above, as a single polygon may not be visible throughout a span.

By altering the algorithm that decides which polygon is visible within a span to handle more cases, we can process a scan line in fewer spans. In Figure 24-3b, for example, spans 1 and 2 could be processed as one: only a single segment falls within the region. Spans 3 and 4 can be treated together,

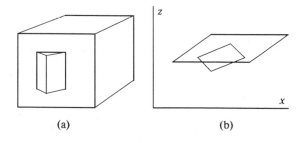

(a)

$z$

$x$

(b)

**Figure 24-5** Penetrating faces: (a) hidden-line view of two intersecting polyhedra; (b) arrangement of segments in the $xz$ plane showing intersecting segments.

provided we disallow penetrating faces or make additional depth comparisons within the span. Watkins' algorithm [500] is capable of handling these larger spans and remembers from one scan line to the next the spans found simple enough to solve.

Scan-line algorithms can also take advantage of depth coherence. A segment's position in the active polygon list (sorted by depth) is unlikely to vary from one scan line to the next. An estimate of this position reduces the number of depth computations required to insert the polygon into the active list.

### Summary

Scan-line algorithms take advantage of coherence between successive scan lines and of span coherence within a scan line. They also simplify the geometric calculations by reducing a three-dimensional problem to a two-dimensional comparison of segments in the $xz$ plane. This geometrical simplification is not without drawback; as we observed in scan-conversion algorithms, very small or very narrow polygons may fall between the scan-line planes.

The performance of scan-line algorithms is primarily related to the complexity of the *visible* image. This behavior was first observed by Watkins [500] and further explored in a survey of several algorithms [466]. Table 24-1, which summarizes the performance of various algorithms, is given at the end of this chapter.

### 24-5 AREA-COHERENCE ALGORITHMS

Area-coherence algorithms try to capitalize on the observation that the image of a typical polygon has similar extent in both $x$ and $y$ directions. The pixels within such an area are coherent in that they show a single surface. Although this is similar to scan-line and span coherence, area algorithms treat $x$ and $y$ directions symmetrically, rather than sorting first in one direction and then in another.

To take best advantage of area coherence, the *windows* tested by the algorithm cannot be fixed in advance but must be selected according to the

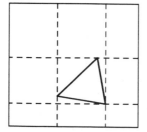 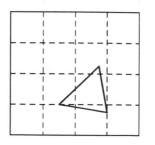

**Figure 24-6** Window selection in area-coherence algorithms: (a) windows chosen according to objects in the image; (b) fixed window arrangement.

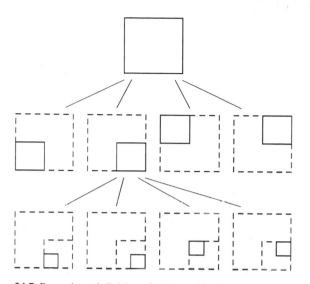

**Figure 24-7** Recursive subdivision of windows by the Warnock algorithm.

complexity of the image. Thus the arrangement of window areas in Figure 24-6a is preferred to the fixed arrangement in Figure 24-6b. The dimensions of the window selected should match the dimensions over which the resulting image is coherent.

### Warnock's Algorithm

Warnock developed one of the first area algorithms, which selects windows by a recursive procedure. The algorithm first tries to "solve" the hidden-surface problem for a window that covers the entire screen. If polygons overlap the window in x or y, a decision procedure is invoked that tries to analyze the relationships between the polygons and generate a display for the window. Simple cases, such as one polygon in the window or none at all, are easily solved.

If a window is too complicated for the decision procedure to display directly, the algorithm divides the window into four smaller windows and recurs, processing each one with the same algorithm. This technique gives rise to a tree of window subdivisions, as shown in Figure 24-7. If a region of the image is very complex, the recursion will force analysis of smaller and smaller windows. The recursion terminates either by eventually finding a window that can be solved or by finding a window that is as small as a single pixel on the screen. In this case, the intensity of the pixel is chosen to represent one of the polygons visible in the pixel.

The decision procedure that analyzes a window takes as input a list of polygons that might be *relevant* to the window. The procedure classifies each polygon into one of three groups:

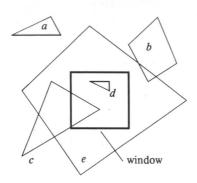

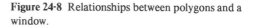

**Figure 24-8** Relationships between polygons and a window.

1. *Disjoint polygons* (*a* and *b* in Figure 24-8). No part of the polygon overlaps the window in *x* or *y*.
2. *Intersector polygons* (*c* and *d* in Figure 24-8). These polygons fall wholly or partly within the window.
3. *Surrounder polygons* (*e* in Figure 24-8). These polygons completely surround the window.

The visibility computation uses this classification to discard any polygons that are *not* relevant to generating a display for the window. Disjoint polygons are clearly not relevant.

The treatment of surrounder polygons is the key step in hidden-surface elimination. Figure 24-9 illustrates how a polygon is determined to be invisible if there is a surrounder and if the surrounder lies closer to the viewpoint than the other polygon. These invisible polygons are removed from the list of relevant polygons. Eliminating these hidden faces is more efficient if the list of potentially relevant polygons is sorted by the depth $z_{min}$ of the vertex closest to

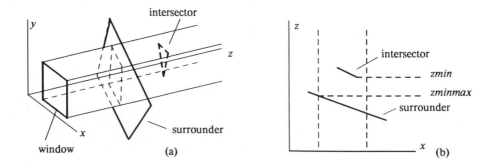

**Figure 24-9** A polygon that surrounds a window hides any intersectors farther from the eye than the plane of the surrounder.

the eye. Whenever the decision procedure encounters a surrounding polygon, it remembers the deepest point of the polygon in the window as $z_{minmax}$. When considering another polygon in the list, if its $z_{min}$ is greater than $z_{minmax}$, it is clearly hidden by the surrounder. Moreover, because the list is sorted by $z_{min}$, all polygons further down the list will also be hidden. Thus the search through the ordered list of polygons may be prematurely terminated by the discovery of a surrounder.

When disjoint and surrounder-hidden polygons have been removed from the list of polygons to process for the window, it may be clear how to generate the image for the window. If no or one polygon remains, the image can be easily generated. If only intersectors remain and they do not overlap in $x$ or $y$, the image can also be generated. If we are unable to decide what should be displayed, the algorithm subdivides the window and recurs.

The analysis of the relationships of polygons to a window greatly speeds the analysis of subwindows. For example, if a polygon surrounds a window, it will surround all subdivisions of that window. If a polygon is disjoint from a window, it will be disjoint from all subwindows and need not even be passed to the decision procedure for the subwindows. Thus, as the recursion goes deeper and the windows get smaller, the lists of polygons that might be relevant to the windows shrink. Eventually the lists become short enough for the window contents to be analyzed and displayed directly.

The computation time of the Warnock algorithm is roughly proportional to the complexity of the final display and not proportional to the complexity of the scene. The amount of computation can be gauged by the number of subdivisions required (Figure 24-10). Subdivisions always result if displayable features lie somewhere within the window being subdivided; therefore computation time is proportional to *visible* complexity. The exact number of subdivisions required is influenced by details of the decision procedure: as more cases are detected and displayed directly, fewer subdivisions are required. Balanced against these savings is increased computation required by the decision procedure to detect the additional cases. An evaluation of the performance of several decision procedures is given in [311].

Although subdivision of the screen is governed by scene complexity, the fixed square geometry of the windows is a source of inefficiency. Another approach might be to try to create subwindows that match the shapes of polygons in the original window. Polygons relevant to the original window will need to be clipped against the polygonal subwindows before being passed to the subwindows for processing. The final output of such an algorithm is a new set of polygons, guaranteed not to overlap in $x$ and $y$, that retain their original depth relationship (Figure 24-11). An algorithm of this sort has been developed by Weiler and Atherton [503]. One additional benefit of the algorithm is that polygons are computed to high precision in object space and turn out to be useful when simulating shadows.

## 24-6 PRIORITY ALGORITHMS

Unlike scan-line and area-coherence algorithms, priority algorithms try to discover depth relationships first and perform $xy$ calculations only after visibility has been determined. These algorithms are similar to the priority algorithms described in Chapter 16 that resolve overlap when scan converting two-dimensional areas.

### Newell, Newell, and Sancha Algorithm

The *painter's algorithm* described in Section 16-3 generalizes to a simple hidden-surface algorithm. The idea is to arrange all polygons in the scene in priority order, based on their depth. Polygons nearer the viewpoint will have higher priority than those far away. After priority has been determined,

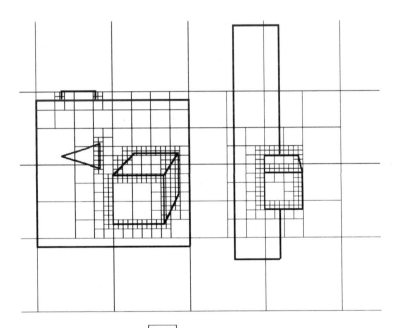

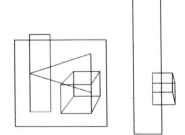

**Figure 24-10** The Warnock algorithm subdivides windows near features that are visible in the image. Note that a single intersector appearing in a window requires no subdivision.

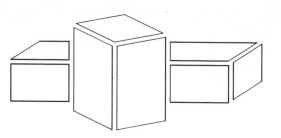

**Figure 24-11** Schematic representation of a polygon-area hidden-surface solution. The output of the algorithm is a set of polygons guaranteed not to overlap in $x$ or $y$.

polygons are scan-converted one at a time into a frame buffer, starting with the polygon of lowest priority. This procedure will generate a correct hidden-surface view provided the priority order is properly computed.

Priority calculations begin by sorting a list of all polygons in the scene by $z_{max}$, the depth of the point on each polygon furthest from the viewpoint. If, after the sort, no two adjacent polygons in the list overlap in depth (see overlap discussion in Section 24-3), the list is in correct priority order. Such a simple priority calculation suffices only for a few scenes, such as a series of planes perpendicular to the viewing direction.

If polygons in the priority list overlap in depth, more careful calculations are required to determine the correct priority order. Consider the last polygon on the list, $P$. If $P$ has no depth overlap with its predecessor in the list, $Q$, $P$ has no depth overlap with *any* polygon in the list and is the polygon of lowest priority. Therefore, its position at the end of the list is correct. More often, $P$ will overlap in depth a set of polygons $\{q\}$ that immediately precede it in the list. Determining this set requires scanning the list backward as long as $P$ overlaps in depth a polygon in the list. Now we try to show that $P$ does not obscure any member of $\{q\}$, that is, that $P$ is already in correct priority order. However, if we find a polygon $Q$ in $\{q\}$ that is obscured by $P$, we shall postulate that $Q$ should have lower priority than $P$ and move it to follow $P$ in the priority list. Figure 24-12 illustrates polygons $P$ and $Q$ that are given initial order $QP$ by the depth sort but are sorted by these more careful calculations into the correct order $PQ$.

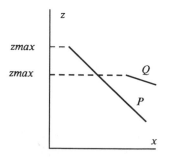

**Figure 24-12** Priority sorting initially gives $Q$ higher priority than $P$, based on $z_{max}$ values. The correct order $PQ$ is determined by more precise depth tests.

The crux of the priority sort is the relation "$P$ obscures $Q$." $P$ does *not* obscure $Q$ if any of the following tests is true:

1. Depth minimax test indicates that $P$ and $Q$ do not overlap in depth and $Q$ is closer to the viewpoint than $P$. This test is actually implemented by the initial depth sort of all polygons and by the way in which $P$ and $\{q\}$ are selected.
2. Minimax test in $xy$ indicates that $P$ and $Q$ do not overlap in $x$ or $y$.
3. All vertices of $P$ are farther from the viewpoint than the plane of $Q$. This test is implemented by substituting $x$ and $y$ coordinates of vertices of $P$ into the plane equation of $Q$, and solving for the depth of $Q$.
4. All vertices of $Q$ are closer to the viewpoint than the plane of $P$.
5. A full overlap test indicates that $P$ and $Q$ do not overlap in $x$ or $y$.

These tests are applied in the order given here, because the later tests are much more complex than the earlier ones.

The "P obscures Q" relation is not entirely sufficient to sort polygons into priority order. Figure 24-13a shows a case in which the "obscures" relation is not transitive: $P$ obscures $Q$, $Q$ obscures $R$, and $R$ obscures $P$. Sometimes $P$ obscures $Q$ *and* $Q$ obscures $P$; a case is illustrated in Figure 24-13b. Both of these cases are manifested as loops in the sorting process. Whenever a polygon is moved in the list, it is marked; if an attempt is made to move it again, it is assumed to be part of a loop. The offending polygon can be divided into two parts to try to resolve the conflict. Figure 24-13c shows the plane of $P$ used to clip the polygon $Q$ into two polygons that will have different priorities with respect to $P$.

This priority algorithm calculates visibility using geometrical criteria rather than the pixel-by-pixel depth comparisons used in the depth-buffer algorithm. The algorithm thus capitalizes on the coherence of polygons in depth to make visibility decisions about polygons as a whole. The priority sort is performed in

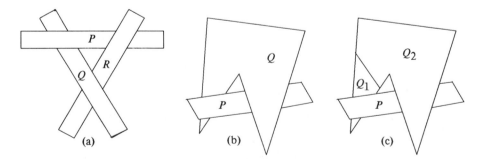

**Figure 24-13** Polygons for which no priority order exists: (a) cyclic overlap; (b) two overlapping polygons. A priority order can be established by splitting one polygon with the plane of another (c).

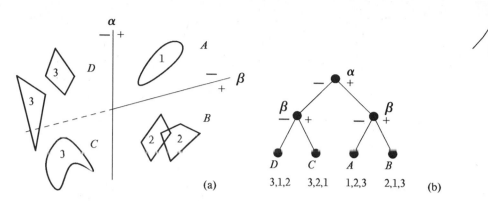

(a)        3,1,2    3,2,1    1,2,3    2,1,3    (b)

**Figure 24-14** Cluster priority. Two separating planes, $\alpha$ and $\beta$, are used to determine the priority order of clusters from the viewpoint location.

object space: the resulting priority list is valid only for a single viewpoint but can be used to generate images at many different scales.

## Other Uses of Priority

The notion of priority is more general than illustrated by Newell, Newell, and Sancha's algorithm. We can order entire parts of a scene, or *clusters*, by priority. The priority order is determined by finding a *separating plane* that separates two clusters but does not intersect any object in either cluster. Of the two clusters, the one on the same side of the plane as the viewpoint will have highest priority. A two-dimensional form of this observation is illustrated in Figure 24-14. Separating planes can be determined manually if clusters never move [427, 511]. Alternatively, the planes can be found dynamically, but the process is intricate [341]. Finding separating planes for clusters is a generalization of comparing two polygons to see which one obscures the other, as in the Newell, Newell, and Sancha algorithm.

Once separating planes have been located, the priority calculation is straightforward. For example, separating planes $\alpha$ and $\beta$ of Figure 24-14a divide space into four regions. If the viewpoint is in region $A$, the cluster priority order is 1, 2, 3; in region $D$, it is 3, 1, 2, etc. These orders are derived by testing on which side of the separating plane the viewpoint lies. If the separating planes and priority orders are precomputed and stored in a tree (Figure 24-14b), we can look up the cluster priority after solving a few plane equations [427].

What are clusters? They can be any collection of parts of the scene localized well enough in space to allow planes to separate them. In the simplest extreme, a cluster is a polygon, and the scheme is identical to the Newell, Newell, and Sancha algorithm. In general, however, a cluster can be arbitrarily complicated, but it must be possible to generate a hidden-surface image of each

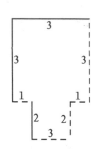

**Figure 24-15** An object with fixed face priority. The location of the viewpoint determines back faces (dashed). Fixed priority assignments determine the priority of remaining faces.

single cluster. Suppose, for example, that each cluster in Figure 24-14 is a complex assembly of polygons. If the viewpoint lies in region $A$, which has priority order 1, 2, 3, we first solve the hidden-surface problem for cluster 3 and write the results into a frame buffer; then we solve and write cluster 2; finally cluster 1 is solved and displayed. Viewed in this way, the cluster technique is a way to subdivide a hidden-surface problem into a number of smaller problems.

Schumacker and co-workers discovered a remarkable property of certain objects: the faces can be assigned a priority order that is correct from any viewpoint [427]. If each cluster contains exactly one of these objects, the priority of each face in the scene is readily determined by computing the cluster priority and then looking up the face priority within the cluster. Figure 24-15 illustrates a top view of an object with fixed face priority. When a viewpoint is determined, all back faces are discarded (dashed lines). The priority numbers of the remaining faces determine which face is visible wherever two or more faces overlap in $x$ or $y$ (in the illustration, faces with higher numbers have higher priority).

Newell [341] has exploited the clustering idea to allow different clusters to be represented by different procedures in the computer, each customized to the kind of object it represents. This allows different objects to have specialized hidden-surface algorithms but lets them all participate in one scene. A sphere, for example, is represented by a procedure that is able to draw its image on the screen, a simpler task than displaying a polyhedral approximation of a sphere. A convex polyhedron has a simple hidden-surface procedure associated with it: simply scan convert all polygonal faces that are not back faces. If a separating plane cannot be found that separates two clusters, Newell's scheme calls on the two clusters to subdivide into smaller or simpler objects that can be tested anew. This subdivision is analogous to splitting overlapping polygons in the Newell, Newell, and Sancha algorithm.

## 24-7 CHOOSING AN ALGORITHM

The preceding sections have described briefly five hidden-surface algorithms: the depth buffer, two scan-line algorithms, Warnock's method, and the Newell,

Newell, and Sancha priority algorithm. Although the depth buffer is certainly the simplest to implement, the others are not difficult. Detailed descriptions of all are available [63, 64, 500, 499, 342, 354].

The algorithms can be extended considerably beyond the descriptions given here, although the extensions add complexity to the algorithms. Each algorithm's tests for visibility can be extended to handle more complex polygon relationships (Watkins' span selection, analysis of a window in the Warnock algorithm, etc.), although the complicated improvements may sometimes slow the algorithm. Scenes with penetrating faces may require special processing in the algorithms: the depth buffer and priority algorithms described here will handle penetrating faces properly, but the scan-line and Warnock algorithms need to be augmented.

Although the algorithms operate only on polygonal models of a scene, the ideas can be adapted to eliminate hidden parts of smooth surfaces. Catmull developed an algorithm based on surface subdivision and a depth buffer [96, 95]. Scan-line algorithms that handle surfaces have been devised by Blinn [55], Whitted [510], and Lane and Carpenter [275]. Many displays of curved surfaces do not use a direct algorithm but operate on polygonal approximations to the surfaces. The final display is made to appear smooth by special shading methods, described in Chapter 25.

Generating images in real time requires an efficient algorithm, in addition to special-purpose hardware to implement it. The earliest equipment of this sort was built by General Electric for NASA's Manned Spacecraft Center in 1968. It is based on a priority algorithm that concurrently scan converts a large number of polygons, selecting the one with the highest priority for display. Watkins' scan-line algorithm is the basis for several real-time systems built more recently by Evans and Sutherland Computer Corp. The frontispiece illustrates an image from one of their systems used for pilot training.

For some applications, hidden-line elimination is preferred to hidden-surface elimination. The two problems have similar overall properties although details of algorithms are different. The Warnock algorithm, for example, is easily adapted to produce line drawings. When a window is discovered to be simple enough to display directly, the *edges* of visible polygons are displayed as lines. If the algorithm ever generates windows that are exactly one screen unit in size, a single dot is displayed by default. Scan-line algorithms can likewise be adapted. Instead of shading segments, lines are displayed corresponding to edges. In some sense, any hidden-surface algorithm can be used to generate a hidden-line view by using a shading rule that makes edges of polygons black and interiors white. In addition to these adaptations, several algorithms have been developed specifically for hidden-line elimination. They concentrate on edges and edge coherence properties to generate a display [466, 404, 10, 193, 189, 294].

The choice of algorithm is not limited to those described here. Many algorithms have been developed, some specialized for certain kinds of images (see Bibliography). Moreover, techniques from existing algorithms can be combined in various ways to design new algorithms. The simple scan-line algorithm introduced in Section 24-4, for example, is simply a combination of the depth-buffer algorithm and the Y-X scan-conversion algorithm described in Section 16-4. Such combinations are often able to exploit various kinds of coherence or to use data structures with particularly efficient implementations of the computer being used. Ideas for additional combined algorithms are given in [466].

## 24-8 SORTING AND COHERENCE

Hidden-line and hidden-surface elimination both seem to require geometrical sorting. All the algorithms we have explored demonstrate explicit sorting steps; other algorithms surveyed in [466] also use sorting as well. The differences between the algorithms relate to the different sorting techniques used and to the order in which depth and lateral sorting are done.

Sorting techniques are chosen to match statistical properties of the data to be sorted. Because the active edge list in a scan-line algorithm is nearly in sort, a bubble sort is a prudent technique to perform the few interchanges necessary to sort it. By contrast, the $y$ bucket sort of edges by topmost scan line in a scan-conversion algorithm is chosen to be insensitive to the order in which edges are inserted, although extracting an edge requires checking a bucket. Clearly a bucket sort for $x$ intersections on a scan line would be desirable only if a great many edges cross a typical scan line.

The properties of a scene determine the characteristics of the geometrical data to be sorted and consequently the performance of the sorting steps. If polygons are well distributed laterally across the screen, a scan-line or area-coherence algorithm may perform best, as they both sort in $xy$ first, thereby reducing the number of items that must be sorted by depth. If, on the other hand, polygons are well distributed in depth, a priority algorithm may be superior. The sorting order may thus help capitalize on a particular statistical property of a scene.

This observation is not as powerful as it seems because many images are isotropic, that is, they have roughly equal distributions of polygon extents in $x$, $y$, and $z$. Consequently, geometrical sorting steps based on each of these coordinates individually are equally effective. Regardless of the sorting order, an algorithm eventually focuses attention on that part of the screen coordinate system where overlaps occur and where visibility decisions must be made (Figure 24-16). If a scene is known to be highly anisotropic, this argument is not valid and one particular sorting order may be superior to the others.

The sorting steps in a hidden-surface algorithm have a strong influence on the performance of the algorithm. Table 24-1 compares estimates of execution time of four algorithms on scenes of 100, 2500, and 60,000 faces. The growth in execution times of the algorithms is primarily attributable to the performance of sorting steps: the sorting algorithms used, the number of items to be sorted, and the complexity of a single comparison operation are all important. Most of the algorithms require more computing time to process more complex scenes because the number of items to sort increases. Although the Newell, Newell, and Sancha algorithm is extremely attractive for small numbers of faces, for a large number of faces the priority sort slows down dramatically. The Warnock and span-coherence algorithms, which operate entirely in image space, seem to have relatively better performance on very complex scenes. Only the depth buffer has uniform performance, attributed to the fact that faces decrease in size as they increase in number. A more detailed characterization of scene complexity and of the performance of the algorithms is given in [466].

**Table 24-1 Estimated execution times of hidden-surface algorithms***

| Algorithm | Number of faces | | | Approximate ratio |
| --- | --- | --- | --- | --- |
| | 100 | 2,500 | 60,000 | 1:25:600 |
| Depth-buffer | 7.5 | 7.5 | 7.5 | 1: 1: 1 |
| Span-coherence | 0.5 | 3 | 64 | 1: 6:120 |
| Warnock | 1.5 | 9 | 43 | 1: 6: 30 |
| Newell, Newell, and Sancha | 0.14 | 1.4 | 71 | 1:10:500 |

* Data from [466].

When implemented on conventional computers, none of these algorithms processes interesting scenes fast enough to be used in interactive applications. However, special-purpose hardware has been built that goes beyond interactive speeds to real-time image generation. When inexpensive parallel processing is available on large-scale integrated circuits, these algorithms can easily make use

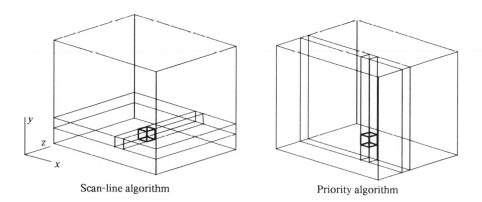

Scan-line algorithm                    Priority algorithm

**Figure 24-16** Sorting order is not as important as it might seem. A scan-line algorithm focuses first on a slab in $y$, then on a span in $x$, and finally on a depth region in $z$. A priority algorithm focuses first in $z$, then in $x$ or $y$. Both explore the same volume.

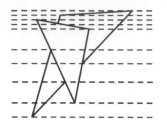

**Figure 24-17** A hidden-line algorithm that scans down the screen, performing depth calculations only when a vertex or edge crossing is encountered.

of the multiple processors to generate images fast enough for interactive systems. Even today, these algorithms are often used to produce final high-quality images of geometric models built interactively.

## EXERCISES

**24-1** In the depth buffer algorithm, how many bits must be allocated to each entry in the *depth* array? How does your answer depend on the properties of the scene being processed?

**24-2** A polygon has a plane equation $ax + by + cz + d = 0$. Suppose that we know the value of $z$ at a point $(x, y)$. What is the easiest way to calculate the value of $z$ at $(x + 1, y)$? At $(x, y + 1)$? If $x$, $y$, and $z$ have 10-bit precision, how much precision is required in your calculations?

**24-3** In the surrounder test, what happens if the sum of the angles subtended by polygon edges is $4\pi$? Can this ever occur?

**24-4** Suggest a method for dealing with extremely small polygons less than one scan line high in a scan-line algorithm.

**24-5** Segments of polygons with a particular depth relationship on one scan-line are likely to have the same relationship on succeeding scan lines. How can this property be used to advantage in a scan-line algorithm? *Hint:* Is it possible to compute the minimum number of scan lines that can be displayed before two segments could possibly change depth order?

**24-6** A scan-line algorithm could be modified to take even greater advantage of scan-line coherence and drastically cut the processing on many scan lines. The idea is that while processing a particular scan line, we estimate the earliest point at which the hidden-surface solution changes, either because an edge terminates (in $y$) or enters or two edges cross. In all scan lines before this critical one, edges may change $x$ position, but the identity of visible segments does not change (Figure 24-17). Explain how this scheme can be made to work. Warnock has suggested that such a technique can be used as a hidden-line elimination algorithm. How is this done?

**24-7** Suppose a hidden-surface algorithm must be chosen that will generate a great many images to make a movie. Consider three cases: (S) the scene is stationary, and only the viewpoint changes; (D) a few objects in the scene move, but the viewpoint is stationary; and (DS) both objects and viewpoint move. What properties would you look for in algorithms to apply to these cases? Which techniques discussed in this chapter seem to be best suited to each case? Can you suggest any additional techniques?

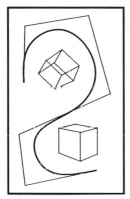

# 25

# SHADING

The realism of a raster-scan image of a three-dimensional scene depends on the successful simulation of shading effects. Once visible surfaces have been identified by a hidden-surface algorithm, a *shading model* is used to compute the intensities and colors to display for the surface. The still-life in the frontispiece illustrates many of the subtle shading effects that can be achieved.

The shading model does not precisely simulate the behavior of light and surfaces in the real world but only approximates actual conditions. In this respect, the shading model is similar to the geometric model. The design of the model is a compromise between precision and computing cost. Trade-offs in a shading model are especially difficult because the properties of the human visual system influence the perception of realism: we must avoid approximations in the model that lead to confusing perceptions by the viewer.

The shading model has two main ingredients, properties of the surface and properties of the illumination falling on it. The principal surface property is its *reflectance*, which determines how much of the incident light is reflected. If a surface has different reflectances for light of different wavelengths, it will appear to be colored. If a surface is textured or has a pattern painted on it, the reflectance will vary with position on the surface. Another surface property that plays a role in shaded pictures is *transparency:* a surface may allow some light to be transmitted through it from behind.

An object's illumination is as important as its surface properties in computing its intensity. The scene may have some illumination that is uniform from all directions, called *diffuse illumination*. In addition, there may be *point sources* of light in the scene; they differ from diffuse lighting in that specular reflections, or *highlights*, appear on surfaces. Finally, the illumination of an object may be partially blocked due to *shadows*.

In addition to modeling these effects, the shading calculation must avoid certain kinds of defects. Some of these arise because of interactions with human vision—Mach bands generated by shading discontinuities are an example. Defects due to improper sampling of the image are also annoying; we discussed in Section 16-2 some measures for avoiding this. Sampling defects are particularly apparent in sequences of frames that show objects in motion. The jagged steps of an improperly sampled edge will appear to move along the edge in distracting ways. The shading model must also deal properly with moving objects, changing their shades in ways consistent with their motion. Inadequacies of a model not apparent in a single image may be disastrous in a sequence of images.

## 25-1 A SHADING MODEL

Shading models determine the shade of a point on the surface of an object in terms of a number of attributes. The shading model can be decomposed into three parts, a contribution from diffuse illumination, contributions for one or more specific light sources, and a transparency effect. Each of these effects contributes shading terms $E$, which are summed to find the total light energy coming from a point on an object. This is the energy a display should generate to present a realistic image of the object. To be precise, the energy comes not from a point on the surface but from a small area around the point. For simplicity, our discussion will refer to the energy coming from a point.

The simplest form of shading considers only diffuse illumination:

$$E_{pd} = R_p I_d \tag{25-1}$$

where $E_{pd}$ is the energy coming from the point $P$ due to diffuse illumination, $I_d$ is the diffuse illumination falling on the entire scene, and $R_p$ is the reflectance coefficient at $P$, which ranges from 0 to 1. Thus the reflectance coefficient relates the energy leaving point $P$ to that arriving. To model colored surfaces, the reflectance coefficient and illumination have separate components in a color coordinate system. If we choose the common red, green, blue system, we might write

$$\begin{aligned}
E_{pd,\text{red}} &= R_{p,\text{red}} I_{d,\text{red}} \\
E_{pd,\text{green}} &= R_{p,\text{green}} I_{d,\text{green}} \\
E_{pd,\text{blue}} &= R_{p,\text{blue}} I_{d,\text{blue}}
\end{aligned} \tag{25-2}$$

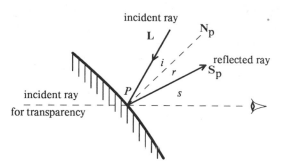

**Figure 25-1** The shading of a point $P$ is determined by reflected and transmitted light. The vector $\mathbf{N_p}$ is normal to the surface at $P$.

In effect, Equation 25-1 becomes a vector equation in which $E$, $R$, and $I$ all have three color components.

A picture that uses diffuse shading alone does not look very realistic, largely because changing the orientation of a surface does not change its shade. Thus, for example, a sphere will have uniform shade throughout and will be perceptually indistinguishable from a disk. Because perfectly diffuse illumination occurs rarely in natural scenes, observers are unaccustomed to its properties. Some diffuse contribution is evident in nearly all natural scenes, however, even though diffuse shading cannot be used as the sole shading effect.

Shading contributions from specific light sources will cause the shade of a surface to vary as its orientation with respect to the light source changes and will also include specular reflection effects. The first of these effects is due to Lambert's law, which states that the energy falling on a surface varies as the cosine of the angle of incidence of the light. Figure 25-1 illustrates a point $P$ on a surface, with light arriving at an angle of incidence $i$, the angle between the surface normal $\mathbf{N}_p$ and a ray to the light source. If the energy $I_{ps}$ arriving from the light source is reflected uniformly in all directions, called *diffuse reflection*, we have

$$E_{ps} = (R_p \cos i)I_{ps} \qquad (25\text{-}3)$$

This equation shows the reduction in intensity of a surface as it is tipped obliquely to the light source. If the angle of incidence, $i$, exceeds 90°, the surface is hidden from the light source and we must set $E_{ps}$ to zero. A sphere shaded with this model will be brightest at the point on the surface between the center of the sphere and the light source and will be completely dark on the half of the surface hidden from the light. This effect, too, is rarely observed in the real world; usually there is a low level of diffuse illumination (Equation 25-1) that prevents the back of the sphere from being completely black.

Specular reflection due to a single light source can be modeled by modifying Equation 25-3. Treating specular reflection requires us to calculate the relationship between the observer, the light source, and the surface, as illustrated in Figure 25-1. The principal reflected ray leaves $P$ with an angle of

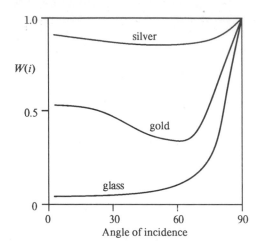

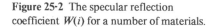

Figure 25-2 The specular reflection coefficient $W(i)$ for a number of materials.

reflection $r$ equal to the angle of incidence. The amount of such light seen by the observer is determined by a specular reflection coefficient $W(i)$ and the angle $s$ between the reflected ray and the observer. Equation 25-3 becomes

$$E_{ps} = [R_p \cos i + W(i)(\cos s)^n]I_{ps} \qquad (25\text{-}4)$$

It is important to note that the specular-reflection component is not sensitive to the "color" of the surface, as modeled by $R_p$. Specular reflections have the same color as the illumination, a property the reader is invited to verify! The reflection coefficient $W(i)$ is a function of the angle of incidence; reflections at a grazing angle reflect a larger percentage of the light (Figure 25-2). The exponent $n$ ranges roughly from 1 to 10 and controls how "shiny" the surface appears. A shiny metallic surface, which produces very small highlight areas, will have a large value of $n$. A dull surface such as a piece of paper will have a small value. The formula is not intended to model physical reflection effects but seems to produce realistic highlights similar to real specular reflections.

If light from several sources falls on a point, Equation 25-4 can be applied to calculate reflected energy contributions from each of them. If an object is in the shadow of one or more light sources, contributions from those sources are not added into the total energy coming from the point.

Technically, the illumination $I_{ps}$ from a point source will decrease as the distance between the light source and $P$ increases. In natural scenes, however, the distance from the source to the scene is large compared with distances within the scene (e.g., the sun illuminating a city). Thus we usually assume the illumination from a source is constant throughout the scene.

Transparency adds a contribution related to the energy arriving at $P$ from behind (Figure 25-1)

$$E_{pt} = T_p E_{pb} \qquad (25\text{-}5)$$

The transmission coefficient $T_p$, which lies between 0 and 1, determines how much light is transmitted at $P$. The energy $E_{pb}$ arriving at $P$ from behind is the result of modeling reflections from another surface in the scene, farther from the eye than $P$.

The total energy arriving at the eye from point $P$ is the sum of the energies from the individual effects:

Diffuse illumination:

$$E_{pd} = R_p I_d$$

Light-source illumination (for each light source):

$$E_{ps} = [R_p \cos i + W(i)(\cos s)^n] I_{ps}$$

Transparency:

$$E_{pt} = T_p E_{pb}$$

Total:

$$E = E_{pd} + \Sigma E_{ps} + E_{pt} \qquad \text{(25-6)}$$

These equations are used to calculate color energies by casting illumination $I$, reflectance $R$, transmission $T$, and the resulting energy $E$ as color vectors.

This model, developed by Bui-Tuong Phong, is a reasonably good basis for shading pictures [77, 76]. Blinn has extended it to produce more accurate highlights [56]. Although the calculations required to implement the model are simple, they will be performed many times in the process of generating a shaded image. The next section explains how the evaluation of $\cos i$ and $\cos s$ can be carried out efficiently. Subsequent sections deal with even more powerful work-saving techniques.

## Calculating Angles

The angles required in the shading model can be determined entirely from the *normal* vector for a surface. As we remarked in Chapter 20, the surface normal of a polygon and its plane equation are closely related. Since plane equations are used in hidden surface elimination, the normal vector is readily available for shading calculations.

Angular calculations are simplified if we assume that the viewpoint and all light sources are infinitely far away from the object in the world coordinate system. Thus a vector to one of these points has a constant direction throughout the scene. For convenience, these vectors are normalized to have unit length. The vector pointing toward the viewpoint in the screen coordinate system is therefore $[0\ 0\ -1]$. A normalized vector $\mathbf{L}$ pointing to a light source will generally be $[a\ b\ c]$, where $a^2 + b^2 + c^2 = 1$. We shall also assume that the surface normal vector $\mathbf{N}_p$ is normalized.

The first term in Equation 25-4 is easily calculated from the normal and a

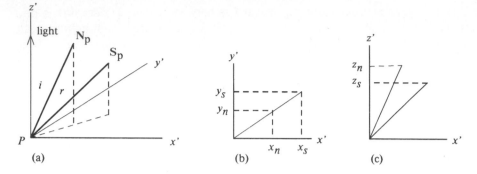

**Figure 25-3** The coordinate system for calculating the direction of the reflected ray $S_p$.

vector to the light source: $\cos i = L \cdot N_p$. This dot product expression requires both $L$ and $N_p$ to be normalized vectors.

The second term is calculated with a method due to Phong.* The method determines the unit vector $S_p$ that points along the reflected ray and then uses this vector to find $\cos s$. Figure 25-3a shows how $S_p$ is calculated. It portrays the same situation as Figure 25-1, but a special coordinate system is added, with origin at $P$ and $z'$ axis pointing toward the light source. The vectors $S_p$ and $N_p$ project onto the $x'y'$ plane with components $(x_s, y_s)$ and $(x_n, y_n)$, respectively. Thus, because these two projections are the same line (Figure 25-3b), we have

$$x_s/y_s = x_n/y_n$$

Along the $z'$ axis, we have:

$$z_n = \cos i$$

$$z_s = \cos(i + r) = \cos 2i = 2(\cos i)^2 - 1$$

Using the relationship $x_s^2 + y_s^2 + z_s^2 = 1$, we find

$$x_s = 2z_n x_n \qquad y_s = 2z_n y_n \qquad z_s = 2z_n^2 - 1$$

These last three equations give the components of the vector $S_p$ in the special coordinate system. We can then find $\cos s = [x_s \quad y_s \quad z_s] \cdot V'$, where $V'$ is a vector pointing toward the viewpoint in the special coordinate system.

The determination of angles is best carried out in the world (or eye) coordinate system, because rays pointing to light sources infinitely far away are

---

*Since Bui-Tuong Phong was Vietnamese, Bui-Tuong was his surname, but phrases like *Phong shading* are now so widespread that the more correct "Bui-Tuong shading" would be confusing.

the same orientation for all points on surfaces in the scene. Thus if all objects in the scene are transformed into a coordinate system in which the $z$ axis points toward the light source, the calculations required to determine cos $s$ are straightforward.

## 25-2 APPLYING THE SHADING MODEL

The shading model given in Equations 25-6, together with methods for computing cos $i$ and cos $s$, lead to a straightforward calculation of the shade of a point on a surface. Even though this computation is not difficult, it may be necessary to perform it very frequently. If we are to compute a shade for each point on a 1024 × 1024 raster, the calculation must be performed over 1 million times. To make matters worse, high-quality images requiring careful shading are often displayed with higher resolution, such as 3000 × 6000 pixels.

These calculations can be reduced by taking advantage of *shading coherence*, that is, the intensity of adjacent pixels is either identical or very nearly so. This observation will allow us to turn the shading calculation into an incremental one and to evaluate surface normals and shading models less frequently. The following sections describe several such techniques.

### Shading Polyhedra

If objects are modeled as plane-faced polyhedra, the intensity of a face is constant throughout the face (Figures 25-4a, 25-5a and b). The plane equation of a face provides a surface normal vector to use in the shading equation. The

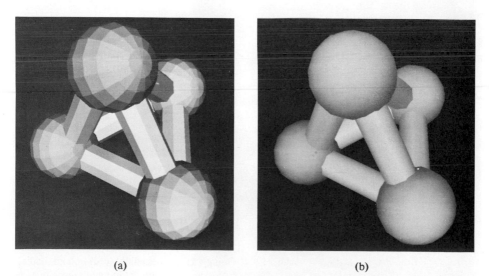

(a)                                           (b)

**Figure 25-4** Two shaded pictures of the same molecular model: (a) applying a constant shade to each face; using smooth shading to achieve the appearance of spheres and cylinders. *Courtesy Univ. of Utah.*

**Figure 25-5** (a,b) Polyhedron shading; (c, d) smooth shading, using Gouraud's technique. Note the shading discontinuities near the lips in (d). *Courtesy University of Utah.*

(d)

(c)

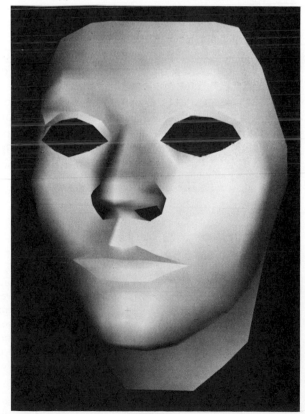

constant shading value can thereafter be associated with the face; whenever a hidden-surface algorithm finds the face visible, this is the intensity value that is passed to the display.

## Smooth Shading

**Gouraud.** If a smooth surface is approximated as a polyhedron in order to simplify hidden-surface elimination, the shading calculation can restore its smooth appearance. Normal polyhedron shading of such images has a disturbing effect on the viewer, even though shading effects such as transparency and highlights can be simulated (Figures 25-4a, 25-5a and b). The smooth shading restores considerable realism to the scene (Figures 25-4b, 25-5c and d). The polyhedral approximation is still evident, however; the edges of the objects contain straight-line segments.

Gouraud introduced smooth shading with a linear-interpolation method illustrated in Figure 25-6 [201]. Normals are computed at the vertices of each face; these normals approximate the normal to the true surface at the vertex. They can be computed from the surface model at the same time the geometry for the polyhedral approximation is derived. Each vertex normal is then used to compute a vertex shade; this value is the precise shade at the vertex.

The shade inside the face is interpolated from the vertex shades. Figure 25-6 shows a scan line that intersects the face to be shaded at $L$ and $R$. The shade at $L$ is a linear interpolation between the shades at $A$ and $B$; the shade at $R$ is interpolated between the shades of $D$ and $C$. Finally, the shade at a point $P$ on the scan line is linearly interpolated between the shades at $L$ and $R$. These simple interpolations can be performed as part of a scan-line hidden-surface algorithm or a tiler process. The shade along an edge is interpolated between vertex shades just as the $x$ coordinate is interpolated; if the shade is expressed as $E = \alpha y + \beta$, the shading interpolation becomes incremental.

Vertex normals can be computed directly from a surface model or by an averaging technique based on face normals (Figure 25-7a). The normal at vertex $V$ is the average of the normals of the faces that surround the vertex.

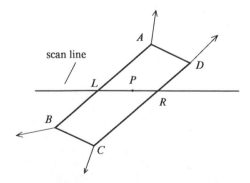

**Figure 25-6** Gouraud shading of a polygon with vertices $ABCD$. The intensity at $L$ is determined by interpolating linearly between intensities at $A$ and $B$, and the intensity at $R$ by interpolating between intensities at $D$ and $C$. The intensity at $P$ is interpolated between intensities at $L$ and $R$.

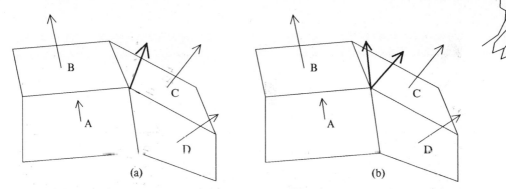

**Figure 25-7** Normal vectors at a vertex are derived by averaging normals of neighboring faces: (a) smooth shading averages all surrounding faces; (b) shading discontinuities are introduced along the B-C and A-D boundaries by averaging only two face normals.

The advantage of normal averaging is that it requires no underlying model of the surface: if a surface is approximated by digitizing a large number of polygonal faces, the smooth effect can still be achieved. The face in Figure 25-5d was generated in this way.

Sometimes the smooth shading across a face boundary must be defeated, in order to show a crease or sharp edge in the object. Figure 25-7b shows two normals computed at a vertex. One, the average of normals A and B, will be used to interpolate shades for faces A and B. The other is used similarly for faces C and D. Thus the A-B and C-D boundaries will be smooth-shaded, but the A-D and B-C boundaries will have discontinuous shading. The lips in Figure 25-5d show a crease generated this way.

The averaging of normals sometimes introduces anomalies that must be corrected. Figure 25-8a shows a series of surfaces and associated averaged normals that are all identical. Gouraud's shading technique will compute a constant shade for these surfaces because all the vertex shades are identical.

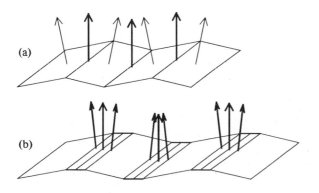

**Figure 25-8** Normal averaging can lead to shading anomalies: (a) all average normals point the same direction, resulting in a constant shade; (b) the error is removed by introducing more polygons.

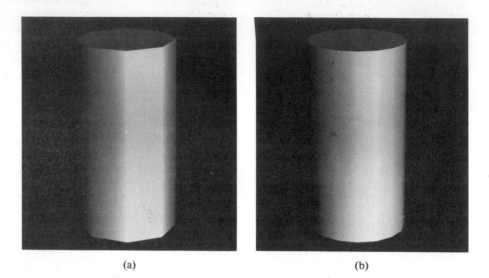

(a)                                                                      (b)

**Figure 25-9** The Mach band effect appears if linear shading interpolation is used. Although image (b) has more faces than (a), the effect is still noticeable. *Courtesy University of Utah.*

The constant shade is very misleading, because the surfaces have different orientations with respect to the light source. Better shading can be achieved by inserting small surfaces near the boundaries (Figure 25-8b) that cause the averaged normals to vary.

The Gouraud shading technique, although very simple, has deficiencies. If smooth shading is used in a motion sequence, the shading appears to change in strange ways. This occurs because the interpolation basis is fixed to the surface of the screen rather than to the surface of the moving object. Highlights generated with this technique are also anomalous—the shape of the highlight is strongly influenced by the shape of the polygons used to approximate the surface rather than the true surface orientation. Another disadvantage of Gouraud shading is that linear shading interpolation may induce the Mach band effect, a perceptual phenomenon due to processing in the human visual system. Discontinuities in the rate of change of shading (i.e., the first derivative) cause the eye to perceive light or dark bands at the discontinuities. Figure 25-9 shows an example of the Mach bands produced by linear shading interpolation. As the number of faces in the model is increased, the magnitude of the discontinuities is reduced, and the band effect is less severe.

**Phong.** A shading technique due to Phong remedies many of the problems with Gouraud shading, although it requires more computation [77, 76]. The idea is to interpolate normal vectors rather than shades and to apply the shading model at each pixel displayed. The scheme is illustrated schematically in Figure

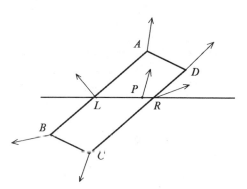

**Figure 25-10** Phong shading of the polygon *ABCD*. The surface normal at *L* is linearly interpolated between true normals at *A* and *B*, that at *R* between *D* and *C*. The normal at *P* is interpolated between normals at *L* and *R*.

25-10. Just as with Gouraud shading, the interpolation scheme fits nicely into scan-line algorithms: the normal along an edge of a face can be expressed as $N_1 y + N_2$, a vector equation that can be implemented with incremental additions. After the normal vector is determined for each point, the shading equation is used to calculate a shade.

Phong also showed how to turn the shading equation (Equation 25-6) into an incremental calculation to reduce the computation required. The result is an interpolation scheme for shades, but the interpolator is more complex than the simple linear interpolator used by Gouraud.

Figure 25-11 illustrates Phong's technique; note the realistic highlights. The champagne glass still exhibits straight contour edges, all that remain of the

**Figure 25-11** Phong's shading of a champagne glass, illustrating transparency and highlight effects. *Courtesy University of Utah.*

**Figure 25-12** A shading anomaly due to interpolation. The shade at point $P$, interpolated between $L$ and $R$, will not necessarily be similar to the shade at the vertex $V$.

underlying polyhedral approximation. Phong's method greatly reduces the disturbing Mach bands, produces more realistic highlights, and largely removes frame-to-frame discontinuities. The method retains an annoying problem also present in Gouraud shading: a concave polygon may introduce shading anomalies. Figure 25-12 shows an example. The shading at $P$ is determined by a normal interpolated between normals at $L$ and $R$. The shading immediately below $P$, however, will be determined by the normal at $V$, which may deviate considerably from the normal calculated for $P$. The discrepancy in the normal vectors will cause a shading discontinuity.

### Shading Each Point Independently

To calculate shading precisely, the normal vector can be computed anew for each point of the display. Although a large number of such calculations is required, they can sometimes be described incrementally. Catmull devised such a scheme for shading bicubic surface patches [96, 95]. The basic operation is subdivision of a surface by parameter value (Figure 25-13). Each of the four corners of the surface is defined by a set of numbers giving the location of the corner, the normal directions, and enough derivative values to subdivide the surface accurately. The subdivision process generates four smaller surfaces and associated normal information. When a surface becomes smaller than a pixel, it is displayed on the screen with a shade calculated from the precise normal vector that has been carried along with the subdivision. This technique generates not only precise normal values but precise values of $x$, $y$, and $z$ in the screen coordinate system. Used with a depth buffer to eliminate hidden surfaces, the method generates displays of smooth surfaces that have properly curved contours.

### Sampling

Shading calculations must be done carefully because they are intrinsically *sampling* the model in the screen coordinate system to generate the display. Proper sampling requires that the shade of a pixel be determined by contributions from a small area around the pixel, not from a single sample point. This same problem crops up in scan-conversion algorithms (Section 16-2).

Proper sampling is required primarily at the edges of surfaces, where shading may change abruptly to that of another surface. Technically, pixels

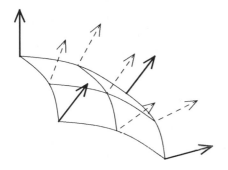

**Figure 25-13** Subdividing a surface patch into four smaller patches allows exact normal vectors to be computed for all points on the surface. These normals are used by the shading model.

within a polygon should be sampled carefully as well, though shading changes so slowly that sampling defects are rarely observed. At edges, however, it is necessary to sum contributions from the several surfaces that fall over a pixel. Figure 25-14 shows a simple case involving two polygons, *a* and *b*. Each polygon has a shade associated with it for each pixel, computed with a shading model. The shade in the pixel, however, is a combination of the shades of the two polygons, governed by the area with which each polygon overlaps the pixel. Thus the shade of pixel 1 might be roughly $0.9E_{a1} + 0.1E_{b1}$, while that of pixel 2 is $0.5E_{a2} + 0.5E_{b2}$.

Area-sampling calculations are tied to hidden-surface elimination techniques. With a scan-line algorithm, it is possible to detect a few simple cases such as in Figure 25-14, and to generate area-sampled displays correctly. These algorithms have available, while processing a span, a list of all other polygons nearby. Thus at an edge where one polygon terminates, the polygon that is just becoming visible can be identified and considered in sampling. The depth-buffer algorithm, however, does not have this property. Polygons or surfaces are written into the depth buffer in arbitrary order, which prevents accurate sampling. Catmull observes that simple approximations are often sufficient to make depth-buffer images adequate [95].

Properly sampling a scene is important when generating a realistic image. When sampling is not performed properly, defects are introduced, called variously *aliasing* and *rastering*. The sampling techniques we have described here and in Chapter 16 are only approximations; precise sampling requires

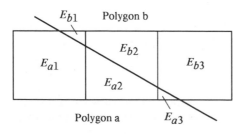

**Figure 25-14** Sampling at an edge separating two surfaces.

complex filtering operations. More information about sampling theory, as it applies to computer graphics, can be found in [127, 128, 94].

**Hardware Considerations**

Careful shading calculations can be spoiled by defects in the hardware used to display an image. A serious defect is noise, either in the delivery of intensity information to a raster-scan CRT or in the deflection system that steers the beam over the pixel array. The size of the spot on the screen must also be adjusted to minimize the perception of the raster array. If the spot is too small, an array of dots is clearly visible; if the spot is too large, the sharpness of the image suffers.

Of more direct concern to shading calculations, however, is the fidelity with which the shading information passed to a display is reproduced on the screen. The shading model specifies precisely the light energy that should be generated at a spot. Nonlinearities in the intensity-control circuits or in the phosphor response can distort the energy actually emitted at a pixel. To combat these effects, the shading calculation must compensate its calculations to account for the hardware effects. This task is easily accomplished with a *compensation table:* given a calculated shade $E$, we find in a table indexed by $E$ a value to store in the frame buffer or send to the display. The table can be built by making photometric measurements of the light emitted by the display for each different intensity value passed to it.

Many raster displays deliberately introduce nonlinearities in the intensity control to broaden the range of intensities that can be displayed. Because the human eye responds roughly to the *logarithm* of the incoming energy, some display designers arrange for the frame buffer value to be roughly proportional to log $E$. This technique enlarges the range of intensities that can be displayed on the screen but forces a shading calculation to compensate for the logarithmic response. It is important to remember that the shading-model and sampling calculations are linear in *energy;* if some other value is to be stored in a frame buffer, the compensation must be done *after* the total energy for the pixel has been determined.

Even more difficult than intensity compensation is accurate color shading, and especially the proper recording of colors on film. The topic is much too intricate to detail here; several references to material on the proper use of color in photography, printing, and computer graphics are [232, 531, 442, 246].

## 25-3 SPECIAL EFFECTS

The basic shading model is often augmented to produce special effects in images. Some of these effects are chosen for artistic value and have no relation to modeling the real world. Others are intended to enhance the realism of the image. Transparency, surface details, shadows, and texture are among these effects. The ideas behind these techniques are briefly surveyed below.

## Transparency

The realistic appearance of the Klein bottle in Figure 25-15 and of the glassware in the frontispiece depends on a simulation of transparency. To add a transparency contribution to the shading model (Equation 25-5), it is necessary to know how much light arrives at a point from behind the surface. This information is obtained easily during the execution of some hidden-surface algorithms. Newell, Newell, and Sancha [342] were the first to experiment with transparency, because their algorithm retains, in the frame buffer, the shade of each point due to polygons already written into the buffer. As a polygon of higher priority is entered, this old shade represents the light arriving from behind. Thus the value of $E_{ph}$ is easily determined from the current frame-buffer contents at point $P$.

Scan-line algorithms can also be adapted to show transparency. Within a span, the algorithm sorts segments by depth. The opaque polygon closest to the observer is found, and its shade is determined. This shade is then modified by any transparent segments that lie between the observer and the opaque surface.

## Surface-Detail Polygons

Often the shade of a surface has more detail than its geometry does. For example, a geometric model of a runway might consist of a single rectangular face. However, the shading of the runway surface is rather complex: painted stripes, markings, and skid marks are among the larger details. These surface details could be modeled as separate polygons, lying "just above" the runway and treated by a hidden-surface algorithm along with all other objects in the scene. This method is to be avoided for two reasons: it needlessly increases the

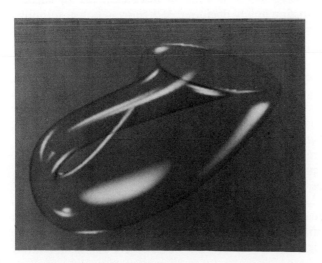

**Figure 25-15** A shaded image of a Klein bottle, showing highlights and transparency. The bottle is modeled with B-spline surfaces. *Courtesy University of Utah.*

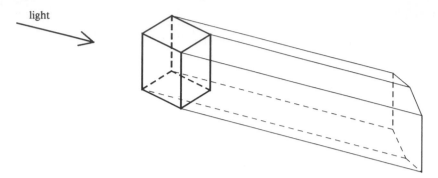

light

**Figure 25-16** The region shadowed by a block is a polyhedron, and can be modeled as a collection of *shadow polygons.*

computation required to eliminate hidden surfaces, and it can introduce errors in the image. If the depth resolution of the hidden-surface algorithm is not sufficient, the algorithm may find the wrong surface to be visible, causing the runway to appear to be on top of its stripes!

Surface details are better treated as shading data than as geometrical data. Wherever a part of the geometric model is determined to be visible (e.g., the runway), the shading algorithm uses surface-detail polygons to generate the shade, in effect providing reflectance values as a function of $x$ and $y$. The Newell, Newell, and Sancha algorithm illustrates how this technique might be applied. The runway polygon is placed in the priority list, with a pointer to a list of surface-detail polygons associated with it. As the algorithm proceeds, the priority list is sorted, testing the runway polygon against others in the list. If the runway polygon must be split, the surface-detail polygons are likewise split, yielding two new runway polygons, each with an associated list of surface details. When the priority sorting finally decides that a runway polygon should be written into the frame buffer, we first tile the runway polygon and then all the associated surface-detail polygons. Thus although these polygons are never involved in priority sorting, they still appear to be on top of the runway.

## Shadows

The shading model is capable of simulating shadows, but it requires that we determine for each point which light sources illuminate the point. The shadow problem is thus quite similar to the hidden-surface problem: we need to determine which faces or parts of faces are visible when viewed from the light source. Several techniques for dealing with shadows have been developed; we shall describe only one.

Prior to hidden-surface elimination, a set of *shadow polygons* is added to the polygons that come from the geometric model of the scene. These polygons are constructed as shown in Figure 25-16. Each edge of an object that is an outline of the object when viewed from the light source is extended to form a shadow polygon. The shadow polygons for one object enclose a volume in which light from the source will be obscured by the object. If several light sources are being simulated, several sets of shadow polygons are generated. Each shadow polygon is tagged with an index that indicates which light source generated it and which object generated it. These polygons are passed to the hidden-surface algorithm along with polygons that represent faces of objects.

As the hidden-surface elimination proceeds, the shadow polygons are used to determine which light sources illuminate a surface. Figure 25-17 shows several spans in a scan-line algorithm, in which two shadow polygons $S_1$ and $S_2$ penetrate an opaque polygon $P$. Suppose both shadow polygons are tagged with identical object and light-source identifications. In span 1, it is clear that a ray from the viewpoint will enter the shadowed region between $S_1$ and $S_2$ and then leave it before hitting $P$; therefore $P$ is not shadowed. In span 2, however, $P$ is encountered within a shadowed region; its shade is thus computed without contributions from the light source that gave rise to the shadow polygons. In general, many shadow polygons will lie between the viewpoint and a face. If an even number of shadow polygons with the same tags is encountered, the face is not shadowed by the object and light source given in the tags. A set of tags encountered an odd number of times indicates that the face is shadowed by the light source given in the tags.

This shadow-generation method is only illustrative of the techniques that have been developed [126, 513]. A particularly interesting approach has been used by Atherton, Weiler, and Greenberg [17]. A comprehensive polygon-clipping technique is used to generate polygons that represent shadows falling on surfaces in the scene. These are then used as surface-detail polygons to modify the shading of shadowed surfaces during hidden-surface elimination. This approach allows many different views of a scene to be generated from a single set of shadow polygons.

### Texture and Reflections

The texture of an object often gives an observer cues to its depth or orientation and is also a valuable ingredient in adding realism to an image. Texture can be

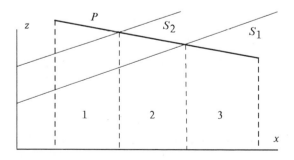

**Figure 25-17** Processing shadow polygons with a scan-line algorithm, illustrating the relationship between an opaque surface $P$ and two shadow polygons $S_1$ and $S_2$.

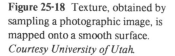

Figure 25-18 Texture, obtained by sampling a photographic image, is mapped onto a smooth surface. *Courtesy University of Utah.*

viewed as a modulation of the reflection coefficients $R_p$ in the shading model, which will change the surface color but will not disturb the flat appearance of the surface. The key lies in finding modulation functions that produce the desired effect. Catmull used reflection coefficients determined by sampling an image to map the image onto the surface (Figure 25-18)[95]. This general idea has been extended by Blinn and Newell to map synthetically generated texture patterns and highlights onto surfaces (Figure 25-19)[60]. Blinn has recently generated pictures that simulate wrinkled and bumpy surfaces by altering the surface normal as well as the reflection coefficients (see the orange in the frontispiece)[57].

## 25-4 CONCLUSION

Much of Part Five has dealt with techniques for producing realistic images of three-dimensional scenes. The perspective drawing, often with hidden parts removed, is the basis on which many other visualization techniques are built. Shading is the culmination of techniques to achieve realism: some viewers have difficulty distinguishing the still-life in the frontispiece from a photograph of an actual scene!

Although hidden-surface and shading techniques produce the most realistic images, they are not necessarily suited to all applications. A user may prefer wire-frame images that are rapidly generated, so that he can quickly select a viewing position that reveals the essential features of the geometric model.

**Figure 25-19** A computer-generated image of a teapot with simulated specular reflections of light entering through a window. *Courtesy University of Utah.*

Sometimes shading is simply an inappropriate visualization technique: the hedgehog image (Chapter 21) reveals properties of a surface that a shading model cannot. In spite of these examples, shaded images have an appeal and a realism that make their use increasingly popular.

## EXERCISES

**25-1** Consider diffuse shading (Equation 25-1) only. If a surface is first oriented perpendicular to the line of sight and is then rotated to become oblique to the line of sight, its intensity does not appear to change. However, the total amount of light energy reaching the eye from the surface does change. How? Why does the surface appear to have constant intensity regardless of its orientation?

**25-2** How would you change the shading model to handle objects that emit light rather than reflect it? Consider point and diffuse sources (e.g., a fluorescent light viewed from a distance of 20 centimeters).

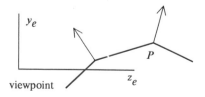

**Figure 25-20** A vertex normal at the edge of an object may point away from the viewer.

**25-3** Can shading calculations be performed in the screen coordinate system? What are the advantages of such a technique? What are the problems? Are there any special cases that make this technique especially attractive?

**25-4** The calculation of cos $i$, as suggested in Section 25-1, is achieved with a dot product, which does not explicitly yield a value for $i$. However, Equation 25-4 requires a value for $W(i)$ to calculate a contribution for specular reflection. How can $W(i)$ be evaluated quickly without calculating $i$?

**25-5** Blinn and Newell [60] have suggested that the calculation of cos $s$ can be simplified greatly by associating with each light source a fictitious light source that will generate specular reflections. This second light source is at an angle halfway between the real light source and the eye. Then Equation 25-4 is expressed as

$$E_{ps} = [R_p(\mathbf{L}{\bullet}\mathbf{N}_p) + W(i)(\mathbf{L'}{\bullet}\mathbf{N}_p)^\eta]I_{ps}$$

where $\mathbf{L}$ and $\mathbf{L'}$ are vectors to the real and fictitious light sources, respectively. Discuss this approach. Does it reduce the computation required to evaluate the shading model? Is it correct or simply a good approximation?

**25-6** Consider Gouraud shading in a situation shown in Figure 25-20. The vertex normal at $P$ actually points *away* from the viewer. What vertex shade will be computed? What sorts of shading errors will result? Does Phong shading avoid this problem? Suggest a solution to the problem.

**25-7** How might the Newell, Newell, and Sancha hidden-surface algorithm be modified to simulate shadows?

**25-8** How would you generate an image that exaggerates changes in surface orientation? Such an image might be used to see if a surface is smooth. How could parameters of the shading model (Equations 25-6) be chosen to achieve this? Would some other shading model be superior? If so, what might it be?

**25-9** Can the idea behind surface-detail polygons be exploited in hidden-line algorithms? If so, how?

**25-10** Analyze the problem illustrated by Figure 25-12. Under what circumstances is the problem absent? Are these cases common or rare? What steps can you suggest to remedy the problem?

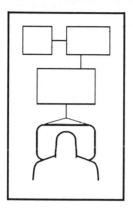

# PART SIX

## GRAPHICS SYSTEMS

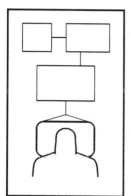

# 26

# DISPLAY PROCESSORS

The remaining three chapters of this book bring together much of the preceding material in discussions of topics of general importance: portability in graphics systems and applications, and the design of user interfaces. These topics could not be discussed properly before because they involve so many different aspects of computer graphics, including graphics package design, interaction, and three-dimensional graphics. One other topic is intimately involved, the design of hardware for computer graphics. The first of these three chapters is therefore devoted to a discussion of graphic displays and how their design is influenced by graphics software requirements.

The focus of this chapter is on display controllers for line-drawing displays. Raster displays are not discussed here, since they were covered in some detail in Chapter 19. The following sections concentrate on the four principal classes of line-drawing display in use today:

1.  The simple refresh line-drawing display, of the kind discussed in Chapter 3;
2.  The storage-tube display, also discussed in Chapter 3;
3.  The unbuffered high-performance display, containing hardware for modeling and transformation;
4.  The buffered high-performance display, similar to the unbuffered variety, but with a refresh buffer in which the transformed picture is stored.

The first two categories of display were covered in Chapter 3; the descriptions that follow build on those given earlier to provide a more thorough discussion of each one.

## 26-1 THE SIMPLE REFRESH LINE-DRAWING DISPLAY

The refresh line-drawing display was one of the earliest types of display to be widely used in interactive graphics. It was developed in the early 1960s and marketed by a number of companies; the most widely used of the early line-drawing displays were probably the Digital Equipment 340 [145] and the IBM 2250 [238]. Since then the line-drawing display has been developed and refined in a number of ways; some of today's displays are extremely powerful instruments for graphical interaction. There has also been continued interest in producing simple refresh line-drawing displays of the type described in Chapter 3.

This simple type of line-drawing display is of interest for two reasons. In the first place it offers an inexpensive basis for simple interactive applications—architectural layout, circuit design, data analysis, and so forth. Second, it is ideally suited to the maintenance of a transformed, segmented display file. Chapters 6 to 8 have discussed the design of software for segmented display-file maintenance; in this section we revisit the simple line-drawing display and discuss its design for the support of such software.

The general arrangement of the simple line-drawing display is shown in Figure 26-1. It consists of a CRT and a *display processor,* i.e., a controller capable of maintaining the refresh cycle more or less unaided by the computer. The display processor reads instructions from memory into an *instruction register,* where they are decoded. Instructions may represent positioning commands, line-generation commands, or commands to reset the address of the next instruction. According to the type of instruction, the data content of the instruction register is copied into one of several other registers that directly control the CRT or the instruction address. These registers include:

*x and y registers,* whose contents are converted into voltages to set the position of the CRT beam;

$\Delta x$ *and* $\Delta y$ *registers,* whose contents generate continuously increasing or decreasing voltages that cause the beam to move in a straight line through the specified displacements in $x$ and $y$;

*A brightness register,* which controls the energy of the CRT beam, thus setting the brightness of the displayed image;

*An instruction address register,* which determines the address of the next instruction fetched from memory.

Figure 26-1 also shows a *control path* from the computer to the display processor. This enables the computer to maintain control over the operation of

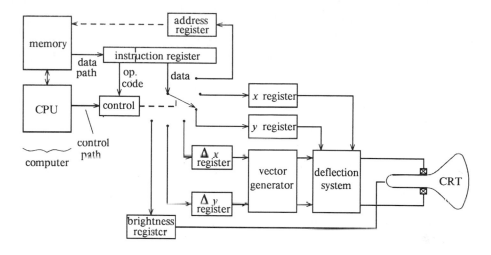

**Figure 26-1**  General arrangement of the simple line-drawing display.

the display processor. In particular the computer must be able to reset the instruction address register and to start and stop the processing of instructions.

In order to support the construction of segmented display files, the display instruction set must include an adequate range of positioning and vector-drawing instructions. Vectors should be specified by the coordinates of the endpoint relative to the starting point (*relative* coordinates); complete segments can then be defined without the use of absolute coordinates, in order to permit dragging and repositioning. It is convenient if vector instructions, which must normally be defined as two separate instruction words, can be stored in non-contiguous addresses, since this facilitates the efficient use of blocks of memory. The instruction set discussed in Chapter 3 and shown in Figure 3-12 permits this by allowing the $\Delta x$ and $\Delta y$ values to be specified independently of the command to generate the vector. Figure 26-2 shows a useful extension to the instruction repertoire, a *short-vector instruction* that allows short vectors to be defined in a single word.

The construction of segmented display files also requires *jump* and *subroutine jump* instructions to reset the instruction address register. The jump instruction is essential as a means of directing the display processor from the end of one block of instructions to the start of the next. The subroutine jump is very useful for segment construction, as described in Section 8-3. Both these instructions must be capable of addressing a large display file, which may

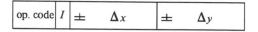

**Figure 26-2** Short vector instruction. The *I* bit controls line intensity.

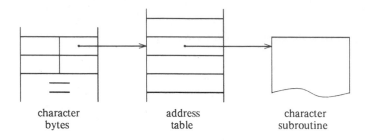

character          address          character
bytes              table            subroutine

**Figure 26-3** Use of an address table to permit a variable character set.

contain in excess of 8000 words of instructions; thus a 14-bit address may be required in these two types of jump instruction.

Text display may be provided by a simple dot-matrix character generator, which reads dot patterns from a read-only memory and displays them at the specified position. More commonly nowadays, text characters are displayed as short vectors; the quality of such characters is better, and it is easier to provide the programmer with the ability to change the character set. For example, the characters may be defined as subroutines and called by means of subroutine jumps. A more compact approach is the use of a *character address table*, a 256-word table containing the subroutine addresses; characters can then be represented in the display file as 8-bit bytes, which are used by the display processor to index the table and call the appropriate subroutine. This technique, first used in the Digital Equipment 338 [144], is shown in Figure 26-3.

Since subroutines can be used both for segment organization and for text display, a multilevel subroutine facility is desirable. The push-down-stack mechanism for the storage of return addresses is the most convenient.

## 26-2 RANDOM-SCAN STORAGE-TUBE DISPLAYS

The storage-tube display was introduced in 1968, at a time when memories for display-file storage were still very expensive. The storage tube's ability to store images internally made it a very inexpensive alternative to the refresh display. Nowadays, with much cheaper memories, the cost savings are less dramatic, but the storage-tube display is functionally somewhat simpler to program than the refresh display and still retains a large following in the computer-graphics community.

As mentioned in Chapter 3, storage-tube displays have generally been designed as display terminals capable of being attached to single-user or multi-access computers in the same manner as alphanumeric terminals. In order to be used in this way, the display must send and receive graphical data in the same format as alphanumeric text. The instruction set given in Figure 3-10 allows vector and text information to be transmitted as 7-bit character bytes. A simple display controller decodes these instructions and passes deflection signals to the storage CRT.

The storage-tube display terminal can be used for graphical interaction, but its effectiveness is limited by the use of a character-based interface and by a lack of feedback capability in the display. Generally it is possible to display a simple cursor on the screen and to maneuver this cursor around with a mouse, joystick, or tablet. To signal an input to the computer, the user presses a key; this transmits the cursor coordinates back to the computer, encoded as a character string. Simple interactive dialogues can be carried out on this basis, but many of the more dynamic techniques described in Chapter 12 are infeasible.

## 26-3 HIGH-PERFORMANCE DISPLAYS

How should hardware best be used to supplement the capabilities of the display processor? This is a question that has intrigued display designers for many years. It is clear that hardware can assist in many of the processes for which we use graphics software, including display-file segmentation, modeling, interaction, and geometric transformations. These potential uses for hardware were evident to many of the early display designers, but the design of graphics software was then only partially understood and could not provide an adequate basis for display design. A 1967 paper by Myer and Sutherland [331] provides a glimpse of the problems then facing the display designer. This entertaining paper drew attention to the tendency to add more and more hardware features to the display; eventually it would resemble a full-scale computer together with a simple display controller, on which the cycle of hardware enhancement could begin again. Myer and Sutherland called this phenomenon the Wheel of Reincarnation.

Now that graphics system design is better understood, it is easier to see how hardware can help. If we examine the sequence of processes by which images are generated by computer and by which human interaction with these images is handled, we find the following seven processes, each of which is a candidate for implementation in hardware:

1. *Display-primitive generation,* such as the generation of arcs and other types of curves;
2. *Segmentation,* i.e., maintaining the separate segments of the display file;
3. *Display-code generation,* i.e., generating display-file instructions from the results of processes 4 to 6 below;
4. *Clipping;*
5. *Geometric transformations,* including both viewing transformations and the more general transformations used in modeling;
6. *Modeling,* in particular traversing a stored model in order to generate an image of it.

The following sections briefly discuss ways of implementing each of these processes in hardware.

### Line- and Curve-Generation Hardware

Hardware can easily be constructed to provide a richer set of graphic primitives. One of the simplest extensions to the hardware is the provision of different line qualities, such as dotted or dashed lines, produced by modulating the beam intensity as each vector is drawn. It is of course important that if the speed of vector generation should vary (as it does in many displays using integrators for vector generation), the rate of intensity modulation must vary too.

Many displays use circle and circular-arc generators. Some employ a simple digital generator, such as the DDA described in Chapter 2; others use a pair of sinusoidal voltage generators. Arc generators require specification of not only the circle's center and radius but also a starting point and endpoint or the equivalent. This means that more decoding logic is required than for a simple circle generator. The arc generator is much more useful, however, since it can be used to display partially clipped circles.

A number of methods have been proposed for the hardware generation of curves. Most of these produce families of curves that include basic conic sections—circular arcs, ellipses, parabolas, etc. They are useful in applications like map display, where the curves do not change once they have been fitted to the data. In curve-modeling applications, such as automobile or aircraft design, it may be necessary to fit the hardware-generated curves to a higher-order modeled curve; this is considerably more complicated than the use of straight-line segments for curve approximation.

### Segmentation Hardware

As we have seen earlier in this chapter, display-file segmentation is easily implemented with the aid of a jump instruction and can be further simplified by the use of subroutine jumps. These two instructions are provided in almost all display processors.

More comprehensive segmentation schemes have been proposed for refresh displays. A design by Guedj [213] included a segment-naming scheme and hardware for creating, modifying, and deleting segments. The Evans and Sutherland Picture System II [164] provides a similar segment-maintenance capability.

### Display Code Generation Hardware

The generation of display instructions from transformed line-segment parameters is one of the simplest processes in the entire output sequence. Little is therefore to be gained by building hardware to perform it, except where both the preceding and the following processes in the sequence are performed by hardware. It then becomes necessary to use a hardware display-code generator. A simple logic circuit creates instructions from the transformed parameters, and an address register indicates where each instruction should be placed in the display file. Display-code generators of this type are used in buffered high-performance displays (see below).

### Clipping Hardware

All line-drawing displays benefit from some form of clipping hardware. If vectors are specified by relative endpoint coordinates, it is always possible to define a vector that extends off the edge of the screen. If no attempt is made to clip the line, the vector-generation hardware will overflow, causing anomalies of one form or another on the screen: the vector may emerge on the opposite side of the screen, or unpleasant streaks may appear along the screen edge.

A very simple form of hardware clipping, known as *scissoring,* is found in some line-drawing displays. A circuit detects when the deflection system moves the beam outside the addressable area of the screen and turns off the beam intensity. When the beam returns to the addressable area, its intensity is turned on again. This is not a particularly satisfactory form of clipping because it allows the deflection system to be driven beyond its limits of linear behavior and therefore tends to throw it out of adjustment. Furthermore the beam spends valuable time tracing out invisible parts of the picture, making the rest of the picture more prone to flicker.

The first hardware clipping device was built in 1968, using the midpoint variant of the Cohen-Sutherland clipping algorithm described in Section 5-2. It was designed to clip both two- and three-dimensional images and was called the *clipping divider* because it included hardware to perform the division required for perspective projection. More recent designs for clipping hardware, many of them based on the clipping divider [451], have tended to use a high-speed general-purpose processor to simplify the control of the device and reduce its cost.

### Transformation Hardware

The transformation of line-endpoint coordinates can be one of the most time-consuming processes in the entire graphic output sequence. From the early days of computer graphics a great deal of effort has been put into the design of transformation hardware [480, 248]. Early designs were either very limited in their range of transformations or were complex and expensive; only with the use of homogeneous matrix techniques has it become possible to produce satisfactory transformation processors.

The forerunner of modern transformation hardware was the matrix multiplier, designed and built in 1968 by Seitz and Sutherland [459]. It used a bank of four parallel multipliers that could multiply a 4-element vector by a $4 \times 4$ matrix in four steps, taking 20 microseconds in all. The matrix multiplier was designed to work in conjunction with the clipping divider (see above), feeding its output to the input registers of the clipping divider in a pipeline fashion. Again, recent matrix multipliers have used much simpler designs based on general-purpose microprogrammed processors.

## Modeling Hardware

The generation of displayed images from a computer model involves traversing the model with a *viewing algorithm* capable of generating the appropriate display representation for each part of the model. This process should ideally be carried out very rapidly, so that the effect of changing the model is quickly made visible on the screen.

The degree to which hardware can be used to speed up the operation of a viewing algorithm depends on the complexity of the algorithm and on the extent to which it changes from one application to the next. In general, application programmers like to have some freedom in their choice of modeling data structure. Often the model contains a lot of information, and its traversal involves fetching data from secondary storage. In either case it is normally impractical to use hardware for model traversal.

The one case where model traversal can appropriately be performed in hardware is where a simple hierarchic model structure can be built from linked lists, without the use of secondary storage. It is then possible to construct the model with the aid of jump and subroutine-jump instructions, as described in Section 10-5. The only hardware requirements are a multil-level subroutine return mechanism, preferably implemented with the aid of a push-down stack, and hardware of the type discussed in the previous section to perform the transformations embedded in the model.

## Hardware for Interaction

Most of the interactive techniques described in Chapter 12 can be programmed on a simple refresh display and require no special hardware assistance. Display-processor designers have from time to time introduced special hardware features in order to make interaction more efficient. Some of these features were designed to improve response under time sharing; Englebart, for example, implemented a set of cursor coordinate registers into which the input device coordinates were deposited automatically; this permitted several cursors to be updated simultaneously by a single time-shared display processor. Many displays have included special features to assist in handling light-pen inputs, such as segment name registers and program access to display coordinate registers. Some displays include special hardware for feedback effects, such as a periodic blinking capability. These features are sometimes useful in non-programmable terminals, since they provide a built-in means of interaction, however primitive. In refresh displays with a dedicated computer attached, there is rarely any need for hardware to assist interaction.

## 26-4  THE UNBUFFERED HIGH-PERFORMANCE DISPLAY

The display-processor designer has, as we have just seen, a large range of processor components at his disposal from which he may select an appropriate set to augment the processor's power, but he is not completely free to choose whatever components he wishes. The display processor's main task is to maintain a high-quality, flicker-free image on the screen, using data stored in its refresh memory. The processes involved in refreshing the screen, whether they include just the fetching and decoding of instructions or extend to include clipping, transformation, and model traversal as well, must be performed in the appropriate sequence, at adequate speeds to prevent flicker. Thus it is not possible to make an arbitrary choice of processes to perform in hardware.

We can reduce the speed requirements for processor hardware by introducing some buffering at the appropriate stage in the output process; the next section discusses this approach to display-processor design. The introduction of buffering requires the inclusion of hardware for display-code generation and segmentation. Without buffering, these two components are not needed.

Unbuffered high-performance displays therefore generally include three components out of the set of seven described above; these three components perform model traversal, geometric transformations, and clipping. The output of the clipping hardware consists of transformed points and vectors that are passed to the display's deflection system. The arrangement of such a display is shown in Figure 26-4.

The first such displays became commercially available in 1968 [459, 215]. One of the most advanced of these displays was the Evans and Sutherland LDS-1, a display system based on the earlier research projects that produced the clipping divider and matrix multiplier. The LDS-1 was designed as a

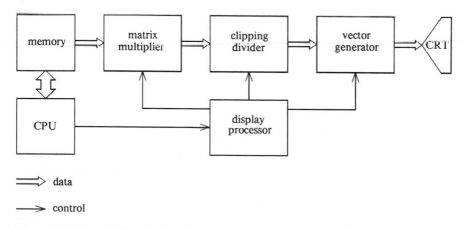

data

control

**Figure 26-4** The unbuffered high-performance display.

*pipeline processor,* i.e., the tasks performed by the various components were carefully sequenced so that as one vector was being displayed, the next was in the process of being clipped, and the next after that was passing through the matrix multiplier. The use of pipelining permitted maximum throughput, but at a considerable increase in hardware complexity and expense.

The LDS-1 display processor also was capable of traversing a very general class of linked-list data structures. The processor contained two push-down stacks, one for return addresses and the other for matrix and windowing data. The processor could read and write all the registers of the matrix multiplier and clipping divider; it could thus load the matrix multiplier with transformations encountered in the model and could perform concatenations with transformations at lower levels in the display-file structure. The matrix multiplier and clipping divider could be used as independent processors, reading and writing data from and to memory, or they could be configured as a pipeline feeding graphical information to the CRT display.

A number of other high-performance displays have been designed with capabilities similar to those of the LDS-1 [215, 490]. Most of these displays do not have the full generality of the LDS-1 and tend to be somewhat restricted in transformation capability or in their ability to be reconfigured as a set of independent processors. What all of these displays lack is the ability to traverse very large data structures, containing 100,000 elements or more. A data structure that is to be used for refresh must contain no more than a few thousand elements, and this is a serious restriction in many design applications. The buffered high-performance display described in the next section was designed to solve this problem.

## 26-5 THE BUFFERED HIGH-PERFORMANCE DISPLAY

The buffered high-performance display differs in two major respects from unbuffered displays like the LDS-1. The most obvious difference is the inclusion of a refresh buffer to hold the transformed data after they have passed through the transformation and clipping stages. A high refresh rate can be maintained out of this buffer, independently of the rate at which the buffer's contents are updated by the prior stages. This places less stringent performance demands on the transformation and clipping components, which can therefore be designed more economically. This indeed is where the second major difference with the LDS-1 lies; the buffered display uses a much simpler *bus-structured* organization of the kind shown in Figure 26-5.

The first buffered high-performance display was the Evans and Sutherland Picture System I. It uses a high-speed general-purpose microprogrammed processor to perform transformations and clipping. It provides a set of registers to store matrices and windowing parameters; these registers can be loaded by the computer controlling the display, and a list of line segments can then be transmitted to the display for transformation and refresh. Line segments, once

computer

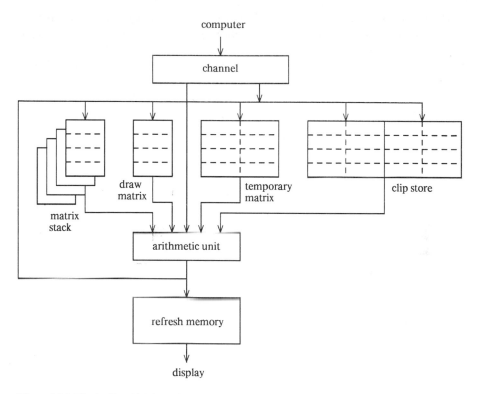

channel

draw
matrix

temporary
matrix

clip store

matrix
stack

arithmetic unit

refresh memory

display

**Figure 26-5** The buffered high-performance display.

transformed and clipped, are packed into vector format and stored in the refresh buffer. Generally a double refresh buffer is provided, so that one buffer can be used for refresh while the other is being filled; in this way a steady picture can be maintained.

The Picture System I differs in one other respect from the LDS-1; the controlling computer, rather than the display processor, is given the task of traversing the model. This permits a free choice of model data structure and allows structures to be kept partly on secondary storage. The only requirement is that lines be passed to the display processor as sequential lists of coordinate pairs.

More recent displays, such as the Vector General 3400 and the Picture System II, have refined the ideas embodied in the Picture System I [164, 491]. The Picture System II contains a refresh buffer that can be segmented, the hardware maintaining a list of segments and their addresses. This permits the display to be used in conjunction with segmented display-file graphics systems.

The high-performance display, whether buffered or not, is a relatively complex output device. Software packages have been developed for these devices [285, 479]; most of them simplify the programming task somewhat but retain access to the special features of the display. Many other types of display have received similar treatment; their graphics packages retain a degree of idiosyncrasy. As a result, application programs developed for one display cannot be run on another. In the next chapter we shall explore this problem and it solutions.

## EXERCISES

**26-1** What characteristics would be required in an inherent display-device memory to prevent it from restricting the device's functional capability?

**26-2** Some display processors have been built with only a partial hardware transformation capabililty, e.g., scaling and translation but no rotation. What are the disadvantages of such a display in terms of using it for general-purpose graphics?

**26-3** In a simple refresh display, what would be the impact of providing only *absolute* line endpoint positioning, i.e., no relative vector coordinates? Would this prevent the implementation of a general-purpose graphics package?

**26-4** Discuss alternative methods of specifying arcs of circles in a display file. Take into consideration (a) the programmer's ease of specifying arcs, and (b) the generation of arcs from clipped circles.

**26-5** How would you generate thick lines on a refresh display? Suggest a hardware solution.

**26-6** In order to incorporate the short vector instruction shown in Figure 26-2 into the display instruction repertoire, an operation code must be assigned to it. The instruction set of Figures 3-12 and 3-16 does not allow for such extension—there are no spare operation codes. How would you modify this instruction set to permit addition of the extra instruction?

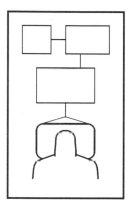

# 27

# DEVICE-INDEPENDENT

# GRAPHICS SYSTEMS

The aim of graphics systems design is to simplify the writing of graphic application programs. The earliest applications were written without the benefit of graphics systems, and were very difficult to write. With the development of higher-level systems in the late 1960's, application programming became much easier. Nowadays it is universal practice to use a graphics package, or some similar system, as the basis for applications development. With this approach, applications take less time to write, and their development demands less skill on the part of the programmer.

This book has devoted several chapters to the design of graphics packages and other systems for applications programming. These systems vary from the very simplest package for plotting two-dimensional pictures on a storage tube display, up to the most complex systems supporting three-dimensional graphic data structures. As the last chapter has shown, graphics systems may be required to support all manner of different display controllers and processors. The result is a very wide range of graphics systems, each supporting a different set of functions and requiring the use of different programming conventions. If an application program is written to use one of these systems, the chances are very remote that it can be run in conjunction with another system. Thus each application program is likely to be dependent on the availability of a specific graphics system; this system in turn tends to require specific hardware on which to run. The program may therefore require major modification before it can be used at another site.

This is the problem of *portability* of graphics applications. It is a problem of considerable importance, for high costs are involved in reprogramming applications at new sites. Furthermore it is quite inconvenient to have to train programmers to use different graphics systems; it would be much more convenient if systems were sufficiently similar that programmers could move from one system to another without the need for retraining. Thus the problem concerns both *program portability* and *programmer portability*.

This chapter discusses methods of achieving portability through proper design of graphics systems. It shows that many of the techniques discussed in earlier chapters, such as display file segmentation, separation of windowing and modeling transformations, and the use of high-level input functions, can contribute to achieving portability. The chapter also discusses the impact on portability of the various display controller designs discussed in the last chapter.

## 27-1 DEVICE INDEPENDENCE

In order to achieve portability in application programs we must design graphics packages to present a uniform interface to the application programmer, no matter what equipment is being used. Whether the output device is a plotter, a storage tube display, or a high-performance refresh display, the programmer should be able to use the same set of functions to generate images.

We use the term *device-independent* to describe such a graphics system. In the course of this chapter we will explore the problem of achieving device independence in graphics packages. Clearly the solution to this problem lies in careful design of the programmer's interface to the graphics package. Behind this interface, the graphics package reconciles the differences between the programmer's interface and the hardware interface to the display device itself. Thus the graphics package must be relatively *device dependent* in its internal design. There are, however, ways of minimizing the amount of device-specific graphics software, that lead to packages that are device-independent, not only in the interfaces they present to the programmer, but also in their own construction.

We must thus be careful, when we use the term "device independence," to indicate the context within which we use it. Most of this chapter is concerned with device independence at the application programming level. Device independence within the actual graphics package is more difficult to achieve, and will be addressed at the end of the chapter.

## 27-2 THE PROGRAMMER'S MODEL OF THE OUTPUT PROCESS

When we build a high-level graphics package for use by application programmers, one of our aims is to hide some of the less important details of the display's construction from the programmer. For example, it is not necessary for the programmer to know that display file segments are stored as linked lists of blocks of 16-bit words; he need only know that each segment represents a logically separate portion of the picture, and that certain segments may be included in the refresh cycle that displays the picture on the screen. Thus instead of trying to explain in complete detail the effect of each graphics function, we can provide the programmer with a simple conceptual *model* of the display process, and explain the meaning of each function in terms of this model.

The use of such a "programmer's model" becomes essential when we try to introduce a degree of device independence into the programmer's interface. We can no longer consider acquainting the programmer with precise hardware details, since these vary from one display to the next. The programmer's model must be designed to accommodate the full range of display equipment that we wish our graphics package to address.

The best conceptual models are those that involve a single, easily understood basic concept. In our search for a suitable model for the graphic output process, we are faced with two alternative concepts from which to choose: the *viewing algorithm* approach, and the *plotter analogy*. Both of these are discussed below. Both have shortcomings that prevent their direct use to form a programmer's model; these shortcomings are discussed, and a more satisfactory model is developed.

## The Viewing Algorithm

We have already encountered the concept of the viewing algorithm in previous chapters. Reduced to its simplest form, it offers a very straightforward approach to interactive graphics. The viewing algorithm is a procedure, implemented either in software or as a hardware processor, that traverses the application data structure, generating a picture that is transformed, clipped, and passed to a refresh CRT. This process, shown in Figure 27-1, is repeated in a continuous manner at a sufficient rate to maintain the picture on the screen flicker-free. When the data structure is modified, the change shows immediately in a fresh picture. This programmer's model thus requires the programmer to devise an appropriate data structure, together with one or more viewing algorithms that will produce suitable pictorial representations of the data. The application program is designed to execute the selected algorithm iteratively to maintain the picture on the screen.

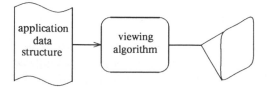

**Figure 27-1** Viewing algorithm model: the display is refreshed directly from the application data structure.

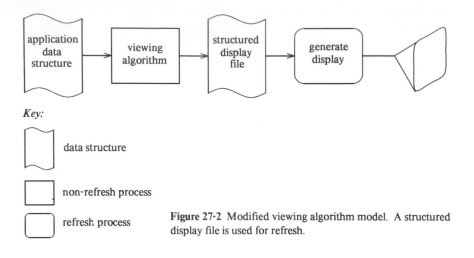

*Key:*

data structure

non-refresh process

refresh process

**Figure 27-2** Modified viewing algorithm model. A structured display file is used for refresh.

The viewing-algorithm approach is thus extremely simple, but is very difficult and expensive to implement. It depends on the ability of the system to traverse the application data structure, to transform and clip all the graphical data found there, and to display them on the screen rapidly enough to maintain a flicker-free image. The only displays capable of supporting such a process are high-performance displays like the LDS-1 (see Section 26-4). As we have seen, these displays restrict the programmer to a simple linked-list data structure that must be held entirely in primary memory. They also limit the programmer to a single graphical representation of the data structure, i.e., a single viewing algorithm. Few applications can be implemented within these constraints.

Rather than abandon the viewing-algorithm model, we can modify it to fit applications with larger, more general data structures. We use a separate *structured display file* to support the refresh process; this structure has the linked-list format required for rapid traversal, and contains only a displayable subset of the application data structure. The application program maintains both structures, and applies a viewing algorithm to the application data structure to generate the structured display file; a more constrained algorithm is then applied repetitively to the display file to produce pictures on the screen (Figure 27-2). This modified version of the viewing-algorithm model has been used in many graphics packages designed for high-performance displays; an example is the set of functions described in Chapter 10 for manipulating groups and items.

### The Plotter Analogy

The plotter-analogy model, as its name suggests, is oriented towards simple display devices and plotters. The programmer treats the display as a device with inherent storage (which it may in fact possess), and generates images by

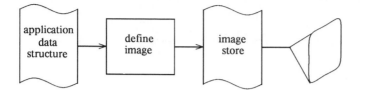

**Figure 27-3** Plotter analogy model.

passing to the display a stream of graphical primitives that are transformed, clipped and stored in the display's inherent *image store*. This process, shown in Figure 27-3, permits the programmer to generate the image in any sequence he wishes, taking as long as necessary. Each primitive passed to the transformation process is added to the stored image, which is thus gradually built up by the application program.

The principal limitation of this model is the lack of a means to modify the contents of the image store selectively. To change the picture, the entire screen is erased, and a fresh picture is created in its entirety. The model treats the display as a nonerasable, plotter-like device whose displayed image cannot be modified by smaller units of picture.

Again we can modify the model to make it less restrictive; as before, we do so by introducing another data structure, this time a *transformed, segmented display file*. The segments of the display file can be created, redefined and deleted selectively; after each set of changes, the image store's contents are regenerated from the display file (see Figure 27-4). The introduction of the display file clearly complicates the programmer's model, but is more in keeping with the use of interactive refresh displays.

## The Gulf

Our overall goal is to devise a programmer's model that leads to a graphics package suitable for a wide range of display equipment. So far, our two models have been oriented towards specific kinds of display: high-performance, unbuffered displays on the one hand, storage-tube displays on the other.

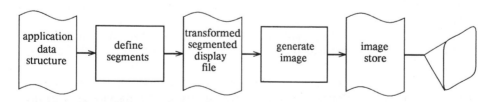

**Figure 27-4** Modified plotter analogy model, with transformed display file.

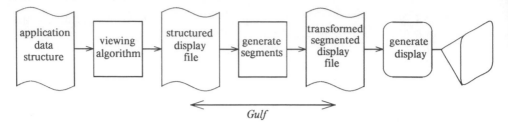

Figure 27-5  Use of viewing algorithm model with a simple refresh display.

Attempts to use one model in conjunction with the other's type of equipment is likely to lead to confusion on the part of the programmer.

To illustrate this problem, let us suppose that we wish to use the viewing algorithm model in conjunction with a simple refresh display possessing no transformation or clipping hardware. As shown in Figure 27-2, a structured display file stores the output of the viewing algorithm process. A transformed display file must also be included to maintain the refresh process, since the display processor is not capable of performing the transformations stored in the structured display file (see Figure 27-5). We are now confronted with a difficult question: what model should we present to the programmer? If we hide from him the existence of the transformed display file, then the segment generation process must be made automatic, so that it appears to be performed continuously. This is clearly a wasteful process, for the entire structured display file must be re-transformed after every change, and a lengthy sequence of updates will follow every set of changes to the structured display file. In such a situation it is better to explain the existence of the transformed display file to the programmer, and let him decide when to update its contents. Unfortunately this requires him to treat certain types of display differently from others: the interface is no longer device-independent.

This is an example of a serious problem in the design of device-independent graphics systems. The root of the problem lies in the varying degree to which displays can perform all the steps in the graphic output process at refresh speed. High-performance displays can perform most of the steps, while low-cost displays can perform very few; those that the display cannot perform must be carried out more slowly by software. At the point where this software hands over its output to the display's hardware, a buffer must be introduced to handle the mismatch in speeds. If all displays required this buffering at the same point in the process, it would be easy to devise a programmer's model. The problem arises when the model requires that buffering occur at one stage (e.g., prior to transformation), but the display requires it at another (e.g., after clipping). A *gulf* is then introduced between the conceptual model of buffering and reality. This gulf, shown in Figure 27-5, must be bridged in some manner, generally by explaining its existence to the programmer.

As we have seen in Chapter 26, different displays introduce buffering at different places. The high-performance, unbuffered display introduces it prior to transformation; the simple refresh display buffers after transformation and clipping; the storage tube buffers at the end of the entire process, when the displayed image has been generated. It might seem impossible to design a programmer's model that would accommodate this wide variation. As we shall see in the next section, it is indeed necessary to exclude certain types of display from use with the model, but this does not prevent the use of both high-performance and low-cost displays.

## A Transformed Display File Model

Chapter 26 has discussed line-drawing display controllers under four separate headings. This discussion provides a basis for the selection of a device-independent programmer's model. We are able to separate displays into four classes, each introducing buffering at a specific point in the output process:

*Storage-tube displays:* buffering occurs after display generation;
*Simple refresh displays:* buffering occurs after transformation and clipping;
*High-performance, unbuffered displays:* buffering occurs before transformation;
*High-performance, buffered displays:* buffering occurs after transformation and clipping.

Our programmer's model can be selected on a basis of compatibility with the four classes of display in this list. As we have just seen, it is very difficult to accommodate, within a single model, two classes of display that buffer on either side of the transformation and clipping stages. Thus we are unlikely to find a model that will allow effective use of both varieties of high-performance display. We must instead choose just one; the obvious choice is the buffered variety, since it includes buffering at the same stage as does the simple refresh display. The remaining class of display, based on the storage tube, buffers at a different stage, and therefore cannot be introduced to the model without creating a "gulf" between the model's buffering at the display file and the display's buffering at the screen. This is not a particularly troublesome gulf, however: it can be bridged by a simple *Update* procedure, that in the storage tube's case transmits display file alterations to the DVST, and in all other cases is a null operation.

Thus it is feasible to base the design of a device-independent graphics system on the programmer's model shown in Figure 27-6, in which the principal data structure internal to the system is a transformed, segmented display file. The model also includes an image store, to permit the use of storage tube displays; the *Update* function of Chapter 7 is used to update the storage tube's contents from the display file. When refresh displays are used, the model specifies that the image contents are always up-to-date with respect to the display file, and the *Update* function has no effect.

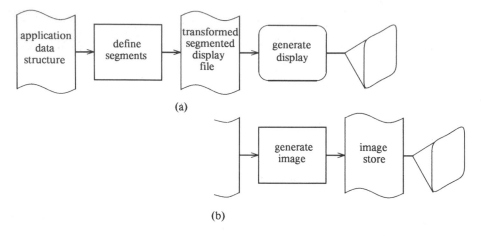

(a)

(b)

**Figure 27-6** Alternative plotter-analogy models: (a) for simple refresh display; (b) for storage-tube display.

The design of a system based on this model involves the solution of a number of difficult problems. The buffered high-performance display, although it fits the model conceptually, in practice often exhibits limitations that make it difficult to use in a device-independent way. For example, it may not be possible to segment the contents of the refresh buffer, or the transformation process may demand fixed-point parameters rather than the floating-point parameters used when transforming by software. While these problems can clearly be solved with the design of more powerful display processors, they currently present a serious problem in the design of device-independent graphics systems. A great deal of care and ingenuity is required in order to make use of high-performance displays in a device-independent way.

In summary, the programmer's model that we have developed for our device-independent graphics system is based on the Plotter Analogy, but includes a transformed display file for better interactive control over the displayed image. This model, shown in Figure 27-6, has been used as the basis of a number of successful graphics packages, several of which have achieved a fair degree of device independence [449, 489]. In certain applications these packages are very convenient and effective. In those involving complex computer models, or special user interfaces, the packages are somewhat cumbersome and restricting. A solution to this problem is to provide a very large number of functions that cover a wide range of requirements. This makes the package bulky and difficult for programmers to understand.

## Modeling Systems

One of the difficulties in designing a graphics system lies in the very wide range of transformations involved in constructing pictures of models, and the relatively restricted range of transformation functions provided by graphics packages. The term "transformation" is used here in a broader context than has been the case in previous chapters. We are concerned not just with geometric transformations, but also with the operations that remove hidden surfaces and produce shaded pictures of solid object models; with operations that produce different styles of plan or elevation from a model of a building; and with graph-plotting functions for the visualization of tabular data. None of these transformations is implicit in the transformed display-file model. Instead this model provides a general $4 \times 4$ matrix transformation capability, useful basically in displaying wire-frame pictures of polygonal objects.

In many applications of three-dimensional computer graphics, a wire-frame display is not a satisfactory visualization technique, and the programmer will use a different, non-linear transformation. Similarly, in two-dimensional applications the programmer may wish to apply non-standard transformations to the data prior to display. In these cases, the generalized geometric transformation capability is not particularly useful. Applications of this kind use a special set of transformations to produce a *world-coordinate system* view of the data, and only then use a more standard form of viewing transformation to create a displayed image.

A more appropriate programmer's model is thus the one shown in Figure 27-7. A specialized set of modeling functions, provided by a separate subroutine package, are used to decompose the application data structure into a picture definition in world coordinates; a general-purpose graphics package is then used to apply the viewing transformation to this picture definition, depositing the transformed and clipped image in the display file. The modeling functions will vary a great deal from one application to the next: in simple applications they may be almost non-existent, while in others they will include a large number of functions for traversing the data structure and generating images. One such set of functions might be those listed in Chapter 10 for manipulating data structures built from groups and items.

The most important aspect of this approach to the programmer's model is its *modularity*. The graphics functions concerned with picture genera-tion—primitive functions, functions for segment manipulation, viewing

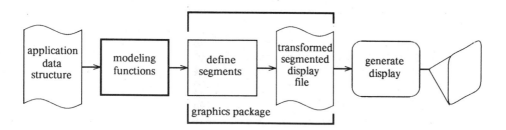

**Figure 27-7** Separation of modeling and graphics functions.

transformation functions—are grouped together as one software module, the graphics system. Modeling functions are separated into another module, the *modeling system.* Different modeling systems can be developed for different applications, but a single graphics system can be expected to handle all picture generation; the graphics system functions can be called by the modeling functions in order to simplify modeling operations.

This modular approach to graphics system design was developed at the Seillac-I workshop on Graphics Methodology, organized by the Graphics Subcommittee of IFIP Working Group 5.2, and held in 1976. The work of this workshop, and its impact on graphics system design, has been documented elsewhere [355].

### Other Software Modules

The modular approach is appropriate as a solution to the modeling problem. It allows us to separate those functions that should be institutionalized for the sake of device-independence (i.e., the graphics functions) from those that should not, since they tend to be application-specific (e.g., the modeling functions). We can apply this methodology to the design of several other modules which also address the needs of specific applications, and which can also be interfaced to the graphics system. These include:

1.  *An input module.* As we have seen in Part Three, and will discuss further in Chapter 28, there are many different styles of input programming. Each style requires a different set of input functions to support it. To cater to these different styles of programming, a set of relatively low-level input functions, such as the *GetEvent* and *PermitEvent* functions of Chaper 13, can be included in the graphics system; various input modules, such as the one described in Chapter 14, can then be developed to support different styles of high-level input function.
2.  *A symbol system.* Many displayed pictures make use of repeated symbols. These can be generated very easily by calling the same set of graphic primitives to generate each symbol instance. In many situations this is a perfectly adequate way of displaying symbols. In some cases it is rather inefficient, however, such as in a situation where a refresh display, with its own local computer, is being used as an "intelligent terminal" to another, remotely located computer. Here, if the speed of communication between the computers is slow, symbol generation is inefficient. A symbol system can be designed that permits symbol definitions to reside in the terminal, thus allowing symbol instances to be specified very efficiently.
3.  *A high-quality text module.* Computer-generated text varies in quality from $5 \times 7$ dot matrices to high-quality photo-typeset material. It is not feasible to include in the graphics system the capability to generate all these different forms of text. A basic text capability should be included in the graphics system, and a separate module should be used to produce higher-quality output.

Other modules, such as map display and graph plotting systems, are also useful for specific types of application. Overall, the modular approach permits powerful, specialized packages to be developed, without encumbering the basic graphics system with complex, seldom-used functions.

## 27-4 GRAPHICS SYSTEM DESIGN

The issues we have discussed so far in this chapter, concerning the programmer's model and the modularization of systems, are perhaps the most important underlying issues in graphics system design. Our discussion has provided us with a resolution of these issues, so that we can now proceed to cover some of the other aspects of graphics system design, including specification of the principal functions. It is of course no coincidence that the programmer's model we have selected, based on the use of a transformed, segmented display file, is in keeping with the material presented in Chapters 6 to 10. This book has been based on a cohesive approach to graphics system design, and we are now able to see the underlying methodology of this approach. As we proceed to a more detailed study of system design issues, we can build on the material of Part Two to a very large extent.

### Graphics Packages and Languages

The applications programmer, in order to design and implement programs that make use of a graphics system, needs some form of programming interface to the system. In general terms, this interface is a *language* in which the programmer defines the algorithms and data structures of the application program. Ideally it should be a *high-level* language, so that the programmer can express algorithms and data structures as he conceives them, rather than in an obscure, machine-oriented representation. Nowadays a large proportion of applications programming is done in high-level languages like PASCAL, Algol 60, Algol 68, and PL/I; facilities of a similarly high level are needed for writing graphics applications.

We can take one of two approaches to the design of a language for graphics applications programming. One is the approach we have used throughout this book: the use of functions or subroutines to access the capabilities of the graphics system. This approach is used in many high-level languages for non-graphical I/O; in Algol or PASCAL, for example, all I/O is performed by means of functions like the following:

*read (f,vl); readln (f);*

The second alternative is to design a programming language with special statements and programming constructs for graphical input and output. A number of such languages have been developed; the most successful have been extensions of existing, well-tried languages, rather than totally new language designs [349, 171]. Language extensions are particularly effective in handling operations that require special program control structures, such as display procedures (see Chapter 10) and statements to handle concurrent input from several devices.

For a device-independent graphics system, however, it is more appropriate to use a package of functions than a set of language extensions. The aim of device independence is, after all, to achieve portability, and the use of a special language leads to the need for special compilers that are unlikely to be plentifully available. The use of a graphics package eases programmer portability too, for it allows the package to be used from a number of different programming languages. Several language-independent graphics packages have been implemented and are in widespread use [115, 489, 198].

### Graphics Package Structure

We have discussed the importance of device independence at the level of the programmer's interface to the graphics package; we have also touched briefly on the need for language independence. Two other forms of independence need consideration in designing the system:

*Device independence within the package:* this permits the package to drive different devices with the minimum of modification for each new device.
*Machine independence:* it should be possible to run the package, not only with different devices, but also on different computers.

Device independence in graphics package design can be achieved by carefully separating those components of the graphics system that are inherently device-dependent from the remaining *common software,* and by giving equally careful attention to the interface between the two parts. Large sections of the package, including transformation and clipping software, can usually be included in the common software.

The most device-dependent parts of the package are likely to be those that contend with the functional characteristics and data formats of the input and output devices. In general, most of the device dependence will tend to lie in the input device polling routines and in the display code generator. Device dependence can be kept to a minimum if interfaces from the common software to these routines are well-designed.

The event queue forms a natural interface between the device-specific code for input polling and the device-independent routines for processing events. Care is needed in the design of the event queue: it must be flexible enough to accommodate the wide variety of input devices used with graphical displays.

The interface to the display code generator may take the form of either an intermediate data structure, or a set of functions within the display code generator, called by the common software. Many plotter-oriented graphics packages use an intermediate data structure, in which the entire image for plotting is stored in a device-independent format; the data structure is then translated to the format required by the device. In an interactive environment this amounts to an extra buffering step, impacting response and requiring additional memory. Intermediate data structures are therefore rarely used in interactive graphics packages, except as "pseudo display files" for off-line plotting, or for storage of images for later re-use.

The use of a functional interface to the display code generator rather than an intermediate data structure implies that the display file is maintained in device-specific format. Within the display code generator, there must be device-specific routines that compile display instructions for addition to the currently open display file segment. One such routine is required for each of the graphical primitives generated by the common software. These primitives are usually a subset of the primitives available to the programmer: dots, absolute vectors, text strings, and arcs of circles. Primitives are passed to the display code generator in clipped form, with coordinates converted to the screen coordinate system. Thus the display code generator need only rearrange the coordinates to conform to display instruction format, and store the resulting instructions in the display file.

Segment manipulation, although conceptually a part of display code generation, can generally be handled by the common software; this has the advantage of greatly decreasing the size of the display code generator. A simple display file format must be used, with as little dependence as possible on special display instructions, such as multi-level subroutine jumps, that may not be present in all displays. The display code generator, when ready to add another instruction word to the display file, passes the word to a routine in the common software; this routine takes care of allocating a fresh block of memory to the segment if the current block should be full. Thus the entire complement of segment manipulating routines, for opening, closing, deleting, posting and unposting segments, resides within the common software. In the case of storage tube displays, segments are constructed in the same way, filling them with actual display instructions that are transmitted to the display by the *Update* function.

Often a single computer installation must support several different types of display. It must be possible for the user of an application program to indicate, when starting execution of the program, the type of display he is using. This requires a flexible mechanism for binding the display code generator to the rest of the program at execution time. The provision of this type of binding mechanism is often one of the most difficult aspects of graphics package implementation.

Machine independence in graphics package design can be achieved by implementing the package in a widely-used language, such as PASCAL, Algol 68 or APL. A number of machine-independent packages have been built in this way, although most of them have been written in FORTRAN. Variations in operating systems, together with minor differences between language dialects, make true machine independence an almost unattainable goal; nevertheless a useful degree of machine independence can be achieved by a good choice of language and by carefully avoiding word-length and I/O dependencies.

## 27-5 FUNCTION SET DESIGN

Many of the functions required in a device-independent graphics package have already been discussed in earlier chapters. This section reviews briefly the set of functions required, and points out some of the special capabilities needed to provide device independence.

A considerable number of compromises must generally be made in designing the function set, in order to accommodate differences amongst displays. Some of the major differences in functional capability can be accommodated within the programmer's model, but there remain a great many minor differences between displays that have similar, but not identical, overall capabilities. Thus one refresh display will support both dashed and solid vectors, while another will support only solid lines but will include an arc generator. We can design the graphics package to support only the common subset of all display capabilities, but we then impose a considerable penalty on those whose display hardware includes useful but non-standard features. A hardware arc-generator, for example, can produce considerable savings in display file size and refresh time, and should therfore be used by the package when it is available.

The simplest solution to this problem is to include functions for all of the more useful graphical operations, whether or not they are commonly available in hardware, and to *simulate* within the graphics software the effect of the hardware that is unavailable. For example, dashed lines are easily simulated by generating an alternating sequence of visible and invisible short vectors. The code to perform such simulations can be incorporated in the common software.

### Application-Program Structure

One very useful concept to apply to the design of graphics functions is that of *application-program structure.* We will recall that the main purpose of device independence is to promote portability in programs. Often we cannot achieve complete portability; we must expect minor changes to be required when a program is moved to another site. For example, one site will permit 8-character function names while another will require names of 6 characters or less. It is usually a simple matter to make these kinds of modification; very little understanding of the design of the program is required.

The type of modification we wish to avoid is the type that involves changing the structure of the application program. This demands a thorough understanding of the program, and must normally be performed by a highly-skilled programmer. Modifications of this type will be required if, for example, the original programmer made extensive use of input functions incorporating special feedback effects. At the new site it may be necessary to provide this type of feedback by means of separate output operations. This will require careful study and alteration of the program.

We can prevent this type of portability problem by designing graphics functions to minimize the need for structural change in application programs. Thus we should attempt to achieve a clean separation between input and output; we should avoid functions that exploit special hardware that is difficult to simulate in software. We should pay particular attention to the design of functions that are likely to affect application-program structure, such as segment-manipulation and input functions.

### Categories of function

The functions required in a device-independent graphics system fall into five categories of function, for graphical primitives, transformations, segment manipulation, input, and overall control. Each of these is discussed briefly below, with references to earlier chapters where appropriate, and with a list summarizing the functions described in these earlier chapters.

1.  *Graphical Primitives.* (Chapter 6) A minimal set of primitive functions will include functions to draw dots, vectors, arcs of circles, and text characters. It should be possible to specify a vector's endpoint either in absolute coordinates or as a relative displacement from the starting point. Some programming systems, such as FORTRAN, require a fixed number of arguments in each function call; this in turn requires separate sets of functions for two- and three-dimensional output. Functions for control of line quality are also useful: dotted or dashed lines, and line intensity or color. Line quality may alternatively be controlled by means of additional parameters to each primitive; this is tedious to program, however, and makes it more difficult to change the line quality of an entire picture part. A minimal set of functions includes:

    *MoveTo* (x,y)
    *LineTo* (x,y)
    *DrawText* (s)

2.  *Transformation functions.* (Chapters 6 and 22) Our programmer's model calls for the inclusion in the graphics package of only those transformation functions needed for picture generation; transformations involved with modeling are excluded. We therefore provide functions for window and viewport specification, together with a set of functions for specifying a three-dimensional viewpoint. Window and viewpoint are specified in the world coordinate system; viewport is defined in screen coordinates, which may vary from device to device. A common approach to the specification

of viewports on screens of different sizes is to use an arbitrary coordinate system, such as inches, and permit the programmer to determine the screen size by inquiry (see below, *Control Functions*).

*SetWindow(wxmin, wymin, wxmax, wymax)*
*SetViewport(vxmin, vymin, vxmax, vymax)*
*SetViewPosition(x, y, z, xd, yd, zd)*

3. *Segment manipulation.* (Chapter 7) A full set of functions for opening, closing, deleting, posting, and unposting segments is required. A function for appending to segments may also be included, but it creates a number of design problems, and is difficult to implement (see Chapter 8).

*OpenSegment(n)*
*CloseSegment*
*DeleteSegment(n)*
*PostSegment(n)*
*UnpostSegment(n)*
*AppendToSegment(n)*

4. *Input functions.* (Chapter 13) A simple set of event-handling functions can be included; these functions may then be used to implement a higher-level input module, separate from the graphics package itself.

*GetEvent(e)*
*PermitEvent(t)*

5. *Control functions.* (Chapter 6) Control functions are very helpful in providing some of the operations and items of information necessary to achieve a high level of portability. One of the most essential control functions is *inquiry,* which enables the program to determine parameters of the display device, and thus to modify viewport parameters or screen layout to suit the display's dimensions. Control functions also permit the selection of different output or input devices, the generation of screen updates or hard copy, and monitoring of error conditions such as exhaustion of free storage.

*ClearScreen*
*InitGraphics*
*Inquire(v)*

The choice and design of functions for a graphics package has been discussed in several publications [353, 355]. A thorough survey of function sets of several widely-used packages has also been published [168], and provides very instructive reading.

## 27-6 CONCLUSION

This chapter has explored some of the issues involved in developing device-independent graphics software. It has shown the need for a well-designed programmer's model of the graphic system, and has developed one on the basis of a simple plotter analogue and a classification of display hardware. A discussion of modeling requirements led to the separation of modeling from the purely graphical functions; this in turn suggested the use of a modular approach to handle other application-specific requirements for graphics software.

The chosen programmer's model, based on the use of a transformed display file, leads to a simple graphics system design. The system is a package of functions, all of which have been discussed in Parts Two, Three and Five. Such a package can be implemented fairly easily for a range of different displays; applications based on the package are therefore likely to be relatively portable.

To achieve absolute portability of applications on a wide scale, a *standard* graphics package is needed. The argument to design and implement such a standard is persuasive, since a wide degree of portability would result, greatly decreasing application programming costs. The most successful interactive application programs are often written without any expectation of wide usage, and would be much more widely useful if based on a standard graphics package. This argument has led to various standardization efforts, including the "Core System" design project of SIGGRAPH, the ACM Special Interest Group on Computer Graphics [533].

These standardization efforts face a number of very difficult problems. Some of these have already been mentioned:

1. The relatively primitive state of development of raster graphics, which makes it inappropriate to propose "standard" ways of using raster displays;
2. The lack of high-performance line-drawing displays that can be treated compatibly with simple refresh displays.
3. The device-dependent and application-dependent nature of input programming.

It is reasonable to suppose that, until these three problems are resolved, few application programs will be fully portable.

Nevertheless we can expect to gain considerably from the adoption, if not of standards, at least of the programmer's model and general methodology presented in this chapter. Graphics packages designed on the basis of the programmer's model will at least exhibit considerable similarity, and applications that use these packages will be portable at the expense of a small amount of fairly straightforward reprogramming by someone with only a rudimentary understanding of the program. Most important of all, a widely accepted set of codes of practice for graphics programming will emerge, and will lead to better understanding between workers in the field and more sharing of ideas. Thus even without true standardization, we stand to gain a great deal from the use of a common graphics methodology.

## EXERCISES

**27-1** Suggest a set of functions for inclusion in a high-quality text display module.

**27-2** Consider the task of designing a graphics package for a set of displays, all of which possess multi-level subroutine capability. How would this affect the design?

**27-3** Make a list of hardware capabilities that one might expect to find in displays, that would affect the design of a device-independent set of primitive functions, e.g., arc generators, blinking. Discuss ways to simulate each capability.

**27-4** Design in detail the common-software function to store a display instruction in the currently open segment of the display file. Note that this will involve checking for block overflow, and occasional free storage allocation.

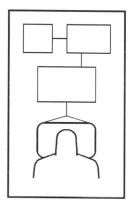

# 28

# USER INTERFACE

# DESIGN

The success with which we design and construct application programs depends on our ability to predict their performance. Some aspects of program performance are quite easy to predict; for example, we can easily estimate a program's capacity in terms of items of data or picture elements. Other aspects of performance such as program size, speed of response, or reliability are less easy to determine and are often the subject of grossly optimistic estimates during program design. The effect of excessive optimism in these estimates is that the program, when complete, fails to meet the original requirements.

No single component of an interactive program is more unpredictable in performance than the *user interface*, i.e., the part of the program that determines how the user and the computer communicate. It is unfortunate that this should be so, for user-interface design has a particularly strong impact on program acceptability as a whole. Our inability to predict user interface performance makes it particularly likely that users will react in unexpected ways when they first use the program. The biggest surprises often occur when the programmer sits down with his first user to explain the operation of the program:

**Programmer:** Now that you've drawn part of the circuit, you might want to change it in some way.

**User:** Yes, let's delete a component. How do we do that?

**P:** Point at the menu item labeled CD.

U: CD?

P: It stands for 'component delete.'

U: Ah. Well, here goes ... hey, what happened?

P: You're in analysis mode: you must have selected AM instead of CD.

U: Funny, I was pointing at CD. How can I get out of analysis mode?

P: Just type control-Q.

U: [types C-O-N-T-R ...]

P: No, hold down the control key and hit Q.

U: Sorry, silly of me ... OK, I'll try for CD again.

P: Maybe aim a bit above the letters to avoid getting into analysis mode—no, not that much above—that's better.

U: Got it!

P: Now point to the component to delete it.

U: OK ... nothing's happening; what am I doing wrong?

P: You're not doing anything wrong; you've deleted the component, but the program hasn't removed it from the screen yet.

U: When will it be removed?

P: When you type control-J to redraw the picture.

U: I'll try it ... there we are; but only part of the component was removed!

P: Sorry, I forgot: you have to delete each half of the component separately. Just point to CD again.

U: Very well ... now what's happened?

P: You're in analysis mode again: type control-Q.

U: Control ... where's that Q? There it is ... hey, why is the screen blank all of a sudden?

P: You typed Q, not control-Q, so the program quit to the operating system. I'm really sorry, but we've lost everything and we'll have to start all over again.

U: [groans] Could we postpone that until next week?

What we see here is an example of a poorly designed *user interface* and the effect it can have on the usefulness of an interactive program. The unfortunate user has to try to remember obscure commands like control-Q and CD, and has difficulty giving the commands correctly. The program often does not respond when the command is given, and when it does respond, the user is often surprised or confused by the result. Minor mistakes by the user can cause disastrous reactions by the program.

It is very important to pay careful attention to the design of interactive user interfaces. Not only are bad user interfaces difficult to learn, but they make programs inefficient to operate even in the hands of experienced users. In extreme cases, of which the example above is typical, an entire application exercise may be invalidated by poor user-interface design: it may prove impossible to train users to operate the program, or the user interface may be so inefficient and unreliable that the cost of using the program cannot be justified.

## 28-1 COMPONENTS OF THE USER INTERFACE

The user interface divides naturally into four components. One of these underlies the other three: this is the *user's model*, the conceptual model formed by the user of the information he manipulates and of the processes he applies to this information. Without this model the user can do little more than blindly follow instructions, like an inexperienced cook following a recipe. The model enables him to develop, even with little or no knowledge of computer technology, a broad understanding of what the program is doing. With the model's help he can anticipate the effect of his actions and can devise his own strategies for operating the program. Sometimes the design of the user's model is simply a matter of simulating as closely as possible a real world system, so that the user need not develop any model of his own. This is what we would do, for example, in designing an aircraft pilot training system. This approach to the user's model does not always work, however, because simulation of the real world often proves inappropriate or difficult.

Once the user has understood the model, he needs *commands* with which to manipulate it. The system of commands we provide is called the *command language* and forms the second component of the user interface. Most of us are familiar with command languages, as many of the machines we use in everyday life—the pocket calculator, the copying machine, the typewriter—have quite extensive systems of commands. That we can learn to use these machines without being conscious of learning a language is a testimonial to the care put into the design of their command languages. Ideally our computer programs should have equally natural command languages.

The third component of the user interface is *feedback*, with which the computer assists the user in operating the program. Feedback comes in many forms: acknowledgement of receipt of commands, explanatory messages, indication of selected objects, and echoing of typed characters. Some forms of feedback are provided mainly to help inexperienced users and can be ignored by experts. On the other hand, some command languages are inherently dependent on feedback; graphical positioning commands, for example, almost always require cursor feedback on the screen in response to the movement of the positioning device.

Feedback helps the user to be sure that his commands are accurately received and fully understood by the program. It tells him little about their real effect. A fourth component, *information display,* is therefore necessary to show him the state of the information he is manipulating. Here we are concerned with organizing the displayed image to convey the information as effectively as possible. The image is a confirmation to the user that his model is correct, and we therefore design it in strict accordance with the model we have chosen. Where the model depends on realism, as in a flight simulator, we must strive for realism in the displayed image; where a more synthetic model is chosen, we may try to reinforce this model by means of well-chosen symbols and graphic imagery in the displayed information.

This subdivision into components is extremely helpful in user-interface design because it enables us both to categorize the problems arising in design and to be more thorough in addressing them. It is also possible to separate the task of user-interface design into smaller subtasks corresponding to the four components. The separation is not a clean one, however, and it is therefore not possible to design any one component independently of the rest. For example, when we design the command language, we must consider what feedback each command should provide, and these feedback techniques must use similar output conventions to information display. As we design these components, we often return to the user's model to make minor alterations to reflect changes in the command language or in information display. Thus we must constantly shift our focus from one component to another as we proceed with the design of the user interface. Nevertheless we can apply separate strategies and design rules to each component and thus ensure that each of the four components will function satisfactorily.

### Task Analysis

The following sections explore in detail each of the four main components of the user interface—user's model, command language, feedback, and information display. Other issues enter into user-interface design and must be kept in mind by the designer. For example, throughout the design process the designer must maintain a realistic estimate of the computing and display resources available to him and must ensure that his user interface design does not overtax these resources. At the same time he must keep in mind the user's needs: these are the main driving force behind the design, and must be clearly defined at the outset.

It is therefore wise to precede the design with a phase of *task analysis* in which the user's needs are studied and a set of functional requirements drawn up. Task analysis often involves interviewing prospective users, measuring their performance, and studying their working environment; the results of these studies must then be analyzed. A written report on the task analysis often forms a starting point for the user-interface design.

Task analysis is in itself a process requiring considerable skill and experience; often it is carried out by specialists who produce a report and then take no further part in the design process. A full discussion of task analysis lies outside the scope of this chapter. Nevertheless the example provided at the end of the chapter will present brief definitions of users' needs such as might be developed by task analysis.

### 28-2  THE USER'S MODEL

As we have already noted, users can be trained to operate interactive programs as if they were following recipes. User's manuals often contain short "recipes" similar to the following example:

*TO PREPARE THE WEEK'S MENU:*
1. Type EDIT MENU.TXT and press the RETURN key.
2. When a basic menu appears on the screen, move the cursor to the word 'Monday-dish' and press the middle mouse button once. The word will be underlined.
3. Press the R key.
4. Type a description of the day's menu; follow it by pressing the ESC key.
5. Repeat steps 2, 3, and 4 for each of the other days.
6. When all five days' menus have been typed, press the H key followed by the ESC key. A printout of the menu will emerge from the printer.
7. Type Q and ESC.

The "recipe" approach to the use of interactive programs has many shortcomings. One of the most serious is its tendency to discourage the user from developing any understanding of the program he is operating, making it most unlikely that he will know what to do if the recipe does not work. For example, the paper may jam in the printer during step 6; should the user then return to step 1 and complete the entire process, or can he simply repeat step 6 after freeing the printer? What should he do if the wrong word is underlined in step 2? To us the answers may be obvious, but to him the menu has no underlying meaning to make one course of action more sensible than another.

To protect the user against such difficulties we must help him develop a conceptual understanding of the program, a *user's model.* In many cases a very simple model, based on nontechnical concepts, is sufficient. For example, we can provide the user of the above recipe with a few helpful facts:

1. The EDIT program allows the user to operate on a *file* of text; to start editing, type EDIT followed by the file name, terminated by RETURN.
2. Any word in the text may be *selected* by pointing to it and pressing the middle mouse button; the selected word is underlined. Making a selection does not alter the text.
3. The program has a small set of commands that may be used at any time: REPLACE (given by typing R), HARDCOPY (H), and QUIT (Q). To complete each command, press the ESC key.
4. The REPLACE command replaces the selected word with the text typed in before pressing the ESC key.

These are perhaps not enough to enable the user to solve all conceivable problems with the EDIT program, but they provide him with a sufficiently rich user's model to understand the purpose of each step in menu preparation.

It is rarely satisfactory to delay development of the user's model until after defining the command set, as we have just done; instead we must consider the user's model from the very outset. In designing the user's model it is helpful to consider these two points:

1. The user's model is a *mental model* and acts as a framework for the development of strategies for operating the program. It is therefore analogous to the grammar of a foreign language: we rely on it in order to communicate successfully. As with a foreign language grammar, the user achieves fluent communication only when he ceases to be conscious of the user's model as a guiding influence; the model has become instilled in his mind.

2. The user's model should employ *familiar concepts*. It is difficult to gain acceptance for a program that presents the user with unfamiliar objects that behave in highly unexpected ways. Instead we should try to use concepts with which the user is familiar: if he is an electronics engineer, we should present him with memory elements, gates, connecting wires and other such objects; if he is an architect, we should allow him to manipulate doors, walls, and windows. The use of familiar concepts makes the user's model more intuitive and easier to learn.

The use of a familiar set of concepts provides us with a good starting point for the user's model design, and we can then proceed to extend and refine the model, keeping it as simple and consistent as possible in order to help the user assimilate it. It is important, however, not to be too literal in copying familiar objects and their behavior. Most environments are too complex or too little understood for complete simulation in an interactive computer program, and so there will be noticeable discrepancies between the real and simulated worlds. It may be difficult for the user to accept these discrepancies in what is basically an extremely accurate simulation. Thus we can simulate a typewriter very accurately on a graphic display, but if we introduce one innovation, such as a backspace key that deletes characters, we may create serious difficulties for the experienced typist who is used to backspacing in order to underline words. It may be better to devise a model somewhat different from the typewriter, so as to avoid these minor points of confusion. A model that differs from reality in a consistent manner throughout is generally better than one that departs from reality in only a few unexpected places.

It is important, when designing the user's model, to give due consideration to the constraints imposed by hardware and system software. The other components of the user interface are directly affected by these constraints: the command language design depends on the availability of input devices, and the choice of feedback techniques is affected by display response. Since the user's model must be consistent with these other components, the constraints that apply directly to the design of these components also apply indirectly to the design of the user's model.

## Objects and Actions

A useful way of representing a user's model, for purposes of discussion and documentation, is as a set of *objects* together with a set of *actions* the user can apply to the objects. Each object is an item of information over which the user has some control; he may be able only to display it and to ask questions about it, or he may be able to modify it, destroy it, and create other objects in its place. Often there is a hierarchic relationship between objects. In a text editor, for example, the simplest object is a single *character*; collections of characters form *words,* words form *lines,* lines form *paragraphs,* paragraphs form *pages,* and a set of pages forms a complete *document.*

Actions are the operations the user can apply to objects. The complete set of actions thus defines the functional capability of the program. Sometimes the actions and objects are *orthogonal;* i.e., any action can be applied to any object. Text editors often allow us to delete characters, words, lines, paragraphs, pages or entire documents. More frequently we find that each action applies only to a specific class of objects.

As we shall see in the pages that follow, there is a close correspondence between the actions of the user's model and the commands that form the command language. This correspondence is not one-to-one, however. Frequently we introduce extra commands to perform common sequences of actions, or we let a single command, with suitable modifiers, perform several different actions. The set of actions defines a *conceptual* set of operations that is adequate to support the application; the command set provides the user with the physical means to carry out these operations.

## Control Objects

The user's model generally contains two kinds of objects: those which are intrinsic to the application and those whose purpose is to assist in the control of the program. The former kind of object we call *intrinsic objects,* the latter *control objects.*

We have encountered many types of control objects in our discussion of interactive techniques in Chapter 12. They include cursors, command menus, selections, scales and guidelines, grids, and many other such artifacts. As in our choice of intrinsic objects we attempt to choose control objects whose behavior is straightforward, consistent and easily assimilated. Actions must apply to control objects as well as intrinsic objects: thus if we provide the user with a displayed grid we may wish to permit him to insert and remove the grid and to change its spacing. Control objects thus add to both the set of objects and the set of actions; we must consider this in our attempts to keep the user's model simple and consistent.

## 28-3 THE COMMAND LANGUAGE

Command languages are found in a great many kinds of computer system, both interactive and noninteractive. Perhaps the most widely used class of command language is the *job control language* (JCL), in which a batch computer system is instructed how to process each of the jobs in a batch. A typical JCL command looks like this:

//JOB DDRUN CORE = 10000 TIME = 1000

Many interactive time-shared systems are operated with similar sets of commands. Each command the user types includes one or more words or characters defining the operation to be performed, together with various operands and modifiers. The user completes the command by striking a terminating key, such as RETURN or ESCAPE, that invokes the operation.

Graphical interaction rarely involves commands of this kind. Instead the user points at menu items, presses buttons, or draws characters for the program to recognize. Sometimes the individual commands of the command language are scarcely apparent: the user inputs a stream of pen positions, some invoking actual operations and some merely providing data. The situation is often further complicated by the use of several different input devices: tablet, alphanumeric keyboard and sometimes function keys as well. Issues like these make graphical command languages more difficult to design than non-graphical ones.

The key to solving such problems lies in recognizing that a command language is more than just a list of commands: it is a true language, in the sense that its constituent commands relate to each other in a systematic way and collectively define a *syntax*. Command languages defined without proper attention to syntax are unlikely to be successful.

The first problem in designing a set of commands is therefore the problem of language design itself. We must define a syntax; we must make sure that this syntax is consistent; we must determine what syntax errors the user can make; and we must make sure that the syntax is sufficiently comprehensive and powerful to satisfy the user's needs. These problems are familiar to those who have studied programming language design, but they are often new to the application programmer. Experience in solving these problems is needed before successful command languages can be designed.

Language design involves consideration not only of syntax but also of *semantics*, i.e., the meaning to be attached to each syntactic construct. The semantics of a command language relates very closely to the user's model. Commands operate on the objects of the user's model, and in many cases their function is to carry out the actions of the model. This relationship simplifies the task of designing a command language from a well-specified user's model; each command corresponds to an action, and the operands of each command are the objects the action affects. Command language design is rarely as simple as this, for it generally starts before the user's model has been completely defined; the two components thus tend to be developed in parallel.

The design of command languages poses one more problem of a rather special nature. The language we design is likely to be used by people with no programming experience, unfamiliar with any command languages more complicated than the command set of a pocket calculator. An interactive computer program may for the first time confront them with an abstract language of considerable complexity, which they must learn in order to be able to use the program. We can alleviate this situation by making the command language very simple (simplicity helps here just as it does in the user's model), but the fact remains that command languages are at first rather mystifying and alien to most novice computer users. In the pages that follow we shall discuss some methods for solving this problem.

## Command Language Design Issues

The objects and actions of the user's model provide a convenient starting point for the design of the command language. They define in an abstract form the operations the user can apply and the operands to which he can apply them. We may view the command language as a concrete representation of the user's model, in which actions are replaced by commands and objects figure as command operands. Given a completely defined user's model, we should therefore be able to derive the command language directly from it, using a simple substitution process. In practice we rarely have the opportunity to design command languages this way since we must generally make certain decisions about the command language in order to complete the design of the user's model. For example, before we can specify that a DELETE action can have multiple operands, we must decide whether it will be feasible to include a multiple-selection capability in the command language. Often the user's model will undergo considerable change as a result of command language design decisions.

How do we make decisions about the design of the command language? The first step is to realize that a number of key issues are involved in the design and must be resolved at an early stage. Four principal issues are these:

1.  *Command modes.* Many interactive programs interpret user actions in two or more different ways according to the state of the program; a text editor, for example, may interpret the letter D as a DELETE operation during one state and as part of some typed-in text in another state. Each such state in which a given operation by the user is interpreted differently by the program is called a command *mode.* The more modes in a command language, the more likely the user is to make mistakes by forgetting which mode he is in. Single-mode command languages avoid this problem completely.
2.  *Selection sequence.* Most applications require selection of command operands; this must be done either before or after the operation itself has been specified. Each approach has certain advantages. They are illustrated in Figure 28-1, showing deletion of a word of text. If selection is performed first, fewer modes result: selection and deletion may be treated as independent operations. If selection is performed afterward, it is less

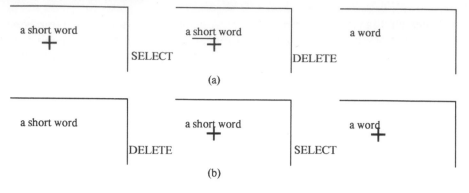

**Figure 28-1** Prefix and postfix commands: (a) selection before command; (b) selection after command.

    ambiguous: specification of the DELETE operation may define what class of item is to be deleted.

3. *Command abort mechanism.* Many commands involve a sequence of two or more steps, and the user may decide in the middle of the sequence that he wishes to retract the command. Often a special "abort" key can be used for this purpose, but in certain cases other techniques must be used. For example, the user may press the pen down on a menu item and change his mind before lifting the pen; he should be permitted to abort the command by moving the pen away from the menu item (see Figure 28-2).

4. *Error handling.* The command language designer must consider how the program should respond to meaningless or erroneous inputs. In many cases errors should simply abort the current command and inform the user of his error. It is important that the user should realize his error: otherwise he may continue with a sequence of commands that are invalidated by the failure of the erroneous command.

    The most important of these issues is the first, concerning command modes, since it affects the stance we take on each of the remaining issues. Consider selection sequence, for example. We may decide that the user should specify operands after giving each command; he gives the DELETE command and then points to the item to be deleted, or he gives the MOVE command, points to an

**Figure 28-2** Aborting a menu command by moving the cursor away from the menu item. Note boldface selection feedback.

item and then indicates its new position. This approach introduces additional command modes because the selection of an item has different effects according to whether it follows a DELETE or a MOVE command. If we wish to achieve a single-mode command language we must generally use prefix selection.

## 28-4 STYLES OF COMMAND LANGUAGE

It is important to preserve *consistency* in command languages. We should not constantly shift the user from one set of input devices to another, for this is very tiring. If we adopt a single-mode command syntax, we should make sure that all commands adhere to it because exceptions can be confusing. Consistency should be obvious so that the user can anticipate the syntax and semantics of unfamiliar commands.

Consistency is most easily achieved by adopting at the outset a particular *style* of command language. In this section we shall discuss a number of different styles, each of which provides a basis for a consistent command language. Our choice of style will depend on a number of factors, including the hardware configuration, the range of objects and actions in the user's model, and the specific requirements of the user. The list presented here is not exhaustive: it merely includes some of the more widely used command-language styles.

### Simple Keyboard Dialogues

Several different command-language styles are in widespread use with alphanumeric terminals. These command languages are of course non-graphical and therefore do not exploit the special properties of graphic displays and input devices. Nevertheless they are occasionally useful in graphical applications.

The simplest such style is the *keyboard dialogue*. The computer prints messages, or *prompts*, to the user, who responds by typing answers on the alphanumeric keyboard. The range of acceptable answers to each prompt is generally quite limited. For example, in response to the prompt, "How many copies?" the program would expect a positive integer, while in response to "Do you wish to proceed?" it would expect "yes" or "no." If the answer lies outside the acceptable range, the program must ask the question again, perhaps indicating what kind of answer it expects: "Do you wish to proceed? (answer yes or no)."

The program's choice of question to ask may depend on the user's response to the previous question; thus it is possible to design quite complex dialogues. Compared with graphical command languages, however, keyboard dialogues are quite inefficient: the user must type many responses to achieve even the simplest results and must be willing to provide information in the exact order requested by the computer. For design applications and other relatively creative tasks the dialogue is unduly restricting; nevertheless it can play a useful part in roles such as logging-in and initialization, where it permits simple interaction to take place without the need for user training.

## Keyboard Command Languages

Although novices find dialogues easy to use, their need for more efficient forms of interaction develops as they become more experienced. A simple way to provide this increase in efficiency is to use a keyboard command language. The user types a single message to the computer containing as much information as would normally be contained in a whole sequence of dialogue responses. To achieve this the user must learn the syntax and semantics of the language; the learning period may be lengthy but is justified if the user is to make extensive use of the program.

In order to shorten the user's learning period and simplify implementation, keyboard command languages generally have a simple syntax. The user types *commands*, each specifying a single action to be taken by the program. For example, he might type

DELETE 1 TO 100

in order to delete items 1 to 100 inclusive. This example illustrates the four basic elements found in keyboard commands:

1. The *verb* (DELETE) specifying what action is to be taken
2. The *operands* (1,100) to which the verb applies
3. *Modifiers* (TO) that indicate how to interpret the operands
4. *Delimiters* (spaces, terminating RETURN) between the elements and between one command and the next.

These items may in some cases be omitted, with the exception of the verb, which must always be present to indicate the action. Sometimes a single item serves more than one function: in the example above, a comma could serve to delimit the two operands and to act as a modifier:

DELETE 1, 100

The verb is usually placed either at the beginning of the command, as in these examples, or at the end. In the QED text editor [143] the verb is usually the last element of a command; the following command would delete lines 1 through 100:

1, 100 DELETE.

Command language syntax is usually *context-free;* i.e., there are no command modes requiring a switch in command syntax. Multiple command modes are sometimes introduced to allow for *subcommands* following the main command. In the TENEX executive language [330], for example, one can invoke a subcommand interpreter by typing a comma at the end of the main command (@ signs are generated by the system):

> @DIRECTORY,
> @@LENGTH
> @@OUTPUT TO FILE: TXTFILES.TTY

Keyboard command languages are useful in graphical applications under two circumstances. Sometimes the keyboard is the only available input device, and it is therefore infeasible to use a graphical command language. In other cases the user must provide many items of numerical or textual data; the use of the keyboard as the sole input device saves him from constantly shifting to and fro between devices.

One additional style of keyboard interaction, which has been used only very rarely in graphical applications, is the use of *natural language*: the user types commands in English (or possibly some other tongue), and the program responds in the same fashion. Generally the speed of response of such systems is very slow, a large amount of processing being required to interpret the user's commands and to formulate replies. Natural-language interaction continues to be the focus of a great deal of research, but for most applications, compared with graphical interaction, it is too inefficient to be a practical alternative.

### Simple Graphical Interaction: Function Keys

In some of the simplest graphical command languages, the use of graphical input is confined to data entry, and commands are given with the aid of a set of function keys. Each key is assigned a specific function, such as DELETE or MOVE, and the operands for each function are specified graphically. Operands may be specified either before or after the function key is pressed. As we have seen, the use of prefix operands is more likely to lead to a single-mode command language.

The use of function keys is less general and less flexible than menu selection, described in the next section. Nevertheless there are certain advantages to the use of function keys:

1. Faster operation is sometimes attainable because no time is lost in selecting the function key; when menus are used, the cursor must often be moved to the far side of the screen in order to select a menu item.
2. Function keys do not take up space on the screen.
3. The function key is conceptually simple and easily understood, particularly if it is labeled with the name of the function it performs.

Not every display installation is equipped with a set of function keys. It is possible to achieve a similar effect, however, by assigning certain alphanumeric keys to act as function keys; thus the D key may be used for deletion, M for moving, and so on. This type of command language is satisfactory provided the keys are used purely as function keys; if they must "double" as keys for text entry, a second command mode is introduced—and with it all the problems associated with multimode command languages.

### Menu-driven Command Languages

A great many interactive graphical programs use menus for command and operand selection. There are several reasons for the popularity of menus. First of all, a menu displays plainly on the screen the full range of options available to the user. Second, it prevents the user from making selections outside this range, and hence solves the problem of erroneous commands. Third, it is very flexible: a menu is easily changed, whereas relabeling a set of function keys or adding an extra key can be time-consuming and expensive. Menus are suitable both for invoking commands and for selecting from a choice of operands; this gives rise to a distinction between *command menus* and *operand menus*.

Chapter 12 has discussed the principal issues in menu design. As we have seen, command menus can spell out each command as a text string, or they can use a graphical, or *iconic,* representation of the command. In the case of operand menus, the use of a graphical menu is more common, since operands are often objects with graphical representations of their own. In application programs with many commands or many different operands, the size of menus becomes a serious problem, and it is normal to use a *multilevel* menu; the first menu selection brings up a second menu, thus allowing the user to select in two steps among as many as 100 different menu items. In extreme cases, menus may have three or more levels. Experienced users can operate such menus very rapidly; they learn the layout of each menu, and after each selection quickly move the cursor to the spot where the desired next selection will appear, thus making it possible to select the item with little or no delay [407].

The first stage in designing a menu-driven command language is to draw up a list of commands and their operands based on the list of actions in the user's model. Once we know the number of commands, we can more easily determine whether a single menu will suffice or whether a multilevel menu scheme must be used. Other factors affect the number of menus required: we may need different menus for different modes of operation of the program (e.g. one for editing and one for analysis); also we may prune certain commands from the menu when they are not needed (e.g., the DELETE command may be omitted when the screen is blank).

As in other command-language designs, it is important to decide whether command operands are to be specified before or after the command is given. If operands precede the command, they must adhere to a set syntax, whereas if they follow the command, it is possible to vary the syntax according to the

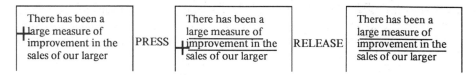

**Figure 28-3** Selecting a contiguous sequence of text lines.

command. For example, after giving the DELETE command the user may point to any number of items to be deleted, whereas the MOVE command may require just a single item selection followed by a new position for the item. Such variation in command syntax may make operation of the program more efficient, but it adds to the user's difficulty in learning to operate the system.

It is therefore best to employ a uniform command syntax, preferably with operand selection preceding the command, since this leads to fewer modes. Where commands require more than one operand, the syntax must permit *multiple selections*. In certain applications, such as text editing, it may be sufficient to allow the user to specify a single sequence of contiguous items, thus standardizing on a single operand per command. Figure 28-3 shows the use of this selection method to manipulate sequences of text. This type of menu-driven command language, in which a single menu is used and each command is preceded by at most one operand selection, is in many respects the most effective for general graphical interaction.

The design of a menu-based user interface involves other issues, such as the layout of menus and the precise feedback provided to menu selections. These will be covered in later sections on feedback and information display.

### Painting Programs

Painting techniques, described in Chapter 12, are useful in a small but significant number of applications: layout of pipework and wiring, simple orthogonal line drawings, and artwork for computer animation.

Most painting programs offer the user a set of *brushes* for use in applying "paint" to the image on the screen. It must be possible to apply different shades or colors of paint, if only to erase mistakes. A black-and-white painting program must therefore provide the user with the means of selecting either black or white paint; a color painting program must offer a wider selection of shades and colors. Often this is done by means of a *palette* of colors, a special menu showing the range of colors available: in order to change the color applied by the brush, the user points to the appropriate color in the palette. Figure 12-40 has shown a typical brush menu and palette for a painting program.

The user, having selected brush and color, paints by pressing down on the stylus and holding the stylus down until the stroke is complete. This simple command syntax can be used for all types of painting, whether freehand or constrained to a grid. Other commands, such as inserting and deleting rectangular images, can be incorporated into the same syntax; special brushes are provided for each of these commands. This style of command language is used in one of the later examples.

### On-Line Character Recognition

On-line character recognition, a powerful interactive technique that can be used to good effect in graphical command languages, has already been discussed in Chapters 12 and 14. The user, instead of selecting points on the screen, draws a character or symbol made up of one or more freehand strokes. The recognition routine attempts to recognize the character by comparing the strokes with those in its dictionary; if it is successful, it returns to the application program the identity of the character, its size, and its screen position.

The main advantage of this style of command language is the large amount of information extracted from each of the user's actions. Thus if the user draws the symbol shown in Figure 28-4a, representing a flowcharting symbol, the program receives enough information to insert in the flowchart a similar symbol of approximately the same size (Figure 28-4b). Another attractive feature of this technique is the user's ability to train the recognizer to accept symbols drawn in the manner most convenient to the user.

On-line character recognition suffers from certain limitations, however, including the following:

1.  Most recognizers, including the Ledeen recognizer described in Chapter 14, are incapable of detecting rotation in symbols. Thus if the same symbol is to be drawn facing up, down, left, or right, it must be defined as four separate symbols. Smaller variations in rotation generally cannot be distinguished by the recognizer.
2.  Size discrimination is also somewhat limited, mainly because it is difficult for the user to draw a symbol freehand to great accuracy. For the user's convenience it is generally necessary to impose a grid, to which sizes and positions are rounded.
3.  Recognizers do not normally respond very rapidly, often waiting ½ second to detect the end of each character and then taking an appreciable fraction

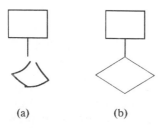

(a)  (b)

Figure 28-4 On-line symbol recognition: (a) hand-drawn symbol; (b) symbol recognized and replaced by program.

of a second to perform recognition. On-line recognition therefore should not be used where very rapid response is required.

4. Most recognizers can distinguish reliably between only 20 to 30 different symbols. If a command language has more than 30 commands, it may not be possible to use on-line recognition effectively.

5. It is sometimes difficult to train people to use a recognizer because they have difficulty drawing characters in the way required by the recognizer and they do not understand the source of their difficulty well enough to retrain the recognizer. This may create a serious obstacle to the novice user.

The repertoire of symbols must be chosen with care in order to avoid the problems listed above. Sometimes it will be necessary to choose symbols that only slightly resemble the object they represent. In particular, if exact rotation is important, it is best to use a single straight line, or some other very narrow symbol, whose angular orientation can be determined from its bounding rectangle. Care is also needed to ensure that symbols can easily be distinguished from each other. To some extent this restricts the degree to which the user can retrain the recognizer, for in so doing he may upset a carefully designed system of symbols.

Command languages that use on-line character recognition rarely require more than one command mode, except for the purposes of training. The user must at any time be able to switch to the training routine, redefine one or more characters by means of a dialogue like that described on page 208, and then switch back to the application. The application program should always retain the updated recognition dictionary until the user's next session.

## 28-5 INFORMATION DISPLAY

The principal argument in favor of the use of graphical displays is their effectiveness in displaying information. Data that would otherwise have to be printed out in numerical form can, with the aid of a display, be plotted as a graph, overlaid on a map, drawn as a network diagram, or displayed as a three-dimensional scene. The power of the graphical display lies not only in the speed with which it can generate such images but also in its flexibility—its ability to present the same data in a variety of ways.

This flexibility poses a problem for the user interface designer: how should information be presented on the display in the most effective manner, i.e., the manner that promotes the most effective interaction between user and computer? This is the central issue in information display as a component of user-interface design. Often the user-interface designer is faced with two or more alternate ways of presenting the same information; furthermore he is constantly confronted with detailed issues in information display, such as choice of line quality, symbol shape and size, position of text labels, and so on. Even minor issues like these can have a significant impact on the success of the user interface design. This section discusses techniques that can lead to more effective information display.

A great deal of research has been conducted on ways of presenting information. Experiments in the psychology of perception have attempted to measure our ability to discriminate between different forms of image [98, 121]; much of this work has been directed toward building models of the human visual process, but a few projects have yielded results that are of interest to the user interface designer. Experiments have also been performed to measure the relative effectiveness of different display organizations and different qualities and styles of text [48].

In the area of general information presentation, some useful work has been done by Bertin [44, 43] and Bowman [66] on graphic design. Bertin's works offer· a careful analysis of the graphic medium in terms of information presentation, with many examples of graphic techniques. Bowman discusses graphic communication under a number of topic headings, again with many examples. One of the most interesting concepts presented his book is the notion of a *grammar* of pictures, i.e., a set of rules that a picture must obey in order to present information effectively; failure to abide by these rules will cause various kinds of misunderstanding on the part of the observer. Many of the ideas of Bertin and Bowman have a direct bearing on user-interface design.

Problems in information display generally relate either to the *overall layout* of the information on the screen or to the *representation of objects,* i.e., the graphical representation of each of the items that appear on the screen. We solve these problems much as we solve other user-interface design problems: by making use of tried and tested solutions and by following established ground rules. Some of these solutions and ground rules are presented in the following discussion.

## Overall Layout

One of the first decisions that must be made regarding information display concerns the utilization of the screen area. Screen space is rather like downtown office space—it is a valuable commodity that we cannot afford to squander. In many applications the screen is simply not large enough, and we must resort to various techniques for presenting selected parts of pictures that are too large and detailed to fit on the screen in their entirety.

The scarcity of screen space is often exacerbated by the need to accommodate menus, prompts and other control objects on the screen. These should be made as compact as possible; where space is at an extreme premium we may resort to erasing them when not when absolutely necessary. For example, error messages are displayed relatively infrequently and therfore need not be allocated permanent space on the screen. Command menus may not be required at all times; it may prove feasible to use a menu that appears only when the user indicates that he is ready to give a command (the technique of displaying the menu near to the cursor, described on page 174, is well suited to this approach). Prompting messages, needed by novice users, may be omitted or curtailed when the user becomes more experienced.

The need to optimize the use of screen space will often argue in favor of giving the user some control over screen layout. This can be achieved through the use of windows, rectangular regions of the screen whose positions and dimensions are set by the user. For example, Figure 28-5 shows a display screen divided into three windows, one for prompts and error messages, a second containing a menu, and a third for application data display. The boundary between windows can be adjusted by the user. Novices will typically enlarge the prompt window to show as much helpful material as possible (Figure 28-5a), while experts will shrink this window so as to maximize the amount of application data displayed (Figure 28-5b).

The screen can be divided both horizontally and vertically into windows, which may overlap in both directions. Figure 17-1a has shown such a set of windows, with several of the windows partly obscured by other windows. This type of user interface requires a fairly extensive set of window manipulation commands.

One advantage of a flexible window manipulation scheme is that it enables the user to rearrange the screen area so as to present the information in a convenient way. If this capability cannot be provided, then the user-interface designer must decide himself how the screen area is to be divided.

## Object Display

Once the overall layout of the screen has been determined, the generation of the displayed image can be treated as a matter of selecting display representations for each kind of object shown on the screen. Representations must be chosen for both intrinsic and control objects: thus we must decide how

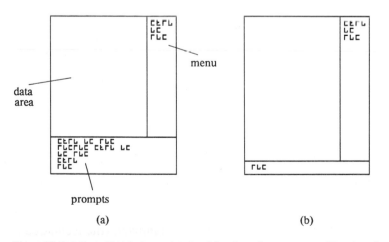

**Figure 28-5** Adjustable windows, showing (a) enlarged prompt area, (b) reduced prompt area.

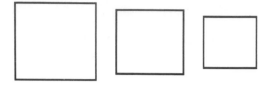

**Figure 28-6** Similar objects that diminish in size appear to recede into the distance.

to show menus, window boundaries, selections, and error information. Representations of objects must accurately display all relevant attributes of the objects, including relationships between objects.

It is in this area of information display that we must pay special attention to the graphic quality of the displayed image. We must design symbols with due consideration of the graphic conventions to which the user may be accustomed. At the same time we must generally be as economical as possible in the use of screen space and image complexity; this often means that we cannot match standard graphic conventions very accurately. Sometimes curved symbols must be drawn with straight lines, or texture paterns must be simplified. Often it is necessary to experiment with different representations in order to find one that satisfies the user.

At all times we must be on guard against making "grammatical" errors in the design of displayed images. The human eye has a tendency to find familiar patterns and graphic meanings in the images we construct; often these are effects that we did not intend. To give an example, if three similar objects are shown side by side with gradually decreasing size from left to right, the viewer may get the impression that the rightmost object is farther away (see Figure 28-6); a similar effect can be caused by intensity variation. The eye also tends to be distracted by unneccessary eccentricities and ornamentation in diagrams, such as the redundant bends in arrows and the attachment points on each of the boxes in Figure 28-7. There is a close analogy here between the grammatical errors we make in constructing pictures and those we make in writing: the error in Figure 28-6 is akin to an error of unintentional association in a sentence, while Figure 28-7 contains errors analogous to the use of flowery language. It is also possible to make the equivalent of spelling mistakes in a picture by

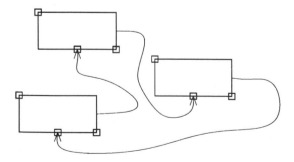

**Figure 28-7** Elaborate curves and excessive attachment points have a distracting effect.

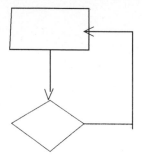

**Figure 28-8** Distracting effect of flaws in execution of a diagram.

allowing minor flaws to appear in the alignment of objects or the shapes of symbols (see Figure 28-8).

The choice of object representation may be fairly obvious, as in electronic circuit layout, or it may involve careful selection from a wide range of alternatives. In the display of multivariate numerical information or of economic data on maps there are, for example, a wealth of different graphical idioms that may be applied. This is a topic that Bertin addresses very thoroughly in his works. He factors graphical representation into six components, or "visual variables," size, shape, orientation, color, shade, and texture, and suggests how these different components can best be applied to the presentation of information.

Information display is an area in which skill in graphic design is a great asset. At the same time it is possible to produce satisfactory results by adhering to some fairly straightforward guidelines: simplicity, economical use of the display, consistency in representation of objects and their attributes, avoidance of grammatical errors, and careful attention to overall layout. Care devoted to the selection of information display techniques pays off handsomely in its effect on the overall quality of the user interface.

## 28-6 FEEDBACK

Feedback is often overlooked as a component of the user interface. In the classical model of man-machine interaction, the user's commands result in alterations to the application data base, which are in turn reflected in changes to the displayed information. The user then issues a fresh command on the basis of these changes. Thus the interaction cycle, according to this model, is a simple matter of an input command followed by an output display of information.

This simple model of the interactive process, shown in Figure 28-9, applies only in cases where the user's command language is very simple and the computer's response is very rapid. In such cases, exemplified by the flight simulator, the user can control the system perfectly well by waiting for the response to each of his commands. If the response is slow, however, this simple process breaks down: the user issues a command and must then wait for a response. During this period of waiting, the user is likely to become

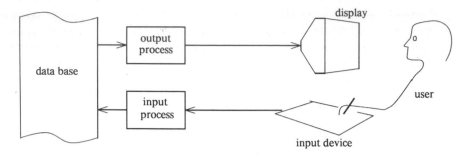

**Figure 28-9** Simple model of the interactive process.

increasingly uneasy about the outcome of his command. Has the computer received it? Should he give the same command again, just in case? Did he give the command correctly? How long should he wait before giving up? These are some of the user's concerns when confronted with a slow-response system.

The purpose of feedback is to supplement the response provided by information display so as to permit more effective interaction. Three principal forms of feedback are:

1.  Feedback from the command interpreting process, informing the user whether the command has been accepted, what stage of executing the command has been reached, and whether an error condition has arisen;
2.  Feedback from the application data base, principally for selection feedback;
3.  Feedback unrelated to command interpretation or to the data base: cursor feedback, character echoing, and so forth.

The relationships between these three forms of feedback, and between them and the simple interaction model, are shown in Figure 28-10. The following sections discuss each form of feedback in turn.

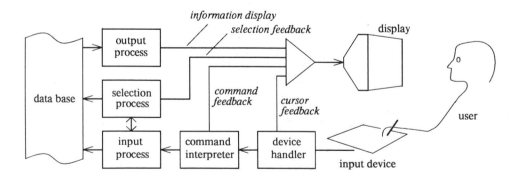

**Figure 28-10** Expanded model of the interactive process showing feedback paths.

One requirement of all forms of feedback is *speed.* If the purpose of the feedback is to confirm receipt of a command or assist in selection, the sooner it is displayed the better. A delay in displaying feedback simply gives rise in the user's mind to the types of question mentioned earlier. In order to display feedback quickly we must make good use of the display hardware's characteristics. On a raster display, for example, it is not easy to change the brightness of a symbol, but it is easy to invert the intensity of each pixel in the symbol's bounding rectangle; inversion therefore provides a fast, simple way of generating selection feedback. In general, feedback techniques must be selected to capitalize on characteristics of the display device.

## Command Feedback

Command feedback, i.e., feedback from the process that interprets the user's commands, is needed for several reasons:

1. It is often feasible to show, by means of feedback, the general effect of the user's next command. If the user points to a menu item and presses down on the stylus or mouse button, feedback can show him which menu item he has selected, so that he can if necessary change his mind before releasing the switch (Figure 28-2).
2. If a command is erroneous in some respect (e.g., it cannot be applied to the selected operand), the user needs an immediate error response. Any delay will make it more difficult for the user to recreate the mental context he needs in order to restate the command. The error message should be brief but should make clear to the user why the command was in error. It should be displayed in a conspicuous place, not in a remote corner of the screen where it will be overlooked. An effective form of error feedback is provided by a change in the shape of the cursor; if there are very few possible error conditions, this may be the only form of error feedback needed.
3. If execution of the command is very slow, the user can benefit from confirmation that the computer is still working on his request. Ideally this feedback should show how many seconds of execution time still remain. If this is not feasible, the user should still be able to check that execution is progressing. A completely unresponsive system can be very disheartening. Command-execution feedback is also useful in reminding the user that the computer is not yet ready for the next command; he can then avoid giving further commands until the system is ready for them. Some systems permit the user to continue to type or input coordinate information ahead of the system; in these systems, some form of confirmation of receipt of input is useful.
4. The user often needs prompts to help him with his next command, particularly in a multimode command language where the choice of permissible commands may not be obvious. Again, the user needs simple,

conspicuous forms of feedback. A printed message may be the most helpful feedback to the complete novice, but once he is more experienced the user will generally find cursor feedback more useful: it requires no shift in his gaze, and is much more noticeable.

Many forms of command feedback serve merely to provide unobtrusive confirmation that the user's commands are being received. A very simple form of feedback is the audible and tactile click from a function key when it is pressed down; this tells the user that the function key command has been transmitted to the computer. The user learns to rely on this click as confirmation and will notice its absence at once. Nevertheless during normal operation the click does not disturb his concentration. Prompts and command execution feedback should if possible always be kept to an unobtrusive level.

## Selection Feedback

It is often difficult to provide adequate feedback during selection operations, for a number of reasons. In the first place, it is not always possible to provide rapid enough feedback. The data base from which the user is selecting may be very large, preventing rapid detection of the object at which the user is pointing. Once the object has been identified, its display representation must be changed in some way to indicate selection. If the user moves the coordinate input device away from the object, selection feedback must be removed, as in menu selection. Clearly we must choose a form of selection feedback that can be displayed and removed very quickly.

A further constraint is the requirement that selection feedback should match the display representation of already selected objects. This representation enables the user to distinguish the selected objects from the rest, and generally takes the form of highlighting or intensity inversion. The feedback provided to the user as he is making the selection should match this representation. Figure 28-11 illustrates a selection sequence that meets this requirement. The objects in question are strings of text, and selected text strings are shown inverted (Figure 28-11a). When the user starts a selection by

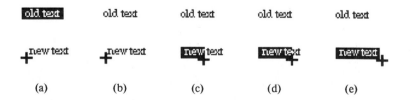

(a)          (b)          (c)          (d)          (e)

**Figure 28-11**  Text selection: (a) previous selection shown inverted; (b) on pressing down, old selection is removed; (c) and (d) as stylus moves, selection is shown inverted; (e) on releasing, selection remains inverted.

pressing down on the stylus, the first action of the system is to de-select any previously selected piece of text (Figure 28-11b). Then, as the user moves the stylus, the extent of the selected text string is shown inverted (Figures 28-11c and d). Finally, when the appropriate text string has been selected, the user lifts the stylus; the inversion remains on the screen to remind the user of the current selection (Figure 28-11e).

Often it is necessary to design the data base with selection feedback in mind, providing rapid access to those attributes necessary for feedback. For example, in a layout program the data base should be organized so that bounding-box coordinates are held in direct access memory, with the remaining attributes of each object held in slower-access memory if necessary. It is then easy to match the input coordinates from the stylus with the closest object and to display a simple form of feedback.

### Application-independent Feedback

A graphics system will generally provide one or two standard forms of feedback. One of the most basic is the feedback of a cursor that follows the coordinate input device. This feedback must be very rapid since even a slight lag between device and cursor movement is noticeable. An analogous form of feedback is the echoing of typed characters; here the need for speed is less extreme.

## 28-7  EXAMPLES

The following two examples work through the steps in user interface design, illustrating many of the issues raised in this chapter. The examples chosen are intentionally very simple (the description of a complete user interface design for an application of any complexity would require a chapter to itself). To simplify the description further, both user interfaces described are designed for the same task, business forms design, but are oriented toward two different types of hardware system. Thus the initial task analysis applies to both examples. The first example is a user interface to a black-and-white raster display and mouse, while the second is for a line-drawing display and tablet.

### Task Analysis

The task for which the two user interfaces are designed is the on-line preparation of artwork for business forms, like the one shown in Figure 28-12. Users are assumed to be members of a graphic arts department who prepare the artwork for new forms on paper *masters*. In a separate process, not included in the application, the masters are photographed, plates are prepared, and the forms are printed. The purpose of the application program is to assist the artist

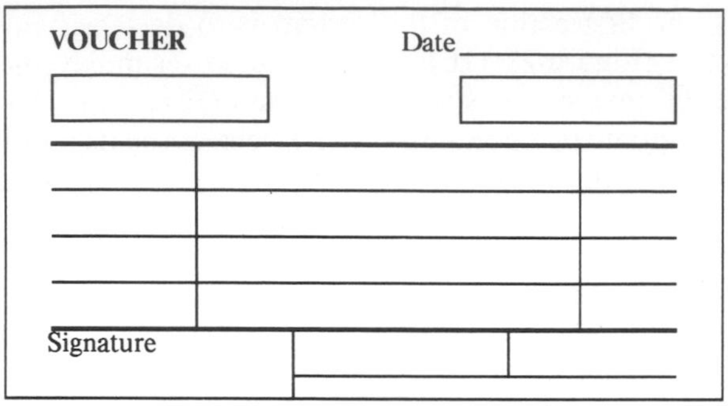

**Figure 28-12** Simple business form.

in preparing masters of new forms and in modifying existing forms when necessary.

Suppose our task analysis has generated the following information:

1. *Sizes of forms.* All forms are designed on standard sizes of paper: 8½ by 11, 8½ by 5½, 5½ by 4¼ inches. Full-sized "landscape" forms, i.e., 11 by 8½-inch forms in which the writing is aligned with the long edge, are not used.
2. *Line quality.* Forms contain solid lines of three thicknesses: 0.01, 0.02, and 0.04 inch.
3. *Text.* Text is included on forms as headings, field labels and instructions. Four different text sizes are used, 8, 10, 12, and 14 point (these are measures of the overall height of the text in *points,* a printer's measure; 1 point is 1/72 inch).
4. *Grid spacing.* For convenience in filling in the forms on a typewriter, lines are to be spaced apart by multiples of 1/6 inch, both horizontally and vertically. More accurate control of text label and heading positioning is required, to about 1/50 inch.
5. *Archiving.* The designer needs to be able to store the artwork for later retrieval and modification.
6. *Hard copy.* After a form has been designed, hard copy must be generated for use as a master.

We shall also assume that the task analysis indicates a need to allow for a considerable amount of trial and error in the process of laying out a form.

### Example 1: Forms Design on a Raster Display

In this example, the user interface is tailored to a high-resolution black-and-white raster display refreshed from a frame buffer memory. The display screen measures about 12 by 12 inches and uses a raster of about 1000 × 1000 pixels. A mouse with two buttons and an alphanumeric keyboard are provided for input, and hard copy is generated on a matrix printer with a resolution of about 200 lines per inch.

**The User's Model**    Since the forms designer's principal activity is the manipulation of lines and text strings, the user's model must provide convenient conceptual models of these two types of information. Our first thought might be to choose straight line segments and text strings as our basic objects, but this ignores the special properties of the raster display as a "painting" surface for freehand and constrained lines. The use of a painting approach to the user interface can simplify the command language and provide the user with a somewhat more flexible tool for artwork generation.

The user's model of the screen surface is therefore of a matrix of dots which the user can set to black or white by means of the painting tools, or *brushes,* with which he is provided. This model applies only to the lines on forms; text strings are represented separately as a different class of object. This enables the user to edit the text and also simplifies the task of printing high-resolution text on the matrix printer.

The two intrinsic objects of the user's model are therefore the raster pixel or *dot,* and the *text string.* A number of control objects are needed to aid in operating the program; they include:

A *drawing area* of the appropriate size, within which the form is designed;
A *type-in buffer* into which text is typed before placing it on the form;
A *text-size menu* for the selection of text size;
A *control menu* for archiving and retrieving forms and for generating hard copy;
An *image buffer,* into which a portion of the form can be copied, with or without the text strings it contains, in order to edit the design.

To complete the user's model we require a set of actions; they include the following:

*Painting and erasing lines* along paths constrained to a 1/6 inch grid;
*Entering and editing text* in the type-in buffer;
*Inserting and deleting text,* inserting from the type-in buffer into the form, deleting in the opposite direction;
*Inserting and deleting rectangular areas* between the drawing area and the image buffer;
*Archiving, retrieving, and printing forms;*
*Setting the size of the drawing area.*

Certain assumptions must be made concerning the command-language design in order to select this set of control objects and actions. For example, the use of a type-in buffer suggests that text will not be typed in and edited directly on the form. Text entry and editing in situ can of course be provided, but this complicates the user interface rather than simplifying it: text may be positioned by its center or its left or right ends, and these positioning constraints applied to text entry must also be applied later to text editing operations. Text entry in situ also requires that the user position the text string before typing it and therefore before its size is known.

The choice of menus is likewise based on an assumption that certain commands and selections will be menu-driven. The use of separate menus for brush selection, text-size selection, and overall control helps the user understand the scope of each operation.

**The Command Language**  The adoption of a painting model for line drawing leads to a very simple, uniform command language. The user defines lines by means of strokes; for each stroke he positions the cursor at the start of the line, presses a mouse button, draws to the other end of the line, and releases the button. The displayed line connects the grid intersections closest to the path of the cursor. One of the mouse buttons is used in adding lines (i.e., in dispensing black ink) while the other erases (with white ink).

The user selects different line thicknesses by pointing to the appropriate brush in the brush menu. Figure 28-13 shows a menu including three line-drawing brushes of different thicknesses, together with brushes for inserting and deleting text and for adding and removing rectangular images. The result is consistent command language, in which one mouse button adds information and the other removes it. Thus if the user draws a stroke starting at point $p_1$ and finishing at $p_2$, the result is as follows, depending on the brush selected:

*Line-drawing brushes:*
> *Insert button.* A sequence of black line segments is drawn connecting $p_1$ to $p_2$, following the gridlines closest to the cursor path.
> *Delete button.* A similar effect, but white line segments are drawn.

*Text brushes:*
> *Insert button.* The contents of the type-in buffer are inserted at $p_1$, positioned by the left end, center, or right end of the string, according to the brush chosen; the position can then be finely adjusted by some fraction of the distance $p_1p_2$.
> *Delete button.* The text string at $p_1$ is deleted. If the cursor is moved away from the string to $p_2$, no deletion occurs.

*Image brush:*
> *Insert button.* The lines in the image buffer are inserted at $p_2$.
> *Delete button.* The lines within the rectangular region with diagonal $p_1p_2$ are deleted into the image buffer.

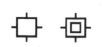

line drawing

text insert/delete

image & image/text insert/delete

**Figure 28-13**  Brush menu.

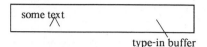

type-in buffer          **Figure 28-14** Type-in buffer and caret.

*Image-and-text brush:*
> *Insert button.* All lines and text in the image buffer are inserted at $p_2$.
> *Delete button.* The lines and text within the rectangle $p_1p_2$ are deleted into the image buffer.

These commands, which are illustrated below in the section on feedback, permit a full range of operations in the contents of the drawing area. The following commands are also required for manipulating the type-in buffer and the form as a whole:

*Placing the type-in caret.* If either mouse button is pressed while the cursor is within the type-in buffer, a text-entry *caret* (Figure 28-14) appears at the nearest position between two characters.

*Text entry and editing.* Any alphanumeric character typed is inserted in the type-in buffer at the caret position; if the BACK-SPACE key is pressed, the character to the left of the caret is removed; the DELETE key erases the entire buffer contents.

*Text size menu.* Selection of one of the sizes in this menu, using either mouse button, changes the size of the text in the type-in buffer and the size of any text entered.

*Set form size.* The size of the drawing area is reset according to the size selected. If the size is reduced so as to exclude certain lines and text strings, they are deleted into the image buffer.

The remaining commands are those for archiving, retrieving and printing forms. They are not always present in the control menu since their use is not always consistent with the state of the drawing area. If the drawing area is empty, for example, it is inappropriate to attempt to archive or print its contents; if the drawing area is not empty, its contents may be destroyed by retrieving another form, so this command is made available only when the drawing area is empty or when its contents have just been archived:

*Retrieve form.* The text in the type-in buffer is used as a name, and the form with this name is retrieved into the drawing area, whose size is reset to the size of the retrieved form.

*Archive form.* The drawing-area contents are archived under the name appearing in the type-in buffer.

*Print form.* The drawing area contents are printed on the matrix printer.

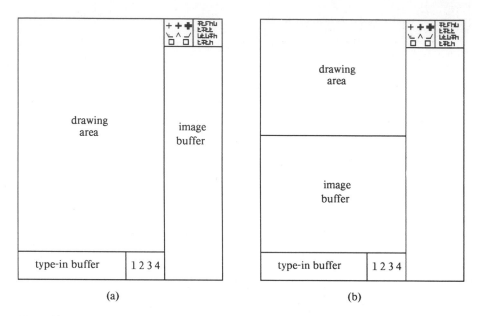

(a)  (b)

**Figure 28-15**  Screen layout for (a) full-sized forms and (b) smaller forms.

**Information display**  A black-and-white raster display is well equipped to display forms consisting of lines and text. It is therefore quite easy to generate suitable display representations of these two principal objects in the user's model. The more difficult aspect of information display is in this instance the design of the overall screen layout.

The main problem in selecting the screen layout is to be able to display simultaneously the drawing area and the image buffer, either of which may be as large as 8½ by 11 inches in size. The 12 by 12 inch screen does not provide enough room for both to be visible; we must therefore choose a solution from the following:

1.  Allow the user to adjust the sizes of the drawing area and image buffer according to the needs of the moment.
2.  Fix the size of each area so that the drawing area is the full size of the form and as much of the image buffer as possible is visible in the remaining space.
3.  Display the entire drawing area and image buffer, if necessary at reduced size.

The simplest of these is the second, in which only part of the image buffer may be visible (Figure 26-15a). In this arrangement the partial image buffer display serves principally as a reminder of the buffer's contents. When smaller form sizes are selected, the entire image buffer can be displayed beneath the drawing area (Figure 28-15b).

An adjustable screen layout can be provided fairly easily by creating a "sensitive" spot on the boundary between the drawing area and the image buffer. The user can point to this spot with the mouse and move it laterally to adjust the widths of the two regions (Figure 28-16). The third layout solution, using a reduced scale for display, is unsatisfactory because at this scale it is difficult to draw and position accurately and the screen lacks the resolution to discriminate between different line widths and text sizes.

The layouts of Figure 28-15 show the three menus positioned according to their function: the brush menu close to the drawing area, the text size menu beside the type-in buffer, and the control menu in the top right-hand corner.

**Feedback** Many of the commands that operate on the drawing area depend on the provision of feedback to the user. For example, when the user deletes or inserts a rectangular image, he must be able to judge its size. Feedback is therefore provided in the following forms:

*Cursor feedback.* The use of different shaped cursors is a very powerful form of feedback, as the user's focus of attention is almost always on the cursor and any change in shape is immediately apparent. Within the drawing area, the cursor shows the shape of the currently selected brush, exactly as it appears in the brush menu. When the cursor moves out of the drawing area its shape changes to an arrow in the type-in buffer, to a circle within menus, and to an x shape elsewhere. During lengthy processing operations the cursor changes to an hour-glass shape. These cursor shapes are shown in Figure 28-17.

*Line drawing.* No feedback is needed during line drawing, provided the display is updated rapidly to show information added or removed.

*Text insertion.* The bounding box of the text string is shown by inverting the rectangle (Figure 28-18).

*Text deletion.* The selected text string is indicated by inverting the pixels within its bounding box (Figure 28-18).

*Image insertion.* The bounding box of the image is shown, with its position rounded to the 1/6 inch grid (Figure 28-19a).

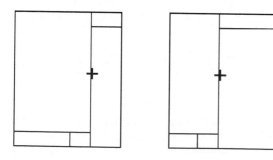

**Figure 28-16** Moving a region boundary by means of a sensitive spot.

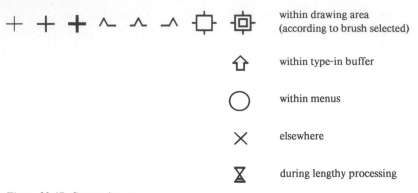

within drawing area
(according to brush selected)

within type-in buffer

within menus

elsewhere

during lengthy processing

**Figure 28-17**  Cursor shapes.

*Image deletion.* The bounding box of the area to be deleted is shown by inverting its pixels (Figure 28-19b).

*Image-and-text manipulation.* The same feedback as in image manipulation can be used without causing confusion.

*Menu selection.* The bounding box of the selected menu item is shown inverted while the mouse button is held down (Figure 28-20).

Some commands may invoke error conditions, and the user must then be alerted to the error. Most errors occur during archiving or retrieval—the user attempts to retrieve a nonexistent form or uses an ill-formed name. Error messages can be displayed in the drawing areas, flashed once or twice by inverting the background, and then removed.

**Refinements to the User Interface**  The user interface just described is perhaps the simplest that will conveniently support the task of forms design. The command language avoids unnecessary command modes and is essentially a single-mode language in the sense that the user can draw, give menu comands or enter text in the type-in buffer interchangeably. The use of different brushes does introduce command modes of a sort, but these are relatively harmless since the cursor feedback makes the user constantly aware of the current mode.

Within this framework, a few user interface refinements can be added. Insertion of images is facilitated if the user can see the entire image as it is dragged around the drawing area; in certain raster displays a second plane of the frame buffer exists for this purpose. The same type of feedback is very helpful in text insertion. Retrieval of forms is made considerably more convenient by the display of a *directory* of names from which the user can select; this also helps prevent the accidental reuse of a name. In making this

**Figure 28-18**   Text insertion and deletion feedback.

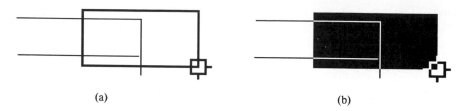

(a)                    (b)

**Figure 28-19**    Image-manipulation feedback: (a) insertion; (b) deletion.

kind of user interface refinement, however, we must guard against adversely affecting the user's model or the command language; the directory is an example of a new control object that must be accommodated with the rest, requires space for its display on the screen, and involves changes to the command language. Extensions of this kind that prove to be inconsistent with the user interface must be avoided.

### Example 2: Forms Design on a Storage Tube Display

Our second example of a user interface design is applied to the same task as the first but differs extensively because of the use of a different output device. In place of a raster display and mouse, we now use a line-drawing storage tube display and tablet. The storage tube, although effective as an information display medium, is not a very powerful interactive device, and this affects the user interface considerably.

In this case we shall assume that the display screen is somewhat smaller, measuring about 10 inches high by 8 inches wide. The tablet stylus has a single switch in the tip, activated by pressing it down on the tablet surface. These two hardware constraints have a considerable effect on the user interface. The description that follows points out these effects: it concentrates mainly on showing how the user interface differs from that of the first example.

**The User's Model**    The painting-style user's model adopted for the first example is not suitable for a line-drawing storage-tube display. Although it is possible to add line segments to the screen in a painting fashion, they cannot be erased in the same way because of the display's limited erase capability. Instead of adopting the same user's model and producing an unsatisfactory command language, we choose a new model better suited to this class of display.

Our new user's model is based on two intrinsic objects, lines and text

**Figure 28-20**    Menu-selection feedback.

strings. The use of lines as objects in place of dots enables the user to edit the form in larger units of information, an important consideration on a storage tube display. A new control object, the *selection,* is introduced: it comprises the lines and text selected by the user for purposes of moving, copying or deleting them. A command menu completes the set of objects; the type-in buffer and image buffer of the previous example are not used since they require relatively frequent updates to the screen's contents.

The exclusion of type-in buffer and image buffer affects the set of actions in the user's model. In particular, we now need to be able to move and copy objects directly on the screen. We therefore require the following set of actions:

> *Inserting lines* whose positions are constrained to a grid
> *Inserting text strings*
> *Selecting* lines and text strings
> *Deleting* the selection
> *Moving* the selection
> *Copying* the selection
> *Archiving, retrieving and printing*
> *Setting the form's size*

This choice of actions produces a somewhat different command language from that of the previous exercise, as we shall now see.

**The Command Language** The previous example used a very uniform command language in which many actions were carried out with a similar stroke-drawing operation, with extensive use of feedback to help the user anticipate the result of each command. The storage tube display does not permit rapid feedback, and we must therefore use a more deliberate form of command language in which the user explicitly specifies each action. This is conveniently done with the aid of the menu: each time the user inserts a line or text string, or deletes, moves or copies the selection, he gives the command by pointing to the menu. Although this produces a relatively slow-moving command language, it results in fewer errors and less confusion on the part of the user.

The menu commands and the syntax within which they are used are as follows:

LINE. Following the command, the user indicates two points, and a horizontally- or vertically-constrained line is drawn between them.

TEXT. The user indicates the position of the left-hand end of the string and then types the string.

SELECT. The user selects any number of lines and text strings by pointing to a spot in the close vicinity of each.

DELETE. The selection is deleted.

MOVE. The user indicates the distance through which the selection is to be moved by specifying two points on the screen.

COPY. This command has the same syntax as the MOVE command.

SET LINE THICKNESS. Three menu items permit selection of one of three thicknesses.

SET TEXT SIZE. Selects between four different text sizes.

SET FORM SIZE. Selects between three form sizes.

PRINT. Generates hard copy on a printer.

ARCHIVE.    The user types a file name followed by a RETURN.

UPDATE.    Blanks the screen and redraws the form and menu.

SHOW SELECTION.    Redraws the selection, as a primitive form of feedback.

The resulting menu has over twenty items in it and is therefore quite large. It is generally necessary to use such large menus in storage tube display user interfaces, however, to avoid the need for frequent menu changes.

**Information Display**    In this example the screen is devoted entirely to the display of the form being designed and the command menu. To prevent the user from trying to position a point within the menu, and thus accidentally invoking a command, the menu is placed in a separate, narrow area on the right-hand side of the screen (Figure 28-21). This leaves an area of about 7½ by 10 inches for the form display. Thus an 8½ by 11 inch form thus cannot be displayed at full size but is scaled down to fit within the available space.

It is not practical to attempt to show lines at their true thickness on the storage tube screen, because it would require drawing several closely spaced parallel lines in order to generate maximum thickness lines. Instead we represent the three different thicknesses symbolically, using dotted lines for the minimum thickness, solid lines for the next and a pair of lines side by side for the maximum thickness.

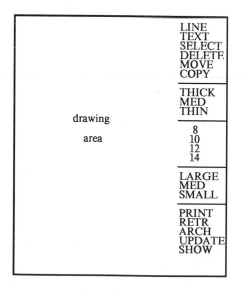

**Figure 28-21** Screen layout for storage-tube display.

**Feedback**  Rapid feedback is not generally feasible on a storage tube display since we normally wish to remove the feedback image just as quickly as we have displayed it and this requires regenerating the entire display.  Feedback in this example is therefore limited to cursor feedback, the display of error messages, and the SHOW SELECTION command, which regenerates the selected items.

## 28-8 CONCLUSION

In this chapter we have explored the design of user interfaces thoroughly enough perhaps to appreciate what a rich and complex subject it is.  User interfaces for interactive graphics-application programs are not a simple matter to design: a number of interrelated issues must be considered.  The designer, in defining the capabilities of the program, must must always be on guard against upsetting the balance of the user interface.

One point which emerges from the worked examples is the impact of hardware characteristics on user-interface design.  For best results, user interfaces must be designed to fit with these characteristics.  Often this means designing the central user's model according to the capabilities of the hardware.  It is of course feasible to design user interfaces that will function on a wide variety of devices, and this is essential for applications that must be portable from one hardware configuration to another.  The design of such user interfaces is relatively difficult, however, and the results are rarely as good as when a specific device is chosen.

Care in the design of user interfaces is always rewarded.  Attention to detail enables us to eradicate the small inconsistencies and flaws that tend to create unforeseen difficulties for the user.  The result of a careful user interface design is that most satisfying and sought-after experience, the knowledge that computer graphics is being used to enhance man's capability and creativity.

## EXERCISES

**28-1**  Return to the original example at the start of the chapter.  Identify each of the flaws in the user interface, relate them to specific user interface components, and suggest better solutions.

**28-2**  The user's model of Example 1 employs one or two unfamiliar concepts.  What are they?  Design a user's model based *entirely* on familiar concepts and develop from it a complete user interface design.

**28-3**  Design a keyboard-controlled command language for the forms-design example.

**28-4**  What user's model changes would be required to permit the simultaneous manipulation of several forms in Example 1?

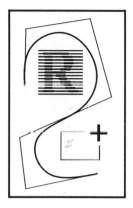

# APPENDICES

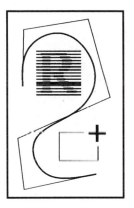

# I

# VECTORS AND

# MATRICES

## I-1 MATRICES

The matrix notation for coordinate transformations is used throughout this book. This section is a summary of some elementary mathematical operations on vectors and matrices. Appendix II contains a discussion of these operations applied to two-dimensional and three-dimensional geometry.

A matrix is an array of elements:

$$A = \begin{bmatrix} a_{11} & a_{12} & a_{13} & \cdot & \cdot & a_{1n} \\ a_{21} & a_{22} & a_{23} & \cdot & \cdot & a_{2n} \\ \cdot & \cdot & \cdot & \cdot & \cdot & \cdot \\ a_{m1} & a_{m2} & a_{m3} & \cdot & \cdot & a_{mn} \end{bmatrix}$$

We shall denote a matrix by an italic upper-case letter, e.g., $A$; its individual elements are denoted $a_{ij}$, where $i$ is the row number and $j$ is the column number of the location of the scalar element. The range of row numbers is from 1 to $m$; column numbers range from 1 to $n$. We shall indicate the number of rows and columns of $A$ with the notation $A_{[m\ n]}$.

Two degenerate cases of matrices occur with $m = 1$ or $n = 1$:

$$\mathbf{b} = [b_{11} \quad b_{12} \quad \ldots \quad b_{1n}]$$

$$\mathbf{c} = \begin{bmatrix} c_{11} \\ c_{21} \\ \cdot \\ c_{m1} \end{bmatrix}$$

The term *vector* is applied to both of these matrices; vectors are denoted by lower-case bold letters. Although **b** is properly called a row vector and **c** a column vector, we shall often adopt a simple notation that uses only one subscript:

$$\mathbf{v} = [v_1 \quad v_2 \quad v_3 \quad \ldots \quad v_l]$$

The number of elements in **v** is indicated by $\mathbf{v}_{[l]}$.

A further degenerate case occurs when both $m$ and $n$ are 1: $A = [a_{11}]$. This construct is *not* equivalent to a scalar with numeric value equal to $a_{11}$.

A matrix can be viewed as a collection of vectors: $A_{[3\ 4]}$ is composed of 3 row vectors, each of length 4. Alternatively, we can imagine $A$ to be composed of 4 column vectors, each with 3 elements. Suppose

$$\begin{aligned} \mathbf{u} &= [u_1 \quad u_2 \quad .. \quad u_l] \\ \mathbf{v} &= [v_1 \quad v_2 \quad ... v_l] \\ \mathbf{w} &= [w_1 \quad w_2 \quad .. \quad w_l] \end{aligned}$$

Then the notation:

$$A = \begin{bmatrix} \mathbf{u} \\ \mathbf{v} \\ \mathbf{w} \end{bmatrix}$$

is shorthand for the full notation:

$$A = \begin{bmatrix} u_1 & u_2 & . & . & . & u_l \\ v_1 & v_2 & . & . & . & v_l \\ w_1 & w_2 & . & . & . & w_l \end{bmatrix}$$

The transpose $A^T$ of an $m \times n$ matrix $A$ is an $n \times m$ matrix:

$$\underset{1 \le i \le m}{\forall} \quad \underset{1 \le j \le n}{\forall} \quad a_{ji}^T = a_{ij}$$

Arithmetic operations on matrices and vectors are defined in terms of arithmetic operations on the *elements* of the matrices or vectors. For example, two matrices $A_{[m\ n]}$ and $B_{[p\ q]}$ are equal (notation: $A = B$) if and only if $m = p$ and $n = q$ and

$$\underset{1 \leq i \leq m}{\forall} \underset{1 \leq j \leq n}{\forall} \quad a_{ij} = b_{ij}$$

The equality is defined on the arithmetic system of which the elements $a_{ij}$ and $b_{ij}$ are part.

Two matrices or vectors can be added, provided they each have the same number of rows and columns: $C_{[m\,n]} = A_{[m\,n]} + B_{[m\,n]}$, where

$$\underset{1 \leq i \leq m}{\forall} \underset{1 \leq j \leq n}{\forall} \quad c_{ij} = a_{ij} + b_{ij}$$

Again, the operation $+$ is defined on the system of elements.

A scalar $s$ multiplied by a matrix $A$ is a new matrix $C$ of the same dimensions as $A$: the multiplication is performed on each element of $A$ to yield an element of $C$, $C_{[m\,n]} = sA_{[m\,n]}$

$$\underset{1 \leq i \leq m}{\forall} \underset{1 \leq j \leq n}{\forall} \quad c_{ij} = sa_{ij}$$

The inner product of two vectors, sometimes called the dot product, is only defined on vectors of the same dimensions. The inner product of $v_{[l]}$ and $w_{[l]}$ is a scalar number:

$$\sum_{i=1}^{l} v_i w_i$$

or, as often seen:

$$\mathbf{v} \bullet \mathbf{w} = [v_1 \quad v_2 \quad \cdots \quad v_l] \begin{bmatrix} w_1 \\ w_2 \\ . \\ w_l \end{bmatrix} = v_1 w_1 + v_2 w_2 + \ldots + v_l w_l$$

The product of two matrices is defined as a generalization of the inner product. The product $C_{[l\,n]}$ of two matrices $A_{[l\,m]}$ and $B_{[m\,n]}$ is computed as follows:

$$\underset{1 \leq i \leq m}{\forall} \underset{1 \leq j \leq n}{\forall} \quad c_{ij} = \mathbf{A}_{i*} \bullet \mathbf{B}_{*j}$$

$\mathbf{A}_{i*}$ is a notation for the $i$th row vector of matrix $A$; $\mathbf{B}_{*j}$ is a notation for the $j$th column vector of matrix $B$. We may write out the inner product:

$$c_{ij} = \sum_{k=1}^{m} a_{ik} b_{kj}$$

Notice the restriction that the number of columns of $A$ must equal the number of rows of $B$. Two matrices which meet this restriction are called *conformal*. Notice also that matrix multiplication is not commutative, i.e., the product $BA$ is not the same as $AB$.

Inspection of the definition of matrix multiplication reveals one special class of matrices $I$, the identity matrices, which, when multiplied by a matrix $A$ conformal to $I$, yields $A$. This matrix class is defined by elements $i_{ij} = \delta_{ij}$:

$$I = \begin{bmatrix} 1 & 0 & 0 & \cdot \\ 0 & 1 & 0 & \cdot \\ 0 & 0 & 1 & \cdot \\ \cdot & \cdot & \cdot & \cdot \end{bmatrix}$$

We can show $AI = IA = A$.

We can define the inverse of $A$, $A^{-1}$, with respect to the identity:

$$AA^{-1} = A^{-1}A = I$$

In order to compute the elements of $A^{-1}$, we need to introduce some new notation.

The determinant of a matrix of scalar elements is a scalar number computed from the elements of the matrix. We define the determinant of the $1 \times 1$ matrix $Z = [z_{11}]$ to be the scalar $z_{11}$. The notation $\det Z$ is used to denote the value of the determinant of $Z$. Let $A_{ij}$ denote the $(n - 1)$ by $(n - 1)$ matrix derived from $A$ by deleting row $i$ and column $j$ from $A$. We proceed to define the determinant of the $n \times n$ matrix $A$ as follows ($n > 1$):

$$\det A = \sum_{i=1}^{n} a_{ij}(-1)^{i+j} \det A_{ij}$$

for some $1 \leq j \leq n$.

A term of the summation above:

$$c_{ij} = (-1)^{i+j} \det A_{ij}$$

is called the *cofactor* of the element $a_{ij}$ of $A$. This expression defines a matrix of cofactors $C$.

We are now prepared to define the inverse $A^{-1}$ of the $n \times n$ matrix $A$:

$$a_{ij}^{-1} = \frac{(-1)^{i+j} \det A_{ji}}{\det A}$$

(Notice the order of subscripts of $A_{ji}$.) The inverse can also be expressed in terms of the matrix of cofactors

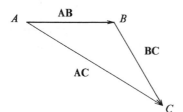

Figure I·1  The vector sum of **AB** and **BC** is **AC**.

$$A^{-1} = \left(\frac{1}{\det A}\right) C^T$$

Notice that the elements of $A^{-1}$ are undefined if $\det A = 0$. In this case, $A$ is called *singular*. In general, inverting matrices with computers is not as easy as described above, because as $\det A$ gets very small, various roundoff errors occur. Furthermore, the alternating signs in the computation of $\det A$ cause numerical problems. Most matrices used for two-dimensional or three-dimensional transformations are very well-behaved; no special numerical techniques are required to invert them. Forsythe and Moler [179] catalog various procedures for computing inverses of near-singular matrices.

### I·2  VECTORS

A vector is a directed line segment. The vector from point $A$ to point $B$ is denoted by **AB**. We often think of points as determined by coordinates in a cartesian coordinate system. If $A$ is at $(x_a, y_a, z_a)$ and $B$ at $(x_b, y_b, z_b)$, then we can represent **AB** by the triple $[(x_b - x_a)\ (y_b - y_a)\ (z_b - z_a)]$. The origin of the coordinate system plays a special role; we equate the vector $\mathbf{v} = [x\ y\ z]$ with the vector **OV**, where $V$ is the point $(x, y, z)$ and **O** is the origin $(0, 0, 0)$.

Vectors **AB** and **BC** add to give **AC**, as shown in Figure I-1. The vector sum $\mathbf{w} = \mathbf{u} + \mathbf{v}$ is defined as a vector of scalar sums:

$$\mathbf{w} = [u_1 + v_1 \quad u_2 + v_2 \ \dots \ u_l + v_l]$$

A scalar $s$ multiplies a vector $\mathbf{v}$:

$$s\mathbf{v} = [sv_1 \quad sv_2 \ \dots \ sv_l]$$

where the scalar multiplications obey normal conventions for real numbers.

A collection of vectors $v_1, v_2, \dots v_n$ is linearly independent if:

$$\alpha_1 v_1 + \alpha_2 v_2 + \dots + \alpha_n v_n = 0$$

only when all the $\alpha_i$ are zero.

The vectors $v_1$, $v_2$, ... $v_n$ *span* the vector space if and only if every vector **m** in the space can be expressed as a linear combination of the $v_i$. For example, the vectors

$$\mathbf{i} = [1 \quad 0 \quad 0] \qquad \mathbf{j} = [0 \quad 1 \quad 0] \qquad \mathbf{k} = [0 \quad 0 \quad 1]$$

span the three-dimensional space of reals because every vector **m** can be represented as:

$$\mathbf{m} = [a \quad b \quad c] = a\mathbf{i} + b\mathbf{j} + c\mathbf{k}$$

If the vectors $v_i$ are linearly independent and span the vector space they are called a *basis* of the vector space. Any $n$ independent $n$-component vectors are a basis for the $n$-dimensional vector space.

Two vectors are said to be orthogonal if and only if their inner product is zero. A basis is said to be an orthogonal basis if every vector of the basis is orthogonal to every other vector of the basis. The basis **i, j, k** given above is orthogonal.

A common use of three-component vectors is for representation of three-dimensional cartesian space. The space is usually defined in terms of the orthogonal basis $[1 \quad 0 \quad 0]$, $[0 \quad 1 \quad 0]$, and $[0 \quad 0 \quad 1]$. Another notation for this basis is the set of unit vectors along the three orthogonal axis directions $x$, $y$, and $z$.

The magnitude or length of a vector is denoted by $|v|$ and is computed by

$$|v| = (v_1{}^2 + v_2{}^2 + \ldots + v_l{}^2)^{\frac{1}{2}}$$

The inner product of two vectors is:

$$\mathbf{v} \bullet \mathbf{w} = |v| \, |w| \cos \theta = v_1 w_1 + v_2 w_2 + \ldots + v_l w_l$$

where $\theta$ is the angle between the two vectors (this angle has intuitive meaning only in two- and three-dimensional spaces).

One special operation on three-dimensional vectors is called the cross product:

$$\mathbf{v} \times \mathbf{w} = [(v_2 w_3 - v_3 w_2) \quad (v_3 w_1 - v_1 w_3) \quad (v_1 w_2 - v_2 w_1)]$$

A helpful mnemonic for this is gained by writing:

$$\begin{bmatrix} v_1 & w_1 & \mathbf{i} \\ v_2 & w_2 & \mathbf{j} \\ v_3 & w_3 & \mathbf{k} \end{bmatrix}$$

The first column is the vector **v**, the second **w**, and the third is a shorthand for the cartesian axis vectors. The evaluation of the determinant of the matrix above gives the cross product.

$$(v_2 w_3 - v_3 w_2)\mathbf{i} + (v_3 w_1 - v_1 w_3)\mathbf{j} + (v_1 w_2 - v_2 w_1)\mathbf{k}$$

Notice that $\mathbf{v} \times \mathbf{w} = -\mathbf{w} \times \mathbf{v}$

The cross product of two vectors $\mathbf{v}$ and $\mathbf{w}$ yields a new *vector*. This vector is orthogonal to $\mathbf{v}$ and $\mathbf{w}$, as can be seen by taking the inner product $\mathbf{v} \cdot (\mathbf{v} \times \mathbf{w}) = 0$, which implies that the angle between $\mathbf{v}$ and $(\mathbf{v} \times \mathbf{w})$ is $90°$ or $270°$. The magnitude of the cross product vector is related to the angle between the two vectors:

$$|\mathbf{v} \times \mathbf{w}| = |\mathbf{v}|\,|\mathbf{w}| \sin \theta$$

As an example of these operations, consider deriving the matrix transformation for three-dimensional vectors which rotates a point through an angle of $\theta$ about the z axis, as shown in Figure I-2. Point $P$ is transformed into $P'$. We have:

$$\mathbf{OP'} = \mathbf{OQ'} + \mathbf{Q'P'} = \mathbf{OQ'} + \mathbf{QP} = \mathbf{OS} + \mathbf{SQ'} + \mathbf{QP}$$

We will compute the three terms of this sum:

1.  Determine **OS**. First compute its magnitude:

$$|\mathbf{OS}| = |\mathbf{OQ'}| \cos \theta = |\mathbf{OQ}| \cos \theta$$

The direction of **OS** is the same as that of **OQ**:

$$\mathbf{OS} = \mathbf{OQ} \cos \theta$$

2.  Determine **SQ'**. First compute its magnitude:

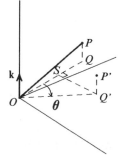

**Figure I-2** Rotation of the point $P$ through an angle $\theta$ about the axis **k**.

$$|SQ'| = |OQ'| \sin \theta = |OQ| \sin \theta$$

The direction is perpendicular to **k** and to **OQ**:

$$SQ = (OQ \times k) \sin \theta$$

3. Determine **Q'P**, which is the same as **QP**. Its magnitude is simply **OP • k** and its direction is parallel to **k**:

$$QP = (OP \cdot k)k$$

Hence

$$OP' = OQ \cos \theta + (OQ \times k) \sin \theta + (OP \cdot k)k$$

Now

$$OQ = OP - (OP \cdot k)k$$

So

$$OP' = OP \cos \theta + (OP \times k) \sin \theta - (k \times k (OP \cdot k) \sin \theta) \\ + (OP \cdot k)(1 - \cos \theta)k$$

The third term is zero because **k** $\times$ **k** is 0. We can finally assemble an expression for **OP'**.

$$OP' = OP \cos \theta + (OP \times k) \sin \theta + (OP \cdot k)(1 - \cos \theta)k$$

Notice that **OP'** is a function of (1) **OP**, (2) the angle of rotation $\theta$, and (3) a unit vector **k** along the axis of rotation. In the development so far, we have made no assumptions about the direction in which **k** points; **k** may in fact represent *any* rotation axis.

We can carry this one step further and derive the 3 $\times$ 3 matrix $R$ which is the transformation of the vector **OP** into **OP'**

$$OP' = OP\ R \qquad \text{or} \qquad [x'\ \ y'\ \ z'] = [x\ \ y\ \ z]R$$

We will assume the axis of rotation **k** to be [0  0  1], aligned with the $z$ axis. Thus we have:

$$OP \cos \theta = [x\ \ y\ \ z] \begin{bmatrix} \cos \theta & 0 & 0 \\ 0 & \cos \theta & 0 \\ 0 & 0 & \cos \theta \end{bmatrix}$$

$$\mathbf{OP} \times \mathbf{k} = [x \quad y \quad z] \begin{bmatrix} 0 & -1 & 0 \\ 1 & 0 & 0 \\ 0 & 0 & 0 \end{bmatrix}$$

$$(\mathbf{OP} \times \mathbf{k}) \sin \theta = [x \quad y \quad z] \begin{bmatrix} 0 & -\sin \theta & 0 \\ \sin \theta & 0 & 0 \\ 0 & 0 & 0 \end{bmatrix}$$

We have

$$(\mathbf{OP} \cdot \mathbf{k}) = [x \quad y \quad z] \begin{bmatrix} 0 \\ 0 \\ 1 \end{bmatrix} = z$$

$$(\mathbf{OP} \cdot \mathbf{k})(1 - \cos \theta) = [x \quad y \quad z] \begin{bmatrix} 0 & 0 & 0 \\ 0 & 0 & 0 \\ 0 & 0 & 1-\cos \theta \end{bmatrix}$$

Substituting into the result for **OP′**:

$$\mathbf{OP'} = \mathbf{OP} \cos \theta + (\mathbf{OP} \times \mathbf{k}) \sin \theta + (\mathbf{OP} \cdot \mathbf{k})(1 - \cos \theta)\mathbf{k}$$

$$\mathbf{OP'} = [x \quad y \quad z] \begin{bmatrix} \cos \theta & -\sin \theta & 0 \\ \sin \theta & \cos \theta & 0 \\ 0 & 0 & 1 \end{bmatrix}$$

This is analogous to Equation 22-2.

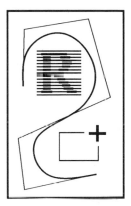

# II

# HOMOGENEOUS

# COORDINATE

# TECHNIQUES

The homogeneous coordinate representations of points, lines, and planes presented in this section are quite useful for describing and manipulating graphical objects. We will discuss only the mathematical aspects of such representations; the mechanics of storing and retrieving object representations in some data structure and of recording relations among objects are ignored.

The term *homogeneous* is applied to the representations described here because the representation for a class of objects involves no explicit constants. For example the equation of a two-dimensional line is $y = mx + b$. The homogeneous equation for the same line is $mx - y + bw = 0$, an equation with three variables. This equation is a representation of the line in a three-dimensional coordinate space.

Homogeneous representation was developed as a geometer's tool for proving theorems of projective geometry. A problem in $n$-space has a corresponding problem in an $(n + 1)$-space. Results in the $(n + 1)$-space are often more easily obtained than those in the $n$-space. The proof in $(n + 1)$-space is then related to the $n$-space problem by projection of the $(n + 1)$-space problem into $n$-space. Thus, although dealing with points at "infinity" in 3-space is difficult, we can deal easily with analogous points in a four-dimensional homogeneous space.

This section follows closely a paper by Roberts [394]. A more formal development of homogeneous coordinate techniques can be found in Maxwell [303, 302]. Homogeneous representations are particularly useful in describing curves and surfaces. A good survey of these techniques is given in [175].

## II-1 HOMOGENEOUS COORDINATES

The homogeneous representation of an object in $n$-space is an object in $(n + 1)$-space. The coordinates in $n$-space are called *ordinary coordinates*, those in $(n + 1)$-space *homogeneous coordinates*. The mapping from $n$-space to $(n + 1)$-space is one-to-many, i.e., there is an infinity of equivalent representations of the $n$-space object in $(n + 1)$-space. The inverse mapping exists, and is called *projection;* there is a many-to-one mapping from $(n + 1)$-space to $n$-space. The projection back into $n$ space can introduce topological changes to the space [386].

A vector in the $(n + 1)$ homogeneous space can be viewed as an $n$-space vector with the addition of one more coordinate to the vector, a scale factor. The homogeneous representation of the two-dimensional point $[x \quad y]$ is $[wx \quad wy \quad w]$ where $w$ is any nonzero scalar which is sometimes called the *scale factor*. The mapping from a homogeneous point $[a \quad b \quad c]$ back to its two-dimensional image is simply $[a/c \quad b/c]$; we divide by the scale factor $c$. An alternate view of the two-dimensional image of $[wx \quad wy \quad w]$ is that it is a projection onto the plane $w = 1$, as shown in Figure II-1.

The transformation matrices developed in Chapter 4 are in fact transformations of homogeneous vectors. The addition of the 1 to the $[x \quad y]$ vector simply creates a homogeneous vector with $w = 1$. The transformations are chosen so that their application to a homogeneous coordinate produces the desired effect on the ordinary coordinates of the point.

Three-dimensional objects are treated analogously: the homogeneous representation of $[x \quad y \quad z]$ is $[wx \quad wy \quad wz \quad w]$ for any $w \neq 0$. A homogeneous point $[a \quad b \quad c \quad d]$ has a three-dimensional image $[a/d \quad b/d \quad c/d]$. The homogeneous transformations given in Chapters 22 and 23 are designed to have the desired effect on the ordinary three-dimensional coordinates of the point.

In describing homogeneous coordinate techniques, it is customary to use the symbols $wx$, $wy$, and $wz$ as dipthongs. That is, $wx$ stands for a single number, not for a multiplication. This notation serves to remind us that the ordinary coordinate $x$ can be derived from the number $wx$ by dividing by $w$.

We observe that multiplying a homogeneous vector by a nonzero scalar constant does not alter its projection in $n$-space. We shall define $n$-space equality with the symbol $\doteq$. Thus, even though two vectors are not $=$, they may be $\doteq$ if one is a scalar multiple of the other. Example: the homogeneous points $[2 \quad 4 \quad 0 \quad 2]$ and $[4 \quad 8 \quad 0 \quad 4]$ are $\doteq$ but not $=$; both project to the two-space point $[1 \quad 2 \quad 0]$.

If the point $(x, y, z)$ is to be transformed by a matrix $M$, we must choose a value of $w$ to form the vector $[wx \quad wy \quad wz \quad w]$ in order to evaluate the product:

$$[w'x' \quad w'y' \quad w'z' \quad w'] = [wx \quad wy \quad wz \quad w] M$$

From a mathematical point of view, the choice of $w$ is not important, provided that $w \neq 0$. In practice, the choice of $w$ may be important. If the calculation of matrix products is performed with fixed-point computer hardware, the familiar problems of overflow and truncation affect the accuracy of the result. Suppose we can represent only integers $-2^{12} \leq x \leq 2^{12} - 1$. The point $x = 0.25$, $y = 0.1$, $z = 10$ cannot be represented if we choose $w = 1$; instead we may choose $w = 20$, and get $[5 \quad 2 \quad 200 \quad 20]$. If we carry this to extremes, and make $w$ reasonably large, we could overflow the maximum allowable integer 4095. However, the homogeneous representation allows us to change $w$ whenever necessary to achieve maximum significance without overflow. For instance, the computation:

$$[5 \quad 2 \quad 200 \quad 20] \begin{bmatrix} 20 & 0 & 0 & 0 \\ 20 & 0 & 0 & 0 \\ 20 & 0 & 0 & 0 \\ 1 & 0 & 0 & 1 \end{bmatrix} = [4160 \quad 0 \quad 0 \quad 20]$$

produces an overflow. We could, however, scale each multiplication by, say, a factor of $1/2$, and get:

$$[5 \quad 2 \quad 200 \quad 20] \begin{bmatrix} 20 & 0 & 0 & 0 \\ 20 & 0 & 0 & 0 \\ 20 & 0 & 0 & 0 \\ 1 & 0 & 0 & 1 \end{bmatrix} \doteq [2080 \quad 0 \quad 0 \quad 10]$$

which represents the same $n$-space point.

## II-2 NOTATION

We shall require a uniform notation for matrices, vectors and scalars throughout the description of manipulation techniques.

*Matrices:* Represented by italic upper-case letters, e.g., $A$.
$\quad$ $A^{-1}$ is the inverse of $A$.
$\quad$ $A^T$ is the transpose of $A$.
*Vectors:* We shall distinguish row vectors and column vectors.
$\quad$ Row vectors: **p,r,v**
$\quad$ Column vectors: $\gamma$, $\lambda$
$\quad$ The transpose of a row vector, $\mathbf{p}^T$, is a column vector.
$\quad$ The transpose of a column vector, $\gamma^T$, is a row vector.
*Scalars:* Other lower-case letters will represent scalars. We shall use three conventions:
$\quad$ 1. $a_{ij}$ are elements of matrix $A$.

2. *s, t* are parametric variables.

3. *x, y, z, w* are specific elements in a vector.

In general, primes (′,″) will be used freely to indicate *transformed* objects, e.g., $\gamma'$ is a column vector, distinct from $\gamma$, but related to $\gamma$ for descriptive purposes.

## II-3 TWO-DIMENSIONAL POINTS AND LINES

1. A two-dimensional point $(x, y)$ is represented by the homogeneous vector $[wx \quad wy \quad w]$, as described above. The 3-vector $[a \quad b \quad c]$ is converted back to ordinary coordinates $(a/c, b/c)$. Any nonzero scalar multiple of the homogeneous representation for a point represents the same two-dimensional point.

2. A line is represented by a column vector:

$$\gamma = \begin{bmatrix} a \\ b \\ c \end{bmatrix}$$

3. The condition that a point $\mathbf{v}$ is on a line $\gamma$ is $\mathbf{v} \cdot \gamma = 0$. This is an inner product, and is equivalent to the scalar equation $a(wx) + b(wy) + c(w) = 0$, where $\mathbf{v} = [wx \quad wy \quad w]$. If $\mathbf{v} \cdot \gamma$ is not zero, then $\mathbf{v}$ does not lie on the line $\gamma$. The sign of $\mathbf{v} \cdot \gamma$ is positive if $\mathbf{v}$ lies on one side of $\gamma$, negative if it lies on the other side. Example:

$$\gamma = \begin{bmatrix} 2 \\ -1 \\ -1 \end{bmatrix} \quad \begin{array}{l} \mathbf{v} = [1 \quad 0 \quad 1] \\ \mathbf{p} = [1 \quad 0 \quad 4] \\ \mathbf{r} = [1 \quad 1 \quad 1] \end{array}$$

Then $\mathbf{v} \cdot \gamma = 1$, $\mathbf{p} \cdot \gamma = -2$, and $\mathbf{r} \cdot \gamma = 0$. The perpendicular distance from a point $\mathbf{v}$ to a line $\gamma$ is determined by $\mathbf{v} \cdot \gamma$ but must be normalized:

$$\text{distance} = (\mathbf{v} \cdot \gamma) \frac{1}{w(a^2 + b^2)^{1/2}}$$

where $\mathbf{v} = [wx \quad wy \quad w]$ and $\gamma^T = [a \quad b \quad c]$.

4. The line $\gamma$ between two points $\mathbf{p}$ and $\mathbf{v}$ is given by:

$$\mathbf{v} = [v_1 \quad v_2 \quad v_3] \qquad \mathbf{p} = [p_1 \quad p_2 \quad p_3]$$

$$\gamma = \begin{bmatrix} p_2 v_3 - p_3 v_2 \\ p_3 v_1 - p_1 v_3 \\ p_1 v_2 - p_2 v_1 \end{bmatrix}$$

Alternatively, we can write $\gamma = v \times p$, the cross product. We can easily verify that both $p$ and $v$ are on the line $\gamma$, i.e., $p \bullet \gamma = 0$ and $v \bullet \gamma = 0$.

5. The point $v$ at the intersection of lines $\gamma$ and $\lambda$ is computed as follows:

$$\gamma^T = [a \quad b \quad c] \qquad \lambda^T = [d \quad e \quad f]$$
$$v = [(fb - ec) \quad (cd - af) \quad (ea - db)] = \gamma \times \lambda$$

Notice that the point $v' = \lambda \times \gamma = -v$ represents the same two-dimensional point as $v$. We can verify that $v \bullet \gamma = 0$ and $v \bullet \lambda = 0$, i.e., $v$ lies on both $\gamma$ and $\lambda$.

6. A transformation $H$ of the 3-space is a $3 \times 3$ matrix. This transformation matrix is of the same form as the transformations described in Chapter 4.

a   A point $v$ is transformed into a point $v'$: $v' = vH$
b   A line $\gamma$ is transformed into a line $\gamma'$: $\gamma' = H^{-1}\gamma$

If we define a line $\gamma$ by the line equation $v \bullet \gamma = 0$, we notice that a transformation of this line preserves the form of the line equation. Suppose a point $v$ is on the line $\gamma$. The line $\gamma$ transforms into $\gamma' = H^{-1}\gamma$; the point $v$ into $v' = vH$. The new point and line are still related by the line equation $v' \bullet \gamma' = 0$. Substituting for $v'$ and $\gamma'$, we have $vHH^{-1}\gamma = 0$, or $v\gamma = 0$, the original line equation.

7. We will demonstrate a transformation $T$ on $(n + 1)$-space homogeneous vectors, which translates points in the space so that $v$ is translated to the origin of the $n$-space, i.e., $vT = [0 \quad 0 \quad v_3]$, where $v = [v_1 \quad v_2 \quad v_3]$:

$$T = \begin{bmatrix} 1 & 0 & 0 \\ 0 & 1 & 0 \\ -v_1/v_3 & -v_2/v_3 & 1 \end{bmatrix}$$

This transformation is similar to the translation transformation given in Chapter 4.

8. The condition that two lines $\lambda$ and $\gamma$ are perpendicular is $(\gamma^T J) \bullet \lambda = 0$, where

$$J = \begin{bmatrix} 1 & 0 & 0 \\ 0 & 1 & 0 \\ 0 & 0 & 0 \end{bmatrix}$$

9. The condition that two lines $\lambda$ and $\gamma$ are parallel is $J\lambda \doteq J\gamma$.

10. The line $\lambda$ which is normal to line $\gamma$ and passes through point $\mathbf{v}$ is computed by:

a. Prepare the translation matrix $T$ from $\mathbf{v}$.
b. $\lambda = TK\gamma$ where

$$K = \begin{bmatrix} 0 & 1 & 0 \\ -1 & 0 & 0 \\ 0 & 0 & 0 \end{bmatrix}$$

Example: if $\gamma^T = [a \quad b \quad c]$, then $\lambda^T = [bv_3 \quad -av_3 \quad (av_2 - bv_1)]$.

11. The line which is parallel to line $\gamma$ and passes through point $\mathbf{v}$ is $\lambda$:

a. Prepare $T$ from $\mathbf{v}$.
b. $\lambda = TJ\gamma$

## II-4 SOLUTION TECHNIQUES

We can illustrate a technique used to derive items 4, 5, 7, 10 and 11. Consider 4: we wish to find $\gamma$ such that $\mathbf{p} \cdot \gamma = 0$ and $\mathbf{v} \cdot \gamma = 0$ both hold, i.e., $[p_1 \ p_2 \ p_3] \cdot \gamma = 0$ and $[v_1 \ v_2 \ v_3] \cdot \gamma = 0$. There is one more degree of freedom left unspecified because of the third homogeneous coordinate—remember that any scalar multiple of a line vector is a line vector which represents the same two-dimensional line. We will therefore be free to choose any value for $c$, such as $[0 \ 0 \ 1] \cdot \gamma = c$. If we define

$$Q = \begin{bmatrix} p_1 & p_2 & p_3 \\ v_1 & v_2 & v_3 \\ 0 & 0 & 1 \end{bmatrix}$$

We can write the matrix equation

$$Q\gamma = \begin{bmatrix} 0 \\ 0 \\ c \end{bmatrix}$$

We can solve this equation by computing the inverse of $Q$. Using the cofactor method described in Appendix I, we have

$$Q^{-1} = \frac{1}{(p_1 v_2 - p_2 v_1)} \begin{bmatrix} v_2 & -p_2 & (p_2 v_3 - p_3 v_2) \\ -v_1 & p_1 & (p_3 v_1 - p_1 v_3) \\ 0 & 0 & (p_1 v_2 - p_2 v_1) \end{bmatrix}$$

which gives

$$\gamma = \frac{c}{(p_1 v_2 - p_2 v_1)} \begin{bmatrix} (p_2 v_3 - p_3 v_2) \\ (p_3 v_1 - p_1 v_3) \\ (p_1 v_2 - p_2 v_1) \end{bmatrix}$$

If we let $c$ be $(p_1 v_2 - p_2 v_1)$ then we have precisely the results of 4. If the determinant $(p_1 v_2 - p_2 v_1) = 0$, then $Q^{-1}$ does not exist. This may occur for two reasons, (1) the original points **p** and **v** are the same point in two dimensions, in which case the line between them is clearly undefined, or (2) our choice for the third degree of freedom was incorrect. To illustrate the second case, consider the line between [2  2  1] and [4  4  1]. Because it passes through the origin, the element $c$ of the line [$a$  $b$  $c$] will be zero. In this case, we should have chosen for the third degree of freedom something like [0  1  0] • $\gamma = 0$. It turns out that the result given in item 4 is correct, regardless of the choice for the third degree of freedom.

As a second example, we shall find a line $\lambda$ which is normal to another line $\gamma$ and passes through the point **v** (item 10). We require that $\lambda \cdot v = 0$ and (from 8), $(\gamma^T J) \cdot \lambda = 0$. We also require a third condition. This arises because there are infinitely many $\lambda$'s which are equivalent descriptions of the line. So we will arbitrarily set [0  0  1] • $\lambda = d$. The three equations may now be written as one matrix equation

$$Q = \begin{bmatrix} v_1 & v_2 & v_3 \\ a & b & 0 \\ 0 & 0 & 1 \end{bmatrix}$$

and

$$Q\lambda = \begin{bmatrix} 0 \\ 0 \\ d \end{bmatrix}$$

Solving, we have

$$\lambda = \frac{d}{(av_2 - bv_1)} \begin{bmatrix} bv_3 \\ -av_3 \\ (av_2 - bv_1) \end{bmatrix}$$

Again, setting $d = av_2 - bv_1$, we get the result of 10. However, suppose $av_2 - bv_1 = 0$; then the inverse of the matrix above does not exist. In this case, we should have made the requirement $[0 \quad 1 \quad 0] \cdot \lambda = d$ instead, and then the matrix would be invertible. We can show that

$$\lambda = \begin{bmatrix} bv_3 \\ -av_3 \\ av_2 - bv_1 \end{bmatrix}$$

is always a solution.

## II-5 THREE-DIMENSIONAL POINTS, LINES, AND PLANES

1. A point in 3-space is a 4-vector $v = [wx \quad wy \quad wz \quad w]$, which is simply an extension of the two-dimensional notation. The three-dimensional point represented by a homogeneous point $[a \quad b \quad c \quad d]$ is the point $[a/d \quad b/d \quad c/d]$. Any nonzero scalar multiple of the homogeneous representation for a point represents the same three-dimensional point.

2. A line can be represented parametrically as a function of the parameter $t$, $v = [t \quad 1]L$, where $L$ is a $2 \times 4$ matrix. Generally, $L$ is formulated so that $t$ ranges from a value of zero at one endpoint of the line to 1 at the other endpoint. Values outside this range represent points on the infinite line through the two endpoints. Lines may also be represented as the intersections of planes, but this representation is not suitable for most applications.

Example: Find the parametric representation of the line through $[1 \quad 0 \quad 1 \quad 1]$ $(t = 0)$ and $[0 \quad 1 \quad 1 \quad 1] \, (t = 1)$. We require

$$[0 \quad 1] \, L = [1 \quad 0 \quad 1 \quad 1]$$
$$[1 \quad 1] \, L = [0 \quad 1 \quad 1 \quad 1]$$

Define the matrix $M$

$$M = \begin{bmatrix} 0 & 1 \\ 1 & 1 \end{bmatrix}$$

The line $L$ can be found by solving the equation

$$ML = \begin{bmatrix} 1 & 0 & 1 & 1 \\ 0 & 1 & 1 & 1 \end{bmatrix}$$

The equation is solved by inverting $M$ and multiplying both sides of the equation by the inverse:

$$L = \begin{bmatrix} -1 & 1 & 0 & 0 \\ 1 & 0 & 1 & 1 \end{bmatrix}$$

Any scalar multiple of $L$, $sL$, yields the same line in three dimensions.

3. A plane is represented by a column vector:

$$\gamma = \begin{bmatrix} a \\ b \\ c \\ d \end{bmatrix}$$

The plane equation (condition that a point $v$ be on the plane $\gamma$) is $v \cdot \gamma = 0$. Actually, $v \cdot \gamma$ is a measure of the distance from $v$ to the plane $\gamma$; it is positive if $v$ lies on one side of the plane and negative if it lies on the other. The actual perpendicular distance from $v$ to $\gamma$ must be normalized:

$$\text{distance} = (v \cdot \gamma) \; \frac{1}{w(a^2 + b^2 + c^2)^{1/2}}$$

where $w = v \cdot [0 \;\; 0 \;\; 0 \;\; 1]^T$. Any nonzero scalar multiple of a plane vector is a vector which represents the same three-dimensional plane. Notice, however, that if the scalar multiplier is less than 0, $v \cdot \gamma$ changes sign.

Plane equations are used frequently in geometric modeling and in hidden-surface algorithms. For these applications, we need to determine the plane equation from a set of points $v_i$, $1 \leq i \leq n$, often the vertices of a polygon. A method due to Martin Newell can be used to compute the three components $a$, $b$, and $c$. Define $j$ to be 1 if $i = n$, otherwise $i + 1$. Then

$$a = \Sigma \, (y_i - y_j)(z_i + z_j)$$
$$b = \Sigma \, (z_i - z_j)(x_i + x_j)$$
$$c = \Sigma \, (x_i - x_j)(y_i + y_j)$$

The value of $d$ can then be determined by requiring one of the points to lie on the plane, i.e., $d = - [x \quad y \quad z \quad 1] \cdot [a \quad b \quad c \quad 0]^T$.

4. Three planes $\gamma_1$, $\gamma_2$, and $\gamma_3$ intersect in one point $v$ such that $v \cdot \gamma_1 = 0$, $v \cdot \gamma_2 = 0$, and $v \cdot \gamma_3 = 0$. Rewriting these three equations, and adding the fourth (scale factor) equation, we have

$$v \begin{bmatrix} & & & 0 \\ \gamma_1 & \gamma_2 & \gamma_3 & 0 \\ & & & 0 \\ & & & 1 \end{bmatrix} = [0 \quad 0 \quad 0 \quad d]$$

(Note that the $\gamma$ vectors fill entire columns of the matrix.) We solve the equation $vQ = [0 \quad 0 \quad 0 \quad d]$ by finding the inverse of $Q$, and setting $v = [0 \quad 0 \quad 0 \quad d]Q^{-1}$. The vector $v$ is thus the bottom row of the inverse of the $4 \times 4$ matrix. If the matrix has no inverse, then either the three planes do not intersect in one point, or the choice of the extra degree of freedom was wrong.

5. Three points $p$, $r$ and $v$ determine a plane $\gamma$ unless all are collinear. We require $p \cdot \gamma = 0$, $r \cdot \gamma = 0$, and $v \cdot \gamma = 0$. The following matrix equation is equivalent:

$$\gamma^T \begin{bmatrix} & & & 0 \\ p^T & r^T & v^T & 0 \\ & & & 0 \\ & & & 1 \end{bmatrix} = [0 \quad 0 \quad 0 \quad d]$$

The matrix will have an inverse if $p$, $r$ and $v$ are not collinear and if the choice for the extra degree of freedom does not make the matrix singular. If the matrix $Q$ can be inverted, we have $\gamma^T = [0 \quad 0 \quad 0 \quad d]Q^{-1}$, where $d$ can be any nonzero number, say det $Q$.

6. Transformations of the $(n + 1)$ homogeneous space are performed with a $4 \times 4$ matrix $H$. This transformation matrix is of the same form as the transformations introduced in Chapter 22.

a.  Points transform as $v' = vH$
b.  Planes transform as $\gamma' = H^{-1}\gamma$
c.  Parametric lines transform as do points: $L' = LH$

7. The translation transformation $T$ is simply an extended form of the two-dimensional form. Letting $v = [v_1 \quad v_2 \quad v_3 \quad v_4]$, we have

$$T = \begin{bmatrix} 1 & 0 & 0 & 0 \\ 0 & 1 & 0 & 0 \\ 0 & 0 & 1 & 0 \\ -v_1/v_4 & -v_2/v_4 & -v_3/v_4 & 1 \end{bmatrix}$$

8. The plane $\gamma$ is parallel to the plane $\lambda$ through a point $v$:

a.  Prepare $T$ from $v$ as in item 7.
b.  $\gamma = TJ\lambda$, where

$$J = \begin{bmatrix} 1 & 0 & 0 & 0 \\ 0 & 1 & 0 & 0 \\ 0 & 0 & 1 & 0 \\ 0 & 0 & 0 & 0 \end{bmatrix}$$

To show that these planes are parallel, we shall consider a point $v$ on $\lambda$, and show that the distance from $v$ to $\gamma$ is constant. We shall use technique 3 for the computation, but the normalization is not necessary: we ensure $w = 1$ by choosing the representation of $v$ accordingly, and note that the remainder of the normalization depends only on the formulation of $\gamma$, and not on $v$. Letting $v = [x \quad y \quad z \quad 1]$, and noting that $[x \quad y \quad z \quad 1] \cdot \lambda = 0$, we have

$$\begin{aligned} [x \quad y \quad z \quad 1]\gamma &= [x \quad y \quad z \quad 1]TJ\lambda \\ &= [(x - v_1/v_4) \quad (y - v_2/v_4) \quad (z - v_3/v_4) \quad 0]\lambda \\ &= [x \quad y \quad z \quad 1]\lambda + 1/v_4[-v_1 \quad -v_2 \quad -v_3 \quad -v_4]\lambda \\ &= 1/v_4[-v_1 \quad -v_2 \quad -v_3 \quad -v_4]\lambda \end{aligned}$$

The last expression is constant, i.e., independent of $x$, $y$, and $z$.

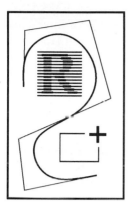

# BIBLIOGRAPHY

This bibliography is intended to serve two purposes: it contains entries for all references made in the text of this book, and it contains additional entries which refer to a spectrum of articles and papers about computer graphics. Because the literature pertaining to computer graphics is immense, the bibliography is rather selective. It concentrates on subjects covered in this book: hardware for input and output, interactive techniques, three-dimensional visualization methods, line-drawing and raster graphics systems, device-independent graphics packages, etc. Applications are covered less well, in part because there are so many.

In order to guide the reader interested in pursuing graphics technology, the bibliography is cross-referenced by subject headings. The paragraphs below attempt to provide brief annotations of the papers. Lists of several references are approximately ordered by pertinence of the paper: especially relevant or readily-available items are given first.

## B-1 Introduction

The flavor of computer graphics is perhaps best represented in an article by Sutherland [460] and two by Licklider [291, 293]. Other papers by these two are inspirational [463, 289, 292], or report on developments in the graphics field [461, 290]. Other survey articles of general interest are [118, 486, 228, 120, 315, 154].

The early days of computer graphics saw the development of some important systems that showed the potential of graphics and inspired many researchers. Sketchpad [462, 323] was an outstanding example. At almost the same time, the power of interactive computing was illustrated by JOSS [438]. The GRAIL project at RAND showed a remarkable integration of interactive graphical functions to create a complete programming environment [155, 156, 383]. The rich environment designed by Englebart applied advanced interactive techniques to help people write documents or work on projects together [158].

Papers of Licklider (particularly [292]) hint at the potential of graphics technology. An early article by Bush [84] is particularly interesting in the light of more recent developments of graphics.

Literature on graphics appears in many places. The Special Interest Group on Graphics of the Association for Computing Machinery (SIGGRAPH-ACM) is the most active organization of graphics professionals. It publishes the journal *Computer Graphics* quarterly and holds an annual conference. The journal *Computer Graphics and Image Processing* is partly devoted to computer graphics. Occasional articles on graphics are published in *Communications of the Association for Computing Machinery* (*CACM*), *Computer Journal, AFIPS National Computer Conference* (*NCC*), and *IFIP Proceedings*. Other journals are oriented toward application areas: *Computers and Graphics* (applications in general), *Computer Aided Design, Computer Graphics and Image Processing.* Several books and conference proceedings have been devoted entirely to computer graphics, and contain good collections of papers: [434, 169, 368, 369].

Films and video tapes are the best way to illustrate an interactive computer graphics program. A survey of films available is [447]. Films that show interactive computer graphics systems in operation are [323, 324, 383, 453, 25, 261, 482]. Films made with the aid of computer animation systems are [116, 25, 318, 38, 435, 153].

### B-2 Display Hardware and Techniques

*Displays.* The technology of display hardware is surveyed in [136]. This reference describes digital and analog control electronics, phosphor characteristics, manufacturing methods, etc. Other material on display systems is contained in [439] and [295]. Trends in display design are described in [351].

The cathode ray tube (CRT) is described in [132, 433, 243]. The Williams tube [512] is of historical interest, used for data storage in Whirlwind [166]. Whirlwind also used a CRT as an output device. Descriptions of some of the newer types of display can be found in the literature: plasma panel [49, 202, 224, 441, 371, 502, 74]; direct view storage tube (DVST) [456, 223, 477]; silicon target tube [377, 378]; liquid crystal displays [124, 281]; the laser display [523]; color plotters [222, 245]. A computer-controlled milling machine for making foam models is described in [178].

*Display processors.* Each kind of imaging technology requires some kind of *controller* or *display processor* to connect it to a computer. Unfortunately, the design of display processors is not adequately documented. A paper that describes the problems faced by the designer and introduces the "Wheel of Reincarnation" is [331]. Interesting processor designs for refresh displays are [163, 164, 501, 144, 86]. Other refresh designs are described in [481, 235, 491, 490, 215, 238]. Tektronix has set the standard in processors for storage-tube terminals, such as [475]. Of historical interest are [27] and [145], which describe early display processor designs.

Raster-scan display controllers are unlike controllers for random-scan displays. They generate video signals, which usually conform to a television standard [370, 509]. Early raster-scan displays were refreshed from rotating disk memories [476, 362, 424], or, equivalently, from semiconductor shift registers [312]. Another early approach used random-scan displays to generate the image, and used video technology to record it and to distribute it to terminals [485, 296]. The random-access frame buffer was explored first by Noll [360]. Decreasing memory prices have made frame buffers increasingly attractive [140, 253, 195, 31, 280]. Some frame buffers have video-generation techniques that allow scaling, translation, or combination of several images [174, 336, 160]. To economize on memory, run-coding techniques have been used [233, 279]. Video-generation hardware designed for characters can be adapted to produce line-drawings [249].

Special hardware techniques have been developed to aid common operations in computer graphics: three-dimensional display [459, 163, 215, 490, 386, 218, 88]; stereoscopic viewing [459, 274, 365, 408, 363]; scan-conversion [101]; hidden-surface elimination and shading [162, 428]. In addition, many of the algorithms mentioned in Section B-6 have been implemented in hardware.

Other articles on display equipment of various kinds are [230, 398, 497, 480, 206, 212, 216, 313].

The *Computer Display Review* [256] gives characteristics of the many displays currently marketed, although often the particularly good or poor features of the display are not readily apparent from the descriptions.

## B-3 Input Hardware and Techniques

Hardware used for input includes tablet devices [135, 71, 474, 484, 431, 374, 322], the SRI mouse [159], and many others. For descriptions of interfaces of tablets to large time-sharing systems, see [131, 194, 334]. Devices which record three-dimensional input information are described in [405, 459, 190, 82, 81]; a brief survey is given in the Appendix of [190]. Experimental devices to impart a kinesthetic sense of "feel" are described in [196, 33]. Evaluations that compare the use of various input devices are presented in [239, 89].

A characterization of interactive techniques is given by Foley and Wallace in [177]; more detail is given in [495]. Specific interactive techniques are often illustrated in movies of graphics programs in action (see Section B-1). Of special note are character recognition methods: a survey of both on-line and off-line methods with a good bibliography appears in [329]; see also [149]. Specific systems of note are [209, 473, 51, 42, 40, 131]. Systems that use character recognition extensively are Grail [383, 155, 156]; also [11, 229, 240]. Signature recognition is described in [220]. Techniques for recognizing and cleaning up freehand sketches are described in [221, 337]. Parsing of line-drawing inputs is described in [437]. A facility for remembering input interactions and selectively re-using them is described in [478]. The light handle technique is described in [344]. See also [457, 462, 265, 159, 239, 158] for input techniques.

### B-4 Graphics Systems

*Packages.* A survey of approaches to designing graphics packages is given in [353]. A large number of current packages are surveyed in [168]. Early noteworthy packages are GRAF [234], GINO [522], and others [85, 519, 425]. Two good examples of packages with structured display files are [58, 198] and [479].

Most modern graphics packages provide some degree of device-independence. Examples are GINO-F [115], Omnigraph [449, 333], GPGS [489], DISSPLA [237], and the ARPA network graphics protocol [452]. Efforts to standardize a device-independent graphics package have resulted in several proposals [355]. In the United States, ACM/SIGGRAPH has proposed a standard *core graphics system*, described in [320, 39, 319, 90], and described in detail in [533]. An implementation is described in [285].

Techniques for building graphics packages for raster displays are less well developed than those for random-scan displays. Two examples are [448, 450].

*Languages.* Many researchers have proposed developing special programming languages or extending existing programming languages to support graphics. Display procedures [349] have been incorporated in Euler-G [352]. Kulsrud's system [270] is also noteworthy. PL/I has been extended for graphics [443]. Other languages are Ambit-G [103, 105, 422], Grin-2 [104], Smalltalk [280, 236], Leap [171, 421, 387], Logo [348], and several others [372, 480, 468, 234, 117, 361].

*Systems.* Graphics applications can be implemented in different programming environments: time-sharing systems, single-user computers, "satellite" systems, or networks. Providing graphics services in time-sharing systems is described in [334, 469, 485, 61, 255]. On single-user machines, graphics may benefit from special support [227].

Large and small computers can cooperate in graphics applications, using a "satellite" arrangement: large calculations are done on a central, shared computer; fast interactive response is provided by a small satellite computer connected directly to the display. Thus parts of the application program reside in each computer. Satellite systems are surveyed in [488]. Graphic-1 [358] and Graphic-2 [104, 357] are prime examples of these systems. Other such systems are described in [398, 123, 522, 480, 384]. A study of the design of such a system is [176].

Another kind of graphics system uses a "remote terminal." Although the hardware arrangement may look deceptively similar to that of a satellite graphics system, there is an important difference: the large computer implements the entire application, while the small computer provides only standard graphical services (i.e., the application programmer is not concerned with programming the terminal). Most frequently, terminals are linked to large computers by low-speed communications, as in the case of the storage-tube terminal. Computer communication networks [406] can be used to link a graphics terminal with a remote computer that implements a particular application. Communication protocols are used to control the display [452].

## B-5 Modeling

Many graphics applications embody *geometric models* that are required to generate images on the display and also to perform calculations and manipulations as part of the application program. Although little has been written about two-dimensional modeling as such, some applications provide good examples [68, 462, 480]; see also [32]. Three-dimensional modeling has attracted considerable attention: techniques are surveyed in [26, 179]. Four comprehensive modeling systems are those of Eastman [151, 150], Braid [69, 70], Voelcker [494, 493], and Baumgart [34, 35, 36]. Some systems concentrate on the input of three-dimensional structures [464, 191, 273]. Procedural models are used in [341, 211]. Additional papers are [326, 109, 366, 367, 454, 498].

*Curves and surfaces.* Techniques for modeling curves and surfaces are surveyed in [181, 183]. Introductory material is [110, 410]. An excellent selection of papers is [29]. Bezier techniques are discussed in [47, 182, 45, 46, 199, 201]. B-splines are described in [200, 393, 394, 138, 396, 93, 529]. A great many spline techniques are used; a good general reference is [2]; specific papers are [356, 267, 3, 6]. Rational cubic curves are described in [119, 283, 185, 113, 4, 111]. Coons surfaces are covered in [119, 184, 282, 283, 181, 13, 12, 14]. Cohen describes curves defined by difference equations [112, 111]. Techniques using quadric surfaces are given in [507, 403, 298, 524]. Additional curve and surface techniques are covered in [277, 297, 28, 148, 271, 314, 5]. If a curve has no intrinsic mathematical representation, points on it may be stored compactly with various encoding techniques [188]. Modeling systems using curves and surfaces are described in [12, 13, 173, 528, 108, 107, 147, 525, 1].

*Data structures.* Modeling is supported by data structures that represent the model and that provide for examining and modifying the model. Data structures for this purpose are surveyed in [514, 204]. The description of the Sketchpad data structure [462] is a good introduction to important considerations in graphics. The LEAP data structures are described in [421, 171, 170]. CORAL, a ring structure, is described in [468] and [402]. The use of relational data structures in graphics is described in [515, 516]. Other papers of interest are [470, 102, 278, 487, 328, 508, 123].

### B-6 Algorithms

A wide range of algorithms and techniques are used to generate images. These methods may be implemented with hardware or software. For example, a line-drawing technique is typically implemented in hardware for a random-scan display processor, but may be implemented in software for use with a frame-buffer display.

*Sampling.* Underlying all image-generation is the theory of sampling, which deals with techniques for sensing and reproducing continuous signals (pictures in our case) with digital approximations. General texts are [214, 219]; applications of the theory to digital signal processing are explored in [381, 364]. Stockham discusses the impact of the human visual system on processing [455]. Papers dealing explicitly with sampling in computer graphics are [129, 127, 128, 440, 94].

*Line and curve generation.* Incremental techniques are used to generate sequences of points on lines and curves. The digital differential analyzer (DDA) is described in [16]; Bresenham's method in [73]; see also [258]. Techniques for generating curves are numerous: evaluating parametric polynomials [276, 97, 397]; circles or conics [72, 226, 133, 134, 112, 373, 19]; techniques designed for hardware implementation [142, 52, 401, 163, 459, 458]; others [113, 251].

*Clipping.* The clipping divider is described in [451]; the "homogeneous" version in [59]. The polygon clipping technique is given in [465]; extensions to arbitrary polygonal clipping regions are given in [503].

*Hidden-line and hidden-surface elimination.* Algorithms for making hidden-line and hidden-surface views are among the most interesting in computer graphics. A good characterization of many of the techniques is given in [466]; a bibliography in [207]. Clark describes modeling techniques well suited to hidden-surface and hidden-line elimination [109].

Historically, hidden-line elimination was the first problem attacked. Roberts devised the first algorithm and spurred activity in the area [404, 354]. The Warnock algorithm can generate line drawings [499, 354, 311]. Many algorithms, following the lead of Appel, compute edge-face intersections [10, 193, 294, 189, 306, 305]. Special techniques can be applied to special situations, such as three-dimensional plots of functions $z = f(x, y)$ [517].

Interest in hidden-surface elimination grew from the desire to produce realistic images on raster displays. General Electric designed the first real-time hidden-surface equipment for NASA simulators [419, 420, 511, 427]. Evans initiated an activity at the University of Utah to search for efficient hidden-surface techniques that could function in real time. The Warnock algorithm is one of the results [499, 354, 311]. Romney developed an early scan-line algorithm [411, 412, 526]. Based on Romney's work, Watkins developed a practical scan-line algorithm that has been implemented in hardware [500, 354]. At almost the same time, Bouknight at the University of Illinois developed a scan-line algorithm [63, 64]. The general priority sort was devised by Newell,

Newell, and Sancha [342] and extended by Weiler and Atherton [503]. Newell's procedural modeling and clustering technique is described in [341]. Other hidden-surface programs of interest are [375, 94, 359, 304, 197, 217, 332]. Extensions to show shadows in scenes are given in [17, 65, 254, 126, 513, 9]. Extensions have also been developed to handle smooth surfaces directly, rather than with polyhedral approximations: quadric surfaces [507, 298, 284, 524]; scan-line algorithms for displaying parametric surfaces [275, 276, 54, 55, 510]; patch subdivision [95, 96]; hidden-line elimination [208]. Techniques developed for hidden-surface elimination have been applied to the hidden-line problem [505].

*Raster algorithms.* Very little information on raster-manipulation techniques has been published. Negroponte gives an overview [336]. Scan-conversion techniques are described in [250, 30] and as part of many hidden-surface algorithms. See also [160, 317].

*Shading.* Shading algorithms are intimately tied to shading models. The models often require careful attention to photometry [7] and color reproduction [531, 165, 232, 527]; for graphics applications see [442, 246]. The shading model given in Chapter 25 is that of Phong [77, 76]; Blinn has extended it [56]. Special shading effects are considered in [60, 57, 95, 96]. Smooth shading interpolation is discussed by Gouraud [201] and Phong [77, 76]. Additional shading information can be found in [375, 298]. Proper sampling techniques for shaded images are discussed in [127, 128, 440, 94].

*Halftones.* Shaded images may be displayed on binary (black/white) output devices with halftone techniques. A survey of computer-oriented techniques is [241]; a historical perspective is given in [266]. Among common algorithms are [175, 409, 37, 242]. Photographic halftone methods are described in [152, 531].

*Computational geometry.* Many calculations required in modeling and viewing techniques require solving geometry problems efficiently—hidden-surface elimination is a good example. The design of algorithms to solve these problems has recently advanced dramatically: many of the techniques are presented in [436]. For specific schemes, see [99, 303, 114, 83].

## B-7 The User Interface

Much has been written on the prospects for fruitful man-machine partnership [291, 292, 293, 289]. Progress in achieving the partnership has been slow, and has not yielded much in the way of principles to guide user interface design. Issues of user-interface design span a broad range of technical disciplines: psychology, human factors, task analysis (an area only now being recognized), computer science, etc. This section is organized into the four topics covered in Chapter 28.

*User's model.* Nothing has been written on this topic as a whole. Example user models can be extracted from existing application programs.

*Information display.* Symbology used in graphics is predominantly borrowed from existing (non-computer) graphical practices. Conventions for circuit diagrams, engineering drawings, and the like are well established. Professional illustrators and graphic artists have developed a far better understanding of the uses of shape, tone and spatial relationships in a diagram than have designers of computer graphics programs. For introductions to graphic design, see [66, 44, 43].

Information displayed to a human being is subjected to complex interpretation by the viewer's visual system. An understanding of that system is required to achieve many visual effects: stereopsis, motion, precise shading and coloration, etc. General texts on perception are [121, 91, 205, 137, 98]. A treatment oriented toward displayed information is [48]. More specialized works are [385, 252, 286, 165, 316, 455]. Optics systems are often used to present light to the eye; see [432, 244].

*Feedback.* Techniques for providing feedback are rarely considered separately from information display.

*Command language.* The command language of a graphics program must take many factors into account: the user's model, feedback provisions, programming methods, etc. The acceptance by the user is especially important: training time, recovery from errors, novice/expert distinctions, performance (i.e., how fast the user can operate the program) are all important.

Command languages can be studied by example: see [12, 68, 239, 407, 11, 159] or other application program descriptions (movies of interactive programs such as Grail [383] are especially revealing).

Programming techniques for implementing command languages have received more attention. Interpreting a command is similar to parsing and interpreting a computer program; many of the methods developed for parsing are consequently applied to command languages. Some attacks on this problem have been designed especially for the kind of interaction prevalent in graphics: the Reaction Handler [345] is the dominant example. Other papers on graphical command language programming are [346, 478, 400, 12, 14, 123]. The text [300] has some relevance to graphics command languages.

Attempts are just beginning to model the performance of users employing complex command languages. This represents a substantial extension of earlier human factors work that is primarily concerned with how humans perform as part of a *control system* (i.e., tasks such as driving an automobile or flying an airplane). Human factors work has provided considerable information about human performance at low-level manipulation tasks (see, for example, [89, 321]; the journal *Human Factors* is a source of many articles on performance of this sort).

## B-8 Applications

There are so many applications of computer graphics that this section can only hint at some of them. As graphics equipment and techniques become more ubiquitous, interactive graphics becomes just another tool of the application designer.

*Diagrams and illustration.* Many early applications of computer graphics had graphical manipulation as their end goal: Sketchpad [462, 323] and its three-dimensional extension [248] are examples. Another early pursuit was the graphical specification of programs [467, 343, 383, 156, 155, 391, 103, 399]. Programs to make illustrations are becoming more popular, as document-processing and office-information applications grow.

*Computer-aided design.* Engineers and designers have long used diagrams to represent their ideas; computer graphics has been extensively used to aid the design process. For overviews of computer-aided design (CAD) see [118, 120]. Circuit design and printed-circuit layout are the topics of [68, 392, 11, 67]. Several commercial systems for circuit design and engineering drafting are available; an example is [11]. Uses in architecture are covered in [325, 340, 338, 339, 335, 347]. Resch has used graphics as an aid to sculpture [389]. The design of ships, airplanes, and automobiles is aided with geometric modeling systems. A description of a cost-effective operational CAD system is [376]. See also [271, 100]. Other papers related to CAD are [418, 480, 416, 494, 350, 257, 12, 13]. See also Section B-5.

The current trend in CAD is away from simple drafting and picture-generation, and toward the construction and management of engineering data-bases. Current work in CAD is reported in the journal *Computer Aided Design* and at an annual *Design Automation Conference.*

*Computer animation.* Animation is used to teach and to entertain; computer processing can be used to manage the large number of pictures that must be generated, to help interpolate between successive frames, or to help draw (or compute) the frames. Computer animation techniques are surveyed in [504]; see also [262, 8]. Baecker developed an early system [22, 23, 24, 25] and extended it to shaded pictures [20]. Knowlton's system is another early and productive one [260, 263, 38, 261]. Other animation efforts are reported in [130, 139, 287, 367, 80, 225]. Uses of animation in education are described or illustrated in [435, 153, 429, 231, 307]. Animations are sometimes the most effective way to see the results of a simulation [122, 496]. The animation of computer programs for instructional purposes is explored in [21, 146, 530]. Artists and filmmakers use computer animation [106, 78, 79, 471]. The television and entertainment industries are beginning to use various forms of computer-generated images [125, 116, 304].

*Mathematical modeling and data analysis.* Interactive programs, many of which use graphics, are used to explore mathematical models of physical processes and to analyze data. Such systems are surveyed in [444]. Examples of modeling systems are [259, 210]. Systems for exploring mathematical topics are [288, 302, 301, 51, 521]. Graphics is used extensively to search for patterns in experimental data [483, 87]. Additional systems are [272, 379, 445, 269].

*Other applications.* Additional applications include: use in programming environments [158, 157, 472, 280]; typography and page layout [267, 141, 299, 482]; simulation (flight or ship navigation) [532, 50, 506]; fast searching of data bases [407, 158, 157]; three-dimensional reconstruction [310]; molecular modeling [172, 518]; pharmacology [92]; education and art [139, 430, 280, 426]; image processing [414, 41, 446]; analysis of moving images [192].

## B-9 Mathematics

The mathematical concepts used throughout this book are described in many standard mathematics texts. An introduction to matrix techniques can be found in [18]. More detailed treatments of analysis techniques are found in [75, 187, 380].

Homogeneous coordinate systems are described fully in [309] and [308], although the treatment is not particularly applicable to graphics (reference [308] depends on [309]). A good introduction for graphics use is [4]. Roberts lists most of the useful constructs in [403]; see also [53]. Topological properties of projective spaces are considered in [395].

Numerical methods for computers are treated in many texts on numerical analysis. References [186, 268, 382] are only a few.

Standard geometry texts describe projective geometries of the type used for perspective display of three-dimensional objects [167, 492].

Abbreviations used in the bibliography listing:

| | |
|---|---|
| ACM | Association for Computing Machinery, 1133 Avenue of the Americas, New York, N.Y. 10036 |
| AFIPS | American Federation of Information-Processing Societies |
| *CACM* | Communications of the Association for Computing Machinery |
| CFSTI | Clearinghouse for Federal Scientific and Technical Information |
| *FJCC* | Fall Joint Computer Conference |
| IEEE | Institute for Electrical and Electronic Engineers, 345 E. 47th St., New York, N.Y. 10017 |
| IFIPS | International Federation of Information-Processing Societies |
| *JACM* | Journal of the Association for Computing Machinery |
| NCC | National Computer Conference, proceedings published by AFIPS Press, Montvale, N.J. |
| NTIS | National Technical Information Service, U.S. Department of Commerce, Springfield, Va. 22161 |
| *SJCC* | Spring Joint Computer Conference |

1. Agin, G. J.: "Representation and Description of Curved Objects," *Stanford Univ., Comput. Sci. Dept.,* STAN-CS-72-305, October 1972.
2. Ahlberg, J. H., E. N. Nilson, and J. L. Walsh: *Theory of Splines and their Applications,* Academic, New York, 1967.
3. Ahuja, D. V.: "An Algorithm for Generating Spline-like Curves," *IBM Syst. J.,* 7(3/4):206, 1968.
4. Ahuja, D. V. and S. A. Coons: "Geometry for Construction and Display," *IBM Syst. J.,* 7(3/4):188, 1968.
5. Akima, H.: "A Method of Bivariate Interpolation and Smooth Surface Fitting Based on Local Procedures," *CACM,* 17(1):18, January 1974.
6. Akima, H.: "A New Method of Interpolation and Smooth Curve Fitting Based on Local Procedures," *JACM,* 17(4):589, October 1970.
7. Akin, R. H. and J. M. Hood: "Photometry," in H. R. Luxenberg and R. L. Kuehn (eds.), *Display Systems Engineering,* McGraw-Hill, New York, 1968.
8. Anderson, S. E.: "Computer Animation: A Survey," *J. Micrograph.,* 5(1).13, September 1971.
9. Appel, A.: "Some Techniques for Shading Machine-Renderings of Solids," *SJCC 1968,* Thompson Books, Washington, D.C., p. 37.
10. Appel, A.: "The Notion of Quantitative Invisibility and the Machine Rendering of Solids," *Proc. ACM Nat. Conf.,* Thompson Books, Washington, D.C., 1967, p. 387.
11. Applicon Inc.: "Computerized Graphic Processing Systems: Systems User's Manual," Applicon, Inc., 154 Middlesex Turnpike, Burlington, Mass. 01803, September 1973.
12. Armit, A. P.: "Computer Systems for Interactive Design of Three-dimensional Shapes," Ph.D. thesis, Univ. Cambridge, November 1970.
13. Armit, A. P.: "Multipatch and Multiobject Design Systems," *Proc. R. Soc. Lond.,* A321(1545):235, 1971.
14. Armit, A. P.: "The Interactive Languages of Multipatch and Multiobject Design Systems," *Comput. Aided Design,* 4(1):10, Autumn 1971.
15. Armit, A. P. and A. R. Forrest: "Interactive Surface Design," *Comput. Graphics 1970,* Brunel University, April 1970.
16. Armstrong, J. R.: "Design of a Graphic Generator for Remote Terminal Application," *IEEE Trans.,* C-22(5):464-468, May 1973.
17. Atherton, P., K. Weiler, and D. Greenberg: "Polygon Shadow Generation," *Comput. Graphics,* 12(3):275, August 1978.
18. Ayres, F.: *Theory and Problems of Matrices,* McGraw-Hill, New York, 1967.
19. Badler, N. I.: "Disk Generators for a Raster Display Device," *Comput. Graphics Image Processing,* 6(6):589-593, December 1977.
20. Baecker, R. M.: "A Conversational Extensible System for the Animation of Shaded Images," *Comput. Graphics,* 10(2):32-39, Summer 1976.
21. Baecker, R. M.: "From the Animated Student to the Animated Computer to the Animated Film to the Animated Student . . .," p. 106 in *Proc. Purdue 1971 Symp. on Appl. Comput. Electr. Eng. Educ.,* Purdue Univ., 1971.
22. Baecker, R. M.: "GENESYS: Interactive Computer-Mediated Animation," p. 97 in J. Halas (ed.), *Computer Animation,* Hastings House, New York, 1974.
23. Baecker, R. M.: "Interactive Computer-mediated Animation," *MIT Project MAC,* TR-61, April 1969.
24. Baecker, R. M.: "Picture-driven Animation," *SJCC 1969,* AFIPS Press, Montvale, N.J., p. 273.
25. Baecker, R. M., L. Smith, and E. Martin: *GENESYS: An Interactive Computer-mediated Animation System,* film available from Digital Computers Group, MIT Lincoln Lab., Lexington, Mass. 02173.
26. Baer, A., C. Eastman, and M. Henrion: "A Survey of Geometric Modeling," *Carnegie-Mellon Univ., Inst. Physical Planning Rep.* 66, March 1977.
27. Ball, N. A., H. Q. Foster, W. H. Long, I. E. Sutherland, and R. L. Wigington: "A Shared Memory Computer Display System," *IEEE Trans.,* EC-15(5):750, October 1966.

28. Barnhill, R. E., J. H. Brown, and I. M. Klucewicz: "A New Twist in Computer Aided Geometric Design," *Comput. Graphics Image Processing*, **8**(1):78–91, August 1978.

29. Barnhill, R. E. and R. F. Riesenfeld (eds.): *Computer Aided Geometric Design*, Academic, New York, 1975.

30. Barrett, R. C. and B. W. Jordan, Jr.: "Scan-conversion Algorithms for a Cell Organized Raster Display," *CACM*, **17**(3):157, March 1974.

31. Baskett, F. and L. Shustek: "The Design of a Low-Cost Video Graphics Terminal," *Comput. Graphics*, **10**(2):235–240, Summer 1976.

32. Baskin, H. B. and S. P. Morse: "A Multilevel Modeling Structure for Interactive Graphic Design," *IBM Syst. J.*, 7(3/4):218, 1968.

33. Batter, J. J. and F. P. Brooks, Jr.: "GROPE-1: A Computer Display to the Sense of Feel," *IFIP 1971*, North-Holland, Amsterdam, p. TA-4-188.

34. Baumgart, B. G.: "A Polyhedron Representation for Computer Vision," *NCC 1975*, p. 589.

35. Baumgart, B. G.: "GEOMED: A Geometric Editor," *Stanford Univ. Comput. Sci. Dept.*, AIM-232, STAN-CS-74-414, May 1974.

36. Baumgart, B. G.: "Geometric Modeling for Computer Vision," *Stanford Univ. Comput. Sci. Dept.*, AIM-249, STAN-CS-74-463, October 1974.

37. Bayer, B. E.: "An Optimum Method for Two-Level Rendition of Continuous-Tone Pictures," *IEEE 1973 Int. Conf. on Communications*, p. 26.11.

38. Bell Telephone Laboratories: *Incredible Machine*, film available from Film Library, Bell Telephone Laboratories, Murray Hill, N.J., 07974.

39. Bergeron, D., P. Bono, and J. D. Foley: "Graphics Programming Using the Core System," *Comput. Surv.*, **10**(4), 1978.

40. Bernstein, M. I. and T. G. Williams: "A Two-dimensional Programming System," *IFIP 1968*, North-Holland, Amsterdam, p. 586.

41. Bernstein, R.: "Digital Processing of Earth Observation Imagery," *IFIP 1974*, North-Holland, Amsterdam, p. 733.

42. Berson, T. A.: "Dynamic Handwriting Recognition by Computer," Ph.D. thesis, Univ. London, May 1977. University Microfilms 77-70026.

43. Bertin, J.: *La Graphique et le Traitement Graphique de l'Information*, Flammarion, Paris, 1977.

44. Bertin, J.: *Semiologie Graphique*, Mouton, Gauthier-Villars, Paris, 1973.

45. Bezier, P.: *Emploi des Machines a Commande Numerique*, Masson et Cie., Paris, 1970.

46. Bezier, P.: "Mathematical and Practical Possibilities of UNISURF," in R. E. Barnhill and R. F. Riesenfeld (eds.), *Computer Aided Geometric Design*, Academic, New York, 1974.

47. Bezier, P.: *Numerical Control—Mathematics and Applications*, A. R. Forrest (trans.), Wiley, London, 1972.

48. Biberman, L. M.: *Perception of Displayed Information*, Plenum, New York, 1973.

49. Bitzer, D. L. and H. G. Slottow: "The Plasma Panel: A Digitally Addressable Display with Inherent Memory," *FJCC 1966*, Spartan Books, Washington, D.C., p. 541.

50. Black, S. R.: "Digital Processing of 3-D Data to Generate Interactive Real-Time Dynamic Pictures," *Proc. Soc. Photo-Optical Instrum. Eng.*, vol. 120, "Three-Dimensional Imaging," August 1977, p. 52.

51. Blackwell, F. W. and R. H. Anderson: "An On-line Symbolic Mathematics System Using Hand-printed Two-dimensional Notation," *RAND Mem.* RM-6018-PR, January 1970.

52. Blatt, H.: "Conic Display Generator Using Multiplying Digital-Analog Converters," *FJCC 1967*, Thompson Books, Washington, D.C., p. 177.

53. Blinn, J. F.: "A Homogeneous Formulation for Lines in 3-Space," *Comput. Graphics*, **11**(2):237–241, Summer 1977.

54. Blinn, J. F.: "A Scan-Line Algorithm for Displaying Parametrically Defined Surfaces," in supplement to SIGGRAPH 78, *Comput. Graphics*, **12**(3), August 1978.

55. Blinn, J. F.: "Computer Display of Curved Surfaces," *Jet Propulsion Lab. Tech. Rep.* 1060-126, October 1978.

56. Blinn, J. F.: "Models of Light Reflection for Computer Synthesized Pictures," *Comput. Graphics*, **11**(2):192, Summer 1977.

57. Blinn, J. F.: "Simulation of Wrinkled Surfaces," *Comput. Graphics*, **12**(3):286, August 1978.

58. Blinn, J. F. and A. C. Goodrich: "The Internal Design of the IG Routines: An Interactive Graphics System for a Large Time-sharing Environment," *Comput. Graphics,* **10**(2):229–234, Summer 1976.
59. Blinn, J. F. and M. E. Newell: "Clipping Using Homogeneous Coordinates," *Comput. Graphics,* **12**(3):245, August 1978.
60. Blinn, J. F. and M. E. Newell: "Texture and Reflection in Computer Generated Images," *CACM,* **19**(10):542, October 1976.
61. Bond, A. H., J. Rightnour, and L. S. Coles: "An Interactive Graphical Display Monitor in a Batch-processing Environment with Remote Entry," *CACM,* **12**(11):595, November 1969.
62. Booth, D. F. and N. Burtnyk: "Simulation of Three-dimensional Objects on a Two-dimensional Computer Display," *Bull. Inf. Proc. Soc. Can.,* 1968.
63. Bouknight, W. J.: "A Procedure for Generation of Three-dimensional Half-toned Computer Graphics Representations," *CACM,* **13**(9):527, September 1970.
64. Bouknight, W. J.: "An Improved Procedure for Generation of Half-tone Computer Graphics Representations," *Univ. Ill., Coord. Sci. Lab.,* R-432, September 1969.
65. Bouknight, W. J. and K. C. Kelley: "An Algorithm for Producing Half-tone Computer Graphics Presentations with Shadows and Movable Light Sources," *SJCC 1970,* AFIPS Press, Montvale, N.J., p. 1.
66. Bowman, W. J.: *Graphic Communication,* Wiley, New York, 1968.
67. Bracchi, G. and M. Somalvico: "An Interactive Software System for Computer Aided Design: An Application to Circuit Project," *CACM,* **13**(9):537, September 1970.
68. Brackett, J. W., M. Hammer, and D. E. Thornhill: "Case Study in Interactive Graphics Programming: A Circuit Drawing and Editing Program for Use with a Storage-Tube Display Terminal," *MIT Project MAC,* TR-63, October 1969.
69. Braid, I. C.: "Designing with Volumes," 2nd ed., Cantab Press, 97 Hurst Park Ave., Cambridge, U.K., 1974.
70. Braid, I. C.: "The Synthesis of Solids Bounded by Many Faces," *CACM,* **18**(4):209–216, April 1975.
71. Brenner, A. E. and P. de Bruyne: "A Sonic Pen: A Digital Stylus System," *IEEE Trans.,* EC–**19**(6):546, June 1970.
72. Bresenham, J. E.: "A Linear Algorithm for Incremental Digital Display of Circular Arcs," *CACM,* **20**(2):100–106, February 1977.
73. Bresenham, J. E.: "Algorithm for Computer Control of a Digital Plotter," *IBM Syst. J.,* **4**(1):25–30, 1965.
74. Brown, F. H. and M. T. Zayac: "A Multi-color Plasma Panel Display," Owens-Illinois, 1971.
75. Browne, E. T.: *Introduction to Theory of Determinants and Matrices,* University of North Carolina Press, Chapel Hill, 1958.
76. Bui-Tuong, Phong: "Illumination for Computer-generated Images," *Univ. Utah Comput. Sci. Dept.,* UTEC-CSc-73-129, July 1973. NTIS ADA-008 786.
77. Bui-Tuong, Phong: "Illumination for Computer-Generated Pictures," *CACM,* **18**(6):311–317, June 1975.
78. Burtnyk, N. and M. Wein: "A Computer Animation System for the Animator," *Proc. 1971 UAIDE Annu. Meet.,* Stromberg Datagraphix.
79. Burtnyk, N. and M. Wein: "Computer-generated Key-Frame Animation," *J. Soc. Motion Pict. Telev. Eng.,* **80**(3):149, March 1971.
80. Burtnyk, N. and M. Wein: "Interactive Skeleton Techniques for Enhancing Motion Dynamics in Key Frame Animation," *CACM,* **19**(10):564, October 1976.
81. Burton, R. P.: "Real-Time Measurement of Multiple Three-dimensional Positions," *Univ. Utah Comput. Sci. Dept.,* UTEC-CSc-72-122, 1972. NTIS AD-762 028.
82. Burton, R. P. and Sutherland I. E.: "Twinkle Box: A Three-dimensional Computer Input Device," *NCC 1974,* pp. 513-520.
83. Burton, W.: "Representation of Many-sided Polygons and Polygonal Lines for Rapid Processing," *CACM,* **20**(3):166, March 1977.
84. Bush, V.: "As We May Think," *Atl. Mon.,* July 1945.

85. California Computer Products, Inc.: "Calcomp Subroutine Package Reference Manual," California Computer Products, Inc., 2411 W. La Palma Ave., Anaheim, Calif. 92801.

86. Callan, J. F.: "Key Decisions in Designing the Picture System," *SID J.*, **11**(1):18, January 1974.

87. Calvert, T. W.: "Projections of Multidimensional Data for Use in Man-Computer Graphics," *FJCC 1968*, Thompson Books, Washington, D.C., p. 227.

88. Capowski, J. J.: "Matrix Transform Processor for Evans and Sutherland LDS-2 Graphics System," *IEEE Trans.*, **C–27**(7):703, July 1976.

89. Card, S. K., W. K. English, and B. Burr: "Evaluation of Mouse, Rate-controlled Isometric Joystick, Step Keys, and Text Keys for Text Selection on a CRT," Xerox Palo Alto Research Center, SSL-77-1, April 1977.

90. Carlbom, I. and J. Paciorek: "Geometric Projection and Viewing Transformations," *Comput. Surv.*, **10**(4), 1978.

91. Carterette, E. C. and M. P. Friedman (eds.): *Handbook of Perception*, Vol. V., *Seeing*, Academic, New York, 1975.

92. Castleman, P. A. et al: "The Implementation of the PROPHET System," *NCC 1974*, p. 457.

93. Catmull, E. and J. Clark: "Recursively Generated B-Spline Surfaces on Arbitrary Topological Meshes," *Comput. Aided Design*, **10**(6), November 1978.

94. Catmull, E. E.: "A Hidden-Surface Algorithm with Anti-aliasing," *Comput. Graphics*, **12**(3):6, August 1978.

95. Catmull, E. E.: "A Subdivision Algorithm for Computer Display of Curved Surfaces," *Univ. Utah Comput. Sci. Dept.*, UTEC-CSc-74-133, December 1974. NTIS A-004968/Ad/A-004973.

96. Catmull, E. E.: "Computer Display of Curved Surfaces," *Proc. IEEE Conf. on Computer Graphics, Pattern Recognition and Data Structure*, May 1975, p. 11.

97. Chaikin, G. M.: "An Algorithm for High-Speed Curve Generation," *Comput. Graphics Image Processing*, **3**:346–349, 1974.

98. Chase, W. G. (ed.): *Visual Information Processing*, Academic, New York, 1973.

99. Chasen, S. H.: *Geometric Principles and Procedures for Computer Graphic Applications*, Prentice-Hall, Englewood Cliffs, N.J., 1978.

100. Chasen, S. H.: "The Introduction of Man Computer Graphics into the Aerospace Industry," *FJCC 1965*, Spartan Books, Washington, D.C., p. 883.

101. Cheek, T. B.: "A Graphic Display System Using Raster-Scan Monitors and Real-Time Scan Conversion," *1973 SID Int. Symp. Dig. Tech. Papers*, May 1973, p. 56.

102. Childs, D. L.: "Description of a Set-theoretic Data Structure," *FJCC 1968*, Thompson Books, Washington, D.C., p. 557.

103. Christensen, C.: "An Example of the Manipulation of Directed Graphs in the AMBIT/G Programming Language," in M. Klerer and J. Reinfelds (eds.), *Interactive Systems for Experimental and Applied Mathematics*, Academic, New York, 1968.

104. Christensen, C. and E. N. Pinson: "Multi-function Graphics for a Large Computer System," *FJCC 1967*, Thompson Books, Washington, D.C., p. 697.

105. Christensen, C., M. S. Wolfberg, and M. J. Fischer: "A Report on AMBIT/G," *Applied Data Research Rep.* CA-7102-2611, -2612, -2613, -2614, February 1971.

106. Citron, J. and J. H. Whitney: "CAMP: Computer Assisted Movie Production," *FJCC 1968*, Thompson Books, Washington, D.C., p. 1290.

107. Clark, J. H.: "3-D Design of Free-Form B-Spline Surfaces," *Univ. Utah Comput. Sci. Dept.*, UTEC-CSc-74-120, September 1975. NTIS A002736/AD/A002736.

108. Clark, J. H.: "Designing Surfaces in 3-D," *CACM*, **19**(8):454, August 1976.

109. Clark, J. H.: "Hierarchical Geometric Models for Visible Surface Algorithms," *CACM*, **19**(10):547, October 1976.

110. Clark, J. H.: "Parametric Curves, Surfaces, and Volumes in Computer Graphics and Computer-aided Geometric Design," NASA Ames Research Center, 1978.

111. Cohen, D.: "Incremental Methods for Computer Graphics," *Dept. Eng. Appl. Math., Harvard Univ.*, ESD-TR-69-193, April 1969.

112. Cohen, D.: "On Linear Difference Curves," *Dept. Eng. Appl. Math., Harvard Univ.*, 1969. Also in *Computer Display Review*, see [256].

113. Cohen, D. and T. M. P. Lee: "Fast Drawing of Curves for Computer Display," *SJCC 1969*, AFIPS Press, Montvale, N.J., p. 297.

114. Comba, P. G.: "A Procedure for Detecting Intersections of Three Dimensional Objects," *JACM*, **15**(3):354, July 1968.

115. Computer Aided Design Centre: "GINO-F User Manual," Issue 2, Computer Aided Design Centre, Cambridge, England, December 1976.

116. Computer Image Corporation: *Caesar*, film available from Computer Image Corporation, 260 South Beverly Drive, Beverly Hills, Calif., 90212.

117. Conn, A. P.: "GRIND: A Language and Translator for Computer Graphics," *Dartmouth Coll., Thayer School of Eng.*, AFOSR-69-2989 TR, June 1969.

118. Coons, S. A.: "Computer Graphics and Innovative Engineering Design," *Datamation*, May 1966, p. 32.

119. Coons, S. A.: "Surfaces for Computer Aided Design of Space Forms," *MIT Project MAC*, TR-41, June 1967.

120. Coons, S. A.: "The Uses of Computers in Technology," *Sci. Am.*, September 1966.

121. Cornsweet, T. N.: *Visual Perception*, Academic, New York, 1970.

122. Cornwell, B.: "Computer Generated Simulation Films," *Inf. Disp.*, **8**(1):21, January 1971.

123. Cotton, I. W. and F. S. Greatorex, Jr.: "Data Structures and Techniques for Remote Computer Graphics," *FJCC 1968*, Thompson Books, Washington, D.C., p. 533.

124. Creagh, L. T., A. R. Kmetz, and R. A. Reynolds: "Liquid Crystal Displays," *1971 IEEE Int. Conv. Dig.*, p. 630.

125. Crow, F. C.: "Shaded Computer Graphics in the Entertainment Industry," *Computer*, **11**(3):11, March 1978.

126. Crow, F. C.: "Shadow Algorithms for Computer Graphics," *Comput. Graphics*, **11**(2):242, Summer 1977.

127. Crow, F. C.: "The Aliasing Problem in Computer-generated Shaded Images," *CACM*, **20**(11):799, November 1977.

128. Crow, F. C.: "The Aliasing Problem in Computer-synthesized Shaded Images," *Univ. Utah Comput. Sci. Dept.*, UTEC-CSc-76-015, March 1976. NTIS AD/A038979/LL.

129. Crow, F. C.: "The Use of Grayscale for Improved Raster Display of Vectors and Characters," *Comput. Graphics*, **12**(3):1, August 1978.

130. Csuri, C. A.: "Real-Time Computer Animation," *IFIP 1974*, North-Holland, Amsterdam, p. 707.

131. Curry, J. E.: "A Tablet Input Facility for an Interactive Graphics System," *Proc. Int. Joint Conf. on Artif. Intell.*, 1969, p. 33.

132. Czech, J.: *The Cathode Ray Tube Oscilloscope*, Interscience, New York, 1957.

133. Danielsson, P. E.: "Comments on a Circle Generator for Display Devices," *Comput. Graphics Image Processing*, **7**(2):300–301, April 1978.

134. Danielsson, P. E.: "Incremental Curve Generation," *IEEE Trans.*, **C-19**:783, September 1970.

135. Davis, M. R. and T. O. Ellis: "The Rand Tablet: A Man-Machine Graphical Communication Device," *FJCC 1964*, Spartan Books, Baltimore, Md., p. 325.

136. Davis, S.: *Computer Data Displays*, Prentice-Hall, Englewood Cliffs, N.J., 1969.

137. Davson, H. (ed.): *The Eye*, Academic, New York, 1962.

138. deBoor, C.: "On Calculating with B-Splines," *J. Approx. Theory*, **6**:50–62, 1972.

139. DeFanti, T. A.: "The Digital Component of the Circle Graphics Habitat," *NCC 1976*, pp. 195-203.

140. Denes, P. B.: "A Scan-Type Graphics System for Interactive Computing," *Proc. IEEE Conf. on Computer Graphics, Pattern Recognition and Data Structure*, May 1975, p. 21.

141. Denes, P. B. and I. K. Gershkoff: "An Interactive System for Page Layout Design," *Proc. ACM Nat. Conf.*, 1974, p. 212.

142. Dertouzos, M. L. and H. L. Graham: "A Parametric Graphical Display Technique for On-line Use," *FJCC 1966*, Spartan Books, Washington, D.C., p. 201.

143. Deutsch, L. P. and B. W. Lampson: "An Online Editor," *CACM*, **10**(12):793, December 1967.
144. Digital Equipment Corporation: "DEC 338 Programmed Buffered Display," Digital Equipment Corporation, Maynard, Mass., 1966.
145. Digital Equipment Corporation: "Type 340 Precision Incremental CRT Display," Digital Equipment Corporation, Maynard, Mass., 1965.
146. Dionne, M. S. and A. K. Mackworth: "ANTICS: A System for Animating LISP Programs," *Comput. Graphics Image Processing*, **7**(1):105–119, February 1978.
147. Dube, R., G. J. Herron, F. F. Little , and R. F. Riesenfeld: "SURFED: An Interactive Editor for Free-Form Surfaces," *Comput. Aided Design*, **10**(2):111–115, March 1978.
148. Dube, R. P.: "Local Schemes for Computer Aided Geometric Design," PhD thesis, Univ. Utah, Dept. of Mathematics, June 1975.
149. Duda, R. O. and P. E. Hart: "Experiments in the Recognition of Hand-printed Text, II: Context Analysis," *FJCC 1968*, Thompson Books, Washington, D.C., p. 1139.
150. Eastman, C., J. Lividini, and D. Stoker: "A Database for Designing Large Physical Systems," *NCC 1975*, p. 603.
151. Eastman, C. M. and M. Henrion: "GLIDE: A Language for Design Information Systems," *Comput. Graphics*, **11**(2):24, Summer 1977.
152. Eastman Kodak: "Halftone Methods for the Graphic Arts," Data Book Q-3, Eastman Kodak Company, Rochester, N.Y., 1968.
153. Educational Development Corporation: *Movies from Computers: An Interim Report*, 1969, and other computer animation films, available from Film Library, Educational Development Corporation, 39 Chapel St., Newton, Mass. 02160.
154. Ellis, T. O., J. F. Heafner, and W. L. Sibley: "Interactive Man-Machine Communications," *Instrum. Control*, **44**(1):92.
155. Ellis, T. O., J. F. Heafner, and W. L. Sibley: "The GRAIL Language and Operations," *RAND Rep.* RM-6001-ARPA, September 1969.
156. Ellis, T. O., J. F. Heafner, and W. L. Sibley: "The GRAIL Project: An Experiment in Man-Machine Communications," *RAND Rep.* RM-5999-ARPA, September 1969.
157. Englebart, D. C. et al: "Computer-augmented Management-System Research and Development of Augmentation Facility," *Stanford Res. Inst.*, RADC-TR-70-82, April 1970.
158. Englebart, D. C. and W. K. English: "A Research Center for Augmenting Human Intellect," *FJCC 1968*, Thompson Books, Washington, D.C., p. 395.
159. English, W. K., D. C. Englebart, and M. L. Berman: "Display-Selection Techniques for Text Manipulation," *IEEE Trans.*, **HFE–8**(1):5, 1967.
160. Entwisle, J.: "An Image-processing Approach to Computer Graphics," *Comput. and Graphics*, **2**(2):111, 1977.
161. Erdahl, A. C.: "Displaying Computer-generated Half-tone Pictures in Real Time," *Univ. Utah Comput. Sci. Dept.*, TR 4-14. NTIS AD-753672.
162. Erdahl, A. C.: "Improved Scene Generator Capability," Final Report NAS-9-14010, Evans and Sutherland Computer Corp., P.O. Box 8700, Salt Lake City, Utah, 84108, October 1977.
163. Evans and Sutherland Computer Corporation: "Line Drawing System Model 1: System Reference Manual," Evans and Sutherland Computer Corp., P.O. Box 8700, Salt Lake City, Utah 84108, 1971.
164. Evans and Sutherland Computer Corporation: "Picture System 2 User's Manual," Evans and Sutherland Computer Corp., P.O. Box 8700, Salt Lake City, Utah, 84108, May 1977.
165. Evans, R. M.: *The Perception of Color*, Wiley, New York, 1974
166. Everett, R. R.: "The Whirlwind I Computer," *Joint AIEE-IRE Conf.*, 1952, *Rev. Electron. Digital Comput.*, February 1952, p. 70.
167. Eves, H.: *A Survey of Geometry*, Allyn and Bacon, Boston, 1965.
168. Ewald, R. H. and R. Fryer (eds.): "Final Report of the GSPC State-of-the-Art Subcommittee," *Comput. Graphics*, **12**(1/2):14, June 1978.
169. Faiman, M. and J. Nievergelt (eds.): *Pertinent Concepts in Computer Graphics*, *Proc. 2nd Univ. Ill. Conf. Comput. Graphics*, University of Illinois Press, Urbana, 1969.

170. Feldman, J. A.: "Aspects of Associative Processing," *MIT Lincoln Lab.* 1965-13, April 1965.
171. Feldman, J. A. and P. D. Rovner: "An Algol-based Associative Language," *CACM*, 12(8):439, August 1969.
172. Feldmann, R. J.: "The Design of Computing Systems for Molecular Modeling," *Ann. Rev. Biophys. Bioeng.*, 5:477–510, 1976.
173. Feng, D. Y. and R. F. Riesenfeld: "A Symbolic System for Computer-aided Development of Surface Interpolants," *Software Pract. Exper.*, 8(4):461–482, July–August 1978.
174. Fisher, M. A. and R. E. Nunley: "Raster Graphics for Spatial Application," *Comput. Graphics*, 9(2):1–8, Summer 1975.
175. Floyd, R. W. and L. Steinberg: "An Adaptive Algorithm for Spatial Gray Scale," *SID 1975 Int. Symp. Dig. Tech. Papers*, p. 36.
176. Foley, J. D.: "An Approach to the Optimum Design of Computer Graphics Systems," *CACM*, 14(6):380, June 1971.
177. Foley, J. D. and V. L. Wallace: "The Art of Natural Graphic Man-Machine Conversation," *Proc. IEEE*, 62(4):462, April 1974.
178. Forrest, A. R.: "A Computer Peripheral for Making Three-dimensional Models," *Automatisme*, 19(6/7):347, June/July 1974.
179. Forrest, A. R.: "A Unified Approach to Geometric Modeling," *Comput. Graphics*, 12(3):264, August 1978.
180. Forrest, A. R.: "Coordinates, Transformations, and Visualization Techniques," *Univ. Cambridge, CAD Group Doc.* 23, June 1969.
181. Forrest, A. R.: "Curves and Surfaces for Computer Aided Design," Ph.D. thesis, Univ. Cambridge, July 1968.
182. Forrest, A. R.: "Interactive Interpolation and Approximation by Bezier Polynomials," *Comput. J.*, 15(1):72, January 1972.
183. Forrest, A. R.: "Mathematical Principles for Curve and Surface Representation," in *Curved Surfaces in Engineering*, I. J. Brown (ed.), IPC Science and Technology Press Ltd., Guildford, Surrey, England, 1972, p. 5.
184. Forrest, A. R.: "On Coons and Other Methods for the Representation of Curved Surfaces," *Comput. Graphics Image Processing*, 1(4):341, 1972.
185. Forrest, A. R.: "The Twisted Cubic Curve," *Univ. Cambridge, Comput. Lab. CAD Doc.* 50, November 1970.
186. Forsythe, G. E. and C. B. Moler: *Computer Solution of Linear Algebraic Systems*, Prentice-Hall, Englewood Cliffs, N.J., 1967.
187. Franklin, J. N.: *Matrix Theory*, Prentice-Hall, Englewood Cliffs, N.J., 1968.
188. Freeman, H.: "Computer Processing of Line-Drawing Images," *Comput. Surv.*, 6(1):57, March 1974.
189. Freeman, H. and P. P. Loutrel: "An Algorithm for the Solution of the Two-dimensional Hidden-Line Problem," *IEEE Trans.*, EC–16(6):784, December 1967.
190. Fuchs, H., J. Duran, and B. Johnson: "A System for Automatic Acquisition of Three-dimensional Data," *NCC 1977*, pp. 49-53.
191. Fuchs, H., Z. M. Kedem, and S. P. Uselton: "Optimal Surface Reconstruction from Planar Contours," *CACM*, 20(10):693, October 1977.
192. Futrelle, R. P.: "GALATEA: Interactive Graphics for the Analysis of Moving Images," *IFIP 1974*, North-Holland, Amsterdam, p. 712.
193. Galimberti, R. and U. Montanari: "An Algorithm for Hidden-Line Elimination," *CACM*, 12(4):206, April 1969.
194. Gallenson, L.: "A Graphics Tablet Display for Use under Timesharing," *FJCC 1967*, Thompson Books, Washington, D.C., p. 689.
195. Genisco Computers Inc.: "GCT-3011 Programmable Graphics Processor," Genisco Computers Inc., Irvine, Calif. 92714.
196. Geyer, K. E. and K. R. Wilson: "Computing with Feeling," *Proc. IEEE Conf. on Computer Graphics, Pattern Recognition and Data Structure*, May 1975, pp. 343-349.

197. Goldstein, R. A.: "The System for Computer Animation by 3-D Objects," *Proc. 1971 UAIDE Annu. Meet.*, Stromberg Datagraphix.
198. Goodrich, A. C.: "Integrated Graphics System User's Guide," Univ. of Michigan, Computing Center Memo 229, Ann Arbor, Mich., January 1976.
199. Gordon, W. J. and R. F. Riesenfeld: "Bernstein-Bezier Methods for the Computer-aided Design of Free-Form Curves and Surfaces," *JACM*, 21(2):293–310, April 1974.
200. Gordon, W. J. and R. F. Riesenfeld: "B-Spline Curves and Surfaces," in R. E. Barnhill and R. F. Riesenfeld (eds.), *Computer Aided Geometric Design*, Academic, New York, 1974.
201. Gouraud, H.: "Computer Display of Curved Surfaces," *Univ. Utah Comput. Sci. Dept.*, UTEC-CSc-71-113, June 1971; NTIS AD-762 018. Abridged version in *IEEE Trans.* C–20(6):623, June 1971.
202. Graff, H. and R. Martel: "A Display Screen with Controlled Electroluminescence," *Information Display*, 2(5):53–57, September 1965.
203. Graham, D. N.: "Image Transmission by Two-dimensional Contour Coding," *Proc. IEEE*, 55(3):336, March 1967.
204. Gray, J. C.: "Compound Data Structures for Computer Aided Design: A Survey," *Proc. ACM Nat. Conf.*, Thompson Books, Washington, D.C., 1967, p. 355.
205. Gregory, R. L.: *Eye and Brain*, 3rd ed., Weidenfeld and Nicholson, London, 1977.
206. Griffin, J.: "Design Considerations for a Low Cost Graphic Computer Terminal: Hardware and Software Compromises," *Int. Conf. Remote Data Process.*, 1969, p. 52.
207. Griffiths, J. G.: "A Bibliography of Hidden-Line and Hidden-Surface Algorithms," *Comput. Aided Design.*, 10(3):203–206, May 1978.
208. Griffiths, J. G.: "A Surface Display Algorithm," *Comput. Aided Design*, 10(1):65–73, January 1978.
209. Groner, G. F.: "Real-Time Recognition of Hand Printed Text," *FJCC 1966*, Spartan Books, Washington, D.C., p. 591.
210. Groner, G. F., R. L. Clark, R. A. Berman, and E. C. DeLand: "BIOMOD: An Interactive Graphics System for Modeling," *FJCC 1971*, AFIPS Press, Montvale, N.J., p. 369.
211. Grossman, D. D.: "Procedural Representation of Three-dimensional Objects," *IBM J. Res. Dev.*, 20(6):582, November 1976.
212. Grover, D. J.: "Low Cost Graphic Display with Serial Access Core," *Comput. Bull.*, 15(1):33, January 1971.
213. Guedj, R. A.: "GRACE: A Sophisticated Graphic Display System," *19th Avionics AGARD Conf. Comput. Disp. Syst.*, NATO, 1970.
214. Guilleman, E. A.: *Theory of Linear Physical Systems*, Wiley, 1963.
215. Hagan, T. G., R. J. Nixon, and L. J. Schaeffer: "The Adage Graphics Terminal," *FJCC 1968*, Thompson Books, Washington, D.C., p. 747.
216. Hambury, J. N., J. Ironside, and G. C. Barney: "An Economical Display System," *Comput. Bull.*, 13(9):314, September 1969.
217. Hamlin, G. and C. W. Gear: "Raster-Scan Hidden Surface Algorithm Techniques," *Comput. Graphics*, 11(2):206, Summer 1977.
218. Hempstead, C. F.: "Motion Perception Using Oscilloscope Display," *Computer Display Review*, see [256].
219. Hendricks, W. A.: *The Mathematical Theory of Sampling*, Scarecrow Press, New Brunswick, N.J., 1956.
220. Herbst, N. M. and C. N. Liu: "Automatic Signature Verification Based on Accelerometry," *IBM J. Res. Dev.*, 21(3):245–253, May 1977.
221. Herot, C. F.: "Graphical Input Through Machine Recognition of Sketches," *Comput. Graphics*, 10(2):97–102, Summer 1976.
222. Hertz, C. H. and A. Mansson: "Color Plotter for Computer Graphics Using Three Electrically Controlled Ink Jets," *IFIP 1974*, North-Holland, Amsterdam, p. 85.
223. Hesse, K. R.: "Improved Memory Tube for Alphanumeric, Graphics and Frame Freezer Applications," *SID Journal*, September-October 1973, p. 19.
224. Hoehn, H. J. and R. A. Martel: "A 60 Line per Inch Plasma Display Panel," *IEEE Trans.* ED–18(9):659, September 1971.

225. Honey, F. J.: "Computer Animated Episodes by Single Axis Rotations," *Proc. UAIDE 1971 Annu. Meet.*, Stromberg Datagraphix. Also in *Purdue Symp. Appl. Comput. Electr. Eng. Educ., Purdue Univ.*, 1971, p. 114.

226. Horn, B. K. P.: "Circle Generator for Display Devices," *Comput. Graphics Image Processing*, 5:280–288, 1976.

227. Hornbuckle, G. D.: "A Multiprogramming Monitor for Small Machines," *CACM*, 10(5):273, May 1967.

228. Hornbuckle, G. D.: "The Computer Graphics/User Interface," *IEEE Trans.*, HFE–8(1):17, March 1967.

229. Hosaka, M. and F. Kimura: "An Interactive Geometrical Design System with Handwriting Input," *IFIP 1977*, North-Holland, Amsterdam, p. 167.

230. Hostovsky, R.: "Design of a Display Processing Unit in a Multi-Terminal Environment," *Univ. Ill. Rep.* 343, July 1969.

231. Huggins, W. H. and D. R. Entwisle: "Computer Animation for the Academic Community," *SJCC 1969*, AFIPS Press, Montvale, N.J., p. 623.

232. Hunt, R. W. G.: *The Reproduction of Color*, 3rd ed., Wiley, New York, 1975.

233. Hunter, G. M.: "Full-Color Television from the Computer, Refreshed by Run Length Codes in Main Memory," *Princeton Univ. Comput. Sci. Lab., Tech. Rep.* 182, April 1975.

234. Hurwitz, A., J. P. Citron, and J. B. Yeaton: "GRAF: Graphical Extensions to FORTRAN," *SJCC 1967*, Thompson Books, Washington, D.C., p. 553.

235. IMLAC Corporation: "IMLAC PDS-1 Users Manual," IMLAC Corporation, Waltham, Mass., 1969.

236. Ingalls, D. H.: "The Smalltalk-76 Programming System Design and Implementation," *Fifth ACM Symp. Prin. Programming Lang.*, January 1978, pp. 9–16.

237. Integrated Software Systems Corp.: "DISSPLA Reference Manual," Integrated Software Systems Corp., San Diego, Calif.

238. International Business Machines Corp.: "IBM 2250 Display Model 3," Form No. A27-2721 0, International Business Machines Corp.

239. Irby, C. H.: "Display Techniques for Interactive Text Manipulation," *NCC 1974*, pp. 247–255.

240. Jarvis, J. F.: "The Line Drawing Editor: Schematic Diagram Editing Using Pattern Recognition Techniques," *Comput. Graphics Image Processing*, 6(5):452–484, October 1977.

241. Jarvis, J. F., C. N. Judice, and W. H. Ninke: "A Survey of Techniques for the Display of Continuous Tone Pictures on Bilevel Displays," *Comput. Graphics Image Processing*, 5(1):13–40, March 1976.

242. Jarvis, J. F. and C. S. Roberts: "A New Technique for Displaying Continuous Tone Images on a Bilevel Display," *IEEE Trans.*, COM–24(8):891–898, August 1976.

243. JEDEC Electron Tube Council: "Optical Characteristics of Cathode Ray Tube Screens," *JEDEC Publ.* 16A, Electronic Institute of America, Washington, D.C., January 1966.

244. Jenkins, F. A. and H. E. White: *Fundamentals of Optics*, McGraw-Hill, 1957.

245. Jern, M.: "Color Jet Plotter," *Comput. Graphics*, 11(1):18, Spring 1977.

246. Joblove, G. H. and D. Greenberg: "Color Spaces for Computer Graphics," *Comput. Graphics*, 12(3):20, August 1978.

247. Johnson, C. I.: "Principles of Interactive Systems," *IBM Syst. J.*, 7(3/4):147, 1968.

248. Johnson, T. E.: "SKETCHPAD III: A Computer Program for Drawing in 3-Dimensions," *MIT Electron. Syst. Lab.*, ESL-TM-173, June 1963. Also in *SJCC 1963*, Spartan Books, Baltimore, Md., p. 347.

249. Jordan, B. W., Jr. and R. C. Barrett: "A Cell Organized Raster Display for Line Drawings," *CACM*, 17(2):70, February 1974.

250. Jordan, B. W., Jr. and R. C. Barrett: "A Scan Conversion Algorithm with Reduced Storage Requirements," *CACM*, 16(11):676, November 1973.

251. Jordan, B. W., W. J. Lennon, and B. C. Holm: "An Improved Algorithm for the Generation of Non-parametric Curves," *IEEE Trans.*, C–22(12):1052–1060, December 1973.

252. Julesz, B. and G. J. Spivak: "Stereopsis Based on Vernier Acuity Cues Alone," *Science*, **157**(3788):563, 1967.

253. Kajiya, J. T., I. E. Sutherland, and E. C. Cheadle: "A Random-Access Video Frame Buffer," *Proc. IEEE Conf. on Computer Graphics, Pattern Recognition and Data Structure*, May 1975, p. 1.

254. Kelley, K. C.: "A Computer Graphics Program for the Generation of Half-tone Images with Shadows," *Univ. Ill. Coord. Sci. Lab.*, R-444, November 1969.

255. Kennedy, J. R.: "A System for Time-Sharing Graphic Consoles," *FJCC 1966*, Spartan Books, Washington, D.C., p. 211.

256. Keydata Corporation: *Computer Display Review*, Keydata Corporation, Watertown, Mass. This review was published annually beginning in 1966, and consisted of reviews of display hardware and selected articles on graphical techniques. Individual articles were retained for several years. The review is now published periodically by GML Associates, 594 Marrett Rd., Lexington, Mass. Articles on graphical techniques are contained in volume 4.

257. Kilgour, A. C.: "Computer Graphics Applied to Computer Aided Design," *Comput. Bull.*, **15**(7):18, January 1971.

258. Klassman, H.: "Some Aspects of the Accuracy of the Approximated Position of a Straight Line on a Square Grid," *Comput. Graphics Image Processing*, **4**:225–235, September 1975.

259. Knott, G. D. and D. K. Reece: "Modelab: A Civilized Curve-fitting System," *Proc. ONLINE 72*, Uxbridge, England, September 1972.

260. Knowlton, K. C.: "A Computer Technique for Producing Animated Movies," *SJCC 1964*, Spartan Books, Baltimore, Md., p. 67.

261. Knowlton, K. C.: *A Computer Technique for the Production of Animated Movies (1967)*, film available from Technical Information Library, Bell Telephone Laboratories, Murray Hill, N.J., 07974.

262. Knowlton, K. C.: "Computer-Animated Movies," in D. Secrest and J. Nievergelt (eds.), *Emerging Concepts in Computer Graphics*, Benjamin, New York, 1968, p. 343.

263. Knowlton, K. C.: "EXPLOR: A Generator of Images from Explicit Patterns, Local Operations, and Randomness," *Proc. 1970 UAIDE Annu. Meet.*, Stromberg Datagraphix, p. 544.

264. Knowlton, K. C.: "Programmer's Description of L-6," *CACM*, **9**(8):616, August 1966.

265. Knowlton, K. C.: "Virtual Pushbuttons as a Means of Person-Machine Interaction," *Proc. IEEE Conf. on Computer Graphics, Pattern Recognition, and Data Structure*, May 1975, pp. 350-351.

266. Knowlton, K. C. and L. Harmon: "Computer-Produced Gray Scales," *Comput. Graphics Image Processing*, **1**(1):1, April 1972.

267. Knuth, D. E.: "Mathematical Typography," *Stanford Univ. Comput. Sci. Dept.*, STAN-CS-78-648, February 1978.

268. Knuth, D. E.: *The Art of Computer Programming*, vol. 1: *Fundamental Algorithms*, vol. 2: *Seminumerical Algorithms*, vol. 3: *Sorting and Searching*, Addison-Wesley, Reading, Mass., 1968–1973.

269. Kubert, B., J. Szabo, and S. Giulieri: "The Perspective Representation of Functions of Two Variables," *JACM*, **15**(2):193, April 1968.

270. Kulsrud, H. E.: "A General Purpose Graphic Language," *CACM*, **11**(4):247, April 1968.

271. Kuo, C.: *Computer Methods for Ship Surface Design*, Longman, 1971.

272. Lafata, P. and J. B. Rosen: "An Interactive Display for Approximation by Linear Programming," *CACM*, **13**(11):651, November 1970.

273. Lafue, G.: "Recognition of Three-dimensional Objects from Orthographic Views," *Comput. Graphics*, **10**(2):103–108, Summer 1976.

274. Land, R. I. and I. E. Sutherland: "Real-Time, Color, Stereo, Computer Displays," *Appl. Opt.*, **8**(3):721, 1969.

275. Lane, J. M. and L. Carpenter: "A Scan-Line Algorithm for the Computer Display of Parametrically Defined Surfaces," Boeing Commercial Airplane Co., Advanced Systems Research and Development Group, Doc. ASRD-2, June 1978.

276. Lane, J. M. and R. F. Riesenfeld: "A Theoretical Development for the Computer Generation and Display of Piecewise Polynomial Surfaces," *IEEE Trans. Pattern Anal. Machine Intell.* to appear.

277. Lane, J. M. and R. F. Riesenfeld: "The Application of Total Positivity to Computer-aided Curve and Surface Design," to appear in *JACM*.

278. Lang, C. A. and J. C. Gray: "ASP: A Ring-implemented Associative Structure Package," *CACM*, **11**(8):550, August 1968.

279. Laws, B. A.: "A Gray-Scale Graphic Processor Using Run-Length Encoding," *Proc. IEEE Conf. on Computer Graphics, Pattern Recognition and Data Structure*, May 1975, p. 7.

280. Learning Research Group: "Personal Dynamic Media," Xerox Palo Alto Research Center, SSL 76-1, 1976. Abridged version in *Computer*, **10**(3):31, March 1977.

281. Lechner, B. J.: "Liquid Crystal Displays," in M. Faiman and J. Nievergelt (eds.), *Pertinent Concepts in Computer Graphics*, University of Illinois Press, Urbana, 1969.

282. Lee, T. M. P.: "A Class of Surfaces for Computer Display," *SJCC 1969*, AFIPS Press, Montvale, N.J., p. 309.

283. Lee, T. M. P.: "Three Dimensional Curves and Surfaces for Rapid Computer Display," *Harvard Univ., Dept. Eng. Appl. Phys.*, ESD-TR-69-189, April 1969.

284. Levin, J.: "A Parametric Algorithm for Drawing Pictures of Solid Objects Composed of Quadric Surfaces," *CACM*, **19**(10):555–563, October 1976.

285. Levine, K.: "Core Standard Graphics Package for the VGI 3400," *Comput. Graphics*, **12**(3):298, August 1978.

286. Levinson, J. Z.: "Psychophysics and TV," in T. S. Huang and O. J. Tretiak (eds.), *Picture Bandwidth Compression*, Gordon and Breach Science Publishers, 1972.

287. Levoy, M.: "A Color Animation System Based on the Multiplane Technique," *Comput. Graphics*, **11**(2):65–71, Summer 1977.

288. Lewis, H. R.: "SHAPESHIFTER: An Interactive Program for Experimenting with Complex-Plane Transformations," *Proc. ACM Nat. Conf.*, 1968, p. 717.

289. Licklider, J. C. R.: "A Picture is Worth a Thousand Words — and It Costs . . .," *SJCC 1969*, AFIPS Press, Montvale, N.J., p. 617.

290. Licklider, J. C. R.: "Man-Computer Communication," in C. A. Cuadra (ed.), *Annu. Rev. Inf. Sci. Technol.*, 3:201, Encyclopedia Britannica, Chicago, 1968.

291. Licklider, J. C. R.: "Man-Computer Partnership," *Int. J. Sci. Technol.*, May 1965.

292. Licklider, J. C. R.: "Man-Computer Symbiosis," *Trans. IRE*, **HFE–1**:4, 1960.

293. Licklider, J. C. R. and W. E. Clark: "On-line Man-Computer Communication," *SJCC 1962*, National Press, Palo Alto, Calif., p. 113.

294. Loutrel, P. P.: "A Solution to the Hidden-Line Problem for Computer-drawn Polyhedra," *IEEE Trans. EC–19*(3):205, March 1970.

295. Luxenberg, H. R. and R. L. Kuehn (eds.): *Display Systems Engineering*, McGraw-Hill, New York, 1968.

296. Macaulay, M.: "A Low Cost Computer Graphic Terminal," *FJCC 1968*, Thompson Books, Washington, D.C., p. 777.

297. MacCallum, K. J.: "Surfaces for Interactive Graphical Design," *Comput. J.*, **13**(4):352, November 1970.

298. Mahl, R.: "Visible Surface Algorithms for Quadric Patches," *IEEE Trans.*, **C–21**(1):1, January 1972.

299. Marcus, A.: "A Prototype Computerized Page-Design System," *Visible Language*, **5**(3):197, 1971.

300. Martin, J.: "Design of Man-Computer Dialogues," Prentice-Hall, Englewood Cliffs, N.J., 1973.

301. Martin, W. A.: "Computer Input/Output of Mathematical Expressions," *2nd Symp. Symb. Algebraic Manip.*, ACM, March 1971, p. 78.

302. Martin, W. A. and R. J. Fateman: "The MACSYMA System," *2nd Symp. Symb. Algebraic Manip.*, ACM, March 1971, p. 59.

303. Maruyama, K.: "A Procedure to Determine Intersections Between Polyhedral Objects," *Int. J. Comp. Inf. Sci.*, **1**(3):255–266, 1972.

304. Mathematical Applications Group, Inc.: "3-D Simulated Graphics," *Datamation*, February 1968.

305. Matsushita, Y.: "A Solution to the Hidden-Line Problem," *Univ. Ill. Dept. Comput. Sci., Doc.* 335, ILLIAC IV, 1969.

306. Matsushita, Y.: "Hidden-Line Elimination for a Rotating Object," *CACM*, **15**(4):245, April 1972.

307. Max, N. L. and W. H. Clifford, Jr.: "Computer Animation of the Sphere Eversion," *Comput. Graphics*, **9**(1):32–39, Spring 1975.

308. Maxwell, E. A.: *General Homogeneous Coordinates in Space of Three Dimensions*, Cambridge Univ. Press, Cambridge, 1951.

309. Maxwell, E. A.: *Methods of Plane Projective Geometry Based on the Use of General Homogeneous Coordinates*, Cambridge Univ. Press, Cambridge, 1946.

310. Mazziotta, J. C. and H. K. Huang: "THREAD (Three-dimensional Reconstruction and Display) with Biomedical Applications in Neuron Ultrastructure and Computerized Tomography," *NCC 1976*, pp. 241-250.

311. McCallister, S. and I. E. Sutherland: "Final Report on the Area Warnock Hidden-Line Algorithm," Evans and Sutherland Computer Corp., Salt Lake City, February 1970.

312. McCracken, T. E., B. W. Sherman, and S. J. Dwyer III: "An Economical Tonal Display for Interactive Graphics and Image Analysis Data," *Comput. and Graphics*, **1**(1):79–94, 1975.

313. McDonald, H. S., W. H. Ninke, and D. R. Weller: "A Direct-View CRT Console for Remote Computing," *Dig. Tech. Pap. Int. Solid State Circ. Conf.*, 1967, p. 68.

314. McLain, D. H.: "Computer Construction of Surfaces through Arbitrary Points," *IFIP 1974*, North-Holland, Amsterdam, p. 717.

315. Meadow, C. T.: *Man-Machine Communication*, Wiley, New York, 1970.

316. Mees, C. E. K.: *The Theory of the Photographic Process*, Macmillan, New York, 1942.

317. Metzger, R. A.: "Computer Generated Graphic Segments in a Raster Display," *SJCC 1969*, AFIPS Press, Montvale, N.J., pp. 161-172.

318. Mezei, L.: *Art From Computers (1971)*, film available from Ontario Communications Authority, 1670 Bayview Avenue, Toronto, Ontario, Canada.

319. Michener, J. and J. D. Foley: "Some Major Issues in the Design of the Core Graphics System," *Comput. Surv.*, **10**(4), 1978.

320. Michener, J. and A. van Dam: "A Functional Overview of the Core System with Glossary," *Comput. Surv.*, **10**(4), 1978.

321. Miller, R. B.: "Response Time in Man-Computer Conversational Transactions," *FJCC 1968*, Thompson Books, Washington, D.C., p. 267.

322. Miller, S. W.: "Display Requirements for Future Man-Machine Systems," *IEEE Trans.* **ED–18**(9):616, September 1971.

323. MIT Lincoln Laboratory: *SKETCHPAD*, film available from Digital Computers Group, MIT Lincoln Laboratory, Lexington, Mass. 02173.

324. MIT Lincoln Laboratory: *The Interactive Circuit Mask Design Program*, film available from Digital Computers Group, MIT Lincoln Laboratory, Lexington, Mass. 02173.

325. Mitchell, W. J.: *Computer-aided Architectural Design*, Petrocelli-Charter, New York, 1977.

326. Miyamoto, E. and T. O. Binford: "Display Generated by a Generalized Cone Representation," *Proc. IEEE Conf. on Computer Graphics, Pattern Recognition, and Data Structure*, May 1975, pp. 385-387.

327. Morland, D. V.: "Computer Generated Stereograms," *Comput. Graphics*, **10**(2):19–24, Summer 1976.

328. Morris, R.: "Scatter Storage Techniques," *CACM*, **11**(1):38, January 1968.

329. Munson, J. H.: "Experiments in the Recognition of Hand-printed Text, I: Character Recognition," *FJCC 1968*, Thompson Books, Washington, D.C., p. 1125.

330. Myer, T. H. and J. R. Barnaby: *TENEX Executive Language*, Bolt Beranek and Newman, Cambridge, Mass., January 1971.

331. Myer, T. H. and I. E. Sutherland: "On the Design of Display Processors," *CACM* **11**(6):410, June 1968.

332. Myers, A.: "An Efficient Algorithm for Computer Generated Pictures," *Ohio State Univ. Comput. Graphics Res. Group*, 1975.

333. National Institutes of Health: "DecSystem-10 Display Systems: Omnigraph," Computer Center Branch, Division of Computer Research and Technology, National Institutes of Health, Bethesda, Maryland, 20014, March 1974.

334. National Institutes of Health: *Guide to the PDP-10 Timesharing System*, Appendix II, Technical Display Information, Division of Computer Research and Technology, National Institutes of Health, Bethesda, Maryland 20014, January 1972.

335. Negroponte, N.: "On Being Creative with Computer Aided Design," *IFIP 1977*, North-Holland, Amsterdam, p. 695.

336. Negroponte, N.: "Raster-Scan Approaches to Computer Graphics," *Comput. and Graphics*, 2(3):179, 1977.

337. Negroponte, N.: "Recent Advances in Sketch Recognition," *NCC 1973*, pp. 663-675.

338. Negroponte, N.: *Soft Architecture Machines*, M.I.T. Press, Cambridge, Mass., 1975.

339. Negroponte, N.: *The Architecture Machine*, M.I.T. Press, Cambridge, Mass., 1970.

340. Negroponte, N. (ed.): *Computer Aids to Design and Architecture*, Petrocelli-Charter, New York, 1975.

341. Newell, M. E.: "The Utilization of Procedure Models in Digital Image Synthesis," *Univ. Utah Comput. Sci. Dept.*, UTEC-CSc-76-218, Summer 1975. NTIS AD/A039 008/LI.

342. Newell, M. E., R. G. Newell, and T. L. Sancha: "A New Approach to the Shaded Picture Problem," *Proc. ACM Nat. Conf.*, 1972, p. 443.

343. Newman, W. M.: "A Graphical Language for Display Programming," in *Spec. Sess. Int. Comput. Graphics Symp., Brunel Univ., Uxbridge, 1968*, Plenum Press, 1969.

344. Newman, W. M.: "A Graphical Technique for Numerical Input," *Comput. J.*, 11(1):63, May 1968.

345. Newman, W. M.: "A System for Interactive Graphical Programming," *SJCC 1968*, Thompson Books, Washington, D.C., p. 47.

346. Newman, W. M.: "An Experimental Display Programming Language for the PDP-10 Computer," *Univ. Utah Comput. Sci. Dept.*, UTEC-CSc-70-104, July 1970. NTIS AD-762 010.

347. Newman, W. M.: "An Experimental Program for Architectural Design," *Comput. J.*, 9(1):21, May 1966.

348. Newman, W. M.: "An Informal Graphics System Based on the Logo Language," *NCC 1973*, pp. 651-655.

349. Newman, W. M.: "Display Procedures," *CACM*, 14(10):651, October 1971.

350. Newman, W. M.: "Raster-Scan Graphics in CAD Systems," CAD Systems, *Proc. IFIP Working Conference on Computer-Aided Design Systems*, North-Holland, Amsterdam, 1977.

351. Newman, W. M.: "Trends in Graphic Display Design," *IEEE Trans.*, C-25(12):1321, December 1976.

352. Newman, W. M., H. Gouraud, and D. R. Oestreicher: "A Programmer's Guide to PDP-10 Euler," *Univ. Utah Comput. Sci. Dept.*, UTEC-CSc-70-105, June 1970. NTIS AD-760 549.

353. Newman, W. M. and R. F. Sproull: "An Approach to Graphics System Design," *Proc. IEEE*, 62(4):471, April 1974.

354. Newman, W. M. and R. F. Sproull: *Principles of Interactive Computer Graphics*, 1st ed., McGraw-Hill, New York, 1973.

355. Newman, W. M. and A. van Dam: "A Brief History of Efforts towards Graphics Standardization," *Comput. Surv.*, 10(4), 1978.

356. Nielson, G. M.: "Multivariate Smoothing and Interpolating Splines," *SIAM J. Numer. Anal.*, 11(2):435, April 1974.

357. Ninke, W. H.: "A Satellite Display Console System for a Multi-access Central Computer," *IFIP 1968*, North-Holland, Amsterdam, p. 962.

358. Ninke, W. H.: "Graphic 1: A Remote Graphical Display Console System," *FJCC 1965*, Spartan Books, Washington, D.C., p. 839.

359. Nishita, T. and E. Nakame: "An Algorithm for Half-toned Representation of Three-dimensional Objects," *Inf. Proc. Japan*, **14**:93, 1974.

360. Noll, A. M.: "Scanned-Display Computer Graphics," *CACM*, **14**(3):143, March 1971.

361. Notley, M. G.: "A Graphical Picture Drawing Language," *Comput. Bull.*, **14**(3):68, March 1970.

362. Ophir, D., S. Rankowitz, B. J. Shepherd, and R. J. Spinrad: "BRAD: The Brookhaven Raster Display," *CACM*, **11**(6):415, June 1968.

363. Ophir, D., B. J. Shepherd, and R. J. Spinrad: "Three-dimensional Computer Display," *CACM*, **12**(6):309, June 1969.

364. Oppenheim, A. V. and R. W. Schafer: *Digital Signal Processing*, Prentice-Hall, Englewood Cliffs, N.J., 1975.

365. Ortony, A.: "A System for Stereo Viewing," *Comput. J.*, **14**(2):140, May 1971.

366. Parent, R. E.: "A System for Sculpting 3-D Data," *Comput. Graphics*, **11**(2):138–147, Summer 1977.

367. Parke, F. I.: "Computer Generated Animation of Faces," *Univ. Utah Comput. Sci. Dept.*, UTEC-CSc-72-120, 1970. NTIS AD-762 022. Abridged version in *Proc. ACM Nat. Conf.*, 1972, p. 451.

368. Parslow, R. D. and R. E. Green (eds.): "Advanced Computer Graphics: Economics, Techniques and Applications," *2nd Int. Comput. Graphics Symp., 1970*, Plenum Press, 1971.

369. Parslow, R. D., R. W. Prowse, and R. E. Green (eds.): "Computer Graphics: Techniques and Applications," *1st Int. Comput. Graphics Symp., 1968*, Plenum Press, 1969.

370. Pearson, D. E.: *Transmission and Display of Pictorial Information*, Halstead Press (Wiley), New York, 1975.

371. Petty, W. D. and H. G. Slottow: "Multiple States and Variable Intensity in the Plasma Display Panel," *IEEE Trans.*, **ED–18**(9):654, September 1971.

372. Pfister, G. F.: "A High Level Language Extension for Creating and Controlling Dynamic Pictures," *Comput. Graphics*, **10**(1):1–9, Spring 1976.

373. Pitteway, M. L. V.: "Algorithm for Drawing Ellipses or Hyperbolae with a Digital Plotter," *Comput. J.*, **10**(3):282–289, November 1967.

374. Pobgee, P. J. and J. R. Parks: "Applications of a Low Cost Graphical Input Tablet," *IFIP 1971*, North-Holland, Amsterdam, p. TA-4-169.

375. Porter, T.K.: "Spherical Shading," *Comput. Graphics*, **12**(3):282, August 1978.

376. Prince, M. D.: *Interactive Graphics for Computer-aided Design*, Addison-Wesley, Reading, Mass., 1971.

377. Princeton Electronic Products: "LITHOCON (TM) Electrical Storage Tube," Princeton Electronic Products, New Brunswick, N.J., 1970.

378. Princeton Electronic Products: "PEP 801 Computer Graphic Terminal," Princeton Electronic Products, New Brunswick, N.J., 1971.

379. Priver, A. S.: "An Interactive Graphic System for Curve Fitting and Editing," *RAND Rep.* P-3766, September 1969.

380. Protter, M. H. and C. B. Morrey, Jr.: *Modern Mathematical Analysis*, Addison-Wesley, Reading, Mass., 1964.

381. Rabiner, L. R. and B. Gold: *Theory and Application of Digital Signal Processing*, Prentice-Hall, Englewood Cliffs, N.J., 1975.

382. Ralston, A. and H. S. Wilf (eds.): *Mathematical Methods for Digital Computers*, Wiley, New York, 1960, 1967.

383. RAND Corporation: *The GRAIL System*, film available from RAND Corporation, 1700 Main St., Santa Monica, Calif. 90406.

384. Rapkin, M. D. and O. M. Abu-Gheida: "Stand-alone/Remote Graphic System," *FJCC 1968*, Thompson Books, Washington, D.C., p. 731.

385. Ratliff, F.: "Mach Bands: Quantitative Studies on Neural Networks in the Retina," Holden-Day, San Francisco, 1965.

386. Rawson, E. G.: "Vibrating Varifocal Mirrors for 3-D Imaging," *IEEE Spectrum*, **6**(9):37, September 1969.

387. Reiser, J. F.: "SAIL," *Stanford Univ. Comput. Sci. Dept.*, STAN-CS-76-574, 1976.

388. Resch, R. D.: "Portfolio of Shaded Computer Images," *Proc. IEEE*, **62**(4):496, April 1974.
389. Resch, R. D.: "The Topological Design of Sculptural and Architectural Systems," *NCC 1973*, p. 643.
390. Richards, M.: "BCPL: A Tool for Compiler Writing and System Programming," *SJCC 1969*, AFIPS Press, Montvale, N.J., p. 557.
391. Richardson, F. K.: "Graphical Specification of Computation," *Univ. Ill. Dept. Comput. Sci. Tech. Rep.* 257, April 1968.
392. Richardson, F. K. and D. R. Oestreicher: "Computer Assisted Integrated Circuit Photomask Layout," in M. Faiman and J. Nievergelt (eds.), *Pertinent Concepts in Computer Graphics*, University of Illinois Press, Urbana, 1969.
393. Riesenfeld, R. F.: "Application of B-spline Approximations to Geometric Problems of Computer-aided Design," *Univ. Utah Comput. Sci. Dept.*, UTEC-CSc-73-126, March 1973. University Microfilms OP 65903.
394. Riesenfeld, R. F.: "Aspects of Modeling in Computer-aided Geometric Design," *NCC 1975*, p. 597.
395. Riesenfeld, R. F.: "Homogeneous Coordinates and Projective Planes in Computer Graphics," *Univ. Utah, Comput. Sci. Dept.*, 1977.
396. Riesenfeld, R. F.: "Non-uniform B-Spline Curves," *Proc. 2nd USA-Japan Computer Conf.*, 1975, p. 551.
397. Riesenfeld, R. F.: "On Chaikin's Algorithm," *Comput. Graphics Image Processing*, **4**(3):304–310, 1975.
398. Rippy, D. E. and D. E. Humphries: "MAGIC: A Machine for Automatic Graphics Interface to a Computer," *FJCC 1965*, Spartan Books, Washington, D.C., p. 819.
399. Robbins, M. F. and J. D. Beyer: "An Interactive Computer System Using Graphical Flowchart Input," *CACM*, **13**(2):115, February 1970.
400. Roberts, L. G.: "A Graphical Service System with Variable Syntax," *CACM*, **9**(3):173, March 1966.
401. Roberts, L. G.: "Conic Display Generator Using Multiplying Digital-Analog Converters," *IEEE Trans.*, **EC-16**(3):369, June 1967.
402. Roberts, L. G.: "Graphical Communication and Control Languages," *Proc. Inf. Syst. Sci. 2nd Cong.*, Spartan Books, Washington, D.C., 1964, p. 211. Also in *Computer Display Review*, see [256].
403. Roberts, L. G.: "Homogeneous Matrix Representation and Manipulation of *N*-dimensional Constructs," *MIT Lincoln Lab.*, MS 1405, May 1965. Also in *Computer Display Review*, see [256].
404. Roberts, L. G.: "Machine Perception of Three Dimensional Solids," *MIT Lincoln Lab.*, TR 315, May 1963. Also in J. T. Tippet, et al (eds.), *Optical and Electro Optical Information Processing*, MIT Press, Cambridge, Mass., 1964, p. 159.
405. Roberts, L. G.: "The Lincoln Wand," *FJCC 1966*, Spartan Books, Washington, D.C., p. 223.
406. Roberts, L. G. and B. D. Wessler: "Computer Network Development to Achieve Resource Sharing," *SJCC 1970*, AFIPS Press, Montvale, N.J., p. 543.
407. Robertson, G., A. Newell, and K. Ramakrishna: "ZOG: A Man-Machine Communication Philosophy," *Carnegie-Mellon Univ., Comput. Sci. Dept.*, August 1977.
408. Roese, J. A. and A. S. Khalafalla: "Stereoscopic Viewing with PLZT Ceramics," *Ferroelectrics*, **10**(1/2/3/4):47–51, 1976.
409. Roetling, P. G.: "Halftone Method with Edge Enchancement and Moire Suppression," *J. Opt. Soc. Am.*, **66**(10):985–989, October 1976.
410. Rogers, D. F. and J. A. Adams: *Mathematical Elements for Computer Graphics*, McGraw-Hill, New York, 1976.
411. Romney, G. W.: "Computer Assisted Assembly and Rendering of Solids," *Univ. Utah Dept. Comput. Sci.*, TR 4-20, 1970. NTIS AD-753 673.
412. Romney, G. W., G. S. Watkins, and D. C. Evans: "Real Time Display of Computer Generated Half-tone Perspective Pictures," *IFIP 1968*, North-Holland, Amsterdam, p. 973.

413. Rose, G. A.: "Computer Graphics Communication Systems," *IFIP 1968*, North-Holland, Amsterdam, p. 211.
414. Rosenfeld, A.: "Picture Processing: 1977," *Comput. Graphics Image Processing*, 7(2):211–242, April 1978.
415. Ross, D. T.: "A Generalized Technique for Symbol Manipulation and Numerical Calculation," *CACM*, **4**(3):147, March 1961.
416. Ross, D. T.: "The AED Approach to Generalized Computer-aided Design," *Proc. ACM Nat. Conf.*, Thompson Books, Washington, D.C., 1967, p. 367.
417. Ross, D. T.: "The AED Free Storage Package," *CACM*, **10**(8):481, August 1967.
418. Ross, D. T. and J. E. Rodriguez: "Theoretical Foundations for the Computer-aided Design System," *SJCC 1963*, Spartan Books, Baltimore, Md., p. 305.
419. Rougelot, R. S.: "The General Electric Computer Color TV Display," in M. Faiman and J. Nievergelt (eds.), *Pertinent Concepts in Computer Graphics*, University of Illinois Press, Urbana, 1969.
420. Rougelot, R. S. and R. A. Schumaker: "General-Electric Real-Time Display," *NASA Rep.* NAS 9-3916.
421. Rovner, P. D. and J. A. Feldman: "The LEAP Language and Data Structure," *IFIP 1968*, North-Holland, Amsterdam, p. 579.
422. Rovner, P. D. and D. A. Henderson, Jr.: "On the Implementation of AMBIT/G: A Graphical Programming Language," *Proc. Int. Joint Conf. Artifi. Intell.*, 1969, p. 9.
423. Ruban, V. G. and P. Luger: "Die Struktur des 4,4'-Dimethoxy-$\alpha,\beta$-diathylstilbens," *Acta Cryst.*, **B31**:2658, 1975.
424. Ruder, D.: "Data Disc Television Display System," *Proc. 1968 UAIDE Annu. Meet.*, Stromberg Datagraphix, p. 338.
425. Rully, A. D.: "A Subroutine Package for FORTRAN," *IBM Syst. J.*, 7(3/4):248, 1968.
426. Scala, J.: "Teaching Art Through Computer Graphics," *NCC 1976*, pp. 185-189.
427. Schumacker, R. A., B. Brand, M. Gilliland, and W. Sharp: "Study for Applying Computer-generated Images to Visual Simulation," *U.S. Air Force Human Resources Lab. Tech. Rep.* AFHRL-TR-69-14, September 1969.
428. Schumacker, R. A. and R. S. Rougelot: "Image Quality: A Comparison of Night/Dusk and Day/Night CGI Systems," *Proc. Image Conf.*, Williams Air Force Base, Arizona, 85224, May 1977.
429. Schwartz, J. L.: "The Computer-generated Film Facility of the Education Research Center," MIT Education Research Center, April 1970.
430. Schwartz, J. L. and E. F. Taylor: "Computer Displays in the Teaching of Physics," *FJCC 1968*, Thompson Books, Washington, D.C., p. 1285.
431. Science Accessories Corporation: "Graf/Pen Sonic Digitizer," Science Accessories Corporation, Southport, Conn., 1970.
432. Sears, F. W.: *Optics*, Addison-Wesley, Cambridge, Mass., 1949.
433. Seats, P.: "The Cathode Ray Tube: A Review of Current Technology and Future Trends," *IEEE Trans.*, **ED–18**(9):679, September 1971.
434. Secrest, T. and J. Nievergelt (eds.): "Emerging Concepts in Computer Graphics," *1967 Univ. Illinois Conf. Comput. Graphics*, Benjamin, New York, 1968.
435. Senses Bureau: *Patchwork 71, a Sampler of Computer Animation in Chemistry (1971)*, film available from Prof. Kent Wilson, The Senses Bureau, Department of Chemistry, University of California, San Diego, La Jolla, Calif. 92037.
436. Shamos, M. I.: *Computational Geometry*, Springer-Verlag, 1979.
437. Shaw, A. C.: "Parsing of Graph-Representable Pictures," *JACM*, 17(3):453–481, July 1970.
438. Shaw, J. C.: "JOSS: A Designer's View of an Experimental On-line Computing System," *FJCC 1964*, Spartan Books, Baltimore, Md., p. 455.
439. Sherr, S.: *Fundamentals of Display System Design*, Wiley, New York, 1970.
440. Shoup, R. G.: "Some Quantization Effects in Digitally Generated Pictures," *SID Int. Symp.*, 1973, p. 58.
441. Slottow, H. G.: "The Plasma Display Panel: Principles and Prospects," *1970 IEEE Conf. Displ. Devices*, p. 57.
442. Smith, A. R.: "Color Gamut Transform Pairs," *Comput. Graphics*, **12**(3):12, August 1978.

443. Smith, D. N.: "GPL/I: A PL/I Extension for Computer Graphics," *SJCC 1971*, AFIPS Press, Montvale, N.J., p. 511.
444. Smith, L. B.: "A Survey of Interactive Graphical Systems for Mathematics," *Comput. Surv.*, 2(4):261, December 1970.
445. Smith, L. B.: "Use of Interactive Graphics to Solve Numerical Problems," *CACM*, 13(10):625, October 1970.
446. Soha, J. M., D. J. Lynn, J. A. Mosher, and D. A. Elliott: "Digital Processing of the Mariner 10 Images of Venus and Mercury," *J. Appl. Photog. Eng.*, 3(2), Spring 1977.
447. Speer, R.: "Sources of Films in the U.S., Canada and Europe," *Comput. Graphics*, 8(3):64, Fall 1974.
448. Sproull, R. F.: "InterLisp Display Primitives," Xerox Palo Alto Research Center, 1977.
449. Sproull, R. F.: "Omnigraph: Simple Terminal-independent Graphics Software," Xerox Palo Alto Research Center, CSL-73-4, 1973.
450. Sproull, R. F. and W. M. Newman: "The Design of Gray-Scale Graphics Software," *Proc. IEEE Conf. on Computer Graphics, Pattern Recognition and Data Structure*, May 1975, p. 18.
451. Sproull, R. F. and I. E. Sutherland: "A Clipping Divider," *FJCC 1968*, Thompson Books, Washington, D.C., p. 765.
452. Sproull, R. F. and E. L. Thomas: "A Network Graphics Protocol," *Comput. Graphics*, 8(3):27, Fall 1974.
453. Stanford Research Institute: *The Augmented Human Intellect Project*, film available from Stanford Research Institute, 300 Ravenswood Ave, Menlo Park, Calif. 94025.
454. Stephenson, M. B. and H. N. Christiansen: "A Polyhedron Clipping and Capping Algorithm and a Display System for Three-dimensional Finite Element Models," *Comput. Graphics*, 9(3):1, Fall 1975.
455. Stockham, T. G.: "Image Processing within the Context of a Visual Model," *Proc. IEEE*, 60(7):828, July 1972.
456. Stotz, R.: "A New Display Terminal," *Comput. Des.*, April 1968.
457. Stotz, R.: "Man-Machine Console Facilities for Computer Aided Design," *SJCC 1963*, Spartan Books, Baltimore, Md., p. 323.
458. Stotz, R.: "Specialized Computer Equipment for Generation of Three-dimensional Curvilinear Figures," *MIT Electron. Syst. Lab.*, ESL-TM-167, January 1963.
459. Sutherland, I. E.: "A Head-mounted Three Dimensional Display," *FJCC 1968*, Thompson Books, Washington, D.C., p. 757.
460. Sutherland, I. E.: "Computer Displays," *Sci. Am.*, June 1970.
461. Sutherland, I. E.: "Computer Inputs and Outputs," *Sci. Am.*, September 1966.
462. Sutherland, I. E.: "SKETCHPAD: A Man-Machine Graphical Communication System," *MIT Lincoln Lab. Tech. Rep.* 296, May 1965. Abridged version in *SJCC 1963*, Spartan Books, Baltimore, Md., p. 329.
463. Sutherland, I. E.: "Ten Unsolved Problems in Computer Graphics," *Datamation*, 12(5):22, May 1966.
464. Sutherland, I. E.: "Three-dimensional Data Input by Tablet," *Proc. IEEE*, 62(4):64, April 1974.
465. Sutherland, I. E. and G. W. Hodgman: "Reentrant Polygon Clipping," *CACM*, 17(1):32, January 1974.
466. Sutherland, I. E., R. F. Sproull, and R. A. Schumacker: "A Characterization of Ten Hidden-Surface Algorithms," *Comput. Surv.*, 6(1):1, March 1974. Abridged version in *NCC 1973*, p. 685.
467. Sutherland, W. R.: "On-Line Graphical Specification of Computer Procedures," *MIT Lincoln Lab. Tech. Rep.* 405, May 1966.
468. Sutherland, W. R.: "The CORAL Language and Data Structure," *Computer Display Review*, see [256].
469. Sutherland, W. R., J. W. Forgie, and M. V. Morello: "Graphics in Time-sharing: A Summary of the TX-2 Experience," *SJCC 1969*, AFIPS Press, Montvale, N.J., p. 629.

470. Symonds, A. J.: "Auxiliary-Storage Associative Data Structure for PL/I," *IBM Syst. J.*, 7(3/4):229, 1968.
471. Talbot, P. A., J. W. Carr, R. R. Coulter, and R. C. Hwang: "Animator: An On-line Two-dimensional Film Animation System," *CACM*, 14(4):251, April 1971.
472. Teitelman, W.: "A Display Oriented Programmer's Assistant," Xerox Palo Alto Research Center, CSL 77-3, 1977.
473. Teitelman, W.: "Real Time Recognition of Hand-drawn Characters," *FJCC 1964*, Spartan Books, Baltimore, Md., p. 559.
474. Teixeira, J. F. and R. P. Sallen: "The Sylvania Tablet: A New Approach to Graphic Data Input," *SJCC 1968*, Thompson Books, Washington, D.C., p. 315.
475. Tektronix, Inc.: *4012 Graphic Computer Terminal*, Tektronix, Inc., Beaverton, Oregon.
476. Terlet, R. H.: "The CRT Display Subsystem of the IBM 1500 Instructional System," *FJCC 1967*, Thompson Books, Washington, D.C., p. 169.
477. Thanhouser, N.: "Intermixing Refresh and Direct View Storage Graphics," *Comput. Graphics*, 10(2):13–18, Summer 1976.
478. Thomas, E.: "The Storing and Reuse of Real-Time Graphical Inputs," Master's Thesis, MIT, Cambridge, Mass., June 1969.
479. Thomas, E. L.: "TENEX E&S Display Software," Bolt Beranek and Newman, Cambridge, Mass., December 1971.
480. Thornhill, D. E., R. H. Stotz, D. T. Ross, and J. E. Ward: "An Integrated Hardware-Software System for Computer Graphics in Time-sharing," *MIT Project MAC*, TR-56, December 1968.
481. Three Rivers Computing Corp.: "Graphic Display Programmer's Guide," Three Rivers Computing Corp., 160 N. Craig St., Pittsburgh, Pa. 15213, June 1978.
482. Tilbrook, D. M., M. Tuori, and R. M. Baecker: "Newswhole: An Interactive Newspaper Pagination System," video tape available from Computer Systems Research Group, Univ. of Toronto, Toronto, Ontario, Canada, 1976.
483. Tukey, J.: *Exploratory Data Analysis*, Addison-Wesley, Reading, Mass., 1977.
484. Turner, J. A. and G. J. Ritchie: "Linear Current Division in Resistive Areas: Its Application to Computer Graphics," *SJCC 1970*, AFIPS Press, Montvale, N.J., p. 613.
485. Uncapher, K. W.: "The RAND Video Graphic System: An Approach to a General User-Computer Graphic Communication System," *RAND Rep.* R-753-ARPA, April 1971.
486. van Dam, A.: "Computer Driven Displays and their Use in Man/Machine Interaction," in F. Z. Alt and M. Rubinoff (eds.), *Advances Comput.*, vol. 7, Academic, New York, 1966.
487. van Dam, A. and D. C. Evans: "A Compact Data Structure for Storing, Retrieving and Manipulating Line Drawings," *SJCC 1967*, Thompson Books, Washington, D.C., p. 601.
488. van Dam, A., G. M. Stabler, and R. J. Harrington: "Intelligent Satellites for Interactive Graphics," *Proc. IEEE*, 62(4):483, April 1974.
489. van den Bos, J., L. C. Caruthers, and A. van Dam: "GPGS: A Device-independent General Purpose Graphic System," *Comput. Graphics*, 11(2):112–119, Summer 1977.
490. Vector General Inc.: "Graphics Display System Reference Manual," Vector General Inc., Canoga Park, Calif., January 1971.
491. Vector General Inc.: "Model 3400 Graphics Display System Reference Manual," Vector General Inc., Woodland Hills, Calif., February 1976.
492. Verdina, J.: *Projective Geometry and Point Transformations*, Allyn and Bacon, Boston, 1971.
493. Voelcker, H. et al: "The PADL-1.0/2 System for Defining and Displaying Solid Objects," *Comput. Graphics*, 12(3):257, August 1978.
494. Voelcker, H. B. and A. A. G. Requicha: "Geometric Modeling of Mechanical Parts and Processes," *Computer*, December 1977, p. 48-57.
495. Wallace, V. L.: "The Semantics of Graphic Input Devices," *Comput. Graphics*, 10(1):61–65, Spring 1976.
496. Walton, J. S. and W. M. Risen, Jr.: "Computer Animation: On-line Dynamics Display in Real Time," *J. Chem. Educ.*, 46(6):334, 1969.

497. Ward, J. E.: "Systems Engineering Problems in Computer-driven CRT Displays for Man-Machine Communication," *IEEE Trans.*, SSC–3(1):47, June 1967.

498. Warner, J. R.: "MIDAS: A Compositional Modeling System," *NCC 1977*, pp. 39-48.

499. Warnock, J. E.: "A Hidden-Surface Algorithm for Computer Generated Half-tone Pictures," *Univ. Utah Comput. Sci Dept.*, TR 4-15, 1969. NTIS AD-753 671.

500. Watkins, G. S.: "A Real-Time Visible Surface Algorithm," *Univ. Utah Comput. Sci Dept.*, UTEC-CSc-70-101, June 1970. NTIS AD-762 004.

501. Watson, R. W., T. H. Myer, I. E. Sutherland, and M. K. Vosbury: "A Display Processor Design," *FJCC 1969*, AFIPS Press, Montvale, N.J., p. 209.

502. Weber, L. F.: "Optical Write-in for the Plasma Display Panel," *IEEE Trans.*, ED–18(9):664, September 1971.

503. Weiler, K. and P. Atherton: "Hidden Surface Removal Using Polygon Area Sorting," *Comput. Graphics*, 11(2):214, Summer 1977.

504. Wein, M. and N. Burtnyk: "Computer Animation," in J. Belzer, A. G. Holzman, and A. Kent (eds.) *Encyclopedia of Computer Science and Technology*, vol. 5, Marcel Dekker, New York, 1976, p. 397.

505. Wein, M., P. Tanner, G. Bechtold, and N. Burtnyk: "Hidden Line Removal for Vector Graphics," *Comput. Graphics*, 12(3):173, August 1978.

506. Weinberg, R.: "Computer Graphics in Support of Space Shuttle Simulation," *Comput. Graphics*, 12(3):82, August 1978.

507. Weiss, R. A.: "Be Vision, a Package of IBM 7090 Fortran Programs to Draw Orthographic Views of Combinations of Planes and Quadric Surfaces," *JACM*, 13(2):194, April 1966.

508. Weizenbaum, J.: "Symmetric List Processor," *CACM*, 6(9):524, September 1963.

509. Wentworth, J W.: *Color Television Engineering*, McGraw-Hill, New York, 1965.

510. Whitted, T.: "A Scan-Line Algorithm for Computer Display of Curved Surfaces," in supplement to SIGGRAPH 78, *Comput. Graphics*, 12(3), August 1978.

511. Wild, E. C., R. S. Rougelot, and R. A. Schumacker: "Computing Full Color Perspective Images," Tech. Inf. Series R71ELS-26, General Electric Electronics Lab., Syracuse, N.Y., May 1971.

512. Williams, F. C. and T. Kilburn: "A Storage System for Use with Binary-Digital Computing Machines," *Proc. IEE*, pt 3, 96:81, March 1949.

513. Williams, L.: "Casting Curved Shadows on Curved Surfaces," *Comput. Graphics*, 12(3):270, August 1978.

514. Williams, R.: "A Survey of Data Structures for Computer Graphics Systems," *Comput. Surv.*, 3(1):1, March 1971.

515. Williams, R.: "On the Application of Relational Data Structures in Computer Graphics," *IFIP 1974*, North-Holland, Amsterdam, p. 722.

516. Williams, R. and G. M. Giddings: "A Picture-building System," *Proc. IEEE Conf. on Computer Graphics, Pattern Recognition, and Data Structure*, May 1975, p. 304.

517. Williamson, H.: "Hidden-Line Plotting Program," *CACM*, 15(2):100, February 1972.

518. Wipke, W. T., S. R. Heller, R. J. Feldmann, and E. Hyde (eds.): *Computer Representation and Manipulation of Chemical Information*, Wiley, New York, 1974.

519. Wiseman, N. E.: "A Note on Compiling Display File from a Data Structure," *Comput. J.*, 11(2):141, August 1968.

520. Wiseman, N. E., H. U. Lemke, and J. O. Hiles: "PIXIE: A New Approach to Graphical Man-Machine Communication," *Proc. 1969 CAD Conf., Southampton, IEE Conf. Pub.* 51, p. 463.

521. Wolfberg, M. S.: "An Interactive Graph Theory System," *Univ. Penna. Moore Sch. Electr. Eng. Rep.* 69-25, June 1969. CFSTI AD-688931.

522. Woodsford, P. A.: "The Design and Implementation of the GINO 3D Graphics Software Package," *Software Pract. Exper.*, 1(4):335, October 1971.

523. Woodsford, P. A.: "The HRD-1 Laser Display System," *Comput. Graphics*, 10(2):68–73, July 1976.

524. Woon, P.: "On the Computer Drawing of Solid Objects Bounded by Quadric Surfaces," *N.Y. Univ. Comput. Sci. Dept. Rep.* TR-403-3, June 1969.

525. Wu, S. C., J. F. Abel, and D. P. Greenberg: "An Interactive Computer Graphics Approach to Surface Representation," *CACM*, 20(10):703, October 1977.

526. Wylie, C., G. W. Romney, D. C. Evans, and A. C. Erdahl: "Halftone Perspective Drawings by Computer," *FJCC 1967*, Thompson Books, Washington, D.C., p. 49.

527. Wyszecki, G. and W. S. Stiles: "Color Science," Wiley, New York, 1967.

528. Yamaguchi, F.: "A Design System for Free Form Objects (FREEDOM)," Tech. Res. Inst., Japan Soc. Promotion of Machine Industry, 1976.

529. Yamaguchi, F.: "A New Curve Fitting Method Using a CRT Computer Display," *Comput. Graphics Image Processing*, 7(3):425–437, June 1978.

530. Yarwood, E.: "Toward Program Illustration," *Univ. Toronto, Comput. Syst. Res. Group, Tech. Rep.* CSRG-84, October 1977.

531. Yule, J. A.: *Principles of Color Reproduction*, Wiley, New York, 1967.

532. —— *Proc. Symp. at CAORF*, 1st, June 1977; 2nd, September 1978. CAORF, Samuels Hall, National Maritime Research Center, Kings Point, N. Y., 11024.

533. —— "Status Report of the Graphics Standards Planning Committee of ACM/SIGGRAPH," *Comput. Graphics*, 11(3), Fall 1977.

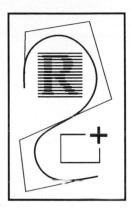

# INDEX